International Commercial Arbitration

An Asia-Pacific Perspective

There has been an exponential rise in the use of international commercial arbitration for resolving international business disputes, yet international arbitration is a scarcely regulated, specialty industry. *International Commercial Arbitration: An Asia-Pacific Perspective* is the first book to explain international commercial arbitration topic by topic with an Asia-Pacific focus.

Written for students and practising lawyers alike, this authoritative book covers the principles of international commercial arbitration thoroughly and comparatively. For each issue it utilises academic writings from Asia, Europe and elsewhere, and draws on examples of legislation, arbitration procedural rules and case law from the major Asian jurisdictions. Each principle is explained in simple language before the text proceeds to more technical, theoretical or comparative content. Real-world scenarios are employed to demonstrate actual application to practice. Readers will also be equipped to deal with the many arbitration issues which are not covered within the various arbitration statutes.

International Commercial Arbitration is an invaluable resource that provides unique insight into real arbitral practice specific to the Asia-Pacific region, within a global context.

Simon Greenberg is Deputy Secretary General of the ICC International Court of Arbitration. He also lectures at the Institute of Political Science of Paris (Sciences Po) and at the University of Aix-Marseille. Simon previously practised international arbitration with firms in Paris and Australia and was formerly the Deputy Secretary General of the Australian Centre for International Commercial Arbitration, first Secretary to the Asia Pacific Regional Arbitration Group and a founding committee member of the Australasian Forum for International Arbitration.

Christopher Kee is Adjunct Professor at the City University of Hong Kong, Honorary Fellow of Deakin University Law School, Melbourne, and Senior Researcher on the Global Sales Law Project, Universität Basel, Switzerland. Christopher currently represents the Asia Pacific Regional Arbitration Group at UNCITRAL and Working Group II meetings, and has served as a Co-Chair of the Australasian Forum for International Arbitration.

Romesh Weeramantry is Associate Professor at the City University of Hong Kong. He has designed and taught courses on international commercial arbitration and investment treaty arbitration at a number of universities in the Asia-Pacific region. Romesh has worked at the Iran-US Claims Tribunal and at the United Nations Compensation Commission and has practised international commercial arbitration at a firm in Geneva. He was a founding Co-Chair of the Australasian Forum for International Arbitration.

International Commercial Arbitration

An Asia-Pacific Perspective

Simon Greenberg
Christopher Kee
J. Romesh Weeramantry

CAMBRIDGE UNIVERSITY PRESS

CAMBRIDGE
UNIVERSITY PRESS

477 Williamstown Road, Port Melbourne, VIC 3207, Australia

Cambridge University Press is part of the University of Cambridge.

It furthers the University's mission by disseminating knowledge in the pursuit of education, learning and research at the highest international levels of excellence.

www.cambridge.org
Information on this title: www.cambridge.org/9780521695701

© Simon Greenberg, Christopher Kee, J. Romesh Weeramantry 2011

This publication is in copyright. Subject to statutory exception and to the provisions of relevant collective licensing agreements, no reproduction of any part may take place without the written permission of Cambridge University Press.

First published 2011

Cover design by Modern Art Production Group
Typeset by Aptara Corp.

A catalogue record for this publication is available from the British Library

National Library of Australia Cataloguing in Publication data
Greenberg, Simon.
International commercial arbitration : an Asia-Pacific perspective / Simon Greenberg
Christopher Kee, J. Romesh Weeramantry
9780521695701 (pbk.)
Includes index.
Arbitration and award–Pacific area.
Arbitration and award, international.
Kee, Christopher.
Weeramantry, J. Romesh
344.0189143091823

ISBN 978-0-521-69570-1 Paperback

Reproduction and communication for educational purposes
The Australian *Copyright Act 1968* (the Act) allows a minimum of one chapter or 10% of the pages of this work, whichever is the greater, to be reproduced and/ or communicated by any educational institution for its educational purposes provided that the educational institution (or the body that administers it) has given a remuneration notice to Copyright Agency Limited (CAL) under the Act.

Cambridge University Press has no responsibility for the persistence or accuracy of URLs for external or third-party internet websites referred to in this publication, and does not guarantee that any content on such websites is, or will remain, accurate or appropriate.

Contents

Foreword   page xv
Preface   xvii
Table of Cases   xix
Table of Statutes   xxxv

1 **Introduction to international arbitration and its place in the Asia-Pacific   1**
   1   Introduction and definition of arbitration   1
   2   A brief history of arbitration   3
       2.1   Ancient history to the birth of modern international law   3
       2.2   Early 20th century: The birth of globalisation and international law   6
       2.3   Post-World War Two: Development of a framework for international arbitration   9
           2.3.1   1958 New York Convention   9
           2.3.2   1965 ICSID Convention   11
           2.3.3   1966 United Nations Commission on International Trade Law (UNCITRAL)   14
           2.3.4   1976 UNCITRAL Arbitration Rules   14
           2.3.5   1985 UNCITRAL Model Law on International Commercial Arbitration   15
   3   Characteristics of arbitration   17
       3.1   Distinction between arbitration and litigation   18
       3.2   Distinction between arbitration and ADR   19
       3.3   Distinction between international arbitration and domestic arbitration   20
       3.4   Key features and overview of arbitration   21
           3.4.1   Arbitration agreement   21
           3.4.2   Arbitrators   21
           3.4.3   Seat of arbitration   22
           3.4.4   Party autonomy and procedure   23
           3.4.5   Finality of outcomes   23
           3.4.6   International enforcement of arbitration agreements and awards   24
           3.4.7   Arbitral institutions   25
       3.5   Sources of international arbitration procedural law and practice   28
           3.5.1   National or domestic sources   29

v

                3.5.2   International legal sources   30
                3.5.3   Supranational and quasi-legal sources   31
    4   International arbitration in the Asia-Pacific   33
        4.1   The growth of international arbitration in the
              Asia-Pacific   33
        4.2   Asian culture and international arbitration   43
                4.2.1   Asian social, religious and political cultural diversity   43
                4.2.2   Asian dispute resolution culture   44

2   Law governing the arbitration and role of the seat   54
    1   Introduction   54
    2   Terminology: Seat or place of arbitration   55
    3   Distinction between the seat of arbitration and venue of
        hearings   55
    4   *Lex arbitri*, arbitral procedural law and arbitration rules   58
        4.1   *Lex arbitri* v arbitral procedural law   60
        4.2   Arbitral procedural law v arbitration rules   63
        4.3   Procedural pyramid   65
    5   Diverging views on link between arbitration proceedings and seat of
        arbitration   66
        5.1   Traditional view   66
        5.2   Delocalised view   68
                5.2.1   Definition   68
                5.2.2   International relations theory and delocalisation   71
                5.2.3   Delocalisation in practice: Relevant legal provisions   72
                5.2.4   Conclusions on delocalisation   78
    6   Choosing the seat of arbitration   80
        6.1   General principles   80
        6.2   Factors to consider in choosing a seat of arbitration   82
        6.3   Changing the seat of arbitration   83
    7   The Model Law as *lex arbitri*   86
        7.1   Asia-Pacific and the Model Law   86
        7.2   Mandatory provisions of the Model Law (1985 text)   88

3   Applicable substantive law   96
    1   Introduction   96
    2   Types of conflict of law issues in international arbitration   96
    3   Determining the law applicable to the substance of the dispute   100
        3.1   Freedom of parties to choose the law   101
        3.2   Applicable law where there is no choice of law by the parties   102
                3.2.1   Arbitration laws and institutional rules regarding applicable law
                        in the absence of party choice   102
                3.2.2   Conflict of laws methodology adopted by international
                        arbitrators   105
        3.3   The law applicable to non-contractual claims   113
                3.3.1   Characterisation of claims as contractual or not   114
                3.3.2   Parties' choice of law applicable to non-contractual claims   115
                3.3.3   Law applicable to torts claims in the absence of choice   116

- 4 Limitations on choice of law: Mandatory laws and public policy   119
- 5 Content of the applicable law   126
- 6 Trade usages   129
- 7 Non-national rules of law and the *lex mercatoria*   131
    - 7.1 Choice of the *lex mercatoria* by the parties   132
    - 7.2 Choice of the *lex mercatoria* by the arbitral tribunal   134
    - 7.3 Discussion of the *lex mercatoria*   135
- 8 Deciding cases without law: *Ex aequo et bono* and *amiable compositeur*   138

4 Arbitration agreement   144

- 1 Introduction   144
- 2 Arbitration agreement   145
    - 2.1 Is an arbitration agreement necessary?   145
    - 2.2 Types of arbitration agreements   146
    - 2.3 Definition and formal requirements of an arbitration agreement   146
        - 2.3.1 General   146
        - 2.3.2 Incorporation by reference   151
- 3 Doctrine of separability   155
    - 3.1 Validity of main contract and arbitration agreement   158
    - 3.2 Law governing main contract and arbitration agreement   159
    - 3.3 Validity of arbitration agreement determined independently of all national laws   163
- 4 Identifying the parties to an arbitration agreement   164
    - 4.1 Non-signatories   164
        - 4.1.1 Alter ego and group of companies   165
        - 4.1.2 Estoppel   167
        - 4.1.3 Assignment   168
    - 4.2 Capacity   169
- 5 Defined legal relationship   170
- 6 Consolidation, joinder and third party notices   172
    - 6.1 Consolidation   174
    - 6.2 Joinder and intervention   175
    - 6.3 Third party notices   178
- 7 Enforcement of arbitration agreements   179
    - 7.1 Existence of a dispute   180
    - 7.2 Attaching conditions   181
- 8 Arbitrability   182
    - 8.1 Subjective arbitrability   182
    - 8.2 Objective arbitrability   186
- 9 Drafting arbitration agreements   189
    - 9.1 Essential elements to include in an arbitration agreement   189
        - 9.1.1 Identity of parties   189
        - 9.1.2 Obligation to arbitrate   189
        - 9.1.3 Subject matter and scope of arbitration   193
        - 9.1.4 Certainty of the seat if designated   193
    - 9.2 Advisable elements to include   194
    - 9.3 Ad hoc or institutional arbitration?   195

    9.4   Multi-tiered arbitration agreements   197
    9.5   What *not* to include in an arbitration agreement   198
    9.6   Pathological arbitration agreements   199

5 Arbitral jurisdiction 202

1   Introduction 202
2   Overview and summary of jurisdictional objections 203
3   Preliminary issues relating to arbitral jurisdiction 205
    3.1   Partial and absolute jurisdictional objections 205
    3.2   Jurisdictional objections raised by a party 206
    3.3   Arbitral tribunal's ex officio examination of jurisdiction 208
    3.4   Appropriate time to decide jurisdiction 209
    3.5   Waiver of the right to invoke an arbitration agreement 211
4   Arbitral tribunal's determination of jurisdiction: Competence-competence rule 214
    4.1   Introduction to the competence-competence rule 215
    4.2   Competence-competence rule and extent of domestic court intervention 218
    4.3   Conclusions on competence-competence 228
5   Arbitral institution's examination of jurisdiction 230
    5.1   Examples in multi-party arbitrations 231
    5.2   Examples in multi-contract arbitrations 233
6   Effects of jurisdictional decisions 233
    6.1   Effect of a court or arbitral institution's prima facie examination of jurisdiction 233
    6.2   Recourse against an arbitral tribunal's jurisdictional decision 234
        6.2.1   Positive jurisdictional decisions 235
        6.2.2   Negative jurisdictional decisions 237
    6.3   Scope of court review of arbitral tribunal's jurisdictional decisions 240
    6.4   Subsidiary orders with negative jurisdictional decisions 242

6 The arbitral tribunal 245

1   Introduction 245
2   Constitution of the arbitral tribunal 246
    2.1   Number of arbitrators 246
    2.2   Procedure for constituting the arbitral tribunal 250
    2.3   Multiparty arbitrations 253
3   Choosing an arbitrator 256
    3.1   Qualifications of an international arbitrator 256
    3.2   Qualities of an arbitrator 260
        3.2.1   Chairpersons and sole arbitrators 261
        3.2.2   Party-nominated co-arbitrators 262
        3.2.3   Pre-appointment interviews 265
4   Formal appointment of arbitrators 266
5   Obligations of arbitrators 267
    5.1   General obligations and potential liability 268
    5.2   Disclosure obligations 270

   5.2.1 General principles of disclosure 270
   5.2.2 IBA Guidelines 271
 6 Challenges to arbitrators 273
  6.1 Challenges for partiality or lack of independence 274
   6.1.1 Impartiality and independence distinguished 274
   6.1.2 Procedure 276
   6.1.3 Assessment of impartiality and independence by arbitral institutions 280
   6.1.4 Assessment of impartiality and independence by domestic courts 282
   6.1.5 The standard for party-nominated co-arbitrators 292
   6.1.6 Impartiality and arb-med or med-arb 293
  6.2 Challenges for misconduct 294
   6.2.1 Definition and procedure 294
   6.2.2 Arbitral institution decisions on misconduct 297
   6.2.3 Court decisions on misconduct 298
 7 Resignation and replacement of arbitrators 301
  7.1 Resignation of arbitrators 301
  7.2 Agreements to replace arbitrators 302
  7.3 Replacement of arbitrators 302

7 Procedure and evidence 304
 1 Introduction 304
 2 Party autonomy 305
  2.1 The principle 305
  2.2 Limits to party autonomy 306
 3 Rules, procedural law and guidelines 308
  3.1 Arbitration rules 308
   3.1.1 Choice of arbitration rules 308
   3.1.2 Differences between institutional and ad hoc arbitration procedure 310
   3.1.3 Failure to object to non-compliance with procedural rules 310
   3.1.4 Applicable version of rules 311
  3.2 IBA Rules of Evidence 312
 4 Core procedural rights and duties 313
  4.1 Right to present case 313
  4.2 Right to equal treatment 315
  4.3 Arbitrators' duty to avoid delay and expense 316
 5 Balancing common law and civil law procedure 318
 6 Arbitral proceedings 322
  6.1 Overview of typical procedural steps 322
  6.2 Initiating the arbitration 323
  6.3 Representation 324
  6.4 Preliminary meeting 325
  6.5 Terms of reference 326
  6.6 Written submissions 326
  6.7 Amendment of claims 328
  6.8 On-site inspections 329

        6.9   Bifurcation and trifurcation   330
        6.10   Party default and non-participating parties   330
        6.11   Expedited arbitration procedures   332
        6.12   Arb-med   333
        6.13   Termination of the proceedings   337
   7   Evidence   337
        7.1   Burden and standard of proof   338
        7.2   Documentary evidence   339
               7.2.1   Document production – Domestic court practice   340
               7.2.2   Document production – Arbitral practice   341
               7.2.3   Court assistance in document production   342
               7.2.4   IBA Rules of Evidence and document production   343
        7.3   Witness evidence   346
               7.3.1   Witness evidence generally   346
               7.3.2   IBA Rules of Evidence and witnesses   348
        7.4   Expert evidence   350
               7.4.1   Party-appointed experts   350
               7.4.2   Tribunal-appointed experts   351
               7.4.3   Witness conferencing   352
   8   Hearings   354
   9   Interim measures   357
        9.1   Tribunal-ordered interim measures   357
               9.1.1   National laws   358
               9.1.2   Arbitral rules   361
               9.1.3   Ex parte preliminary orders   361
        9.2   Court assistance   363
   10 Security for costs   369
   11 Privacy and confidentiality   371

8 The award: Content and form   379
   1   Introduction   379
   2   Deliberations and decision-making   379
   3   Content, form and effect of arbitral awards   382
        3.1   Formalities   382
        3.2   Reasons for the award   383
        3.3   Signature, place and date   386
        3.4   Time limits   386
        3.5   Drafting an arbitral award   388
        3.6   Scrutiny of the draft award   389
        3.7   Finality   390
        3.8   Notification or deposit of award   392
   4   Definition of an arbitral award   392
   5   Types of awards   395
        5.1   Final awards   395
        5.2   Partial awards   396
        5.3   Interim or provisional awards, orders or measures   396
        5.4   Consent awards   398
        5.5   Default awards   399

5.6   Domestic, non-domestic, foreign and international awards   400
  5.7   Majority decisions, separate or dissenting opinions   401
6 Costs   403
  6.1   Costs of the arbitration v parties' costs   404
  6.2   Payment of costs: By which party and in what proportion?   404
  6.3   Sealed offers   406
  6.4   Arbitrators' fees   407
  6.5   Taxation of costs   408
7 Correction and interpretation of awards   409

9 The award: Challenge and enforcement   411
  1 Introduction   411
  2 Finality of awards   412
  3 Challenging awards   415
    3.1 State control over awards at seat of arbitration   415
    3.2 Setting aside awards   417
      3.2.1 Setting aside at seat of arbitration   417
      3.2.2 Setting aside foreign awards   418
      3.2.3 Model Law setting aside grounds and their exclusivity   419
      3.2.4 Elaboration or qualification of Article 34 grounds   422
      3.2.5 Failure to make a timely objection   424
      3.2.6 Setting aside jurisdictional decisions   424
    3.3 Time limits   425
    3.4 Consequences of challenge   426
  4 Recognition of awards   427
  5 Enforcement of New York Convention awards   427
    5.1 Implementation of the New York Convention   431
    5.2 Enforcement at the seat of arbitration   436
    5.3 Bilateral and multilateral enforcement agreements   436
    5.4 Application of the New York Convention   437
      5.4.1 Scope   437
      5.4.2 Reciprocity reservation   440
      5.4.3 Commercial reservation   441
      5.4.4 Documents required for enforcement   443
    5.5 Temporal issues   444
      5.5.1 Retroactivity of New York Convention   444
      5.5.2 Time limits   444
      5.5.3 Delays in enforcement   445
  6 Enforcement refusal grounds   447
    6.1 Overlap of the New York Convention with Articles 34, 35 and 36 of the Model Law   450
    6.2 Article V(1) of the New York Convention   451
      6.2.1 Party incapacity or agreement invalidity   451
      6.2.2 Violation of due process   453
      6.2.3 Excess of jurisdiction   455
      6.2.4 Irregularity in procedure or composition of arbitral tribunal   457
      6.2.5 Award not yet binding or set aside   459

    6.3 Article V(2) of the New York Convention 461
      6.3.1 Arbitrability 461
      6.3.2 Public policy 461
   6.4 Adjournment of enforcement proceedings (New York Convention Article VI) 467
  7 Non-New York Convention enforcement 468
  8 Execution of awards 470
  9 Other enforcement issues 471
   9.1 *Forum non conveniens* 471
   9.2 State responsibility for illegal court interference with award 471
   9.3 State immunity 473

10 Investment treaty arbitration 477

  1 Introduction 477
  2 International investment law 478
  3 Investment treaties 479
  4 The International Centre for Settlement of Investment Disputes (ICSID) 482
   4.1 Background and structure of ICSID 482
   4.2 ICSID jurisdiction 483
   4.3 Requirement of an 'investment' 483
   4.4 Nationality 485
   4.5 Choice of law 486
   4.6 Consent to ICSID arbitration 487
   4.7 Additional facility 488
  5 Assessment of the ICSID Convention 488
   5.1 Advantages 489
   5.2 Disadvantages 489
   5.3 Innovative features 491
     5.3.1 Exclusion of diplomatic protection and investor's direct rights 491
     5.3.2 ICSID's self-contained procedure 492
     5.3.3 Exhaustion of domestic remedies not required 493
  6 Substantive rights and protections under investment treaties 493
   6.1 Expropriation 494
   6.2 Fair and equitable treatment 495
   6.3 Full protection and security 496
   6.4 Arbitrary or discriminatory treatment 496
   6.5 National treatment 497
   6.6 Most favoured nation treatment 498
   6.7 Umbrella clauses 499
  7 Remedies 500
   7.1 Compensation for expropriation 500
   7.2 Compensation for non-expropriatory treaty breaches 500
   7.3 Costs 501
   7.4 Interest 501

    8   Annulment of ICSID awards   502
    9   Enforcement of ICSID awards   503

Appendix 1 Asia-Pacific arbitral institutions at a glance 505
Appendix 2 Selected arbitral institutions 512
Appendix 3 List of UNCITRAL Model Law countries 514
Appendix 4 List of parties to the New York Convention 1958 515
*Appendix 5 Selected list of Asia-Pacific arbitration legislation and
          instruments* 517
Glossary 518
Index 527

Foreword

It is a great pleasure for me to contribute a foreword to this book. Arbitration in the Asia-Pacific region has been a central interest of mine for over two decades. I have been involved as an arbitrator, teacher and administrator. Furthermore, the three authors are persons well known to me and I have observed the development of their careers in international arbitration with great interest.

There are now many books on international commercial arbitration. What distinguishes this work from others in the field is its regional perspective. The development of international arbitration in Asia has been quite spectacular. Singapore and Hong Kong now rival London, Paris, Geneva and New York as major centres of international commercial arbitration. The number of arbitrations in south Asia, south-east Asia, east Asia and China is rapidly increasing. Thus Asia is developing as a centre for services including dispute resolution services as well as an economic powerhouse.

This book is written primarily for students of international arbitration in Asian universities and for lawyers who have a practice or interest in arbitration in Asia. It presents, within a broad compass, an overview of the principal aspects of international commercial arbitration. True to its focus, each topic is illustrated by reference to arbitration laws, rules, institutions and secondary writings in the region. The book is much more than a brief overview of international commercial arbitration. Each topic is examined in depth and the text is written in a clear and attractive style. While the book has an Asian perspective, it is not written in a parochial way. In addition to references to laws and cases from the region there are also frequent references to well-known materials from outside Asia.

The first chapter presents a panorama of international commercial arbitration, defining arbitration, exploring the history of arbitration and elucidating its development. The principal conventions, laws and rules are noted and there is an overview of the key features of international arbitration. Other matters discussed are arbitral institutions, sources of procedural law and practice and an introduction to international arbitration in the Asia-Pacific region which includes an interesting discussion of Asian social, religious, political and cultural diversity. The following chapters explore the classic aspects of international arbitration including the governing law, the arbitration agreement, jurisdiction, the tribunal, procedure and the award. Although the book deals with international commercial arbitration there is a chapter on investment treaty arbitration. The book is supported by a number of most useful appendices.

The authors themselves, although comparatively young, have accumulated a wealth of experience in international commercial arbitration. Simon Greenberg, now the Deputy Secretary General of the ICC International Court of Arbitration, was an arbitration practitioner in a leading commercial law firm and has experience of international arbitration in Europe as well as the Asia-Pacific region. He was previously the Deputy Secretary General of the Australian Centre for International Commercial Arbitration and the First Secretary to the Asia-Pacific Regional Arbitration Group. His expertise in international commercial arbitration is widely recognised.

Christopher Kee has a strong academic background. He is an adjunct professor at the City University, Hong Kong and is a Senior Researcher at the University of Basel. Previously he taught international arbitration at an Australian law school.

Romesh Weeramantry is Associate Professor at the City University of Hong Kong, teaching international commercial arbitration, investment treaty arbitration and international law. He has had wide international experience at the Iran-United States Claims Tribunal and the United Nations Compensation Commission in Geneva. He has also published widely and is involved with a number of arbitral organisations.

I congratulate the authors on producing an excellent book with a unique focus. It is most informative and well written and will, I am confident, be useful not only to students and practitioners in the region but also to lawyers in other parts of the world who wish to know more about arbitration in Asia.

Michael Pryles
Chairman
Singapore International Arbitration Centre

Preface

International arbitration is firmly established worldwide as a distinct discipline. A major component of its exponential growth in the last 15–20 years emanates from the Asia-Pacific region.[1] In Chapter 1 we describe an Asia-Pacific arbitration craze that includes sharp increases in the case loads of its major arbitral institutions, a raft of important legislative changes, and a flurry of other regionally focussed international arbitration activity.

In its traditional centres (mainly Europe and more recently North America), international arbitration has grown into an important industry for the legal profession and has consequently become an essential subject for university legal studies. Numerous textbooks have emerged in response, but until now none focuses on the Asia-Pacific. There are several practitioners' guides on specific Asia-Pacific jurisdictions, but no book addresses the region in a subject-by-subject textbook style.

When we embarked on this project, we believed there was a need for an Asia-Pacific focused international arbitration textbook. The 2008 financial crisis has reinforced that belief. Adrian Winstanley, writing in *The Asia Pacific Arbitration Review 2009* (a Global Arbitration Review publication), captured the essence of this increased need when he observed:

> We have, then, had the most piercing of wake-up calls, which must surely lead to a new global economic order, at the heart of which will, once again, be the great tiger economies of the Asia-Pacific, which have had not only to rethink economic strategy regarding their export markets and foreign investments, but also to manage the expectations of their huge populations for improvements in their quality of life, while minimising the environmental impact of growing consumer demands. And it is in addressing these twin problems that new industries and services will emerge and grow, and out of which, for better or for worse, another generation of arbitral work will emerge.

Our book does not purport to provide an extensive overview of any individual arbitration law. A practitioner is unlikely to find in it everything he or she wants to know about a particular jurisdiction. Rather, the aim is to spice the teaching of general principles of international arbitration with strongly Asia-Pacific flavours.

---

[1] We principally focus on the following jurisdictions: Australia, China (Mainland), Hong Kong, India, Indonesia, Japan, Korea (Republic of), Malaysia, New Zealand, the Philippines and Singapore. From time to time we also give examples from other jurisdictions.

It is almost trite to observe that private international arbitration is a dynamic discipline. The law and practice of it in the Asia-Pacific evolved dramatically as we wrote this book. We would never have got through the research without assistance from numerous people. Special thanks are due to Karen Allardice, Amrita Biswas, José Caicedo, Rachel Carter, Jacqueline Chang, Rahul Chatterji, Vicky Chung, Romain Dupeyré, Kun Fan, Julien Fouret, Alain Hosang, Sophie Hottlet, Kevin Kee, Winki Lam, Vincent Lee, Ruth Lemaire, Jacky Man, Michael McAllister, Luke Nottage, Brar Harprabdeep Singh, Aurélie de Raphelis Soissan, Tamela Smith, Andrew Sykes, Candy Tang, Hélène van Lith, Claire Wilson, Megan Valsinger-Clark, Sophia Yang and Philip Yang. Professor Wang Guiguo of City University of Hong Kong requires particular mention for providing a research grant. We acknowledge various other institutions, generally our employers, who kindly supported and/or tolerated the project: Basel University, City University of Hong Kong, Deakin University, Dechert LLP, International Chamber of Commerce, and Keelins Lawyers. We are also grateful to the many colleagues with whom we discussed ideas and issues; and to our family and friends for putting up with it all. Finally, we thank all the individuals we worked with at Cambridge University Press.

The end product (with the exception of the index and tables) is our creation and we accept full responsibility for its errors of substance. Any views expressed are personal to us, and cannot be attributed to any of our respective institutions. We should note that at the proof stage of the book, a number of important developments occurred. The revision of the UNCITRAL Arbitration Rules was completed, SIAC launched its 2010 Rules and the IBA released its 2010 Rules on the Taking of Evidence in International Arbitration. We have attempted to refer to these new rules or revisions where possible but time constraints prevented us from including any detailed or considered analyses. We have done our best to ensure accuracy. This was particularly challenging where information was only available in a language none of us understands. At times it was necessary to refer to unofficial translations from public sources. We also acknowledge that we are not specialist practitioners in each jurisdiction covered. Local advice should be sought about the particularities of individual jurisdictions. Finally, we all initially trained as common law lawyers and the influence of that background may well be lurking in the following pages.

We hope that this book proves a useful and informative contribution to the exciting world of international arbitration in the Asia-Pacific.

Simon Greenberg
Christopher Kee
Romesh Weeramantry

Table of Cases

Ad Hoc International Arbitrations

Petroleum Dev (Trucial Coast) Ltd v Sheikh of Abu Dhabi (award of 28 August 1951) reprinted in (1952) 1 *Int'l & Comp LQ* 247   8, 136–7

Australia

Able Demolitions & Excavations v State of Victoria [2004] VSC 511   289
ACD Tridon Inc v Tridon Australia Pty Ltd [2002] NSWSC 896   188
ACN 006 397 413 Pty Ltd v International Movie Group (Canada) Inc [1997] 2 VR 31   448
Age Old Builders Pty Ltd v Swintons Pty Ltd [2003] VSC 307   191
American Diagnostica Inc v Gradipore (1998) 44 NSWLR 312   56, 60
Angela Raguz v Rebecca Sullivan(2000) 50 NSWLR 236   56–7
Ansett Australia Ltd (Subject to a Deed of Company Arrangement) v Malaysian Airline System Berhad (2008) 217 FLR 376   182
Antclizo Shipping Corp v Food Corp of India [2008] unreported, Supreme Court of Western Australia   445
Australian Granites v Eisenwerk Hensel Beyreuth GmgH [2002] Qd R 461   64
BHP Billiton Ltd v Oil Basins Ltd [2006] VSC 402   259, 384, 385
Brali v Hyundai Corp (1988) 84 ALR 176   468
Clough Engineering Ltd v Oil & Natural Gas Corporation Ltd [2007] FCA 881 (7 June 2007); [No. 2] [2007] FCA 927 (19 June 2007); [No. 4] [2007] FCA 2110 (21 December 2007); [2008] FCA 191 (29 February 2008); [2008] FCAFC 136 (22 July 2008)   120, 121–2, 367–8
Comandate Marine Corp v Pan Australia Shipping Pty Ltd [2006] FCAFC 192   113, 183, 185
Commonwealth of Australia v Cockatoo Dockyard Pty Ltd [1995] 36 NSWLR 662   374
Commonwealth Development Corporation (UK) v Montague [2000] QCA 252   243–4, 326, 408
Conagra International Fertiliser v Lief Investments (1997) 141 FLR 124; [1998] NSWSC 481   152–3
Corvetina Technology Ltd v Clough Engineering Ltd, Corvetina Technology Ltd v Clough Engineering Ltd [2004] NSWSC 700   464
Elders CED Ltd v Dravo Corporation [1984] 59 ALR 206   188
Electra Air Conditioning BV v Seeley International Pty Ltd [2008] FCAFC 169   186

Enterra Pty Ltd v ADI Ltd [2002] NSWSC 700   301
Esso Australia Resources Ltd v The Honourable Sidney James Plowman (1995) 183 CLR 10   33, 194, 371, 373–4
Ferris v Plaiser (1994) 34 NSWLR 474   158
Gascor v Ellicott [1997] 1 VR 332   288–9, 290
Gordian Runoff Limited v Westport Insurance Corporation [2010] NSWCA 57   385
Hewitt v McKensey [2003] NSWSC 1186   140
Hi-Fert Pty Ltd v Kiukiang Maritime Carriers [1998] 159 ALR 142   113, 171, 183
ICT Pty Ltd v Sea Containers Ltd [2002] NSWSC 77   26
Incitec Ltd v Alkimos Shipping Corp (2004) ALR 558   183
International Movie Group Inc (IMG) v Palace Entertainment Corp Pty Ltd (1995) 128 FLR 458   448
Liverpool City Council v Casbee Pty Ltd [2005] NSWSC 590   190
LKT Industrial Berhad (Malaysia) v Chun [2004] NSWSC 820   409
Mond v Berger [2004] VSC 150   269
O'Brien v Tanning Research Laboratories Inc (1988) 14 NSWLR 601   182
Oil Basins Ltd v BHP Billiton Ltd [2006] VSC 402; [2007] VSCA 255   260, 384–5
Paxton Enterprises Pty Ltd v Brancoe Australia NL [2000] WASC 273   169
Pindan Pty Ltd v Uniseal Pty Ltd [2003] WASC 168   288
PMT Partners Pty Ltd (in liq) v Australian National Parks & Wildlife Service (1995) 184 CLR 301   190, 193
QH Tours Ltd v Ship Design & Management (Aust) Pty Ltd (1991) 104 ALR 371   156
Resort Condominiums International Inc v Bolwell (1993) 118 ALR 655; (1995) XX YBCA 628   393, 397, 439–40, 448, 464
Reganam Pty Ltd v Crossing [2007] NSWSC 582   301
Savcor Pty Ltd v State of New South Wales (2001) 52 NSWLR 587   190
Sea Containers Pty Ltd v ICT Pty Ltd [2002] NSWCA 84   299–300
Seeley International Pty Ltd v Electra Air Conditioning BV [2008] FCA 29   185–6
Thoroughvision Pty Ltd v Sky Channel Pty Ltd & Anor [2010] VSC 139   386
Toyo Engineering Corp v John Holland Pty Ltd [2000] VSC 553   468
Transfield Philippines Inc v Pacific Hydro Ltd [2006] VSC 175   106, 118–19, 183
TV New Zealand v Langley Productions Ltd [2000] 2 NZLR 250   374
Walter Rau Neusser Oel Und Fett AG v Cross Pacific Trading Ltd [2005] FCA 1102   188
Webb v The Queen [1993] 181 CLR 41   283

Bangladesh

Bangladesh Air Service (Pty) Ltd v British Airways PLC, (1998) XXIII YBCA 624   432

Bermuda

Sojuznefteexport (SNE) v Joc Oil Ltd (1990) XV YBCA 384   158

Brunei

L & M Prestressing Sdn Bhd v Engineering Construction Pte Ltd [1991] BNHC 39   183
Royal Brunei Airlines Sdn Bhd v Philip Tan Kok Ming [1993] BNHC 18   164

Canada

Coderre v Coderre (2008) QCCA 888   142–3
H & H Marine Engine Services Ltd v Volvo Penta of the Americas Inc [2009] BCSC 1389   215, 217
Inforica Inc v CGI Information Systems and Management Consultants Inc [2009] ONCA 642   397
Noble China Inc v Lei Kat Chong [1998] CanLII 14708   381
United Mexican States v Metalclad Corporation (2001) BCLR (3rd) 359, 5 ICSID Reports 236   492

China

Reply of Supreme People's Court to the Query about the Arbitration Clause in the Sales Contract between *Baoyuan Trade Co v Yu Jianguo*, (Civil 4, Miscellaneous), No. 38 (2007)   161
China Henan Import-Export Co v Xinquan Trade Ltd, Supreme Court, (Civil, Economic), Final, No. 48 (2000)   169
Reply of Supreme People's Court to the Non-enforcement Decision by Yulin Intermediate Court against Dongxun Investment Co., Ltd (Civil 4, Miscellaneous), No. 24 (2006)   189
Duferco SA v Ningbo Arts & Crafts Import and Export Co Ltd, Decision of 22 April 2009, ICC award 14006/MS/JB/JEM   452
Reply of Supreme People's Court regarding the Request of Haikou Intermediate People's Court for Refusal to Recognize and Enforce the Arbitral Award of the Arbitration Institute of Stockholm Chamber of Commerce, (Civil, 4 Miscellaneous), No. 12 (2001)   463, 465
Reply of Supreme People's Court to the Request for Enforcement of a UK Arbitral Award by Hanjin Shipping Co., Ltd (Civil 4, Miscellaneous), No. 53 (2005)   154
Heavy Metal case: Reply of the Supreme People's Court in the matter regarding the Request by Beijing First Intermediary People's Court to Refuse Enforcement of Arbitral Award [1997] Jing Ta No. 35   465
Reply of Supreme People's Court in the matter regarding the Request by *Hemofarm DD v Jinan Yongning Phamaceutical Co Ltd* (Civil, 4 Miscellaneous), No. 11 (2008)   456–7
Reply of Supreme People's Court in the matter regarding *Hong Kong Heung Chun Cereal & Oil Food, Co Ltd v Anhui Cereal & Oil Food Co Ltd* for Enforcement of a HKIAC Arbitral Award, (Civil, 4 Miscellaneous), No. 9 (2003)   435, 446, 451
Mitsui & Co (Japan) v Hainan Province Textile Industry Corporation (2001) Min Si Ta Zi No. 12, China's Supreme People's Court   465
People's Insurance Company of China, Guangzhou Branch v Guangdong Guanghe Power Co Ltd, China's Supreme People's Court, (Civil 4), (Final), No. 29 (2003)   307
PepsiCo Inc. v Sichuan Pepsi-Cola Beverage Co. Ltd., Chengdu Intermediate People's Court (Civil), First Instance, No. 912 (2005), decision dated 30 April 2008   459
PepsiCo Investment (China) Ltd. v Sichuan Province Yun Lu Industrial Co. Ltd., Chengdu Intermediate People's Court (Civil), First Instance, No. 36 (2006), decision dated 30 April 2008   459
Raw Sugar case: *ED & F Man (HK) Co., Ltd. v China National Sugar & Wines Group Corp.*   465

Revpower Ltd v Shanghai Far East Aerial Technology Import and Export Corporation, (Unreported)   445–6
Reply of Supreme People's Court to the Request of Enforcement of Arbitral Award made in England by Swiss Bangji Co., Ltd (Civil 4, Miscellaneous), No. 47 (2006)   167
Wuxi Woco-Tongyong Rubber Engineering Co Ltd v Zueblin Int'l GmbH, Wuxi Intermediate People's Court (Civil, 3), Final, No. 1 (2004), decision dated 19 July 2006   197, 438, 451–2
Wuxi Woco-Tongyong Rubber Engineering Co Ltd v Zueblin Int'l GmbH, Supreme People's Court (Civil, 4 Miscellaneous), No. 23 (2003), decision dated 8 July (2004)   451–452
Zhong Chen International Engineering Contracting Co. Ltd v Beijing Construction Engineering Group Co. Ltd, 18 May 2001, Beijing Second Intermediate People's Court (Economic and Arbitration), No. 657 (2001), decision dated 18 April 2001   226

England

AIG Capital Partners Inc v Kazakhstan [2005] EWHC 2239; [2006] All ER (Comm) 11   474, 476
Albon (trading as N A Carriage Co) v Naza Motor Trading SDN BHD [2007] 2 All ER 1075   157
Ali Shipping Corporation v Shipyard Trogir [1998] 2 All ER 136   372
Amazonica Peruana SA v Compania Internacional de Seguros del Peru [1988] 1 Lloyd's Rep 116   57–8, 60
Arenson v Gasson Bechman Rutley [1997] AC 405   192
ASM Shipping Ltd v TTMI Ltd [2005] EWHC 2238 (Comm)   289
Associated Electric and Gas Insurance Services Ltd v European Reinsurance Co of Zurich [2000] UKPC 11   374, 375
AT & T Corporation and Lucent Technologies Inc v Saudi Cable Co [2000] EWCA (Civ) 154   283–4
AWG Group Ltd (formerly Anglian Water Plc) v Morrison [2006] EWCA (Civ) 6   284
Bank Mellat v Helliniki Techniki [1984] QB 291   78
Black Clawson International Ltd v Papierwerke Waldhof-Aschaffenberg [1981] 2 Lloyd's Rep 446   59
Bremer Handelsgesellschaft v Westzucker [1981] 2 Lloyd's Rep 130   385
C v D [2008] 1 All ER (Comm) 1001   160
Campbell v Edwards [1976] 1 WLR 403   192
Channel Tunnel Group v Balfour Beauty Ltd [1993] 1 All ER 664   59, 368
Christopher Brown v Genossenschaft Oesterreichischer Waldbesitzer Holzxirtschaftsbetriebe Registrierte GmbH [1954] 1 QB 8; [1953] 2 All ER 1039   468
Conder Structures v Kvaerner Construction Ltd [1999] ADRLJ 305   295
Coppee-Lavalin SA/NA & Voest-Alpine AG v Ken-Ren Chemicals & Fertilisers Ltd [1994] 2 All ER 449   32, 78
Czarnikow v Roth Schmidt [1922] 2 KB 478   242
Dallah Estate and Tourism Holding Company v The Ministry of Religious Affairs, Government of Pakistan [2009] EWCA (Civ) 755   241–2, 412
Department of Economics, Policy & Development of the City of Moscow v Bankers Trust Company and International Industrial Bank [1991] 2 All ER 890   372

Emmott v Michael Wilson & Partners Ltd [2008] EWCA (Civ) 184   372
F P Waring (UK) Ltd v Administracao Geral Do Acucar E Do Alcool EP [1983] 1 Lloyd's Rep 45   259
Falkingham v Victorian Railways Commissioner [1900] AC 542   468
Fiona Trust & Holding Corporation v Privalov [2007] 4 All ER 951   183, 185
Gater Assets Ltd v Nak Naftogaz Ukrainiy [2007] 2 Lloyd's Rep 588   10
Hagop Ardahalian v Unifert International SA [1984] 2 Lloyd's Rep 84   298
Harbour Assurance Co (UK) Ltd v Kansa General International Insurance Co Ltd, [1993] QB 701   156
Hassneh Insurance Co of Israel v Mew [1982] 2 Lloyd's Rep 243   372–3
Helow v Advocate General [2007] CSIH 5   291
Hiscox v Outhwaite [1992] 1 AC 562   386
Hussman (Europe) Ltd v Al Ameen Dev & Trade Co [2000] EWHC 210 (Comm)   127
International Bulk Shipping & Service v Minerals Trading Corp [1996] 1 All ER 1017   445
Ipswich Borough Council v Fisions PLC [1990] Ch 709   258
Jones v Ministry of Interior al Mamlaka Al Arabiya AS Saudiya (Kingdom of Saudi Arabia) [2006] UKHL 26; [2007] 1 AC 270   474
Jones v Sherwood Computer Services Inc [1992] 1 WLR 277   192
Laker Airways Inc v FLS Aerospace Ltd [1999] 2 Lloyd's Rep 45   283
Law Debenture Trust Corp Plc v Elektrim Finance BV [2005] 1 All ER 476   193
London & Leeds Estates v Paribas Ltd (No.2) [1995] EGLR 102   375
Nikko Hotels (UK) Ltd v MEPC (1991) 28 EG 86   192
Peterson Farms Inc v C & M Farming Ltd [2004] EWHC 121 (Comm)   166
Porter v Magill [2002] 2 AC 357   284, 285
Premium Nafta Products Ltd v Fiji Shipping Company Ltd [2007] 2 All ER (Comm) 1053, an appeal from *Fiona Trust & Holding Corporation v Privalov* [2007] 4 All ER 951   32, 159, 183, 185
R v Abdroikov, R v Green and R v Wilkinson [2008] 1 All ER 315   284
R v Bow Street Metropolitan Stipendiary Magistrate, ex parte Pinochet Ugarte (1991) 1 All ER 557   276, 473, 474
R v Gough [1993] AC 646   283
R v Sussex Justices; Ex Parte McCarthy [1924] 1 KB 356   283
Re Catalina (Owners) and Norma M V (Owners) [1936] 61 Lloyd's Rep 360   276
Shashoua v Sharma [2009] EWHC 957 (Comm)   56
Shell Egypt West Manzala GmbH and Shell Egypt West Qantara GmbH v Dana Gas Egypt Ltd (Formerly Centurion Petroleum Corporation) [2009] EWHC 2097 (Comm)   413
Smith Stone and Knight v Birmingham Corporation [1939] 4 All ER 116   166
Soleimany v Soleimany [1999] 3 All ER 847   467
Stargas SPA v Petredec Ltd (The Sargasso) [1994] 1 Lloyds Rep 412   468
Sumukan Ltd v Commonwealth Sectretariat [2007] EWCA (Civ) 1148   289
Tracomin SA v Gibbs Nathaniel (Canada) Ltd [1985] 1 Lloyd's Rep 586   249, 283
Union of India v McDonnell Douglas Corporation [1993] 2 Lloyd's Rep 48   55, 59, 60–1
Westacre Investments Inc v Jugoimport-SPDR Holding Co Ltd, [1999] 3 All ER 864   466–7
Zermalt Holdings SA v Nu-life Upholstery Repairs Ltd [1985] 2 EGLR 14   259

European Court of Justice

Eco Swiss v Benetton [1999] ECR 3055   33, 124

France

American Bureau of Shipping (ABS) v Copropriété Jules Vernes, Cour de cassation (Chambre civile 1), 26 June 2001, (2001) 3 *Revue de l'arbitrage* 529; (2007) XXXII Yearbook Commercial Arbitration 290   227

Braspetro Oil Services (Brasoil) v Management and Implementation of the Great Man-Made River Project (GMRA), Paris Court of Appeal, 1 July 1999, (1999) 4 *Revue de l'arbitrage* 834; (1999) XXIV Yearbook Commercial Arbitration 296   440

Communaute urbaine de Casablanca v Degremont, Cour de cassation (Chambre civile 1), 15 June 1994, (1995) 1 *Revue de l'arbitrage* 88   387

Creighton v Ministère des Finances de l'État du Qatar et a., Cour de cassation (Chambre civile 1), 6 July 2000, (2001) 1 *Revue de l'arbitrage* 114; (2000) XXV Yearbook Commercial Arbitration 458; (2000) *Journal de droit international* (Clunet) 1054   475

Gatoil v National Iranian Oil Company, Paris Court of Appeal, 17 December 1991, (1993) 2 *Revue de l'arbitrage* 281   100

Golshani v Islamic Republic of Iran Cour de cassation (Chambre civile 1), 6 July 2005, (2005) 4 *Revue de l'arbitrage* 993   167

Hilmarton Ltd v Omnium d traitment et de valorisation (OTV), Cour de cassation (Chambre civile 1), 23 March 1994, (1994) 2 *Revue de l'arbitrage* 327; (1995) XX Yearbook Commercial Arbitration 663   69–70, 74, 460

Isover-Saint-Gobain v Dow Chemical France, Paris Court of Appeal, 21 October 1983, (1984) 1 *Revue de l'arbitrage* 98   33

J&P AVAX v Tecnimont SPA, Paris Court of Appeal, 12 February 2009, (2009) 1 *Revue de l'arbitrage* 187   271, 290–1

La Marocaine de Loisirs v France Quick, Cour de cassation (Chambre civile 1), 8 July 2009, (2009) 2 *Revue de l'arbitrage* 360   167

Menicucci v Mahieux, Paris Court of Appeal, 13 December 1975, (1977) 2 *Revue de l'arbitrage* 147; (1976)   163

Merial v Klocke Verpackungs – Service GMBH, Cour de cassation (Chambre civile 1), 3 February 2010, case n° 08-21288, 2010 Bulletin civil   167

Ministère tunisien de l'Equipement v Bec Frères, Paris Court of Appeal 24 February 1994, (1995) 2 *Revue de l'arbitrage* 275; (1997) XXII Yearbook Commercial Arbitration 682   100

Municipalité de Khoms El Mergeb v société Dalico, Cour de Cassation (Chambre civile 1), 20 December 1993, (1994) *Revue de L'Arbitrage* 116   32

PT Putrabali Adyamulia v Rena Holding et al, Cour de cassation (Chambre civile 1), 7 January 1992, (1992) 3 *Revue de l'arbitrage* 470; (1993) XVIII Yearbook Commercial Arbitration 1400   460, 461–7

Siemens AG and BKMI Industrienlagen GmbH v Dutco Construction Company, Cour de Cassation (Chambre civile 1) 7 January 1992 (1992) 3 *Revue de l'arbitrage* 470; (1993) XVIII Yearbook Commercial Arbitration 1400   33, 254–5

SM Bloc'h et fils v SM Delatrae Mockfjaerd, Paris Court of Appeal, 17 January 1984, (1984) 4 *Revue de l'arbitrage* 498   387

SNF SAS v Chambre De Commerce Internationale, Paris Court of Appeal, 22 January 2009, (2009) XXXIV Yearbook Commercial Arbitration 263   269
Société d'études et représentations navales et industrielles (Soerni) v Air Sea Broker, Cour de cassation (Chambre civile 1), 8 July 2009, (2009) 3 *Revue de l'arbitrage* 529   163, 164–70
SA Thalès Air Défense v GIE Euromissile et autres, Paris Court of Appeal, 18 November 2004, (2005) 3 *Revue de l'arbitrage* 751   124

Germany

German Coffee Association (Panamanian buyer) v Papua New Guinean Seller, 28 September 1992, Rechtsprechung kaufmännischer Schiedsgerichte, vol. 5, Section 3B   199

Hong Kong

Agro Industries (P) Ltd v Texuna International Ltd (1993) XVIII YBCA 396   463
Apex Tech Investment Ltd v Chuang's Development (China) Ltd [1996] 2 HKLR 155   455
CCECC (HK) Ltd v Might Foundate Development Ltd [2001] HKCU 916   298
Charteryard Industrial Ltd v Incorporated Owners of Bo Fung Gardens [1998] 4 HKC 171   300
China Nanhai Oil Joint Service Corp v Gee Tai Holdings Co Ltd (1995) XX YBCA 671   449, 458
China Ocean Shipping Co v Mitrans Shipping Co Ltd [1995] HKCA 604   166
Daily Win Engineering Ltd v The Incorporated Owners of Greenwood Terrace [2001] HKC 1252   220
Deacons v White & Case Ltd Liability Partnership [2004] 1 HKLRD 291   286
FG Hemisphere Associates v Democratic Republic of Congo [2010] 2 HKC 487   474
Gay Construction Pty Ltd v Caledonian Techmore (Building) Ltd [1994] 2 HKC 562   153–4
Getwick Engineers Ltd v Pilecon Engineering HCA 558/2002 (unreported)   183
Gingerbread Investments Ltd v Wing Hong Interior Contracting Ltd HCCT 14/2008   298, 396–7
Grandeur Electrical Co Ltd v Cheung Kee Fung Cheung Construction Co Ltd [2006] HKCU 1245   190
H Smal Ltd v Goldroyce Garment Ltd [1994] 2 HKC 526   149
Hebei Import & Export Corp v Polytek Engineering Co Ltd [1999] 1 HKLRD 665   10, 414, 426, 451, 462, 463–4, 467
Jiangxi Prov'l Metal & Minerals Imp & Exp Corp v Sulanser Co [1995] 2 HKC 373   155
Jung Science Information Technology Co Ltd v ZTE Corporation HCCT 14/2008; [2008] HKCU 1127   284, 286, 287–8, 381
Karaha Bodas Co Llc v Perusahaan Pertambangan Minyak Dan Gas Bumi Negara (Pertamina case) [2003] 380 HKCU 1   60, 62–3, 70, 77–8, 418, 460
Kin Yat Industrial Co Ltd v MGA Entertainment (HK) Ltd [2007] HKCU 435   221
Lee Hong Dispensary Superstore Co Ltd v Pharmacy and Poisons Board [2007] HKCU 379   285–6
Leviathan Shipping Co v Sky Sailing Overseas Co [1998] 4 HKC 347   368
Mayers v Dlugash [1994] 1 HKC 755   192

Milibow Assets Ltd v Dooyan Hong Kong Ltd [2001] HKCU 767   192
Newmark Capital Corporation Ltd v Coffee Partners Ltd [2007] HKCU 241   183–4
Ng Yat Chi v Max Share Ltd [2005] HKCU 69   286
Ocean Park Corporation v Proud Sky Co Ltd [2007] HKCU 1974   221
Pacific Crown Engineering Ltd v Hyundai Engineering and Construction Co Ltd [2003] 3 HKC 659   221
Paklito Investment Ltd v Klockner East Asia Ltd [1993] 2 HKLR 39   414, 455
Parkson Holdings Ltd v Vincent Lai & Partners (HK) Ltd [2008] HKCU 1985   153
PCC Limited v Interactive Communications Service Ltd [2003] 3 HKC 659   221
PCCW Global Ltd v Interactive Communications Service Ltd [2007] 1 HKC 327   220–1
Private Company Triple V Inc v Star (Universal) Co Ltd, Sky Jade Enterprises Group Ltd, [1995] HKCU 27   165
Sam Ming City Forestry Economic Co v Lam Pun Hung Trading as Henry Company, Unreported decision, Court of Appeal, 27 June 2001, CLOUT Case 448   457
Société Nationale d'Operations Petrolières de la Cote d'Ivoire Holding v Keen Lloyd Resources Ltd [2004] 3 HKC 452   460
Suen Wah Ling t/a Kong Luen Construction Engineering Co v China Harbour Engineering Co (Group) [2008] HKCU 570   286
Tai Hing Cotton Mill Limited v Glencore Grain Rotterdam, [1996] 1 HKC 363   181
The Incorporated Owners of Sincere House v Sincere Company Ltd [2005] HKLT 18; [2007] 2 HKC 424   220
The Owners of and/or other Persons entitled to sue in respect of cargo lately laden on board the ship or vessel Yaoki v The Owners of and/or Demise Charterers of the ship or vessel & Quotyaoki & Quot and the ships or vessels listed in schedule hereto [2006] HKCU 765   154
Tommy Cp Sze & Co v Li & Fung (Trading) Ltd [2003] 1 HKC 41   183, 190
Tsang Yuk Ching T/A Tsang Ching Kee Eng Co v Fu Shing Rush Door Joint Venture Co Ltd [2003] HKCU 1072   153
Werner A Bock KG v N's Co Ltd [1978] HKLR 281   458
Winbond Electronics (HK) Ltd v Achieva Components China Ltd [2007] HKCU 1514   149
Xu Yi Hong v Chen Ming Han [2006] HKCU 1663   183

ICC International Court of Arbitration

Case No. 1472, in (1973) *Revue de l'Arbitrage* 122   131
Case No. 4132 in S Jarvin, Y Derains and JJ Arnaldez, *Collection of ICC Arbitral Awards 1974–1985,* ICC Publishing, 1990, p. 164, at p. 167   122
Case No. 4367, *Yearbook of Commercial Arbitration,* 1986, p. 134   212
Case No. 5721, in S Jarvin, Y Derains and JJ Arnaldez, *Collection of ICC Arbitral Awards 1986–1990,* ICC Publishing, 1994, p. 401, at p. 404   130
Case No. 6320, in S Jarvin, Y Derains and JJ Arnaldez, *Collection of ICC Arbitral Awards 1991–1995,* ICC Publishing, 1997, p. 577, at p. 584   122
Case No. 6379, in S Jarvin, Y Derains and JJ Arnaldez, *Collection of ICC Arbitral Awards 1991–1995,* ICC Publishing, 1997, p. 134, at p. 142   122
Case No. 6515, in S Jarvin, Y Derains and JJ Arnaldez, *Collection of ICC Arbitral Awards 1996–2000,* ICC Publishing, 2003, p. 241, at p. 243   130–1
Case No. 6516, in S Jarvin, Y Derains and JJ Arnaldez, *Collection of ICC Arbitral Awards 1996–2000,* ICC Publishing, 2003, p. 241, at p. 243   130–1

Case No. 6840, *Collection of ICC Arbitral Awards*, vol. III., p. 470   213
Case No. 7074, in S Jarvin, Y Derains and JJ Arnaldez, *Collection of ICC Arbitral Awards 1996–2000*, ICC Publishing, 2003, p. 32, at p. 51   122
Case No. 9479, (2001) 12(2) *ICC International Court of Arbitration Bulletin* 67, at p. 68   131

India

Ace Pipeline Contracts Private Ltd v Bharat Petroleum Corporation Ltd (2007) 5 SCC 304   92, 252–3, 255
Agri Gold Exims Ltd v Sri Lakshmi Knits and Wovens, Civil Appeal No. 326 of 2007, 2007 (1) *Arb LR* 235   225
Badat & Co Bombay v East India Trading Co AIR 1964 SC 538   469
Bhatia International v Bulk Trading SA (2002) 4 SCC 105   77, 225, 366, 418
Citation Infowares Ltd v Equinox Corporation, Arbitration Application No. 8 of 2008   252
Compagnie de Saint-Gobain – Pont à Mousson v Fertilizer Corporation of India, High Court of Delhi, (1977) II YBCA 245   440
Daelim Industrial Co v Numaligarh Refinery Ltd, High Court of Gauhati, Arbitration Appeal No. 1 of 2002 (24 August 2006)   423
Firm Ashok Traders v Gurumukh Das Saluja (2004) 3 SCC 155   365
Fuerst Day Lawson v Jindal Exports Ltd (2001) 6 SCC 356   470
Indian Oil Corp Ltd v Langkawi Shipping Ltd, High Court of Bombay, (2004) *Arb LR* 568   423
M/s V/O Tractoroexport Moscow v M/s Tarapore and Co (*Tractoroexport* case) [1971] AIR 1   85–6
McDermott International Inc v Burn Standard Co Ltd (2006) 11 SCC 181   423
Max India Ltd v General Binding Corporation, Dehli High Court, 6 May 2009   40, 225, 366, 367
Municipal Corporation of Delhi v Jagan Nath Ashok Kumar (1987) 4 SCC 497   338
N Radhakrishnan v Maestro Engineers (2009) Supreme Court, No. 7019   187
National Thermal Power Corporation v The Singer Company, (1993) XVIII YBCA 403   438
Oil and Natural Gas v Saw Pipes Ltd (2003) 5 SCC 705   77, 420, 422–3, 465
Renusagar Power Co Ltd v General Electric Corp [1994] AIR 860 1994 SCC Supl. (1) 644; (1995) XX YBCA 681   462–3
RM Investments Trading Co Pty Ltd v Boeing Co (1994) 5 SCC 541   442
SBP v Patel Engineering (2005) 8 SCC 618   33, 224–5, 236, 238
Shin-Etsu Chemical Co Ltd v Aksh Optifibre Ltd (2005) 7 SCC 234   160, 222, 223, 224, 225
Sime Darby Engineering SDN BHD v Engineers India Ltd, Arbitration Petition 3/2009   247, 248
Smita Conductors Ltd v Euro Alloys Ltd, Indian Supreme Court, (2002) XXVII YBCA 482   462
Sundaram Finance Ltd v NEPC India Ltd (1999) 2 SCC 479   365
Union of India v Popular Construction Company (2001) 8 SCC 470   425
Union of India v Tecco Trichy Engineers & Contractors (2005) 4 SCC 239   425
Uttam Wires & Machines Pty Ltd v State of Rajasthan 1990 AIR (Del) 72   192
Venture Global Engineering v Satyam Computer Services Ltd (2008) SCALE 214 (2008) 4 SCC 190; [2008] INSC 40   77, 225, 366, 418, 423

Indonesia

Ascom Electro AG v PT Manggala Mandri Sentosa, Supreme Court, 22 September 1993   401
ED & F Man (Sugar) Ltd v Yani Haryanto, in (2002) 68 Arbitrator 106   465
Himpurna v Indonesia Doc A in 15 Mealey's Int'l Arb Rep., Jan 2000   41
Navigation Maritime Bulgare v PT Nizwar (1986) XI YBCA 508   432

International Centre for the Settlement of Investment Disputes (ICSID)

Aguas del Tunari SA v Bolivia, Decision on Jurisdiction, 21 October 2005, (2005) 20 ICSID Rev-FILJ 450   486
Amco Asia v Indonesia, ICSID Case No. ARB/81/1, 24 ILM 365 (1985)   36, 374, 479, 502
Asian Agricultural Products Ltd v Sri Lanka, Award, 27 June 1990, ICSID Reports 245   487, 496
Autopista Concesionada de Venezuela CA v Venezuela, Award, 23 September 2003, 10 ICSID Reports 309   501
Bayindir Insaat Ticaret Ve Sanayi AS v Pakistan, Decision on Jurisdiction, 14 November 2005   498
CME Czech Republic BV v Czech Republic, Partial Award, 13 September 2001, 9 ICSID Reports 121   479, 496
CMS Gas Transmission Co v Argentine Republic, Award, 12 May 2005, (2005) 44 ILM 1205   351, 490
Compañia del Desarrollo de Santa Elena SA v Costa Rica, Award, 17 February 2000, 5 ICSID Reports 153   501
Fedax N V v Venezuela, Decision on Jurisdiction, 11 July 1997, 5 ICSID Reports 186, (1998) 37 ILM 1378   485
Feldman v Mexico, Award, 16 December 2002, 7 ICSID Reports 341   497
Generation Ukraine Inc v Ukraine, 16 September 2003, 10 ICSID Reports 240   482, 488, 501
Gruslin v Malaysia, 27 November 2000, 5 ICSID Reports 484   485
Holiday Inns SA v Morocco, ICSID Case No. ARB/72/1   482
Hrvatska Elektropivreda v Slovenia, ICSID Case No. ARB/05/24, Tribunal's Ruling of 6 May 2008   275
Klöckner Industrie-Anlagen GmbH v Cameroon, ICSID Case No. ARB/81/2   502
Lauder v Czech Republic, Final Award, 3 September 2001, 9 ICSID Reports 66   490, 497
LG & E Energy Corp v Argentina, Decision on Liability, 3 October 2006, (2007) 46 ILM 36   487, 490
Loewen Group v United States, Decision on Hearing of Respondent's Objection to Competence and Jurisdiction, 5 January 2001   374, 493
Maffezini v Spain, Decision on Jurisdiction, 25 January 2000, 5 ICSID Rep 387   480, 498
Malaysian Historical Salvors Sdn Bhd v Malaysia, Decision on the Application for Annulment, 16 April 2009   484
Metalclad Corp v United Mexican States, Award of 20 August 2000, 5 ICSID Reports 209   374, 494–5

MTD Equity Sdn Bhd & MTD Chile SA v Chile, Award, 25 May 2004, 44 ILM 91   480, 499
Petrobart Ltd v Kyrgyz Republic, Award II, 29 March 2005, 13 ICSID Reports 387   501
Plama Consortium Ltd v Bulgaria, Decision on Jurisdiction, 8 February 2005, 44 ILM 721   498
Saipem SpA v Bangladesh, Decision on Jurisdiction, 21 March 2007   278, 350, 472–3
Salini v Morocco, Decision on Jurisdiction, 23 July 2001, 6 ICSID Reports 400   484
SD Myers Inc v Canada, Partial Award, 13 November 2000, 8 ICSID Reports 18, 40 ILM 1408   497
Société Générale de Surveillance SA v Pakistan (SGS v Pakistan), 6 August 2003, 8 ICSID Reports 406   482, 499
Société Générale de Surveillance SA v Philippines (SGS v Philippines), 29 January 2004, 8 ICSID Reports 518   499
Soufraki v United Arab Emirates, Award on Jurisdiction, 7 July 2004, 12 ICSID Reports 158   485
Southern Pacific Properties (Middle East) Ltd v Egypt, Decision on Jurisdiction, 3 ICSID Reports 112   487
Tecnicas Medioambientales Tecmed SA v Mexico, Award, 29 May 2003, 10 ICSID Reports 133, (2004) 43 ILM 133   495–6
Tokois Tokelės v Ukraine, Decision on Jurisdiction, 29 April 2004, 20 ICSID Rev-FILJ 205   403, 486
TSA Spectrum de Argentina SA v Argentina, Decision on Jurisdiction, 21 October 2005, (2005) 20 ICSID Rev-FILJ 450   486

International Court of Justice

Barcelona Traction, Light and Power Company Ltd (1970) ICJ Reports 3   491

Iran-US Claims Tribunal

Dadras International v Islamic Republic of Iran (1995) 31 Iran-US CTR 127   314–15, 338
Phillips Petroleum Co Iran v Iran (1989) 21 Iran-US CTR 79   500
R J Reynolds Tobacco Co v Iran (1984) 7 Iran-US CTR 181   501
Rockwell International Systems Inc v Government of the Islamic Republic of Iran (1989) 23 Iran-US CTR 150   328
Sedco Inc v National Iranian Oil Co (1987) 16 Iran-US CTR 282   408, 409
W Jack Buckamier v Islamic Republic of Iran (1992) 28 Iran-US CTR 53   339
William J Levitt v Islamic Republic of Iran 27 Iran-US CTR 164   345

Japan

KK Descente v Adidas-Salomon AG, 26 January 2004, Tokyo District Court, 1847 Hanrei Jiho 123   421
Undisclosed Plaintiff v Cosmo Futures Co Ltd, 16 May 2003 – Sapporo District Court 199

Xinan Co of China Technology Export-Import Co v Kyoei Boeki KK, 27 January 1994, 853 Hanrei Taimuzu 266, (1995) XX YBCA 742   452
Zhe-jiang Provincial Light Industrial Products Import & Export Corp v Takeyari K K, (1997) XXII YBCA 744   437
Zhong Guo Hua Gong Kian Sh Quig Dao Gong v Color Chemical Industry KK, 25 August 1999, Dist. Ct Yokohama, (2002) XXVII YBCA 515   462

Korea (Republic of)

Adviso NV v Korea Overseas Construction Corporation, 14 February 1995, Supreme Court, (1996) XXI YBCA 612   462, 463
GKN case, 10 April 1990, Korean Supreme Court, 89 Daka 20252   454

Malaysia

Aras Jalinan Sdn Bhd v TIPCO Asphalt Company Ltd, ILO Case 15609   367
Bauer (M) Sdn Bhd v Daewoo Corp [1999] 4 MLJ 545   152, 208
Bina Puri Sdn Bhd v EP Engineering Sdn Bhd [2008] 3 MLJ 564   152
Bintulu Development Authority v Pilecon Engineering Bhd [2007] 2 CLJ 422   167, 168
Boustead Trading (1985) Sdn Bhd v Arab Malaysia Merchant Bank Bhd [1995] 3 MLJ 331   168
Darshan Singh v Farid Kamal Hussain [2005] 3 MLJ 502   286
Dato' Tan Heng Chew v Tan Kim Hor [2006] MLJU 11   286
Ganda Edible Oils Sdn Bhd v Transgrain Bv [1988] 1 MLJ 428   130
Government of India v Cairn Energy India Pty Ltd, [2003] 1 MLJ 348   464
Harris Adacom Corporation v Perkom Sdn Bhd (1993) 3 MLJ 506   169, 466
Jan De Nul NV v Inai Kiara Sdn Bhd [2006] 3 CLJ 46   113, 183
Lai Sing Kejuruteraan (M) Sdn Bhd v Ten Engineering Sdn Bhd [1997] MLJU 197   168
Majlis Peguam Malaysia v Raja Segaran [2005] 1 MLJ 15   286
Malaysia v Zublin Muhibbah Joint Venture [1990] 3 MLJ 125   324–5
Perbadanan Kemajua Negeri Perak v Asean Security Paper Mill Sdn Bhd [1991] 3 MLJ 309   168
Seraya Sdn Bhd v Government of Sarawak [2007] MLJU 0595   286
Sineo Enterprise Sdn Bhd v Jayarena Construction Sdn Bhd [2005] MLJU 216 (High Court)   300–1
Sri Lanka Cricket v World Sports Nimbus Pte Ltd, [2006] 3 MLJ 117   434
Tan Kim Hor v Tan Chong & Motor Co Sdn Bhd [2003] 2 MLJ 278   286
Usahasama SPNB-LTAT Sdn Bhd v Borneo Syndegy (M) Sdn Bhd [2009] MLJU 0001   152

Netherlands

Bursa Büyüksehir Belediyesi v Güris Insaat VE Mühendislik AS, 2008, Netherlands Court Reports [NJ 2009, 6]   402
Himpurna v Indonesia, Doc A in 15 *Mealey's Int'l Arb Rep.*, Jan 2000   41
Patuha v Indonesia, Doc B in 15 *Mealey's Int'l Arb Rep.*, Jan 2000   41
Republic of Indonesia v Himpurna California Energy Ltd (Bermuda) September 1999, (1999) 4 *ASA Bulletin* 583   41

New Zealand

Amaltal Corp Ltd v Maruha (M3) Corp Ltd [2004] 2 NZLR 614   463
Auckland Casino Ltd v Casino Control Authority [1995] 1 NZLR 142   284
Banks v Grey District Council [2004] 2 NZLR 19   292
Bowport Ltd v Alloy Yachts International [2004] 1 NZLR 361   183
Casata Ltd v General Distributors Ltd [2006] 2 NZLR 721   404
CBI NZ Ltd v Badger Chiyoda [1989] 2 NZLR 669   58, 60
Downer-Hill Joint Venture v Government of Fiji [2005] 1 NZLR 554   464–5
Gold and Resource Developments (NZ) Ltd v Doug Hood Ltd [2000] 3 NZLR 318   258
Grey District Council v Banks [2003] NZAR 487   279, 296
Lindow v Barton McGill Marine Ltd (2002) 16 PRNZ 796   370
Methanex Motunui Ltd v Spellman [2004] 1 NZLR 95   33, 93, 170, 259, 416, 421
Mount Cook (Northland) Ltd v Swedish Motors Ltd [1986] 1 NZLR 720   183
Muir v Commissioner of Inland Revenue [2007] 3 NZLR 495   284–5
Pickens v Templeton [1994] 2 NZLR 718   269
Reeves v One World Challenge [2006] 2 NZLR 184   463
Sensation Yachts Ltd v Darby Maritime Ltd, Auckland High Court, 16 May 2005   368
Todd Energy Ltd v Kiwi Power (1995) Ltd, High Court, Wellington, CP 46/01, 29 October 2001   180
Tolmarsh Development Ltd v Stobbs [1990] LVC 835   292

Pakistan

Hitachi Ltd v Mitsui & Co and Rupali Polyester (2000) XXV YBCA 486, 10 June 1998   418

Permanent Court of International Justice (PCIJ)

Chorzow Factory (Germany) v Poland, Merits, (1928) PCIJ Series A, no. 17, p. 47   500–1

Philippines

Heritage Park v Construction Industry, CA-G.R SP No. 86342, 9 February 2005   169
Jorge Gonzales v Climax Mining Ltd, G.R. No. 161957/ G.R. No. 167994 [2007] PHSC 6   145
Luzon Hydro Corporation v Baybay and Transfield Philippines Inc (2007) XXXII YBCA 456   406, 418, 420, 466
National Union Fire Insurance Company of Pittsburgh Pa/American International Underwriter (Phil) Inc v Stolt-Niesen Philippines Inc and Court of Appeals, 184 SCRA 682, G.R. No. 87958, 26 April 1990   153
Transfield Philippines Inc v Luzon Hydro Corporation and Australia and New Zealand Banking Group Ltd and Security Bank Corporation, GR No. 146717, 19 May 2006   213–14

Singapore

ABC Co v Owners of the Ship or Vessel 'Q', Admiralty in Rem no. 251 of 1995, High Court of Singapore, 9 May 1996   203–5
ABC Co v XYZ Co Ltd [2003] SGHC 107   420, 425
Aloe Vera of America Inc v Asianic Food (S) Pte Ltd [2006] 3 SLR 174   167, 187, 415, 447, 451, 461
Anwar Siraj v Ting Kang Chung [2003] 2 SLR 287   298
Black and Veatch Singapore Pty Ltd v Jurong Engineering Ltd [2004] SGCA 30   311
Bovis Lend Lease Pte Ltd v Jay-Tech Marine & Project Pte Ltd [2005] SGHC 91   196
Builders Federal (Hong Kong) Ltd and Joseph Gartner & Co v Turner (East Asia) Pte Ltd in (1988) 2 Malaysian Law Journal 280; and (1988) 5(3) Journal of International Arbitration 139   324
Concordia Agritrading Pte Ltd v Cornelder Hoogewerff (Singapore) Pte Ltd [2001] 1 SLR 222   152
Dalian Hualiang Enterprise Group Co Ltd v Louis Dreyfus Asia Pte Ltd [2005] 4 SLR 646   181, 221–2
Dermajaya Properties Sdn Bhd v Premium Properties Sdn Bhd [2002] 2 SLR 164   60, 64, 65, 308
Dongwoo Mann and Hummel Co Ltd v Mann and Hummel GmbH [2008] SGHC 67   420
Evergreat Construction Co Pte Ltd v Presscrete Engineering Pte Ltd [2006] 1 SLR 634   192
Front Carriers Ltd v Atlantic & Orient Shipping Corp [2006] 3 SLR 854   367
Government of the Republic of the Philippines v Philippine International Air Terminals Co Inc [2007] 1 SLR 278   420
Hainan Machinery Import & Export Corporation v Donald & McArthy Pte Ltd [1996] 1 SLR 34; (1997) XXII YBCA 771   10, 331–2
Insigma Technology Co Ltd v Alstom Technology Ltd [2009] 1 SLR 23   196, 199, 200–1, 241
Jevaretnam v Lee Kuan Yew [1992] 2 SLR 310   285
John Holland Pty Ltd v Toyo Engineering Corp [2001] 2 SLR 262   60, 64
Jurong Engineering Ltd v Black & Veatch Singapore Pte Ltd [2004] 1 SLR 333   184
Koh Bros Building and Civil Engineering Contractor Pte Ltd v Scotts Development (Saraca) Pte Ltd [2002] 4 SLR 748   294
Louis Dreyfus v Bonarich International (Group) Ltd [2005] 4 SLR 646   181, 214
Luzon Hydro Corp v Transfield Philippines [2004] 4 SLR 705   352, 388, 390–1
Mitsui Engineering & Shipbuilding Co Ltd v Easton Graham Rush [2004] 2 SLR 14   296
Myanma Yaung Chi Oo Co Ltd v Win Win Nu [2003] SGHC 124   373
NCC International AB v Land Transport Authority of Singapore [2008] SGHC 186   247, 248
Newspeed International Ltd v Citus Trading Pte Ltd [2003] 3 SLR 1   414–15
Northern Elevator Manufacturing Sdn Bhd v United Engineers (Singapore) Pte Ltd (No.2) [2004] 2 SLR 494; [2004] SGCA 11   413
Philippines v Philippine International Air Terminals Co Inc [2007] 1 SLR 278   80–1, 161–3
PT Asuransi Jasa Indonesia (Persero) v Dexia Bank SA [2007] 1 SLR 597   23, 209–11, 237, 238, 393, 395, 412, 420, 462

PT Garuda Indonesia v Birgen Air [2002] 1 SLR 393   33, 55, 56, 57–8, 59, 60, 83–4
Re Shankar Alan S/O Anant Kulkarni [2006] SGHC 194   285
Sabah Shipyard (Pakistan) Ltd v Government of the Islamic Republic of Pakistan [2004] 3 SLR 184; [2004] SGHC 109; [2004] 1 CLC 149   206
Soh Beng Tee v Fairmount [2007] SGCA 28   453–4
Swift-Fortune Ltd v Magnifica Marine SA [2006] SGCA 42; [2006] 2 SLR 323 (High Court)   367
Tang Boon Jek Jeffrey v Tan Poh Leng Stanley [2001] 3 SLR 237   391–2, 393
Tang Kin Hwa v TCM Practitioners Board [2005] 4 SLR 604   285
Turner v Builders Federal [1988] 1 SLR 532   276, 285, 288
VV v VW [2008] SGHC 11   467
Win Line (UK) Ltd v Masterpart (Singapore) Pte Ltd [2000] 2 SLR 98   167
WSG Nimbus Pte Ltd v Board of Control for Cricket in Sri Lanka [2002] 3 SLR 603   190
Yee Hong Pte Ltd v Powen Electrical Engineering Pte Ltd [2005] 3 SLR 512   295–6

Sweden

Bulgarian Foreign Trade Bank Ltd v A1 Trade Finance Inc, Swedish Supreme Court, 27 October 2000, in (2000) 15 *Int'l Arb Rep* B-1   374
Czech Republic v CME Czech Republic BV, Svea Court of Appeal, Sweden, Case No. T 8735–01, 9 ICSID Reports 439   382, 492

Switzerland

A Ltd v B SA, 10 June 2003 (unreported Swiss Supreme Court decision)   300
Cañas v ATP Tour, ATF 133 III 235, 240/241/242 (2007)   415
Fomento de Construcciones y Contratas SA v Colon Container Terminals SA, (2001) ATF 127 III 279   213
Foundation M v Bank X, Swiss Federal Tribunal, 29 April 1996, ATF 122 III 139, 1996; ASA News Bull 527   227

United States

Baker Marine Ltd v Chevron Ltd, 191 F 3d 194, 197 n. 3 (2d Cir. 1999)   70
Bergesen v Joseph Muller Corp, 710 F 2d 928 (2d Cir. 1983)   439
Brandeis Intsel Ltd ve Calabrian Chemicals Corp, 656 Fed Sup 160 (SDNY 1987)   420
Buckeye Check Cashing Inc v Cardegna, 546 US (2006)   227
Chromalloy Aeroservices Inc (US) v The Arab Republic of Egypt, 939 F Supp 907 (DDC 1996)   69–70, 74, 78, 460
Coutinho Caro & Co USA Inc v Marcus Trading Inc, (2000) WL 435566   447
Europcar Italia SpA v Maeillano Tours Inc, 156 F 3d 310 (2d Cir. 1998)   467–8
Gulf Petro Trading Co v Nigerian National Petroleum Corp, 512 F 3d 742 (5th Cir. 2008)   440
Hall Street Associates, LLC v Mattel Inc, 128 S.Ct. 1396 (2008)   24, 32, 94, 420–1
Hasbro Inc v Catalyst USA Inc, 367 F 3d 689 (2004)   387
Hobart v Drogan 35 US 108 (1836)   5

Jacada (Europe) Ltd v International Marketing Strategies Inc, 401 F 3d 701 (6th Cir. 2005)   **436, 439**
M & C Corp v Erwin Behr GMBH & Co KG, 87 F 3d 844 (6th Cir. 1996)   **420**
Mitsubishi Motors v Soler Chrysler-Plymouth, [1985] 105 Supreme Court Reports 3346   **32, 120, 121–2**
Monegasque de Reassurances SAM v Nak Naftogaz of Ukraine, 311 F 3d 488 (2d Cir. 2002)   **417–24**
Parsons & Whittemore Overseas Co Inc v Societe General de l'Industrie du Papier, 508 F 2d 969 (2nd Cir. 1974)   **462**
Publicis Communication and Publicis SA v True North Communications Inc, 206 F 3d 725 (7th Cir. 2000)   **393, 440**
Sandvik AB v Advent Int. Corp, 220 F 3d 99 (3d Cir. 2000)   **218, 227**
Southern Seas Nav Ltd v Petroleos Mexicanos of Mexico City, 606 F Supp 692 (SDNY 1985)   **398, 440**
Termorio SA v Eltranta SP, 487 F 3d 928 (DC Cir. 2007)   **70**
Thomson-CSF SA v American Arbitration Association and Evans & Sutherland Computer Corporation, 64 F 3d 773 (2d Cir 1995)   **165**
United States v Panhandle Eastern Corporation, 118 FRD 346 (D Del 1988)   **374**
Weizmann Institute of Science v Neschis, 229 F Supp 2d 234 (SDNY 2002)   **468**
Wilko v Swan, 346 US 427 (1953)   **420**

Vietnam

Tyco Services Singapore Pty Ltd v Leighton Contractors (VN) Ltd, Judgment No. 02/PTDS, 21 January 2003, Court of Appeal of the Supreme People's Court of Vietnam, Ho Chi Minh City   **442, 465–6**

Table of Statutes

Australia – Commonwealth
   Carriage of Goods by Sea Act 1991
      188
   Foreign States Immunities Act 1985
      475
   Insurance Contracts Act 1984   188
   International Arbitration Act 1974
      30, 64, 65, 174, 181, 219, 252,
      269, 336, 397, 404, 432, 434, 436,
      441, 444, 448
   Trade Practices Act 1974   121, 171
Australia – State/Territory Uniform Legislation
   Commercial Arbitration Acts   140, 218, 225, 336
Australia – New South Wales
   Commercial Arbitration Act   56, 140
Australia – Victoria
   Commercial Arbitration Act   225, 259–60
   Domestic Building Contracts Act 1995   191

Bangladesh
   Arbitration Act 2001   139

Brunei
   Arbitration Act 2001   517

Canada
   Quebec Code of Civil Procedure   142

China (Mainland)
   Arbitration Law of the PRC 1994
      101–2, 139, 156, 161, 187, 194, 197, 212, 225–7, 231, 248, 262, 360, 420, 425, 432–3
   Arrangement Concerning Mutual Enforcement of Arbitral Awards between the Mainland [China] and the Hong Kong Special Administrative Region (MOU)   435, 465
   Civil Procedure Law   417–24
   Criminal Law   470
   Interpretation of Supreme People's Court on Certain Issues Relating to the Application of the Arbitration Law of the PRC of 23 August 2006   150, 156, 161, 169, 183, 197, 447
   Notice of the Supreme People's Court on Handling by People's Courts of Relevant Issues Pertaining to Foreign-Related Arbitration and Foreign Arbitration of 28 August 1995   517
   Notice of the Supreme People's Court on Matters Relating to Setting Aside of Foreign-Related Arbitral Awards by the People's Courts of 23 April 1998   517
   Regulations of the Supreme People's Court concerning Issues in Relation to Enforcement by the People's Court   443–4
   Supreme People's Court Notice on the Implementation of China's Accession to the Convention on the Recognition and Enforcement of Foreign Arbitral Awards of 10 April 1987   449, 517

Denmark
    Arbitration Act   127

England
    Arbitration Act 1996   23, 107, 157,
        218, 225, 241, 260, 295, 391, 413
    State Immunity Act 1978   476

Hong Kong (China)
    Arbitration (Appointment of
        Arbitrators and Umpires) Rules
        (Cap 341B)   517
    Arbitration Ordinance (Cap 341)
        62, 77, 126, 149, 150, 174, 252,
        269, 314–15, 316, 335, 342, 345,
        365, 368, 370, 405
    Arbitration (Parties to New York
        Convention) Order (Cap 341A)
        517

India
    Aircraft Act   188
    Arbitration Act 1940   61
    Arbitration and Conciliation Act
        1996   8, 77, 102, 103, 134, 188,
        209, 213, 214, 222–5, 235, 236–7,
        238, 252, 335, 348, 365–7, 418,
        422, 423, 425, 426, 434, 444, 445,
        469
    Atomic Energy Act   188
    Carriage by Air Act   188
    Foreign Awards (Recognition and
        Enforcement) Act 1961
        433
    Specific Relief Act   188

Indonesia
    Arbitration and Dispute Resolution
        Act (No 30 of 1999)   104,
        139, 187–8, 257, 383, 423,
        443
    Code of Civil Procedure   63

Japan
    Arbitration Law (Law No 138 of
        2003)   76, 105, 134, 187,
        207–8, 209, 219, 252, 270, 302,
        443
    Code of Civil Procedure   342

Korea (Republic of)
    Arbitration Act (amended by Act No
        6626 of 20 January 2002)   134,
        188, 343, 390, 392, 425–6, 432,
        453, 469
    Civil Enforcement Act   419–21
    Civil Procedure Act   342, 469

Malaysia
    Arbitration Act 1952   78
    Arbitration Act 2005   75, 98, 101,
        102, 132, 139, 174–5, 180, 219,
        251, 269, 360, 368, 394, 400–1,
        407, 434
    New York Convention on the
        Recognition and Enforcement of
        Foreign Arbitral Awards Act 1985
        434

Netherlands
    Arbitration Act   127

New Zealand
    Arbitration Act 1996   38, 170, 174,
        180, 182, 225, 235, 237–8, 252,
        269, 368, 373, 394, 413, 421, 463
    Arbitration Amendment Act 2007
        38, 147, 149, 370, 375–6
    Fair Trading Act 1986   171
    Insurance Law Reform Act 1977
        188

North Korea
    External Economic Arbitration Law
        1994   257, 517

Pakistan
    Presidential Ordinance   433–4

Philippines
    Alternative Dispute Resolution Act
        2004   2, 187, 214, 252, 394, 433
    Republic Act No 876 (The
        Arbitration Law)   213, 214
    Republic Act No. 9285   447

Singapore
    Civil Law Act   367
    International Arbitration Act 2002
        (Cap 143A)   64–5, 174–5, 181,

219, 235, 251, 269, 295, 296, 308,
348, 360, 363, 365, 367, 391–2,
394, 395, 427, 444, 466
State Immunity Act 1979   474

Sri Lanka
Arbitration Act (No 11 of 1995)
104, 129, 187, 190–1, 218, 222

Switzerland
Private International Law Act 1987
105, 106, 209, 415

Taiwan
Arbitration Law (2002)   258, 517

Thailand
Arbitration Act BE 2545 (2002)
360, 444, 517

United States
Federal Arbitration Act   94, 420–1,
439

Vietnam
Civil Procedure Code   465
Ordinance on Commercial
Arbitration (No
08/2003/PL-UBTVQH of 25
February 2003)   139, 360,
405

Introduction to international arbitration and its place in the Asia-Pacific

1 Introduction and definition of arbitration

Over the past 20–30 years, international arbitration has become by far the most popular mechanism for resolving international commercial disputes in the Asia-Pacific and globally. International arbitration is exceptionally effective because of its flexibility, neutrality, finality, and enforceability. It is flexible because parties are accorded enormous freedom to choose the manner in which their dispute is decided. They can, for example, agree on the seat of arbitration, the identity of the arbitrators, the applicable law, the number of written briefs (if any), the number of oral hearings or meetings (if any), and whether there will be expert or factual evidence. The neutrality of arbitration principally relates to separating the dispute resolution mechanism from any of the parties' countries and from any political interference. Parties can, for example, select a seat of arbitration, applicable law and arbitrators from a country that is neutral with respect to all parties. Arbitration is final because domestic legal systems generally do not permit any appeal from arbitrators' awards, and allow only very limited review of such awards on procedural grounds. Arbitration is enforceable thanks to its recognition in virtually all domestic laws and thanks to several international treaties. Arbitral awards may be enforced using the enforcement mechanisms of state courts in most countries throughout the world. As we will see, the study of international arbitration is exciting, innovative, creative, and yet sometimes complex.

In this chapter, after briefly defining arbitration in the introduction, we set out its historical evolution in Section 2. Section 3 summarises the characteristics of international arbitration as we know it today, including the sources of international arbitration law, thus introducing the concepts which are addressed in

1.1

1.2

1

much greater detail throughout the book. Finally, Section 4 explains the role, status and culture of international arbitration in the Asia-Pacific region.[1]

1.3 A definition of arbitration can be found in any dictionary. A straightforward and accurate definition is that provided in *Black's Law Dictionary* which defines arbitration as '[a] method of dispute resolution involving one or more neutral third parties who are usually agreed to by the disputing parties and whose decision is binding'.[2] This identifies the core elements which are applicable even in the most advanced forms of international commercial arbitration. It states that arbitration:

(i) is a 'method of dispute resolution' (arbitration is simply a procedure or method for resolving disputes);
(ii) 'involving one or more neutral third parties' (the notion that all of the arbitrators be neutral, independent and impartial is an essential feature of arbitration);
(iii) 'who are usually agreed to by the disputing parties' (appointment of the arbitrator or arbitral tribunal by agreement of the parties, or by some agreed method, is one of the most important, defining features of arbitration; more generally, party consent is essential to all aspects of arbitration);
(iv) 'whose decision is binding' (there would be limited value in arbitration if a party to an arbitration agreement could subsequently refuse to comply with its obligation to arbitrate or could refuse to honour the arbitrator's decision. The binding nature of arbitral decisions (called 'awards') has been facilitated by the law, which is comprised of both domestic laws and international treaties. The law provides a framework to ensure that arbitration agreements and arbitral awards are legally enforceable).

1.4 There are many different types of arbitration, and even different species of international commercial arbitration. The most common is sometimes called 'New York Convention arbitration' because the awards are enforced pursuant to the procedures set out in the 1958 New York Convention on the Recognition and Enforcement of Foreign Arbitral Awards ('New York Convention'). However, 'New York Convention arbitration' as a name is inaccurate because it omits a small number of private arbitrations in countries that are not signatories to the New York Convention. Some call this kind of arbitration simply 'commercial arbitration' but we prefer 'international commercial arbitration' to distinguish it from domestic arbitration.

---

1 This book focuses on the following Asia-Pacific jurisdictions: Australia, China (Mainland), Hong Kong, India, Indonesia, Japan, Korea (Republic of), Malaysia, New Zealand, the Philippines and Singapore. However, examples from other jurisdictions are mentioned from time to time.
2 *Black's Law Dictionary*, 8th edn, Thomson West, 2004, p. 112. A similar definition can be found in any dictionary or in the various books on arbitration. See, e.g. the discussion of the definitions in J-F Poudret and S Besson, *Comparative Law of International Arbitration*, 2nd edn, Thomson, 2007, paras 1–3, who conclude that 'arbitration is a contractual form of dispute resolution exercised by individuals, appointed directly or indirectly by the parties, and vested with the power to adjudicate the dispute in the place of state courts by rendering a decision having effects analogous to those of a judgment'. Another useful definition is found in Section 3(d) of the Philippines Alternative Dispute Resolution Act 2004: '"Arbitration" means a voluntary dispute resolution process in which one or more arbitrators, appointed in accordance with the agreement of the parties, or rules promulgated pursuant to this Act, resolve a dispute by rendering an award.'

International commercial arbitration may be contrasted with 'ICSID arbitration' which is the most common type of 'investment arbitration'. ICSID arbitrations arise under the 1965 Washington Convention on the Settlement of Investment Disputes between States and Nationals of Other States ('ICSID Convention'). A distinctive feature of ICSID arbitration is that one party must be a state (i.e. government) or a state entity. States can also be parties to international commercial arbitrations.[3] Although ICSID arbitration differs from international commercial arbitration in several respects, especially concerning the applicable substantive law and recourse against and enforcement of awards, there are numerous similarities in terms of procedure and practice.

1.5

This book focuses principally on international commercial arbitration, which is the main form of international arbitration, but much of the book also applies to ICSID arbitration. The sections that are specific to ICSID arbitration are the brief history of ICSID at Section 2.3.2 below and the description of the main features of ICSID in Chapter 10.

1.6

2 A brief history of arbitration

2.1 Ancient history to the birth of modern international law

International arbitration has seen enormous growth in the last 40–50 years and has unquestionably become the preferred method for resolving international commercial disputes both in the Asia-Pacific and worldwide. However, the concept of parties referring to a neutral third party of their choice for the resolution of disputes between them is very much older and dates back to ancient times. Arbitration is said to have existed 'long before law was established, or courts were organised, or judges had formulated principles of law'.[4]

1.7

Recourse to arbitration indeed seems natural: when two people wish to resolve a difference between them, an instinctive reaction is to turn to a mutually respected third person, such as a tribal elder. It is therefore not surprising that arbitration was practised in ancient times in all corners of the globe.

1.8

Arbitration in China can be traced back to about 2100–1600 BC.[5] Mediation gained an even stronger foothold in China because of Confucianism. Confucius is

1.9

---

[3] In fact, most arbitrations involving state parties are international commercial arbitrations rather than ICSID arbitrations. In 2009, for example, 78 of the ICC International Court of Arbitration's 817 new cases involved a state or state entity. By comparison, ICSID's total number of new cases for the year 2009 was 25. Moreover, arbitrations involving states are often entirely ad hoc, for example using the UNCITRAL Arbitration Rules, and/or partially administered by the Permanent Court of Arbitration in The Hague.
[4] F Kellor, *American Arbitration, Its History, Functions and Achievements 1*, Harper & Brothers, 1948, p. 3. For an excellent collection of resources on the history of arbitration see D Roebuck, 'Sources for the History of Arbitration: A Bibliographical Introduction', (1998) 14(3) *Arbitration International* 237.
[5] Xu Chuanbao, *Traces of International Law in Prior Qing Period*, 1931, pp. 254–255, cited in Kay Zhongjun Ch'ien, MK McCardell and H Yu, *Rights and Remedies: A Comparison of Consumer Law in China and Hong Kong*, Intern Publications by Civic Exchange, 2004, p. 20; Jingzhou Tao, *Arbitration Law and Practice in China*, 2nd edn, Kluwer Law International, 2008, p. 1 et seq briefly discusses the history of arbitration in China from 1912 onwards. For a more recent era see RK Wagner, 'Magistrate Justice, Proto-arbitration and Foreign-trader Driven Litigation Reforms: Aspects of Commercial Dispute Resolution in Late Imperial and Early Republican

said to have believed that conflict and litigation were sources of great disharmony which in turn damaged social relationships.[6] Arbitration was also popular in ancient Egypt; it has been said that until about the mid-20th century, around 80% of all disputes would be settled out of court by recourse to a respected and popular elder chosen for his wisdom, integrity and standing in the community.[7] India also has an ancient history of resolving disputes in a three-tiered structure that is comparable to modern-day arbitration. This system continued through until the British arrived in India and made significant changes to the judicial system.[8]

1.10 Early examples of arbitration from the West include ancient Greece, in particular for the resolution of maritime disputes with trading partners such as the Phoenicians and between Greek city states, and ancient Rome.[9] Arbitration was the preferred method for resolving civil disputes in Europe during the Middle Ages. It was also used to resolve colonial power struggles between states, such as to define the zones of influence among colonial empires in the 15th and 16th centuries. Western states would often turn to the Pope to arbitrate such issues, giving the arbitral award an almost divine authority. Known examples include the arbitral decision rendered in 1493 by Pope Alexander VI which clarified borders between Portuguese and Spanish colonies in the Pacific Ocean and paved the way for the linguistic division of Latin America between Spanish and Portuguese.[10] It also clarified land ownership division in India.[11] International disputes were also frequently referred to other sovereigns who acted as arbitrators in the resolution of those disputes.[12]

1.11 Arbitration was not without its critics as it developed in the West. Some felt that the idea of private justice was an affront to a nation state's judicial system.

China', 3 September 2008, unpublished LLM dissertation, School of Oriental and African Studies, University of London (on file with authors).
  6 ES Reinstein, 'Finding a Happy Ending for Foreign Investors: The Enforcement of Arbitration Awards in the People's Republic of China', (2005–2006) 16 *Indiana International and Comparative Law Review* 37.
  7 AS El-Kosheri, 'Is There a Growing International Arbitration Culture in the Arab-Islamic Juridical Culture?', (1996) *ICCA Congress Series* 47 at pp. 47–8. See also D Roebuck, 'Cleopatra Compromised: Arbitration in Egypt in the First Century BC', (2008) 74 *Arbitration* 263.
  8 V Raghavan, 'New Horizons for Alternative Dispute Resolution in India', (1996) 13(4) *Journal of International Arbitration* 5, at pp. 6–7. See also the transcript of a speech by the then President of India, Shri KR Narayanan: Speech by the President of India at the Inauguration of the International Council for Commercial Arbitration Conference – New Delhi, 2 March 2000; Introduction by Fali S Nariman, President of ICCA and Vice Chairman of the International Court of Arbitration of ICC, published in 17(5) *Journal of International Arbitration* 153. The President speaks of Mohandas Karamchand Gandhi and Buddha as espousing the values of arbitration.
  9 See generally C Reus-Smit, 'The Constitutional Structure of International Society and the Nature of Fundamental Institutions', (1997) 51(4) *International Organization* 555, who discusses the use of arbitration to resolve interstate disputes; G Murray, 'Reactions to the Peloponnesian War in Greek Thought and Practice', (1944) 64 *The Journal of Hellenic Studies* 1, at p. 5; HT King and MA LeForestier, 'Arbitration in Ancient Greece', (1994) 49 *Dispute Resolution Journal* 38; D Roebuck and B de Loynes de Fumichon, *Roman Arbitration*, Holo Books, 2004; and D Roebuck, *Ancient Greek Arbitration*, Holo Books, 2001.
  10 See A Gautier, *100 dates qui ont fait le monde: 3000 ans de mondialisation*, Studyrama, 2005, p. 157.
  11 A Gordon, *La vie du pape Alexandre VI. et de son fils Cesar Borgia*, ed. Pierre Mortier, 1732, p. 104. See also F Despagnet, *Cours de Droit International Public*, ed. L Larose 1894, p. 702.
  12 PA Merlin, *Répertoire universel et raisonné de jurisprudence*, H Tarlier, 1825, p. 28. An interesting book that reproduces numerous ancient treaties in which third party sovereigns were appointed as arbitrators is WG Grewe, *Fontes Historiae Iuris Gentium/Sources Relating to the History of the Law of Nations*, Walter de Gruyter, 1995.

In England in 1609, Sir Edward Coke held that an arbitration agreement was 'by the law and of its own nature countermandable'.[13] More than 200 years later, a similar comment can be found in United States jurisprudence. The United States Supreme Court in 1836 somewhat patronisingly referred to an arbitral tribunal as 'a mere amicable tribunal'.[14] One US commentator reflecting on the judicial view of arbitration at that time has noted that 'a dispute settled by an arbitrator could be appealed to an American court and essentially be treated as though it had never been investigated before'.[15]

1.12 The lack of specific legal recognition given to arbitrators' decisions, and in particular the inability to enforce arbitration agreements was indeed its historical weakness. For example, the English Arbitration Act 1697 allowed either party to the dispute to withdraw its consent to arbitrate right up to the point when the arbitrator's decision was issued.

1.13 Despite such early scepticism of arbitration, and despite its mere partial recognition and enforceability by the law, recourse was still had to it. It is interesting to note, for example, that George Washington's will contained an arbitration clause providing that any dispute about interpretation of its wording should be resolved by a panel of three arbitrators.[16]

1.14 The first international commercial arbitration of the modern era is often said to be the Alabama Claims Arbitration[17] which took place in the aftermath of the American Civil War. The US claimed that Britain had violated neutrality obligations under international law by allowing the battle ship CSS *Alabama* to be constructed in Britain in full knowledge that it would enter into service with the Confederacy.[18] As a consequence, the US asserted that Union merchant marine and naval forces had suffered heavy direct and indirect damages.[19] After years of unsuccessful US diplomatic initiatives to obtain compensation, it was agreed in the Treaty of Washington 1871 that the claims would be resolved by a five-member arbitral tribunal sitting in Geneva.[20] The arbitral tribunal issued its

---

13 *Vynior's Case*, 8 Cohe. Rep 81b, 82a, 77 Eng Rep 597, 599 (England, King's Bench).
14 *Hobart v Drogan* 35 US 108 (1836) (US Supreme Court) at p. 119.
15 BL Benson, 'An Exploration of the Impact of Modern Arbitration Statutes on the Development of Arbitration in the United States', (1995) 11 *Journal of Law, Economics and Organization* 479, at p. 484.
16 'My Will and direction expressly is, that all disputes (if unhappily any should arise) shall be decided by three impartial and intelligent men, known for their probity and good understanding; two to be chosen by the disputants – each having the choice of one – and the third by those two. Which three men thus chosen, shall, unfettered by Law, or legal constructions, declare their sense of the Testators intention; and such decision is, to all intents and purposes to be as binding on the Parties as if it had been given in the Supreme Court of the United States.' Cited www.gwpapers.virginia.edu/documents/will/text.html.
17 This is the name given to the claims in the Treaty of Washington 1871.
18 The CSS *Alabama*'s story, beginning with the manner in which it was commissioned and armed through to its naval battles and its ultimate demise, is extraordinary. It involves many acts of subterfuge and culminates in a sea battle witnessed by thousands of people standing on the French coastline. See, e.g. T Bingham, 'The Alabama Claims Arbitration', (2005) 54 *International & Comparative Law Quarterly* 1; EC Bruggink, 'The Alabama Claims', (1996) 57 *Alabama Lawyer* 339; EB Canfield, 'Alabama's Defeat Was No Surprise', (2004) 18(4) *Naval History* 43.
19 Charles Sumner, then Chairman of the Senate Foreign Relations Committee, argued that British aid to the Confederacy had prolonged the Civil War by two years and indirectly cost the US hundreds of millions or even billions of dollars (Sumner suggested US$2.125 billion). Some Americans adopted this argument and suggested that Britain should offer Canada to the US as compensation.
20 The arbitrator appointment process was relatively straightforward but interesting: 'one shall be named by Her Britannic Majesty; one shall be named by the President of the United States; His Majesty the King of

decision in September 1872, ordering Britain to pay the US some $15.5 million[21] in compensation for direct damages suffered. The claims for indirect damages were rejected. Unlike international arbitrations these days, delivery of the award was accompanied by a gunnery salute.

1.15   The Alabama Claims dispute prompted the global recognition of international arbitration and the development of certain principles of international arbitration as we know them today. It also helped trigger a movement towards codifying international law to facilitate peaceful solutions to international disputes.[22] The Alabama Claims can be considered a precursor to The Hague Conventions of 1899 and 1907 (which instituted the Permanent Court of Arbitration), and perhaps even part of the inspiration for aspects of the League of Nations, the International Court of Justice and the United Nations.

2.2 Early 20th century: The birth of globalisation and international law

1.16   The seeds of international commercial arbitration as we know it today were sewn in the late 19th and early 20th centuries as a response to growing international trade, mainly in Europe, and the desire for an internationally enforceable, commercially sensible mechanism to resolve disputes. Robert Briner and Virginia Hamilton explain:[23]

> As nations increasingly affirmed their sovereignty and international trade outgrew its former structures, the dispute resolution mechanisms developed within trade associations began to prove inadequate. The group pressure that had formerly been such an effective means of ensuring enforcement of arbitral awards lost its power, and there were no specific legal means of compulsion to take its place.

1.17   Arbitral institutions contributed substantially to the growth of international arbitration during this period. The London Court of International Arbitration ('LCIA') was established in 1892 (then called the London Chamber of Arbitration). The *Law Quarterly Review* at that time reported that 'this Chamber is to have all the virtues which the law lacks. It is to be expeditious where

---

Italy shall be requested to name one; the President of the Swiss Confederation shall be requested to name one; and His Majesty the Emperor of Brazil shall be requested to name one.' (Preamble, Treaty of Washington 1872).
21 This would correspond to about £160 million in 2005, Bingham op. cit. fn 18. For further discussion on the Alabama claims see also S Hilmer, 'The Alabama Claims – The Origins of International Arbitration', (2008) July *Asian Dispute Review* 87.
22 According to one leading international arbitrator, the peace movement of the late 19th and 20th centuries 'considered international adjudication and arbitration as a substitute for war in settling international conflicts', K-H Böckstiegel, 'The Role of Arbitration within Today's Challenges to the World Community and to International Law', (2006) 22(2) *Arbitration International* 165, at p. 171.
23 R Briner and V Hamilton, 'The History and Purpose of the [New York] Convention' in E Gaillard and D Di Pietro, *Enforcement of Arbitration Agreements and International Arbitral Awards, the New York Convention in Practice*, Cameron May, 2008, p. 3. See also Yasuhei Taniguchi, 'Is There a Growing International Arbitration Culture? – An Observation from Asia', (1996) 8 *ICCA Congress Series* 31, at pp. 38–39.

the law is slow, cheap where the law is costly, simple where the law is technical, a peacemaker instead of a stirrer-up of strife.'[24] The LCIA was followed by establishment of the Chartered Institute of Arbitrators in 1915. The first edition of the Institute's journal *Arbitration*, published in February 1916, reported that it was formed 'at the instance of members of those professions whose services are usually invoked for the purpose of acting as Arbitrators in commercial matters... with a view to their corporate association, both for their own benefit and the interest of the general public'.[25]

1.18 The International Chamber of Commerce ('ICC') was established in 1919 by a group of international businessmen who called themselves 'Merchants of Peace'. They quickly realised that an effective mechanism for resolving international business disputes would foster growth in international commerce and assist in achieving world peace. The ICC began administering international disputes in 1921 and had dealt with 15 such cases before the ICC International Court of Arbitration ('ICC Court') was created in 1923. The ICC Court's mission was to foster international trade by providing a framework for the resolution of international commercial disputes.

1.19 Various ICC congresses in the early 1920s called strongly for better legal recognition of arbitration, which was rapidly gaining popularity among international businessmen. The following resolution was adopted at an ICC Congress in Rome in March 1923:[26]

> The International Chamber of Commerce considers that for the purpose indicated in the preceding resolutions it is desirable that one or more international conventions should be negotiated with the least possible delay, to embrace the largest possible number of States, particularly those of commercial importance. Such conventions should pledge the contracting States to recognise and make effective arbitration clauses in international commercial contracts, and to provide that if two parties of different nationalities agree to refer disputes that may arise between them to arbitration, an action brought by either party in any country shall be stayed by the Court, provided that the Court is satisfied that the other party is, and has been, willing to carry out the arbitration.

1.20 This and other pressure prompted the League of Nations to adopt the 1923 Geneva Protocol on Arbitration Clauses, the first genuine international treaty specifically concerned with commercial arbitration. It provided for the recognition of arbitration agreements and awards. It also offered a mechanism for the enforcement of an arbitral award in the jurisdiction that it was made, but did not facilitate the enforcement of an arbitral award made outside the enforcing jurisdiction, i.e. foreign arbitral awards. Foreign awards, if recognised at all,

---

24 E Manson, 'The City of London Chamber of Arbitration', (1893) 9 *Law Quarterly Review* 86.
25 (1916) 1(2) *Arbitration* 2.
26 International Chamber of Commerce, Resolutions Adopted at the Second Congress, Rome, March 1923, Brochure no. 31, at 37, cited in Briner and Hamilton, op. cit. fn 23, p. 5. Briner and Hamilton provide a captivating account of the lobby for legal recognition of arbitration during this period.

1.21 The Geneva Protocol was followed by the much wider 1927 Geneva Convention on the Execution of Foreign Arbitral Awards. This convention sought to improve on the 1923 Geneva Protocol by extending the scope of the recognition and enforcement of awards to all contracting states. In other words, it was not limited to enforcement of awards made in the enforcing court's own state (as was the case under the 1923 Geneva Protocol). While this assisted with the enforcement of foreign awards, a significant weakness of the two Geneva conventions was that neither the US nor USSR were parties. In addition, the language of these treaties was far from ideal, with various shortcomings and unclear provisions.[27] Neither of these treaties has much practical effect today, either in the Asia-Pacific or elsewhere, because they have been superseded by the New York Convention.[28]

1.22 A particularly interesting example of an international arbitration in the pre-World War Two period is the *Abu Dhabi* oil case.[29] It concerned an oil concession granted by the Sheik of Abu Dhabi to a foreign private company in 1939. The dispute arose over the geographical limits of the concession holder's oil extraction rights. The two arbitrators appointed under the arbitration agreement chose Lord Asquith as their 'umpire' because they could not agree on the outcome of the case. Lord Asquith made a controversial decision regarding the law applicable to the dispute. While acknowledging that Abu Dhabi law would ordinarily apply since the contract was signed and to be performed in Abu Dhabi, Lord Asquith concluded that:[30]

> [the Sheik, an] absolute, feudal monarch... administers a purely discretionary justice with the assistance of the Koran; and it would be fanciful to suggest that in this very primitive region there is any settled body of legal principles applicable to the construction of modern commercial instruments.

1.23 Applying 'principles rooted in the good sense and common practice of the generality of civilised nations – a sort of "modern law of nature"',[31] Lord Asquith determined that the subsoil of the territorial belt was included in the concession agreement. In favour of the Sheik of Abu Dhabi, however, Lord Asquith found that the concession holder had no rights with regard to the subsoil outside the territorial belt on the Continental Shelf.

---

27 Briner and Hamilton, op. cit. fn 23, pp. 7–8; A Redfern, M Hunter, N Blackaby and C Partasides, *Law and Practice of International Commercial Arbitration*, 4th edn, Sweet and Maxwell, 2004, paras 1–146, 3–4 and 10–22. See also V Petocha, 'Geneva Convention on the Execution of Foreign Arbitral Awards', (1986–1987) 1 *World Arbitration Reporter* 11.
28 Article VII(2) of the New York Convention states that 'The Geneva Protocol on Arbitration Clauses of 1923 and the Geneva Convention on the Execution of Foreign Arbitral Awards of 1927 shall cease to have effect between Contracting States on their becoming bound and to the extent that they become bound, by this Convention'. For domestic legislation implementing these treaties see, as an example, Sections 53–60 of the Indian Arbitration and Conciliation Act 1996.
29 *Petroleum Dev (Trucial Coast) Ltd v Sheikh of Abu Dhabi* (award of 28 August 1951), reprinted in (1952) 1 *International and Comparative Law Quarterly* 247.
30 Ibid., at 250–251.
31 Ibid., at 251.

Lord Asquith's award was made from an excessively Western perspective and would not be acceptable in the globalised world of international arbitration today.

2.3 Post-World War Two: Development of a framework for international arbitration

The outbreak of World War Two halted international business. However, its immediate aftermath saw huge economic growth and trade, particularly from the 1950s onwards when global commerce between private parties began to flourish. This was stimulated by various post-war initiatives at the international level, including the establishment of the International Bank for Reconstruction and Development (later renamed the World Bank) and International Monetary Fund in 1944; and the establishment of the General Agreement on Tariffs and Trade (usually called the 'GATT') in 1947.

2.3.1 1958 New York Convention

Perhaps the most important milestone in the entire history of international commercial arbitration was the adoption of the New York Convention. Its completion in 1958 cannot be viewed in isolation as a sudden act of innovation. It was a product of the developments described above and further lobbying by the international business and legal communities since the early 20th century.

The ICC played a significant role in the lobbying process of the 1950s, including submitting to the United Nations a 'Preliminary Draft Convention' on the recognition and enforcement of international arbitral awards and agreements.[32] The ICC's proposal for an international award that was not subject to any control by the courts of the place of arbitration proved to be unacceptable to most states. The United Nations Economic and Social Council ('ECOSOC') instead produced its own draft convention for the enforcement of foreign awards.[33] ECOSOC's draft was debated by representatives of some 40 countries at the 'Conference on International Commercial Arbitration', also known as the New York Conference, held at United Nations Headquarters in New York from 20 May to 10 June 1958.[34] After the first week of this conference, the Dutch delegation submitted a substantially altered version of Articles III to V of the ECOSOC draft.[35] Thereafter,

---

[32] See AJ van den Berg, *The New York Convention of 1958: Towards a Uniform Interpretation*, Kluwer Law International, 1981, p. 7 and Briner and Hamilton, op. cit. fn 23, pp. 8–9.
[33] United Nations Economic and Social Council, Draft Convention on the Enforcement of Foreign Arbitral Awards, UN Doc E/2704 and Corr 1.
[34] See generally Briner and Hamilton, op. cit. fn 23, pp. 13–19. For the Summary Records of the New York Conference, see UN Doc E/Conf 26/SR 1–25; and for other preparatory materials of that conference, including suggested amendments to the ECOSOC draft and reports of the Working Parties, see UN Doc E/Conf 26/7 and L 7–63. These documents are reproduced in G Gaja, *International Commercial Arbitration: The New York Convention*, Oceana Publications Inc, 1978–1980, Part III. See also www.uncitral.org.
[35] United Nations Economic and Social Council, United Nations Conference on International Commercial Arbitration, 'Consideration of the Draft Convention on the Recognition and Enforcement of foreign arbitral Awards (Item 4 on the Agenda) – Netherlands: amendments to Draft Convention; UN Doc /CONF.26/L.17 (26 May 1958).

the conference continued its deliberations using the Dutch proposals as the basis for discussions. A Working Party was appointed and prepared a revised draft in the light of the discussions.[36] That version, with some further modifications, was adopted by the conference on 10 June 1958 by 35 votes to none, with four abstentions.[37]

1.28 The final text of the New York Convention was not quite as business-friendly as some lobbyists might have wished, but was nonetheless a remarkable achievement given the diversity of cultural and political interests that ultimately consented to it.

1.29 The New York Convention facilitates the recognition and enforcement of foreign arbitral awards and agreements. It is said to have a pro-enforcement bias. There are many reasons for this bias but two are paramount. First, a major object and purpose of it is 'to encourage and liberalise the process of recognition and enforcement of awards by decreasing the scope for obstruction by national courts and laws'.[38] The second reason is due to the principle of comity. As Justice Prakash stated in the Singapore High Court decision of *Hainan Machinery Import & Export Corporation v Donald & McArthy Pte Ltd*:[39]

> the principle of comity of nations requires that the awards of foreign arbitration tribunals be given due deference and be enforced unless exceptional circumstances exist. As a nation which itself aspires to be an international arbitration centre, Singapore must recognise foreign awards if it expects its own awards to be recognised abroad.

1.30 If the party against whom enforcement of an award is sought does not resist enforcement, the procedure should be very straightforward and akin to quasi-administrative proceedings.[40] There are very limited grounds in Article V on which a party can resist enforcement.[41]

1.31 Twenty-five states were parties to the New York Convention by the end of 1958. Since then, numerous others have signed, bringing the total number of parties at the time of writing to approximately 145.[42] States seeking to portray themselves as players on an international commercial market, and wishing to attract foreign investment, readily adopted it. The growing number of parties meant that the New York Convention in turn expanded its geographical reach and, consequently, the advantages that it offered. It became vital to the expansion of cross-border trade and investment and caused a dramatic shift in the way that

---

[36] United Nations Economic and Social Council, United Nations Conference on International Commercial Arbitration, Consideration of the Draft Convention on the Recognition and Enforcement of Foreign Arbitral Awards (Item 4 on the Agenda), UN Doc E/CONF.26/L.43 (New York Convention draft of Working Party no. 3) (3 June 1958).
[37] United Nations Economic and Social Council, United Nations Conference on International Commercial Arbitration, Summary Record of the Twenty-fourth Meeting, UN Doc E/CONF.26/SR.24 (12 September 1958).
[38] R Garnett and M Pryles, 'Recognition and Enforcement of Foreign Awards under the New York Convention in Australia and New Zealand', (2008) 25 *Journal of International Arbitration* 899, at 904.
[39] [1996] 1 SLR 34, at para 45; (1997) XXII *Yearbook of Commercial Arbitration* 771. See also *Hebei Import & Export Corp v Polytek Engineering Co Ltd* [1999] 1 HKLRD 665.
[40] These are the words of Lord Justice Rix in *Gater Assets Ltd v Nak Naftogaz Ukrainiy* [2007] 2 Lloyd's Rep 588 at 603, para 72.
[41] Enforcement of awards is dealt with briefly below at Section 3.4.6, and in much more detail in Chapter 9.
[42] A list of parties to the New York Convention is provided at Appendix 4.

international business disputes are resolved. One reason for its success is that it had no real competitor – there was no comparable convention providing for the international recognition and enforcement of domestic court judgments.[43]

1.32 By the time the New York Convention was completed, further interesting arbitrations were taking place in Asia. An example of a West Asian arbitration in the early post-World War Two era is the famous *Aramco* case of 1963. It concerned an oil concession granted to the Arabian American Oil Company ('Aramco') by the Kingdom of Saudi Arabia in 1933. Aramco purportedly reserved the contractual right to determine how it would transport the oil that it extracted, including the right to engage foreign tankers. However, in 1954 the Kingdom of Saudi Arabia granted a Saudi company a 30-year right of priority for the export of any Saudi oil. The parties agreed to refer their dispute to an arbitral tribunal seated in Geneva and chaired by George Sauser-Hall, a Swiss international arbitrator. Finding Saudi law insufficient to deal with the complexity of the concession agreement, the arbitral tribunal resorted to the parties' agreed fallback choice of law: international customs relating to the petroleum industry, general principles of law and international law. The arbitral tribunal held for Aramco. This led the Saudi Government swiftly to enact a decree prohibiting arbitration of any dispute involving Saudi state entities. The decree left Saudi Arabia virtually off the international arbitration map until it become a party to the ICSID Convention in 1980 and the New York Convention in 1994.

1.33 The growth of international arbitration since the New York Convention can be seen in various ways. ICC statistics are insightful. Viewed at 10 year intervals, the ICC Court saw 29 new arbitrations filed in the year 1960, 56 in 1970, 152 in 1980, 251 in 1990, 541 in 2000 and 817 in 2009. Furthermore, over one-third of the more than 17 000 arbitrations that the ICC has administered since 1923 were in the last 10 years, demonstrating the recent exponential growth of international arbitration.

1.34 The New York Convention's success sparked related developments at the international legal level. These included the 1965 ICSID Convention, the 1966 United Nations Commission on International Trade Law ('UNCITRAL') and its 1976 Arbitration Rules and, of particular importance in the Asia-Pacific, the 1985 UNCITRAL Model Law on International Commercial Arbitration ('Model Law'). Each of these is discussed in turn.

2.3.2 1965 ICSID Convention

1.35 The ICSID Convention was formulated under the auspices of the World Bank to facilitate a specialised method of international dispute settlement: investment

---

[43] If parties to a dispute have entered into a specific choice of court agreement, the Hague Convention on Choice of Court Agreements, completed in 2005, provides for the recognition and enforcement of civil and commercial court judgments internationally in a manner similar to the New York Convention for arbitral awards. At the time of writing, the Convention had not yet entered into force because it had not been ratified or acceded to by the required number (three) of states. Mexico is the only country to have acceded to it. Both the US and the European Community have signed the Convention and are expected to ratify it soon.

treaty arbitration.[44] The claimant in this form of arbitration is a private party that is a national of one state and the respondent is a foreign state ('host state') in which the private party has invested. The treatment of the investor or its investment by the host state is typically the subject matter of the dispute.

1.36 In the first half of the 20th century, investment disputes multiplied as a result of vast land reforms, nationalisations, repudiation of government concessions in Central America, the rise of socialism from 1917, and World War One. Following World War Two, socialism expanded, with certain industries being nationalised in France and the UK for instance, former colonies sought independence and many petroleum and mining concessions were nationalised.[45] This environment of political risk for investors prompted a movement towards the creation of instruments to protect foreign investments (e.g. the 1948 Havana Charter, the 1948 Bogota Economic Agreement and the 1949 ICC International Code of Fair Treatment for Foreign Investors). However, these early attempts were not successful.

1.37 A growing desire emerged to encourage foreign investment in developing countries so as to boost their economies. This met with resistance from many developing countries which wanted to avoid becoming economically dependent on foreign companies. These states expressed a strong desire to exercise their sovereignty over their natural resources. To address the problems associated with these issues, two Harvard professors (Louis Sohn and Richard Baxter) published in 1961 a Draft Convention on the International Responsibility of States for Injuries to Aliens.[46] Although this document did not become a treaty, it was an important first step towards creating a legal framework for the protection of foreign investors. In 1962, the UN General Assembly adopted the famous Resolution 1803 (XVII) entitled Permanent Sovereignty over Natural Resources. It recognises the permanent sovereignty of states over their natural resources and determines that nationalisations are lawful only when appropriate compensation is paid to foreign investors whose assets are expropriated. The OECD also contributed to establishing a satisfactory legal environment for foreign investment with its 1962 Draft Convention on the Protection of Foreign Property.[47] This Draft Convention was not accepted by less developed OECD members (such as Greece, Portugal and Turkey) because they considered some of its provisions to be heavily in favour of capital exporting interests.[48]

1.38 The World Bank, a key player in the field of foreign investment and development, was the institution that managed to produce a groundbreaking solution that was internationally acceptable.[49] The World Bank's staff, notably its General

---

[44] The ICSID Convention and investment treaty arbitration are dealt with in more detail in Chapter 10.
[45] For more details on the history of foreign investment see RD Bishop, J Crawford and WM Reisman, *Foreign Investment Disputes: Cases, Materials and Commentary*, Kluwer Law, 2005, Chapter 1.
[46] See L Sohn and R Baxter, 'Responsibility of States for Injuries to the Economic Interests of Aliens', (1961) 55 *American Journal of International Law* 545.
[47] (1963) 2 *International Legal Materials* 241.
[48] P Muchlinski, *Multinational Enterprises and the Law*, Oxford University Press, 2007, p. 657.
[49] C Schreuer, *The ICSID Convention: A Commentary*, Cambridge University Press, 2001, pp. 1–11.

Counsel, Aron Broches, prepared a draft convention in 1962 embodying a unique concept – it was a convention dealing exclusively with dispute resolution procedure and did not touch on matters of substance. Four regional consultations with legal experts were conducted in Africa, the Americas, Asia and Europe to discuss this draft.[50] In the light of these consultations, government experts, World Bank staff and its Executive Directors worked at improving the original draft. The final text of the ICSID Convention was approved by the bank's Executive Directors on 18 March 1965 and entered into force on 14 October 1966. As of mid 2010, 144 states were parties to the ICSID Convention, including most of the prominent trading nations in the Asia-Pacific region.[51]

1.39 A remarkable innovation of the ICSID Convention was that it gave rights to investors to make direct claims against a state or state entity. Traditionally, private parties did not have standing to bring claims by themselves against states before international courts or tribunals because only states were recognised as subjects of international law.[52] Seeking assistance from the investor's home state through the mechanism of diplomatic protection was also inadequate, partly because state to state relations involve a multitude of other political, military and economic priorities and compromises.[53]

1.40 The prior unsuccessful attempts at concluding a convention that protected foreign investment raises a question as to why the ICSID Convention was accepted so readily by states. One of the main reasons is that it did not establish the substantive rights to be accorded to foreign investors. It established only a procedural mechanism by which disputes between foreign investors and host states could be resolved. Binding arbitration is used as a means to provide redress to foreign investors that have suffered loss or damage as a result of the acts or omissions of the host state. As discussed in Chapter 10, the substantive rights granted to investors are dealt with in separate, multilateral or bilateral investment treaties.

1.41 The ICSID Convention established the International Centre for Settlement of Investment Disputes (ICSID), which administers investment treaty arbitrations that fall within the ICSID Convention's jurisdictional scope. The ICSID Convention also deals with the annulment and enforcement of awards rendered by ICSID arbitral tribunals.

1.42 In its first 30 years, ICSID handled a humble average of one case per year but since 1995 the number has grown significantly. Most awards rendered under the auspices of ICSID are now published and have significantly contributed to the development of the law on foreign investment and to some extent international arbitration practice.

---

50 Ibid., pp. 2–3.
51 India, Taiwan and Vietnam are notable exceptions. A list of ICSID Convention states is available at http://icsid.worldbank.org.
52 Some exceptions to this rule in the 1950s were the holders of petroleum concession contracts in the Middle East who, with contractual clauses consenting to ad hoc arbitration, were given the right to take the granting state directly to arbitration.
53 Diplomatic protection is briefly discussed in Chapter 10, Section 5.3.1.

2.3.3 1966 United Nations Commission on International Trade Law (UNCITRAL)

1.43   In 1966, the General Assembly of the United Nations established UNCITRAL.[54] It was established amid a climate of expanding world trade in the 1960s with a mandate to advance the harmonisation and unification of international trade law. It originally comprised a committee of representatives of 29 states elected for a term of six years. Membership has now expanded to 60 states representing all geographic regions and principal economic and legal systems in the world. Although only member states make Commission decisions, non-member states ('observer states') and non-government organisations also participate in the drafting of UNCITRAL documents. UNCITRAL has developed a wide range of conventions, model laws and other instruments relevant to procedural and substantive aspects of international trade law.[55] It has accordingly played a key role in the development of international arbitration.

1.44   UNCITRAL refers preparatory work to various working groups.[56] At present there are six working groups each tasked with work in one of the areas for which UNCITRAL is responsible. Working Group II has focused on the topic of international arbitration since 2000. It comprises representatives from the 60 UNCITRAL member states. Other interested states and non-governmental organisations are invited to participate as observers. As a consequence, a wealth of knowledge and practical experience is utilised by Working Group II. At the time of writing, Working Group II has just completed its revision of the UNCITRAL Arbitration Rules. It took on this task after it had completed the 2006 version of the UNCITRAL Model Law on International Commercial Arbitration. The revision of the Model Law was a very involved process and took a number of years. Working Group II has also prepared an interpretative instrument regarding Article II(2) of the New York Convention.

2.3.4 1976 UNCITRAL Arbitration Rules

1.45   An UNCITRAL initiative of particular importance to international commercial arbitration was the 1976 UNCITRAL Arbitration Rules. These flexible rules apply as though they are incorporated into the parties' contract when parties to an arbitration agreement expressly select them. They were innovative in many ways when they were released in 1977, and have stood the test of time. They have been used for some of the largest and most politically sensitive international commercial arbitrations in history.

1.46   Certain features of the UNCITRAL Arbitration Rules soon gained substantial international acceptance and became part of a body of generally accepted

---

54 Resolution 2205(XXI) of 17 December 1966, General Assembly of the United Nations.
55 We mention only the 1976 Arbitration Rules and the 1985 Model Law, but UNCITRAL has developed several other arbitration related instruments and many documents relating to other areas of international trade law. See www.uncitral.org.
56 See, e.g. UN Doc A/CN.9/676 'UNCITRAL rules of procedure and methods of work – Note by the Secretariat', available at www.uncitral.org/pdf/english/commissiondocs/a-cn9–676.procedural.guidelines. draft%2028%20February%2009.pdf.

principles of international commercial arbitration. They have also been a source of considerable inspiration for the rules of international arbitral institutions seeking to adopt these globally accepted principles. Some institutions adopted the UNCITRAL Arbitration Rules verbatim, granting themselves certain supervisory functions like default appointment of arbitrators, whereas others used them as inspiration for their own rules.

The UNCITRAL Arbitration Rules gained considerable exposure due to their use (in a slightly varied form) by the busiest single arbitral tribunal ever: the Iran-United States Claims Tribunal. The Iran-United States Claims Tribunal was established pursuant to the Algiers Declarations of 19 January 1981 to deal with the aftermath of the 1979 Iranian Revolution. It has dealt with literally thousands of claims involving disputes mostly between nationals of the US and the Iranian government. According to one source, 'as of April 2006, the Tribunal had issued over 800 awards and decisions – a total of 600 awards (including partial awards and awards on agreed terms), eighty-three interlocutory and interim awards, and 133 decisions – in resolving almost 4,000 cases'.[57] A significant contribution of this tribunal to arbitral practice is that its decisions and orders applying the UNCITRAL Arbitration Rules to a multitude of situations were made publicly available, thus creating a body of decisions that has been described as a 'gold mine of information for perceptive lawyers'.[58] A number of books have reported and commented on these decisions.[59]

1.47

Just prior to this book being completed, UNCITRAL adopted the 2010 UNCITRAL Arbitration Rules. It is understood that these rules will be effective from 15 August 2010 for arbitration agreements made after that date. The 1976 UNCITRAL Arbitration Rules will however remain relevant for arbitration agreements concluded before that date, and in particular for bilateral investment treaties concluded before that date.

1.48

2.3.5 1985 UNCITRAL Model Law on International Commercial Arbitration

One of the most significant global legislative spin-offs of the New York Convention, particularly for Asia, was the Model Law.[60] The Model Law is a suggested

1.49

---

[57] CS Gibson and CR Drahozal, 'Iran-United States Claims Tribunal Precedent in Investor-State Arbitration', (2006) 23(6) *Journal of International Arbitration* 521, at p. 521.
[58] HM Holtzmann, 'Some Lessons of the Iran-United States Claims Tribunal' in *Private Investors Abroad: Problems and Solutions in International Business* (1987) 16–1 at 16–5, cited in Gibson and Drahozal, ibid., at p. 521.
[59] See, e.g. D Caron, L Caplan and M Pellonpää, *The UNCITRAL Arbitration Rules – A Commentary*, Oxford University Press, 2006; S Baker and M Davis, *The UNCITRAL Arbitration Rules in Practice: The Experience of the Iran-United States Claims Tribunal*, Kluwer, 1992; J van Hoff, *Commentary on the UNCITRAL Arbitration Rules: The Application by the Iran-United States Claims Tribunal*, Kluwer, 1991.
[60] On the relationship between the New York Convention and the UNICTRAL Model Law see R Sorieul, 'The Influence of the New York Convention on the UNCITRAL Model Law on International Commercial Arbitration', (2008) 2(1) *Dispute Resolution International* 27. At the time of writing, Sorieul had recently been appointed Director, International Trade Law Division, United Nations Office of Legal Affairs and Secretary of UNCITRAL.

text for domestic jurisdictions to adopt as their own arbitration law. Any jurisdiction is free to use it as the basis for its national legislation, with or without any modifications it may desire.[61]

1.50 The Model Law has no independent force of law. If it is adopted by a state, it applies as law in that state only because the state has enacted it as part of its own domestic law. The fact that UNICTRAL prepared the Model Law does not give it the force of international law. It must therefore be contrasted with conventions like the New York and ICSID Conventions which constitute international treaty law applicable among the respective state parties. The Model Law is simply a recommended template that may be copied verbatim or adapted in drafting a country's domestic law.

1.51 The drafters of the Model Law gathered the most important principles that are necessary in an arbitration law and formulated one cohesive instrument. Many of these important principles were already reflected in arbitration laws worldwide, and/or were inspired by the New York Convention and to some extent the UNCITRAL Arbitration Rules. Two overarching principles behind the Model Law are (i) that it allows for a very significant degree of procedural flexibility – the parties to the arbitration can agree on virtually any procedure – and (ii) it greatly restricts the role of domestic courts in the arbitral process. The Model Law text 'is usually held up as the template signifying ideal balance between arbitral and curial authority'.[62]

1.52 After setting out the key features of the Model Law, the Indian Supreme Court in a decision of 2005 conveniently summarised UNCITRAL's purpose in creating a harmonised arbitration law:[63]

> All these [features of the Model Law] aim at achieving the sole object to resolve the dispute as expeditiously as possible with the minimum intervention of a Court of Law so that trade and commerce is not affected on account of litigations before a Court. [The] United Nations established [UNCITRAL] on account of the fact that the General Assembly recognised that disparities in national laws governing international trade created obstacles to the flow of trade. The General Assembly regarded [UNCITRAL] as a medium which could play a more active role in reducing or removing the obstacles. [UNCITRAL], therefore, was given a mandate for progressive harmonization and unification of the law of International Trade.

1.53 At the time of writing, more than 60 states, including most of the Asian jurisdictions that are the focus of this book, have based their arbitration laws on the

---

[61] For more on the background to the Model Law see 'Report of the [UN] Secretary-General: Possible Features of a Model Law on International Commercial Arbitration', 14 May 1981, UN Doc A/CN.9/207, (1981) XII *Yearbook of the United Nations Commission on International Trade Law*.

[62] R Morgan, 'Abandoning Colonial Arbitration Laws in Southeast Asia – II: Background and Commentary', (2000) 15(7) *Mealey's International Arbitration Report* 44. See also JK Schaefer, 'Abandoning Colonial Arbitration Laws in Southeast Asia – I: An Analytical History', (2000) 15(7) *Mealey's International Arbitration Report* 30, at p. 35, who describes the Model Law as having been 'developed by international experts as a role model for developing countries when modernizing their arbitration law'.

[63] *Shin-Etsu Chemical Co Ltd v Aksh Optifibre Ltd* (2005) 7 SCC 234 (Supreme Court of India, judgment of Justice YK Sabharwal). See also M Sornarajah, 'The UNCITRAL Model Law: A Third World Viewpoint', (1989) 6(4) *Journal of International Arbitration* 7, who examines in a now somewhat dated article whether the Model Law is really suitable for adoption by developing countries.

Model Law.[64] The benefits of this for international companies and their legal advisors should be obvious. It has created a harmonised, consistent approach to domestic arbitration laws based on an excellent precedent developed by some of the world's experts on international commercial arbitration.

1.54 There are many economically important states which have not chosen to use the Model Law as their arbitration law. For example, certain European jurisdictions with a long, solid history of arbitration, like France and Switzerland, have not adopted it. The UK (except Scotland) and US (at the Federal level and all but a few states) are other notable exceptions. Notwithstanding that these countries have not adopted the Model Law, when one examines their arbitration laws, it is clear that many of the general principles enshrined in the Model Law can also be found in those laws.

1.55 The Model Law was revised by UNCITRAL's Working Group II in July 2006. Given its nature as a Model Law, this revision cannot affect the law applicable in those states that have already used the unrevised Model Law as a basis for their laws. The new amendments only apply to the extent that an individual state specifically chooses to adopt them. New Zealand, Singapore and Australia are the only countries in this region which have adopted the 2006 revisions, but Hong Kong is likely to do so in the imminent amendments to its arbitration law. It would not be at all surprising if other Asia-Pacific jurisdictions follow in the near future.

1.56 The fact that harmonisation of arbitration laws is one of the major goals of the Model Law is reflected in Article 2A of the 2006 version of the Model Law. It provides:

> (1) In the interpretation of this Law, regard is to be had to its international origin and to the need to promote uniformity in its application and the observance of good faith.
> (2) Questions concerning matters governed by this Law which are not expressly settled in it are to be settled in conformity with the general principles on which this Law is based.

1.57 The Model Law is thus to be interpreted from an international standpoint, taking into account the principles behind it, rather than from a domestic standpoint. This is to encourage a consistent interpretation among different states.

3 Characteristics of arbitration

1.58 Arbitration was defined in Section 1 above. The present section first distinguishes arbitration from related dispute resolution mechanisms and distinguishes domestic from international arbitration (Sections 3.1–3.3). It then outlines the key features of arbitration (Section 3.4) which are developed in greater detail throughout this book.

---

64 A list of arbitration laws based on the Model Law is provided at Appendix 3.

3.1 Distinction between arbitration and litigation

1.59 Aside from arbitration, the other form of legally binding commercial dispute resolution is litigation in a domestic court. There are numerous differences between litigation and arbitration, including:

(i) International litigation takes place in a court that derives its competence from the application of sometimes cumbersome international jurisdiction rules. Commercial parties are accorded some freedom to choose the court, but that choice is restricted by the inconsistent rules of various courts. Furthermore, it is not uncommon that litigation relating to the same dispute is commenced in more than one domestic court that is competent to hear the case, thus creating a duplication or multiplicity of proceedings. Conversely, in international arbitration the seat or place of arbitration is chosen by the parties, without the restrictions that can apply to the choice of a court in international litigation proceedings. The parties can choose virtually any place in the world they wish as the seat of their arbitration. In practice they usually choose a seat that is neutral as concerns the parties and which has a legal framework that is conducive to arbitration.[65]

(ii) In litigation, a judge is assigned to the case by the court. The parties therefore cannot select the judge who will determine their dispute. In arbitration, however, the parties are free to choose the arbitrator(s), enabling them to choose people with the appropriate expertise, cultural neutrality, or other desired skills or characteristics.[66]

(iii) In litigation the procedure is fixed or otherwise determined by the rules of the particular court. In arbitration the parties have enormous flexibility to choose the kind of procedure that they wish to adopt for their arbitration. There are very few limits on that choice. The parties can, for example, agree on a procedure that is much cheaper and faster than litigation.[67]

(iv) In litigation the proceedings are usually open to the public. International commercial arbitration is a matter concerning only the parties to the particular dispute. It is therefore possible for arbitrations to be kept confidential from outsiders. This is important for business disputes where the leaking of commercial information can be devastating. However, the confidential nature of arbitration is somewhat diluted when support from courts is needed, for example where parties seek curial support or seek to enforce arbitral awards. In many jurisdictions the pleadings and evidence submitted to a court, even if related to a confidential arbitral process, become part of the public record.[68]

(v) In litigation the parties usually have one or more levels of appeal from the initial judgment if a party wishes to challenge that judgment.

---

[65] Issues concerning the seat of arbitration are addressed in Chapter 2.
[66] Issues concerning arbitrators are addressed in Chapter 6.
[67] Procedure is dealt with in Chapter 7, which also explains the limits to party autonomy.
[68] The confidentiality of arbitration is dealt with in Chapter 7. ICSID arbitration awards are generally public but the proceedings are confidential. ICSID is addressed in Chapter 10.

International arbitral awards are, with a few exceptions, final. The only means of recourse is an application for setting aside the award on narrow procedural grounds.[69]

(vi) Enforcing a foreign arbitral award is generally much easier than enforcing a foreign court judgment by virtue of the New York Convention.[70]

3.2 Distinction between arbitration and ADR

1.60 ADR procedures, such as mediation and conciliation,[71] are a friendlier means to resolve disputes. 'ADR' can stand for either 'alternative' or 'amicable' dispute resolution.[72] We prefer the latter to distinguish the nature of these procedures from arbitration and litigation.

1.61 In ADR, parties work together with an experienced third person with the aim of reaching an amicable settlement or other solution. Often the parties' settlement will be recorded in the form of a written agreement. Because everyone has participated in forming the agreement, it is hoped that it will be complied with voluntarily. If not, the agreement may be enforceable as a matter of contract law. However, an agreement reached during an ADR procedure is not an arbitral award so it cannot be enforced under the New York Convention. Nevertheless, a settlement agreement reached in the course of arbitral proceedings can be drawn up in the form of an award by consent so that it can be enforced under the New York Convention.[73]

1.62 The consensual nature of ADR processes must be distinguished from the binding procedures in arbitration and litigation. The key difference is that in the latter the outcome is decided by the arbitrator or judge rather than by agreement of the parties. Further, a judge's decision or arbitrator's award is final (subject to any rights of appeal) and binding. Also, parties can be forced to participate in arbitration or litigation proceedings at the risk of a binding decision against them if they do not. A party can to some extent be required to attempt an ADR procedure but it cannot be forced to accept a settled outcome – no decision can be *imposed* in ADR, it is rather *proposed*. In arbitration and litigation the decision of a third party is imposed, unless the parties reach a settlement agreement in the course of the arbitration, which quite often occurs.[74]

---

69 Setting aside of arbitral awards is dealt with in Chapter 9.
70 Enforcement of awards is dealt with in Chapter 9. See also footnote 43 above concerning The Hague Convention on Choice of Courts Agreements.
71 Arb-med is addressed in Chapter 7, Section 6.12. See also the articles by Wong Yan Lung, 'The use and Development of Mediation in Hong Kong' and M Dewdney, 'Party-Mediator and Lawyer-Driven problems in Mediation', (2008) *Asian Dispute Review*, at pp. 54 and 57 respectively.
72 Arbitration could be considered as an alternative to the courts but strictly speaking it is not a form of alternative dispute resolution.
73 See, e.g. ACICA Rules Article 35.1; HKIAC Rules Article 32.1; SIAC Rules Article 27.7; 1975 UNCITRAL Arbitration Rules Article 34.1; KCAB International Rules Article 34; JCAA Rules, Rule 54.2; ICC Rules Article 26.
74 For example, from 2003–2008, an average of 47% of ICC arbitrations were withdrawn by the parties before the arbitral tribunal issued its final award. Approximately 65% of those withdrawals were in the early stages of the arbitrations, before the ICC Terms of Reference were finalised.

1.63 If ADR leads to a resolution of the dispute, it is generally much cheaper, faster and less disrupting for business than seeing through to conclusion a binding procedure such as arbitration or litigation. A successful ADR process also has the advantage of better preserving business relationships. For most kinds of commercial disputes, it is therefore well worth exploring ADR options both before launching arbitration or litigation proceedings, and even during such proceedings. At the end of the day, however, commercial parties need the protection of a fallback binding dispute resolution option. The best fallback option for international disputes is international arbitration.

3.3 Distinction between international arbitration and domestic arbitration

1.64 This book concerns international rather than domestic arbitration. Many jurisdictions in the Asia-Pacific have different laws that apply to domestic as opposed to international arbitrations, or at least different provisions of the same law that apply to each. Typically, laws on domestic arbitration:
  (i) leave less room for the parties to determine the arbitral procedure and applicable laws;
  (ii) provide more possibilities for recourse, such as appeal, from the resulting award; and
  (iii) permit a greater degree of domestic court involvement.

1.65 Whether an arbitration is domestic or international depends on the definition provided in the law applicable to that question. Usually the relevant law is that of the seat of arbitration. If the seat of arbitration's law distinguishes between international and domestic arbitrations, then it should provide a definition of each. Thus an international or domestic arbitration is one that is defined as such by the law of the seat of arbitration.

1.66 A typical example of a definition of international arbitration is that found in the Model Law. Article 1(3) of the Model Law provides:

> An arbitration is international if:
> (a) the parties to an arbitration agreement have, at the time of the conclusion of that agreement, their places of business in different States; or
> (b) one of the following places is situated outside the State in which the parties have their places of business: (i) the place of arbitration if determined in, or pursuant to, the arbitration agreement; (ii) any place where a substantial part of the obligations of the commercial relationship is to be performed or the place with which the subject-matter of the dispute is most closely connected; or
> (c) the parties have expressly agreed that the subject-matter of the arbitration agreement relates to more than one country.

1.67 Article 1(3)(c) of the Model Law is very broad indeed. It effectively allows parties to agree that their arbitration is international, thus opting into the law or provisions of law applicable to international arbitrations in the jurisdiction

3.4 Key features and overview of arbitration

3.4.1 Arbitration agreement

Since party consent is the very essence of arbitration, an arbitration agreement is perhaps its most essential feature. Without an arbitration agreement there can be no arbitration.[75]

By entering into an arbitration agreement the parties principally do two things: first, they agree to oust (or at least significantly restrict) the jurisdiction of the domestic court(s) that would ordinarily be competent to decide their dispute; second, they agree to authorise an arbitral tribunal to decide that dispute instead. These are sometimes called, respectively, the negative and positive effects of an arbitration agreement. The extent of these two effects is determined by the language of the arbitration agreement itself because an arbitral tribunal's jurisdiction is limited to what the parties have granted it.[76]

When parties agree to arbitrate, they typically do so in one of two ways. The most common is at the time of negotiating a contract. The parties can insert an arbitration clause into their contract which provides for the resolution of future disputes by arbitration. The other occasion is in the form of a submission agreement after a dispute has arisen. Here the parties refer their pre-existing dispute, or some part of it, to arbitration.

An arbitration agreement is a binding, <u>contractual</u> arrangement between the parties. It may at first seem trite to emphasise the word contractual but it is important. An arbitration agreement is a contract, the nature of which is much like any other contract. But a feature of an agreement to arbitrate is that it is, in effect, specifically enforceable. If a party refuses to participate in the arbitration, it will nonetheless be bound by the arbitrator's award. Furthermore, as noted above, by agreeing to arbitrate a party loses its right to litigate the merits of the dispute in court.

3.4.2 Arbitrators

Having highly professional, efficient and impartial arbitrators is essential to an efficient, satisfying international arbitration.[77]

An underlying feature and key advantage of arbitration is that the parties can choose the arbitrator(s). This inspires confidence in the process and enables parties to choose people with appropriate expertise. It is often said that the very best arbitral tribunals are those where the parties have been able to agree on the

---

[75] Arbitration agreements are dealt with in Chapter 4. ICSID arbitration is sometimes described as 'arbitration without privity' because of the nature of establishing the consent to arbitrate. This is discussed in Chapter 10.
[76] Given the importance of consent, there are frequently disputes about the extent of an arbitral tribunal's jurisdiction. Jurisdiction in arbitration is dealt with in Chapter 5.
[77] Issues surrounding the appointment and removal of arbitrators are dealt with in Chapter 6.

identity of all of its members. Of course it often happens that, by the time a dispute arises, the parties cannot agree. That is why arbitration agreements, arbitration rules and arbitration laws provide a fallback or default appointment mechanism. Typically, if there are to be three arbitrators then each side nominates one and, if the parties cannot agree on the chairperson's identity, he or she is appointed by the default mechanism. If there is to be a single arbitrator, a similar default mechanism applies if the parties cannot agree on the arbitrator.

1.74 In general, there are no qualifications required in order to sit as an arbitrator. It is not necessary to have legal training or a legal qualification. Parties sometimes choose an engineer or other technical person whose expertise relates to the issues of the case. In practice though, most international arbitrators have a legal background or solid experience in the law.

1.75 The parties' choice of arbitrators is limited by mandatory legal requirements, particularly that all arbitrators be and remain impartial and independent from the parties. This requirement is reflected in virtually all arbitration rules and laws and applies as an internationally accepted overriding rule of international arbitration practice. Arbitrators who are not independent can be removed by the relevant supervising institution or court.

3.4.3 Seat of arbitration

1.76 The seat (or place) of arbitration is an important legal concept. The seat's law provides the supporting legal framework for the arbitration. Its courts may be called on to provide assistance during the arbitration. Its courts also have exclusive jurisdiction to hear an action to set aside the arbitral award.[78]

1.77 The seat of arbitration is usually chosen by the parties. The parties can choose virtually any place they wish, and in practice they often choose a seat that is neutral vis-à-vis all parties. Thus, for example, for a contract involving one party from Hong Kong and another from India, the arbitration clause might select Singapore as the seat of arbitration because it is neutral, geographically convenient for both parties, has an excellent arbitration law, and has efficient courts in case supportive measures are needed. Many other jurisdictions in the Asia-Pacific also have excellent arbitration laws and courts. Parties should ensure that the chosen seat of arbitration has a good law on arbitration and that it is a signatory to the New York Convention.

1.78 It is not necessary that any person involved in the arbitration actually lives or works at the seat of arbitration, or that anyone has had any connection with it or even ever visited it. Nor is it necessary that any part of the arbitration proceedings – such as the hearings and meetings – actually takes place there. The seat simply functions as the jurisdiction that provides the legal framework for the arbitration.

---

78 Issues concerning the seat of arbitration and setting aside of the award are addressed in Chapters 2 and 9, respectively.

3.4.4 Party autonomy and procedure

It was noted above that consent is a fundamental aspect of international arbitration. Consent implies choice. International arbitration provides many choices to the parties, ranging from the seemingly trivial to the more fundamental. 1.79

The first choice the parties make is the choice to resolve their disputes by arbitration. The second might be the seat of arbitration, discussed above. Another is to choose the law that will apply. 1.80

Choice of law issues in international arbitration can be interesting.[79] This is primarily because in international arbitration there is no *lex fori* (law of the forum). Although the law of the seat of arbitration provides the legal backbone of the arbitration, it does not generally provide the arbitration with a system of conflict of laws rules. Many different laws might be relevant in an international arbitration, applicable to various issues in the case. In international arbitration the parties can even choose that the arbitrators will apply general principles of international commercial law, or principles of fairness and equity (*amiable composition*) in resolving their dispute. 1.81

Another choice, and one of the major advantages of arbitration over litigation, relates to procedure. In litigation the procedure is fixed or otherwise determined by the rules of court. In arbitration there is enormous flexibility for the parties to choose the kind of procedure that they wish to adopt for their arbitration. There are very few limits on that choice. For example, the parties can and frequently do agree on a set of arbitration procedural rules, such as the rules of an arbitral institution.[80] If so, those rules will apply somewhat contractually – as though they have been incorporated into the parties' contract by reference. Notwithstanding the choice of any rules, the parties can agree to any kind of procedure they wish, such as short and cheap or long and detailed; with expert assistance or without; with an oral hearing or without; with witnesses or not, etc.[81] 1.82

3.4.5 Finality of outcomes

Finality is another major advantage of international arbitration over litigation. In general, and in all jurisdictions that are the focus of this book, there is no appeal from an award issued in an international arbitration. In most arbitration laws the only recourse against an international arbitral award is an application to set aside the award. This is clearly stipulated in Article 34 of the Model Law.[82] 1.83

The bases for setting aside an award are narrow, relating for example to whether there was a valid arbitration agreement, whether the parties had capacity, whether the arbitrator was independent and impartial, and whether the 1.84

---

79 Choice of law in international arbitration is discussed in Chapter 3.
80 Arbitral institutions are discussed below in Section 3.4.7.
81 Procedure is dealt with in Chapter 7, which also explains the legal limits to party autonomy.
82 Unlike the English Arbitration Act 1996, the Model Law does not provide an avenue for any appeals at all, even arising from a question of law. As an example of a case confirming this, see the Singapore decision of *PT Asuransi Jasa Indonesia (Persero) v Dexia Bank SA* [2007] 1 SLR 597 (Singapore Court of Appeal). Recourse from awards is dealt with in Chapter 9. The only recourse against an ICSID award is by way of an amendment procedure, which is discussed in Chapter 10.

procedure was fair and equitable to all parties. An award can also be set aside where it breaches rules of international public policy.

1.85 The question of whether or not an appeal (in addition to a setting-aside procedure) is available is determined by the law of the seat of arbitration. The laws of some jurisdictions, notably England,[83] do allow a limited form of appeal. The laws of several jurisdictions in the Asia-Pacific allow a limited form of appeal under their legislation applying to domestic but not international arbitrations.

1.86 If the law provides that an application for setting aside is the only form of recourse available, it is generally accepted that the parties are not permitted – even by express agreement – to authorise a more extensive appeal. This was confirmed recently by the US Supreme Court.[84] It can therefore be said that finality is an underlying and perhaps even mandatory feature of international arbitration.

3.4.6 International enforcement of arbitration agreements and awards

1.87 Another key advantage of arbitration over international litigation is that it is generally much simpler to enforce an arbitral award abroad than it is to enforce a court judgment abroad.[85] Enforcement is effective in arbitration principally due to the New York Convention, a brief history of which has been provided above. The New York Convention obliges contracting states, through their courts, to do two things: (i) enforce arbitration agreements and (ii) enforce foreign arbitral awards.

1.88 Enforcement of arbitration agreements means that if a party begins court proceedings in a New York Convention country and the opposing party contests that court's jurisdiction on the basis of the arbitration agreement, the court must stay its own proceedings and refer the parties to arbitration unless it finds that the arbitration agreement is null and void, inoperative or incapable of being performed.[86] It does not matter where the chosen seat of arbitration is – it can be within the same country or abroad. This mechanism greatly reduces the chances of court proceedings taking place in parallel to arbitration proceedings.

1.89 Enforcement of awards means using the procedures and mechanisms of domestic courts to ensure compliance with the award if a party refuses to honour it voluntarily. Basically, any New York Convention party is obliged to recognise and enforce a foreign award without imposing procedures more onerous than those that apply to the enforcement of court judgments rendered in the enforcing country. There are very narrow grounds on which a court can refuse to enforce an award under the New York Convention. These are almost

---

[83] See Section 69 of the English Arbitration Act 1996.
[84] *Hall Street Associates, LLC v Mattel Inc*, 128 S Ct 1396, 2008 (US Supreme Court).
[85] Enforcement of awards is dealt with in Chapter 9. Concerning enforcement of foreign court judgments, see above footnote 43 regarding The Hague Convention on Choice of Courts Agreements.
[86] Enforcement of arbitration agreements is dealt with in Chapter 4. The extent to which a court will consider the existence of an arbitration agreement in referring the parties to arbitration is dealt with in Chapter 5.

identical to those mentioned above for setting aside an arbitral award under the Model Law.[87]

An arbitral award can be enforced in any country that is a party to the New York Convention where the losing party has assets. If the place where enforcement is sought is not one of the approximately 145 New York Convention signatory countries, enforcement is trickier. Enforcement may, however, be facilitated by another bilateral or regional enforcement treaty that is similar to the New York Convention. It might alternatively be facilitated by the jurisdiction's own laws.[88]

3.4.7 Arbitral institutions

An arbitral institution is an organisation that provides services in connection with arbitration proceedings. Certain leading arbitral institutions have in addition assumed a role of industry regulators, setting standards and developing soft law for arbitration. They may also organise conferences and training sessions for arbitrators and lawyers. Arbitral institutions have contributed significantly to the growth of international arbitration and their popularity is such that a discussion of the key features of arbitration would be incomplete without them.[89]

When considering the sociological aspects of international commercial arbitration in 1982, Ottarndt Glossner said of the arbitral institution:[90]

> It is a matter of definition what the arbitration institution means.... In any case, much depends on the organisation of the arbitration institution. There must be enough qualified persons to handle the matter and to deal with the task of administering arbitration proceedings, in short there must be a well equipped infrastructure, an experienced routine in the mechanics of handling the subjects and the individuals and of the legal appraisal of the cases.... it is essential that they provide a smooth handling machinery, that they stay away from undue influence, that if such influence is exercised there is room for challenge of such practice and that arbitration awards which are the consequence of improper handling can be set aside. If these guarantees are granted, an arbitration institution can be valued on the same level as a law court.

The level of service offered by an arbitral institution depends entirely on the institution and can range from simple appointment of a default arbitrator to full supervision and monitoring from the beginning to the end of the proceedings. The services offered by institutions operating at the latter end of that spectrum may include:

(i) checking that there is a prima facie arbitration agreement (certain institutions only);
(ii) appointing arbitrators if a party fails to appoint one, or if the two party-appointed arbitrators (or the parties themselves) cannot agree on the chairperson (or sole arbitrator);

---

[87] The New York Convention refusal grounds are dealt with in Chapter 9.
[88] Enforcement of awards in non-New York Convention countries is dealt with in Chapter 9.
[89] Information on Asia-Pacific and other arbitral institutions is provided in Appendix 1. Certain Asia-Pacific arbitral institutions are also discussed in Section 4 below.
[90] O Glossner, 'Sociological Aspects of International Commercial Arbitration', (1982) 10 *International Business Law* 311, at p. 313.

(iii) removing and replacing an arbitrator who has become unable to complete his or her role for any reason;
(iv) deciding challenges as to the independence and/or impartiality of an arbitrator;
(v) keeping an up-to-date file on the arbitration proceedings;
(vi) scrutinising the arbitration award before it is finalised (certain institutions only); and
(vii) managing the administrative and financial aspects of the arbitration.

1.94 An institution's role in relation to financial aspects of the arbitration can be very valuable. The institution not only saves the arbitral tribunal time, as with several of the features listed above, but also acts as an intermediary between the arbitral tribunal and the parties, removing the need for them to deal with each other directly on the delicate issue of the arbitrators' fees.[91]

1.95 The cost of the services provided by an arbitral institution and the manner in which they are calculated are important points of difference among arbitral institutions. Another important difference is the method used by each institution to determine arbitrators' fees. The institution's fees are commonly calculated as a percentage of the amount in dispute, but may alternatively be fixed as a lump sum irrespective of the amount in dispute (particularly where minimal service is provided) or based on an hourly rate. While there are significant differences in the fees charged by institutions, these must be assessed against the extent and quality of services offered. The key question is whether the institution offers value for money. If the institution charges high fees, then the parties should expect highly qualified, efficient staff offering excellent supervisory services.

1.96 The two most common approaches to determining arbitrators' fees are by hourly rate, either agreed with the parties or fixed by the institution, or by a fee calculated as a regressive percentage of the amount in dispute. Both these types of fees vary and depend on the approach adopted by each institution. Fees calculated on the amount in dispute have the advantage of predictability and proportionality. These fees can be estimated with reasonable certainty at the outset of the arbitration and will be proportionate to the value of the dispute. On the other hand, hourly rates have the advantage of certainty for the arbitrators since the value of a dispute does not necessarily provide a reliable indication of the amount of time required by the arbitrators to dispose of a case. In addition, parties choosing an institution which applies a fee scale based on the amount in dispute should ensure that the institution applies the scale with some degree of flexibility so that the arbitrators are not grossly overpaid or grossly underpaid. Similarly, parties choosing an institution applying an hourly rate should ensure that someone (either the institution or the parties) carefully checks

---

91 In this sense see *ICT Pty Ltd v Sea Containers Ltd* [2002] NSWSC 77 (Supreme Court of New South Wales, Australia), and the discussion of the case in S Greenberg, 'Latest Developments in International Arbitration Down Under', (2003) 7(2) *Vindobona Journal* 287, at p. 294. In that case, an entire arbitral tribunal was removed for misconduct because the arbitrators tried to force the parties to agree to pay hearing cancellation fees.

the reasonableness of the hours claimed, as one should do when obtaining any service based on an hourly rate.

Parties should be very wary of fee structures which appear to provide low remuneration for arbitrators. Good international arbitrators are usually senior professionals accustomed to receiving fees at least equivalent to the upper end of the fees charged for their profession in their home jurisdiction. If the fee structure is too low, the parties are unlikely to be able to retain appropriately qualified arbitrators, or if they do, those arbitrators may not be willing to dedicate the amount of time required to deal with the case properly. 1.97

With the exception of arbitrations seated in mainland China, it is not mandatory in this region to engage an arbitral institution. The alternative to institutional arbitration is ad hoc arbitration, where no institutional administration is involved.[92] In an ad hoc arbitration, some of the services otherwise provided by the institution are undertaken by the arbitral tribunal itself and/or the courts at the seat of arbitration. 1.98

Ad hoc arbitration works well when all parties (and their lawyers) are cooperative. However, by the time a dispute has reached the stage of arbitration it often transpires that at least one party no longer wants to cooperate. There are numerous examples of dilatory tactics which, if used in an ad hoc arbitration, could cause serious delays and costs. Well-established arbitral institutions can deal quickly and efficiently with many such tactics. As Thomas Carbonneau explains:[93] 1.99

> [Ad hoc arbitration] places a substantial burden upon the parties to cooperate in the circumstances of dispute. The expectation of cooperation is likely to be unrealistic. Moreover, arbitral institutions have a good professional track record and have significant experience in the administrative aspects of arbitrations. Unless the parties themselves have substantial expertise in the arbitration process, institutional arbitration becomes a virtual necessity. Also, an award rendered under the auspices of a recognized arbitral institution may have a greater likelihood of enforcement for reasons of institutional reputation. The real question involves choosing among the arbitral institutions.

As Carbonneau notes, if the arbitration was administered by an experienced, reputable institution, this will increase the overall chances of successful recognition and enforcement of a resulting award. The staff of the top institutions have the experience and training necessary to provide legal and administrative support. They can answer arbitrators' and parties' questions, thus increasing the chances that the procedure will not be subject to a valid challenge. Some institutions also scrutinise draft arbitral awards to ensure, so far as possible, that the award is enforceable. Arbitration under the auspices of an experienced 1.100

---

[92] The Permanent Court of Arbitration in The Hague provides some support for ad hoc arbitrations under the UNCITRAL Arbitration Rules, such as appointment of default arbitrators.
[93] TE Carbonneau, 'The Exercise of Contract Freedom in the Making of Arbitration Agreements', (2003) 36 *Vanderbilt Journal of Transnational Law* 1189, at p. 1207.

1.101 institution that scrutinises the award therefore provides the best chances of securing an enforceable outcome.

1.101 For all of the above reasons, it is not surprising that a study on the views of in-house counsel at leading multinational corporations published in 2008 found that '86% of awards that were rendered over the last ten years were under the rules of an arbitration institution, while 14% were under ad hoc arbitrations'.[94] This confirms anecdotal evidence from arbitration practitioners that institutional arbitration is preferred over ad hoc arbitration. The same study showed that on a global level the ICC remained the preferred institution, with 45% of participating corporations preferring the ICC. This was followed by the AAA-ICDR (16%) and the LCIA (11%).[95] In terms of case numbers, that study found that AAA-ICDR was the most frequently used arbitral institution.[96] Asia-Pacific corporations participating in the study were found to prefer submitting their disputes to CIETAC, ICC or LCIA arbitration.[97]

1.102 One very important point must be kept in mind in relation to arbitral institutions: like many aspects of arbitration procedure, an institution can only be utilised if the parties have specifically chosen to use it. It is not possible for an institution to administer an arbitration unless the parties have agreed. Since it is usually difficult for parties to agree after a dispute has arisen, institutions are normally chosen in advance, for example in an arbitration clause contained in a contract.

3.5 Sources of international arbitration procedural law and practice

1.103 International commercial arbitration procedural law[98] arises from private (as opposed to public) international law so it always has some connection to one or various domestic legal systems. In that sense it is not truly international in the way that public international law operates *between* sovereign states. However, the practice and culture of international arbitration procedure has made it *transnational*. This is due to the nature of the sources of international arbitration procedural law, including the fact that various international conventions and widely adopted model laws are involved and that there are supranational practices.

---

[94] PricewaterhouseCoopers and Queen Mary College, *International Arbitration: Corporate Attitudes and Practices 2008*, 2008, p. 15. Similar results were obtained in a prior version of that study: PricewaterhouseCoopers and Queen Mary College, *International Arbitration: Corporate Attitudes and Practices 2006*, 2006, p. 12.
[95] PricewaterhouseCoopers and Queen Mary College, 2008, ibid., p. 15. Similar results were obtained in a prior version of that study: PricewaterhouseCoopers and Queen Mary College, 2006, ibid., p. 12.
[96] Ibid. (2008 version of the study).
[97] Ibid.
[98] This section addresses the sources of international arbitration *procedural* law, rather than issues relating to the determination and application of the *substantive* law that the arbitrators will apply in deciding a case. The latter is the subject of Chapter 3 of this book.

Thus international commercial arbitration unquestionably transcends national boundaries. Put differently, it:[99]

1.104

> lies between international and national law, private and public law, substantive and procedural law, and, in a wider perspective, between the science of law (the jurisprudentia of the Roman jurisconsults), economics and politics.

Furthermore:[100]

1.105

> The attraction that the study and practice of international commercial arbitration has for lawyers is due not only to the sometimes considerable material interests at stake. It is also due in large part to the intellectual appeal of a concept that lies at the crossroads of almost all areas of law, both substantive and methodological, defying the compartmentalization that nowadays all too often results from the excessive specialization and narrow technicalization that have become the dominant trends in modern scholarship. Indeed, the very problems international commercial arbitration has to deal with mean that the only way of resolving many of the difficulties with which it is confronted is by reflecting on the most fundamental questions likely to arise within the context of a legal system: justice, including its forms and aims; judiciality, including its sources and nature; the structure of the legal system *and the purposes of law*.

Different experts have different methods of explaining the sources of international arbitration law and practice. In our view there are at least three general categories of sources. These are:

1.106

(i) national or domestic sources;
(ii) international legal sources; and
(iii) supranational quasi-legal sources.

International arbitration lawyers and arbitrators regularly use all three sources when dealing with issues that arise in arbitrations.

1.107

3.5.1 National or domestic sources

The national or domestic sources are the international arbitration laws of each domestic jurisdiction which is involved in an international arbitration. The most important is the international arbitration law of the seat of arbitration. Each country has its own law on international arbitration.

1.108

Most of the Asia-Pacific jurisdictions that are the focus of this book have adopted laws based on the Model Law. As explained above,[101] the Model Law is a template arbitration law which any state is free to adopt and/or modify. It forms the basis of the arbitration laws in more than 60 states worldwide.[102]

1.109

Domestic case law on arbitration matters, especially in common law countries, is also a source of domestic international arbitration law. The case law needs to be considered together with the statutory laws.

1.110

---

99 E Silva Romero, 'ICC Arbitration and State Contracts', (2002) 13(1) *ICC International Court of Arbitration Bulletin* 34, p. 34.
100 B Oppetit, *Théorie de l'arbitrage*, PUF, 1998, p. 109. This English translation of Oppetit's French text was made by Silva Romero ibid., p. 34.
101 Section 2.3.5.
102 A list of countries whose arbitration laws are based on the Model Law is provided at Appendix 3.

1.111   The other relevant national or domestic legal system which is a relevant source of procedural law in a given arbitration is that of any likely place that the arbitral award may need to be enforced. While not directly applicable, international arbitrators will take this law into consideration to some degree to ensure that the award can be enforced there.

3.5.2 International legal sources

1.112   The Model Law is not an international law. It applies as national law only in the states that have adopted it. International conventions (also referred to as treaties) are different. An international convention attains the status of international law usually when it is ratified by the minimum number of states necessary for it to enter into force. Ordinarily, an international convention that has entered into force regulates the relations only between those state parties to it.

1.113   An international convention may also have domestic effect because individuals may be able to rely on the treaty provisions before domestic courts. To give a treaty domestic effect, the state party to the convention must usually implement the terms of the convention in its territory by enacting domestic legislation. As an example, in Australia the New York Convention has been implemented through the International Arbitration Act 1974. This domestic enactment enables Australian courts to entertain enforcement proceedings based on the New York Convention, which is an international law.

1.114   An important distinction between an international convention and a model law is that a state adopting a model law can decide to modify any term it chooses. International conventions cannot be modified by the country signing them, except to the extent that the convention permits modifications or reservations.

1.115   The most important international convention in relation to international commercial arbitration is the New York Convention. The Geneva Conventions of 1923 and 1927, although now almost obsolete, are also international legal sources of arbitration law. Regional conventions are also relevant. These include the 1961 European Convention on International Commercial Arbitration and the 1975 Inter-American Convention on International Commercial Arbitration, but they do not affect the Asia-Pacific region.

1.116   Other international sources that should be mentioned are free trade agreements and investment treaties. Examples include the 2003 Singapore-Australia Free Trade Agreement, the 2009 Agreement Establishing the ASEAN-Australia-New Zealand Free Trade Area and the 2005 Agreement Between the Government of the Republic of Singapore and the Government of the Republic of Indonesia on the Promotion and Protection of Investments. These become international law as between the parties to them. The breach of a free trade agreement or an investment treaty obligation may give rise to an international arbitration between a state party to that treaty and an investor that is a national of the other (or another) state party. Breach of treaty obligations where two states are involved might alternatively give rise to a case before the world's international court – the International Court of Justice.

All of the above international treaties or conventions are international legal sources of arbitration law. 1.117

3.5.3 Supranational and quasi-legal sources

To understand supranational and quasi-legal sources one needs to think much more broadly about the law than one does in domestic legal practice. Moreover, the notion and concept of supranational sources are understood more naturally by civil lawyers than common lawyers. Civil legal systems are generally more familiar with the concept of 'soft laws'. These include documents, texts, academic articles, working groups, studies, international practices etc. They all form an important part of the law and practice of international arbitration but are not strictly *law* at all. 1.118

The simplest example might be the rules of international arbitral institutions. These are not law. They will only apply if the parties have adopted them as part of their contract. Thus they apply as contractual provisions rather than law. However, the worldwide existence and use of these rules have created standards of practice which influence arbitration procedures even when the rules in question do not apply contractually in a given case. Thus a party or arbitrator might refer to a well-known provision of the UNCITRAL Arbitration Rules as reflecting a general principle of international commercial arbitration, even though the UNCITRAL Arbitration Rules do not directly apply as a matter of contract to the arbitration in question. 1.119

Similarly, although the Model Law only becomes law once it is adopted by a state, it is also a supranational source of arbitration law given that it was developed by a highly respected international organisation (UNCITRAL) and has been subsequently adopted by so many countries. This means that even if the Model Law is not applicable in a particular arbitration its provisions can, like the UNCITRAL Arbitration Rules example given above, be used as an expression of the general principles of international arbitration law. The Model Law is therefore a supranational source of international arbitration law both (i) because so many arbitration laws are based on it and (ii) because it is a reflection of general principles of international arbitration law. 1.120

Another important supranational source is comprised of journal articles, books and other publications by experts. Articles and books will often be cited by arbitral tribunals in their awards and by lawyers in their legal briefs. They might, for example, be cited as authority for a proposition in relation to arbitral practice to support a party's position as to what procedure an arbitral tribunal should adopt. A notable annual publication is the International Council for Commercial Arbitration's ('ICCA') Yearbook of Commercial Arbitration. It has been an important source of arbitral jurisprudence since it was first published in 1976. It reproduces extracts of arbitral awards, court decisions on arbitration, court decisions on multilateral arbitration conventions, commentary on court decisions on the New York Convention, and updates on developments in arbitration law and practice, including investment treaty arbitration. 1.121

1.122 Several supranational sources of arbitration law result from industry self-regulation. These include arbitral and other institutions (such as ICCA and the International Bar Association ('IBA')) which conduct conferences, organise working groups and committees, publish arbitration awards, and accordingly become a source of authority regarding the practice of international arbitration. These various associations, committees and working groups often produce documents which become important parts of arbitration practice. The 1999 IBA Rules on the Taking of Evidence in International Commercial Arbitration (which were updated in 2010) and the 2004 IBA Guidelines on Conflicts of Interest in International Arbitration are good examples of supranational sources of international arbitration law developed by IBA working groups. Similarly, the ICC Commission on Arbitration publishes the results of special studies on particular aspects of arbitration. An example is the ICC Report on Drafting Arbitral Awards. All of these rules, guidelines and publications are not law in the sense that they do not govern any international arbitration proceedings unless the parties specifically agree to adopt them. However, when a highly esteemed group of international lawyers have painstakingly formulated such guidelines or rules, arbitrators will be tempted to be guided by the practices set out in them even if they do not apply specifically in a given case.

1.123 The production of these guidelines and rules etc. is sometimes criticised as reducing the flexibility of arbitration and making it too formalistic and 'judicialised'. On the other hand, some consider that such documents are sufficiently flexible and provide invaluable guidance to those who have less experience in arbitration. Providing such guidance for parties, arbitrators and lawyers helps to maintain quality and equality in the arbitral process. It is akin to a right of access to the law.[103]

1.124 Seminal cases from national jurisdictions constitute another supranational source of arbitration law. Although these will not be binding on a foreign arbitral tribunal, they may be persuasive and have the effect of changing international arbitration practices. A seminal case may trigger working groups or studies such as those mentioned above, and/or the writing of academic articles. A few examples of well-known domestic court decisions on arbitration include the US Supreme Court decisions of *Mitsubishi v Chrysler*[104] and *Hall Street v Mattel*;[105] the English House of Lords decisions of *Coppee-Lavalin v Ken-Ren*[106] and *Premium Nafta v Fiona Trust*;[107] the French Cour de Cassation decisions of

---

[103] For an interesting discussion of the pros and cons of soft law in international arbitration, see W Park, 'The Procedural Soft Law of International Arbitration' in LA Mistelis and JDM Lew (eds), *Pervasive Problems in International Arbitration*, Kluwer, 2006, p. 141 et seq.
[104] *Mitsubishi Motors v Soler Chrysler-Plymouth* (1985) 105 Supreme Court Reports, 3346.
[105] *Hall Street Associates, LLC v Mattel Inc*, 128 S Ct 1396, 2008 (US Supreme Court).
[106] *Coppee-Lavalin SA/NA & Voest-Alpine AG v Ken-Ren Chemicals & Fertilisers Ltd (in liq)* [1994] 2 All ER 449.
[107] *Premium Nafta Products Ltd v Fili Shipping Co Ltd* [2007] 2 All ER (Comm) 1053 on appeal from *Fiona Trust & Holding Corporation v Privalov* [2007] 4 All ER 951.

Dalico,[108] *Dow Chemicals*[109] and *Dutco*;[110] and the European Court of Justice decision of *Eco Swiss v Benetton*.[111] From the Asia-Pacific, some examples are the Australian High Court decision of *Esso v Plowman*;[112] the New Zealand High Court decision of *Methanex Motunui Ltd v Spellman*;[113] the Singapore Court of Appeal decision of *PT Garuda Indonesia v Birgen Air*;[114] and the Indian Supreme Court decision of *SBP v Patel Engineering*.[115] These decisions have all triggered discussion and analysis of arbitration principles and led to the development of practices, rules changes and/or soft law.

Published international arbitral awards are also a supranational source of arbitration law. For example, the ICC publishes in various places extracts of ICC arbitral awards; the awards issued by the Iran-United States Claims Tribunal are reported in over 30 volumes; and there is a burgeoning body of published investment treaty arbitration awards. Although no system of binding precedent applies in international commercial arbitration, certain of these published awards or a series of similar arbitral decisions are sometimes considered as persuasive authority by arbitral tribunals.

1.125

Supranational sources of arbitration law and practice are not binding in the sense that they are not strictly law. However, they can have an important influence on the conduct and outcome of arbitration proceedings – that is both the manner in which lawyers plead their cases and the manner in which arbitrators take their decisions – and, albeit to a lesser extent, the conduct and outcome of domestic court proceedings.[116]

1.126

4 International arbitration in the Asia-Pacific

4.1 The growth of international arbitration in the Asia-Pacific

As noted above, Asia has an ancient history of arbitration that can be traced back to about 2100–1600 BC whereas international arbitration as we know it today developed mainly in the West, especially Europe, as a consequence of thriving international trade creating the need for a reliable system to resolve international commercial disputes.[117] Asia did not have the same political and

1.127

---

108 *Municipalité de Khoms El Mergeb v Société Dalico*, 20 December 1993, Cour de Cassation (1re Ch. Civ.), [1994] *Revue de L'Arbitrage* 116.
109 *Société Dow Chemical France v Société Isover – Saint-Gobain*, 21 October 1983, Cour d'appel de Paris, [1984] *Revue de L'Arbitrage* 98; 110 *Journal du droit international* (Clunet) 899, 1983; 9 *Yearbook of Commercial Arbitration* 131, 137, 1984.
110 *Siemens AG and BKMI Industrienlagen GmbH v Dutco Consortium Construction Co*, Cour de Cassation (1re Ch Civ) 7 January 1992.
111 (1999) ECR 3055.
112 *Esso Australia Resources Ltd v The Honourable Sidney James Plowman* (1995) 183 CLR 10.
113 [2004] 1 NZLR 95.
114 *PT Garuda Indonesia v Birgen Air* [2002] 1 SLR 393 (Singapore Court of Appeal).
115 *SBP & Co v Patel Engineering* 2005 8 SCC 618.
116 See generally Park, op. cit. fn 103, p. 141 et seq.
117 See Section 2.1 above.

transnational economic climate in the late 18th and early 19th centuries. It also has a traditionally less confrontational approach to dispute resolution and less rigid approach to the interpretation of contractual obligations.[118] These factors, among others, delayed the growth of international arbitration in this region. But as we will see below an 'arbitration craze'[119] in the last 20–30 years has made up for that initially slow growth.

1.128　Asia did experience some international arbitrations in the early 19th century, particularly in its trade disputes with parties from Europe. It is interesting to note that the ICC Court administered its first case involving an Asian party in its inaugural year, 1923. The claimant was Thai, the respondents were from the US and Portugal, and the dispute related to the delivery of lanterns. In addition, as noted above, several states from this region were parties to the first international instrument facilitating international arbitration: the 1923 Geneva Protocol on Arbitration Clauses. Asia-Pacific signatories included then British colonies such as Sri Lanka (at that time called Ceylon), Myanmar (at the time called Burma), New Zealand and India, as well as Japan and Thailand. The parties to the 1927 Geneva Convention on the Execution of Foreign Arbitral awards were similar, excluding Japan. Some early examples of Asian arbitration institutions include those of Japan (1950)[120], China (1956), and India (1965).

1.129　The Asia-Pacific international arbitration climate has changed dramatically in the last 20–30 years. The region is now a major user of international arbitration, with at least 500 international arbitrations taking place here each year. The background to that growth should be considered alongside the Asian international economic climate and legal framework.

1.130　With Japan taking the lead, Asia started to gain international economic significance after World War Two, and saw particularly impressive economic growth in the last few decades, up until the 2008 financial crisis. Japan's success spread to South Korea, Malaysia, Singapore, Thailand, and Taiwan. China and India are now among the world's top economies. Cambodia is the latest country to become one of Asia's economic hotspots, attracting investment from neighbours such as China, Korea, Japan, Singapore and Malaysia. Cambodia's economy grew at an average rate of 9.8% from 2003–2008. Asia is also home to two of the world's principal commercial and financial centres: Singapore and Hong Kong, which have consequently become two of the world's most prominent and effective seats for international arbitrations.

1.131　Much of the regional growth in the last few decades has been connected to strong international trading, exports and inward investment to develop infrastructure. An obvious consequence of this kind of economic growth is increased international commercial transactions. These included simple international sale

---

118 The influence of culture on the development of international arbitration in Asia is discussed below at Section 4.2.
119 Taniguchi speaks of the Asian 'arbitration craze': Yasuhei Taniguchi, 'The Changing Attitude to International Commercial Dispute Settlement in Asia and the Far East', (1997) *Arbitration and Dispute Resolution Law Journal* 67, at p. 70.
120 It should be noted that the date given in Appendix 1 is for the JCAA, which was established in 1953.

of goods and services transactions, construction of manufacturing facilities and technology transfers. Infrastructure projects have been particularly strong in the Asia-Pacific in the past 10–15 years. With these transactions came related commercial activities: international financing, cooperation mechanisms like joint ventures and shareholders' agreements, and mergers and acquisitions. International transactions sometimes lead to international commercial disputes; and that creates a need to resolve them in a manner that is commercially sensible and legally recognisable throughout the globe. As a result of this need, the Asia-Pacific was on its way to becoming an important international commercial arbitration region by the early 1990s; and since then it has blossomed. This can be seen in several ways.

First, numerous Asian legal systems are now 'arbitration-friendly' (i.e. providing a legal system that is supportive of arbitration), the courts and legislators being conscious of the need to keep abreast of international developments. Almost all are parties to the New York Convention.[121] Concerning local international arbitration laws, there has been a raft of legislative changes based on the internationally recognised Model Law. Between 1990 and 2006, legislation based on the Model Law was adopted in Bangladesh, Cambodia, Hong Kong, Macau, India, Japan, Korea, Malaysia, The Philippines, Singapore, Sri Lanka, Thailand, Australia and New Zealand. New Zealand was the first country in the world to adopt the 2006 amendments to the Model Law. Hong Kong is expected to adopt the 2006 amendments in late 2010 or early 2011[122] and both Singapore and Australia adopted some of these amendments in 2010.[123] It is also anticipated that the individual states and territories of Australia will shortly adopt the Model Law as their arbitration laws, to replace rather outdated uniform State legislation. Vietnam passed a new, more modern arbitration law in mid 2010, which takes effect from January 2011. The law was inspired by the Model Law but does not reflect all of its provisions. India's law ministry in early 2010 released a consultation paper on proposed amendments to the arbitration law in India. Meanwhile Taiwan, while not adopting the Model Law, enacted an arbitration-friendly law in 1998. Similarly, several key principles in the 1994 Chinese arbitration law appear to have been inspired by the Model Law.

The widespread adoption of the Model Law was an essential ingredient for the growth of arbitration in this region. Morgan describes it as having been critical:[124]

---

[121] Australia, Bangladesh, Brunei Darussalam, Cambodia, China, Hong Kong, India, Indonesia, Japan, Laos People's Democratic Republic, Malaysia, Nepal, New Zealand, Pakistan, Philippines, Republic of Korea, Singapore, Sri Lanka, Thailand and Vietnam.

[122] The proposed amendments are summarised by L de Germiny, 'Arbitration Law reform in Hong Kong: Furthering the UNCITRAL Model Law', (2008) July *Asian Dispute Review* 73. The second reading speech of the Bill is expected to take place in October 2010.

[123] In Singapore the major changes relate to the definition of 'arbitration agreement', court-ordered interim measures and the designation of an officer of an arbitration institution to authenticate arbitration agreements and awards. In Australia, the International Arbitration Amendment Bill was passed by the Commonwealth Parliament. It modernises and corrects certain aspects of the Act to make Australian international arbitration law more arbitration-friendly including, like Singapore, the definition of arbitration agreements and interim measures.

[124] Morgan, op. cit. fn 62, p. 47. See also M Hwang and S Lee, 'Survey of South East Asian Nations on the Application of the New York Convention', (2008) 25(6) *Journal of International Arbitration* 873, who confirm

Being visibly a model law jurisdiction or having the UNCITRAL model law as a 'trademark' over territories' arbitration law, is critically important from the standpoint of attracting international arbitration business to an arbitration centre. This was a clear motivation to Hong Kong and Singapore.

1.134 The Asia-Pacific now stands out as *the* principal Model Law region of the world, with the highest concentration of Model Law countries. This shows its commitment, at a regional as well as national level, to developing a sound climate for efficient international dispute resolution, in turn facilitating healthy international trade.

1.135 As regards investor-state arbitration, the Asia-Pacific had an early start – one of the earliest ICSID awards concerned an Asian state.[125] Thereafter, this type of arbitration was slow to take off in this region. Much like international commercial arbitration, there appears to be a lag in Asia-Pacific practice compared to Europe and the Americas. Most Asia-Pacific states have ratified the ICSID Convention, with the exceptions of Thailand and India. Many have, in addition, ratified a considerable number of bilateral investment treaties ('BITs'). Nonetheless, compared with other regions, ICSID arbitration claims against states from the Asia-Pacific have so far been relatively infrequent. Similarly, in comparison with other regions, there is a relative paucity of ICSID arbitration claims instituted by Asia-Pacific companies or nationals. Given the number of investment treaties signed in this region, it is to be expected that the Asia-Pacific will in due course follow the prodigious rise of investment arbitration around the globe.[126]

1.136 Singapore and Hong Kong are the leading arbitration jurisdictions in the Asia-Pacific, resulting from several factors including geographic convenience, prominence as global financial centres, English as the main business language, excellent international arbitration laws, and efficient, supportive, corruption-free courts. Both cities are unquestionably viewed as world-renowned seats for international arbitration and are regularly chosen as the seat even when they have no connection whatsoever to the dispute or any of the parties involved. Both cities are constantly looking for ways to keep these reputations, as can be seen from recent developments in each jurisdiction.

1.137 In April 2008, the Singapore Government announced two new developments intended to make the country more attractive for international arbitration: a tax incentive for firms carrying out international arbitration work with hearings in Singapore and a work pass exemption for those entering Singapore for arbitration and mediation services. In mid-2009, a state-of-the-art, purpose-built arbitration hearing centre called Maxwell Chambers opened for business. It houses regional offices of international arbitration institutions such as the Singapore International Arbitration Centre ('SIAC'), the International Centre for Dispute Resolution ('ICDR'), the ICC Court, and the Permanent Court of Arbitration

that the Model Law's widespread adoption is 'one prominent factor' in the recent growth of arbitration in South-East Asia. See also Sornarajah, op. cit. fn 63.
125 *Amco Asia Corp v Republic of Indonesia*, ICSID Case No. ARB/81/1, Award of 20 November 1984.
126 See generally L Nottage and R Weeramantry, 'Investment Arbitration for Japan and Asia: Five Perspectives on Law and Practice', *Sydney Centre for International Law Working Paper*, no. 21, March 2009 at www.law.usyd.edu.au/scil/WorkingPapers.html.

('PCA') as well as arbitration bodies such as the Singapore Institute of Arbitrators. In mid-2009, the Singapore Government also announced that it would be revising Singapore's arbitration law to make it even more arbitration-friendly, and to include several of the 2006 amendments to the Model Law. The International Arbitration (Amendment) Act 2009 came into force on 1 January 2010.

Hong Kong's importance was confirmed when the ICC Court decided in 2008 to open an office of its Secretariat there, fully integrating the ICC into the Asia-Pacific network of international arbitral institutions. It is the first time in the ICC Court's history (i.e. since 1923) that the Secretariat will have case administration staff based outside ICC Headquarters in Paris. Although Hong Kong is now a part of China, its laws and courts still operate according to the English legal system. After its handover to China in 1997, one arbitration-related problem arose because the New York Convention ceased to apply to the enforcement of Hong Kong awards in mainland China and vice versa. While this caused some initial concerns, it was resolved by the Memorandum of Understanding on the Arrangement Concerning the Mutual Enforcement of Arbitral Awards between mainland China and Hong Kong, signed on 20 June 1999. The arrangement confirmed the general enforceability of Hong Kong arbitral awards in mainland China and set out a detailed procedure (including time limits) for seeking enforcement. Mainland China and Macau subsequently signed a similar agreement called the Arrangement on Reciprocal Recognition and Enforcement of Arbitral Awards.[127] Hong Kong is currently undertaking a major review of its arbitration laws and will likely adopt most of the 2006 Model Law amendments.[128]

A number of arbitration institutions have evolved or been rejuvenated in the Asia-Pacific over the last 20–30 years. Many have recently modernised their arbitration rules, adopting sound international standards. The Hong Kong International Arbitration Centre ('HKIAC') amended its rules in 2008. The new HKIAC Administered Rules represent a comprehensive overhaul of its former version which incorporated the 1976 UNCITRAL Arbitration Rules. Other updates include the Japan Commercial Arbitration Centre ('JCAA') in 2008 (which also amended its rules for administering UNCITRAL arbitrations in 2009), SIAC in 2007 and again in 2010, Korean Commercial Arbitration Board ('KCAB') in 2007,[129] Australian Centre for International Commercial Arbitration ('ACICA') in 2005 (which also released rules for expedited arbitration in 2008)[130], Indonesian Arbitration Board ('BANI') in 2003, and Kuala Lumpur Regional Centre for Arbitration ('KLRCA') in 2003 with a revision in 2008 and a further revision in 2010 adopting the 2010 UNCITRAL Arbitration Rules. In 2008, the Beijing Arbitration Commission ('BAC') modernised its 2001 rules so that parties can select

---

[127] For a detailed account of the development of Hong Kong as an arbitral centre through to 2002 see N Kaplan, 'Arbitration in Asia – Developments and Crises – Part 1', (2002) 19(2) *Journal of International Arbitration* 163.
[128] The proposed amendments are summarised by de Germiny, op. cit. fn 122.
[129] Under Article 41 of the Korean Arbitration Act, arbitration institutions must obtain the approval of the Chief Justice of the Korean Supreme Court to establish or amend arbitration rules.
[130] For a discussion of the ACICA Rules see L Nottage and R Garrett (eds), *International Arbitration in Australia*, Federation Press, (forthcoming 2010), Chapter 4. Sydney also unveiled a new international disputes hearing and facilities centre in August 2010.

arbitrators who are not on BAC's ordinary panel for international cases and can agree on increased remuneration for foreign arbitrators. The China International Economic and Trade Arbitration Commission ('CIETAC') Rules were amended six times between 1989 and 2005, and now exist in English as well as Chinese. Finally, the LCIA set up a branch office in Delhi, India in early 2009, and released its special India arbitration rules in early 2010.

1.140 The Arbitrators and Mediators Institute of New Zealand ('AMINZ') established in 2007 an innovative private arbitration appeals tribunal ('AAT'). It was given legislative enactment by the Arbitration Amendment Act 2007, which amended New Zealand's Arbitration Act 1996. Parties can agree to allow appeals on questions of law to the AAT. The system is supervised by the AMINZ Court of Arbitration, which acts as an appointing authority. The parties' agreement to use the AMINZ AAT system implies a waiver of the possibility of appeal to the New Zealand High Court in relation to both the original award and the award rendered by the AAT.[131]

1.141 Apart from arbitral administering institutions, related associations and organisations have sprung up to accommodate and serve the exponentially growing arbitration industry in the Asia-Pacific. In our view, three of the most significant are the Asia-Pacific Regional Arbitration Group ('APRAG'), the Australasian Forum for International Arbitration ('AFIA') and the Vis (East) Moot Competition, which are each explained below.

1.142 APRAG was established in 2004 as a regional federation of arbitration associations. Its membership consists of approximately 30 arbitral institutions and organisations. APRAG promotes an awareness of international arbitration and, in so doing, aims to improve professional standards and knowledge. It holds conferences related to arbitration and publishes a quarterly newsletter with information about developments in the region. It also has observer status at UNCITRAL Working Group II. More information about APRAG and copies of its newsletters can be found at www.aprag.org.

1.143 AFIA was also established in 2004 as a networking and educational forum for the next generation of Asia-Pacific arbitration practitioners. The object of AFIA is principally to introduce and promote international arbitration to younger practitioners in a non-intimidating manner. It holds three or four symposia each year, which have so far taken place in Hong Kong, Kuala Lumpur, Melbourne, Seoul, Shanghai, Singapore and Sydney. AFIA symposia are not like conferences and are conducted in an informal manner. More information can be found at www.afia.net.au.

1.144 Another sign of the Asia-Pacific's prominence was the launch of the Willem C Vis (East) International Arbitration Moot Competition in 2002. Since its inception, it has been held every year in Hong Kong. It is a sister competition to the

---

131 For a general explanation of the AMINZ AAT, see S Williams, 'Arbitration Appeals Tribunal', New Zealand Arbitration Day, 30 November 2007, LexisNexis; and the accompanying critique by S Fitzgerald, 'Arbitration Appeals Tribunal – A Commentary', New Zealand Arbitration Day, 30 November 2007, LexisNexis.

most prestigious and best attended international arbitration event for law students and their professors. To this day, the Vis Moot has been held only in Hong Kong and Vienna, Austria. In 2010, 75 law schools from 17 different countries around the globe competed in the Vis (East) Moot.

Apart from APRAG, AFIA and the Vis (East) Moot, there are numerous signs of this growth in arbitration support associations. The East Asian Branch of the Chartered Institute of Arbitrators, established in 1972, also plays a role in the education of arbitrators. Other examples include the ICC Court's opening of a representative office in Asia in 1997[132] (initially in Hong Kong but now in Singapore); the launch in 2002 of a large and active Intercollegiate Negotiation and Arbitration Competition held each December in Tokyo; the creation in 2003 of an Arbitration Council in Cambodia, followed by the decision in 2009 to establish Cambodia's first arbitral institution, the National Arbitration Centre, which will be supported by the IFC, a member of the World Bank Group; the establishment in 2007 of the Karachi Centre for Dispute Resolution; and the creation in 2008 of an Asian Chapter of the ICC Young Arbitrators' Forum.[133] Finally, international arbitration has been added to the curricula of most leading universities in the Asia-Pacific in the last 10–15 years.

1.145

All this healthy activity has contributed to substantial growth in the number of cases submitted to Asia-Pacific arbitral institutions. For example, HKIAC had a humble nine cases in its inaugural year 1985; 273 international arbitrations in 2003; and 309 international arbitrations in 2009. In 1993, SIAC had 20 cases. In 2003 it received 41 new international arbitrations and 114 in 2009. CIETAC handled 37 cases in 1985, and in 1995 that figure was over 1000. CIETAC's international case load has also increased. Between 2001 and 2008 it has steadily received between 422 and 562 new international cases each year, with 559 in 2009. The Beijing Arbitration Commission, with 11 international cases in 2000, received 72 in 2009. Between 2000 and 2008, KCAB received an average of 55 cases per year, with 78 international arbitrations in 2009.

1.146

The ICC's statistics show marked growth in its arbitrations from this region. In 1980, only 22 parties to ICC arbitrations (or 4.7% of all parties to ICC arbitrations for that year) came from South and East Asia and Oceania.[134] Ten years later, in 1990, that figure had increased by more than five times to 111 parties (or 11.2%); in 2000 it rose to 152 parties (or 11.6%). By 2009, the number of South and East

1.147

---

[132] It should be noted that this is a marketing office, and is to be distinguished from the Hong Kong office of the ICC Court's Secretariat which opened in 2008, as mentioned above.
[133] An active Regional Coordinating Committee was appointed for the Asian Chapter in October 2008. Its three members are based in Tokyo, Hong Kong and Mumbai. It is responsible for the development of ICC YAF in Asia and organises events and develops networks for younger lawyers and in-house counsel. More information can be found at www.iccyaf.org.
[134] In the ICC's statistical system, South and East Asia includes Bangladesh, Brunei, Cambodia, China (People's Republic)/ Hong Kong, India, Indonesia, Japan, South Korea, North Korea, Lao, Malaysia, Maldives, Nepal, Pakistan, Philippines, Singapore, Sri Lanka, Taiwan ROC, Thailand and Vietnam. Oceania includes Australia, Cook Islands, Fiji, Marshall Islands, New Zealand, Northern Mariana Island, Papua New Guinea, Vanuatu and Western Samoa.

Asia and Oceania parties had reached 284 (or 13.5%).[135] Similar growth trends can be seen with respect to the location of ICC arbitration seats. In 1980, no ICC arbitrations were seated in South and East Asia and Oceania. In 1990 eight ICC arbitrations were seated in the region (or 3.2%); and in 2000 there were 13 (or 10.7%). That figure had increased six fold by 2009 when 78 new ICC arbitrations (or 12.4%) were seated in the region. Those 78 cases were seated in 11 different countries but the most common Asia-Pacific seat for ICC arbitrations is Singapore (38 arbitrations in 2009 or 6.03% of all 2009 ICC cases worldwide).

1.148   At the time of writing, all Asia-Pacific arbitration institutions, including the ICC's Hong Kong branch, reported growth for the first half of 2010. The institutions put this growth partly down to disputes having increased as a consequence of the global economic recession, but it confirms the extent to which parties to Asia-Pacific related disputes are choosing arbitration as their preferred method of dispute resolution.

1.149   Despite all these encouraging signs, certain regional jurisdictions still have some distance to go before they can offer an arbitration-friendly legal environment. Some countries are not yet parties to the New York Convention. These include Myanmar and Taiwan.[136] Furthermore, ratifying the New York Convention does not guarantee enforcement of foreign arbitral awards. Problems can be faced enforcing awards in China, Thailand, India, Indonesia and Vietnam, which have all ratified the New York Convention. In a study on the views of in-house counsel at leading multinational corporations published in 2008, the respondents perceived China, India and Russia as the three countries that are most hostile to enforcement of foreign arbitral awards.[137]

1.150   Courts in India, Indonesia and the Philippines have on occasions purported to assert jurisdiction to set aside awards not made in those jurisdictions.[138] This conflicts with the universal principle of international arbitration law, reflected in the Model Law, that only a court at the seat of arbitration can set aside an

---

[135] The very small change in the percentage figures between 1990 and 2008 shows that there was a comparable increase in the number of parties to ICC arbitrations from other parts of the world. Details on ICC statistics can be found in the ICC's Published Statistical Reports for each year. See, e.g. '2009 Statistical Report', (2010) 21 *ICC International Court of Arbitration Bulletin* 5.

[136] Taiwan has not been able to adopt the New York Convention because it is not recognised as an independent state by the United Nations. However, it has reciprocal enforcement agreements or understandings with various states.

[137] PricewaterhouseCoopers and Queen Mary College, 2008, op. cit. fn 94, p. 11. The report states that 'China was the country cited most often with India and Russia also considered as potentially problematic territories'. See also Maniruzzaman who speaks of various problems he perceives to be facing international arbitration in Asia, including problems with enforcing awards in certain jurisdictions (AFM Maniruzzaman, 'Arbitration of International Oil, Gas and Energy Disputes in Asia', (2004) 1(1) *Transnational Dispute Management*). Like Maniruzzaman suggests for much of Asia, Kaplan considers that the core problem in China is the lack of proper education for judges and to some extent lawyers; see N Kaplan, 'Arbitration in Asia – Developments and Crises – Part 2', (2002) 19(3) *Journal of International Arbitration* 245, at pp. 245–247.

[138] For a more positive perspective on India see S Kachwaha, 'The Arbitration Law of India: A Critical Analysis', (2005) 1 *Asian International Arbitration Journal* 105. The recent decision of *Max India Ltd v General Binding Corporation* (Delhi High Court, 6 May 2009) is also encouraging. While not a Supreme Court decision, it takes a more arbitration-friendly approach to the jurisdiction of Indian courts over the conduct of arbitrations seated outside India. Moreover, India's law ministry in early 2010 released a consultation paper on proposed amendments to the arbitration law. One of the reasons for this consultation paper was to examine this very issue, assertions of jurisdiction over foreign-seated arbitration proceedings.

international arbitral award.¹³⁹ Furthermore, Indonesian, Indian, Bangladeshi and Pakistani courts have on occasion issued injunctions to prevent arbitrations from proceeding despite agreements to arbitrate disputes.

1.151 One famous example from Indonesia involved the courts injuncting the three arbitrators (in addition to the parties) from any further steps in an arbitration in which the Indonesian government was the respondent. The penalty for breach of the order was set at US$1 million per arbitrator per day! The arbitral tribunal decided to move the arbitration hearings to The Hague, but the Indonesian member of the arbitral tribunal was 'strongly discouraged' from attending the hearings by his embassy officials in The Netherlands and was sent back to Indonesia.¹⁴⁰ Decisions like this have prompted comments to the effect that there are 'no realistic chances of Indonesia qualifying as an international arbitration venue in the near future. An arbitration venue needs political, economic and legal stability. Regrettably, all of these requirements are currently absent in Indonesia'.¹⁴¹

1.152 Both India and the Philippines have enacted arbitration-friendly legislation but their courts have occasionally strayed from universally accepted principles of arbitration practice. This shows that an effective arbitration statute alone is not sufficient; states must take measures to ensure that arbitration legislation and conventions are applied in line with the international principles on which they are based.¹⁴² Hwang and Lee summarise this problem well, and point to the encouraging general trend away from it:¹⁴³

> The reality, however, is that curial interference has occurred in spite of ostensible support of arbitration and express support in legislation. While the right phrases have been used and repeated, the actual judicial practice has sometimes demonstrated overreach and an approach that can be said to be more visceral than cerebral. Part of it can be attributed to overcoming residual historical distrust of arbitration. The other part may be attributed to a misplaced sense of judicial parochialism and perhaps unfamiliarity with the arbitration process. However, on the whole, we do see a growing trend towards pro-arbitration sentiments and practices pursuant to the increasing

---

139 Article 36(1)(a)(v) of the Model Law and Article V(1)(e) of the New York Convention also refer to the setting aside of awards 'under the law of which' the award was made, but that has very little practical significance because the law under which the award was made is almost always that of the seat of arbitration. See Chapter 9, Section 6.2.5.
140 *Himpurna v Indonesia* and *Patuha v Indonesia* appear as Docs A and B in 15 *Mealey's International Arbitration Report*, Jan 2000. The arbitral tribunal's interim and final awards are extracted in AJ van den Berg (ed), *Yearbook of Commercial Arbitration*, Kluwer Law, 2000, pp. 11–432. See also MF Schaad, 'The Abduction of an Arbitrator – A Disturbing Account of a State's Attempts to Derail an International Arbitration', (1999) 4 *ASA Bulletin* 511 and the judgment of the Dutch Court (District Court, The Hague, Civil law division – President; judgment in summary proceedings of 21 September 1999, docket number 99/1142 *Republic of Indonesia v Himpurna*) in 4 *ASA Bulletin* 583, 1999. See also the discussion in J Werner, 'When Arbitration Becomes War – Some Reflections on the Frailty of the Arbitral Process in Cases Involving Authoritarian States', (2000) 17(4) *Journal of International Arbitration* 97.
141 Schaefer, op. cit. fn 62, p. 36.
142 In the Philippines, the legislature has taken the right approach. Section 25 of the Alternative Dispute Resolution Act 2004 states that 'In interpreting the Act, the court shall have due regard to the policy of the law in favour of arbitration'. However this has not prevented some questionable decisions from the Philippines. For some interesting comments on the teething problems of modern international arbitration in India, see FS Nariman 'Finality in India: the Impossible Dream', (1994) 10 *Arbitration International* 4, at p. 373.
143 Hwang and Lee, op. cit. fn 124, p. 876.

enactment of arbitration legislation adopting the Model Law, coupled with reduced hostility to, and growing judicial acceptance of, arbitration as an alternative...

1.153 Thankfully, horror stories do not occur in the courts of most Asia-Pacific jurisdictions. However, problems associated with judges that are still learning about international arbitral law and practice can happen anywhere. For example, certain Australian courts – while not being hostile towards arbitration – have made decisions which misapply well-established arbitration principles. One court incorrectly held that by selecting arbitral institutional rules parties had excluded the Model Law,[144] and another ordered the reopening of a factual question in the process of enforcing a foreign arbitral award.[145]

1.154 China's arbitration law includes a further unique barrier because ad hoc (non-institutional) arbitrations are not permitted if seated in China. Furthermore, there are doubts as to whether foreign institutions qualify as institutions under Chinese law. On the positive side, Chinese courts do enforce arbitral awards rendered outside China, even if made in an ad hoc arbitration or one administered by a foreign institution.[146] In a letter dated 25 October 2007, the Supreme People's Court specifically stated that ad hoc arbitration awards made in Hong Kong are enforceable in China. A related notification was issued by the Supreme People's Court in January 2010, further increasing confidence in the success of this initiative. In 2007, China took steps towards modernising aspects of its arbitration law. In April 2008 it signed a free trade agreement with New Zealand, including a commitment to arbitration for the resolution of investment disputes if the investor agrees to use domestic review procedures lasting no more than three months. The FTA also includes the competence-competence rule, which ordinarily does not apply in China.[147] Furthermore, having concluded upwards of 120 BITs, China is second only to Germany in the number of BITs any single country has concluded.[148] Finally, in June 2009 the Supreme People's Court issued new directions expected to liberalise and improve the flexibility of mediation by permitting mediation that is not conducted under the auspices of an arbitral institution.

---

144 See the discussion of *Australian Granites v Eisenwerk Hensel Beyreuth GmbH* [2001] 1 Qd R 461 in Chapter 2, Section 4.2.
145 See *Corvetina Technology Ltd v Clough Engineering Ltd.* [2004] NSWSC 700.
146 See a summary of points for the advantages of arbitration over litigation in China listed in J McLaughlin, K Scanlon and C Pan, 'Planning for Commercial Dispute Resolution in Mainland China', (2005) 16 *American Review of International Arbitration* 133, at p. 141. Furthermore, it has been reported that between 2000 and 2008, 58 foreign awards have been recognised and enforced in China and 12 foreign awards have been refused. Most refusals related to the arbitration agreement and the arbitral procedure (reported by G Huangbin 'Overview of Commercial Arbitration in China' during the ALB-SIAC Workshop on Effective Dispute Resolution in China of 26 June 2008, held in Singapore). See also Johnson Tan, 'A Look at CIETAC: Is it Fair and Efficient?', Jones Day, Hong Kong, www.chinalawandpractice.com/Article/1693224/Search/Results/A-Look-at-CIETAC-Is-it-Fair-and-Efficient.html?Keywords=johnson+tan. This article examines a survey of American companies, which apparently shows that they think CIETAC arbitrations are just as fair as arbitrations with institutions outside China.
147 See Article 154 of the China-New Zealand FTA. On the competence-competence rule and its application in China and other Asia-Pacific jurisdictions, see Chapter 5.
148 See *International Investment Rule Making: Stocktaking, Challenges and the Way Forward*, UNCTAD Series on International Investment Policies for Development (2008), UN Doc UNCTAD/ITE/IIT/2007/3, p. 24.

1.155 The problems mentioned above are for the most part in the process of being rectified effectively. The international arbitration community, and particularly that in the Asia-Pacific, is successfully taking steps towards better educating legislatures, judiciaries, lawyers and companies in those jurisdictions where it is necessary. The trend for law schools in the Asia-Pacific to offer international arbitration on their curricula should ensure that the future generation of practitioners will be well versed in arbitration.

1.156 Finally, for cultural, political or other reasons, arbitration has not taken off to the extent that might have been expected within one of Asia's superpowers: Japan. Nottage points out that Japanese companies often now include arbitration clauses in their cross-border contracts and appear regularly in arbitral and court proceedings around the world, but that 'arbitration has failed to take root in Japan'. He cites a key reason as being a general disinterest by the Japanese government but says that the modern, effective, international (and domestic) arbitration law adopted in 2004 might well change this, attracting 'perhaps larger and more complex matters where Japan's mania for minutiae could actually become a comparative advantage.'[149] Another historical reason might be an unexpected side effect of limits on foreign lawyers practising in Japan,[150] although an amendment in 1996 clearly allows them to represent clients in international arbitrations, and full profit-sharing partnerships with Japanese lawyers have been permitted since 2004.

4.2 Asian culture and international arbitration

1.157 A question is often raised about differences in the dispute resolution approaches or cultures between different countries and regions and the impact of those differences on international arbitrations. Given that the Asia-Pacific is now a vibrant region for international arbitrations to take place, in this section we examine the influence of Asian culture on international arbitration and the influence of the Western, particularly Continental European, approach.

4.2.1 Asian social, religious and political cultural diversity

1.158 The Asian countries and cultures that are the focus of this book are extraordinarily diverse. They are arguably far more diverse than in other regions of the world with established international arbitration environments. Asia is probably more diverse than Europe for example, even counting Central and Eastern Europe. One need only consider the diversity of Asian languages and religious influences. There is also intense cultural diversity within many Asian countries, notably China, India, Indonesia and Japan.

1.159 All this intra-country and inter-country diversity adds to the seemingly impossible task of proclaiming common threads between Asian cultures. What is

---

149 L Nottage, 'Japan's New Arbitration Law: Domestication Reinforcing Internationalisation?' (2004) 7(2) *International Arbitration Law Review* 54, at p. 55 and generally.
150 Taniguchi, 1997, op. cit. fn 119, pp. 71–72.

certain is that Asian culture is very different from Western culture. As Taniguchi elegantly puts it:[151]

> Even the Far East, including China, Korea and Japan which have been heavily influenced by Confucianism for centuries, is not uniform. Each country has a language and culture distinctively different from that of others. When we view broader Asia, it is impossible to characterise it except as being 'non-Western'. Even the degree and nature of non-Westernness vary country to country. Moreover, some countries like Singapore are multicultural.... Nevertheless, for an Asian, Asia is Asia. We Asians feel more at home in Asia than in Europe or in America. Despite all kinds of differences we still seem to share more in common with other Asians than with non-Asians.

1.160 Any comparison of social, religious or political cultures is, in any event, outside the scope of this book. What we rather comment on in this section is the culture of dispute resolution and mainly international arbitration in Asia.[152]

4.2.2 Asian dispute resolution culture

1.161 History and culture strongly influence the law as well as commercial and business practices. There is little doubt that each Asian sociopolitical environment has influenced the development of its own unique approach to dispute resolution and evolution of a legal system. The diversity between Asian cultures has in turn created substantial, corresponding diversity between dispute resolution and legal systems.

1.162 As others explain:[153]

> Certainly we can identify some shared cultural and legal traditions across the region, such as those of Islamicization in parts of South East Asia or the Sinitic roots of law and legal culture in North East Asia. The customary law developed within ethnic groups that transcends national borders such as those of commercial networks in the Chinese Diaspora is a supra-national phenomenon. The rise of lawyers and multi-jurisdictional law firms in Asia is also likely to lead to some convergence of forms and techniques for high-value cross-border transactions within Asia. However, at the foundational level if we compare contemporary legal systems and approaches to law in Australia and Taiwan; in Japan and Indonesia; or in Mongolia and Hong Kong SAR, we are still struck by dramatic differences. It is very difficult to identify any common cultural and legal norms or sources of positive laws that are uniformly shared from the former Soviet Far East to Sulawesi, even though there are dense linkages in subgroups, such as those sharing a common colonial heritage. Nonetheless there is no organic relationship linking the cultural and legal histories of all the countries loosely identified as 'Asia'.

1.163 While we attempt to identify major influences on the legal systems and international dispute resolution cultures of Asia, we are conscious of the brevity of

---

151 Taniguchi, 1996, op. cit. fn 23, p. 67.
152 We focus on South and East Asia itself here, to the exclusion of former British colonies that are physically in the region like Australia and New Zealand, which took British culture and, as we will see further below, helped to spread the influence of European arbitration culture into Asia.
153 VL Taylor and M Pryles, 'The Culture of Dispute Resolution in Asia' in M Pryles (ed), *Dispute Resolution in Asia*, 3rd edn, Kluwer Law International, 2006, p. 7. See also at p. 1 where they speak of the 'economic and political factors that influence the design of legal institutions and constitute drivers for legal convergence and divergence within individual Asian jurisdictions today'.

attention given to these issues, and of the risks of generalisation and subjectivity. Furthermore, we focus on the culture of international commercial arbitration, while there are of course many other uses for arbitration in a domestic context, to which our comments may not apply.

First, it is often said that Asia has a history of and preference for amicable rather than adversary forms of dispute resolution. One reason is that in certain Asian cultures preserving business relationships is considered more important than winning an individual dispute.[154] Taniguchi notes that:[155]

1.164

> The dispute resolution culture can be subdivided into the 'litigation culture', the 'arbitration culture', and the 'conciliation (negotiation/mediation) culture'. The western world is traditionally characterized, to varying degrees, by the litigation culture, perhaps with the United States and Germany at the extreme end of the scale. Asia, especially East Asia, is known for its emphasis on conciliation. For centuries, a conciliation culture comprising a variety of forms has flourished there.... Litigation was condemned as a moral wrongdoing to the society and to the other party. A good judge was not supposed to give a judgment but to try to bring about a good conciliation.

Kim, writing from the perspective of Confucian-influenced South Korea, observes that:[156]

1.165

> under Confucian tradition, well educated persons should be governed by the concept of 'li', which establishes social norms... 'li' is ethical and persuasive in nature, not compulsive and legalistic. In contrast, 'law'... is compulsive and punitive in nature, and below 'li' in importance, since it is required only for such persons who are so poorly educated that they are unable to resolve a *dispute* through the ethical principals of 'li'.

Similarly, Nottage refers to the comparatively low levels of civil litigation in Japan and points out that 'the Japanese "do not like law"', and prefer negotiation and settlement'. But this may not be directly determined by culture. He says that another view is that 'the Japanese can't like law', because of institutional barriers such as costs and delays in bringing suit – although such barriers may themselves reflect some widely-shared cultural preferences. A third view is that 'the Japanese are made not to like law', with narrower elite groups (big business, conservative politicians and bureaucrats) controlling socio-economic change by diverting cases away from courts into opaque mediation systems. But a fourth view instead argues that the law matters – 'the Japanese do like law'. Low levels of new case filings are tied to the predictability of the Japanese legal system. People 'rationally settle because they know what they can get in court but can get

1.166

---

154 For a detailed explanation of the difference between Eastern and Western cultures of dispute resolution, see SF Ali, 'Approaching the Global Arbitration Table: Comparing the Advantages of Arbitration as Seen by Practitioners in East Asia and The West', (2009) 28 *Review of Litigation* 791, particularly at p. 803 et seq.
155 Taniguchi, 1996, op. cit. fn 23, at p. 31. See also at p. 36 ('What I call the "conciliation culture", on the other hand, is based on a diametrically opposed ideology. It stems from a deep mistrust in any pre-set rules of law and the concept of right as an absolute entitlement.')
156 Grant Kim 'East Asian Cultural Influences' in M Pryles and M Moser (eds), *The Asian Leading Arbitrators' Guide to International Arbitration*, JurisNet, 2007, pp. 27–28. See also M Pryles and M Moser's 'Introduction' in the same book at p. 2 and, regarding China, Jingzhou Tao, op. cit. fn 5, pp. 10–100; Bobby Wong, 'Traditional Chinese Philosophy and Dispute Resolution', (2000) 30 *Hong Kong Law Journal* 304, at p. 306. For a more detailed analysis see SF Ali, op. cit. fn 154, at p. 812 et seq.

it more cheaply and quickly in a non-court setting'. Such differing perspectives can arguably be applied not only to explain patterns in commercial arbitration, but also investment arbitration involving Japanese or other Asian parties.[157] In a detailed study of the reasons behind the Japanese business world's apparent adversity to litigation, Tony Cole contends that Japan's arbitration framework does not suffer from the alleged institutional obstacles identifiable in court litigation, thus rejecting the second view noted by Nottage. Cole analyses the litigation adversity with reference to Japanese cultural issues and the relationship between the law and society.[158]

1.167 Whatever the reason behind it, a preference for softer, conciliatory mechanisms is known to lie behind the Asian culture of dispute resolution, at least historically. After a thoughtful analysis, Ali concludes that:[159]

> The unique underpinnings of the concept of dispute resolution in East Asia have had a long lasting impact on its legal system and continue to impact the process of arbitration in the region. In comparison, Western emphasis on a clear 'winner' and 'loser' and limited emphasis on compromise has given rise to institutional bifurcation of conciliation and arbitration processes.

1.168 However, Kim points out that Asian jurisdictions have become much more litigious in recent years, as reflected, among other indicators, in the increased case loads of Asian arbitral institutions.[160] He also observes, in our view quite correctly, that it is not clear whether a presumed traditional preference for amicable forms of dispute resolution would have any influence on international arbitrations in Asia and/or involving Asian parties.[161]

1.169 That background might have an impact in some instances – particularly where all of the parties, their lawyers and the arbitrators are from one or more Asian cultures where mediation is ingrained as the norm. The arbitration might even take on a kind of hybrid between arbitration and mediation (so-called 'arb-med')[162] that is rarely seen in Western arbitrations but is said to be more popular in this region.[163] This might also explain why many of the region's Model Law

---

[157] Nottage, op. cit. fn 149, at p. 55; and generally Nottage and Weeramantry, op. cit. fn 126. See also Taniguchi, 1997, op. cit. fn 119, p. 67.
[158] T Cole, 'Commercial Arbitration in Japan: Contributions to the Debate on Japanese "Non-Litigiousness"', (2007) 40(1) *New York University Journal of International Law and Politics* 30, available at SSRN: http://ssrn.com/abstract=1083371; also recently published online at *Transnational Dispute Management* (September 2009, www.transnational-dispute-management.com).
[159] SF Ali, op. cit. fn 154, particularly at pp. 827–828.
[160] The increased case loads of Asian arbitral centres, and indeed numerous other evidence of sustained growth in arbitration in Asia was described above at Section 4.1, thus confirming Kim's point (op. cit. fn 156) in this regard.
[161] Kim, op. cit. fn 156, p. 26.
[162] Maniruzzaman, op. cit. fn 137, see generally and at p. 2. See also A Ye, 'Commentary on Integrated Dispute Resolution Systems in the PRC', (2004) 12 *ICCA Congress Series* 478, pp. 478–483, and G Kaufmann-Kohler and F Kun, 'Integrating Mediation into Arbitration : Why it Works in China', (2008) 25 *Journal of International Arbitration* 479. The concept of arb-med is discussed in Chapter 7.
[163] See, e.g. T Sawada, 'Hybrid Arb-Med: Will West and East Never Meet?', (2003) 14(2) *ICC International Court of Arbitration Bulletin* 29, at p. 36 ('Asian countries rather than countries in the West have created laws more positive to hybrid Arb-Med.'); J Trappe, 'Conciliation in the Far East', (1989) 5 *Arbitration International* 173; Wang Guiguo, 'The Unification of the Dispute Resolution System in China: Cultural, Economic and Legal Contributions', (1996) 13 *Journal of International Arbitration* 2, at pp. 5–9; S Lubman, 'Dispute Resolution in China after Deng Xiaoping: "Mao and Mediation" Revisited', (1997) 11 *Columbia Journal of Asian Law* 229;

countries have enacted provisions in their domestic legislation enabling arb-med procedures.[164] Despite these assertions and legislative developments, at the time of writing arb-med was still infrequently practised in international arbitration proceedings in the Asia-Pacific, with the exception of China.

Generally, once arbitration has been commenced the parties must accept that they have a legal dispute. The embarrassment of not being able to rely on 'li' (as described in Kim's quotation above) would therefore irreversibly have occurred. For that reason, it is sometimes even said that Asian parties are less likely to settle their dispute *after* having commenced litigation or arbitration, whereas Western parties often do settle after proceedings are commenced.[165] Thus while the common Asian stereotype of reluctance to litigate may reduce the number of arbitrations that is commenced (although there is no concrete empirical or even unequivocal anecdotal evidence for this), the culture of international arbitration once it begins is not, in our view, necessarily affected by it in a systematic – as opposed to occasional or individual – manner.

1.170

It is even possible that the historical dislike of harsh, legal confrontation has transformed into a preference for non-court based dispute resolution; that is, a preference for arbitration over litigation. Pryles and Taylor, while wary of generalisations about a preference for non-confrontational dispute resolution in Asia,[166] consider that:[167]

1.171

> The perceived 'Asian' preference for non-court dispute resolution is pragmatic, as much as cultural. In most of Asia courts do not provide dispute resolution services that are market-responsive, reliable or reciprocal. For these reasons commercial arbitration remains a default choice in most cross-border transactions in the region.

It seems that the explanation offered by Pryles and Taylor might hold true in Indonesia. Karen Mills notes that 'Indonesia is not, on the whole, a litigious culture. [Its] underlying philosophy, Pancasila, calls for deliberation to reach a consensus and discourages contention'. But she concludes that the reluctance to use Indonesian courts is more generally based 'upon the uncertainty and unpredictability of court judgments and the inordinate amount of time it can take to reach a final and binding decision through the judicial system'.[168]

1.172

Leaving aside Confucian and other historical traditions, one cannot ignore that Asian legal and business cultures were strongly influenced by their colonial

1.173

Wang Wenying, 'The Role of Conciliation in Resolving Disputes: A PRC Perspective', in M Pryles and M Moser (eds), *The Asian Leading Arbitrator's Guide to International Arbitration*, JurisNet, 2007, p. 501.
164 See S Harpole, 'The Role of the Third Party Neutral when Arbitration and Conciliation Procedures are Combined: A Comparative Survey of Asian Jurisdictions', in Pryles and Moser (eds), ibid., p. 526. Concerning arb-med procedures, see Chapter 7.
165 See, e.g. Taniguchi, 1997, op. cit. fn 119, p. 69 who notes that once litigation or arbitration has commenced Japanese parties 'have become by that point emotionally offended by each other's recalcitrant attitude', and whereas around 95% of US court cases settle before trial, that figure is around 50% in Japan.
166 Taylor and Pryles, op. cit. fn 153, p. 3.
167 Ibid., pp. 15–16.
168 K Mills, 'Indonesia', *International Handbook of Commercial Arbitration*, Arb. Suppl 47, 2006, p. 47. See also Schaefer, op. cit. fn 62, p. 36 ('arbitration is the only realistic form of dispute resolution in Indonesia. The courts, especially the provincial courts, have a bad reputation.')

past. The particular European empire which colonised each Asian country shaped the growth of its legal system significantly, arguably more so than anything pre-colonisation.[169] Several Asian legal systems were British colonies or otherwise saw a strong influence from the common law (e.g. Singapore, Hong Kong, Australia, New Zealand, Brunei, Malaysia, India and Bangladesh) while others inherited civil law traditions (e.g. Japan, South Korea, China, Taiwan, Thailand, Indonesia, Vietnam and Laos). The Philippines and Sri Lanka can be put into both categories. Many Asian jurisdictions were also influenced by associated political or economic (socialist, democratic, capitalist etc.) and/or religious (Hindu, Buddhist, Muslim, Christian etc.) factors.

1.174   Pryles and Taylor correctly note that 'today we can still classify Asian legal systems by their predominant source of law; former colonial influence (or voluntary borrowing) and contemporary religious or ideological influence' and that despite the diverse range of social, religious, political and legal influences, 'the point here is that most [Asian] systems fit within more than one category'.[170] The overlap in those colonial influences on South-East Asian dispute resolution cultures has been analysed in closer detail elsewhere.[171]

1.175   Those varying colonial influences combined with radical cultural differences to begin with have left so much diversity in Asian legal systems and attitudes to the law that it is almost futile to compare their general dispute resolution cultures. When it comes to comparing international arbitration cultures, however, the task is simplified by the heavy influence of Europe, which is the ultimate source of the legal and practical framework for international arbitration culture worldwide.

1.176   As explained above,[172] Asia now has several thriving domestic or regional arbitration centres and a thriving international arbitration culture. But today's arbitration craze did not happen overnight and without guidance from the other side of the world. When considering the culture of international arbitration in Asia, one therefore cannot ignore broader, historical international influences. The most significant in this sense is that modern international arbitration evolved in the West. As Taniguchi notes:[173]

> There has been, however, a distinct 'commercial arbitration culture' in the West, and through the reception of the western legal system by the non-western world, arbitration

---

169 See generally Morgan, op. cit. fn 62, p. 41. See also the previous article in the same journal by Schaefer, op. cit. fn 62, p. 30. Schaefer examines the reasons for abandoning colonial arbitration laws in favour of internationally recognised laws such as the Model Law.
170 Taylor and Pryles, op. cit. fn 153, p. 8.
171 See generally Morgan, op. cit. fn 62, and the previous article in the same journal by Schaefer, op. cit. fn 62. Schaefer examines the reasons for abandoning colonial arbitration laws in favour of internationally recognised laws such as the Model Law.
172 Section 4.1.
173 Taniguchi, 1996, op. cit. fn 23, pp. 33, 35–36. See also Taniguchi, 1997, op. cit. fn 119, p. 67 ('Assuming that there is a distinctive "dispute resolution culture" in Asia, such culture may collide with the Euro-American culture as the economic and other contact increases and globalization progresses in all aspects of human life.') and p. 68 ('A fair guess is that Asian businessmen have learned how to do business with Europeans and Americans. Until some 20 years ago, a Japanese defendant was willing to settle at any cost if sued in an American court. Today, they are ready to fight and will settle only when an offer is reasonable.').

has become a legitimate method of dispute resolution virtually everywhere in the world with a varying degree and scope of its application.... The present trend appears to be towards a single international arbitration culture. The New York Convention of 1958 has been extremely instrumental in bringing about a uniform standard for international arbitral practice. UNCITRAL has also made a great contribution toward the unification of arbitration law and arbitration rules, although some of the major centers of international commercial arbitration, namely Paris, London and New York, do not seem directly affected. Nobody can deny the fact that these developments have contributed greatly to the formation of a single arbitration culture. This culture is now going to cover the world.

International arbitration mainly developed in Europe and has been quasi-codified by predominantly European-based or European-influenced international organisations and associations.[174] That is not to say that Asia-Pacific practitioners have not influenced the way that arbitration developed in Europe (as well as in this region). They certainly have, particularly in recent times, as will be explained further below. But the principal historical academic and practical contributors were Europeans or at least European educated. 1.177

For example, the best examples of quasi-codification have come from UNCITRAL, ICCA, the ICC, and the IBA. While these are all truly international bodies these days, they have European influenced origins. These 'supra-national sources' of arbitration law are rarely binding (one exception is the Model Law if it is actually adopted as law) but rather guide arbitration practice. They have guided Asian arbitration practice just like they have guided it in the rest of the world. 1.178

Academic writings are another major supra-national source of international arbitration practice. Until about 20 years ago, by far the most influential academic publications measured by quantity and quality emanated from Europe. While we now see significant academic contributions coming from other regions, the European origins have heavily influenced the content of those contributions. Like in any academic discipline the origins shape what is to follow both directly, through citations, discussions and analysis of prior seminal works, and indirectly by shaping opinions and views of educated authors. 1.179

The same can be said for other ways in which knowledge and expertise about international arbitration is disseminated. Conferences and seminars are hugely popular in international arbitration. They provide fora for less experienced practitioners to learn and for their more experienced colleagues to share their knowledge and to network by acting as speakers and teachers. Once again, while there are now strong regional influences in these events, especially in recent years in Asia, many speakers and many experiences shared still come from Europe or the Americas. 1.180

---

174 See in that respect the discussion of the history of international arbitration (Section 2 above) and the sources of international arbitration law (Section 3.5 above). See also, generally, Y Dezalay and BG Garth, *Dealing in Virtue: International Commercial Arbitration and the Construction of a Transnational Legal Order*, University of Chicago Press, 1996, who explain in detail that international arbitration was created in Europe by a group of European 'grand old men'.

1.181   Another way that knowledge is shared is through formal education. Asian students may study arbitration in Europe or North America.[175] Similarly, academics from such regions regularly teach in Asia. The traditional methods of teaching arbitration emerge from its European origins. There is very steady growth in the number of dedicated international arbitration courses at universities in this region. The traditional methods of arbitration are also taught when Asian practitioners gain experience in law firms and arbitral institutions abroad and then bring that knowledge home.

1.182   International arbitration – again of a historically European style – became the norm in the US as its economy boomed and its companies became the world's most influential players in a globalised commercial market place. The economic force of the US meant that its international business practices influenced the rest of the world and especially developing countries which strived for stability and, in particular, inward investment. Pryles and Taylor point out that 'much of the aid provided for legal infrastructure development by [Western states] is predicated on the idea that the new commercial law developed will be modelled on a western scheme and will be, therefore, transparent and familiar to western investors and trade partners'.[176] Commercial conditions of that kind mould the evolution of legal structures towards what is familiar to the West.

1.183   With growing investment in Asia from Western cultures, expatriate professionals started relocating there. These individuals in turn influenced the way that Asia did business. Global commercial law firms followed. The influence in Asia of major law firms from Western cultures (i.e. from the US, UK and Australia) has been significant concerning foreign investment, commercial deals and, consequently, international arbitration culture. Many law firms have even sent experienced arbitration partners to Asia to build up the practice. Such individuals, bringing with them the way that they were taught or practised arbitration, may act as arbitrators, conference speakers, part-time academics, and publish articles etc., again influencing the development of arbitration.[177]

1.184   This Western influence on international arbitration culture in Asia should not be seen as negative. To the contrary, it could be considered as having helped to attract foreign investment in certain Asian economies, particularly in public interest areas of infrastructure, resources and utilities, and assisted local businesses in their exporting activities by making them savvier and more attractive to foreign business partners. Moreover, international commercial arbitration is an inherent part of today's globalisation and modernisation process that is transforming the entire world. While modern international arbitration had its origins in the West, its growth and global utilisation are detaching it (or perhaps have now detached it) from those origins, making it difficult to link arbitration – in

---

[175] Kim confirms that Korean lawyers traditionally went to Europe (in particular Germany) to study given that the Korean legal system was civil law based but now they tend to go to the US. (Kim, op. cit. fn 156, p. 31).
[176] Taylor and Pryles, op. cit. fn 153, p. 10.
[177] See RP Alford, 'The American Influence of International Arbitration', (2003) 19 *Ohio State Journal on Dispute Resolution* 69, at p. 80 et seq.

its current form – to any one tradition or region. It is not a form of clandestine Western imperialism but an integral part of the universal modernisation process, which serves to facilitate international trade and commerce. As Samuel P Huntington elegantly notes, 'modernisation... strengthens [non-Western] cultures and reduces the relative power of the West. In fundamental ways, the world is becoming more modern and less Western'.[178] International arbitration as a species of modernisation strengthens non-Western economies and reduces the East-West divide.

In any event, all of this Western influence has not prevented Asia from developing to some extent its own uniquely Asian variation of international arbitration. In order to appreciate how that occurred, it should be recalled that a major benefit of international arbitration is that its flexibility enables it to adapt to a literally infinite combination of cultural requirements. Conversely, domestic courts are parochial in the sense that in an international dispute the procedures will be very familiar to one side and completely foreign to the other. 1.185

Experienced international arbitrators are generally adept at creating an atmosphere that is culturally acceptable to both sides in a dispute.[179] That cultural acceptance could result from the arbitrator designing a procedure that is at least partially culturally familiar for both sides, and/or because the arbitrator adopts a culturally neutral, international arbitration approach to procedure. The latter theory may well be gaining popularity but an ability to identify and appreciate cultural differences remains essential, both for the arbitrators and lawyers involved in arbitrations. Kim explains that:[180] 1.186

> multiculturalism is a strength of international arbitration because it promotes acceptance of international arbitration by multiple cultures, allows the tribunal to combine the best features of diverse cultures, and helps to promote a fair result that takes into account the cultures of the parties involved.

Indeed, the best international arbitral tribunals are those where all of the arbitrators are open to all kinds of cultures. Thus it is possible that a previously sought after cultural *neutrality* has been transformed into a desire for cultural *empathy* and acceptance, while avoiding any unnecessary parochial influence. A keen awareness of other cultures will always be an essential ingredient of an efficient international arbitration. Good practitioners must develop a vision of the culture of each individual arbitration, considering the parties themselves, including the individuals within the companies who are representing those parties, as well as the lawyers, witnesses and other arbitrators or experts. The best international arbitration lawyers and arbitrators are people who take all of those aspects into account for each arbitration proceeding and adapt their behaviour accordingly. 1.187

---

178 SP Huntington, *The Clash of Civilizations and the Remaking of World Order*, Simon and Schuster, 1997, p. 78.
179 See generally R Goodman-Everard, 'Cultural Diversity in International Arbitration – A Challenge for Decision-Makers and Decision-Making', (1991) 7(2) *Arbitration International* 155.
180 Kim, op. cit. fn 156, p. 48.

1.188   The individuals involved in any particular arbitration are the key to optimising the procedural flexibility that international arbitration offers. They shape and mould the procedure and accordingly have the greatest say, and the greatest influence, on the way that any culture can affect it.

1.189   Kaplan notes the important influence that arbitrators and counsel have:[181]

> How [do cultural differences] affect the arbitration itself? The answer to that question, to a great extent, lies in the personality of the arbitrators and of counsel. An American lawyer appearing for [an] American contractor ... will be very wise to behave calmly, politely, but firmly. He should not take on the assumed cultural attributes of his clients. He should cross-examine politely and courteously – just what is not expected of him.
>
> It seems to me that at the arbitration, it is the cultural attributes of counsel that are often more crucial than that of the client. I am sure one could take the very same dispute and have it tried with two different sets of lawyers and end up with two completely different arbitrations with perhaps two differing results.

1.190   Kim considers that arbitrators have the greatest influence:[182]

> The avenue by which culture is likely to have the greatest impact is through the arbitrators. This is because the arbitrators have the power to decide the dispute and control the proceedings, and thus have the greatest influence over the arbitration. Experienced international arbitrators have some familiarity with and sensitivity to multiple cultures. Nevertheless, arbitrators tend to be influenced by their own culture.

1.191   In considering how Asian parties, arbitrators and lawyers will shape international arbitrations, one must also keep in mind the evolving preferences of transnational companies. Given the contemporary multicultural nature of both international business and international arbitration practices, parties' priorities appear to be evolving. Many now consider factors like time and cost efficiency, specially tailored procedures, expertise, and international enforcement of outcomes to be more important than an appearance of cultural neutrality. These preferences are reflected in the global acceptance of harmonised arbitration procedural laws, with legislators preferring to support international trade by adopting a law that is universally familiar rather than one that is individually tailored to the particularities of the country concerned.

1.192   We accordingly agree with Taniguchi that:[183]

> the Asian trend is clearly toward a more internationalised international commercial arbitration. True, internationalisation of the international arbitration sounds funny. But it is particularly important in Asia in order for an arbitration to be accepted internationally.... Internationalisation does not necessarily mean the abandonment of traditional characteristics as long as they are agreeable with internationalisation. If

---

[181] Kaplan, op. cit. fn 137, at p. 255.
[182] Kim, op. cit. fn 156, p. 19. He correctly notes at p. 36 that 'of course, East Asian culture is less likely to influence an arbitration if no East Asian arbitrators or counsel are involved, and the place of arbitration is outside of East Asia'.
[183] Taniguchi, 1997, op. cit. fn 119, p. 67, at p. 74. See also M Pryles and M Moser, 'Introduction' in M Pryles and M Moser (eds), *The Leading Arbitrators' Guide to International Arbitration*, JurisNet, 2007, p. 13.

successful an international commercial arbitration with an acceptable Asian flavour will enhance the use of Asian arbitration.

1.193 Accordingly, in our view the craze for international arbitration combined with the peculiarities of Asian culture and the adaptability of international arbitration procedure has left Asia with its own flavour of international arbitration culture. The evolution of that flavour was a key inspiration for this book.

1.194 Finally, this section has focused mainly on the culture or approach to international arbitration proceedings conducted by arbitrators rather than the culture of domestic court judges in Asia who may be dealing with international arbitration issues. The latter will apply their own procedures, rules and laws in a way that reflects their legal system and education and social or cultural environment. Lawyers pleading before judges will usually be from the same jurisdiction as the judges and have a similar legal education and social and cultural background. Domestic court proceedings are therefore heavily influenced by individual parochial culture.

1.195 Nonetheless, in our view the Asia-Pacific international arbitration environment has influenced the way that courts and national jurisdictions operate in relation to arbitration matters. A simple example is the widespread adoption of the Model Law. Another is the fact that several jurisdictions, supported by their legislators and judiciaries, are now competing between each other as seats of arbitration. Another is that the sheer growth of arbitration in the Asia-Pacific has helped to develop in many regional domestic court judges a respect for international commercial arbitration and an increasingly sophisticated understanding of its subject matter. The influence of Asian international arbitration culture on its courts, and a growing Asian approach by the courts, will be demonstrated indirectly throughout the following chapters of this book.

2

Law governing the arbitration and role of the seat

1 Introduction

2.1 This chapter examines how, why and on what basis the process of international commercial arbitration is legally permitted. It also covers the main practical functions of the seat of arbitration.

2.2 The seat (or place) of arbitration is the jurisdiction in which an arbitration takes place legally. This must be distinguished from the location of any physical hearings or meetings that are held as part of the arbitration proceedings. The hearings or meetings do not necessarily have to be held at the seat of arbitration.

2.3 It is essential to appreciate the connection between arbitration proceedings and the laws of the seat of arbitration. The different theories relating to this connection arise from the delicate interplay between a state's powers (particularly state judicial powers), an arbitral tribunal's powers and the freedom of parties to choose how their disputes are determined. At times these interests may conflict and there is potential for the law and/or the courts of the seat of arbitration to constrain the flexible and pragmatic qualities of arbitration. To gain a deeper understanding of these conflicting circumstances, recourse to theory and legal doctrine is unavoidable.

2.4 In Section 2 we discuss whether to use the term 'seat' or 'place' referring to the jurisdiction to which the arbitration is legally attached. In this book we mainly use 'seat.' In Section 3 we distinguish between the seat of arbitration and the place or venue of hearings. Section 4 examines the different laws and rules which regulate international arbitration proceedings. They are the *lex arbitri*, arbitral procedural law and arbitration rules. In Section 5 we explore two broad categories of legal theory relating to the connection between arbitration proceedings and the seat of arbitration. The first is the traditional or jurisdictional view and the second is the delocalised or contractual view. Each of these theories has many nuances and is worthy of an entire dissertation, but the present discussion is limited to the fundamental aspects of each. We then move to the practical considerations of choosing a seat of arbitration in Section 6. Finally, Section 7 provides an overview of the mandatory aspects of the Model Law.

2 Terminology: Seat or place of arbitration

The phrases 'seat of arbitration' and 'place of arbitration' are often used interchangeably to mean the legal jurisdiction to which an arbitration is attached.[1] It has been suggested that the two terms may have evolved from linguistic differences in English and French.[2] The term 'seat' is sometimes said to reduce confusion with the 'place' where an arbitration hearing might physically occur. There is a variety of arbitration instruments that use the term 'place'[3] but 'seat' is becoming increasingly common, particularly in the Asia-Pacific region.[4] The growing preference for 'seat' is demonstrated by SIAC's switch from using 'place' in the second edition of its Rules to 'seat' in its third edition.[5] The HKIAC Rules also refer to the 'seat' rather than the 'place' of arbitration.[6] The ACICA Rules generally use 'seat', but 'place' has been utilised to refer to the location where the award is made, so as to avoid any potential conflict with the New York Convention, which uses the word 'place'.

An arbitration will be conducted according to the arbitration law at the seat of arbitration (*lex arbitri*), even if hearings or other meetings are held elsewhere. Under no circumstances should the terms 'seat' or 'place' of arbitration be confused with the venue, location or place of hearings, as explained in the next section.

2.5

2.6

3 Distinction between the seat of arbitration and venue of hearings

As noted above, the seat or place of arbitration is the primary legal jurisdiction to which the arbitration is attached. It is the *legal* location of an arbitration

2.7

---

1 *PT Garuda Indonesia v Birgen Air* [2002] 1 SLR 393 at 399 (Singapore Court of Appeal).
2 See e.g. *Union of India v McDonnell Douglas Corporation* [1993] 2 Lloyd's Law Reports 48. Justice Saville's judgment in that English Commercial Court case discusses the submissions made by counsel for both parties on this point.
3 See, e.g. UNCITRAL Arbitration Rules, UNCITRAL Model Law, ICC Rules and SIAC Rules (1997), KCAB International Rules, ICA Rules, PDRCI Arbitration Rules, BAC Rules, Model Law and New York Convention.
4 See e.g. the SIAC Rules (2007), HKIAC Rules, ACICA Rules and Swiss Rules. See also M Hwang and Fong Lee Cheng, 'Relevant Considerations in Choosing the Place of Arbitration', (2008) 4(2) *Asian International Arbitration Journal* 195, at p. 195.
5 The 2010 SIAC Rules also use the word seat.
6 HKIAC Rules Article 15.

proceeding. This must be distinguished from the *physical* location of any arbitration hearings and meetings.[7] Hearings and meetings may be held at any convenient location. In this regard it is useful to remember that 'an arbitration proceeding does not only comprise of the oral hearing and the submission [to arbitration]. It encompasses an entire process, commencing from the appointment of the arbitrator or arbitrators to the rendering of the final award'.[8] It is possible that during an arbitration none of the participants (arbitrators, lawyers, parties, witnesses etc.) ever travels to the seat of arbitration. In practice, however, hearings and meetings are often held at the seat.

2.8   Virtually all arbitration laws and rules expressly permit arbitration hearings to be held in a location other than the seat of arbitration. For example, Article 20(2) of the Model Law provides that regardless of the seat of arbitration 'the arbitral tribunal may, unless otherwise agreed by the parties, meet at any place it considers appropriate for consultation among its members, for hearing witnesses, experts of the parties, or for inspection of goods, other property or documents'.

2.9   The Supreme Court of New South Wales, Australia, commented on Article 20(2) of the Model Law in *Angela Raguz v Rebecca Sullivan*.[9] This case involved an arbitration arising from the 2000 Sydney Olympic Games. The seat of arbitration was Geneva (as is the case for all arbitrations under the auspices of the Court of Arbitration for Sport) but the hearings were to be held in Sydney, being the venue of the Olympics that year. The Court of Appeal observed:[10]

> Commentators have pointed out that Article 20 [of the Model Law] makes sense when it is understood that there is a vital distinction between the so-called place (or seat) of arbitration and the place or places where the arbitrators may hold hearings, consultations .... The common law recognises this distinction...
>
> This legislative history reinforces the propriety of confining the words 'arbitration in a country other than Australia' in s 40(7) of the [New South Wales Commercial Arbitration Act] as connoting the technical meaning of a 'seat' or 'place' of arbitration, a well-established concept in and for the purposes of arbitration with an international aspect. We would therefore reject the plaintiff's submission that the expression refers to the place of hearing of a particular arbitration. If that were correct, the application of ss 38, 39 and 40 could change with a temporary change of hearing venue rather than exist as a statutory framework applicable or not applicable as the case may be to an arbitration agreement from its outset. It is inconceivable that those who drafted s 40 would have contemplated this.

---

7 These concepts were briefly touched on in the New South Wales Supreme Court case of *American Diagnostica Inc v Gradipore* (1998) 44 NSWLR 312, however that discussion focused on the ability to conduct the arbitration physically at a location other than the seat. See also the English Court of Appeal decision of *Shashoua v Sharma* [2009] EWHC 957 (Comm).
8 *PT Garuda Indonesia v Birgen Air* [2002] 1 SLR 393 at 402 (Singapore Court of Appeal).
9 (2000) 50 NSWLR 236. For a discussion of this case and in particular an explanation of how agreements to exclude appeals and other exclusionary agreements operate pursuant to the domestic arbitration regime when applied to international arbitrations in Australia, see S Barrett-White and C Kee, 'Enforcement of Arbitral Awards Where the Seat of the Arbitration is Australia – How the Eisenwerk Decision Might Still Be a Sleeping Assassin' (2007) 24(5) *Journal of International Arbitration* 515.
10 (2000) 50 NSWLR 236, paras 97, 102, 103.

In our opinion the legislature was concerned with the legal place of the arbitration, not the physical place of the arbitration. The legislative scheme was primarily concerned with commercial disputes. Such disputes may involve commercial activities that are physically located in different locations. They are the subject of a single arbitration agreement, which is intended to encompass hearings in the various locations at which disputes could arise. Indeed, it may be convenient to conduct hearings in more than one physical location in the course of a particular dispute. It is, in our opinion, likely that the legislature intended to allow parties to commercial agreements to select a single legal place of arbitration and to leave the choice of the physical location of hearings to the felt necessities of a specific dispute.

Importantly, the fact that an arbitration hearing is held outside the seat of arbitration does not and cannot of itself change the legal seat of arbitration. This was confirmed by the Singapore Court of Appeal in *PT Garuda Indonesia v Birgen Air*. The Court of Appeal observed:[11] 2.10

> It should be apparent from art 20 [Model Law] there is a distinction between 'place of arbitration' and the place where the arbitral tribunal carries on hearing witnesses, experts or the parties, namely the 'venue of the hearing'. Where parties have agreed on the place of arbitration, it does not change even though the tribunal may need to hear witnesses or do any other things in relation to the arbitration in a different location.

The Singapore Court of Appeal rejected an argument by PT Garuda that the parties had changed the place of arbitration from Jakarta to Singapore by holding their hearings in Singapore. Singapore was the venue of the hearings but the place of arbitration remained Jakarta. On this issue the Singaporean judgment cites with approval a passage from Lord Justice Kerr in *Naviera Amazonica Peruana SA v Compania Internacional de Seguros del Peru*.[12] In the cited passage Lord Justice Kerr is in fact quoting from the first edition of Redfern and Hunter's *Law and Practice of International Commercial Arbitration*. That book expanded the explanation of this point in later editions, but the original passage as cited remains succinct and elegant:[13] 2.11

> there is only one 'place' of arbitration. This will be the place chosen by or on behalf of the parties; and it will be designated in the arbitration agreement or the terms of reference or the minutes of proceedings or in some other way as the place or 'seat' of the arbitration. This does not mean, however, that the arbitral tribunal must hold all its meetings or hearings at the place of arbitration. International commercial arbitration often involves people of many different nationalities, from many different countries. In these circumstances, it is by no means unusual for an arbitral tribunal to hold meetings – or even hearings – in a place other than the designated place of arbitration, either for its own convenience or for the convenience of the parties or their witnesses... It may be more convenient for an arbitral tribunal sitting in one country to conduct a

---

11 *PT Garuda Indonesia v Birgen Air* [2002] 1 SLR 393, at 399. See also the discussion of changing the seat at Section 6.3.
12 [1988] 1 Lloyd's Rep 116 (English Court of Appeal).
13 A Redfern and M Hunter, *Law and Practice of International Commercial Arbitration*, 1st edn, Sweet & Maxwell, 1986, p. 69, quoted in [1988] 1 Lloyd's Rep 116 at 120.

hearing in another country – for instance, for the purpose of taking evidence... In such circumstances, each move of the arbitral tribunal does not of itself mean that the seat of the arbitration changes. The seat of the arbitration remains the place initially agreed by or on behalf of the parties.

4 *Lex arbitri*, arbitral procedural law and arbitration rules

2.12 *Lex arbitri*, arbitral procedural law, and arbitration rules are all terms referring to provisions that regulate, among other matters, the procedure of an international arbitration. The differences between them are important to understand but sometimes difficult to grasp. The terms are often used incorrectly or interchangeably. In the following paragraphs we briefly define each, before distinguishing the terms in Sections 4.1–4.3.

2.13 The Latin phrase '*lex arbitri*' means the law of the arbitration.[14] The *lex arbitri* is not directly chosen by the parties. When the parties choose country Y as the seat, the automatic consequence, without the need for express words, is that aspects of country Y's laws and legal framework become the *lex arbitri*.[15] This point was clearly made by the Singapore Court of Appeal in *PT Garuda Indonesia v Birgen Air*,[16] referred to above. In that circumstance the court had been called upon to determine the *lex arbitri* and whether the parties had changed the seat of arbitration from Indonesia to Singapore. The Court of Appeal stated: 'Clearly, if it was established that the parties had agreed to change the "place of arbitration" to Singapore, <u>then it must follow</u> that the curial law would be Singapore law'[17] (emphasis added).

2.14 The *lex arbitri* legitimises and provides a general legal framework for international arbitration. The relevant law itself might be found in an independent statute on international arbitration or it might be a chapter in another law, such as a civil procedure code or a law also governing domestic arbitration. However, the *lex arbitri* of a given jurisdiction can also include other statutes and codes (even those not specifically dealing with arbitration), and case law which relates to the basic legal framework of international arbitrations seated there. If the seat of arbitration is, for example, Hong Kong, then the *lex arbitri* constitutes those provisions of Hong Kong's laws which, among other things, permit the resolution of disputes in Hong Kong by way of arbitration rather than by Hong Kong court litigation. Other general features of the *lex arbitri* are that it gives (with

---

14 *Lex arbitri* refers to the law of arbitration generally; *lex loci arbitri* can be used once a specific arbitration and or seat has been identified. However, most practitioners simply use *lex arbitri* all the time.
15 A Redfern, M Hunter, N Blackaby and C Partasides, *Law and Practice of International Commercial Arbitration*, 4th edn, Sweet & Maxwell, 2004, at para 2–19; J-F Poudret and S Besson, *Comparative Law of International Arbitration*, 2nd edn, Thomson, 2007, at para 113.
16 [2002] 1 SLR 393.
17 *PT Garuda Indonesia v Birgen Air* [2002] 1 SLR 393 at 402. On this point, see also the New Zealand Court of Appeal decision in *CBI NZ Ltd v Badger Chiyoda* [1989] 2 NZLR 669.

certain exceptions) parties the freedom to choose the law and rules to apply and it indicates what types of matters cannot be arbitrated.[18]

In some ways, the *lex arbitri* is to an arbitration proceeding what the *lex fori* is to a domestic national court. However, although the *lex arbitri* and the *lex fori* perform certain similar functions for arbitration and domestic national courts respectively, they are different and should not be confused. One such difference relates to the application of conflict of laws rules and mandatory rules of law, both of which are discussed in Chapter 3.[19] Arbitration does not have a *lex fori*.[20] It is therefore unfortunate that there are continuing lines of English authority which use the expression *lex fori* when in reality they are referring to the *lex arbitri*. This authority has influenced common law courts in this region.[21]

2.15

The procedural law sets out the parameters of the procedure and support for international arbitration. It provides, for example, mandatory rules about how arbitration can be conducted. These include rules requiring equal treatment, due process and the independence of arbitrators. One way to conceptualise the differences between the *lex arbitri* and procedural law is to consider the *lex arbitri* as governing matters external to the arbitration and the procedural law as governing matters internal to the arbitration procedure (but excluding substantive issues).[22]

2.16

Having explained *lex arbitri* and procedural law, the final category is procedural rules or arbitration rules. These are rules chosen by the parties that relate to the mechanism and processes of arbitration. They typically regulate the conduct of the arbitration from its initiation until a final award is rendered, and can be likened to the civil procedure rules of a court. Arbitration rules comprise the rules of an arbitral institution, ad hoc arbitration rules such as the UNCITRAL Arbitration Rules, and rules that are tailor-made and agreed to by the disputing parties. Arbitration rules generally apply as a matter of contract – not law – although default arbitration rules are usually found in procedural laws. Typical arbitration rules, such as those of arbitration institutions, generally cover the practical aspects of how to commence an arbitration and to see it through until the end. The subject matter of rules include provisions on filing a request for arbitration, answering the request for arbitration, appointing arbitrators, challenging non-neutral arbitrators, removing non-performing arbitrators, the arbitral tribunal's procedural powers and basic rules relating to hearings and the taking of evidence.

2.17

---

18 See the discussion in Chapter 3, Section 3.1.
19 See the discussion in Chapter 3, Section 3.2 (conflict of laws) and Section 4 (mandatory laws).
20 Poudret and Besson, op. cit. fn 15 at para 114.
21 The expression *lex fori* is used to describe the seat of the arbitration in cases such as *Black Clawson International Ltd v Papierwerke Waldhof-Aschaffenberg AG* [1981] 2 Lloyd's Rep 446 (Queen's Bench, Commercial Court) through to *C v D* [2007] EWCA Civ 1282 (English Court of Appeal). It was also used in the Singaporean decision of *PT Garuda Indonesia v Birgen Air* [2002] 1 SLR 393 (Singapore Court of Appeal).
22 This distinction was explained in *Union of India v McDonnell Douglas* [1993] 2 Lloyd's Rep 48 (Queen's Bench, Commercial Court). See also *Channel Tunnel Group v Balfour Beatty Ltd* [1993] 1 All ER 664, 683 (Lord Mustill, House of Lords).

4.1 *Lex arbitri* v arbitral procedural law

2.18 The arbitral procedural law and the *lex arbitri* are rarely separated.[23] For this reason, many people do not distinguish between *lex arbitri* and procedural law, or alternatively use the terms as synonyms.[24] While this approach is understandable, it is nevertheless problematic and better avoided. Redfern and Hunter observe that 'the lex arbitri is much more than a purely procedural law'.[25] As explained above the *lex arbitri* is the law that gives the arbitration its nationality and legal validity. An example of a non-procedural issue that is determined under the *lex arbitri* is objective arbitrability.[26]

2.19 The potential for confusion and need for a clear distinction arise from the fact that arbitrating parties in some jurisdictions may select an arbitral procedural law that is different from the *lex arbitri*. This means that the parties may seat their arbitration in one jurisdiction and choose the procedural law of a different jurisdiction. It is vital to remember that, as Born explains, 'the [foreign] procedural law will not ordinarily supplant, but rather operate within the arbitration legislation of the arbitral seat'.[27] While theoretically and legally possible,[28] choosing a foreign procedural law can create many practical problems. For example, to which courts would the parties have recourse to seek an interim measure or to set aside an arbitral award? Assuming the proper courts in which to bring these applications are identified, which jurisdiction's procedural laws would those courts apply?

2.20 There is English authority on point that may be instructive, at least for common law jurisdictions. Lord Justice Kerr clearly recognised in *Naviera Amazonica Peruana SA v Compania Internacional de Seguros del Peru* as early as 1988 that 'there is equally no reason in theory which precludes parties to agree that an arbitration shall be held at a place or in country X but subject to the procedural laws of Y'.[29] In *Union of India v McDonnell Douglas Corporation*[30] the

---

[23] *CBI NZ Ltd v Badger Chiyoda* [1989] 2 NZLR 669 (New Zealand Court of Appeal); *American Diagnostica Inc v Gradipore Ltd* (1998) 44 NSWLR 312 (New South Wales Supreme Court); *John Holland Pty Ltd v Toyo Engineering Corp* [2001] 2 SLR 262 (Singapore High Court); *Dermajaya Properties Sdn Bhd v Premium Properties Sdn Bhd* [2002] 2 SLR 164 (Singapore High Court); *PT Garuda Indonesia v Birgen Air* [2002] 1 SLR 393 (Singapore Court of Appeal).
[24] For example, Justice Burrell in the Hong Kong High Court decision of *Karaha Bodas Co Llc v Perusahaan Pertambangan Minyak Dan Gas Bumi Negara (also known as Pertamina)* [2003] 380 HKCU 1, at p. 8 stated that 'A variety of expressions are used to describe this such as lex arbitri, curial law and procedural law. For consistency I shall use the expression lex arbitri'.
[25] Redfern, Hunter et al, op. cit. fn 15, at para 2–19.
[26] See the discussion in Chapter 4 Section 8.2.
[27] G Born, *International Commercial Arbitration*, Kluwer, 2009, at p. 1315. Born devotes considerable effort to explaining the need to distinguish between the arbitral procedural law and the law of the place of the arbitration. His analysis is well reasoned. It would therefore be unfortunate if he were interpreted as suggesting that parties could choose their *lex arbitri*. At p. 1346, Born states that the suggestion that parties could not choose two *lex arbitri* is incorrect. It is apparent from his following discussion that he is referring to the selection of procedural laws, and not the law of the seat of the arbitration (i.e. *lex arbitri*).
[28] Whether it is legally possible depends on the *lex arbitri*, the ultimate framework law regulating all arbitrations seated in the jurisdiction. See Redfern, Hunter et al, op. cit. fn 15, at para 2–20; see also L Nottage and R Garnett (eds), *International Arbitration in Australia*, Federation Press, forthcoming 2010, Chapter 2.
[29] [1988] 1 Lloyd's Rep. 116, at p. 120 (English Court of Appeal).
[30] [1993] 2 Lloyd's Rep 48.

Queen's Bench Division of the Commercial Court was asked to determine the *lex arbitri* where the arbitration clause selected London as the seat of arbitration but expressly identified the Indian Arbitration Act 1940 as applicable. Justice Saville noted that English law admitted the theoretical possibility of parties choosing the procedural law notwithstanding a contradictory choice of seat:[31]

> It is clear from the authorities cited above that English law does admit of at least the theoretical possibility that the parties are free to choose to hold their arbitration in one country but subject to the procedural laws of another, but against this is the undoubted fact that such agreement is calculated to give rise to great difficulties and complexities.

2.21 This situation highlights some of the complexities in trying to choose a different procedural law from the *lex arbitri*. Justice Saville, having referred to a variety of significant legal authorities, was concerned by the 'great difficulties and complexities'[32] of such an approach and the 'potentially unsatisfactory method of regulating ... arbitration procedures'.[33] Nonetheless, he held that 'if the Court were convinced that the parties had chosen the procedural law of another country, then it might well be slow to interfere with the arbitral process'.[34] Given the grave dangers, however, Justice Saville ultimately concluded that choosing a foreign procedural law could not have been the parties' intentions. He held that in this particular case the parties must have intended the Indian Arbitration Act to regulate only the internal conduct of the arbitration (i.e. to apply like arbitration rules and not as procedural law), and English law to govern the external supervision of the arbitration by the courts.

2.22 The decision implies that if parties desire a foreign procedural law to govern their arbitration, they should say so in very clear language. But, as noted above, it is difficult to imagine why parties would want to choose foreign procedural law given the risks and complexities. Nowadays, there is far less need to take such risks because so many countries have modern arbitration legal systems, whether based on the Model Law or otherwise.

2.23 There are perhaps two scenarios where the choice of a foreign procedural law might be warranted. The first is when the award will need to be enforced in a specific and known non-New York Convention signatory country. Choosing that jurisdiction's procedural law to govern the conduct of a foreign arbitration might (though with no guarantee) provide recourse to the enforcement procedures in that law, without the need to seat the arbitration in that jurisdiction. The second is when the chosen arbitral seat has a less than modern arbitration legal system but is chosen nevertheless to avoid award enforcement problems based on a 'reciprocity reservation' that a state has made when concluding in the New York

---

31 Ibid., at 50.
32 Ibid., at 50–51.
33 Ibid., at 51.
34 Ibid.

Convention.³⁵ Even in these scenarios, choosing a foreign procedural law would raise complex legal issues and is ill-advised.³⁶

2.24 Very few courts in the Asia-Pacific appear to have directly considered the possibility of parties choosing a foreign arbitral procedural law to apply in their arbitration. The Hong Kong High Court decision of *Karaha Bodas Co Llc v Perusahaan Pertambangan Minyak Dan Gas Bumi Negara (also known as Pertamina)*³⁷ should be interpreted as addressing this possibility, although a literal reading of the decision might at first be confusing. This decision is particularly relevant to a number of the issues discussed in this chapter but requires some interpretation. The case is a classic example of the confusion that can arise when the terms *lex arbitri* and procedural law are used incorrectly or synonymously.

2.25 In the *Pertamina* case, Justice Burrell had been faced with an application resisting enforcement of an arbitral award. One of the grounds on which enforcement could be refused was Section 44(2)(f) of the Hong Kong Arbitration Ordinance; this section corresponds directly with Article V(1)(e) of the New York Convention. Pursuant to these provisions enforcement can be refused if the party resisting enforcement establishes 'that the award has not yet become binding on the parties, or has been set aside or suspended by a competent authority of the country in which, <u>or under the law of which</u>, it was made' (Emphasis added).

2.26 In the extracted passages of Justice Burrell's judgment below, he appears to suggest that it is possible for parties to seat their arbitration in one jurisdiction and then to choose a different *lex arbitri* to govern their arbitration. Notwithstanding that Justice Burrell cites from English authorities, for the reasons we explained above, it is in our view, as a matter of definition, not possible to choose a different *lex arbitri*. We respectfully submit that the decision should be understood as confirming that parties can choose a foreign procedural law, i.e. other than the procedural law of the *lex arbitri*. This interpretation would not have affected the outcome of the decision in this particular case. Furthermore this interpretation is consistent with Article V(1)(e) of the New York Convention, which many authors such as Lew, Mistelis and Kröll note may be seen as 'manifesting the potential for challenging an award in a place other than the place of arbitration'.³⁸

2.27 When read as if concerning the application of a different procedural law, as we suggest it should be, Justice Burrell's analysis provides very useful and practical guidance:³⁹

---

35 See the discussion in Chapter 9, Section 5.4.2.
36 Hwang and Fong Lee Cheng, op. cit. fn 4, at p. 216.
37 [2003] 380 HKCU 1.
38 JD Lew, LA Mistelis and SM Kröll, *Comparative International Commercial Arbitration*, Kluwer Law International, 2003, para 25–16; see also Born, op. cit. fn 27, at pp. 1339–1341. In his discussion of this issue, Born refers to a number of cases from India, Pakistan and Indonesia (including the *Pertamina* case discussed here), where courts have purported to set aside awards even though those jurisdictions were not the seat of arbitration (certain of these decisions and others are discussed in Chapter 9, Section 3.2.2). Born criticises those particular decisions but concludes that 'it should in principle be for the parties . . . to determine whether they wish a particular national court to consider annulment applications', at p. 1340.
39 *Karaha Bodas Co Llc v Perusahaan Pertambangan Minyak Dan Gas Bumi Negara (also known as Pertamina)* [2003] 380 HKCU 1, at p. 15.

From the wealth of authority cited by both counsel on this issue can be gleaned the following starting point: 'The curial law' (lex arbitri) is normally, but not necessarily, the law of the place where the arbitration proceedings are held'. . . 'The place' plainly refers to the legal seat of the arbitration (here Geneva) not a random city of convenience for the arbitrators (here Paris). For the normal situation not to apply there must be strong pointers to the contrary. Such pointers as there may be in this case cannot, in my view, be regarded as strong when put in context and balanced against the following factors.

(1) Had the parties wanted to, expressly, depart from the norm they could have said so in the contracts but they did not. The contracts are specific as to the substantive law (Indonesian) but silent as to the lex arbitri [procedural law].

(2) The drafters of the contracts were explicit on many matters such as the choice of a neutral place (Geneva), the adoption of the UNCITRAL rules in the arbitration and the choice of Indonesian law as the law of the contracts. It is not a difficult inference to draw that had Pertamina insisted on an express provision stating that the lex arbitri [procedural law] was to be Indonesian law, the contracts would not have been signed. I find it irresistible that the choice of Geneva as the 'place' was also a choice that it was the formal 'seat' in the legal sense. By the same token it is plain that the choice of an independent neutral seat of arbitration carried with it an intention to be bound by the lex arbitri of that place.

. . .

(4) Pertamina, as evidence of 'strong pointers' to rebut the presumption rely, inter alia, on the fact that the contracts themselves are 'replete with references to the provisions of Indonesian law'. The expression 'replete with' somewhat overstates the position but they point out that the contracts expressly provide for the modification of, in particular, four Articles of the Indonesian Code of Civil Procedure. Article 650.2 (appointment of arbitrators) and 620.1 (time limit on arbitrations) have been modified, Article 631 (authority to arbitrators to decide on 'amiables compositeurs') has been invoked and Article 641 (rights of appeal) has been waived.

4.2 Arbitral procedural law v arbitration rules

There is usually an overlap between procedural laws and arbitration rules. As noted above, the former will also provide default procedural rules, in case the parties have not otherwise agreed. Normally arbitration rules specifically chosen by the parties will override those provided in a procedural law, except to the extent that the latter are mandatory.

Pryles explains the difference between procedural law and arbitration rules as follows:[40]

2.28

2.29

It is true that the arbitral procedural law may deal with many matters concerning the conduct of an arbitration which can be addressed in procedural rules selected by the parties to apply to the arbitration. In a sense, therefore, the arbitral procedural law may deal with matters which the parties have failed to address, either by not selecting any arbitration rules (institutional or otherwise) or because those rules are deficient. Where the parties do select arbitral rules, they are likely to prevail over the 'fall-back' [default] provisions made by the law governing the arbitral procedure. This is because

---

[40] M Pryles, 'Exclusion of the Model Law', (2001) 4(6) *International Arbitration Law Review* 175, at p. 177.

the latter will be regarded as non-mandatory and liable to be displaced by the parties' express provision to the contrary. But, some provisions of the arbitral procedural law will be different in nature to those contained in arbitral rules selected by the parties, be they institutional or ad hoc. For example, the arbitral procedural law may prescribe the degree of judicial supervision of the arbitration, including appeals and applications to set-aside an award. The arbitral procedural law may also provide for judicial assistance in aid of an arbitration, for example, the issue of a subpoena requiring a witness to attend the hearing. Plainly, these are matters which cannot be the subject of contractual rules agreed by the parties and incorporated into the arbitration clause.

2.30 *Australian Granites v Eisenwerk Hensel Beyreuth GmbH*[41] is a decision of the Queensland Court of Appeal in Australia that found an express choice by parties of ICC arbitration demonstrated an intention to exclude the Model Law under Section 21 of the Australian International Arbitration Act.[42] Singapore legislation has similar Model Law opt-out provisions and a similar decision was subsequently made in the Singapore High Court – *John Holland Ltd v Toyo Engineering Ltd*[43] which essentially adopted the Queensland Court of Appeal position.

2.31 Both of these decisions were incorrect because it is not inconsistent with the Model Law to choose a set of institutional arbitration rules to apply in an arbitration. Choosing institutional rules is permitted within the scope of Article 19(1) of the Model Law.[44] To the extent any inconsistencies exist between the Model Law and the chosen rules, the latter will apply, so long as they do not conflict with mandatory provisions of either the Model Law or of the law of the seat.

2.32 Following the Singaporean case mentioned above, the Singapore Government moved quickly to amend Section 15 of the Singapore International Arbitration Act as well as shortly thereafter introducing Section 15A:

> (1) It is hereby declared for the avoidance of doubt that a provision of rules of arbitration agreed to or adopted by the parties, whether before or after the commencement of the arbitration, shall apply and be given effect to the extent that such provision is not inconsistent with a provision of the Model Law or this Part from which the parties cannot derogate.
>
> (2) Without prejudice to subsection (1), subsections (3) to (6) shall apply for the purposes of determining whether a provision of rules of arbitration is inconsistent with the Model Law or this Part.

---

41 [2001] Qd R 461, but overruling see *Cargill International SA v Peabody Australian Mining Ltd* [2010] NSWSC 887.

42 Section 21 of the Australian International Arbitration Act will be amended in 2010, however prior to that amendment it provided:

Settlement of dispute otherwise than in accordance with Model Law
If the parties to an arbitration agreement have (whether in the agreement or in any other document in writing) agreed that any dispute that has arisen or may arise between them is to be settled otherwise than in accordance with the Model Law, the Model Law does not apply in relation to the settlement of that dispute.

43 [2001] 2 SLR 262. See also *Dermajaya Properties Sdn Bhd v Premium Properties Sdn Bhd* [2002] 2 SLR 164 (Singapore High Court).

44 For a discussion of this see Pryles, op. cit. fn 40. See also S Greenberg, 'ACICA's New International Arbitration Rules', (2006) 23(2) *Journal of International Arbitration* 189, at p. 192; Barrett-White and Kee, op. cit. fn 9.

(3) A provision of rules of arbitration is not inconsistent with the Model Law or this Part merely because it provides for a matter on which the Model Law and this Part is silent.
(4) Rules of arbitration are not inconsistent with the Model Law or this Part merely because the rules are silent on a matter covered by any provision of the Model Law or this Part.
(5) A provision of rules of arbitration is not inconsistent with the Model Law or this Part merely because it provides for a matter which is covered by a provision of the Model Law or this Part which allows the parties to make their own arrangements by agreement but which applies in the absence of such agreement.
(6) The parties may make the arrangements referred to in subsection (5) by agreeing to the application or adoption of rules of arbitration or by providing any other means by which a matter may be decided.
(7) In this section and section 15, 'rules of arbitration' means the rules of arbitration agreed to or adopted by the parties including the rules of arbitration of an institution or organisation.

2.33 This section makes clear that a choice of arbitral rules is not tantamount to excluding the Model Law. In late 2009, the Australian government introduced a bill to amend Australia's international arbitration laws.[45] As part of those amendments Section 21 has been revised. Despite this likely amendment, it remains advisable that parties arbitrating in Australia include in their arbitration agreement an indication that the Model Law is still to apply despite the choice of institutional rules. The ACICA Rules have adopted this approach in Article 2(3).[46]

4.3 Procedural pyramid

2.34 As the differences between the *lex arbitri*, arbitral procedural laws and arbitration rules can be conceptually difficult it may be useful to visualise their relationship as a pyramid.

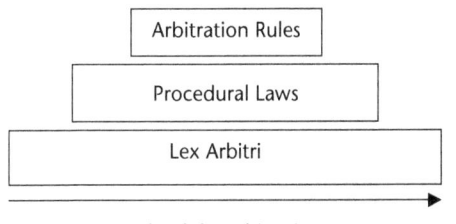

```
        ┌──────────────────────┐
        │  Arbitration Rules   │
      ┌─┴──────────────────────┴─┐
      │     Procedural Laws      │
    ┌─┴──────────────────────────┴─┐
    │         Lex Arbitri          │
    └──────────────────────────────┘
    ─────────────────────────────▶
         Life of the arbitration
```

2.35 This pyramid shows that the *lex arbitri* is the foundation on which the arbitration is built. Procedural laws are the next layer, and then finally arbitration rules. To the extent that any layer overlaps with one that is below it in the pyramid, it will normally take precedence over the lower layer except where relevant provisions of the lower layer are mandatory.

---

45 Australian International Arbitration Amendment Bill 2009. See also *Cargill International SA v Peabody Australia Mining Ltd* [2010] NSWSC 887 at para 91 which found the *Eisenwerk* decision 'plainly wrong'.
46 ACICA Rules Article 2.3 reads 'By selecting these Rules the parties do not intend to exclude the operation of the UNCITRAL Model Law on International Commercial Arbitration'.

2.36 As an illustration of the order of this hierarchy, assume that the *lex arbitri*'s own arbitral procedural law may contain provisions regarding the default appointment of arbitrators. Assume that the parties choose a foreign arbitral procedural law which contains different default procedures and the parties also choose arbitration rules which have a third default method. In this situation, it is the default mechanism in the chosen arbitration rules that will apply. However, mandatory provisions of the *lex arbitri* or procedural law will displace the chosen arbitration rules if those arbitration rules conflict with the mandatory provisions.

5 Diverging views on link between arbitration proceedings and seat of arbitration

2.37 Lively theoretical debate has ensued about the extent to which arbitration proceedings are linked to and constrained by the seat of arbitration's laws and courts. We briefly introduce two broad legal theories explaining this link, the traditional and delocalised theories, before developing them from the perspective of international relations theory. We then consider the legal and practical reality of delocalisation based on international norms and laws, before finally discussing where these theories leave us today.

5.1 Traditional view

2.38 The traditional or jurisdictional view is that every private, commercial arbitration must be attached to a legal seat of arbitration. That is, it must be attached to some existing legal jurisdiction. According to this view, the seat of arbitration is the jurisdiction that gives legitimacy and legality to the arbitration proceedings and the resulting award. Consequently, without the international arbitration law of the seat (i.e. the *lex arbitri*), which permits arbitration to take place, any arbitration proceeding would not exist legally.

2.39 The traditional view is based on accepted legal theories that date back at least as far as the 1600s in Western cultures. In Eastern cultures these debates are even older.[47] The Peace of Westphalia (1648) is widely considered to represent the birth of the nation-state system that exists today. Decades of religious conflict in Europe were put to an end by the signing of two peace treaties that comprised the Peace of Westphalia. This divided Europe into various states and emphasised the supreme power of the sovereign ruler over the territory of his or her respective state. Accordingly, each state was obliged, under the principle of state sovereignty, to respect the independence and integrity of other

---

[47] Arguments of this kind have been espoused in Eastern cultures as far back as Mencius (also known as Meng Zi) whose works collectively known as The Mencius were published after his death in c289 BCE.

states. A vital and central feature of state sovereignty was said to be jurisdiction, which 'concerns the power of a state to affect people, property and circumstances ... [and] is an exercise of authority which may alter or create or terminate legal relationships and obligations'.[48]

2.40 A consequence of this particular conception of sovereignty is that states are the highest authority regulating the lives and activities of private individuals and companies. In other words, states are exclusively empowered to regulate anything and everything that occurs within their boundaries.[49]

2.41 With this background, quite early in the development of international arbitration as a discipline of law, Francis Mann suggested that in reality there was no such thing as an *international* arbitration – arbitration had to be connected to and controlled by a domestic legal system. Two quotes from Mann illustrate his views particularly well:[50]

> It would be intolerable if the country of the seat could not override whatever arrangements the parties may have made. The local sovereign does not yield to them except as a result of the freedoms granted by himself.

> Is not every activity occurring on the territory of a State necessarily subject to its jurisdiction? Is it not for such State to say whether and in what manner arbitrators are assimilated to judges and, like them, subject to the law? Various States may give various answers to the question, but that each of them has the right to, and does, answer it according to its own discretion cannot be doubted.

2.42 His arguments and reasoning at first appear both logical and plausible. If the sovereign state is the highest authority and it has exclusive power to make and enforce laws relating to persons, property or events within its territory, it stands to reason that it is only because of the laws of the seat that the arbitration agreement (and ultimately the arbitration award) gains legal recognition. According to the traditional view, an arbitration agreement, like any contract, has no legal effect unless some domestic law gives it effect. The *lex arbitri* thus regulates and limits the arbitration proceedings in any way its lawmakers wish. Markham Ball explains this as follows:[51]

> Arbitration is not a separate, free-standing system of justice. It is a system established and regulated pursuant to law, and it necessarily bears a close relationship to a nation's courts and judicial system.

However, as we will see below, this is not the only view.

---

48 MN Shaw, *International Law*, 5th edn, Cambridge University Press, 2003, at p. 572.
49 The rise of international organisations like the World Trade Organization and groupings like the European Union now challenge this conception.
50 FA Mann, 'Lex Facit Arbitrum' in P Sanders (ed), *International Arbitration: Liber Amicorum for Martin Domke*, Martinus Nijhoff, 1967, pp. 161–162. Mann's arguments are reflected in more recent commentaries. See generally R Goode, 'The Role of the Lex Loci Arbitri in International Commercial Arbitration', (2001) 17(1) *Arbitration International* 19.
51 M Ball, 'The Essential Judge: the Role of the Courts in a System of National and International Commercial Arbitration', (2006) 22 *Arbitration International* 73.

5.2 Delocalised view

5.2.1 Definition

2.43 The delocalised or contractual conception of arbitration is that no link need exist between the seat of arbitration and arbitration proceedings taking place in that jurisdiction. Arbitration proceedings are said to gain their legitimacy and existence from the parties' contract. The principal consequence of this is that arbitration proceedings should be free from any interference from local courts and local laws at the seat of arbitration. The only domestic courts that can interfere are those asked to enforce a resulting arbitral award. It is only these enforcement courts that need to give the arbitral award state recognition because that is required before state-backed mechanisms can be deployed to enforce and execute the award. Before an award is enforced, it exists simply as an extension of the parties' contract.

2.44 In 1983, Jan Paulsson wrote an article entitled 'Delocalisation of International Commercial Arbitration: When and Why it Matters'.[52] It has become one of the most cited articles in the debates on delocalisation. The article was a defence of a series of papers Paulsson had written previously which developed the idea of delocalised arbitration. His earlier papers had evoked a range of responses, including the description 'dangerous heresy'.[53] In defence to this description, Paulsson explained:[54]

> What this critique misses is that the delocalised award is not thought to be independent of any legal order. Rather, the point is that a delocalised award may be accepted by the legal order of an enforcement jurisdiction although it is independent from the legal order of its country of origin.

2.45 Paulsson accordingly clarified that delocalisation does not mean that arbitration proceedings exist on their own and outside any domestic legal order. Rather, they are attached to a domestic legal order but only to the jurisdiction (or jurisdictions) where enforcement of the award is sought. They are not attached to the legal order of the seat of arbitration and should not be subjected to its laws or courts.

2.46 The focus on the enforcement jurisdiction made considerable practical sense, as at that time the only truly harmonised aspect of international arbitration was enforcement – thanks mainly to the New York Convention. This was a time before the Model Law and its adoption into national legal systems. Although today there is still no single unified system of international arbitration law, there is a considerably greater degree of consistency. Arguably, there is less need for the delocalisation debate today than there was back in the 1980s when international arbitration laws had not yet begun to converge.

---

52 J Paulsson, 'Delocalisation of International Commercial Arbitration: When and Why it Matters', (1983) 32 *International and Comparative Law Quarterly* 53.
53 As Paulsson notes, this was a description used by W Park in his paper 'The Lex Loci Arbitri and International Commercial Arbitration', (1983) 32 *International and Comparative Law Quarterly* 21.
54 Paulsson, op. cit. fn 52, at p. 57.

2.47 The delocalisation thesis is well illustrated with regard to mandatory laws, which may be described as a catalyst for the development of the delocalisation theory. Mandatory laws are laws that have public policy characteristics that contracting parties cannot exclude by agreement. They can apply whenever there is a strong link between the facts of a case and the jurisdiction in which the mandatory laws exist, even if that jurisdiction's law is not ordinarily the applicable law in the case.[55]

2.48 There would be no particular difficulty with mandatory laws if every state's mandatory laws were the same. But since they are not, conflicts inevitably arise from the application of peculiar domestic mandatory laws. One such conflict arises where a certain mandatory law exists in the *lex arbitri* but does not exist in the jurisdiction of the law governing the contract. From the perspective of the traditional view of arbitration (discussed above), it might be argued that a mandatory law of the seat should be applied by virtue of the simple fact that it is a law of the seat. From a delocalised viewpoint, however, the mere fact that arbitration is seated in a given jurisdiction should not of itself be sufficient for its mandatory laws to apply. There would have to be a strong factual nexus between the potentially applicable law and the underlying dispute itself.

2.49 After a flurry of largely academic activity in the early 1980s the delocalisation debate was enlivened in the mid-1990s by several cases. The best known are *Hilmarton v OTV*[56] and *Chromalloy v Egypt*.[57] Both of these cases involved arbitral awards that had been set aside by courts at the seat of arbitration but which were still enforced in other countries. They illustrate the practical attraction of a delocalised approach because the reasons for the awards being set aside at the seats of arbitration were not considered relevant in the jurisdictions where enforcement was granted.

2.50 In the first case, Hilmarton sought recovery of commissions it claimed to have earned by securing business for OTV in Algeria. The seat of arbitration was in Switzerland. The arbitral tribunal found the contract unenforceable because it contravened Algerian laws relating to bribery and corruption. It accordingly rejected Hilmarton's claims. Upon Hilmarton's application, the Swiss Federal Supreme Court set aside the award, finding that the arbitrators ought not to have considered Algerian law. But French courts – in decisions ultimately appealed to and confirmed by France's highest court – nonetheless recognised the award. The Cour de Cassation controversially observed:[58]

> the award made in Switzerland was an international award which was not integrated into the legal system of that State, meaning that the award's existence remained established despite its having been set aside and that its recognition was not contrary to international public policy

---

[55] Mandatory laws are addressed and explained in Chapter 3, Section 4.
[56] Cass. le civ., Mar. 23, 1994, 1994 *Revue de L'Arbitrage*. 327 (French Cour de Cassation).
[57] 939 F Supp 907 (DDC 1996) (US District Court of the District of Columbia).
[58] Authors' translation from French. Cour de Cassation decision of 23 March 1993. See *Revue de L'Arbitrage*, 1994.327, note Ch. Jarrosson; *Bull civ*, I, no. 104, p. 79; *Journal du droit international (Clunet)*, 1994.701, note E Gaillard.

2.51   The Cour de Cassation later refused enforcement of subsequent (contradictory) awards in the same case. These subsequent awards had been rendered by the arbitrators as a consequence of their first award having been set aside by the Swiss courts.

2.52   In *Chromalloy*, courts in both France and the District of Columbia, USA, enforced an international arbitral award that had been set aside by the courts of the seat of arbitration – in this instance Cairo, Egypt. Chromalloy had been successful in the arbitration and sought to enforce the award in the District of Columbia. At the same time the Government of Egypt, having lost the arbitration, managed to set aside the award in Cairo on the basis that the arbitrators had applied Egyptian administrative law rather than civil law. Courts in both the District of Columbia and France enforced the award despite Egypt's argument that the award no longer existed under Egyptian law. The District of Columbia court noted that the parties had agreed to exclude all forms of recourse against the arbitral tribunal's awards and that error of law was not a basis to refuse enforcement of a foreign arbitral award.[59]

2.53   Both decisions were based on the notion that where an award contravenes the public policy of the seat of arbitration but not that of the enforcement country, the award can still be enforced. These cases, and others taking the same approach, show a tendency to favour the law of the state in which enforcement is sought over that of the seat of arbitration. They thus lend support to a delocalised conception of international arbitration. However, while French case law continues to support the *Hilmarton* approach,[60] subsequent US cases have retreated towards the traditional line, refusing to enforce awards set aside at the seat of arbitration.[61]

2.54   Delocalisation supporters say that the only role courts at the seat of arbitration should have is to assist the arbitration with the procedural tasks that arbitrators cannot undertake. These include, for example, issuing urgent interim protection orders, subpoenas for witnesses or discovery orders in respect of third parties, appointing arbitrators where the parties have not done so, or removing non-performing arbitrators.[62]

---

59 *Chromalloy Aeroservices Inc (US) v The Arab Republic of Egypt* 939 F Supp 907 (DDC 1996) (US District Court of the District of Columbia).
60 Cass. 1ère civ., *PT Putrabali Adayamulia v Rena Holding*, 29 June 2007, case No. 06-13.293; see also M Haravon, 'Enforcement of Annulled Foreign Arbitral Awards: The French Supreme Court Confirms the Hilmarton Trend', (2007) 22(9) *Mealey's International Arbitration Report* 1.
61 US cases which supported the *Chromalloy* approach include *Karaha Bodas Co v Perusahaan Pertambangan Minyak Dan Gas Bumi Negara*, 335 F 3d 357, 367 (5th Cir 2003) (US Court of Appeals); *Baker Marine Ltd v Chevron Ltd*, 191 F 3d 194, 197 n. 3 (2d Cir 1999) (US Court of Appeals); more recent authority has adopted a different view; see e.g. *Termorio SA v Eltranta SP*, 487 F 3d 928 (D.C. Cir 2007). In his extensive discussion of this issue, Born is very critical of the *Termorio* decision; see Born, op. cit. fn 27, p. 2685. See also for discussion D Freyer, 'United States Recognition and Enforcement of Annulled Foreign Arbitral Awards: The Aftermath of the Chromalloy Case', (2000) 17(2) *Journal of International Arbitration* 1. For further references to other countries, see Nottage and Garnett, op. cit. fn 28, Chapter 10.
62 If the parties have opted for institutional arbitration, tasks in connection with arbitrator appointment and removal are typically performed by the chosen institution, so courts may not be needed for those purposes. However, institutions cannot subpoena witnesses, issue interim protective relief, or perform similar functions.

5.2.2 International relations theory and delocalisation

Without expressly addressing it, the delocalisation debate in international arbitration contains numerous parallels with the discipline known as international relations theory. Yet the relationship between international arbitration and international relations theory has remained relatively unexplored. Some basic principles of international relations are reviewed below because this helps to understand delocalisation and contribute to the debate.[63]

2.55

Theories of international relations attempt to explain and predict the way humans and society interact on an international level. The main focus of most of the various theories is the actions of nation states, however the relative importance of nation states differs according to different theories. International relations theory emerged as a discipline in its own right in the second half of the 20th century. The study of modern international arbitration began in earnest at about the same time – although both international relations and international arbitration can claim histories spanning hundreds of years. In a very general sense the various theories of international relations can be grouped into categories. This discussion will only examine two: Realism and Liberal Internationalism.

2.56

Realism (or variations of it) has dominated international relations scholarship over the years. The essential premise of Realism is that nation states exist in an anarchical system with no guarantees of survival. As a result, the pursuit of power is an inevitable and crucial part of international relations. Originally this was manifested by a quest for military might. However, with the spread of capitalism it has also come to mean the attainment of economic power. Realism seeks to draw its strength from looking at what is actually happening; its focus is on reality or at least a reflection of it.

2.57

Partly as a consequence of basing itself on 'reality', Realism completely embraces the notion that states are sovereign. Sovereign states are also accepted by the majority of the other significant theories of international relations such that it can safely be said that traditional international relations theory confirms the theory of state sovereignty. A consequence of pure sovereignty is the absence of an overarching authority to control the actions or interactions of states.[64] Because each state is sovereign, none has the right to interfere with the domestic laws and policies of another. Domestic laws and policies are made by the state and followed by those within it. Therefore citizens of a state can do only what is either expressly permitted by the laws of the state or not otherwise prohibited by

2.58

---

[63] For the purposes of this book, we provide no more than a very brief introduction to international relations. We make a number of generalisations that do no justice to the intellectual endeavours of international relations theorists.
[64] International conventions and treaties might be seen as impinging on the traditional notion of sovereignty. Traditional supporters of sovereignty dismiss this by arguing that a state's decision to sign a treaty is a consensual one, and therefore a nation state does not lose sovereign power by signing a treaty. Such an interpretation may have been previously true, however it must now be questioned in light of the emergence of genuine international organisations such the World Trade Organization, to name but one example.

those laws. Realism's emphasis on sovereignty therefore supports the traditional or jurisdictional view.

2.59 Thus when delocalisation advocates argue against the traditional view that international arbitration is attached to the seat of arbitration, they are not just arguing against it in the context of arbitration, but also against the Realism school's understanding of how the world interacts. To battle with any level of success, the delocalised view must itself have an equally developed theoretical analogy. That analogy can be found in the international relations theory of Liberal Internationalism.

2.60 Liberal internationalism is a term used to encompass a wide variety of thought within the field of international relations theory. However, fundamental to all brands of liberal thought is the primacy of the individual. Nation states exist and have power, but they do so because that is the collective will of the individuals who band together to form that state.

2.61 Characterisation of the delocalisation view strongly reflects a liberal internationalist perspective. The legitimacy of the parties' decision to resolve their dispute by arbitration comes from their agreement to do so. They as individuals have the power to make that decision. Whether a state – embodying the view of the collective society – subsequently decides to enforce the outcome of the arbitration is a different matter. It may be that the subject matter of the dispute is considered illegal or immoral in the enforcing state, and thus the award should not be enforced. However that is a different issue; the main point is that the contracting parties should not be required to integrate their arbitration and resulting award into a state's legal system until such time as they want to use a legal system to assist them by enforcing a resulting award. Liberal internationalist theories therefore support the delocalisation view.

2.62 Today, nation states are increasingly acting in ways that challenge the traditionally accepted understanding of state sovereignty. A decline in the sociopolitical acceptance of sovereignty is likely to lead to a greater willingness to accept the idea of delocalised arbitration.

5.2.3 Delocalisation in practice: Relevant legal provisions

2.63 The proposition that no link is needed between the seat of arbitration and arbitration proceedings is initially attractive. It is also attractive to consider that arbitration relies on a national court only at the place of award enforcement and during enforcement proceedings. These propositions imply that international arbitration is truly international.

2.64 Despite the theoretical attractions of delocalisation, it is important to keep in mind what the laws say and what domestic courts will do. The legal effectiveness of international arbitration depends principally on laws that facilitate the enforcement of international arbitration agreements and awards, that is mainly the New York Convention, and subsidiarily the various domestic *lex arbitri* which permit, legitimise and positively support international arbitration. It is the combination of those legal sources which has elevated international arbitration to a superior and preferred mechanism for resolving international business disputes. Both the New York Convention and domestic international arbitration laws should therefore be considered.

Article V of the New York Convention provides some support for delocalisation but simultaneously throws it into doubt. Article V(2) provides: 2.65

> recognition and enforcement of an arbitral award may also be refused if the competent authority in the country where recognition and enforcement is sought finds that (a) the subject matter of the difference is not capable of settlement by arbitration under the law of that country or (b) the recognition or enforcement of the award would be contrary to the public policy of that country.

The reference to 'that country' is of course the country where enforcement is sought. Thus the New York Convention expressly recognises that a court asked to enforce an award applies its own laws in deciding whether the subject matter was capable of settlement by arbitration and applies its own views on (international) public policy.[65] 2.66

This simultaneously appears to promote both a traditional and a delocalised view. From the delocalisation perspective, the article allows one state (the enforcing state) to prefer its own laws over those of the seat. This runs contrary to the traditional view of sovereignty, which is based, among other things, on mutual recognition of a foreign state's power and sovereign rights. From a traditionalist's perspective, however, there is nothing unusual about a sovereign state limiting the kinds of arbitration awards that it is willing to enforce. 2.67

Article V(1) of the New York Convention provides some support for delocalisation but more for the traditional conception of international arbitration. It states in relevant part: 2.68

> Recognition and enforcement of the award may be refused [upon] proof that:
> (a) ... the [arbitration] agreement is not valid under the law to which the parties have subjected it or, failing any indication thereon, under the law of the country where the award was made; or ...
> (d) The composition of the arbitral authority or the arbitral procedure was not in accordance with the agreement of the parties, or, failing such agreement, was not in accordance with the law of the country where the arbitration took place; or ...
> (e) The award has ... been set aside or suspended by a competent authority of the country in which, or under the law of which, that award was made;

Article V(1)(a) and (d) thus give primacy to the parties' agreement, at first appearing to support delocalisation. Yet in the absence of agreement on the matters dealt with in Articles V(1)(a) and (d), the enforcing court must refer to (a) 'the law of the country where the award was made' or (d) 'the law of the country where the arbitration took place', both meaning in practice the law of the seat of arbitration, rather than its own law. As a matter of treaty law under the New York Convention, these references back to the law of the seat 2.69

---

[65] A distinction should be drawn between domestic and international public policy. See the discussion in Chapter 9, Section 6.3.2.

provide support for the proposition that there is a legal link between the seat of arbitration and the arbitrations that take place there. However, the mere fact that the legal link can be displaced by party agreement on a different law reduces its significance. Article V(1)(e) can be read to lend support to either view. On the one hand it empowers a court to refuse enforcement of an award which has been set aside or suspended at the seat of arbitration, regardless of the reasons for that setting aside or suspension. This creates a link to the seat of arbitration. On the other hand, the fact that the enforcement court has a discretion[66] (rather than an obligation) to refuse enforcement in these circumstances means that that link with the seat is tenuous.

2.70   The fact that proponents of both sides of the delocalisation debate refer to Article V is therefore unsurprising. As Hong-Lin Yu has noted, Article V(1)(e) can be read in conjunction with Article VII to find support for delocalisation:[67]

> [The] Hilmarton and Chromalloy cases make a substantial link between Article V(1)(e) and Article VII of the [New York] Convention. Not only do they endorse the concept of delocalisation theory applied in [other cases], but also stress the significance of the 'more favourable right principle' established in Article VII of the Convention and its interplay with Article V(1)(e). They believe that the language used in Article VII was intended to facilitate the development of international commercial arbitration, rather than placing obstacles in its path. Furthermore, due to the lack of negative language in Article VII, they believe that the draftsmen did not exclude the possibility of using Article VII as the basis for recognising or enforcing an award which has been set aside in its country of origin on the ground that this particular provision allows a party to rely on more favourable domestic law as far as recognition or enforcement of arbitral awards are concerned.

2.71   The use of Article VII in this way also finds support in UNCITRAL's 2006 recommendation, which provides that this article 'should be applied to allow any interested party to avail itself of rights it may have, under the law or treaties of the country where an arbitration agreement is sought to be relied upon, to seek recognition of the validity of such an arbitration agreement'.[68]

2.72   The most significant barrier to the pure delocalisation view is found in Article I of the New York Convention:

> This Convention shall apply to the recognition and enforcement of arbitral awards made <u>in the territory of a state</u> other than the state where the recognition and enforcement of such awards are sought. (Emphasis added)

2.73   Thus in order to be enforced under the New York Convention an award must have been made in the *territory of a state* and not in some supranational space.

---

[66] All of the grounds for refusing recognition under Article V are discretionary.
[67] Hong-Lin Yu, 'Is the Territorial Link Between Arbitration and the Country of Origin Established by Articles I and V(1)(e) Being Distorted by the Application of Article VII of the New York Convention?', (2002) 5 *International Arbitration Law Review* 196, at p. 203.
[68] Recommendation regarding the interpretation of Article II, para 2, and Article VII, para 1 of the Convention on the Recognition and Enforcement of Foreign Arbitral Awards, done in New York, 10 June 1958, adopted by the United Nations Commission on International Trade Law on 7 July 2006 at its thirty-ninth session. UN Doc A/6/17.

Hong-Lin Yu accordingly notes:[69] 2.74

> By linking Article I and V(1)(e) of the Convention, the arguments emphasising the territorial link between arbitration and the place of arbitration have won the support of most academics and practitioners involved in international commercial arbitration who have been using Article V(1)(e) of the Convention as the shield against any movement towards the concept of 'delocalisation' or 'denationalisation' of international commercial arbitration.

It is not particularly surprising that arguments supporting both sides of the debate can be grounded in the provisions of the New York Convention. The fact that both sides of the debate rely heavily on the New York Convention confirms the importance of referring to laws to resolve the debate in the first place. 2.75

As noted above, the other laws to consider are the various domestically enacted *lex arbitri*. One of the most pure forms of delocalised international commercial arbitration in the Asia-Pacific region, and indeed the world, was found in Malaysia's former arbitration law. Prior to the 2005 Malaysian Arbitration Act, where the seat of arbitration was in Malaysia and the parties had chosen to adopt the Arbitration Rules of the Kuala Lumpur Regional Centre for Arbitration, the law did not permit any recourse at all from arbitral awards.[70] This extraordinary provision meant, in effect, that Malaysia permitted purely delocalised arbitration in which the Malaysian courts had no power to review international arbitral awards even if the seat of arbitration was in Malaysia. The only means of recourse for a party dissatisfied with the award was to wait for the successful party to try to enforce it and in response resist that enforcement attempt.[71] 2.76

Apart from the old Malaysian law, no other Asia-Pacific country's laws support pure delocalisation. Malaysia's 2005 Arbitration Act is based on the Model Law, similar to most arbitration laws in the Asia-Pacific. Drafting of the Model Law was completed by UNCITRAL in 1985, some 27 years after the conclusion of the New York Convention. Its provisions relating to enforcement of awards (Article 36) mirror those of the New York Convention (Article V) so that the same comments explained above concerning recognition of delocalisation in Article V of the New York Convention apply more or less mutatis mutandis to the Model Law. 2.77

Apart from those similarities with the New York Convention, the Model Law provides for a highly unsupervised or delocalised form of international arbitration with minimal intervention from courts. As Kaufmann-Kohler has noted, one of the Model Law's 'main purposes was to free the proceedings from the 2.78

---

69 Hong-Lin Yu, op. cit. fn 67, at p. 197.
70 Section 34(1) of the Malaysian Arbitration Act 1952 reads:

> Notwithstanding anything to the contrary in this Act or in any other written law but subject to subsection (2) in so far as it relates to the enforcement of an award, the provisions of this Act or other written law shall not apply to any arbitration held under the Convention on the Settlement of Investment Disputes Between States and Nationals of Other States 1965 or under the United Nations Commission on International trade Law Arbitration Rules 1976 and the Rules of the Regional Centre for Arbitration at Kuala Lumpur.

71 For commentary on this section, see H Arfazadeh 'New Perspectives in South East Asia and Delocalised Arbitration in Kuala Lumpur', (1991) 8(4) *Journal of International Arbitration* 103.

constraints of local law, so as to avoid the parties' expectations from being frustrated by conflicting provisions of such law'.[72] This is also reflected in UNCITRAL reports leading up to the establishment of the Model Law:[73]

> Probably the most important principle on which the model law should be based is the freedom of the parties in order to facilitate the proper functioning of international commercial arbitration according to their expectations. This would allow them to freely submit their disputes to arbitration and to tailor the 'rules of the game' to their specific needs. It would also enable them to take full advantage of rules and policies geared to modern international arbitration practice as, for example, embodied in the UNCITRAL Arbitration Rules.

2.79 However, it is clear that the Model Law does not support fully delocalised arbitration. The best example is Article 34 of the Model Law, which empowers a court at the seat of arbitration to set aside an arbitral award made in that seat if certain conditions are met. If the Model Law recognised fully delocalised arbitration, it would not permit applications to set aside an award. Moreover, Article 34(2)(b) of the Model Law provides additional grounds for setting aside an award if the dispute was not capable of settlement by arbitration under the law of the seat of arbitration or is in conflict with the public policy of the seat of arbitration. This directly links an award to the local laws on arbitrability and public policy, and again casts doubt on the acceptance of delocalisation (although the concepts of arbitrability and public policy should be interpreted from an international and not domestic perspective).[74]

2.80 In the Asia-Pacific, the Model Law has not been adopted by all states without modification. We can find – to use Matthew Secomb's phrase – 'shades of delocalisation';[75] that is differences in the adoption and modification of the Model Law and differences in the attitudes of courts, mainly relating to the level of court intervention. On the one hand, states may have increased the role of courts beyond what is permitted in the Model Law. In this vein there is criticism from one commentator regarding the 2003 Japanese Arbitration Law. Although that enactment is based on the Model Law:

> Japanese district courts have a wider jurisdiction than most. Whilst the leer of the Model Law is clearly set out in art 4 of the New Law – 'No court shall intervene with respect to any arbitral proceedings except where so provided in this Law' – its spirit is perhaps less faithfully observed by the provisions which follow.[76]

---

72 G Kaufmann-Kohler, 'Identifying and Applying the Law Governing the Arbitration Procedure – The Role of the Law of the Place of Arbitration', (1998) 9 *ICCA Congress Series* 336, at p. 355.
73 'Report of the Secretary-General: possible features of a model law on international commercial arbitration' UN Doc A/CN.9/207, at para 17.
74 In relation to arbitrability see Chapter 4, Section 8 and in relation to public policy see Chapter 9, Section 6.3.2.
75 M Secomb, 'Shades of Delocalisation – Diversity in the Adoption of the UNCITRAL Model Law in Australia, Hong Kong and Singapore', (2000) 17(5) *Journal of International Arbitration* 123.
76 D Roughton, 'A Brief Review of the Japanese Arbitration Law', (2005) 1(2) *Asian International Arbitration Journal* 127, at p. 131. It should be noted that Roughton appears to be in the minority with this characterisation of Japan's Arbitration Law; see, e.g. L Nottage, 'Japan's New Arbitration law: Domestication Reinforcing Internationalisation?', (2004) 7(2) *International Arbitration Law Review* 54.

On the other hand, domestic courts can decide to restrict the freedom of international arbitration and thereby restrict the delocalised character of the Model Law. Examples of this kind of restriction are usually found in those cases where an attempt is made to set aside an award.

Several Indian Supreme Court decisions have attracted considerable attention and commentary in this general regard. Often cited cases are *Oil and Natural Gas Corp v Saw Pipes Ltd*,[77] *Bhatia International v Bulk Trading S.A.*,[78] and *Venture Global Engineering v Satyam Computer Services Ltd*.[79] In the *Saw Pipes* decision, the Supreme Court had been called on to consider and apply Section 34 of the Indian Arbitration and Conciliation Act 1996. This section, except for two aspects, mirrors Article 34 of the Model Law.[80] Section 34 of the Indian legislation and Article 34 of the Model Law limit the grounds on which an award may be set aside. Critics of the *Saw Pipes* decision have described it as adding 'a new "judge-made" ground'[81] by allowing a court to consider whether the decision was patently illegal. The decisions in *Bhatia* and *Venture Global* suggest that the Indian Supreme Court has the power to set aside foreign awards, that is awards made in seats of arbitration outside India. In the *Venture Global* decision, enforcement was not even sought in India so the link with that jurisdiction was very tenuous.[82]

2.81

An understanding (albeit limited) about general attitudes to delocalisation can be found in Asia-Pacific court decisions. One example is the High Court of Hong Kong judgment in *Karaha Bodas Co LLC v Perusahaan Pertambangan Minyak Dan Gas Bumi Negara (also known as Pertamina)*.[83] We referred to this case earlier in the chapter.[84] Enforcement of the award in Hong Kong was resisted by Pertamina on the basis that Indonesian courts had already set aside the award. Justice Burrell found as both a matter of fact and law that the seat of arbitration had been Geneva, Switzerland. Since an award can only be set aside at the seat of arbitration (or by a court pursuant to whose laws the award was made), he held that the Indonesian decision was irrelevant and did not allow Pertamina to invoke Section 44(2)(f) of the Hong Kong Arbitration Act (the equivalent of Article V(1)(e) of the New York Convention). In the course of his reasoning, by

2.82

---

77 2003 (5) SCC 705. For commentary on the decision see FS Nariman, 'Judicial Supervision and Intervention' in M Pryles and M Moser (eds), *Asia's Leading Arbitrators' Guide to International Arbitration*, JurisNet, 2007, at p. 353; S Kachwaha, 'Enforcement of Arbitration Awards in India', (2008) 4 *Asian International Arbitration Journal* 64; S Sharma, 'Public Policy Under the Indian Arbitration Act In Defence of the Indian Supreme Court's Judgment in ONGC v Saw Pipes', (2009) 26(1) *Journal of International Arbitration* 133; P Nair, 'Surveying a Decade of the "New" Law of Arbitration In India', (2007) 23(4) *Arbitration International* 699.
78 (2002) 4 SCC 105. See also the discussion in Chapter 9, Section 3.2.2 of this book.
79 (2008) SCALE 214. See also the discussion in Chapter 9, Section 3.2.2 of this book.
80 Unlike the Model Law, pursuant to Section 13(5) of the Arbitration and Conciliation Act 1996, where parties have unsuccessfully challenged an arbitrator, they must wait until the award has been delivered before they can pursue that challenge by way of an action to set aside. Similarly, pursuant to Section 16(6), a party objecting to an arbitration agreement must also bring a setting aside action.
81 Kachwaha, op. cit. fn 77, at p. 68.
82 See generally S Sattar, 'National Courts and International Arbitration: A Double-edged Sword?', (2010) 27 *Journal of International Arbitration* 51.
83 [2003] 380 HKCU 1.
84 See discussion in Section 4.1.

way of obiter dictum, Justice Burrell referred to the Hong Kong courts' discretion to enforce an award despite its having been set aside at the seat:[85]

> Secondly, had Pertamina come within [Section 44] (2)(f) or (3), KBC's task in persuading the court to exercise its discretion [to grant enforcement] would have been more difficult. The issues under (2)(f) and (3) are more fundamental and more important in nature. Normally, a court would be inclined not to exercise the discretion in such circumstances. In this case, however, the balance would have been tipped against the norm for just one reason. That reason being the lateness of the emergence of Pertamina's contentions. The argument that the lex arbitri arbitration [sic] is Indonesian law and the complaint that the political risk policy was not disclosed, can both be described as '11th hour' challenges. Such lateness would, in my judgment, dilute the strength of the arguments to the extent that it would have been appropriate to exercise the discretion to, nonetheless, enforce the award.

2.83 Hong Kong judges therefore seem to be at least open to the possibility of a delocalised, *Chromalloy*,[86] approach to enforcing arbitration awards set aside at the seat of arbitration in certain cases. It was not necessary for the court in *Pertamina* to decide the issue in this case, since it had rejected Pertamina's argument that the *lex arbitri* was Indonesian law. Even if Indonesian law applied as the *lex arbitri*, the circumstances of this case were peculiar given Pertamina's delay in raising the argument that the award had been set aside.

2.84 More specific guidance for common law jurisdictions can also be found in powerful statements of English courts in *Coppee-Lavalin v Ken-Ren*.[87] Lord Mustill made very clear that delocalisation was inconsistent with the arbitration law of England. He was following the decision in *Bank Mellat v Helliniki Techniki*, where Justice Kerr explained:

> despite suggestions to the contrary by some learned writers under other systems, our jurisprudence does not recognise the concept of arbitral procedures floating in the transnational firmament, unconnected with a municipal system of law.[88]

2.85 Finally, although no delocalised system exists for international commercial arbitration, a delocalised approach has been adopted by the ICSID Convention for arbitrations between foreign investors and states.[89] That Convention excludes any review of ICSID arbitral awards by domestic courts and does not allow domestic courts to employ grounds (such as in Article V of the New York Convention) as a basis for refusing the enforcement of ICSID awards.

5.2.4 Conclusions on delocalisation

2.86 In its purest form, delocalisation means independence and complete disassociation of international arbitration proceedings from the jurisdiction and control

---
85 [2003] 380 HKCU 1, at para 69.
86 See the discussion of this case in Section 5.2.1.
87 *Coppee-Lavalin SA/NV v Ken-Ren Chemicals & Fertilizers Ltd (in liq)* [1994] 2 All ER 449 (House of Lords).
88 *Bank Mellat v Helliniki Techniki SA* [1984] QB 291, at p. 301 (English Court of Appeals, Civil).
89 See the discussion in Chapter 10, Section 5.3.2. A form of purely delocalised arbitration also existed in Malaysia before 2005. See Section 34(1) of the Malaysian Arbitration Act 1952.

of courts until such time as an award needs to be enforced. The previous section demonstrates that pure delocalisation does not exist (except in ICSID arbitrations) because it is inconsistent with the international instruments that constitute the legal framework for international arbitration.

2.87 But the delocalisation debate has certainly influenced aspects of international arbitration practice. It has fuelled a movement away from control by the courts at the seat of arbitration, away from the application of peculiar mandatory substantive laws of the seat, and away from overly strict or rigid arbitration laws that constrain party autonomy and the flexibility of the arbitral process. A good example of delocalisation's influence on the enactment of laws is the Model Law, which as explained above and elsewhere throughout this book,[90] provides for very limited court interference and a very high degree of party autonomy.

2.88 It may therefore be concluded that while pure delocalisation does not exist, a more diluted and pragmatic form does. In this diluted form, domestic laws and courts have bowed to legislative and/or practitioner pressure to take a more hands-off approach to arbitrations seated in their jurisdiction. The effect is that delocalised (or nearly delocalised) arbitration can be practised in certain jurisdictions if the law and courts of those jurisdictions so permit. Take as an example the former Malaysian arbitration law, referred to above, which expressly permitted purely delocalised arbitration. It is sometimes argued that this amounts to a combination of the delocalised and traditionalist conception of arbitration or a 'hybrid' approach because the law of the seat effectively permits delocalisation.[91]

2.89 In this diluted or hybrid form, delocalisation must still depend on the level of interference permitted by the laws and courts of the seat of arbitration. It may consequently be said that the control over delocalisation by the laws of the seat of arbitration is consistent with the traditionalist or jurisdictional reasoning but fundamentally inconsistent with delocalisation. As long as there is a provision in the *lex arbitri* which permits something, then that provision is itself a form of attachment to the seat of arbitration and displaces truly delocalised arbitration.

2.90 In other words, when analysing the hybrid approach from a theoretical perspective, a fundamental problem emerges. The hybrid approach is not a hybrid at all but rather a more or less modified restatement of the traditional view. Even on the basis of the so-called hybrid there is an essential link to the seat of the arbitration. We can conclude from a traditional line of reasoning that delocalisation is not a phenomenon in its own right, but rather permitted by the state.

2.91 Notwithstanding these theoretical conclusions, we consider the delocalisation debate to have had a very positive effect on the success of international arbitration by decreasing the level of court interference at the seat of arbitration and reducing the application of otherwise irrelevant local mandatory laws. Although

---

90 See Chapters 7 and 9 generally.
91 A Barraclough and J Waincymer, 'Mandatory Rules of Law in International Commercial Arbitration', (2005) 6 *Melbourne Journal of International Law* 205, at p. 210.

the increasingly widespread use of the Model Law and similar arbitral laws have removed the perceived need for delocalisation, it is likely that the debate will continue.

6 Choosing the seat of arbitration

6.1 General principles

2.92 The parties to an arbitration are free to agree on the seat at any time. Usually, it is agreed in the arbitration agreement. If not, it might be agreed later. The freedom to choose the seat of arbitration is widely recognised by institutional arbitration rules.[92] Such rules simply restate a fundamental right that parties have been granted by virtually all *lex arbitri*.[93]

2.93 It is very rare that arbitration rules deny the parties any freedom to choose the seat. Rule 12 of the Rules of Arbitration of the Bangladesh Council of Arbitration appears to be an exception.[94] The seat of arbitration must be in Bangladesh, with the precise location determined by the Council. The seat can be outside Bangladesh only if international parties are involved. Rule 42 of the Rules of Arbitration of the Indian Council of Arbitration is similar. While the approach adopted by both these sets of rules is uncommon, it is not itself a restriction on party autonomy nor particularly surprising. Usually, the parties will have acted autonomously by choosing the arbitral rules in the first instance, and it can be expected that they were familiar with the contents of their chosen rules. The parties can thus be said to have chosen the seat of arbitration, albeit indirectly by choosing those rules.

2.94 The best way to record an agreed seat of arbitration is to state simply that 'the seat of arbitration will be x' or 'the place of arbitration will be x', specifying both the city and country. However, there is no mandatory form of wording necessary to indicate a choice of seat. For example, if an arbitration agreement states words to the effect 'the arbitration will be held in x' or 'the arbitration shall take place at x' or 'the dispute shall be decided by arbitration in x' or even 'the arbitrators shall convene in x', etc., it should be presumed that x was the intended seat of arbitration rather than simply the intended place where the meetings or hearings will be held.

2.95 An issue of this kind was considered in the Singapore High Court decision of *Philippines v Philippine International Air Terminals Co Inc*.[95] The court decision

---

[92] For example: ACICA Rules Article 19; KCAB International Rules Article 17; SIAC Rules, Rule 18; PDRCI Rules Article 18; LCIA Rules Article 16; ICC Rules Article 14.
[93] For example, Article 20(1) of the Model Law provides that 'The parties are free to agree on the place of arbitration'.
[94] Rule 12.1: 'The place or venue of arbitration shall be Bangladesh. The Arbitration proceedings shall be held at such place or places in Bangladesh as the Council may determine having regard to the convenience of the Arbitrators and the parties. In a case in which one or both of the parties are from overseas, the arbitration proceedings may also be held at any place outside Bangladesh at the discretion of the Council.'
[95] [2007] 1 SLR 278.

relates to an action to set aside a partial award. This case involved a construction contract between a private company and the Government of the Philippines. The arbitration agreement specifically distinguished between disputes regarding actual construction works issues (which were to be resolved by domestic arbitration in the Philippines) and all other disputes (which were to be resolved by ICC arbitration in Singapore).[96] The partial award dealt with the law governing the arbitration procedure and the proper law of the arbitration agreement. In the partial award, the arbitration agreement's reference to Singapore as the place of arbitration was considered. To the arbitral tribunal, it appeared that Singapore was designated as the place of arbitration because it was a neutral venue for the resolution of disputes given one of the parties was the Government of the Philippines. As such, Singapore was not simply a more convenient venue to hold hearings than the Philippines. The arbitral tribunal ultimately determined that both the law governing the procedure of the arbitration and the law governing the arbitration agreement was the law of Singapore rather than the law of the Philippines.

2.96 Failing party agreement, the seat may be determined by an arbitral institution, by a court or by the arbitral tribunal itself. Arbitration laws and rules provide default mechanisms for determining the seat. For example, Article 20 of the Model Law provides:

> The parties are free to agree on the place of arbitration. Failing such agreement, the place of arbitration shall be determined by the arbitral tribunal having regard to the circumstances of the case, including the convenience of the parties.

2.97 Institutional rules generally follow one of three approaches where the parties have not agreed on the seat. The first approach prescribes a default seat which can be changed by party agreement. The second approach empowers the arbitral tribunal to decide where the parties have not otherwise agreed and the third gives that power to the institution. Most institutional rules in the Asia-Pacific create a presumption in favour of the jurisdiction where the institution is situated.

2.98 The first approach identified can be seen in both the HKIAC Rules and the ACICA Rules. HKIAC Rules Article 15 states:

> The seat of all arbitrations conducted under these Rules shall be the Hong Kong Special Administrative Region of the People's Republic of China, unless the parties have expressly agreed otherwise.

2.99 ACICA Rules Article 19.1 provides that if the parties cannot agree on the seat, it will be Sydney, Australia. The PDRCI Rules in the Philippines provide for the arbitral tribunal to decide in the absence of party choice, but with a presumption in favour of Manila. Similarly, Article 18 of the KCAB International Rules provides

---

[96] The arbitration agreement provided that 'All disputes, controversies or claims arising from or relating to the construction of the Terminal and/or Terminal Complex or in general relating to the prosecution of the Works shall be finally settled by arbitration in the Republic of the Philippines following the Philippine Arbitration Law or other relevant procedures. All disputes, controversies or claims arising in connection with this Agreement except as indicated above shall be finally settled under the Rules of Arbitration of the International Chamber of Commerce by three (3) arbitrators appointed in accordance with the said Rules. The place of arbitration shall be Singapore and the language of the arbitration shall be English.'

that if the parties fail to agree the seat will be Seoul unless the arbitral tribunal decides that another place is more appropriate.

2.100 Among those that provide for the institution to decide are the SIAC Rules. Absent party agreement, SIAC Rule 18 designates Singapore unless the SIAC Registrar determines that another seat is more appropriate. In contrast, Article 14(1) of the ICC Rules provides for the ICC Court to decide in the absence of party choice, with no presumption in favour of a particular place. ICC arbitrations take place literally all over the world. In 2009, they took place in 101 cities across 53 different countries.

2.101 Having the institution decide the seat has several advantages over giving the task to the arbitral tribunal. First, the seat is quickly determined without much fuss. Second, the seat may be determined before the arbitral tribunal is constituted, meaning that the seat can be taken into consideration when choosing, in particular, the presiding arbitrator or sole arbitrator to ensure that he or she is geographically proximate and familiar with its laws.

6.2 Factors to consider in choosing a seat of arbitration

2.102 Some might cynically suggest that the most important factors when choosing a seat of arbitration depend on whom you ask. The parties' lawyers will probably want a seat the location of which is easily accessible and which has an arbitration law with which they are familiar. The parties themselves may be interested in the neutrality of the venue and the financial costs of arbitrating there. Everybody involved might consider it important that the seat of arbitration be the place of residence of the chairperson of the arbitral tribunal or the sole arbitrator. This may reduce costs and ensure that the chairperson has a good knowledge of the local arbitration law.

2.103 Realistically, the most important factor is the presence of laws and courts that are favourable to international arbitration.[97] First, the seat should be a party to the New York Convention. This is important for enforcement of any resulting award in other New York Convention countries because many jurisdictions have adopted the New York Convention with reciprocity reservations.[98] Second, the seat's arbitration law should provide for the desired level of judicial interference and control (that is, the desired level of delocalisation). The trend in modern international arbitration laws such as Model Law jurisdictions is for a very limited degree of judicial control, or highly delocalised arbitration proceedings. Further, the quality of the judiciary and the court system should be considered. If it becomes necessary during arbitration proceedings to approach a court for assistance, will that court be able to deal with the matter quickly, efficiently and predictably?

---

97 Hwang and Fong Lee Cheng op. cit. fn 4, at p. 201; JB Tieder Jr., 'Factors to Consider in the Choice of Procedural and Substantive Law in International Arbitration', (2003) *Journal of International Arbitration* 393.
98 For further explanation of these reservations see Chapter 9, Section 5.4.2.

Geographic and infrastructure convenience should be the second main criteria after the quality of the legal system and courts. The seat of arbitration should be geographically convenient for most people who will be involved in an arbitration; that is parties, witnesses, arbitrators and lawyers. Also important is that there are international flights and facilities such as appropriate hotels and rooms for conducting the arbitration hearings.

The third consideration concerns the neutrality of the seat. Usually contracting parties will prefer a seat that is outside the jurisdictions of any contracting party. The ability to choose a totally neutral seat – that is a seat with no connection whatsoever to the parties or the underlying dispute – is one of the many advantages of international arbitration over litigation. In international litigation it is rarely possible for parties simply to select any court that they want to resolve their dispute. Depending on the rules of that particular court, there usually has to be a connection between the court and the parties or the dispute in order for the court to accept jurisdiction. This is not true for arbitration. There is often no requirement that the chosen seat of arbitration be in any way linked to one of the parties or the underlying transaction.

6.3 Changing the seat of arbitration

Once the seat of arbitration has been agreed or decided, as a general rule it can be changed only by agreement of all of the parties. If the arbitration has already begun, such an agreement would in practice need to be made in consultation with the arbitral tribunal itself.

The decision to change the seat of arbitration can be a complex one and should not be taken lightly. The arbitral tribunal and parties should take care to ensure that no unexpected legal consequences of a changed seat inadvertently occur. For example, a party may subsequently attempt to derail the newly seated arbitration by raising issues of *res judicata* or a similar principle. It might be argued that by moving to a new seat, a new and legally distinct arbitration has commenced. To avoid this sort of argument, measures could be taken by both the parties and the arbitral tribunal. The parties may enter into an agreement clearly indicating their intent to move the seat but otherwise to preserve their respective rights and positions. The arbitral tribunal might decide to close formally the first arbitration with an award that expressly preserves the status quo.

The question of whether parties had decided to change the seat of their arbitration arose in the Singaporean Court of Appeal decision of *PT Garuda Indonesia v Birgen Air*.[99] As was noted above, in this case one party argued that the seat of arbitration had been moved from Indonesia to Singapore. The court acknowledged that in theory the parties could make such an agreement but found in that particular instance that they had not.[100]

---

99 [2002] 1 SLR 393.
100 Ibid., at paras 23–95.

> The place of arbitration is a matter to be agreed by the parties. Where they have so agreed, the place of arbitration does not change even though the tribunal may meet to hear witnesses or do any other things in relation to the arbitration at a location other than the place of arbitration. ...
>
> Thus the place of arbitration does not change merely because the tribunal holds its hearing at a different place or places. It only changes where the parties so agree. ...
>
> While the agreement to change the place of arbitration may be implied, it must be clear. This is in the interest of certainty.

2.109   Importantly, and as emphasised in the second paragraph quoted above, the fact that hearings were held in Singapore rather than Indonesia was not in and of itself sufficient evidence of an agreement to move the seat of arbitration.

2.110   If there is no party agreement to change the seat, it is nearly impossible to have it changed. In order to determine the mechanism for changing it, consideration would need to be given to how the seat was initially fixed. If initially fixed by an arbitral institution, such as ICC or SIAC, or by the arbitral tribunal itself, changing the seat may be possible by making a very well-reasoned request to that body.

2.111   However, if the seat of arbitration was initially agreed by the parties, attempting to change it would be very difficult should one party disagree. As Justice Allsop, then of the Australian Federal Court, observed: '[g]enerally speaking, a party, having bargained for a place of dispute resolution, should not have to go into its private reasons for agreeing to that place and for not wanting to litigate elsewhere'.[101]

2.112   Indeed the chosen seat could be considered a condition of the consent to arbitrate. A court order to change the seat would give rise to an argument that the arbitration proceedings were not conducted in accordance with the parties' agreement. Failing to follow the parties' agreement exposes a resulting arbitral award to attack. For example, Article 34(2) of the Model Law provides that an award can be set aside if 'the arbitral procedure was not in accordance with the agreement of the parties'. The same rule is found in Article V(1)(d) of the New York Convention, providing a ground on which to resist enforcement of an award.

2.113   The only circumstance in which an agreed seat of arbitration could be changed under protest of one party is when the agreement on the initial seat has become frustrated or impossible. A sufficient ground would appear to be that subsequent to the agreement on the seat of arbitration some legal or physical impediment had arisen which prevented the parties from seating their arbitration at the chosen location. For example, there could be a significant political or legal change in the chosen jurisdiction which makes arbitrating there unworkable or impossible. If the legal or physical impediment were strong enough, changing the seat should not invalidate the fundamental consent to arbitrate and thus invalidate the entire arbitration agreement. It may rather be considered that the parties, at

---

101 *Incitec Ltd v Alkimos Shipping* (2006) ALR 558, at p. 566.

the time of agreeing on a certain seat, could not have contemplated the changed circumstances and that the fundamental agreement to arbitrate disputes prevails over the agreed seat.

2.114 Determining which courts would have jurisdiction to hear an application to change a previously agreed seat of arbitration is not straightforward. A court at the initial seat would appear the most competent. However, if the initially chosen seat were frustrated by some legal or physical impediment, it is likely that reference to its courts would be complicated if not also impossible. One would therefore have to try the courts of the proposed new seat.

2.115 We are not aware of any examples where a court has changed the seat of an arbitration. A former justice of the Supreme Court of New South Wales Court of Appeal in Australia, Andrew Rogers, has discussed a number of cases in which courts from around the world have refused applications to change the seats of arbitrations on alleged *forum non conveniens* bases. He states in relation to *M/s V/O Tractoroexport Moscow v M/s Tarapore and Co* ('*Tractoroexport*')[102] that 'India is the only country in which successful applications have been made to secure arbitral hearings away from the agreed forum'.[103] We are, with respect, unable to agree with his interpretation of *Tractoroexport*.

2.116 The factual circumstances of *Tractoroexport* demonstrate in part why we disagree. The contract involved an Indian and a Russian company. An arbitration agreement called for arbitration under the auspices of the Foreign Trade Arbitration Commission of the USSR Chamber of Commerce, Moscow. The Indian company commenced proceedings in the Madras High Court alleging breach of contract. Very soon after, the Russian company initiated arbitral proceedings in Moscow, entered an appearance under protest in the Madras High Court, and sought a stay of those proceedings on the basis of the arbitration agreement. The Indian company countered by seeking an injunction preventing the Russian company from continuing the arbitration in Moscow. Through each level of appeal the Indian company was successful. The stay of proceedings was refused and the Russian company was injuncted from proceeding with arbitration in Moscow.[104] On a majority decision of the Indian Supreme Court, the Russian company's appeal was finally dismissed.

2.117 That is where the judgment ends. The court did not compel the parties to arbitrate in India. Indeed the judgment appears simply to allow the Indian party to continue its breach of contract claim in the Indian courts.

2.118 Rogers refers to obiter dicta made by the majority to support his interpretation:[105]

---

[102] AIR 1971 SC 1.
[103] A Rogers, 'Forum Non-conveniens in Arbitration', (1988) *Arbitration International* 240, at p. 253.
[104] The stay was refused on the basis that the arbitration proceedings had begun after the court proceedings. It involved a very narrow interpretation of the then Indian statute that enacted the New York Convention. That statute has since been repealed and the matter would be one for the Arbitration and Conciliation Act 1996. It is also curious that the court's ability to injunct the Russian company does not appear to have been addressed until the ultimate appeal before the Supreme Court.
[105] As quoted in Rogers, op. cit. fn 103, at p. 253.

The current restrictions imposed by the Government of India on the availability of foreign exchange of which judicial notice can be taken will make it virtually impossible for the Indian Firm to take its witnesses to Moscow for examination before the Arbitral tribunal and to otherwise properly conduct the proceedings there. Thus, the proceedings before that Tribunal are likely to be in effect ex parte. The High Court was, therefore, right in exercising discretion in the matter of granting an interim injunction in favour of the Indian Firm.

2.119 Rogers notes that:[106]

It seems harsh indeed that meeting the test of impossibility should be insufficient to avoid the forum selection clause on the basis of the principle of forum non conveniens.

2.120 However, the reality is that the Indian courts did not change the seat of arbitration: they merely refused to stay their own court proceedings. They refused the stay mainly because of an erroneous interpretation of Article II of the New York Convention, and not on what Rogers describes as *forum non conveniens* grounds.

2.121 We do not consider the Indian company's arguments to have been *forum non conveniens* related in any event. An argument that the agreed seat is no longer appropriate or possible affects the validity and enforceability of the agreement on that seat of arbitration. That is why we have suggested above that the only circumstance in which a seat of arbitration could be changed is where the agreement on the initial seat has become practically, physically or legally frustrated or impossible to perform.

7 The Model Law as *lex arbitri*

7.1 Asia-Pacific and the Model Law

2.122 We now turn to consider the Model Law and the role it has played in the Asia-Pacific. This discussion focuses principally on mandatory law issues, and relates to a general level. Other texts and journal articles can be consulted for individual country analysis.[107] Many Asian jurisdictions have separate laws dealing

---

[106] Ibid., p. 254.
[107] See, e.g.: Asia-Pacific generally – M Pryles (ed), *Dispute Resolution in Asia*, 3rd edn, Kluwer Law, 2006; PJ McConnaughay (ed), *International Commercial Arbitration In Asia*, JurisNet, 2004; D Jones, 'Recent Developments in International Commercial Arbitration', (2008) 11 *International Trade and Business Law Review* 83; Australia – Nottage and Garnett, op. cit. fn 28; China – Jingzhou Tao, *Arbitration Law and Practice in China*, 2nd edn, Kluwer Law, 2008; JA Cohen, DR Fung, N Kaplan, P Malanczuk and SH Wang, *Arbitration in China: A Practical Guide*, Sweet & Maxwell Asia, 2004; Hong Kong – MJ Moser and Teresa YW Cheng, *Hong Kong Arbitration: A User's Guide*, Kluwer Law International, 2004; K Sanger, B Segorbe and J Niu, 'Arbitration in Greater China: Hong Kong, Macau and Taiwan', (2007) 24(6) *Journal of International Arbitration* 651; India – Nair, op. cit. fn 77; Japan – T Nakamura 'Arbitration' in L Nottage (ed), *Japan Business Law Guide*, CCH, 2009; Malaysia – S Rajoo and WSW Davidson, *The Arbitration Act 2005: UNCITRAL Model Law as applied in Malaysia*, Sweet & Maxwell Asia, 2007; New Zealand – T Kennedy-Grant 'The New Zealand Experience of the UNCITRAL Model Law: A Review of the Position as at 31 December 2007', (2008) 4(1) *Asian International Arbitration Journal* 1; Vietnam – Hop X Dang, 'Towards a Stronger Arbitration Regime for Vietnam', (2007) 3(1) *Asian International Arbitration Journal* 80.

with international arbitration,[108] or arbitration in general with special provisions for international arbitration.[109] These statutes mainly regulate issues that include:

(i) questions concerning the formal validity of an arbitration agreement;
(ii) basic, default structure concerning the nomination and removal of arbitrators;
(iii) fundamental (often mandatory) procedural rules, such as the requirements of arbitrator independence, natural justice and procedural fairness;
(iv) formal and substantive requirements for arbitral awards;
(v) the mode of recourse against arbitral awards; and
(vi) the recognition and enforcement of arbitration agreements and arbitral awards.

This is by no means an exhaustive list and it is important that each country be considered individually.

2.123 Globalisation, increased international trade and the substantial growth of international arbitration have led to numerous jurisdictions adopting international arbitration laws. This in turn has led to international scrutiny and discussion of those laws and increasing uniformity among arbitration laws. This process has been greatly assisted by the Model Law. As noted in Chapter 1, the Model Law text has no independent legal status whatsoever.[110] It is simply a suggested model of an international arbitration law recommended by UNCITRAL. Any jurisdiction can adopt the Model Law partially or entirely and with any modifications it chooses.

2.124 The Model Law was prepared in 1985 and covers broadly the elements listed above as typical to arbitration laws. At the time of writing, it had been used as a basis for the arbitration laws of about 60 jurisdictions around the world. It is particularly prominent in the Asia-Pacific. Within this region most jurisdictions have based their legislation on the Model Law.[111]

2.125 UNCITRAL revised the Model Law in 2006. The revisions do not affect in any way the laws in force in the jurisdictions that have already adopted the 1985 text, or any part of it. At the time of writing only Australia, (Florida, USA), Ireland, Mauritius, New Zealand, Peru, Rwanda, Singapore and Slovenia have adopted all or some of the 2006 amendments. Hong Kong is understood to be in the process of passing legislative amendments.[112]

---

108 For example Australia, Hong Kong (although it is expected consolidation into a single system will occur in 2010), Singapore and Pakistan.
109 Brunei, China, India, Indonesia, Japan, Korea, the Philippines, Malaysia and New Zealand. Sri Lanka has one Act which makes very little distinction between domestic and international arbitration.
110 See the discussion in Chapter 1, Section 2.3.5.
111 A list of countries whose arbitration laws are based on the Model Law is provided at Appendix 3.
112 The arbitration law reforms currently before the Hong Kong Legislative Council, if adopted, will mean that both domestic and international arbitration will be governed by a single system.

7.2 Mandatory provisions of the Model Law (1985 text)

2.126 The principle of party autonomy in international arbitration dictates that parties should be free to agree on the procedure of their arbitrations. However, like all laws the Model Law contains mandatory provisions. Mandatory provisions of arbitral procedural law apply irrespective of party choice when an arbitration is seated in a particular jurisdiction.

2.127 Despite early proposals to do so the Model Law does not contain a list of mandatory provisions.[113] The UNCITRAL Working Group that formulated the Model Law reported that the group considered it 'desirable to express the non-mandatory character in all provisions of the final text which were intended to be non-mandatory'.[114] By implication therefore one could assume that unless an article of the Model Law contains the phrase 'unless otherwise agreed by the parties', or something similar, then the article will be mandatory. However, as explained in the quote from Holtzmann and Neuhaus below, this would be a dangerous assumption, and making a determination on that basis alone would be unwise.

2.128 The issue is certainly difficult, as can be evidenced by the significant deliberations of the UNCITRAL Working Group on this topic alone. In their commentary on the development of the Model Law, Holtzmann and Neuhaus say of mandatory provisions:[115]

> The proposal for an Article listing such mandatory provisions was initially made during the Working Group's second session on the Model Law[116] and was subsequently adopted by the Group.[117] The Secretariat then raised some doubts as to the wisdom of such an Article, on the ground that such a provision was not needed and was subject to drafting difficulties.[118] It noted that the great majority of Articles that were intended to be nonmandatory had been drafted so as to indicate their nonmandotry [sic] nature, and suggested that words such as 'unless otherwise agreed by the parties' be added to the few remaining articles that were thought to be nonmandatory.[119] The Working Group adopted this approach, but with a significant caveat: it stated in its Report that '[i]t was understood' that the decision to express the nonmandatory character of those provisions 'did not mean that all those provisions of the model law which did not express their non-mandatory character were necessarily of a mandatory nature.'[120] The proposal for an Article listing the mandatory Articles of the Law was not revived during the Commission's session.

---

[113] In the report of the working group on its seventh session, it is noted that the working group agreed that an article listing mandatory provisions should not be included, despite its appearance in earlier drafts, UN Doc A/CN 9/246–6 (March 1984) at para 176.
[114] UN Doc A/CN 9/246–6 (March 1984) at para 177.
[115] H Holtzmann and J Neuhaus, *A Guide to the UNCITRAL Model Law on International Commercial Arbitration: Legislative History and Commentary*, Kluwer, 1989, p. 1120, (original footnotes included).
[116] See Second Working Group Report, A/CN 9/232, paras 77, 181, p. 1150 infra. (Original footnote.)
[117] Fourth Working Group Report, A/CN.9/245, para 175, p. 1151 infra. (Original footnote.)
[118] See Fourth Secretariat Note, A/CN.9/WG.II/WP.50, para 9, pp. 1151–52 infra. One example of the drafting difficulties was that a number of the provisions of the Law granted a freedom to the parties, accompanied by supplementary rules to apply in the absence of agreement. Here, the Secretariat said, 'the question of mandatory nature seems to be a philosophical one and ... redundant'. Ibid. (Original footnote.)
[119] Ibid. (Original footnote.)
[120] Fifth Working Group Report, A/CN.9/246, para 177, pp. 1152–53 infra. At the same time, the Working Group suggested that the Commission might wish to express the nonmandatory character of other provisions,

Perhaps the best test as to whether a Model Law provision is mandatory is to ask whether to alter it would in some way alter a fundamental and innate quality of international arbitration. This test is appropriate only for the Model Law and would not be suited to determine mandatory procedural laws imposed by the various applicable laws at the seat of an arbitration. In a domestic environment, mandatory laws usually deal with matters of public policy – an area the Model Law drafters intentionally avoided.[121]   2.129

A benefit of the proposed test is that it allows for degrees of autonomy or varying flexibility within the actual articles of the Model Law. It may be possible to vary some otherwise mandatory articles in such a way as to preserve the fundamental or innate nature of arbitration. An example of this can be found in Article 11(4) and is indeed contemplated by that article. The mandatory feature of the provision is a process designed to prevent one party from stalling or frustrating the arbitration. The article provides for recourse to the courts if necessary but also acknowledges that the parties may have determined an alternative procedure that achieves the same result. Therefore, even though the parties are free to alter the appointment process, they cannot do so to the extent that the resulting change enables a party to block all means to appoint an arbitrator. Such a change would bestow upon a recalcitrant party the power to stall the arbitration completely.   2.130

On the basis of the proposed test, we examine a number of specific articles in the Model Law to determine whether they were intended to be mandatory. Of course circumstances or modifications of the Model Law in specific jurisdictions mean that this discussion may not apply in the same way to all jurisdictions: 2.131

Article 1 Scope of application

(1) This Law applies to international commercial arbitration, subject to any agreement in force between this State and any other State or States.
(2) The provisions of this Law, except articles 8, 9, 35 and 36, apply only if the place of arbitration is in the territory of this State.
(3) An arbitration is international if:
   (a) the parties to an arbitration agreement have, at the time of the conclusion of that agreement, their places of business in different States; or
   (b) one of the following places is situated outside the State in which the parties have their places of business:
      (i) the place of arbitration if determined in, or pursuant to, the arbitration agreement;
      (ii) any place where a substantial part of the obligations of the commercial relationship is to be performed or the place with which the subject-matter of the dispute is most closely connected; or

---

since it was 'the prevailing view, adopted by the Working Group … that it was desirable to express the non-mandatory character in all provisions of the final text which were intended to be nonmandatory'. Ibid. (Original footnote.)

[121] Although Articles 34 and 36 of the Model Law refer to public policy, they do not make any attempt to characterise what constitutes matters of public policy.

(c) the parties have expressly agreed that the subject-matter of the arbitration agreement relates to more than one country.
(4) For the purposes of paragraph (3) of this article:
   (a) if a party has more than one place of business, the place of business is that which has the closest relationship to the arbitration agreement;
   (b) if a party does not have a place of business, reference is to be made to his habitual residence.
(5) This Law shall not affect any other law of this State by virtue of which certain disputes may not be submitted to arbitration or may be submitted to arbitration only according to provisions other than those of this Law.

2.132 This article is not typically included in a list of mandatory provisions. However it must, at least in part, be mandatory. Article 1 states when the Model Law applies. Although parties may subsequently derogate from particular articles, they cannot prevent the application of the Model Law under Article 1 as to do so would create a paradox. If the Model Law itself gives the parties the power to amend non-mandatory terms, logically it must apply before any amendment is legally possible.

2.133 As a matter of practice this is a largely unnecessary theoretical question, but it does point to a real conflict of laws issue. It is important always to identify properly the actual source of a power to act. Commonly in arbitration the power to amend – or even exclude altogether – the Model Law is found in the legislation that introduces it. As the source of the power is the Act and not the Model Law itself the paradox does not arise.

Article 7 Definition and form of arbitration agreement (1985 version)

1. 'Arbitration agreement' is an agreement by the parties to submit to arbitration all or certain disputes which have arisen or which may arise between them in respect of a defined legal relationship, whether contractual or not. An arbitration agreement may be in the form of an arbitration clause in a contract or in the form of a separate agreement.
2. The arbitration agreement shall be in writing. An agreement is in writing if it is contained in a document signed by the parties or in an exchange of letters, telex, telegrams or other means of telecommunication which provide a record of the agreement, or in an exchange of statements of claim and defence in which the existence of an agreement is alleged by one party and not denied by another. The reference in a contract to a document containing an arbitration clause constitutes an arbitration agreement provided that the contract is in writing and the reference is such as to make that clause part of the contract.

2.134 In the 1985 version of the Model Law Article 7 provides a definition and stipulates form requirements for an arbitration agreement. Although Article 7(2) is couched in the language of a mandatory term, it fails the test proposed above, and consequently is not strictly mandatory. This view is supported by the fact that in the 2006 revision of the Model Law, Article 7 Option II does not refer to writing at all. Whether or not the agreement is in writing has no impact on the very nature of arbitration, that is to say that the arbitral process will not be fundamentally changed if it arises out of an oral agreement. However, it is included in this list because, as a matter of practice, it would generally be advantageous for an arbitration agreement to be in writing or evidenced in writing. While some jurisdictions permit oral arbitration agreements,[122] the New York Convention requires an arbitration agreement to be in writing in order to have the award enforced.

Article 8(1) Arbitration agreement and substantive claim before court

1. A court before which an action is brought in a matter which is the subject of an arbitration agreement shall, if a party so requests not later than when submitting his first statement on the substance of the dispute, refer the parties to arbitration unless it finds that the agreement is real and void, inoperative or incapable of being performed.

Article 8(1) of the Model Law imposes a mandatory stay of court proceedings where a valid arbitration agreement exists. Other commentators have suggested that this is a mandatory article.[123] Applying the test proposed above, an innate aspect of arbitration is that arbitration agreements must be enforceable. A party should not be permitted to renege on its initial promise to arbitrate. It is of course different if both parties subsequently agree not to arbitrate their dispute, in which case neither Article 8 nor the entire Model Law apply at all.

2.135

Articles 11(4) and (5) Appointment of arbitrators

4. Where, under an appointment procedure agreed upon by the parties,
   (a) a party fails to act as required under such procedure, or
   (b) the parties, or two arbitrators, are unable to reach an agreement expected of them under such procedure, or
   (c) a third party, including an institution, fails to perform any function entrusted to it under such procedure,
   any party may request the court or other authority specified in article 6 to take the necessary measure, unless the agreement on the appointment procedure provides other means for securing the appointment.
5. A decision on a matter entrusted by paragraph (3) and (4) of this article to the court or other authority specified in article 6 shall be subject to no appeal. The court or other authority, in appointing an arbitrator, shall have due regard to any qualifications required of the arbitrator by the agreement of the parties and to such considerations as are likely to secure the appointment of an independent and impartial arbitrator and, in the case of a sole or third arbitrator, shall take into account as well the advisability of appointing an arbitrator of a nationality other than those of the parties.

---

122 For example, New Zealand Arbitration Act 2006, Article 7, Schedule 1.
123 See, e.g. A Broches, 'UNCITRAL – Commentary On The Model Law' in J Paulsson (ed), *International Handbook on Commercial Arbitration*, Suppl 11, Kluwer, 1990. It is possible innocently to misinterpret Broches on this point. At p. 92 he states 'I submit that the only mandatory provisions concerning the conduct of the proceedings, other than Article 18, are Article 24(2) and (3) and Article 27 (g.v.)'. In this statement he is only referring to those articles concerning the conduct of the proceedings and not to the Model Law as a whole.

2.136 As noted above[124] Article 11(4) is mandatory in so far as its purpose is to ensure that the arbitration proceeds, and cannot be frustrated by an unwilling participant. Broches confirms that, notwithstanding the wording of the last sentence of Article 11(4), parties cannot contract out of the court specified by Article 6 as an appointing authority of last resort.[125]

2.137 Article 11(5) refers to the mandatory requirements that arbitrators be impartial and independent.[126] These are fundamental to the prospect of the parties receiving equal treatment and a fair hearing – both essential characteristics of arbitration. However, where parties have agreed on institutional arbitration rules which contain a test for securing an arbitrator's independence or impartiality, any domestic court considering a challenge should take into consideration, when applying its own rules on impartiality and independence, that the parties have expressed a view on the appropriate test.

Article 12(1) Grounds for challenge

1. When a person is approached in connection with his possible appointment as an arbitrator, he shall disclose any circumstances likely to give rise to justifiable doubts as to his impartiality or independence. An arbitrator, from the time of his appointment and throughout the arbitral proceedings, shall without delay disclose any such circumstances to the parties unless they have already been informed of them by him.

2.138 Article 12(1) is not mandatory, however it is identified in this list because it might at first sight be considered such.[127] The problem lies in the different subject obliged to act under that article – the arbitrator as opposed to the parties.

2.139 The article places an obligation of disclosure on the arbitrator and not on either of the parties to the arbitration agreement. If the parties agreed that the arbitrator need not make any disclosures, this would not relieve the arbitrator of the obligation, but may prevent the parties from later objecting to that failure to disclose. Thus in a practical sense the effect of the article can be avoided. This should not be understood, however, as a waiver of the right to object to an arbitrator who is not independent. It is very unlikely that parties would be permitted to waive that right in advance of receiving the relevant information.[128] If a party came into information regarding a lack of independence, by a means other than an arbitrator disclosure, then a challenge could be brought.

---

124 See para 2.130.
125 Broches op. cit. fn 123, at p. 56.
126 However an interesting view of the independence of an arbitrator requirement was taken in the Supreme Court of India decision *Ace Pipeline Contracts Private Ltd v Bharat Petroleum Corporation Ltd*, (2007) 5 SCC 304. In that case, an arbitration clause which named a representative of one party as the arbitrator was upheld. This case is explored further in Chapter 6, Section 2.2.
127 Broches takes the view that this is a mandatory provision, see Broches, op. cit. fn 123, at p. 59.
128 However, see the Supreme Court of India decision *Ace Pipeline Contracts Private Ltd v Bharat Petroleum Corporation Ltd*, (2007) 5 SCC 304 discussed in Chapter 6, Section 2.2.

Article 18 Equal treatment of parties

The parties shall be treated with equality and each party shall be given a full opportunity of presenting his case.

Article 18 can be described as a true cornerstone of arbitration. As an illustration of the importance of this provision, in the New Zealand decision of *Methanex Motunui Ltd v Spellman*,[129] the Court of Appeal in Wellington found that a clause purporting to exclude a right of review for a breach of natural justice would be an impermissible attempt to derogate from Article 18.

2.140

Article 24(2) and (3) Hearings and written proceedings

2. The parties shall be given sufficient advance notice of any hearing and of any meeting of the arbitral tribunal for the purposes of inspection of goods, other property or documents.
3. All statements, documents or other information supplied to the arbitral tribunal by one party shall be communicated to the other party. Also any expert report or evidentiary document on which the arbitral tribunal may rely in making its decision shall be communicated to the parties.

Article 24(2) relates to giving the parties sufficient notice of hearings and meetings. It is simply an extension of the principle embodied in Article 18. Without due notice a party will not be in a position to present its case properly.

2.141

It has been suggested by Aron Broches[130] that Article 24(3) is also mandatory. The basic obligation in this article is that '[a]ll statements, documents or other information supplied to the arbitral tribunal by one party shall be communicated to the other party'.

2.142

Article 34 Application for setting aside as exclusive recourse against arbitral award

1. Recourse to a court against an arbitral award may be made only by an application for setting aside in accordance with paragraphs (2) and (3) of this article.
2. An arbitral award may be set aside by the court specified in article 6 only if:
    (a) the party making the application furnishes proof that:
        (i) a party to the arbitration agreement referred to in article 7 was under some incapacity; or the said agreement is not valid under the law to which the parties have subjected it or, failing any indication thereon, under the law of this State; or
        (ii) the party making the application was not given proper notice of the appointment of an arbitrator or of the arbitral proceedings or was otherwise unable to present his case; or
        (iii) the award deals with a dispute not contemplated by or not falling within the terms of the submission to arbitration, or contains decisions on matters beyond the scope of the submission to arbitration, provided that, if the decisions on matters submitted to arbitration can be separated from those

---

129 [2004] 3 NZLR 454.
130 Broches, op. cit. fn 123, at p. 92.

not so submitted, only that part of the award which contains decisions on matters not submitted to arbitration may be set aside; or
  (iv) the composition of the arbitral tribunal or the arbitral procedure was not in accordance with the agreement of the parties, unless such agreement was in conflict with a provision of this Law from which the parties cannot derogate, or, failing such agreement, was not in accordance with this Law; or
 (b) the court finds that:
  (i) the subject-matter of the dispute is not capable of settlement by arbitration under the law of this State; or
  (ii) the award is in conflict with the public policy of this State.
3. An application for setting aside may not be made after three months have elapsed from the date on which the party making that application had received that award or, if a request had been made under article 33, from the date on which that request had been disposed of by the arbitral tribunal.
4. The court, when asked to set aside an award, may, where appropriate and so requested by a party, suspend the setting aside proceedings for a period of time determined by it in order to give the arbitral tribunal an opportunity to resume the arbitral proceedings or to take such other action as in the arbitral tribunal's opinion will eliminate the grounds for setting aside.

2.143   Article 34 of the Model Law deals with applications to set aside awards. Lew, Mistelis and Kröll state that '[i]n principle, court control over an arbitration award in challenge proceedings can never be excluded'.[131] Some jurisdictions do, however, allow parties to limit the power of courts to set aside awards.[132] Those exceptions aside, Article 34 can be considered mandatory. Additionally, it is uncertain whether parties would be permitted to add further grounds upon which courts could review or set aside an award, such as error of law. In a 2008 US Supreme Court decision *Hall Street Associates LLC v Mattel Inc*,[133] it was held that parties could not add grounds to those stated in the Federal Arbitration Act. How countries in this region would react when faced with the same issue is not clear, especially as the domestic arbitration laws of several jurisdictions (which international parties can opt into) generally permit expanded grounds of judicial review and/or appeals.

Article 35 Recognition and enforcement

1. An arbitral award, irrespective of the country in which it was made, shall be recognized as binding and, upon application in writing to the competent court, shall be enforced subject to the provisions of this article and of article 36.
2. The party relying on an award or applying for its enforcement shall supply the duly authenticated original award or a duly certified copy thereof, and the original arbitration agreement referred to in article 7 or a duly certified copy thereof. If the

---
131 Lew, Mistelis and Kröll, op. cit. fn 38, at para 25–67.
132 For example, Article 1717(4) of the Belgium Judicial Code. See also Article 192 of the Swiss Statute on Private International Law and the decision of the Swiss Federal Tribunal (ATF 133 III 235, 240/241/242).
133 128 S Ct 1396, 2008 (US Supreme Court).

award or agreement is not made in an official language of this State, the party shall supply a duly certified translation thereof into such language.

Article 35 sets out one of the fundamental tenets of arbitration, its binding and enforceable nature. As discussed in the context of Article 34, parties are not able to undermine this principle by permitting the courts to review awards on grounds other than those provided by the law. It is therefore mandatory. 2.144

3

Applicable substantive law

1 Introduction

3.1 This chapter concerns the identification of the law that applies in an international arbitration. Various laws may apply to different aspects of the dispute.

3.2 After providing an overview of the types of choice of law issues that arise in international arbitration (Section 2), the remainder of this chapter focuses on the law applicable to the merits or substance of the parties' dispute. It first examines how an arbitral tribunal should determine the applicable law (Section 3). It then considers other issues such as mandatory laws, which apply regardless of the otherwise applicable substantive law (Section 4), how an arbitral tribunal should determine the content of the applicable law (Section 5), the compulsory application of the terms of the contract and trade usages (Section 6), the possibility of applying national rules of law or the *lex mercatoria* (Section 7), and finally the possibility for international arbitrators to decide cases based on principles of fairness and justice without reference to law (Section 8).

3.3 The treatment of applicable law issues in investment arbitrations under the ICSID Convention is completely different from international commercial arbitration. It is addressed in Chapter 10, Section 4.5.

2 Types of conflict of law issues in international arbitration

3.4 Determining the applicable law in an international litigation matter (i.e. before a state court) can be very complex, yet seductively interesting from an academic perspective. It involves an analysis of the interaction between different legal systems and their rules for determining the applicable law, usually referred to as 'conflict of laws rules' or 'private international law rules'. Indeed, it has been observed that:[1]

> The realm of the conflict of laws is a dismal swamp, filled with quaking quagmires and inhabited by learned but eccentric professors who theorise about mysterious matters in a strange and incomprehensible jargon. The ordinary court, or lawyer, is quite lost when entangled in it.

3.5 It might be thought that these conflict of laws complications would not exist in a system such as international commercial arbitration, one of the features and benefits of which is to do away with excess formality. This is not, however, entirely correct. While resolving conflict of laws issues in international arbitration is certainly more flexible than in international litigation, there is arguably an additional complication which does not exist in state courts: in international commercial arbitration there is no fallback legal forum or the *lex fori*. *Lex fori* means literally the law of the forum; it is the law of the jurisdiction where a domestic court proceeding is taking place. Among other matters, such a legal system provides the courts of that jurisdiction with fallback conflict of laws rules for determining the law that applies in a case involving foreign elements.

3.6 The *lex fori* should be distinguished from the *lex arbitri* which, as explained in Chapter 2, is the law regulating arbitration at the seat of the international arbitration (which is not necessarily its physical location but where it legally takes place). International arbitration proceedings have no *lex fori* because they are not connected to the seat of arbitration in the same way that domestic court proceedings are connected to the forum.[2] In particular, although the *lex arbitri* provides the legal backbone of the arbitration it does not provide a system of conflict of laws rules. So when an arbitral tribunal has to decide a question of applicable law, it does not have a fixed conflict of laws regime at its disposal.[3] Moreover, any and all elements which may precede or be a necessary part of resolving conflict of laws questions in domestic courts are undefined in international arbitration.

3.7 With that background, it is useful first to consider briefly the conflict of laws issues faced by a judge in domestic litigation proceedings. In international litigation, there are primarily two types of conflict of laws questions: First, which

---

[1] WL Prosser, 'Interstate Publication', (1953) 51 *Michigan Law Review* 959 at p. 971, cited in E Gaillard, 'The Role of the Arbitrator in Determining the Applicable Law' in LW Newman and RD Hill (eds), *The Leading Arbitrators' Guide to International Arbitration*, Juris Publishing, 2004, p. 185.
[2] Some authors consider that the seat of arbitration is the *lex fori*, but the prevailing view is that there is no *lex fori* in international arbitration. One of the early proponents of this view was Y Derains, 'L'application cumulative par l'arbitre des systèmes de conflit de lois intéressés au litige', (1972) *Revue de l'arbitrage* 99, at p. 102.
[3] As explained in Section 3.2.1.4 below, both the Japanese (Article 36) and South Korean (Article 29(1)) arbitration laws are exceptions because they include a conflict of laws rule for arbitrators in determining the governing contractual law in the absence of party choice. These rules are, however, very flexible and do not cover all conflict of laws issues that might arise, as do domestic conflict of laws rules when there is a *lex fori*.

law governs the procedure? Second, which law governs the parties' substantive rights?

3.8 The law governing the procedure in international litigation is necessarily that of the forum, i.e. the law of the jurisdiction where the court is situated or the *lex fori*; and the applicable rules of procedure are those of the court hearing the case. In other words, once a litigant brings court proceedings, the litigant usually has no choice as to the applicable procedural law or rules.

3.9 As to the law governing the parties' substantive rights, the judge will apply the substantive law of the *lex fori* unless there is a foreign element in the case and the conflict of laws rules of the *lex fori* otherwise direct the judge. Domestic conflict of laws rules are definitive in the manner that they determine the law applicable to any given situation. They may allow the litigating parties to choose the governing law, in which case the judge would apply the parties' chosen law. The conflict of laws rules might also include international, regional or bilateral conventions on applicable law. Several international conventions on applicable law have been prepared by the Hague Conference on Private International Law[4] but no Asia-Pacific states are parties to any such convention relevant in civil and commercial matters. There are also various regional conventions on applicable law, notably in Europe,[5] but again there are none in the Asia-Pacific. Whether their source is from an international or regional convention or purely domestic, conflict of laws rules are essentially part of the *lex fori* and will be applied accordingly. Any and all other conflict of laws questions that may arise in international litigation – to determine for example which law governs the parties' capacity to contract – are resolved definitively by those same conflict of laws rules.

3.10 In international arbitration, many more choice of law issues can arise than in international litigation. It is possible that a different law will govern each issue, thus creating a 'soup' of potentially relevant laws. The potential choice of law issues include:[6]

(i) Which law governs the arbitral procedure?
(ii) Which law governs the individual reference to or instance of arbitration?
(iii) Which law governs the arbitration agreement?
(iv) Which law governs supervisory, supportive, and enforcement measures?
(v) Which law governs a party's legal capacity?
(vi) Which law governs the parties' substantive rights?

Each of the above issues is addressed in turn.

---

[4] An example relevant to civil and commercial matters is the Convention of 2 October 1973 on the Law Applicable to Product Liability, which has been adopted by most European Community states. A list of these Hague Conference conventions is available on its website: www.hcch.net.
[5] For example, the 1980 Rome Convention on the Law Applicable to Contractual Obligations, which was recently superseded for European Community countries by EC Regulation No. 593/2008 on the Law Applicable to Contractual Obligations. There is also EC Regulation No. 864/2007 on the Law Applicable to Non-Contractual Obligations.
[6] These are similarly listed in M Pryles, 'Choice of Law Issues in International Arbitration', February 1997 *The Arbitrator* 260. See also generally A Chantara-opakorn, 'Dealing with Conflict of Laws in International Commercial Arbitration under the ICC Arbitration Rules and the Arbitration Act of Thailand', (2007) January *Asian Dispute Resolution* 5.

The question of the law governing the arbitral procedure has been dealt with in Chapter 2. As explained in that chapter, the international arbitration procedural law at the seat of arbitration normally applies. Alternatively, the parties may be free to choose a different procedural law.[7] 3.11

The law governing an individual reference or instance of arbitration means the procedural law governing a given submission to arbitration. Put another way, it is the procedural law that governs a particular dispute which has been referred to arbitration. A contract could lead to several separate disputes that might in turn give rise to several separate referrals to arbitration. It is possible – although unlikely – that a different arbitration procedural law will apply to each instance of arbitration. 3.12

The interesting question of which law governs an arbitration agreement is dealt with in Chapter 4.[8] For the purposes of this chapter it is sufficient to note two things. First, an arbitration agreement in the form of a clause in a broader commercial contract is considered to be an agreement separate and independent from the contract containing it. One consequence of this division is that the arbitration clause might be governed by a law other than the law governing the contract itself. The second point to note is that since an arbitration agreement is a contract, similar principles and methods can be used to determine which law governs an arbitration agreement as are used to determine which law governs any contract. This means that the choice of law methodology for contracts that is set out in the present chapter has some relevance to determining the law governing an arbitration agreement. 3.13

Supervisory, supportive and enforcement measures in an international arbitration are all proceedings that ordinarily take place before domestic courts. The law governing those measures depends on the law where they are sought, that is the *lex fori*, including the conflict of laws rules at that place. During arbitration proceedings, parties and arbitrators should keep in mind jurisdictions where enforcement may take place, so as to make efforts to ensure that the resulting award is valid and enforceable under the law of such fora.[9] 3.14

A party's capacity (for example to enter into a contract and/or an arbitration agreement) will generally be governed by its *lex personum* (personal law), that is the law of its nationality, even if a different law applies to the merits of the parties' dispute. For a company, that will be the law of the place of incorporation or place of business. For a state (i.e. a government), however, international arbitrators may in some circumstances find it inappropriate to apply that state's own law to the question of its capacity to contract internationally. A company is a legal person created under the laws of a state with powers that are limited by those laws. In contrast, a state possesses international legal personality, is capable of exercising rights and bears obligations under international law. When entering into a contract with a foreign party, it cannot be assumed that a state possesses 3.15

---

7 See Chapter 2, Section 4.1.
8 See Chapter 4, Section 3.2.
9 See further Chapter 7, Section 9 (relating to interim measures of protection) and generally Chapter 9.

100   INTERNATIONAL COMMERCIAL ARBITRATION

capacity that is limited by its own law.[10] Whether a party has validly entered into a contract or arbitration agreement may alternatively be determined by the law governing that contract or arbitration agreement.[11]

3.16   The question of which law governs the merits of the dispute is the focus of the rest of this chapter. As we will see, if the parties have not chosen the governing law, the answer is occasionally provided by the law of the seat of arbitration, but more generally has evolved by arbitration practice and academic studies. Even in those domestic jurisdictions where a fixed rule applies, international arbitral tribunals tend to follow international practice in applying such rules.

3 Determining the law applicable to the substance of the dispute

3.17   In some international arbitrations, the parties and arbitrators never actually refer to the substantive law at all. Even where there is a choice of law clause in the contract providing for the application of a specified law, the arbitral tribunal might not find it necessary to refer expressly to the law because the case can be decided directly by reading the contract clauses, perhaps supplemented by 'trade usages' of the particular industry.[12] Nonetheless, even if the law is not specifically referred to, every contract has to be governed by some law or rules of law.[13] The question is which law?

3.18   Article 28 of the Model Law is illustrative of provisions which address the question of applicable substantive law in international arbitration. It provides:

> *Article 28. Rules applicable to substance of dispute*
> (1) The arbitral tribunal shall decide the dispute in accordance with such rules of law as are chosen by the parties as applicable to the substance of the dispute. Any designation of the law or legal system of a given State shall be construed, unless otherwise expressed, as directly referring to the substantive law of that State and not to its conflict of laws rules.
> (2) Failing any designation by the parties, the arbitral tribunal shall apply the law determined by the conflict of laws rules which it considers applicable.

---

10 A state or state-controlled entity may not invoke its sovereignty or internal law to deny contractual consent. This is a consequence of the general principles of *pacta sunt servanda* and *bona fides* (see for example principle 38 of the 'List of Principles, Rules and Standards of the Lex Mercatoria', in KP Berger, *The creeping codification of the Lex Mercatoria*, Kluwer Law International, 1999, p. 296. The rule has been described as a general principle of international arbitration, see E Gaillard and J Savage (eds), *Fouchard Gaillard and Goldman on International Commercial Arbitration*, Kluwer Law International, 1999, n. 21, p. 322 et seq. See also relevant French cases: Cour d'Appel de Paris, *Gatoil v National Iranian Oil Company*, 17 December 1991, 1993 *Revue de l'arbitrage* p. 281 and Cour d'Appel de Paris, *Ministère tunisien de l'equipement v Bec Frères*, 24 February 1994, 1995 *Revue de l'arbitrage* 275. A similar principle is found in public international law, see International Law Commission, *Articles on Responsibility of States for Internationally Wrongful Acts*, 2001, UN Doc A/56/10, Articles 3 and 32, p. 170, para 4.85.
11 A party's capacity to enter into an arbitration agreement is considered in Chapter 4, Section 4.2.
12 Trade usages are dealt with below at Section 6.
13 Unless the parties agree that an arbitrator can decide as *amiable compositeur*, which is rare. See below Section 8.

(3) The arbitral tribunal shall decide ex aequo et bono or as amiable compositeur only if the parties have expressly authorized it to do so.

(4) In all cases, the arbitral tribunal shall decide in accordance with the terms of the contract and shall take into account the usages of the trade applicable to the transaction.

3.19 The question of applicable substantive law in international arbitration can be divided into two distinct scenarios. The first is where the parties to the dispute have chosen an applicable law, as foreseen by Article 28(1) of the Model Law (see Section 3.1 below), and the second is where they have not chosen the law, as foreseen in Article 28(2) of the Model Law (see Section 3.2 below). A related question is the law applicable to non-contractual claims raised during arbitration proceedings (see Section 3.3 below).

3.20 The matters referred to in Article 28(3) and 28(4) of the Model Law are addressed elsewhere in this chapter.[14]

3.1 Freedom of parties to choose the law

3.21 The most important rule for determining the applicable substantive law in international arbitration is that the parties are free to choose it. This principle is reflected in the Model Law Article 28(1), which was set out above, and in virtually all arbitration rules and laws.[15]

3.22 The parties' choice of law is usually made in the contract itself, but can be made at any time, even after a dispute arises. Practice shows that arbitrating parties usually exercise their right to choose the applicable law. For instance, in 2009 parties chose the applicable law in 88% of arbitrations before the ICC International Court of Arbitration.[16]

3.23 In international arbitration, the parties are generally not restricted in their choice of applicable law. There is no requirement, for example, that the chosen law has some connection to the parties or to the dispute.[17]

3.24 Choice of law is, however, restricted for international arbitrations in China. Article 7 of the Chinese Arbitration Law does not mention freedom to choose the law, but provides simply that 'in arbitration, disputes shall be resolved on the basis of facts, in compliance with law and in an equitable and reasonable

---

14 See respectively Sections 8 and 6 below.
15 The arbitration laws of most Asia-Pacific jurisdictions include an identical or similar provision to Article 28(1) of the Model Law with the exception of China, which is discussed below. Section 30(2) of Malaysia's Arbitration Act has a slight but significant difference, substituting 'rules of law' for 'law' in the first sentence (see the discussion below in Section 7). Among the institutional rules, one exception is the SIAC Rules, which do not include a provision relating to the applicable substantive law. Most SIAC arbitrations are seated in Singapore so the fallback would be Article 28(1) of the Model Law which applies in Singapore without modification. The 2010 SIAC Rules now include a provision on applicable law at Article 27.
16 This figure hovered between 77% and 87% from 2000 to 2008. The percentage seems to be increasing gradually but steadily over the years. ICC statistics can be found in the ICC's Published Statistical Reports for each year. See, e.g. '2009 Statistical Report', (2010) 21 *ICC International Court of Arbitration Bulletin* 1.
17 See, e.g. Y Derains and E Schwarz, *A Guide to the ICC Rules of Arbitration*, 2nd edn, Kluwer, 2005, p. 238 (They cite ICC case number 4154 as stating that: 'The principle of autonomy – widely recognized – allows the parties to choose any law to rule their contract, even if not obviously related to it.')

manner'. This provision is complemented by the treatment of applicable law in the Chinese law of contracts, which limits the types of contracts for which parties can choose the law, even if there is a foreign element in the case. The combined effect of these provisions is that parties may choose the applicable law only for certain types of contractual disputes that are submitted to arbitration seated in China.[18]

3.25 Domestic arbitration laws also sometimes contain restrictions. For example, Section 28(1)(a) of the Indian Conciliation and Arbitration Act 1996 provides that where the arbitration is 'other than an international commercial arbitration' Indian law will be the substantive law irrespective of party choice.[19]

3.26 The other limitation on the parties' choice of law is so-called 'mandatory laws', which apply regardless of the parties' chosen law. These are addressed below.[20] Apart from the exceptions just mentioned, it follows that if the parties have chosen the law, the arbitral tribunal must respect that choice, whatever it may be. It is only if they have not chosen the law, or if their choice is limited to certain aspects of the dispute, that a conflict of laws analysis becomes necessary.

3.2 Applicable law where there is no choice of law by the parties

3.27 Where the parties have not agreed on the governing law, the arbitral tribunal has to determine it by some form of conflict of laws analysis. As noted above, conflict of laws issues in international arbitration can be complex yet interesting. Despite this, conflict of laws in international arbitration has not been the subject of significant court decisions or academic studies in the Asia-Pacific region. The regional treatment in arbitration laws and rules is addressed below (3.2.1), before moving on to a discussion of the conflict of law methods used by international arbitrators generally (3.2.2). The latter section draws significantly on material from outside this region given the scant regional treatment.

3.2.1 Arbitration laws and institutional rules regarding applicable law in the absence of party choice

3.28 An arbitral tribunal's power to decide the law where the parties have not agreed on it is recognised in almost all arbitration rules and laws. There are several categories of approaches among the laws and rules in the Asia-Pacific region. These are addressed in turn.

---

18 See Jingzhou Tao, *Arbitration Law and Practice in China*, Kluwer, 2008, p. 101.
19 A similar provision exists for domestic arbitrations in Section 30(1) of the Malaysian Arbitration Act. India's arbitration law has a more restrictive definition of an 'international arbitration' than the Model Law, referring to the place of incorporation rather than principal place of business of any foreign party. Section 2(1)(f)(iii) of the Indian Conciliation and Arbitration Act may offer some prospect that the choice of law intentions of parties are followed because it refers to central management and control outside India. Parties should nonetheless be aware of Section 28(1)(a) when setting up locally incorporated project specific subsidiaries in India.
20 Mandatory laws are the subject of Section 4 below.

3.2.1.1 *'Conflict of laws rules' and 'direct' approaches*

3.29 The first and most common approach among Asia-Pacific arbitration laws is that used in Article 28(2) of the Model Law, which empowers the arbitral tribunal to select the 'conflict of laws rules it considers appropriate'.[21] A second approach, which is very common in arbitral institutional rules in the region, allows the arbitral tribunal to choose an 'appropriate' law.[22] The latter is often referred to as the 'direct' approach because it does not require the arbitral tribunal to apply a set of conflict of laws rules. Examples of possible conflict of laws rules that could be referred to under the direct approach are provided below.[23]

3.30 Arbitral tribunals applying the direct approach will undoubtedly have conscious or unconscious recourse to their knowledge and experience of private international law.[24] One author believes that 'the arbitrators de facto use conflict of laws considerations even if they are not aware of doing so.'[25]

3.31 If the direct approach applies, it certainly does not relieve the arbitral tribunal from having to reason and justify its decision as to which law applies, as has occasionally been suggested.[26] The arbitral tribunal must still engage in some form of analysis, which should logically be based on conflict of laws principles. Indeed, for the choice of a law to be 'appropriate', the necessary implication is that conflict of laws rules should be applied in some way or another because they are the most pertinent rules to make such a choice. It would not be at all satisfactory if arbitrators could directly choose a law without due consideration and justification. One expert on international arbitration is highly critical of the suggestion that the direct approach could be understood as to relieve the arbitrators from applying any conflict of laws analysis. He says it 'leaves the parties' substantive rights to turn on subjective, unarticulated instincts of individual arbitrators and does little to further interests of predictability or fairness'.[27]

3.32 In practice, provided that an arbitral tribunal applying the direct approach justifies its decision, there is unlikely to be a practical difference between it and an approach that uses a set of conflict of laws rules. Experienced international

---

21 Article 28(2) of the Model Law was set out above. That provision applies unmodified, or similarly, in Hong Kong, Singapore, Korea, New Zealand, the Philippines and Australia. Discussed below in this section are the unusual provisions of India, Malaysia, China, Indonesia and Sri Lanka.
22 Most Asian institutional rules follow the direct approach. See, e.g. Article 34.1 of the ACICA Rules, Article 25.1 of the KCAB International Rules, Article 15 of the BANI Rules, and Rule 6 of the Indian Arbitration Centre Rules. The different approach of Article 31(1) of the HKIAC Rules is addressed below. In addition to being found in many institutional rules, this direct method is found in one regional arbitration law, that of India. Section 28(1)(b)(iii) of the Indian Conciliation and Arbitration Act provides: 'failing any designation of the law . . . by the parties, the arbitral tribunal shall apply the rules of law it considers to be appropriate given all the circumstances surrounding the dispute.'
23 See Section 3.2.2.8 below.
24 Gaillard and Savage, op. cit. fn 10, para 1550.
25 B Wortmann, 'Choice of Law by Arbitrators: The Applicable Conflict of Laws System', (1998) 14(2) *Arbitration International* 97, at p. 101.
26 See, e.g. JD Lew, LA Mistelis and SM Kröll, *Comparative International Commercial Arbitration*, Kluwer Law International, 2003, paras 14–59.
27 G Born, *International Commercial Arbitration: Commentary and Materials*, 2nd edn, Transnational Publishers, 2001, p. 531. This comment is repeated in G Born, *International Commercial Arbitration*, Kluwer, 2009, p. 2137.

arbitrators tend to prefer the direct method because it is more straightforward, but the outcome should logically be the same either way.

3.2.1.2 *Requiring the application of the substantive law of seat of arbitration*

3.33 Indonesia and Sri Lanka appear to have adopted the approach of requiring arbitral tribunals to apply their respective local laws in the absence of a different choice by the parties.[28] The Indonesian Arbitration Law is unique in the Asia-Pacific in that it does not provide any indication as to how an arbitral tribunal should determine the law in the absence of party choice. Article 56(2) provides simply that 'the parties are entitled to designate the choice of law to be applied to the resolution of disputes which may arise, or which have arisen, between or among them'. It therefore appears that Indonesian law would apply as the fallback if another law has not been chosen. The Sri Lankan Arbitration Act contains an unusual provision at Section 24(3), the effect of which is that the parties would have to empower an arbitral tribunal specifically to decide the applicable law in the absence of party choice. The consequences of the parties not having so authorised the arbitral tribunal are not stated, but once again its language suggests that Sri Lankan law applies as the default.

3.2.1.3 *Requiring the application of the conflict of laws rules of the seat of arbitration*

3.34 Two Asian jurisdictions require the arbitral tribunal to apply the seat of arbitration's conflict of laws rules if the parties have not chosen the applicable law. One is China.[29] The second appears to be Malaysia, depending on how its relatively recent arbitration law will be interpreted. Malaysia's Arbitration Act 2005 is based principally on the Model Law, but has modified several provisions. Article 28(2) of the (unmodified) Model Law provides: 'Failing any designation by the parties, the arbitral tribunal shall apply the law determined by the conflict of laws rules which it considers applicable'. (Emphasis added) However, Section 30(4) of the Malaysian Arbitration Act is different: 'Failing any agreement [by the parties], the arbitral tribunal shall apply the law determined by the conflict of laws rules'. The Malaysian Arbitration Act thus omits 'which it considers applicable' while maintaining the definite article 'the' before 'conflict of laws rules'. The only linguistically loyal interpretation of Section 30(4) would be that 'the' is referring to Malaysian conflict of laws rules, thus suggesting that the arbitral tribunal must apply them.

3.35 While that interpretation is linguistically correct, it is possible that this drafting in the Malaysian law was an oversight and that Section 30(4) will be interpreted

---

[28] This was also the position in the UK before it was rejected in *Compagnie d'Armement Maritime SA v Compagnie Tunisienne de Navigation SA* [1971] AC 572, at p. 596.

[29] For China, if the nature of the contract is such that the parties may choose the law (see the discussion above at Section 3.1) and they have not chosen it, it must be determined by the arbitral tribunal applying Chinese conflict of laws rules. The usual conflict of laws rule that will be applicable points to the law with the closest connection to the contract (see Jingzhou Tao, op. cit. fn 18, at p. 103, who also sets out the Chinese guidelines for determining which law is most closely connected to a contract).

liberally. There do not appear to be any court decisions or published arbitral awards on this point as yet.

3.2.1.4 Requiring the application of the law with the closest connection to the dispute

Two Asia-Pacific jurisdictions mandate a fixed conflict of laws rule for arbitrators to apply where the parties have not chosen the applicable law. Article 36(2) of the Japanese Arbitration Law provides: 'Failing agreement as provided in the preceding paragraph, the arbitral tribunal shall apply the substantive law of the State with which the civil dispute subject to the arbitral proceedings is most closely connected.' A rule with similar effect is found in Article 29(1) of the South Korean Arbitration Act.[30] Arguably, such laws do not leave international arbitrators the usual freedom to select the applicable law by any method they wish.[31] An analysis of this choice of law rule as applied by international arbitral tribunals is provided below.[32]

3.36

3.2.2 Conflict of laws methodology adopted by international arbitrators

As noted earlier, when there is an international element in a case before a domestic court, fixed conflict of laws rules in the *lex fori* direct the judge on how to determine the applicable law. As we have seen in the previous section, this is not true for international arbitrators because international arbitrations have no *lex fori* and the vast majority of arbitration legislation and rules leave arbitrators with great flexibility and little guidance. The question is how the arbitral tribunal will determine the applicable law within the scope of its broad discretion. A decision about which law applies may have a direct impact on the parties' substantive rights. Surprisingly, however, there is notable diversity in approaches adopted by arbitrators. Leading practitioners who have written separately on the subject claim to report on the 'common methods', yet different practitioners report different methods as being common.[33]

3.37

This section first explains that domestic courts tend not to interfere with conflict of laws decisions made by arbitral tribunals, before setting out the methodologies commonly used by international arbitrators to determine the applicable law.

3.38

---

30 See also Article 31 of the HKIAC Administered Rules and Rule 41(2) of the JCAA Rules. A similar rule applies in Switzerland, Germany, Italy and Mexico.
31 However, Blessing submits in relation to the equivalent Swiss provision that there is no such restriction: 'Clearly, it would not be incompatible with Article 187 (1) [of the Swiss Private International Law Act] to operate the voie directe advocated by a number of scholars and practitioners.' He appears to make this assertion on the basis that finding the closest connection is at the heart of every set of conflict rules anyway. See M Blessing, 'The New International Arbitration Law in Switzerland: A Significant Step Towards Liberalism', (1988) 5(2) *Journal of International Arbitration* 9, at p. 59.
32 See below Section 3.2.2.6.
33 The spread of methods is reported in S Greenberg 'The Law Applicable to the Merits in International Arbitration', (2004) 8 *Vindobona Journal* 315. The following discussion in this chapter draws on various aspects of that article.

3.2.2.1 *Absence of court interference in arbitral tribunal's conflict of laws decisions*

3.39 There is nothing in either the grounds for setting aside awards or the grounds for resisting their enforcement that empowers a court to review an arbitral tribunal's decision as to the applicable law.[34] As a result, such decisions can be considered like those relating to the substance of the dispute, meaning that they are not subject to any review by the courts.

3.40 In practice, courts tend not to interfere in the power of arbitrators to decide the law even where the determination of law could affect the court's jurisdiction to decide claims under mandatory domestic laws. For example, in *Transfield Philippines Inc v Pacific Hydro Ltd*,[35] an ICC arbitral tribunal sitting in Singapore decided that Transfield's claims for misleading and deceptive conduct and negligent misrepresentation were governed by the laws of the Philippines, thus rejecting Transfield's contention that those claims were governed by Australian trade practices legislation. Transfield later sought to bring those claims in the Supreme Court of Victoria, Australia, contending that the claims were no longer capable of settlement by arbitration because the arbitral tribunal had declined to hear them. Justice Hollingworth held:[36]

> 71. The ... arbitral tribunal held that [Transfield's] claims for misleading and deceptive conduct and misrepresentation were governed by the law of the Philippines and the [Australian trade practices legislation was] not applicable to the arbitral proceeding. The arbitral tribunal gave thorough consideration to the approach it should adopt to the selection of the applicable law, and found that 'the preponderance of claims put forward are clearly rooted in a contract governed by the law of the Philippines.'
>
> ...
>
> 73. ... it would not be appropriate for an Australian court to adjudicate claims for misrepresentation under Australian statutes dealing with misleading and deceptive conduct, once the arbitral tribunal had determined, applying appropriate choice of law rules, that such claims are governed by the law of the Philippines. To do so would lead to a multiplicity of proceedings, usurp the jurisdiction of the tribunal and deny the intention of the parties as expressed by them in the arbitration agreement.

3.41 Practice and doctrine have developed various solutions for resolving conflict of laws issues in international arbitration. These vary in flexibility, rigour and appropriateness for an international environment. Some of the major themes are assessed in the following sections.

3.2.2.2 *Substantive law of the seat of arbitration*

3.42 A now very outdated approach was for arbitrators to apply the substantive law of the seat of arbitration. It was thought that if parties had not chosen the substantive

---
34 See Article 34 of the Model Law (or its equivalent) and Article V of the New York Convention. The setting aside and enforcement of awards are addressed in Chapter 9.
35 See, e.g. *Transfield Philippines Inc v Pacific Hydro Ltd* [2006] VSC 175, Supreme Court of Victoria, Australia, per Justice Hollingworth.
36 Ibid., at para 73.

law but had chosen the seat of arbitration, the choice of seat implied a choice of the same substantive law.

This solution is simple and predictable. However, parties choose the seat of arbitration for a variety of reasons, such as its international arbitration (procedural) laws, its neutrality, the quality of its courts, geographic convenience, and relevant infrastructure.[37] The seat of arbitration often has no further connection whatsoever with the underlying transaction. It would therefore be artificial to presume either (i) that the parties implicitly wanted the seat's law to be the substantive law or (ii) that it would be an appropriate law to apply by virtue only of the fact that it is the law of the seat of arbitration. Finally, this method is even less relevant when an arbitral institution, or the arbitral tribunal, has decided the seat of arbitration rather than it having been agreed by the parties. In such circumstances, there is no compelling basis for assuming any implicit choice by the parties in favour of that law. 3.43

3.2.2.3 *Conflict of laws rules of the seat of arbitration*

A related, but much better, method is for the arbitral tribunal to apply the domestic conflict of laws rules of the seat of arbitration. This has historically been one of the most commonly used methods for resolving conflict of laws questions in international arbitration. It was the solution recommended by the Institute of International Law as early as 1957[38] and was used in England prior to the enactment of its Arbitration Act 1996. 3.44

From a practical perspective, using the seat of arbitration's conflict of laws rules is convenient. It not only provides a solution to establishing the law applicable to the contract, but also provides a comprehensive set of rules to resolve any other conflict of laws question that may arise. For example, the same conflict of laws rules could be used to determine the law applicable to non-contractual claims that are raised in the arbitration.[39] 3.45

Theoretical support for this method is found in the juridical conception of international arbitration. According to this theory, international arbitrators act under the legal auspices of the domestic jurisdiction where the seat of arbitration is located. But the international trend towards delocalisation – even in its softer form – rejects the notion of relying on the seat of arbitration as a fallback legal system. Delocalisation supports detachment of arbitration proceedings from the national legal jurisdiction where they take place.[40] Applying delocalisation 3.46

---

37 See further Chapter 2, Section 6, on selecting the seat of arbitration.
38 *Annuaire de l'Institut du Droit International 1957*, at p. 469. This recommendation did not gain state support and was not adopted.
39 See the discussion of the law applicable to non-contractual claims at Section 3.3 below.
40 Chapter 2, Section 5 which examines the juridical and delocalised conceptions of international arbitration. Examples of discussions of delocalisation are J Paulsson, 'Delocalisation of International Commercial Arbitration: When and Why it Matters', (1983) 32 *International and Comparative Law Quarterly* 53; P Mayer, 'The Trend Towards Delocalisation in the last 100 years', presented in The Internationalisation of International Arbitration, the LCIA Centenary Conference, London, 1995, pp. 37–46. And against delocalisation: R Goode, 'The Role of the Lex Loci Arbitrii in International Commercial Arbitration', (2001) 17(1) *Arbitration International* 19.

theory, the conflict of laws rules of the seat of arbitration would be considered inappropriate. Another more practical problem is that domestic conflict of laws rules are developed with national and sometimes political interests in mind. They may not be well suited for use in a truly international dispute.[41]

3.47 On balance, despite some notable support for using the seat of arbitration's conflict of laws rules,[42] we agree with the majority of commentators who oppose such an approach.[43] The approach is out of touch with the truly transnational character of international arbitration, ignores the fact that domestic conflict of laws rules may not be well suited or adapted to international arbitrations, limits the flexibility that is such a commendable feature of international arbitration, and fails to address the situation where the parties have failed to agree on the seat of arbitration (meaning that the seat would have to be determined by the *lex arbitri*, arbitral rules or arbitral institution).

3.2.2.4 *Cumulative application of the conflict of laws rules connected to the dispute*

3.48 The cumulative method involves applying all of the domestic conflict of laws rules connected to a particular dispute to see whether they converge and result in the application of one substantive law.[44] For example, consider a dispute between a party from India and a party from Thailand in relation to a project that took place in the Philippines. Applying the cumulative method, the arbitral tribunal would need to examine the conflict of laws rules of India, Thailand and the Philippines to see whether, in the circumstances of the case, they would all lead to the application of the same substantive law.

3.49 When performing the cumulative method, the domestic conflict of laws rules of each jurisdiction should be applied exactly as a judge of that state would apply them. For example, if the various conflict of laws rules all designated the law with the 'closest connection to the dispute', that phrase should be applied in the same way it is applied by judges in the jurisdictions where those laws have been enacted.[45] Any less rigorous interpretation would be inaccurate.

---

[41] Lew, Mistelis and Kröll, op. cit. fn 26, paras 17–41.
[42] See for example P Nygh and M Davies, *Conflict of Laws in Australia*, 7th edn, LexisNexis, 2002, p. 233 describing it as a 'strong presumption'; O Lando, 'The Law Applicable to the Merits of the Dispute' in JDM Lew (ed), *Contemporary Problems in International Arbitration*, Kluwer Law International, 1986, p. 101; Born, 2009, op. cit. fn 27, pp. 2138–2143.
[43] Most contemporary commentators consider this method is outdated. See, e.g. the considerable authority cited by P Fouchard, E Gaillard and B Goldman, *International Commercial Arbitration*, Kluwer Law International, 1999, para 1541. The historical, traditional arguments are in B Goldman, 'Les conflits de lois dans l'arbitrage international de droit privé' (1963) 109 *Recueil des Cours* 351.
[44] A seminal article on this method is Derains, 1972, op. cit. fn 2, p. 99. See also *Korean Seller v Jordanian Buyer* ICC Case No. 6149, (1995) XX *Yearbook of Commercial Arbitration*, 41–57.
[45] M Blessing, 'Regulations in Arbitration Rules on Choice of Law' (1994) 7 *ICCA Congress Series* 391, at p. 411. Furthermore, in order to apply domestic conflict of laws rules correctly, the arbitrator would have to take into account that jurisdiction's attitude towards the doctrine of 'renvoi'. Renvoi is a technical conflict of laws concept that is beyond the scope of this book. In brief, the doctrine deals with whether or not a foreign jurisdiction's conflict of laws rules are taken into account when applying that jurisdiction's laws. Properly applying renvoi could help achieve a convergence when using the cumulative method, but may also complicate the process.

3.50 Surprisingly enough, it is not uncommon for the cumulative method to result in convergence.[46] This is because domestic conflict of laws rules rely on a finite number of connecting factors.[47] For example, it is common to find a conflict of laws rule which says that, absent party choice of law, a contract is to be governed by the law with which it has the closest connection. Common threads are also found in subsets of that rule. For example, in many legal systems there is a presumption that the law with the closest connection to a sale of goods contract is the law of the seller's place of business.[48] Thus, even if the conflict of laws rules are themselves not the same, the different rules may nonetheless lead to the application of the same substantive law.

3.51 If convergence is not initially achieved, a slightly more complicated variation of this method is to sidestep the conflict of laws convergence and look directly for convergence of substantive legal solutions from the different potentially applicable laws. In this situation, the arbitral tribunal would need to examine whether the legal outcome is the same regardless of which potentially applicable law is applied. Whenever there is a dispute about which law applies, it is not uncommon for arbitrators to analyse the parties' substantive rights under several potentially applicable laws in any event, by way of prudence, and to give further support to their reasoning.

3.52 If convergence of solutions is ultimately found, the cumulative method is very sound theoretically. Successful application of it means that the interests of the states connected to the case are respected. This may in turn increase the enforceability of the resulting award.[49] It also removes any perceived subjectivity or arbitrariness arising from the flexibility left to international arbitrators to decide which law applies.

3.2.2.5 *General principles of private international law*

3.53 This method involves the arbitral tribunal applying 'general principles' of private international law or conflict of laws.[50] Despite historical calls for a 'supranational' system,[51] there is no universally accepted set of conflict of laws rules. This means that the exact nature of these general principles is often debated.

3.54 An arbitral tribunal using this method has several alternatives. It might compare the conflict of laws rules of the domestic legal systems connected to the dispute to establish common themes. In doing so, it would be looking for general principles of private international law as between the jurisdictions connected to the case, rather than general principles of private international law throughout

---

46 As noted by Born, 2009, op. cit. fn 27, p. 2129.
47 Although in a slightly different context, the major trends in connecting factors and the weights attached to them are summarised by Blessing, 1994, op. cit. fn 45, p. 414.
48 See, e.g. Article 3 of the Convention of 15 June 1955 on the Law Applicable to International Sales of Goods and Article 4(1)(a) of EC Regulation No. 593/2008 on the Law Applicable to Contractual Obligations.
49 See Chapter 9 regarding enforcement of awards generally. If a state's conflict of laws rules have been respected there are less likely to be issues of public policy that may derail the enforcement process.
50 As noted above, 'private international law' is another name for conflict of laws rules.
51 Goldman advocated the need for such an approach as early as 1963, see Goldman, op. cit. fn 43, p. 415.

the world. Another possibility is to extract general principles from international or regional conventions on private international law, such as the 1980 Rome Convention on the Law Applicable to Contractual Obligations ('Rome Convention')[52] and the various Hague Conventions.[53] Finally, some arbitral tribunals simply announce what they consider to be a general principle of private international law based on their own experience.

3.55 There are no international or regional conventions on conflict of laws that apply in the Asia-Pacific, but those applicable in Europe, such as the Rome Convention, could be considered for general guidance. In that respect, Giardini suggests that much more importance should be given to regional conventions on private international law as evidence of general principles. He says that arbitrators should use conventions like the Rome Convention to back up other methods and reduce arbitrariness.[54]

3.56 Other commentators note the growing acceptance of general principles of private international law,[55] while others criticise them as too unpredictable because of inconsistency in determination.[56] One author suspects that 'purporting to use the conflict laws of international law is, in reality, nothing more than a veiled attempt to allow the arbitrators to choose any substantive law they wish'.[57]

3.57 Indeed, while individual arbitrators may have their own views about what does or does not constitute a general principle of private international law, it is not clear the extent to which general principles exist from a truly international perspective. Apart from some very general rules, like the 'closest connection' rule for contracts, there are few universally accepted conflict of laws rules, even for determining the law applicable to contractual obligations. Any individual arbitrator's view about what constitutes a general principle is likely to be clouded by his own background and experience, thus leading to unpredictability.

3.2.2.6 *Law with the closest connection to the dispute*

3.58 The freedom granted to international arbitrators by arbitration rules and laws means that they can decide to adopt a very simple method, like determining which law has the closest connection to the dispute. As noted above, this rule is often found in domestic legal systems for determining the law applicable to contracts and is one of the few general principles of private international law. It has also been adopted by international conventions such as the Rome Convention.

---

[52] This was recently superseded for European Community countries by EC Regulation No. 593/2008 on the Law Applicable to Contractual Obligations. See also EC Regulation No. 864/2007 on the Law Applicable to Non-Contractual Obligations.
[53] An example relevant to civil and commercial matters is the Convention of 2 October 1973 on the Law Applicable to Product Liability, which has been adopted by most EC states. A list of the conventions prepared by the Hague Conference on Private International Law is available on its website: www.hcch.net.
[54] A Giardina, 'International Conventions in Conflict of Laws and Substantive Law', (1994) 7 *ICCA Congress Series* 459, at p. 459.
[55] J Lew, 'Relevance of Conflict of Laws Rules in the Practice of Arbitration', (1994) 7 *ICCA Congress Series* 447, at p. 451.
[56] See, e.g. Born, 2001, op. cit. fn 27, p. 531. However, Born's more recent treatise points out simply that 'there is as yet no such body of international conflict of laws rules'; see Born, 2009, op. cit. fn 27, p. 2132.
[57] SJ Toope, *Mixed International Arbitration*, Grotius Publications, 1990, p. 51.

Although this method may seem straightforward, it is not always easy to   3.59
determine which law has the closest connection to a dispute. In fact, it is precisely
this question which conflict of laws rules generally seek to answer. They purport
to direct judges to the law with the closest connection. Take, for example, a
dispute arising from a simple sale of goods transaction involving companies
from different countries. Company A sells and promises to deliver goods to
Company B. B pays the price but A does not deliver anything. B sues A. There
is no logical reason why either A's or B's law is more closely connected to the
dispute. As noted above, many conflict of laws rules create a presumption in
favour of the application of the law of the seller's place of business. An arbitral
tribunal that decides to apply (or is required to apply) the law with the closest
connection to the dispute might well have to refer to general principles of private
international law in any event, in order to apply the closest connection rule. If
so, this effectively means going back to square one – i.e. the relevant conflict of
laws rule.

3.2.2.7 Implied intent

Some consider that international arbitrators should attempt to discern the par-   3.60
ties' implicit choice of law. One experienced practitioner considers that, from his
experience, implied intent is sometimes so obvious that it cannot be ignored,[58]
while another finds the idea of searching for an implied intent artificial.[59] It is
indeed difficult to see any difference between applying an objective criterion,
such as connecting factors, and searching for a virtually hypothetical implied
intent. It would seem that the same factors are applied either way.

Various theories of presumed intent have nonetheless developed. One exam-   3.61
ple is the 'implied negative choice' theory[60] according to which if parties from
different states have not agreed on the applicable law in their contract, it is
presumed that each party specifically rejected the national law of the opposing
party. The argument is that during negotiations each party would have proposed
its own law. The absence of a choice of law clause in the final contract means the
other party must have rejected this proposal.

This implied negative choice theory is dubious because the absence of a con-   3.62
tractual choice of law does not necessarily mean the parties could not agree. If a
party wanted to reject a law specifically, it could have tried to negotiate a clause
that said so in the contract. Parties may simply prefer to leave the choice of law
up to the arbitral tribunal to make once the substance of a particular dispute
is known. What is more, applying this theory would often rule out the law that
should naturally apply. In a sale of goods case, for example, it would be artificial
to rule out the law of both parties' places of business simply because neither was
specified as the applicable law in the contract.

---

58 Blessing, 1994, op. cit. fn 45, p. 407.
59 AFM Maniruzzaman, 'Conflict of Laws Issues in International Arbitration: Practice and Trends', (1993) 9(4) *Arbitration International* 371, at p. 371.
60 Blessing, 1994, op. cit. fn 45, p. 407.

3.63   From a theoretical perspective, if genuine evidence of contractual intent can be found, it should be applied. Otherwise, however, the theories of implied intent seem to be superficial if the same connecting factors would be used for a more objective method anyway.

3.2.2.8 Selecting a set of conflict of laws rules

3.64   As indicated above,[61] Article 28(2) of the Model Law and almost all Asia-Pacific arbitration laws require the arbitral tribunal to choose and apply 'conflict of laws rules', while most regional institutional rules allow arbitral tribunals directly to choose the law that they 'consider appropriate' without passing via conflict of laws rules.

3.65   If an arbitral tribunal must choose a set of domestic conflict of laws rules, there are several which could logically be considered. One is the conflict of laws rules of the seat of arbitration, addressed above.[62] Another possibility is the conflict of laws rules of the place where the award is likely to be enforced. However the place of enforcement is rarely a certainty.

3.66   Another option is to apply the conflict of laws rules of the jurisdiction that would have been competent but for the arbitration clause.[63] However, this is extraordinarily complex and has been strongly rejected by commentators.[64] Usually, several jurisdictions would find themselves competent (except, perhaps, where there is an effective applicable international convention on judicial competence, such as in European Community countries). Moreover, the answer might turn on where the action was first commenced, something about which the arbitral tribunal could only speculate. Finally, one reason parties choose arbitration is to find a more neutral dispute resolution forum than the one that would ordinarily be competent.[65]

3.67   Better conflict of laws rules include those of the place of contractual performance, those of a jurisdiction with some element common to the parties, such as common residence, domicile or nationality, or those of the jurisdiction with the closest connection to the dispute. One might wonder, however, how an arbitrator would decide between these possibilities.

3.2.2.9 Conclusions on methods adopted by international arbitrators; a preferred approach

3.68   The cumulative method, if it works, is the most rigorous and acceptable approach. It should satisfy the parties, it is theoretically justified because it is international, and it increases the enforceability of the resulting arbitral award by respecting

---

61 See above Section 3.2.1.1.
62 See above Section 3.2.2.3.
63 According to Wortmann, op. cit. fn 25, p. 105, this method was first proposed and examined by the Italian jurist Dionisio Anzilotti in 1906.
64 Blessing, 1994, op. cit. fn 45, p. 412.
65 P Lalive, 'Les règles de conflit de lois appliquées au fond du litige par l'arbitre international siégeant en Suisse', (1976) Revue de l'arbitrage 157, at p. 161.

the interests of the states connected to the dispute. The disadvantage of this method is that it can be complex and does not always result in convergence.

3.69 If the cumulative method fails, the next best option is debatable. There is comfort in the security and certainty of the choice of law rules of the seat of arbitration. As noted above, however, we consider the seat of arbitration's conflict of laws rules inappropriate, mainly because there is often no connection whatsoever between the seat of arbitration and the underlying substantive dispute.

3.70 In our view, the preferred approach failing successful application of the cumulative method is to apply the general principles of private international law, established by eliciting common themes from the conflict of laws rules of the jurisdictions connected to the substance of the dispute. If an appropriate general principle of private international law cannot be established, a fallback rule should be to apply the law with the closest connection to the underlying substantive dispute, taking into account the particular claims that the parties have raised.

3.71 Given the uncertainty of the determination of applicable substantive law in international commercial arbitration, some guidance would be welcome to assist arbitrators in this process. This would be especially useful for arbitrators who do not have expertise in the specialised discipline of the conflict of laws. Rather than attempting an international convention, however, a set of soft guidelines would be preferable. These could provide guidance without being proscriptive to the detriment of flexibility.

3.3 The law applicable to non-contractual claims

3.72 Normally, arbitration clauses are drafted broadly enough to include non-contractual claims within the jurisdiction of the arbitral tribunal. Contractual choice of law clauses are often narrower, referring expressly to the contract. For example, a typical choice of law clause might be drafted in the following terms: 'this contract shall be governed by and construed in accordance with the laws of X', while a typical arbitration clause is broader, such as: 'all disputes arising out of or relating to this contract shall be decided by arbitration...'. Thus, read literally, a choice of law clause generally does not cover all claims that potentially fall within the scope of an arbitration agreement.[66] Furthermore, there is no guidance on this in arbitration rules or laws. This raises the

---

[66] Numerous courts have found arbitration clauses that are even narrower than the example given above as sufficiently broad to cover tort claims. For example, the Korean Supreme Court has held that an arbitration agreement submitting 'legal disputes regarding this contract' to arbitration was broad enough to cover tort claims (91 Da 17146, 14 April 1992, cited in Seung Wha Chang, 'Article V of the New York Convention and Korea', (2008) 25 *Journal of International Arbitration* 865, at p. 868). Such clauses are, however, occasionally read down so as not to cover torts. See, *Jan De Nul NV v Inai Kiara Sdn Bhd* [2006] 3 CLJ 46, where the Malaysian Court of Appeal found that tort claims were not covered by an arbitration clause which referred to 'any dispute or difference arising out of and/or in connection with this agreement'. The Malaysian Court of Appeal referred with approval to the Full Federal Court of Australia decision of *Hi-Fert Pty Ltd v Kiukiang Maritime Carriers* [1998] 159 ALR 142. Aspects of the *Hi-Fert* decision related to this issue were specifically overruled by the Full Federal Court in *Comandate Marine Corp v Pan Australia Shipping Pty Ltd* [2006] FCAFC 192. See also the discussion of this point in Chapter 4, Section 8.1.

question as to which law applies to non-contractual claims that are raised in an arbitration.

3.73   Complex contractual disputes might give rise to any number of non-contractual claims. Examples of these are restitution, unjust enrichment, *culpa in contrahendo*, and torts, including statutory torts like antitrust or trade practices claims. Claims based on any of these doctrines could well be governed by a law different from the law governing the contract. It certainly should not be assumed that the contractual law will govern non-contractual claims simply because those claims are somehow connected to the contractual relationship.

3.74   Surprisingly little attention has been given to the law applicable to non-contractual claims in arbitration.[67] It is possible that when a non-contractual issue arises, lawyers and arbitrators fail to recognise that a different law might apply to it. They might not properly identify the differences. As will be seen below, in many cases the law applicable to non-contractual claims will be the same law that governs the contract. But in other cases it can be different, and it may well be to the distinct advantage of one party to argue that a different law applies.

3.3.1 Characterisation of claims as contractual or not

3.75   The first step in determining whether a different law might apply to a given claim is to characterise the claim as contractual or otherwise. If it is a contractual claim, the applicable contractual law should apply. If not, the issue of applicable law needs to be considered separately.

3.76   It is not always evident whether a particular claim is based in contract, tort or otherwise. Sometimes claims can be dressed up as one or the other, depending among other things on whether the party making the claim sees some advantage in having a different law apply to it. Domestic legal systems generally provide established rules enabling the judge to characterise claims. Those rules are part of the *lex fori* (i.e. the legal system where the court is situated). But an international arbitrator has no *lex fori* because, as noted above,[68] the laws of the seat of arbitration do not constitute a *lex fori*. An international arbitrator must therefore decide which characterisation rules to use, if any, in order to characterise the claims.

3.77   To ensure consistency and eliminate overlap, the chosen characterisation system must be consistent with the law governing the contract.[69] It has been suggested that claims should be characterised by a cumulative application of all the characterisation rules of the jurisdictions connected, or possibly connected,

---

[67] One eminent private international law professor has commented, following a speech on this topic, that: 'You have explored a subject that is new; it seems that there has never been a study on those problems of [the law applicable to] tort and extra-contractual responsibility in arbitration.' (Authors' translation from original French). See P Lagarde, 'Débats' in C Reymond, 'Conflits de lois en matière de responsabilité délictuelle devant l'arbitre international', (1991) [1988–1989] *Travaux du Comité Français de Droit International Privé* 97, at p. 107. We are not aware of more recent studies on this subject although, as addressed below, the law applicable to non-contractual claims generally is the subject of a new European Community Regulation.
[68] See above Section 2.
[69] Reymond, op. cit. fn 67, p. 99.

to the dispute and, if that does not work, by using general principles of private international law.[70]

3.78 In our view, the best characterisation rules to ensure harmony with the contractual law are those of the law governing the contract. The contractual law necessarily has a close connection to the dispute. Using its characterisation rules will eliminate inconsistencies and overlaps. This approach also avoids the complexities of the cumulative approach and the uncertainty associated with general principles of private international law.

3.3.2 Parties' choice of law applicable to non-contractual claims

3.79 As noted above,[71] the parties' ability to choose the law governing their contract is of paramount importance in international arbitration. It is also a widely recognised general principle of private international law and applied by domestic courts all over the world. But it is not clear whether the same principle applies to empower the parties to choose the law to govern non-contractual claims.

3.80 Experts' views are mixed. At least one commentator is confident that, as a matter of policy, parties can choose the law applicable to torts after the tort has occurred. He is less decisive as to whether parties can choose the law before a tort occurs, but concludes that they probably can.[72] On the other hand, a leading treatise states that 'according to traditional private international law thinking, the principle of party autonomy does not apply [to non-contractual claims]'.[73]

3.81 There are logical reasons why party autonomy may be restricted in relation to the law governing non-contractual claims. Contracts regulate the relationship between private, consenting parties. Tort law is mandatory and formulated by legislators in order to attribute responsibility and provide compensation specifically outside contractual relationships. A tort may even affect third parties' rights, such that a choice of law for a tort claim between two parties may impact the rights of others. Furthermore, certain statutory torts are designed to protect the common good (e.g. relating to anti-trust, environmental protection, safety of employees, etc.). It would not be acceptable if contracting parties could circumvent mandatory laws designed to improve or protect a nation's society as a whole by choosing a foreign law as applicable.[74]

3.82 These policy considerations do not seem to be reflected in international arbitration legislation. Arbitration laws tend not to prohibit – at least expressly – parties from choosing the law to govern tort claims. For example, Article 28(1) of the Model Law states: 'The arbitral tribunal shall decide the dispute in accordance with such rules of law as are chosen by the parties as applicable to the

---

[70] Reymond, op. cit. fn 67, p. 112.
[71] See Section 3.1 above.
[72] W Kuhn, 'Express and Implied Choice of the Substantive Law in the Practice of International Arbitration', (1994) 7 *ICCA Congress Series* 380, at p. 387.
[73] Gaillard and Savage, op. cit. fn 10, para 1530.
[74] See further the discussion of mandatory laws at Section 4 below.

substance of the dispute.'[75] (Emphasis added) 'Dispute' is broad enough to cover tort claims, but it is possible that some courts will interpret it narrowly.

3.83   Support for the view that parties can choose the law governing non-contractual claims, even in advance of the facts giving rise to the claim, can be found in the recent European Community Regulation on the Law Applicable to Non-contractual Obligations ('Rome II Regulation'), which entered into force on 12 January 2009. The Rome II Regulation obviously has no direct applicability in any Asia-Pacific jurisdiction, but arbitrators may take it into account because it is the first significant regional convention of its kind and was prepared by some of the world's foremost experts in private international law. Article 14(1) of the Rome II Regulation expressly permits parties to choose the law governing non-contractual claims both '(a) after the event giving rise to the damage occurred; or (b) where all the parties are pursuing a commercial activity, also by an agreement freely negotiated before the event giving rise to the damage occurred'. Thus in the European Community commercial parties can choose the law to govern existing or future non-contractual claims. Nonetheless, Articles 14(2) and 14(3) of the Rome II Regulation ensure that, despite such freedom of choices, mandatory domestic laws and European Community laws cannot be avoided. We expect that international arbitrators and even courts in the Asia-Pacific will find the rules of the Rome II Regulation of some guidance for international matters, unless they conflict with general principles of private international law in the jurisdiction concerned.

3.84   Despite the right to choose the law governing non-contractual claims, it is very rare that parties to arbitration proceedings do so expressly, whether before or after the relevant events occur. If the contract contains a clause designating the contractual law, that clause may be broad enough to cover non-contractual claims. This is a matter of interpretation. But, as noted above, choice of law clauses tend to be narrow, referring specifically to the contract.

3.85   Nonetheless, it could be considered that contractual choice of law clauses should be read broadly, with a presumption that the parties intended to choose the same law for all claims relating in any way to the contract. The parties might have intended that the contractual choice of law would apply to any dispute relating to the contract. An arbitral tribunal could therefore perhaps find that the parties implicitly chose the same law for their non-contractual claims. Furthermore, the contractual law will be practical, convenient and closely connected to the dispute.

3.3.3 Law applicable to torts claims in the absence of choice

3.86   Without a choice of law for non-contractual claims, a convenient approach is to invoke the conflict of laws rules applicable under the contract's governing law to determine the law governing the non-contractual claims.[76] From a practical

---

75 This is equivalent in most arbitration laws and rules in Asia and elsewhere.
76 As preferred by Lalive, op. cit. fn 65, p. 164.

point of view, using the contractual law's conflict of laws rules ensures perfect harmony of legal solutions. The substantive laws of the chosen jurisdiction are applied to the contract and the same jurisdiction's conflict of laws rules are used to determine other applicable laws.

This method is attractive but has one problem in cases where the contractual law has been chosen by the parties. Contractual choice of law clauses generally exclude the conflict of laws rules of the jurisdiction designated. They often say, for example: 'This Agreement shall be governed by and construed in accordance with the laws of X without regard, however, to its conflict of laws rules....' Article 28(1) of the Model Law gives the same effect to any contractual choice of law clause to which the Model Law applies: 'Any designation [by the parties] of the law or legal system of a given State shall be construed, unless otherwise expressed, as directly referring to the substantive law of that State and not to its conflict of laws rules'. The exclusion of local conflict of laws rules is designed to prevent the frustration of the parties' agreement on the applicable law because those rules may, in contrast to the agreement, designate another law. 3.87

It might, however, be assumed that the exclusion of local conflict of laws rules is intended only to avoid an unexpected law applying to the contract. Arguably, these exclusions are not intended to prevent an arbitral tribunal using those conflict of laws rules for other issues, such as determining the law applicable to non-contractual claims. 3.88

Apart from applying the conflict of laws rules of the law governing the contract, there are other possible methods for determining the law governing non-contractual claims. The arbitral tribunal could establish the applicable law using a method analogous to any of those described above for establishing the law governing contracts where the parties have not chosen it.[77] In complex commercial torts, there will rarely be convergence among the conflict of laws rules connected to the dispute, thus making the cumulative approach difficult to achieve. As regards the general principles of private international law applicable to non-contractual claims, there is very little global uniformity in approaches. Claude Reymond suggests applying the law of the centre of gravity of a tort.[78] As Peter Nygh explains, such an approach:[79] 3.89

> makes the choice of law dependent on the number of contacts the parties, the events and the issue have with the several jurisdictions involved in an interstate or international incident, and gives the controlling voice to the jurisdiction with the most important 'contacts.' In that jurisdiction the 'centre of gravity' of the tort is said to lie.

Once again, guidance might alternatively be sought from the Rome II Regulation which sets out the European Community's view on the law governing non-contractual claims. Its basic rule is (Article 4(1)): 3.90

---

[77] See Reymond, op. cit. fn 67, p. 104 and Gaillard and Savage, op. cit. fn 10, para 1531.
[78] Reymond, op. cit. fn 67, p. 104.
[79] P Nygh, 'Some Thoughts on the Proper Law of a Tort', (1977) 26(4) *International and Comparative Law Quarterly* 932, at p. 933.

the law applicable to a non-contractual obligation arising out of a tort/delict shall be the law of the country in which the damage occurs irrespective of the country in which the event giving rise to the damage occurred and irrespective of the country or countries in which the indirect consequences of that event occur.

3.91 There are various special circumstances and exceptions to this rule stipulated in the Rome II Regulation. Of particular relevance to international commercial arbitration is Article 4(3):

> Where it is clear from all the circumstances of the case that the tort/delict is manifestly more closely connected with a country other than that indicated in [Articles 4(1) and 4(2)], the law of that other country shall apply. A manifestly closer connection with another country might be based in particular on a pre-existing relationship between the parties, such as a contract, that is closely connected with the tort/delict in question.

3.92 Arbitrators and lawyers in the Asia-Pacific, especially if they come from or were trained in civil law countries, might well be guided by the Rome II Regulation's approach. Common lawyers may be less interested because Rome II was drafted from a predominantly civil law perspective.

3.93 An example of an arbitral tribunal determining the law applicable to non-contractual claims in this region occurred in *Transfield Philippines Inc v Luzon Hydro Corporation Ltd*.[80] The dispute related to the construction of a hydro-electric power station in Northern Luzon, the Philippines. The subcontractor, Transfield Philippines Inc. ('TPI'), commenced arbitration against the contractor, Luzon Hydro Corporation ('LHC'), and sought various relief under the contract. In accordance with the arbitration clause, the seat of the ICC arbitration was Singapore and a contractual choice of law clause stipulated that the contract was governed by the laws of the Philippines.

3.94 In addition to its contractual claims, TPI raised claims for pre-contractual misleading and deceptive conduct and negligent misrepresentation by LHC's directors about what TPI might expect in relation to the project. It contended primarily that those claims were governed by Australian trade practices legislation rather than Philippines law, on the basis that the relevant misrepresentations and misconduct had occurred in Australia. The arbitral tribunal ruled on the issue of applicable law in its first partial award as follows:[81]

> ... the claims for misleading and deceptive conduct are governed by the law of the Philippines under either of two alternative approaches. The first is to apply the law of the Philippines directly without recourse to choice of law rules ('voie directe'). Alternatively if the governing law is to be selected indirectly through the application of a choice of law rule, the arbitral tribunal determines that the appropriate choice of law rule (application of the law most closely connected with the claim) also leads to the selection of the law of the Philippines.

---

[80] See, e.g. *Transfield Philippines Inc v Pacific Hydro Ltd* [2006] VSC 175 (Supreme Court of Victoria, Australia).
[81] Page 24 of the arbitral tribunal's first partial award dated 18 February 2002, cited in *Transfield Philippines Inc v Pacific Hydro Ltd* [2006] VSC 175, at para 68 (Supreme Court of Victoria, Australia).

[TPI] has indicated that it will institute court proceedings in Australia if this arbitral tribunal does not determine claims under the [Australian trade practices legislation]. [TPI] has submitted that resort to two tribunals is undesirable. The arbitral tribunal agrees. However, this consideration is not of itself sufficient to warrant the application of a law which the tribunal considers in all the circumstances, not to be appropriate to the dispute between the parties. Further, this tribunal notes that [TPI] has also sought damages for misrepresentation under the law of the Philippines. The claim for misrepresentation will still proceed in this arbitration but will be determined in accordance with the law of the Philippines.

3.95 The arbitral tribunal did not appear to ground its decision on the fact that TPI's non-contractual claims were covered by the contractual choice of law clause. Rather, it held that Philippines law governed the claims because it was the appropriate law or, alternatively, by virtue of a general principle of private international law because it was the law most closely connected to the claims.

3.96 Given the uncertainty of using the cumulative approach or trying to establish general principles of private international law applicable to non-contractual claims, in our view, as a general rule it is best to use the contractual law's conflict of laws rules (discussed above in this section). That legal system will not only provide characterisation rules, but also a system of conflict of laws rules that can be applied to any and all conflict of laws issues that may arise. Alternatively, an arbitral tribunal might use the Rome II Regulation for guidance as to the general principles of private international law for torts.

4 Limitations on choice of law: Mandatory laws and public policy

3.97 Mandatory laws are imperative provisions of law that are imposed on arbitrating parties regardless of their choice of law. They constitute a limitation on the general principle that parties are free to choose the applicable law. It is rare in practice that a mandatory law will apply. One may apply only if the legal system to which the mandatory law belongs cannot be ignored by virtue of some close connection that legal system has to the facts of the underlying dispute <u>and</u> the mandatory law itself was intended to be applied in the circumstances of the case, including, where relevant, extraterritorially.

3.98 In a seminal article on the topic, Pierre Mayer explains that:[82]

> a mandatory rule (loi de police in French) is an imperative provision of law which must be applied to an international relationship irrespective of the law that governs that relationship. To put it another way: mandatory rules of law are a matter of public policy (ordre public), and moreover reflect a public policy so commanding that they must be applied even if the general body of law to which they belong is not competent

---

[82] P Mayer, 'Mandatory Rules of Law in International Arbitration', (1986) 2(4) *Arbitration International* 274, at p. 274. See further generally (2009) 18(1–2) *American Review of International Arbitration* which is a special edition of this journal focusing on mandatory laws in international arbitration and litigation, including several articles by leading scholars and practitioners.

by application of the relevant rule of conflict of laws. It is the imperative nature per se of such rules that make them applicable.

3.99 Mandatory laws only exist when there is a fundamental and unavoidable public policy objective at stake. A classic example that could interfere with a commercial relationship is anti-trust or competition laws.[83] States enact anti-trust laws to encourage competition for the protection of consumers. If commercial parties were able to avoid complying with anti-trust laws by simply choosing a different law to govern their contract, this would completely frustrate the broad, policy objectives behind anti-trust laws.

3.100 That said, a mandatory competition law (or any other mandatory law) will not apply simply because the dispute is somehow related to the legal system which enacts that law. There must be a real connection to the underlying transaction that would trigger the law's application. Thus, for example, if an arbitration between parties from China and Singapore in relation to the acquisition of a company in the Philippines happens to have its seat of arbitration in Australia, there is no ground whatsoever to apply mandatory Australian competition or trade practices laws. On the facts given, there would be no connection between those laws and the underlying transaction.

3.101 Other classic examples of mandatory laws relate to criminal law, corruption, money-laundering, racial or gender discrimination, environmental protection, and employment law.

3.102 The concept of mandatory laws is not generally seen in statutes relating to arbitration or in arbitration rules. There are no references to them in the Asia-Pacific arbitration laws or institutional rules. References to mandatory laws can sometimes be seen in regional or international conventions on applicable law. The recent European Community Regulation on the Law Applicable to Contractual Obligations ('Rome I Regulation'), which entered into force for European Community countries at the end of 2009, provides various rules for determining the law applicable to contracts, based on its predecessor the Rome Convention. It also reserves the possibility for courts to apply mandatory laws regardless of the applicable contractual law. While this obviously has no direct application in the Asia-Pacific, Article 9 provides a useful definition of mandatory laws that may guide arbitrators in this region:

> 1. Overriding mandatory provisions are provisions the respect for which is regarded as crucial by a country for safeguarding its public interests, such as its political, social or economic organisation, to such an extent that they are applicable to any

---

[83] In the famous *Mitsubishi v Soler* case (1985) 105 S Ct 3346, the US Supreme Court confirmed that issues arising from US anti-trust legislation were capable of settlement by arbitration, laying down a principle that has been followed in numerous other jurisdictions and which has enhanced the efficacy of dispute resolution by arbitration. By confirming the arbitrability of such issues, a related question arose about whether and to what extent mandatory competition laws that are not part of the law governing the contract must be applied. See also See DF Donovan and AKA Greenawalt, 'Mitsubishi after Twenty Years: Mandatory Rules before Courts and International Arbitrators', in LA Mistelis and JDM Lew (eds), *Pervasive Problems in International Arbitration*, Kluwer, 2006, p. 42 et seq.

situation falling within their scope, irrespective of the law otherwise applicable to the contract under this Regulation.
2. Nothing in this Regulation shall restrict the application of the overriding mandatory provisions of the law of the forum.
3. Effect may be given to the overriding mandatory provisions of the law of the country where the obligations arising out of the contract have to be or have been performed, in so far as those overriding mandatory provisions render the performance of the contract unlawful. In considering whether to give effect to those provisions, regard shall be had to their nature and purpose and to the consequences of their application or non-application.

3.103 A regional example of a court applying a mandatory law in the context of arbitration proceedings can be found in a series of Federal Court of Australia decisions in *Clough Engineering Ltd v Oil & Natural Gas Corporation Ltd*.[84] Clough had won a tender from Oil & Natural Gas to develop oil and gas fields off the coast of India. The contract was governed by Indian law and included an arbitration clause with the seat of arbitration in India. Before arbitration was commenced, Clough sought an injunction from the Australian Federal Court to prevent certain Australian banks from paying out on an unconditional performance bond with a value of 10% of the contract price which Clough had procured in favour of Oil & Natural Gas in order to secure the contract. Clough argued that the Federal Court had jurisdiction to issue the injunction for several reasons, including the fact that it had claims against Oil & Natural Gas under mandatory provisions of the Australian Trade Practices Act. The connection between these claims and Australia was that the relevant written communications that amounted to Oil & Natural Gas's allegedly unconscionable conduct had been received in Australia and the damage, alleged to be the unconscionable calling of the performance bonds, would occur in Australia.

3.104 Justice Gilmour, referring to various authorities, noted:[85]

> The [Trade Practices Act] is 'a public policy statute'. Its operation cannot be ousted by private agreement. 'Parliament passed the [TPA] to stamp out unfair or improper conduct in trade or in commerce; it would be contrary to public policy for special conditions such as those with which this contract was concerned to deny or prohibit a statutory remedy for offending conduct under the [TPA]': . . . . Any attempt to contract out of the remedies conferred by the Act may be void . . . .

3.105 Justice Gilmour granted an ex parte interim injunction in favour of Clough. He must have been satisfied that there was at least a prima facie case for applying mandatory trade practices laws despite acknowledging that this was contrary to the parties' choice of Indian substantive law and arbitration seated in India. The

---

[84] [2007] FCA 881 (7 June 2007); [No. 2] [2007] FCA 927 (19 June 2007); [No. 4] [2007] FCA 2110 (21 December 2007); [2008] FCA 191 (29 February 2008); [2008] FCAFC 136 (22 July 2008).
[85] *Clough Engineering Ltd v Oil and Natural Gas Corporation Ltd* [2007] FCA 881 (7 June 2007), at para 41.

injunction was ultimately set aside, as confirmed on appeal to the Full Court of the Australian Federal Court.[86]

3.106 While it is not uncommon that mandatory laws are asserted in the context of international arbitrations, they are rarely applied. Examples of how arbitral tribunals have dealt with these issues can be found in ICC jurisprudence:

(i) *ICC Case No. 4132 (1983)* – A supply and purchase agreement was governed by Korean law but European antitrust law was considered. The arbitral tribunal recognised that antitrust and fair trade laws possessed a public policy character. It ultimately held, however, that since the agreement did not affect trade between EU Member states, only Korean law was relevant.[87]

(ii) *ICC Case No. 6320 (1992)* – The arbitrators accepted that US mandatory laws prohibiting corruption could apply extraterritorially to a contract governed by Brazilian law. However, a condition (which was not met in this case due to lack of factual, geographic proximity to the US) would be that the particular rule relating to corruption reflected 'an important and legitimate interest' of the US.[88]

(iii) *ICC Case No. 6379 (1990)* – The arbitral tribunal would not allow Italian law, which had been chosen by the parties to govern their contract, to be disregarded in favour of Belgian distributorship law, which provides that it must be applied to exclusive distributorship agreements producing effects in all or part of Belgium.[89]

(iv) *ICC Case No. 7047 (1994)* – The parties entered into a contract governed by Swiss law for sales assistance in support of various products. In an attempt to avoid liability for non-performance of its obligations, the defendant relied on regulations in the country where the contract was to be performed, which prohibited the use of intermediaries in that field of activity. The arbitral tribunal rejected the defendant's argument on the grounds that 'the parties are entitled to submit their legal relations to whatever law they choose, and to exclude national laws which would apply in the absence of a choice. Consequently the provision of the law thus excluded can only prevail over the chosen law in so far as they are matters of public policy'.[90] The asserted laws were not, according to the arbitral tribunal, matters of public policy.

3.107 The above examples demonstrate the high burden of a connection to the underlying dispute that a party seeking to assert the application of a mandatory law must establish. Mandatory laws are not, and should not be, applied readily, but

---

[86] *Clough Engineering Ltd v Oil and Natural Gas Corporation Ltd* [2008] FCAFC 136 (22 July 2008).
[87] Award in *ICC Case No. 4132*, in S Jarvin, Y Derains and JJ Arnaldez, *Collection of ICC Arbitral Awards 1974–1985*, ICC Publishing, 1990, p. 164 at p. 167.
[88] Award in *ICC Case No. 6320*, in S Jarvin, Y Derains and JJ Arnaldez, *Collection of ICC Arbitral Awards 1991–1995*, ICC Publishing, 1997, p. 577 at p. 584.
[89] Award in *ICC Case No. 6379*, in ibid., p. 134 at p. 142.
[90] Award in *ICC Case No. 7074*, in S Jarvin, Y Derains and JJ Arnaldez, *Collection of ICC Arbitral Awards 1996–2000*, ICC Publishing, 2003, p. 32 at p. 51.

only where there is a real connection to the dispute and real public policy issues at stake.

It is sometimes said that there are two kinds of mandatory laws, those of a domestic nature and those of an international nature. We do not find the distinction especially useful because the real question should be whether a particular mandatory law is in fact mandatory in the given circumstances, particularly taking into account the location of the conduct (i.e. the relevant aspect of performance of the contract) which potentially offends the law. If the distinction is made, however, it will be important[91] because only international mandatory laws should affect international arbitrations. As Voser notes, 'a domestic mandatory rule can only have the quality of an international mandatory rule if the enacting state itself wants it to be applied in international situations'.[92]

3.108

A question arises as to whether an arbitral tribunal should apply a mandatory law only when a party has requested its application or whether it may do so of its own initiative, i.e. ex officio. It is one thing for an arbitral tribunal to go beyond the parties' choice of law agreement and apply, on one party's request, a mandatory law, the application of which is disputed by the opposing party. An even more delicate question is whether arbitrators should consider applying a mandatory law on the arbitral tribunal's own initiative when neither party has requested the application of that law.

3.109

This conundrum leads authors Barraclough and Waincymer wisely to point out that 'arbitrators confronted with mandatory rules questions find few easy answers'.[93] The authors argue that the issue will remain unclear until the nature of arbitration (judicial or contractual) is resolved one way or the other. Not surprisingly, Professor Pierre Mayer's seminal 1986 article identifies the same central, intellectual debate as being at the core of whether to apply mandatory laws. Mayer notes that arbitrators 'would . . . be confronted, unlike the national judge, with a conflict between the will of the State having promulgated the mandatory rule of law, on the one hand, and on the other hand, the will of the parties from which indeed his authority is derived'.[94]

3.110

Professor Mayer focuses on when and to what extent arbitrators (i) may apply mandatory laws, (ii) are obliged to do so and (iii) if so, which mandatory laws. He says that if a party invokes the mandatory law, the arbitral tribunal would at least be required to consider applying it. If, however, neither party has referred to the mandatory law, but its existence nonetheless comes to the arbitral tribunal's

3.111

---

91 See generally N Voser, 'Current Development: Mandatory Rules of Law as a Limitation on the Law Applicable in International Commercial Arbitration', (1996) 7 *American Review of International Arbitration* 319.
92 Ibid., p. 347.
93 A Barraclough and J Waincymer, 'Mandatory Rules of Law in International Commercial Arbitration', (2005) 6 *Melbourne Journal of International Law* 205, at p. 243. See also more recently J Waincymer, 'International Commercial Arbitration and the Application of Mandatory Rules of Law', (2009) 5(1) *Asian International Arbitration Journal* 1.
94 Mayer, op. cit. fn 82, p. 275. See also P Mayer, 'Effect of International Public Policy in International Arbitration' in Mistelis and Lew, op. cit. fn 83, p. 141 et seq. See also the discussion of delocalisation in Chapter 2, Section 5.2.

attention, or is simply obvious, the tension between the judicial and contractual nature of arbitration intensifies. If arbitration is characterised as purely contractual, then the arbitral tribunal should do nothing that the parties have not requested of it. If proceeding in this way offends an arbitrator's professional integrity he should resign. But if the nature of arbitration is considered to be quasi-judicial, then arbitrators owe duties to the state. In that latter scenario, one may ask to which state(s) an arbitral tribunal owes a duty; the state of the seat of arbitration, the applicable substantive law, the parties' nationalities, or another?

3.112   Apart from the Australian example given above, there are few examples of courts in the Asia-Pacific dealing with the application of mandatory laws in international arbitration.[95] These issues have, however, come to the attention of domestic European courts as well as the European Court of Justice ('ECJ') in the context of EC competition laws. In the famous *Eco Swiss v Benetton*[96] case, the contract contained a choice of law clause selecting Dutch law to govern the contract and an arbitration clause providing for arbitration of all disputes or differences under the rules of the Netherlands Arbitration Institute. Eco Swiss obtained an award in its favour of just over US$26 million. Benetton sought to set aside the award in the Netherlands on the basis that the underlying agreement was contrary to EC competition law. The competition law in question had not been raised by either party during the arbitration. The Dutch court submitted several questions to the ECJ, one being whether an arbitral tribunal had a duty ex officio to apply EC competition laws. The ECJ avoided answering that question directly, but held that a Dutch court could, during setting aside proceedings, examine whether EC competition law had been respected. This means that if mandatory competition laws are not dealt with by the arbitral tribunal, an award can still be set aside if it contravenes such laws. Following this decision, a prudent arbitral tribunal, in the interests of increasing the enforceability of its award, ought to consider raising and addressing such mandatory competition laws during the arbitration.

3.113   Also interesting is the Paris Court of Appeal decision of *Thales v Euromissile*[97] which, among other issues, proceeded on the assumption that an arbitral tribunal could raise a competition law issue ex officio. A subsequent decision of the Swiss Federal Tribunal cast confusion on the matter. The Federal Tribunal doubted that competition law was per se of a sufficiently public policy character to be raised as a basis to set aside an arbitral award. On the one hand, this means that arbitrators may be reluctant to raise competition laws ex officio. On the other hand, however, it means that if an arbitrator considers the competition law to be mandatory he or she may wish to apply it in the place of a domestic judge so that the parties cannot escape the application of these laws.[98]

---

[95] See, however, the hypothetical example given in the conclusion of Waincymer, op. cit. fn 93, p. 39.
[96] (1999) ECR 3055.
[97] 18 November 2004, Paris Court of Appeal, *Case No. 2002/60932*.
[98] See C Partasides and L Burger, 'The Swiss Federal Tribunal's Decision of 8 March 2006: A Deepening of the Arbitrator's Public Policy Dilemma', (2006) 3 *Concurrences*, p. 26, which discusses all three of these cases.

Another factor influencing whether an arbitral tribunal should apply a manda- 3.114
tory law is its source, i.e. which jurisdiction it comes from. Domestic judges dealing with an international litigation case may apply mandatory laws of their own jurisdiction (the *lex fori*) that are applicable in international matters even if the dispute is governed by a foreign substantive law. Whether or not domestic judges will apply foreign international mandatory laws that are not part of the *lex fori* depends on the *lex fori*'s conflict of laws rules and its rules regarding the application of foreign mandatory laws. For countries within the EC, the above-cited Article 9 of the Rome II Regulation provides for the application of mandatory laws that are neither part of the *lex fori* nor the *lex contractus* (law governing the contract).

Once again, a difficulty in relation to conflict of laws issues in international 3.115
arbitration is that there is no *lex fori* and the rules of the *lex arbitri* are of limited relevance.[99] Nonetheless, lawyers and international arbitrators should be alert to any jurisdictions where mandatory laws may be relevant. It is obvious that if a party asserts an international mandatory law that is part of the *lex contractus*, the arbitral tribunal must apply it. But if the mandatory law arises from some other legal system connected to the dispute, the matter is more complex. Potential mandatory laws arise from any jurisdiction which has a close factual connection to the transaction at the heart of the dispute.

Authors Barraclough and Waincymer contend that there are four categories 3.116
of mandatory laws which are not (or should not be) controversial. These are: (i) laws which legitimately create a force majeure for one of the parties, (ii) laws implementing transnational public policy, (iii) mandatory rules of the *lex contractus*, and (iv) mandatory procedural rules of the *lex arbitri* that are applicable to international arbitrations.[100]

Perhaps most contentious is mandatory substantive laws of the *lex arbitri*. 3.117
These are potentially applicable, but in reality they may have no connection to the underlying transaction. As in the example of competition laws given above, mandatory laws of the *lex arbitri* should be applied very sparingly.

Voser convincingly objects to the application of any mandatory laws (procedu- 3.118
ral or substantive) at the seat of arbitration. Her analysis of the European and US conflict of laws approaches to applying mandatory laws leads her to recommend that arbitral tribunals apply an approach 'based on the Continental European theory of Special connection of mandatory rules ('Sonderanknupfungstheorie')'.[101] In Voser's view, this approach ensures the application of genuine mandatory rules of all concerned states. She asserts that the seat of arbitration is acknowledged as having a close relationship for any mandatory procedural laws, but not mandatory laws that apply to the merits of the case, unless the seat has some other connection to the dispute. Her rationale is the absence of a *lex fori* – arbitral tribunals are not an organ of the state and are therefore under no obligation to

---

99 See above Section 2; see also Chapter 2, Section 5.2, on the delocalisation debate.
100 Barraclough and Waincymer, op. cit. fn 93, p. 218.
101 Voser, op. cit. fn 91, p. 345.

apply the public policies of that state. A fundamental premise of Voser's argument is that the mandatory laws of all sufficiently interested states are to be treated equally. Since an arbitral tribunal does not itself belong to any state, all mandatory laws, including those of the seat of arbitration, are 'foreign' and relevant (or irrelevant) to the same extent.[102]

3.119 As should be clear from this section so far, we tend to agree with Voser. The point is whether or not the mandatory law has a genuine factual connection to the issue it seeks to regulate. The *lex arbitri*'s mandatory laws should always be kept in mind because there is a risk that a judge in subsequent setting aside proceedings will see his own mandatory laws as prevailing and apply them as international public policy. Nonetheless, the mere fact that an arbitral award could possibly be set aside is insufficient for an arbitral tribunal to decide to apply a law that it otherwise determines to be irrelevant, if doing so would affect a party's substantive rights. An arbitral tribunal should do what it finds to be correct as a matter of law in the circumstances. It should not be excessively constrained by hypothetical predictions as to future decisions of state courts. Barraclough and Waincymer's advice is a sound conclusion:

> For arbitrators who want a present workable solution for their daily practice, there do appear to be two feasible alternatives. There is a restrictive approach that applies mandatory rules only in the accepted categories... or alternatively an approach that gives arbitrators a broad discretion... [A]t present, giving arbitrators a broader discretion, on balance, seems to be the most attractive of determining mandatory rules' applicability.

5 Content of the applicable law

3.120 So far this chapter has focused on determining which law applies to a dispute. Once the law is established, an arbitral tribunal has to determine its content. Given the diverse range of countries across which an international arbitration may span, it very often happens that some or all of the arbitrators are not specialists in the applicable law. It is also not uncommon that none of the parties' lawyers are specialists in the applicable law either. A question therefore arises as to how an international arbitrator should establish the content of the law.

3.121 Once again, this issue differs in international arbitration in contrast with domestic litigation. A domestic court will have a well established body of rules relating to the manner in which foreign law is established and dealt with. There are no such rules in international arbitration, once again because there is no fallback *lex fori*. No Asia-Pacific arbitration laws or rules contain guidance as to how foreign law is to be established.[103] Arbitrators therefore have considerable

---

[102] Ibid., p. 338.
[103] Apart from simple confirmations of an arbitrator's power to decide how to ascertain the law. See, e.g. Section 2GB(6) of the Hong Kong Arbitration Ordinance, which provides that 'In conducting arbitration proceedings, an arbitral tribunal may decide whether and to what extent it should itself take the initiative in ascertaining the facts and the law relevant to those proceedings'. Some laws do provide guidance or a

freedom to establish it in the manner they deem fit,[104] provided always that the parties' fundamental due process rights are respected.

After considering numerous questions and issues relating to how an international arbitral tribunal should determine the content of the applicable law, a special task force on this topic, appointed by the International Law Association's International Commercial Arbitration Committee, summarised them in the following four 'overarching and thematic questions':[105] 3.122

  i. How should arbitrators acquire information about the contents of the applicable law?
  ii. How should arbitrators interact with the parties about the contents of the applicable law?
  iii. How should arbitrators make use of the information they receive about the contents of the applicable law?
  iv. How should arbitrators address situations that may call for special treatment regarding the contents of the applicable law?

The task force, after analysing various domestic court approaches to determining the content of foreign laws, concluded that domestic approaches are unsuitable for international arbitration. It proceeded to assess the issues relevant to arbitral tribunals before concluding among other things that:[106] 3.123

> a balanced approach is the most acceptable general approach to the determination of the contents of the applicable law in international commercial arbitration. Arbitrators should primarily rely on the parties to articulate legal issues and to present the law, and disputed legal issues. They should give parties appropriate directions in relation thereto and should give appropriate weight to information so obtained.

The point made here about the arbitrators relying principally on the parties to articulate legal issues is important. While arbitral tribunals may be permitted some limited scope to apply provisions of the governing law that have not been specifically plead by a party (the '*jura novit curia*' principle, well known in civil law countries), they cannot stray too far from the pleadings and apply statutes, cases or principles of law that the parties would not reasonably have expected them to apply.[107] 3.124

---

mechanism for arbitrators to determine the content of law. See, e.g. Article 1044 of the Dutch Code of Civil Procedure and Section 27(2) of the Danish Arbitration Act.
104 There is English authority suggesting that where the seat of arbitration is in England or Wales, an arbitral tribunal should apply the England and Wales approach to determining the content of foreign law, see *Hussman (Europe) Ltd v Al Ameen Dev & Trade Co* [2000] EWHC 210 (Comm). There are multiple reasons why this view should not be preferred, which reasons are analogous to our arguments as to why the theories of applying the seat of arbitration's substantive law or choice of law rules is inappropriate, see Sections 3.2.2.2 and 3.2.2.3 above.
105 *Ascertaining the Contents of the Applicable Law in International Commercial Arbitration*, International Commercial Arbitration Committee of the International Law Association, October 2008, available at www.ila-hq.org/en/committees/index.cfm/cid/19, at p. 7.
106 Ibid., p. 22.
107 These limits have recently been analysed in Swiss case law. On 9 February 2009 (Case reference 4A-400/2008), the Swiss Federal Tribunal set aside an award of the Court of Arbitration for Sport (CAS) because one of the bases of the CAS's decision was a law that had not been pled by the parties and was inapplicable in any event. See also an earlier Federal Tribunal decision which, after confirming that arbitrators sitting in Switzerland can apply a law not specifically pled by the parties (*jura novit curia*), distinguished contractual

3.125   The task force also produced a (non-binding but guiding) list of recommendations for arbitrators faced with the task of determining the content of the applicable law. They are summarised below:[108]
   (i) Arbitrators should identify the potentially applicable laws and rules and ascertain their contents insofar as it is necessary.
   (ii) In ascertaining the contents of the applicable law and rules, arbitrators should respect due process and public policy and avoid bias or appearance of bias.
   (iii) When it appears to the arbitrators that the contents of the applicable law might be significant, they should promptly raise that topic with the parties and establish appropriate procedures as to how the contents of the law will be ascertained.
   (iv) Rules governing the ascertainment of the contents of law by national courts are not necessarily suitable for arbitration given the fundamental differences between international arbitration and litigation before national courts.
   (v) Arbitrators should primarily receive information about the contents of the applicable law from the parties.
   (vi) Arbitrators should not introduce legal issues – propositions of law that may bear on the outcome of the dispute – that the parties have not raised.
   (vii) Arbitrators are not confined to the parties' submissions about the contents of the applicable law but may question the parties about legal issues and about their submissions and evidence on the contents of the applicable law. They may also review sources not invoked by the parties relating to those legal issues and may, in a transparent manner, rely on their own knowledge as to the applicable law.
   (viii) Before rendering a decision or an award, arbitrators should give parties a reasonable opportunity to be heard on all legal issues. They should not give decisions that might reasonably be expected to surprise the parties, or that are based on legal issues not raised by or with the parties.
   (ix) In ascertaining the contents of a potentially applicable law or rule, arbitrators may consider and give appropriate weight to any reliable source, including statutes, case law, submissions of the parties' advocates, opinions and cross-examination of experts, scholarly writings and the like.
   (x) If arbitrators intend to rely on sources not invoked by the parties, they should bring those sources to the attention of the parties and invite their comments.
   (xi) If in the course of deliberations arbitrators consider that further information about the contents of the applicable law is necessary to the disposition

provisions which had not been pled. It held that an arbitral tribunal cannot decide a case based on a contractual clause that the parties had not discussed (30 September 2003, 4P 100/2003, (2004) 22 *ASA Bulletin* 574).
108 These are partially quoted and partially summarised and/or paraphrased. For the full citation of this list see 'Ascertaining the Contents of the Applicable Law in International Commercial Arbitration', International Commercial Arbitration Committee of the International Law Association, October 2008, available at www.ila-hq.org/en/committees/index.cfm/cid/19, p. 22 et seq.

of the case, they should consider reopening the proceedings to enable the parties to make further submissions.

(xii) In disputes implicating rules of public policy or other mandatory rules, arbitrators may be justified in taking measures appropriate to determine the applicability and contents of such rules, including by independent research.

3.126 In practice, disputes about the manner in which the content of the applicable law should be determined are rare. The usual approach is for the parties' lawyers to plead the content of that law, with or without the assistance of a legal expert. In many cases, the parties' dispute can be resolved by establishing the facts and then directly applying the parties' contract. Express referral to the law is not always necessary.

6 Trade usages

3.127 The term 'trade usages' refers to the way that business is conducted in a particular trade or industry. Regardless of what the applicable law is and whether or not it has been determined, an arbitral tribunal may need to consider relevant trade usages to give appropriate context to the facts, contract and applicable law.

3.128 Most arbitration rules and laws require arbitral tribunals to take into account trade usages in reaching their decisions. For example, Article 28(4) of the Model Law provides that 'In all cases, the arbitral tribunal shall decide in accordance with the terms of the contract and shall take into account the usages of the trade applicable to the transaction'.[109] Applying trade usages is also a general principle of international commercial law.[110]

3.129 The importance of trade usages is emphasised and well explained in the context of ICC arbitration by Craig, Park and Paulsson:[111]

> Reference to trade usages may frequently fill gaps in the applicable law, since usages in the world of international commerce may frequently develop more rapidly than the law.
>
> ...
>
> The application of trade usages is consistent with the primacy of contractual terms. Usages may be deemed incorporated into the contract as a matter of specific intent (for

---

[109] This applies unmodified, or equivalently, in Hong Kong, Singapore, Korea, New Zealand, Malaysia, India, Japan, the Philippines and Australia. Sri Lanka is different. According to Section 24(4) of its Arbitration Act, 'the arbitral tribunal shall decide according to ... trade usages only if the parties have expressly authorised it to do so'. (Emphasis added) Neither the Chinese nor Indonesian arbitration laws refer to trade usages. Most arbitration institutional rules provide something similar to Article 28(4) of the Model Law.

[110] See, e.g. Article 1.9(2) of the UNIDROIT Principles of International Commercial Contracts (2004 edn). See also CR Drahozal, 'Commercial Norms, Commercial Codes, and International Commercial Arbitration', (2000) 33 *Vanderbilt Journal of Transnational Law* 79, at p. 109, observing 'that the requirement [to consider trade usages] is not one that results simply from national substantive contract laws'.

[111] W Craig, WW Park and J Paulsson, *International Chamber of Commerce Arbitration*, 3rd edn, Oceana Publishing, 2000, pp. 330–332. See also S Bainbridge, 'Trade Usages in International Sales of Goods: An Analysis of the 1964 and 1980 Sales Conventions', (1984) 24 *Virginia Journal of International Law* 619.

instance, if reference is made in the contract to Incoterms, or contracting regulations), or by implication (a custom is not referred to but is deemed by the arbitrators to have been within the contemplation of the parties). In this sense trade usages can be said to be internal to the contract and an expression of what the parties intended or can be deemed to have intended.

3.130   In *Ganda Edible Oils Sdn Bhd v Transgrain Bv*, the Malaysian Supreme Court of Civil Appeal was asked to consider whether the arbitrator had based the award on trade usages, which the court found had not occurred. In the course of judgment, the court observed:[112]

> One has to understand what is meant by 'custom of trade' before dealing with the subject. A custom is a particular rule which has existed either actually or presumptively from time immemorial and obtained the force of law in a particular locality. It is distinguishable from particular trade or local usages which have been imported as express or implied term [sic] into commercial or other contracts..... The arbitrator may apply his own knowledge of the usage, but before that can be done, there must be sufficient material for its inclusion. It follows that where persons execute a contract under circumstances governed by usage, the usage, when proved, must be considered as part of the agreement. In general, every usage must be notorious, certain and reasonable and must not offend against the intention of any statute. By notorious, it means that it has acquired such notoriety in a particular branch of trade or business or amongst the class of persons who are affected by it, that any person who enters into a contract affected by the usage must be taken to have done so with the intention that the usage should form part of the contract. By certainty, usage is required to be as certain as the written contract itself. It must be uniform and reasonable before it can be imported into a contract.

3.131   An abundance of ICC and other arbitral case law confirms that industry specific trade usages must be used to complement the content of the applicable law and the contract. In some instances, arbitral awards have gone further by holding that, in addition to industry specific trade usages, there are general trade usages in international commerce which are analogous to general principles of international commercial law. Such usages may be considered relevant in addition to the applicable law. A few examples may be cited from ICC jurisprudence:

(i) In *ICC Case No. 5721* (1990), the arbitral tribunal found that: 'Article 13(5) of the [1975] ICC Arbitration Rules invites the Tribunal to take account of trade usages and the contractual stipulations. From that perspective, the Tribunal is allowed to make reference to the lex mercatoria... the Tribunal therefore bases its decision on the general notion of good faith in business and the usages of international trade.'[113]

(ii) In *ICC Cases Nos. 6515 and 6516* (1994), the contract provided for the application of Greek law. The arbitral tribunal held that 'it results from

---

[112] [1988] 1 MLJ 428, at p. 430.
[113] Award in *ICC Case No. 5721*; in S Jarvin, Y Derains and JJ Arnaldez, *Collection of ICC Arbitral Awards 1986–1990*, ICC Publishing, 1994, p. 401 at p. 404 (informal translation from the original in French).

the combination between the provisions of the second paragraph of the arbitral clauses, of Art. 2 [rectius 1] in the Greek Civil Code and of Art. 13(5) in the [1975] ICC Rules of Arbitration that the arbitral tribunal must primarily resort to Greek law and subsidiarily to the relevant usages of international trade, if and when needed'.[114]

(iii) In *ICC Case No. 9479* (1999), the contract was governed by New York law. The arbitral tribunal held: 'the Arbitral Tribunal finds any question concerning the validity of the Agreement must be decided under the Law of the State of New York. Any other question will have to be decided according to the provisions of the Agreement in the light of, and, in case of need, supplemented by the usages of international trade. Whenever necessary, the Arbitral Tribunal will have regard to international public policy.'[115]

(iv) Finally, in *ICC Case No. 1472*, the arbitral tribunal noted: 'considering that, in the case under consideration, the contracts were signed in Paris, French national law should apply, supplemented, if necessary, by international custom and practice governing international contracts.'[116]

While these awards suggest a fairly broad interpretation of the term 'trade usage', as noted above it is normally limited to customs specific to a particular trade or industry, or specific to a course of dealing between the disputing parties. As to the content of trade usages, it is up to any party who wants to rely on a trade usage to prove its existence and meaning. This can be done in many ways, such as through trade publications and guidelines and/or by expert witness testimony. Provided that the *lex arbitri* permits the arbitral tribunal to use trade usages,[117] such usages are often considered more important than the applicable law itself.[118] The arbitral tribunal must take them into account. 3.132

7 Non-national rules of law and the *lex mercatoria*

Given the inherently transnational nature of the international commercial disputes that are decided by international arbitration, one may wonder whether domestic laws are suitable substantive laws to apply. A series of academic studies and the application by international arbitrators of non-national general 3.133

---

114 Award in *ICC Case No. 6515 and 6516*, in Jarvin, Derains and Arnaldez, op. cit. fn 90, p. 241 at p. 243 (informal translation from the original in French).
115 Final Award in Case 9479, (2001) 12(2) *ICC International Court of Arbitration Bulletin* 67, at p. 68.
116 Cited in Y Derains, 'Le statut des usages du commerce international devant les juridictions arbitrales', (1973) *Revue de l'arbitrage* 122.
117 As noted by P Bernardini 'International Arbitration and A-National Rules of Law', (2004) 15(2) *ICC International Court of Arbitration Bulletin* 58, at p. 65, the application of trade usages must be permitted by the law of the seat of arbitration.
118 G Aksen, 'The Law Applicable in International Arbitration – Relevance of References to Trade Usages' in (1994) 7 *ICCA Congress Series* 470; Derains, 1972, op. cit. fn 2, p. 99.

principles of international commercial law (or the so-called 'lex mercatoria')[119] has led to considerable debate on the topic.[120]

7.1 Choice of the *lex mercatoria* by the parties

3.134 Parties to international arbitration proceedings are generally permitted to select a non-national system of law to govern their dispute. This possibility is implicitly recognised in the Model Law. The language of Article 28(1) should be recalled:

> The arbitral tribunal shall decide the dispute in accordance with such <u>rules of law</u> as are chosen by the parties as applicable to the substance of the dispute. Any designation of <u>the law or legal system of a given State</u> shall be construed, unless otherwise expressed, as directly referring to the substantive law of that State and not to its conflict of laws rules. (Emphasis added)

3.135 The reference to 'rules of law' in the first sentence should be distinguished from 'the law or legal system of a given State' in the second sentence. The former logically includes any rules of law, state-based or otherwise,[121] while the latter concerns the situation where the parties have chosen a domestic legal system.[122]

3.136 Section 30(2) of the Malaysian Arbitration Act deviates from Article 28(1) of the Model Law by substituting 'rules of law' for 'the law', which would exclude non-national rules of law. Since most institutional arbitration rules allow parties to select 'rules of law',[123] one may wonder how this Malaysian provision will be interpreted when the parties have chosen such a set of institutional rules. Ordinarily, chosen rules prevail over non-mandatory provisions of the *lex arbitri*. But since the Malaysian legislators appear to have deliberately modified Article 28(1) to restrict the parties' choice of law, choosing a set of institutional rules may be insufficient to reinstate that free choice.

3.137 A party agreement on a non-national system of law to govern a contract can be made in a countless number of ways, including references to the *lex mercatoria*, general principles of international trade law, etc. A typical example is the following clause which was contained in a contract relating to the supply

---

119 The concept of the *lex mercatoria*, or law of merchants, dates back to the Middle Ages, but was revived in modern times by scholars like B Goldman, 'Frontiers du droit et "lex mercatoria"', (1964) 9 *Archives de Philosophie du Droit* 177.
120 For a clear overview of these debates and issues see generally M Pryles, 'Application of the Lex Mercatoria in International Commercial Arbitration', (2003) 18(2) *Mealey's International Arbitration Report* 1.
121 Note that some commentators question whether Article 28(1) was intended to allow parties to choose the *lex mercatoria*. See, e.g. HM Holtzmann and JE Neuhaus, *A Guide to the UNCITRAL Model Law on International Commercial Arbitration: Legislative History and Commentary*, Kluwer, 1989, pp. 766–769 and D Caron, L Caplan and M Pellonpää, *The UNCITRAL Arbitration Rules – A Commentary*, Oxford University Press, 2006, p. 128 suggesting that 'rules of law' is limited to established texts or conventions, but excludes unwritten laws like the *lex mercatoria*.
122 Article 28(1) of the Model Law applies unmodified, or similarly, in Australia, Hong Kong, Singapore, New Zealand, India, Japan, the Philippines and South Korea. Malaysia is discussed below.
123 A provision equivalent to Article 28(1) of the Model Law in the sense of allowing parties to choose 'rules of law' exists in most Asia-Pacific institutional rules. Exceptions are Article 34.1 of the ACICA Rules ('the law') and Article 15(1) of the BANI Rules ('the law').

of energy between an Asian state-owned energy provider and a foreign private company, which stipulated that:

> Any questions relating to this contract which are not expressly or implicitly settled by the provisions contained in this contract shall be governed by the principles of law generally recognized in international trade as applicable to international distribution contracts, with the exclusion of national laws.

3.138 In another interesting example, the parties appear to have sought the application of the principles of law common to both of their legal systems, and failing such common principles by a form of *lex mercatoria* applicable in 'civilised nations':

> The signatories base their relations with respect to this Agreement on the principles of goodwill and good faith. Taking into account their different nationalities, this Agreement shall for the purpose of arbitration be given effect and shall be interpreted and applied in conformity with principles of law common to [Country A] and [Country B] and, in the absence of such principles, then in conformity with the principles of law normally recognized by civilized nations in general, including those which have been applied by international tribunals.

3.139 A non-national system of law should not be agreed to without careful consideration. While it may appear attractive in the context of a transnational negotiation to select as the governing law something like 'the principles of law normally recognised by civilised nations in general', such attractiveness comes at the price of certainty and predictability. What is a civilised nation? Does the notion of a civilised nation change in time or is it stagnant? Where do we find the principles of law recognised by civilised nations? What is the impact of 'normally' – does it mean that the arbitrators can find a principle of law but then choose not to apply it?

3.140 For all these reasons, it is not surprising that while parties are generally permitted to choose a non-national system of law, they rarely do. In the five-year period from 2004 and 2008, parties in ICC International Court of Arbitration administered arbitrations agreed that their dispute would be governed by general principles of international commercial law, the *lex mercatoria*, the UNIDROIT Principles of International Commercial Contracts, or some equivalent in a total of only 19 choice of law clauses.[124] This figure is insignificant given that the ICC Court's total case load over that same period was 2937 arbitrations. The low figure shows that the excitement about the *lex mercatoria* in certain academic circles far outweighs its practical utility and significance. On the other hand, it shows that the *lex mercatoria* is not an esoteric concept that is never used. This is also confirmed by the fact that, despite the relatively infrequent choice of the

---

124 We refer to 'choice of law clauses' rather than 'arbitrations' intentionally here as there are slightly more choice of law clauses than arbitrations. Furthermore, the figure of 19 does not include agreements indicating that the 1980 UN Convention on the International Sale of Goods should apply (25 such choice of law clauses in that period), or other international conventions (such as 'The Hague Convention on Law' and the 'Geneva Convention', each chosen once), or attempts by parties to choose regional laws (such as 'OHADA law' (OHADA being the Organisation pour l'Harmonisation en Afrique du Droit des Affaires) and 'European Economic Community law', each chosen twice), nor does it include the choice of *ex aequo et bono/amiable compositeur*, which is dealt with in Section 8 below.

lex mercatoria as governing law, it is more frequently referred to by arbitrators to fill gaps in a domestic law or to support general findings in their decisions that are based on some domestic law.

7.2 Choice of the *lex mercatoria* by the arbitral tribunal

3.141 Aside from the ability of parties to choose a non-national system of law, it is theoretically possible for an arbitral tribunal to decide to apply non-national law where the parties have failed to choose the governing law. This is not considered to be permitted in Model Law jurisdictions. In contrast to Article 28(1) of the Model Law, which allows the parties to choose 'rules of law', Article 28(2) restricts the arbitral tribunal's selection in the absence of party choice to 'the law...'. When reading Articles 28(1) and 28(2) together, it seems that the intention was to restrict arbitrators to selecting a domestic law. This interpretation is supported by commentators.[125]

3.142 Some jurisdictions in this region have gone further than Article 28(2) of the Model Law to ensure that the arbitral tribunal cannot select non-national laws in the absence of party choice. Article 36(2) of the Japanese Arbitration Law limits arbitrator choice to 'the substantive law of the State...'.[126]

3.143 India has gone the opposite direction, modifying the Model Law in such a way as to empower arbitrators to select non-national laws. Section 28(b)(iii) of the Conciliation and Arbitration Act provides that, in the absence of party choice, the arbitral tribunal 'shall apply the rules of law it considers to be appropriate given all the circumstances'. (Emphasis added)

3.144 Most Asia-Pacific institutional rules follow the Model Law approach in this regard, with the exception of HKIAC, KCAB and ACICA. The HKIAC and KCAB Rules allow arbitral tribunals to select 'rules of law'. This is interesting since the arbitration laws of neither Hong Kong nor Korea permit this under their equivalent of Article 28(2) of the Model Law. Article 34(1) of the ACICA Rules is very curious. It provides that 'The Arbitral Tribunal shall apply the law designated by the parties as applicable to the substance of the dispute. Failing such designation by the parties, the Arbitral Tribunal shall apply the rules of law which it considers applicable'. (Emphasis added) Thus it appears that the ACICA Rules restrict party choice to 'the law', whereas arbitrators may choose 'rules of law'. This may well be a drafting oversight.[127]

3.145 While arbitral tribunals are sometimes permitted to select non-national rules of law, they should think carefully before doing so.[128] The rarity (noted above)

---

125 See, e.g. Holtzmann and Neuhaus, op. cit. fn 121, pp. 764–772.
126 Article 29(2) of the Korean Arbitration Act similarly refers to 'the law of the State...'. For comments on the *lex mercatoria* from the Japanese perspective see L Nottage 'Practical and Theoretical Implications of the Lex Mercatoria for Japan: CENTRAL's Empirical Study on the Use of Transnational Law', (2000) 4 *Vindobona Journal* 132.
127 This point is taken up and discussed further, and with a suggested solution, in Chapter 4 of L Nottage and R Garnett (eds), *International Arbitration in Australia*, Federation Press, forthcoming 2010.
128 For some examples of arbitral awards where arbitral tribunals have decided to apply, or reject the application of, the *lex mercatoria*, see Pryles, op. cit. fn 120, p. 16 et seq.

of parties choosing non-national rules in their contracts, as mentioned earlier, suggests that international businesses are not especially fond of them, probably because of the absence of certainty and depth in their content.

It is more acceptable for arbitral tribunals to apply – but still with considerable caution – non-national rules of law or general principles of international commercial law to substitute, fill gaps in or even occasionally to interpret domestic laws.[129] As noted in the previous section, international arbitrators occasionally also apply the *lex mercatoria* as a trade usage, although doing so is rare.

3.146

7.3 Discussion of the *lex mercatoria*

There is a rich and romantic academic debate about the content and even existence of so-called bodies of law such as the *lex mercatoria*. It is certain that – if it exists – the *lex mercatoria* is a law. An arbitrator applying it is not somehow authorised to apply his own view on the general principles of law. Nor can he apply general notions of fairness and justice without reference to law.[130] He must rather search out and determine the content of the *lex* on a particular point and then apply it, just as he would apply a domestic law. This is well explained by Lord Mustill:[131]

3.147

> The *lex mercatoria* is a *lex*, albeit not yet perfected. It creates norms which an arbitrator must seek out and obey in every case to which the *lex* applies. Whether the reason for its application is understood to be an express or implied agreement between the parties, or the concept that it forms the essential juridicial context of the bargain, there is no room here for the arbitrator to impose his own ideas, unless of course they happen to coincide with the rules of the *lex mercatoria*: for if he does so, he falsifies the transaction. Naturally, everyone hopes that the *lex mercatoria* will in every case yield a solution which will seem fair to all. But even if this expectation is disappointed, the *lex mercatoria* must still prevail; otherwise it would not be a law. Thus, since the prime maxim of the *lex mercatoria* is *pacta sunt servanda*; an arbitrator who smoothes the corners of a contract which seem to him too sharp is not complying with his mandate.

There have been various attempts effectively to codify the *lex mercatoria*. One is the UNDROIT Principles of International Commercial Contracts, first published in 1996 and then revised in 2004, with a further revised version currently being prepared. They set out basic principles of contractual formation, interpretation and obligations in a somewhat civil law influenced manner, but in a user-friendly, flexible, logical structure. Like most soft law in international arbitration, the UNIDROIT Principles have no independent force of law unless parties expressly select them, in which case they apply quasi-contractually. They are also occasionally applied by arbitrators as a restatement of the *lex mercatoria*.

3.148

---

129 See in this regard KP Berger, *International Economic Arbitration*, Kluwer, 1993, p. 563; J-F Poudret and S Besson, *Comparative Law of International Arbitration*, 2nd edn, Thomson, 2007, para 696; Lew, Mistelis and Kröll, op. cit. fn 26, para 18–42; Craig, Park and Paulsson, op. cit. fn 111, p. 623.
130 See Section 8 below on *ex aequo et bono* and *amiable composition*.
131 M Mustill, 'The New Lex Mercatoria: The First Twenty-five Years', (1988) 4(2) *Arbitration International* 86, at p. 103.

136   INTERNATIONAL COMMERCIAL ARBITRATION

Another well-known attempt at codification is German Klaus Peter Berger's book *The Creeping Codification of the Lex Mercatoria* (Kluwer, 1999), which formed the basis for his more recent and commendable CENTRAL Transnational Law Database, which describes itself as 'the world's first' in providing 'international practitioners and academics with an easy-to-use online knowledge & codification platform for transnational commercial law, the New Lex Mercatoria'.[132]

3.149   While these attempts at codification are truly impressive, one may wonder about their global utility. It is quite possible that the content of the *lex mercatoria* varies according to the peculiarities of the parties and the particular dispute in question. For example, the content of the *lex mercatoria* might be different when a question of law arises between parties from Thailand and Indonesia, as compared to the same question of law arising between parties from Singapore and Hong Kong, or parties from Germany and France. The point is well summarised by a former Chief Justice of New South Wales, Australia:[133]

> It seems to me that [the *lex mercatoria*] equates universality with only the European world. This alleged universal law merchant held no sway in India, or China and even less in the less developed or undiscovered parts of the world. Thus, the cry of universality must surely ring hollow. In much the same way, the new *lex mercatoria* can hardly be said to bear the imprint of universality. Is it seriously suggested that the trade usages of the highly sophisticated international conglomerates in the Western world are to be found or accepted in less developed commercial societies? It seems to me that there is a new *lex mercatoria* in the same very confined way that there was once in the Middle Ages.

3.150   It should also be noted in this regard that the whole concept (or at least the alleged substantive content) of the *lex mercatoria* is sometimes criticised as being overly Westernised, designed to enable Western multinationals to escape local laws that that are unhelpful to them.[134] Such criticisms may well derive from some rather one-sided historical applications of a so-called *lex mercatoria*. A good example is Lord Asquith's infamous decision in the *Abu Dhabi* oil arbitration.[135] His decision on the proper law of the contract was critical to the outcome of the case. Applying conflict of laws principles, Lord Asquith acknowledged that Abu Dhabi law would be appropriate because the contract was made in Abu Dhabi and was to be performed there. He concluded, however, that:[136]

---

132 See www.tldb.net. See also UNILEX, at www.unilex.info, which provides cases and materials on the UNIDROIT Principles and also KP Berger (ed), *The Practice of Transnational Law*, Kluwer Law International, 2001.
133 A Rogers, 'Contemporary Problems in International Commercial Arbitration', (1989) *International Business Lawyer* 154, at p. 158.
134 See, e.g. Toope, op. cit. fn 57, p. 96 who describes the *lex mercatoria* as an effort to 'legitimize as law the economic interests of Western corporations' and M Sornarajah, 'The UNCITRAL Model Law: A Third World Viewpoint', (1989) 6(4) *Journal of International Arbitration* 7 ('Third World countries are likely to be more wary of encroachments on their sovereignty in the name of transnational mercatorialism than other states') and at p. 16 ('The so-called lex mercatoria is a creation of a coterie of Western scholars and arbitrators who have loaded it with norms entirely favourable to international business', 'it could become the vehicle for the introduction of norms that are inimical to the interests of developing countries').
135 *Petroleum Dev (Trucial Coast) Ltd v Sheikh of Abu Dhabi*, (1952) 1 *International and Comparative Law Quarterly* 247. Some background to this case was provided in Chapter 1, para 1.22.
136 Ibid., at pp. 250–251.

[the Sheik, an] 'absolute, feudal monarch'... administers a purely discretionary justice with the assistance of the Koran; and it would be fanciful to suggest that in this very primitive region there is any settled body of legal principles applicable to the construction of modern commercial instruments.

3.151 Lord Asquith decided to apply 'principles rooted in the good sense and common practice of the generality of civilised nations – a sort of "modern law of nature"'. He declined to apply English law directly, but presumptuously determined that 'some of its rules are... so firmly grounded in reason, as to form part of this broad body of jurisprudence' and are 'principle[s] of ecumenical validity' and 'mere common sense'.[137] Using this 'modern law of nature', Lord Asquith applied the English rule which 'attributes paramount importance to the actual language of the written instrument in which the negotiations result' and determined the case predominantly in favour of the English oil concession holder.

3.152 Lord Asquith's characterisation of Middle Eastern law as primitive was controversial. El-Kosheri criticises it as a 'lack of sensitivity towards the national laws of developing countries', blaming it on 'ignorance, carelessness or... unjustified psychological superiority complexes'.[138]

3.153 As hinted at above, doubt is sometimes cast on the very existence of the *lex mercatoria*. Indeed it can be argued that its existence has not been necessary because domestic laws have always regulated private commercial dealings. This can be contrasted with the public international law sphere where the inapplicability of private law has led to the evolution of 'customary international law' to regulate the conduct between nation states. On the other hand, while the traditional subjects of public international law (states) are different from those in private international law (individuals, companies and states acting as commercial entities), there is no reason why customary laws should not also have evolved for transnational commercial law. We therefore consider it difficult to deny the existence of a *lex mercatoria* in some form.

3.154 The main drawback of the *lex mercatoria* is uncertainty in the determination of its content. If it exists, then its content could not possibly be temporally, geographically or circumstantially stagnant, but should rather be considered as dynamic, depending, among other factors, on the parties' backgrounds and the peculiarities of their commercial relationship. Given the almost infinitely diverse combination of these variants, once the appropriate principles of law are established, it would be surprising if their depth to resolve complex commercial questions is really adequate. In other words, while it might set forth general principles, trying to establish the content of detailed, technical provisions of the *lex mercatoria* seems futile.

3.155 Starting from the unquestionable principle that it would be inappropriate for Western companies (or anyone else for that matter) to impose on non-Westerners their own view of what commercial law should be, the main perceived benefit

---
137 Ibid., at p. 251.
138 AS El-Kosheri, 'Is There a Growing International Arbitration Culture in the Arab-Islamic Juridical Culture?', (1996) 8 *ICCA Congress Series* 47, at p. 48.

of using the *lex mercatoria* must be to guarantee *pacta sunt servada* and to ensure that international dealings are resolved in a way that recognises their international character, rather than by applying potentially rigid and occasionally ill-suited domestic laws. If that is the goal, then the *lex mercatoria* is not necessary for achieving it. That goal is achieved in any event because wise international arbitration lawyers and arbitrators focus on the contract and the parties' relationship and will apply domestic laws in an internationally sensible way. Moreover, provisions such as Article 28(4) of the Model Law, discussed in the previous section, help to preserve *pacta sunt servada* and a common sense approach to resolving international commercial disputes. It might therefore be the case that parties should draft their contracts carefully and choose their lawyers and arbitrators wisely rather than selecting a somewhat elusive *lex mercatoria*. For all these reasons, the minimal use of the *lex mercatoria* these days is unsurprising.

8 Deciding cases without law: *Ex aequo et bono* and *amiable compositeur*

3.156 Both the Model Law and most institutional arbitration rules permit an arbitral tribunal to decide a case as '*ex aequo et bono or as amiable compositeur*'.[139] In brief, this means deciding a case based on principles of fairness and justice without necessarily following the law. The terms '*ex aequo et bono*' and '*amiable compositeur*' have much the same meaning. The concept they represent can alternatively be referred to as '*general principles of justice and fairness*'.[140] For the purposes of this discussion we mainly use the term *ex aequo et bono*.

3.157 Deciding disputes *ex aequo et bono* is very rarely permitted in domestic courts.[141] Courts must apply the law. The possibility for parties to empower an arbitral tribunal to decide *ex aequo et bono* is therefore an advantage of arbitration over litigation. *Ex aequo et bono* may be preferable where the parties consider that the law is not well suited or is insufficiently evolved to meet their particular needs and/or where a key priority is to preserve their long-term business relationship. Agreements on *ex aequo et bono* are therefore more common in long-term contracts than short-term contracts.

---

[139] Article 28(3) provides in full: 'The arbitral tribunal shall decide ex aequo et bono or as amiable compositeur only if the parties have expressly authorized it to do so.' This applies unmodified, or in a very similar form, in Australia, Hong Kong, Singapore, New Zealand, India, Japan, the Philippines and South Korea. Other domestic laws are dealt with below. An equivalent provision exists in the following institutional rules: KLRCA, SIAC, HKIAC Administered, BANI, JCAA, KCAB. Article 34.2 of the ACICA Arbitration Rules adds a requirement that deciding in this way be consistent with the applicable procedural law: 'The Arbitral Tribunal shall decide as amiable compositeur or ex aequo et bono only if the parties have, in writing, expressly authorized the Arbitral Tribunal to do so <u>and if the law applicable to the arbitral procedure permits such arbitration</u>.'(Emphasis added)
[140] This is the language used in Section 24(4) of the Sri Lankan Arbitration Act.
[141] An exception for certain UK courts is noted in the Final Report of the ICC Commission on Arbitration's Task Force on Amiable Composition and *ex aequo et bono*, September 2008, pp. 9–10.

3.158 Several arbitration laws in this region go against the norm and do not permit arbitral tribunals to decide based on *ex aequo et bono*. The Model Law has been modified in Malaysia and Bangladesh such that there is no provision about deciding *ex aequo et bono* or similar in the arbitration legislation of these two states. One commentator has suggested, in respect of Bangladesh, that deciding *ex aequo et bono* would be possible provided that the chosen arbitration rules allow it.[142] The rationale for this view is that the law is simply silent on the issue rather than prohibitive. We are not entirely convinced by this suggestion. When a jurisdiction bases its law on the Model Law but deliberately omits a provision such as this, as is the case for Malaysia and Bangladesh, it might well be considered that the legislators intended to exclude the possibility for parties to refer disputes to an *ex aequo et bono* decision.

3.159 Another law which does not allow *ex aequo et bono* is that of Vietnam. The Vietnamese Ordinance on Commercial Arbitration requires that disputes submitted to arbitration be resolved according to law,[143] saying nothing about *ex aequo et bono*, *amiable compositeur*, or similar. This has led one commentator to conclude that deciding as *amiable compositeur* may not be permitted in Vietnam.[144]

3.160 Where the law or arbitration rules allow decisions based on *ex aequo et bono*, the parties must expressly request and authorise the arbitral tribunal to proceed in this manner. Thus Article 28(3) Model Law provides that 'the arbitral tribunal shall decide ex aequo et bono or as amiable compositeur <u>only if the parties have expressly authorized it to do so</u>'. A similar requirement for an express agreement can be found in most Asia-Pacific arbitration laws[145] with two exceptions.

3.161 The first exception is Article 56 of the Indonesian Arbitration Law which provides simply that 'The arbitrator or arbitration tribunal shall render its decision based upon the relevant provisions of law, or based upon justice and fairness'. There is no express requirement for an agreement of the parties. The second exception is China. According to Jingzhou Tao, while the Chinese arbitration law does not refer to *ex aequo et bono* in the same way that the Model Law does, Chinese arbitration commissions are empowered to render decisions based on such equitable principles, and it is in fact impossible for the parties to request the arbitral tribunal to ignore such principles and decide the case strictly according to law. He concludes, however, that an arbitral tribunal cannot ignore the law altogether as it might be able to do under the Model Law.[146]

3.162 Despite the exceptions just mentioned, party agreement is normally required to authorise the arbitral tribunal to decide *ex aequo et bono*. While there is no

---

142 AFM Maniruzzaman, 'The New Law of International Commercial Arbitration in Bangladesh: A Comparative Perspective', (2003) 14 *American Review of International Arbitration* 139, at p. 163.
143 See Articles 3(2) and 7(2) of the 2003 Vietnamese Ordinance on Commercial Arbitration.
144 Hop X Dang, 'Towards A Stronger Arbitration Regime For Vietnam', (2007) 1 *Asian International Arbitration Journal* 80, at p. 95.
145 See above footnote 139.
146 See Jingzhou Tao, op. cit. fn 18, pp. 105–106, also referring to Hu Li, 'Arbitration *ex aequo et bono* in China', (2000) 66(3) *Arbitration* 188. See also Article 43(1) of the CIETAC Rules which provides that 'The arbitral tribunal shall independently and impartially make its arbitral award on the basis of the facts, in accordance with the law and the terms of the contracts, with references to international practices and in compliance with the principle of fairness and reasonableness'.

form requirement for such an agreement,[147] it is prudent for arbitral tribunals to ensure that the agreement is clear, specific and either made in writing or evidenced in writing. In *Hewitt v McKensey*,[148] Hewitt sought to set aside an arbitral award before the Supreme Court of New South Wales, Australia, on various grounds including that the arbitrator had acted as *amiable compositeur* without authorisation from the parties. The sole arbitrator's award stated that the parties had authorised him to act as *amiable compositeur* during a preliminary conference at which the procedure for the arbitration was discussed. However, Hewitt testified during the setting aside proceedings that neither he nor his solicitor, who had been present at the preliminary conference, could recall that agreement having been reached. The judge concluded that, in the circumstances, there was insufficient evidence that the parties had authorised the arbitrator to act as *amiable compositeur*, noting:[149]

> The passage that I have just quoted [about the preliminary conference] was followed by a statement that [the arbitrator] 'would prepare minutes containing his directions, which he would circulate to the parties'. One would have thought that something as important as an agreement [to act as amiable compositeur] even if not in writing... would have been recorded in those minutes had it been struck at the preliminary conference.

3.163   The judge consequently found that the sole arbitrator had misconducted himself. The request to set aside the award was ultimately rejected though because the judge was not convinced that the sole arbitrator would have reached a different conclusion on the merits had he applied the law rather than acting as *amiable compositeur*.

3.164   One may wonder what *ex aequo et bono* actually means for the arbitrator's decision-making process. For the avoidance of doubt, it is useful at this point to distinguish *ex aequo et bono* from the *lex mercatoria*, which was discussed in the previous section. The *lex mercatoria* is a body of law, only no universally accepted written version of it exists. If the *lex mercatoria* is the applicable law, the arbitral tribunal must first work out its relevant content and then apply it, just as it would apply some domestic law once its content is determined. On the other hand, deciding a case *ex aequo et bono* is certainly not the same as applying a law or even 'gap filling' mechanisms for contracts. It is also not the same as applying principles of 'equity' in the sense of the common law doctrine and remedy. Making a determination *ex aequo et bono* is a distinct approach to dispute resolution which must be separated from the law and any mechanisms that might be contained in it. Thus Lord Mustill has noted that 'the essence of

---

147 One exception is that under Section 22 of the uniform Australian state Commercial Arbitration Acts, which occasionally apply to international arbitrations in Australia, the parties must agree in writing in order for the arbitrator to decide the case 'by reference to considerations of general justice and fairness'.
148 *Hewitt v McKensey* [2003] NSWSC 1186 (16 December 2003).
149 Ibid., at para 54. It should be noted that this arbitration was governed by the New South Wales Commercial Arbitration Act which does require, at Section 22, that an agreement for the arbitrator to act as *amiable compositeur* must be in writing. The judge considered it unnecessary for him to decide the effect of there not having been a written agreement since there was insufficient evidence of an oral agreement in any event.

amiable composition is to dispense the arbitrator from the duty of enforcing any system of law'.[150]

When deciding *ex aequo et bono*, an arbitrator is thus relieved from applying the law. Rather than turning to the law, the arbitral tribunal should apply common commercial sense, making its decisions based on what it deems to be fair and reasonable, taking into account the peculiarities of the parties' relationship. While the arbitral tribunal is still required to provide reasons for its decisions, the reasoning need not be legal reasoning but should rather be based on principles of fairness and justice. It has been said that if an arbitrator acting as *ex aequo et bono* wishes to rely on and apply the law, he must explain and justify why he is doing so.[151] 3.165

In a detailed analysis of *ex aequo et bono*, Trakman explains that:[152] 3.166

> If the adjudicative decision is to be 'fair', it must be fair against the background of the practical reasonableness of the respective claims of the parties. If it is to be 'just', it must produce consequences that are just in light of customs and usages that are related to the interests of those parties. If it is to be practically reasonable, it must be reasonable in light of the interdisciplinary context surrounding the dispute, not because of the wholly personal conceptions of fairness of whosoever happens to be the adjudicator.
>
> ...
>
> In particular, the process of deciding *ex aequo et bono* is grounded in notions of common sense, practical expediency and fairness that are not necessarily attributed to law. Ultimately, internal limits upon discretion *ex aequo et bono* depend on a functional not a formal process of reasoning. They hold that, no matter how informal and expeditious, adjudicative proceedings should be transparent and applied evenhandedly to the parties.
>
> ...
>
> the foundations of ex aequo et bono are situated in realistic decision-making that is directed at resolving practical but often complex problems. The decision-maker is bound neither to apply nor to disregard the law as a matter of principle, but to exercise discriminating judgment on the practical reasons by which to decide each case. Those practical reasons are informed by specific patterns of fact, by identifiable party practices and by applicable customs and usages. The practical reasons that guide decisions ex aequo et bono may also justify adopting alternative processes of dispute resolution, including but not limited to those that are provided for by law.

While arbitrators deciding *ex aequo et bono* need not apply the law, there is some debate as to whether they should apply the terms of the parties' contract literally, or whether they may digress from those terms. One expert contends that 3.167

---

150 Mustill, op. cit. fn 131, p. 103.
151 Detailed guidelines on how an arbitrator acting *ex aequo et bono* should conduct himself and the arbitration are provided in 'Amiable Composition: Report of ICC France Working Group', *International Business Law Journal/Revue de Droit des Affaires Internationales*, Article No. 6 of Dec 2005, pp. 753–768.
152 L Trakman, 'Ex Aequo et Bono: De-mystifying an Ancient Concept', (2007) *University of New South Wales Faculty of Law Research Series* 39, at Sections V, VI and VII respectively (footnotes omitted). L Trakman is the former Dean of Law at the University of New South Wales, Australia. See also M Rubino-Sammartano, 'Amiable Compositeur (Joint Mandate to Settle) and Ex Bono et Aequo (Discretional Authority to Mitigate Strict Law): Apparent Synonyms Revisited', (1992) 9(1) *Journal of International Arbitration* 5.

'the better view, adopted by a majority of commentators and other authorities, is that arbitrators may depart from the terms of the parties' contract in fashioning a fair and equitable result, provided that they do not rewrite the structure of the agreement'.[153] However, this does not seem to sit comfortably with the Model Law. Article 28(4) of the Model Law provides that 'in all cases' the arbitral tribunal must decide in accordance with the contract and trade usages. The positioning of Article 28(4) numerically *after* Article 28(3) suggests that Article 28(4) applies to and limits Article 28(3).

3.168 This issue was examined in a case before the Court of Appeal of Quebec, Canada, interpreting the equivalent article of the Quebec Code of Civil Procedure, which is based on the Model Law.[154] The main issue was whether the arbitrator, under Article 944.10(3) of the Code of Civil Procedure, had exceeded his mandate of *amiable compositeur* when he decided to ignore two provisions of the parties' contractual accounting formula. The court affirmed that the arbitrator had indeed exceeded his powers. As such, it found that Article 944.10(3) applies both to an 'ordinary' arbitrator as well as one acting as *amiable compositeur*. Although an arbitrator is entitled to a certain degree of discretion[155] when acting as *amiable compositeur*, he cannot remove or rewrite provisions in the parties' contract, unless the parties have explicitly authorised him to do so.[156] In the course of her judgment, Judge Bich noted:[157]

> Par. 66 The difference between an 'ordinary' arbitrator and an arbitrator acting as amiable compositeur therefore rests mainly on the fact that the former is bound to apply the rules of law, mainly the 'rules of positive law',... regardless whether the law in question is mandatory, whereas the latter, who is still bound by rules of public policy, including the rules of natural justice, can, on the basis of equity, interpret the applicability of non-mandatory laws or can even decide to depart from them in a manner conforming to the general principles of law....
>
> ...
>
> Par. 99 The power of amiable composition cannot, and should not, call into question the fact that an arbitrator's primary role is to adjudicate disputes and not to substitute his own views for those of the parties in renegotiating disputed contractual clauses.
>
> Par. 100 Although there is a fine line between contractual interpretation and contractual revision with a view to adapting the contract to changed circumstances, it should be highlighted that granting the power of amiable composition does not ipso facto grant a power of adaptation. The parties must be explicit if they intend to grant that power to the arbitrator.

3.169 The Court of Appeal's approach seems sensible. First, it conforms with the plain language of Article 28(4) of the Model Law. Second, it is legally logical.

---

153 Born, 2009, op. cit. fn 27, p. 2242. See also the discussion in the Final Report of the ICC Commission on Arbitration's Task Force on Amiable Composition and *ex aequo et bono*, September 2008, p. 12 et seq.
154 *Coderre v Coderre* (2008 QCCA 888), Court of Appeal of Quebec, 13 May 2008. Article 944.10 of the Quebec Code of Civil Procedure is almost identical to Article 28 of the Model Law except that it omits Article 28(1).
155 Ibid., see particularly at para 95.
156 Ibid., see particularly at paras 82–87 and 98.
157 Authors' own translation from the original French.

International arbitration is essentially contractual so arbitrators should, so far as possible, limit themselves to what the parties have agreed. That is true regardless of the applicable law or whether the arbitral tribunal has been authorised to decide *ex aequo et bono*. In general the parties' true intentions should prevail over the plain language of a contractual clause, a rule of contract interpretation that is recognised in some form in most legal systems. But it would seem to us that only in an extreme case of unfairness should an arbitrator deciding *ex aequo et bono* ignore or modify the terms of the parties' contract, unless the arbitrator has been explicitly authorised to do so.

3.170 As also indicated in the extract from Judge Bich's judgment above, there are other legal limits to what an arbitrator deciding as *ex aequo et bono* can do. He or she is of course still limited by public policy and mandatory rules of law, just as an arbitrator applying the law is so limited.

3.171 In practice, parties very rarely expressly empower an arbitral tribunal to decide *ex aequo et bono* or similar.[158] Perhaps parties and their legal advisors prefer the structure and perceived predictability of the law and are comforted by the fact that international arbitrators will generally strive to ensure that the outcomes of their decisions are fair. Nonetheless, *ex aequo et bono* clauses may be to the distinct advantage of parties where the law is not well suited to their relationship. More guidance – such as that from the Quebec decision mentioned above – may provide parties with increased confidence in *ex aequo et bono* in the future.

---

[158] The ICC International Court of Arbitration received approximately three new arbitrations each year from 2003–2008 where the parties agreed that the arbitrator would decide the case *ex aequo et bono* or similar. In one ICC case in 2010, the parties decided to change their choice of law (originally a state law) for amiable composition mid way through the arbitration proceedings, after a partial award had been issued but before a final award was issued.

4

Arbitration agreement

1 Introduction

4.1   Arbitration agreements embody the consent of the parties to submit their disputes to arbitration. In essence they oust the jurisdiction of domestic courts to decide certain disputes and instead empower an arbitral tribunal to resolve those disputes. The extent and scope of these two functions are dependent on the words of the arbitration agreement and the laws governing both that agreement and the arbitration proceedings. The arbitration agreement is especially important in determining the jurisdiction and powers of an arbitral tribunal.

4.2   Some suggest that arbitration agreements are so powerful that they are supranational and beyond domestic laws. The French courts have on occasion adopted this position. They have held that an arbitration agreement is independent of all national laws and forms a supranational source of authority for arbitral jurisdiction.

4.3   This chapter begins with a general discussion of the form and formal requirements of arbitration agreements in Section 2. Section 3 explains the concept of the doctrine of separability, which concerns the separation of an arbitration clause from the contract in which it is contained. Section 4 moves on to consider the issues of identity, non-signatories and capacity, following which Section 5 addresses the requirement of a defined legal relationship. The focus of the chapter then turns to the issues of consolidation, joinder and intervention of third parties in Section 6. Section 7 considers the enforcement of arbitration agreements. Section 8 covers the important topic of arbitrability and distinguishes between subjective arbitrability and objective arbitrability. Finally Section 9 addresses the drafting of arbitration agreements.

2 Arbitration agreement

2.1 Is an arbitration agreement necessary?

The short answer is yes: an arbitration agreement is necessary in order to institute arbitration proceedings. The Philippines Supreme Court (among many others) has stated this in clear and simple language:[1]   4.4

> Disputes do not go to arbitration unless and until the parties have agreed to abide by the arbitrator's decision. Necessarily, a contract is required for arbitration to take place and to be binding.

Every international commercial arbitration requires an arbitration agreement. Arguably, there are exceptions where no arbitration agreement exists but where the parties are treated as though one had been concluded between them. For example, the definition of arbitration agreements in Article 7(2) of the Model Law includes 'an exchange of statements of claim and defence in which the existence of an agreement is alleged by one party and not denied by another'. An arbitration could thus be based on the failure to deny an arbitration agreement even if that agreement did not in fact exist. Similarly, arbitrations may take place without an arbitration agreement if an estoppel or similar legal doctrine operates to preclude a party from denying the existence of an arbitration agreement. This may occur when that party fails to object to the absence of an agreement during the early stages of an arbitration or because, on the basis of a party's conduct, it would be unfair for that party to deny the existence of an arbitration agreement. The effect of estoppel on arbitration agreements is discussed below.[2]   4.5

Furthermore, in some domestic jurisdictions, the law provides for so-called 'compulsory arbitration'. This refers to the court practice of compelling parties to submit their dispute to arbitration whether or not the parties have signed an arbitration agreement.   4.6

Another exception occurs in the context of investor-state arbitration. The state's consent to arbitrate may be given in a bilateral or multilateral treaty, such as the 1988 Agreement between the Government of Australia and the Government of the People's Republic of China on the Reciprocal Encouragement and Protection of Investments,[3] or the North American Free Trade Agreement.[4] In this situation there is no direct arbitration agreement between the state and an investor who institutes arbitration against that state. The consent to arbitrate is derived in two separate phases. The state provides its consent in the provisions of the treaty and the investor's consent is deemed to be provided when   4.7

---

1 *Jorge Gonzales v Climax Mining Ltd*, G.R. No. 161957/ G.R. No. 167994 [2007] PHSC 6.
2 See Section 4.2.1.
3 Signed and entered into force on 11 July 1988, (1988) *Australian Treaty Series* no. 14.
4 Signed 12 December 1992, entered into force 1 January 1994, 32 *International Legal Materials* 296 and 605.

it institutes arbitration proceedings pursuant to the treaty. Consequently, an arbitration takes place in the absence of a direct arbitration agreement between the parties. Jan Paulsson has famously described this type of dispute resolution as 'arbitration without privity'.[5] Investor-state arbitration is examined in Chapter 10.

2.2 Types of arbitration agreements

4.8 Arbitration agreements may be concluded before or after the dispute arises. The latter are called 'submission agreements'. In practice, most arbitration agreements are contained in contracts. Submission agreements are relatively rare because once a dispute arises one side may see an advantage in arbitration while the other refuses to arbitrate in order not to give the first side an advantage and/or to delay resolution of the case.

4.9 If the arbitration agreement is in the form of a clause contained in a substantive contract (which is the norm), the arbitration agreement will generally be considered as having been formed at the same time as the contract is formed. However, despite the identical time of formation and the fact that the arbitration agreement is a clause of the substantive contract, the arbitration agreement is normally treated as an agreement separate from the rest of the contract.[6] This means that it is possible for an arbitration agreement to have been made even though the substantive contract in which that agreement is contained never came into existence. In these circumstances the arbitration agreement is preserved to resolve a dispute relating, for example, to the formation of the substantive contract.

2.3 Definition and formal requirements of an arbitration agreement

2.3.1 General

4.10 The 1985 version[7] of Article 7 of the Model Law provides a useful definition of arbitration agreements. However, it must be recalled that the particular form requirements may vary from country to country.

> *Article 7. Definition and form of arbitration agreement*
> (1) 'Arbitration agreement' is an agreement by the parties to submit to arbitration all or certain disputes which have arisen or which may arise between them in respect of a defined legal relationship, whether contractual or not. An arbitration

---

5 J Paulsson, 'Arbitration without Privity', (1995) 10 *International Centre for Settlement of Investment Disputes Review – Foreign Investment Law Journal* 232.
6 See Section 3.
7 This is the version of the Model Law that is most prevalent. At the time of writing only Australia, (Florida, USA), Ireland, Mauritius, New Zealand, Peru, Rwanda, Singapore and Slovenia have implemented some or all of the 2006 Model Law amendments. Hong Kong is understood to be in the process of passing legislative amendments. See also the discussion of the Model Law in Chapter 2.

agreement may be in the form of an arbitration clause in the contract or in the form of a separate agreement.
(2) The arbitration agreement shall be in writing. An agreement is in writing if it is contained in a document signed by the parties or in an exchange of letters, telex, telegrams or other means of telecommunication which provide a record of the agreement, or in an exchange of statements of claim and defence in which the existence of an agreement is alleged by one party and not denied by another. The reference in a contract to a document containing an arbitration clause constitutes an arbitration agreement provided that the contract is in writing and the reference is such as to make that clause part of the contract.

The 1985 Model Law Article 7(2) was directly inspired by the New York Convention. Articles II(1) and (2) of the New York Convention use much of the same language.[8]   4.11

From the plain language of Article 7(2) of the 1985 Model Law and Article II of the New York Convention it appears essential that a valid arbitration agreement be in writing. However, this is not quite correct. A distinction should be drawn between a requirement which, if not satisfied, renders an arbitration agreement void (sometimes called a solemn form requirement); and a requirement which is not a condition but an evidentiary rule making it difficult to prove the existence or validity of the arbitration agreement (sometimes called a proof form requirement). Reading closely it can be seen that both the Model Law and the New York Convention require that an arbitration agreement be <u>evidenced</u> in writing.[9] An oral arbitration agreement could therefore be valid and enforceable if the consent of all parties was recorded in writing.   4.12

The writing requirement was further relaxed in the 2006 version of the Model Law. In that version, two optional texts for Article 7 are provided. The second does not stipulate any writing requirement whatsoever: 4.13

Option I

Article 7. Definition and form of arbitration agreement
(1) 'Arbitration agreement' is an agreement by the parties to submit to arbitration all or certain disputes which have arisen or which may arise between them in respect of a defined legal relationship, whether contractual or not. An arbitration agreement may be in the form of an arbitration clause in a contract or in the form of a separate agreement.

---

8 New York Convention Article II provides:
1. Each Contracting State shall recognize an agreement in writing under which the parties undertake to submit to arbitration all or any differences which have arisen or which may arise between them in respect of a defined legal relationship, whether contractual or not, concerning a subject matter capable of settlement by arbitration.
2. The term 'agreement in writing' shall include an arbitral clause in a contract or an arbitration agreement, signed by the parties or contained in an exchange of letters or telegrams.

9 For a contrary view on the New York Convention, see JF Poudret and S Besson, *Comparative Law of International Arbitration*, 2nd edn, Thompson, 2007, at para 188.

(2) The arbitration agreement shall be in writing.
(3) An arbitration agreement is in writing if its content is recorded in any form, whether or not the arbitration agreement or contract has been concluded orally, by conduct, or by other means.
(4) The requirement that an arbitration agreement be in writing is met by an electronic communication if the information contained therein is accessible so as to be useable for subsequent reference; 'electronic communication' means any communication that the parties make by means of data messages; 'data message' means information generated, sent, received or stored by electronic, magnetic, optical or similar means, including, but not limited to, electronic data interchange (EDI), electronic mail, telegram, telex or telecopy.
(5) Furthermore, an arbitration agreement is in writing if it is contained in an exchange of statements of claim and defence in which the existence of an agreement is alleged by one party and not denied by the other.
(6) The reference in a contract to any document containing an arbitration clause constitutes an arbitration agreement in writing, provided that the reference is such as to make that clause part of the contract.

Option II

Article 7. Definition of arbitration agreement

'Arbitration agreement' is an agreement by the parties to submit to arbitration all or certain disputes which have arisen or which may arise between them in respect of a defined legal relationship, whether contractual or not.

4.14 The note accompanying the 2006 version of the Model Law observes that the movement away from a strictly enforced writing requirement reflects modern realities:[10]

> It was pointed out by practitioners that, in a number of situations, the drafting of a written document was impossible or impractical. In such cases, where the willingness of the parties to arbitrate was not in question, the validity of the arbitration agreement should be recognized. For that reason, article 7 was amended in 2006 to better conform to international contract practices. In amending article 7, the Commission adopted two options, which reflect two different approaches on the question of definition and form of arbitration agreement. The first approach follows the detailed structure of the original 1985 text.... It follows the New York Convention in requiring the written form of the arbitration agreement but recognizes a record of the 'contents' of the agreement 'in any form' as equivalent to traditional 'writing'. The agreement to arbitrate may be entered into in any form (e.g. including orally) as long as the content of the agreement is recorded. This new rule is significant in that it no longer requires signatures of the parties or an exchange of messages between the parties.... It also states that 'the reference in a contract to any document' (for example, general conditions) 'containing an arbitration clause constitutes an arbitration agreement in writing provided that the reference is such as to make that clause part of the contract'. It thus clarifies that applicable contract law remains available to determine the level of consent necessary for a party to become bound by an arbitration agreement allegedly made 'by reference'.

---

[10] UNCITRAL Model Law on International Commercial Arbitration 1985, with amendments as adopted in 2006, United Nations Publication, Sales No. E.08.V.4 (2008), at 28.

The second approach defines the arbitration agreement in a manner that omits any form requirement.

4.15 Even prior to its adoption of the 2006 revision to the Model Law, New Zealand expressly recognised arbitration agreements made orally and similarly recognises any resulting award.[11] The language of the New Zealand statute, '[a]n arbitration agreement may be made orally or in writing,' is expressed inclusively. This position can be contrasted with the negative phrasing of Hong Kong's Arbitration Ordinance, Section 2AC of which expressly states that for the purpose of that Ordinance an agreement is not an arbitration agreement if it is not in writing.[12] This is a subtle but significant drafting difference – the latter may be considered an example of a solemn form requirement as explained above.[13] However, fortunately Section 2AC has been interpreted very liberally. In the Hong Kong District Court decision of *Winbond Electronics (HK) Ltd v Achieva Components China Ltd* it was noted:[14]

> H Smal Ltd. v Goldroyce Garment Ltd. [1994] 2 HKC 526, 529 where it was said that 'There is no basis for arguing that the arbitration agreement can be established by a course of dealings or the conduct of the parties... unless there is a record whereby the defendant has in writing assented to the agreement to arbitrate.' In view of the present Section 2AC, what was there said or held is no longer the law – the arbitration agreement may now be established by a course of dealings or conduct of the parties provided there is reference to terms (of arbitration) that are in writing.

4.16 As the quoted passage indicates, the statute in Hong Kong was amended between these two decisions. Somewhat appropriately, Neil Kaplan commented on *H Smal Ltd v Goldroyce Garment Ltd* in a lecture given approximately two years later, and after he had retired from judicial service. Kaplan said of the decision:[15]

> I venture to suggest that this decision, even if technically correct, produces an absurd result which is inconsistent with commercial reality. There was no doubt that the parties entered into a contract which was contained in or evidenced by the written order and B's conduct. Why on earth should the arbitration clause in the contract require to be established by any higher degree of proof than the basic contractual terms themselves? I hasten to add that I am not advocating the bringing within the New York Convention of oral agreements to arbitrate. All I am suggesting is that on the facts of the case under discussion there are sufficient legal theories available which could lead to a form of words which would bring the case not only within the Model Law but also the New York Convention.

---

11 New Zealand Arbitration Act 1996 Article 7(1), Schedule 1. 'An arbitration agreement may be made orally or in writing. Subject to [section 11], an arbitration agreement may be in the form of an arbitration clause in a contract or in the form of a separate agreement.'
12 Section 2AC(1) of the Hong Kong Arbitration Ordinance states 'An agreement is not an arbitration agreement for the purposes of this Ordinance unless it is in writing'.
13 See para 4.12.
14 [2007] HKCU 1514, at 6.
15 N Kaplan, 'Is the Need for Writing as Expressed in the New York Convention and the Model Law Out of Step with Commercial Practice?', (1996) 12(1) *Arbitration International* 28, at p. 30.

4.17 In response to the sorts of criticisms and observations made by Kaplan, UNCITRAL formulated the 'Recommendation regarding the interpretation of article II, paragraph 2, and article VII, paragraph 1, of the Convention on the Recognition and Enforcement of Foreign Arbitral Awards, done in New York, 10 June 1958, adopted by the United Nations Commission on International Trade Law on 7 July 2006 at its thirty-ninth session'. In relevant part it states:

> Taking into account also enactments of domestic legislation, as well as case law, more favourable than the Convention in respect of form requirement [sic] governing arbitration agreements, arbitration proceedings and the enforcement of arbitral awards,
>
> Considering that, in interpreting the Convention, regard is to be had to the need to promote recognition and enforcement of arbitral awards,
> 1. *Recommends* that article II, paragraph 2, of the Convention on the Recognition and Enforcement of Foreign Arbitral Awards, done in New York, 10 June 1958, be applied recognizing that the circumstances described therein are not exhaustive.

4.18 Kaplan's view is attractive, especially his rhetoric as to 'Why on earth should the arbitration clause in the contract require to be established by any higher degree of proof than the basic contractual terms themselves?' Ultimately, the role of the writing requirement is to assist in proving that an arbitration agreement exists and the terms of that arbitration agreement. So long as that proof can be established, then there appears to be no reason to place a significantly higher burden on a party trying to establish the existence or content of an arbitration agreement than one trying to establish the existence or content of any other contractual obligation.[16] The evolution in the Model Law and UNCITRAL's guidance on interpretation are therefore to be commended.

4.19 Whereas the discussion above considers the policy behind the 'in writing' requirement, we now turn to consider what 'in writing' actually means. Increasingly, countries are expanding the definition of writing to include examples of newer forms of communication, such as electronic communications. These clarifications are usually drafted to remove doubt.[17] Hong Kong adopted a different approach by defining writing as 'includ[ing] any means by which information can be recorded'.[18] The writing requirement must necessarily be understood with reference to its underlying purpose, and interpreted according to technology and business practices that prevail today, not those that existed over 50 or 25 years ago when, respectively, the New York Convention and the Model Law were originally drafted.

---

16 A view shared by JD Lew, LA Mistelis and SM Kröll, *Comparative International Commercial Arbitration*, Kluwer Law International, 2003, para 7–9.
17 For instance, the specific addition of electronic communications, found in Article 1 of the Supreme People's Court's Interpretation of Several Issues regarding the Application of the Arbitration Law of the PRC (FaShi [2006] No. 7), the Australian International Arbitration Amendment Act 2010, and Singapore International Arbitration (Amendment) Act 2009 to note just a few examples. However, specific note should be taken that the Singaporean amendments only apply to Part II of the Singapore International Arbitration Act and not Part III. The Explanatory Statement which accompanies the Bill states that the distinction is because Part III deals with the New York Convention which does not have a modernised definition of an arbitration agreement.
18 Hong Kong Arbitration Ordinance, Section 2AC(4).

2.3.2 Incorporation by reference

Difficulties can arise when the arbitration agreement is said to have been incorporated by reference. This situation arises where parties have not included an arbitration agreement in their own contract, but merely include a reference to another document which contains an arbitration agreement. The question is whether the arbitration agreement in the other document is binding on the parties to the contract. 4.20

Although some arbitration laws provide guidance, the question of whether or not a clause has been properly incorporated must ultimately be considered in light of the law governing the arbitration agreement. Born notes that different jurisdictions have adopted different approaches to this issue. After commenting that most jurisdictions will recognise the incorporation of an arbitration clause where it has been specifically drawn to the attention of a party, he observes that where there is a general reference to the other document as a whole, 'there is little apparent uniformity among different national legal regimes'.[19] As we explain below, there appears to be a consistent approach adopted by the majority of countries within the Asia-Pacific region. 4.21

Where we find Born persuasive is that the question of incorporation by reference should not in any way be confused with or influenced by the doctrine of separability. That doctrine is dealt with in detail in the next section. Essentially, it treats an arbitration clause in a contract as a separate and independent agreement from the contract containing it. Born notes that some might incorrectly assume that because the arbitration agreement is considered separate, it could not as a matter of construction be incorporated without some specific reference.[20] Indeed, denying that an arbitration agreement has been incorporated by reference on this reasoning alone would be insufficient. 4.22

The general issue of incorporation by reference has come before different national courts in this region on a number of occasions. It typically arises in the context of an application to stay court proceedings. The factual scenarios often involve charterparty agreements and bills of lading, where reference is made in the bill of lading to the charterparty agreement – and the arbitration agreement is found in the charterparty agreement. Although there have been some exceptions, the general approach adopted in the Asia-Pacific region is that it is not necessary to refer specifically to the arbitration agreement for it to be incorporated by reference. The test is simply whether the parties intended to incorporate the arbitration agreement. A specific reference, while not strictly necessary, is nevertheless advisable to avoid sometimes lengthy arguments on the point. 4.23

---

19 G Born, *International Commercial Arbitration*, Kluwer, 2009, p. 700. For other commentaries on this issue in a European context, see V Van Houtte, 'Consent to Arbitration through Agreement to Printed Contracts: The Continental Experience', 2000 16(1) *Arbitration International* 1; L Huber, 'Arbitration Clauses "by Reference"', *ASA Special Series No. 8* (December 1994), pp. 78–88; M Blessing, 'The New International Arbitration Law in Switzerland: A Significant Step Towards Liberalism', (1988) 5(2) *Journal of International Arbitration* 9, at p. 30.
20 Born, ibid., p. 703.

4.24　Traditional arguments for requiring a specific written reference reflect a belief that an arbitration agreement is particularly special because it precludes avenues of state judicial recourse. As Born has noted this reasoning has been discredited in the context of international arbitration. He further states:[21]

> ... international arbitration is adopted in large part to avoid the resulting jurisdictional disputes and confusion, which frequently deprive one or both parties of effective access to a judicial forum or legal remedy. Accordingly, whatever the rule in domestic cases, there is no satisfactory basis for imposing any heightened proof requirement for establishing the existence of international arbitration agreements.

4.25　The Malaysian Court of Appeal decisions in *Bauer (M) Sdn Bhd v Daewoo Corp*,[22] and *Bina Puri Sdn Bhd v EP Engineering Sdn Bhd*[23] endorse the view that the test is one of intent, with or without express wording. In the latter case, Justice Gopal Sri Ram was called upon to consider the incorporation of an arbitration clause in the absence of specific wording. Following a review of various authorities, he observed:[24]

> The principle then to be distilled from the decided cases is this. Whether a term or a clause in one contract has been incorporated in another depends on the facts and circumstances of each case. There may be express incorporation or incorporation by conduct.

4.26　The subsequent Malaysian High Court case of *Usahasama SPNB-LTAT Sdn Bhd v Borneo Synergy (M) Sdn Bhd*[25] has also adopted this test. Similarly, Justice Lim Teong Qwee of the Singaporean High Court stated in *Concordia Agritrading Pte Ltd v Cornelder Hoogewerff (Singapore) Pte Ltd*:[26]

> I think it is a question of construction in each case. There must be a clear intention to incorporate an arbitration clause. If the words of incorporation are specific that intention may well have been clearly expressed.

4.27　In *Conagra International Fertiliser v Lief Investments*,[27] Justice Rolfe of the New South Wales Supreme Court considered a long line of authorities from both Australian and UK courts. The judgment contains an enlightening discussion of those authorities. Although not personally convinced, Justice Rolfe reached the view, based on the weight of authority, that specific reference was required to incorporate an arbitration agreement pursuant to Australian law. His Honour's preferred position would have been to determine simply on a case by case basis whether the parties had intended to incorporate the term absent a specific

---

21 Ibid., p. 647.
22 [1999] 4 MLJ 545. This is an interesting case because although the Court of Appeal agreed with the trial judge that the parties had not incorporated an arbitration agreement into their contract, it then found that the acts of the respondent in participating in the arbitration estopped it from subsequently denying the arbitrator's jurisdiction. For a further discussion of this point see Section 4.2.1.
23 [2008] 3 MLJ 564.
24 Ibid., at 571.
25 [2009] MLJU 0001.
26 [2001] 1 SLR 222 at 228.
27 (1997) 141 FLR 124.

reference. This is akin to the approach adopted by the Malaysian courts noted above. The *Conagra* decision was appealed to the New South Wales Court of Appeal. That court found that no terms had been incorporated. However it also observed that 'if the parties had agreed to the incorporation of the terms and conditions of Sinochem's standard contract and these could have been identified with certainty, [then] there was no textual or policy consideration'.[28] Therefore the position in Australia (at least for New South Wales) should now be simply a question of intent without the need for any particular wording.

Likewise, it appears that South Korea follows the same approach. The South Korean Supreme Court has noted that as a general rule explicit reference is required, but:[29]   4.28

> for an effective incorporation to take place an assignee (a holder) of the bill of lading knew or should have known about the existence of such an arbitration clause to be incorporated and an arbitration clause should not contradict with the other terms and conditions of the bill of lading after being incorporated; moreover, such arbitration clause of vessel hiring contract should be phrased comprehensively so that an arbitration clause of vessel hiring contract covers not only disputes arising between an owner of vessel and a vessel hiring person, but also applies to a holder of bill of lading.

The exception outlined above renders this position as simply a question of fact – did the parties intend to incorporate the arbitration agreement?   4.29

The 1990 decision of the Philippines Supreme Court in *National Union Fire Insurance Company of Pittsburg Pa/American International Underwriter (Phil) Inc v Stolt-Nielsen Philippines Inc and Court of Appeals*[30] similarly states that no explicit reference is required:[31]   4.30

> It is settled law that the charter may be made part of the contract under which the goods are carried by an appropriate reference in the Bill of Lading [...]. This should include the provision on arbitration even without a specific stipulation to that effect. The entire contract must be read together and its clauses interpreted in relation to one another and not by parts.

In the 2008 Hong Kong Court of First Instance decision of *Parkson Holdings Ltd v Vincent Lai & Partners (HK) Ltd*,[32] Justice Burrell accepted that an arbitration clause in a domestic arbitration had been incorporated notwithstanding the absence of explicit wording to that effect. This decision accorded with the position he had taken in the 2003 case of *Tsang Yuk Ching T/A Tsang Ching Kee Eng Co v Fu Shing Rush Door Joint Venture Co Ltd*.[33] In his 2003 decision Justice Burrell quoted the passage below from *Gay Construction Pty Ltd v Caledonian Techmore*   4.31

---

28 [1998] NSWSC 481 per Sheller JA.
29 Supreme Court Decision 2000Da70064 [2003] KRSC 1 (10 January 2003). This quotation is taken from the website of the South Korean Supreme Court, http://library.scourt.go.kr/jsp/html/decision/2.4. 2000Da70064.htm. However, it should be noted that the site warns that the translation is provisional and subject to revision.
30 184 SCRA 682 (G.R. No. 87958 April 26, 1990). See also E Lizares, *Arbitration in the Philippines and the Alternative Dispute Resolution Act of 2004*, EPL Publications, 2004, at pp. 63–64.
31 184 SCRA 682 at 687.
32 [2008] HKCU 1985.
33 [2003] HKCU 1072.

*(Building) Ltd.*³⁴ This was a case involving an international arbitration and in which the Hong Kong High Court considered Article 7 of the Model Law. In *Gay Construction* Justice Kaplan (as he then was) stated:³⁵

> To require a specific reference to the arbitration clause would be far too restrictive and clearly was not intended by those drafting the Model Law.

4.32 There have been cases in Hong Kong which appear to take a contrary view; however, they can be distinguished as not being exactly on point.³⁶ In light of the persuasive decisions delivered by Justices Kaplan and Burrell referred to above, it can be said that the test in Hong Kong, like those countries discussed above, is simply a question of whether there was an intention to incorporate the arbitration clause, and there is no requirement that there be a specific reference.

4.33 Proceedings under the New York Convention to enforce an award are another context in which incorporation of an arbitration clause by reference raises difficulties. Article II(2) of the New York Convention does not refer directly to incorporation by reference. It states:

> (2) The term 'agreement in writing' shall include an arbitral clause in a contract or an arbitration agreement, signed by the parties or contained in an exchange of letters or telegrams.

4.34 As Di Pietro notes:³⁷

> Article II does not deal directly with incorporation of arbitration clauses by reference. Therefore, it is unclear whether Article II(2) only applies to cases where the arbitration clause is contained in the documents exchanged by the parties or whether it also applies to cases where:
> (a) although the documents exchanged do not contain an arbitration clause, nonetheless, they make express reference to an arbitration clause contained in another document (a so-called *relatio perfecta*); or
> (b) the documents exchanged by the parties do not contain an arbitration clause but make reference to a document containing one, although there is no express reference to it in the exchange of documents (a so-called *relatio imperfecta*).
> ... the prevailing case law seems to support the argument that the exchange of documents described under Article II(2) should be read as entailing scenario (a) above. Whether scenario (b) applies is much more controversial.

---

34 [1994] 2 HKC 562.
35 Ibid., at 566.
36 See, e.g. *Owners of and/or other Persons entitled to sue in respect of cargo lately laden on board the ship or vessel Yaoki v Owners of and/or Demise Charterers of the ship or vessel & Quotyaoki & Quot and the ships or vessels listed in schedule hereto* [2006] HKCU 765. At para 14 the court suggests that '[t]he general discussion on this subject in Carver shows that incorporation of [an] arbitration clause is possible if sufficiently clear words exist in the bill of lading incorporation provision and the intention to incorporate such clause is clear'. The court in this case was being asked to consider whether an exclusive jurisdiction clause had been incorporated. Applying the rationale established for arbitration agreements, it found that such a reference had not been incorporated. The court was further asked to consider whether a vague reference to terms could override a clear and express intent to arbitrate. It found that it could not. For China, see also Reply of Supreme People's Court to Request for Enforcement of a UK Arbitral Award by Han Jin Shipping Co., Ltd (Civil 4, Miscellaneous), No. 53 (2005).
37 D Di Pietro, 'Incorporation of Arbitration Clauses by Reference', (2004) 21(5) *Journal of International Arbitration* 439, at p. 441.

In the context of an enforcement proceeding, Di Pietro refers to the *Jiangxi Prov'l Metal & Minerals Imp & Exp Corp v Sulanser Co*[38] decision of the Supreme Court of Hong Kong. In that case the court reasoned that the omission in Article II(2) of the word 'only' meant that the definition in that provision was not exhaustive. Di Pietro observes that this reasoning may not sit as well with the other language versions of the Convention, such as the French and Spanish versions which do use terms equivalent to 'only'.[39]

3 Doctrine of separability

The doctrine of separability treats an arbitration agreement contained in a contract as a separate agreement from the contract itself. The Supreme Court of the Philippines has noted:[40]

> The doctrine of separability, or severability as other writers call it, enunciates that an arbitration agreement is independent of the main contract. The arbitration agreement is to be treated as a separate agreement and the arbitration agreement does not automatically terminate when the contract of which it is part comes to an end.

The doctrine is supported by case law[41] and arbitration rules.[42] As the following discussion demonstrates it is also found in arbitration laws. Even if it were not so supported, the compelling logic of the doctrine would make it difficult to present a reasoned argument against it.[43]

Article 16(1) of the Model Law codifies the doctrine of separability as follows:

Article 16 – Competence of arbitral tribunal to rule on its jurisdiction
1. The arbitral tribunal may rule on its own jurisdiction, including any objections with respect to the existence or validity of the arbitration agreement. For that purpose, an arbitration clause which forms part of a contract shall be treated as an agreement independent of the other terms of the contract. A decision by the arbitral tribunal that the contract is null and void shall not entail ipso jure the invalidity of the arbitration clause.

---

38 [1995] 2 HKC 373.
39 Di Pietro, op. cit. fn 37, p. 442, n 7 which states: 'The French version of art. II(2) reads: "[o]n entend par 'convention écrite' une clause compromissoire insérée dans un contrat, ou un compromis, signés par les parties ou contenus dans un échange de lettres ou de télégrammes."' The phrase 'on entend', which in this context can be translated into the English 'it is understood' seems much narrower than the phrase 'shall include' employed in the English version and seems also to contradict what was advocated in the decision taken by the Supreme Court. Similar observation [sic] can be made with reference to the Spanish version according to which: '[l]a expresión "acuerdo por escrito" denotará una cláusula compromisoria incluida en un contrato o un compromiso, firmados por las partes o contenidos en un canje de cartas o telegramas'. Also here, the verb 'denotar', which can be translated into the English 'to denote', seems to challenge the interpretation advocated by the Supreme Court in Hong Kong.
40 *Jorge Gonzales, et al. v Climax Mining Ltd., et al.* GR No. 161957, 22 January 2007, citing P Capper, *International Arbitration: A Handbook*, Informa Legal Publishing, 2004, p. 12.
41 *Comandate Marine Corp v Pan Australia Shipping Pty Ltd* [2006] FCAFC 192; *Fung Sang Trading Ltd v Kai Sun See Products and Food Co Ltd* [1992] HKCU 380; *H Smal Ltd v Goldroyce Garment Ltd* [1994] 2 HKC 526; T Tateishi, 'Inquisitorial Approach in Dispute Resolution – A Japanese Way to Mete Out Justice', 44 *WaveLength – Bulletin of the Japan Shipping Exchange Inc* 8, at pp. 14–15 citing Heisei 10 (wa) 3851; Hanrei Jiho no. 1707.
42 See, e.g. HKIAC Rules Article 20.2; SIAC Rules, Rule 25.1; ACICA Rules Article 24.2.
43 However, see A Baron, 'Arbitration and the Fiction of Severability', (1999) 19 *Australian Bar Review* 50, at pp. 50–66 and discussion below.

4.39   Within this region, most laws on separability follow the Model Law example. However, in the past China was considered a notable exception. Article 19 of the Chinese Arbitration Law was previously criticised as 'one of the most ambiguous provisions of the [Arbitration Law]', providing only 'partial separability'.[44] Now this law must be interpreted in the light of the Supreme People's Court's Interpretation of Several Issues regarding the Application of the Arbitration Law of the PRC.[45] As a consequence 'the arbitration agreement is now unconditionally independent and, accordingly, an arbitral tribunal has the jurisdiction over the dispute even if the existence and effect of the main contract is questioned'.[46]

4.40   Without the doctrine of separability, or some equivalent, the entire arbitral process could be frustrated – a party wanting to avoid arbitration could simply assert that the contract was void and therefore go to court. But the doctrine of separability is not without its critics. Some commentators disagree with the present manifestation of the doctrine of separability, describing it as a legal fiction that favours commercial pragmatism over logic.[47] Others support the importance of the doctrine in general but dispute its application where there is an allegation that the contract never existed at all.[48] These two criticisms are discussed in turn below.

4.41   The core problem identified by those arguing that the doctrine is a legal fiction is that if a contract is void ab initio then as a matter of law it never had any effect; necessarily implying that the arbitration agreement never had any legal effect either. In our view it is incorrect to describe the doctrine of separability as a legal fiction. The argument fails to recognise modern forms of contracting such as point by point negotiation. All that is necessary is a finding that the parties intended to treat their arbitration agreement separately. There has been some debate about whether this would need to be explicit. However, it seems likely that implicit presumptive intent is sufficient.[49]

4.42   Those who argue against separability in cases of disputed existence of the contract then turn their attention to the actual language of the arbitration agreement. They contend that if the arbitration agreement refers to a contractual relationship then there is a problem. According to them, even if the parties intended their arbitration agreement to survive, its scope is limited to disputes relating to the contract which never came into existence. There is certainly logic to this

---

44 Gu Weixia, 'China's Search for Complete Separability of the Arbitral Agreement', (2007) 3 *Asian International Arbitration Journal* 163, at p. 168 citing Lianbin Song, Jian Zhao and Hong Li, 'Approaches to the Revision of the 1994 Arbitration Act of the People's Republic of China', 2003(2) *Journal of International Arbitration* 169, at p. 181.
45 FaShi [2006] No. 7.
46 Gu Weixa, op. cit. fn 44, at p. 188. See also Wan Exiang and Yu Xifu, 'Latest Evolution in the Judicial Intendence Mechanism over Arbitration in China,' (2008) 3(2) *Front Law China* 181, at 172.
47 Baron, op. cit. fn 43.
48 See, e.g. A Redfern, M Hunter, N Blackaby and C Partasides, *Law and Practice of International Commercial Arbitration*, 4th edn, Sweet & Maxwell, 2004, para 5–43. Contrast with E Gaillard and J Savage (eds), *Fouchard Gaillard Goldman on International Commercial Arbitration*, Kluwer Law International, 1999, p. 201 who found it necessary to state explicitly that contrary to other texts they did not distinguish between void/voidable contracts and those that never existed.
49 See *QH Tours Ltd v Ship Design & Management (Aust) Pty Ltd* (1991) 104 ALR 371 per Justice Foster; *Harbour Assurance Co (UK) Ltd v Kansa General International Insurance Co Ltd* [1993] QB 701 per Lord Justice Ralph Gibson, as cited by Baron, op. cit. fn 43.

assertion but it will not apply if the arbitration agreement is found to cover disputes about formation of a contract, or claims relating to pre-contractual gains or expectations – *quantum meruit* or *culpa in contrahendo* for example. To determine this question, the arbitral tribunal, or court as the case may be, will need to consider as a matter of fact what was the parties' intended scope of the arbitration agreement. In doing so, consideration should be given to the language of and law governing the arbitration agreement,[50] and the evidence led by the parties.

Some authors appear to suggest that for the purposes of the separability doctrine it is necessary to distinguish between cases in which a contract originally existed but thereafter was terminated or voidable and cases where there was never a contract from the beginning. Similarly, some courts in the US have demonstrated a preference to decide the existence or otherwise of an arbitration agreement when the existence of the entire contract is also in question.[51] The practical reasons behind this distinction are at best questionable. One possible explanation for the view can be found in the interpretation of the English Arbitration Act 1996. Section 9(4) of that Act states that 'on an application under this section the court shall grant a stay unless satisfied that the arbitration agreement is null and void, inoperative, or incapable of being performed'. While its key operative language is identical to Article 8(1) of the Model Law and Article II of the New York Convention, Section 9(4) has been interpreted to mean that a court must first find that an arbitration agreement actually exists before it will order a stay.[52]   4.43

This interpretation should not be extended to international arbitration generally, and in particular not to Model Law countries despite the identical language in Article 8(1). Article 16(1) of the Model Law specifically empowers the arbitral tribunal to decide 'any objections with respect to the <u>existence</u> or validity of the arbitration agreement'. (Emphasis added). In contrast, Section 30 of the English Arbitration Act 1996, which sets forth the competence-competence rule[53] in that jurisdiction, empowers the arbitral tribunal to decide 'whether there is a valid arbitration agreement' and 'whether the arbitral tribunal is properly constituted', without mentioning existence.   4.44

---

50 See Section 8.1, in particular the discussion of how different phrases can have different meanings when interpreted according to different laws.
51 T Várady, C Barceló and A von Mehren, *International Commercial Arbitration – A Transnational Perspective*, 3rd edn, Thomson, 2006, at p. 90, citing *Sandvik AB v Advent International Corp*, 220 F 3d 99 (3d Cir 2000) (Party seeking stay of court action in favour of arbitration claimed container contract did not come into existence because its purported signatory did not have authority. It nevertheless sought to rely on the arbitration clause in the container contract. The Third Circuit Court of Appeals refused to apply the separability concept and ruled that a court decision on the existence of the contract was a prerequisite to sending the parties to arbitration.).
52 See *Albon (trading as N A Carriage Co) v Naza Motor Trading SDN BHD* [2007] 2 All ER 1075. In this case the court was asked to stay proceedings in favour of an arbitration seated in Malaysia. The party resisting the stay application alleged that the signature on the arbitration agreement was a forgery. The court refused to stay the proceedings on the ground that it was not satisfied that an arbitration agreement actually existed. See commentary on the decision – N Pengelley, 'Albon v Naza Motor Trading: Necessity for a Court to Find that there is an Arbitration Agreement Before Determining that it is Null and Void', (2008) 24 *Arbitration International* 171.
53 The competence-competence rule is explained in Chapter 5, Section 4.

4.45 The doctrine of separability simply instructs the inquirer to treat the arbitration agreement separately from the main contract for the purposes of determining its existence and validity. If the alleged main contract never existed, then it might well be that the arbitration clause never existed either. Consequently the existence of the arbitration agreement still needs to be considered. Take for example a situation where one party (Buyer) puts forward to another (Seller) an offer to enter a sales contract which contains an arbitration agreement. Buyer purports to withdraw or revoke its offer, while at the same time Seller purports to accept it. Seller now claims that a sales contract exists which Buyer denies. If the sales contract does exist, then so will the arbitration agreement. But even if the sales contract does not exist, the arbitration agreement may still exist as the parties may still have intended to have any dispute resolved by arbitration. Thus the doctrine of separability applies to situations where the main contract existed but was terminated or voidable, as well as situations where it is alleged that the main contract never came into existence.

4.46 Three broad consequences may follow from the application of the doctrine of separability: the arbitration agreement's validity is considered separately from the main contract's validity (which we have touched on in the discussion above); 'juridical autonomy', meaning that a different law may apply to the arbitration agreement than that which applies to the substantive contract; and finally there is an aspect of autonomy from all laws. Although this last aspect is not generally found in Asia-Pacific international arbitration jurisprudence it has influenced arbitral practice and doctrine. These three points will be discussed in turn.

3.1 Validity of main contract and arbitration agreement

4.47 When parties conclude a contract containing an arbitration agreement, they are in effect concluding two separate agreements. In the words of Judge Schwebel, formerly of the International Court of Justice, '[w]hen the parties to an agreement containing an arbitration clause enter into that agreement, they conclude not one but two agreements, the arbitral twin of which survives any birth defect or acquired disability of the principal agreement'.[54] In a 1994 New South Wales Court of Appeal decision, former Justice Kirby (then President of that court) adopted the following explanation:[55]

> validity of the arbitration clause does not depend upon the validity of the remaining parts of the contract in which it is contained. This allows an arbitration tribunal to declare a contract invalid and yet retain its jurisdiction to decide a dispute as to the consequences of such invalidity provided that the arbitration clause is valid as a separate entity and is sufficiently broad in its wording so as to cover non-contractual disputes.

4.48 As a consequence, the arbitral tribunal can determine whether the main contract is valid, or even whether it exists, without contradicting its own jurisdiction.[56] As

---

[54] S Schwebel, *International Arbitration: Three Salient Problems*, Grotius Publications, 1987, pp. 2–3.
[55] *Ferris v Plaister* (1994) 34 NSWLR 474 quoting a passage from *Sojuznefteexport (SNE) v Joc Oil Ltd*, (1990) XV *Yearbook of Commercial Arbitration* 384.
[56] The power of arbitrators to rule on their own jurisdiction is discussed in Chapter 5, Section 4.

suggested above, the reasons for this are logically compelling. If the arbitration clause were part of the main contract, the arbitration clause would not come into existence unless the main contract did, and would be terminated when the main contract terminates. Further, separability in this context avoids a paradox. If the arbitration clause were part of the main contract, and one party contended that the main contract was void, an arbitral tribunal may not be able to decide that allegation because if it finds that the contract was void, the basis of its power to make that decision would never have existed.

Thus the validity of an arbitration clause must be considered as a question separate from the validity of the contract containing that arbitration clause. Moreover, the arbitral tribunal remains competent not only to determine its own jurisdiction but also to determine the validity or existence of the substantive contract. This concept has important ramifications. The arbitration agreement can for example survive the novation, nullity, or termination of the main contract. The House of Lords has noted:[57]   4.49

> The arbitration agreement must be treated as a 'distinct agreement' and can be void or voidable only on grounds which relate directly to the arbitration agreement. Of course there may be cases in which the ground upon which the main agreement is invalid is identical with the ground upon which the arbitration agreement is invalid. For example, if the main agreement and the arbitration agreement are contained in the same document and one of the parties claims that he never agreed to anything in the document and that his signature was forged, that will be an attack on the validity of the arbitration agreement. But the ground of attack is not that the main agreement was invalid. It is that the signature to the arbitration agreement, as a 'distinct agreement', was forged. Similarly, if a party alleges that someone who purported to sign as agent on his behalf had no authority whatever to conclude any agreement on his behalf, that is an attack on both the main agreement and the arbitration agreement.

> On the other hand, if (as in this case) the allegation is that the agent exceeded his authority by entering into a main agreement in terms which were not authorized or for improper reasons, that is not necessarily an attack on the arbitration agreement. It would have to be shown that whatever the terms of the main agreement or the reasons for which the agent concluded it, he would have had no authority to enter into an arbitration agreement. Even if the allegation is that there was no concluded agreement (for example, that terms of the main agreement remained to be agreed) that is not necessarily an attack on the arbitration agreement. If the arbitration clause has been agreed, the parties will be presumed to have intended the question of whether there was a concluded main agreement to be decided by arbitration.

3.2 Law governing main contract and arbitration agreement

As an arbitration clause in a contract is an agreement separate from that in which it is contained, the determination of the law that governs the arbitration clause and that which governs the contract must also be separate. Since the two agreements have different purposes, it is quite conceivable that a different   4.50

---

[57] *Premium Nafta Products Ltd v Fiji Shipping Company Ltd* [2007] 2 All ER (Comm) 1053, at paras 17 and 18 per Lord Hofmann.

law applies to each. This does not mean that the governing laws are necessarily different, but rather that they might be different.

4.51 Much like the practice that exists in relation to commercial contracts, parties are free to choose the law that governs their arbitration agreement.[58] This freedom of choice is implicitly recognised in the Model Law and the New York Convention. Article 34(2)(a) of the Model Law and Article V(1)(a) of the New York Convention refer to the determination of the validity of an arbitration agreement 'under the law to which the parties have subjected it'. There is no doubt that parties are free to choose the law that governs their arbitration agreement, even if it is a different law from that governing the main contract or from the *lex arbitri*. In practice, however, parties very rarely express a choice as to the law that governs the arbitration agreement so a question arises as to how it is to be determined.

4.52 Following England's lead, common law jurisdictions have historically applied a rebuttable presumption that the law governing the main agreement will also govern the arbitration agreement. It is indeed only a presumption.[59] However that position, in England at least, appears to be changing. In the English Court of Appeal decision of *C v D*, Lord Justice Longmore speaking for the entire court said by way of obiter dictum:[60]

> if there is no express law of the arbitration agreement, the law with which that agreement has its closest and most real connection is the law of the underlying contract or the law of the seat of arbitration. It seems to me that . . . the answer is more likely to be the law of the seat of arbitration than the law of the underlying contract.

4.53 The Indian case of *Shin-Etsu Chemical Co Ltd v Aksh Optifibre Ltd* expounds an interesting hybrid between the common and (as explained below) civil law positions, but nevertheless highlights the fact that a different law can apply to the arbitration agreement:[61]

> This question of choice of law has been conclusively decided by the judgment of this court in National Thermal Power Corporation v. Singer Company, where it was observed: 'The proper law of the arbitration agreement is normally the same as the proper law of the contract. It is only in exceptional cases that it is not so even where the proper law of the contract is expressly chosen by the parties. Where, however, there is no express choice of the law governing the contract as a whole, of the arbitration agreement as such, a presumption may arise that the law of the country where the arbitration is agreed to be held is the proper law of the arbitration agreement. But that is only a rebuttable presumption.'

4.54 It makes a lot of sense that the presumption, in as much as there is one, should be in favour of the law of the seat of arbitration. It is generally in accord with the

---

58 An explanation of the extent to which arbitrating parties are free to choose the law governing their contract is provided in Chapter 3, Section 3.
59 M Pryles, 'Choice of Law Issues in International Arbitration', (1997) 63(3) *Arbitration – The Journal of the Chartered Institute of Arbitrators* 200, at p. 202; see also *Sonatrach Petroleum Corporation (BVI) v Ferrell International Ltd* [2002] 1 All ER (Comm) 627 (Queen's Bench, Commercial Court).
60 [2007] EWCA Civ 1282 at para 22.
61 (2005) 7 SCC 234, at pp. 268–269 (Supreme Court of India).

approach adopted in a number of civil law countries[62] including China,[63] and arguably also in the USA.[64] The substantive law, if determined by the application of conflict of laws rules, is selected because of the connection that that law has to the substance of the principal contractual obligations under the contact. For example, in a contract dealing with the construction of a facility in Indonesia, the choice of Indonesian law would seem most relevant given its close connection to the characteristic performance (i.e. construction) in Indonesia. If we were to apply that same principle – i.e. looking for the law with the closest connection to the characteristic obligation – to determine the law governing the arbitration agreement, would we end up with the same law? The characteristic or principal obligation under an arbitration agreement is an obligation to arbitrate disputes. The obligation to undertake the procedure of arbitration to resolve one's disputes appears much more closely related to the place that that procedure will happen – that is the legal place of that procedure, in other words the seat of arbitration. The performance will occur at the seat of arbitration and therefore the obligation is most closely connected to that place and that law.

Moreover, if the parties have chosen a seat of arbitration that is outside the place of the substantive contractual law, the parties could be considered to have indicated an intention to separate their substantive obligations under the contract from their obligations in relation to arbitration. There might be a very good reason for this. Take the Indonesian project example just given. In that case, if Indonesian law governed the arbitration agreement that agreement would be subjected to certain peculiarities of Indonesian Arbitration law which are not quite in line with international arbitration standards. On the other hand, if the parties had chosen a Singapore seat of arbitration, Singapore law should be presumptively considered (i.e. if the parties have not expressly chosen a law to govern the arbitration agreement) as governing all aspects of the dispute resolution process. It would be reasonable to expect that Singapore law was intended to govern this part of the agreement to avoid the Indonesian particularities mentioned above. 4.55

The Singapore High Court decision of *Philippines v Philippine International Air Terminals Co Inc*[65] is an example of just how significant this the choice of law to govern an arbitration agreement can be. In that case, a contract between the Philippines Government and a private foreign consortium operating through a Philippines incorporated company provided for ICC arbitration with the seat in Singapore. The contract also included a choice of law clause providing that it 4.56

---

62 See Born, op. cit. fn 19, pp. 470–475 referring particularly to Japan, Germany, Switzerland and Sweden, but Born also notes that the approach is not uniformly settled. See also Poudret and Besson, op. cit. fn 9, at para 300 noting authority from Belgium and Italy in favour of the main contract law presumption.
63 Under Chinese law the position has been settled in favour of applying the law of the seat, or in the absence of a seat being designated, the law of the forum, Article 16 of the Supreme People's Court's Interpretation of Several Issues regarding the Application of the Arbitration Law of the PRC (FaShi [2006] No. 7); Reply of Supreme People's Court to the Query about the Arbitration Clause in the Sales Contract between *Baoyuan Trade Co v Yu Jianguo*, (Civil 4, Miscellaneous), No. 38 (2007). See also Wan Exiang and Yu Xifu, op. cit. fn 46, at p. 190.
64 Redfern, Hunter, et al, op. cit. fn 48, para 2–91. But see also Born, op. cit. fn 19, p. 485 et seq; and Poudret and Besson, op. cit. fn 9, para 300, n 716a.
65 [2007] 1 SLR 278.

was to be governed by Philippines law. The Philippines Government challenged jurisdiction, arguing that since the entire contract had been invalidated by the Philippines Supreme Court there was no arbitration agreement. A preliminary question for the arbitral tribunal was which law governed the arbitral proceedings and the arbitration agreement.

4.57   The arbitral tribunal delivered a partial award finding that it had jurisdiction. The reported judgment is a challenge to that award before the Singapore courts. After first accepting the doctrine of separability,[66] the arbitral tribunal went on to consider whether an arbitration agreement could have a proper law different to that of the main agreement. Having found that it could, the arbitral tribunal was then required to determine what law governed the arbitration agreement in this instance. The arbitral tribunal found that Singapore law governed both the arbitration agreement and the arbitral proceedings. This was despite the choice of Philippines law as the law governing the main contract, despite the fact that both parties were Filipino, and despite the fact that the contract related to a project carried out entirely in the Philippines. According to the arbitral tribunal, although all relevant connecting factors pointed to the Philippines, the fact that parties had deliberately chosen ICC arbitration seated in Singapore indicated that the parties preferred a law other than that of the Philippines to govern their dispute resolution clause and the related process.

4.58   If Philippines law had been found to govern the arbitration it seems likely that there would have been no arbitration agreement and consequently no arbitral jurisdiction as a result of decisions already taken by the Philippines Supreme Court. In this case, the advantage of the principle that a different law can govern the arbitration agreement should therefore be obvious. As the Arbitral Tribunal held:[67]

> In the opinion of the arbitral tribunal a strong implication arises that the parties not only removed non-construction and Works disputes from the jurisdiction of the Philippines but also intended that the obligation to arbitrate these disputes should not be referred to the law of the Philippines. In other words, by designating Singapore and the ICC Rules in contrast to the other arbitration obligation appertaining to construction and Works disputes, the parties implied a choice of Singapore law to govern the arbitration agreement as well as the arbitral proceedings for nonconstruction and Works disputes.
>
> One further point can be made. Mustill and Boyd state that if the choice lies between two systems of law, one of which would uphold the arbitration agreement and the other would not, the former may be preferred. A question may arise in this case as to whether the arbitration agreement is valid under the law of the Philippines in view of the decision of the Supreme Court of the Philippines holding that the ARCA is void ab initio. This factor also inclines towards construing the agreement to arbitrate disputes in Singapore as governed by the law of Singapore.

---

[66] One of the grounds of appeal in the case was that the Government of the Philippines was taken by surprise when the arbitral tribunal made a determination on the doctrine of separability. Dismissing this objection Judge Prakash found that such a determination was implicit in the issue of determining the validity of the arbitration agreement. [2007] 1 SLR 278 at 287.
[67] Partial Award, paras 84 and 85 as extracted in [2007] 1 SLR 278 at 283.

The Singapore court dismissed the challenge to the partial award, and although noting that it was not necessary for it to comment on the process adopted by the arbitral tribunal, it nevertheless indicated its endorsement of that process.

Once the law governing the arbitration agreement has been identified, the arbitration agreement must be interpreted according to that law. An exception to this position may be found in France as described in the following section.

3.3 Validity of arbitration agreement determined independently of all national laws

Some French decisions from the mid 1970s prompted discussion about whether an arbitration agreement needs to be governed by any law at all. The theory was that the existence and validity of an arbitration agreement should be determined simply by looking at the facts of the case in order to establish the parties' intentions. Reference to any governing law was considered unnecessary.

The French position was first espoused in the 1975 decision of the Court of Appeal of Paris in the case of *Menicucci*. The Court of Appeal held:[68]

> it is sufficient, for determining objections to the arbitral tribunal's competence, to note that taking account of the autonomy of the arbitration agreement in an international contract, that agreement is valid independently of the reference to any state law.

Several French cases have followed this decision or reached a similar result, most recently in the 2009 decision of *Soerni v ASB*,[69] but it continues to be the subject of academic debate. In their analysis of *Menicucci* and cases that followed, Poudret and Besson observe that the prevailing opinion among French authors supports the rule.[70] However, Poudret and Besson persuasively criticise it, noting that the approach contradicts the need for connecting factors found in Article V(1)(a) of the New York Convention.[71]

An approach which seeks to determine the validity of an arbitration agreement independently of all national laws has notions of delocalisation at its heart.[72] When expressed as the simple proposition that a court should only examine whether the parties agreed to arbitrate – which is a question of fact not law – it at first sounds attractive. However, when carefully considered this approach cannot be endorsed as it is not a question of fact at all. Rather it is simply saying

---

68 *Menicucci*: Paris, 13 décembre 1975, *Revue de l'arbitrage*, 1977.147, note Ph Fouchard; *Journal du droit international (Clunet)*, 1977.107, note E Loquin; *Revue critique de droit international privé*, 1976.506, note B Oppetit.
69 Cour de Cassation, Première chambre civile, 8 July 2009. See also L Graffi, 'Securing Harmonized Effects of Arbitration Agreements Under the New York Convention', (2006) Spring *Houston Journal of International Law* 718 citing the *Dalico* (1993) and *Bomar Oil* (1993) decisions.
70 Poudret and Besson, op. cit. fn 9, para 182.
71 Ibid. For discussion on the New York Convention see Chapter 9, Section 6.2.1 of this book.
72 See Chapter 2, Section 5.2.1.

that as a matter of law (i.e. French law), consent is the only element required to determine that there is an arbitration agreement. Thus although the rule is clothed in language of an international material rule, in reality it is applied as a domestic legal concept and part of French law.

4.65 It therefore comes as no surprise that Asia-Pacific courts have not adopted the same approach. Courts and arbitral tribunals in this region seek to establish a governing law for the arbitration agreement, on the basis of which validity is then considered.

4 Identifying the parties to an arbitration agreement

4.66 As arbitration is based on consent, an arbitration agreement can bind only those who are parties to it. The question of identity of the parties to an arbitration agreement can arise when a party to the arbitration agreement seeks to enforce that agreement against another entity which contests that it is a party to the arbitration agreement or vice versa, that is where a party to the arbitration agreement denies that another entity is a party to that arbitration agreement.

4.67 An example of the latter is found in the High Court of Brunei decision *Royal Brunei Airlines Sdn. Bhd. v Philip Tan Kok Ming*.[73] The defendant was attempting to stay litigation proceedings commenced against him by invoking an arbitration agreement. The defendant was not a signatory to the arbitration agreement himself, but had provided a guarantee in favour of one of the signatories. Chief Justice Roberts of the Brunei High Court stated:[74]

> It seems to me to follow, from the fact that neither an assignee of a debt nor a surety is bound by an arbitration award, that it would not be open to the court to stay proceedings before it in either event, since neither the assignee nor the surety could properly be said to be acting 'through or under' the assignor or the principal debtor.
>
> ...
>
> I do not consider that it is reasonable to stay these proceedings. The effect of such a stay would be to make Tan subject to an arbitration agreement to which he was not a party.

4.1 Non-signatories

4.68 The consensual nature of arbitration has been repeatedly emphasised throughout this chapter, and indeed throughout this book. It is so important that as a general rule written evidence is required to establish an arbitration agreement. However, a strict signature requirement would not accommodate the realities of cross-border trade, multinational companies and the inevitable temporal

---

[73] *Royal Brunei Airlines Sdn Bhd v Philip Tan Kok Ming* [1993] BNHC 18.
[74] Ibid.

evolution of corporate structures and ownership. Courts, arbitral tribunals and commentators have developed numerous theories that may bind non-signatories to an arbitration agreement. Several of these theories were conveniently set out in the 1995 US decision of *Thomson-CSF SA v American Arbitration Association and Evans & Sutherland Computer Corporation*.[75] The court recognised five theories whereby a non-signatory could be bound by an arbitration agreement:[76]

(i) *Incorporation by reference*. This has been discussed elsewhere in the context of the formalities of an arbitration agreement.[77]
(ii) *Assignment/Assumption*. As the name suggests, this describes the circumstance when a non-signatory assumes or takes over one party's obligations under a contract. Together with taking on any potential liability, the non-signatory may also assume the remedial right (and obligation) to arbitrate. This is discussed at Section 4.1.3.
(iii) *Agency*. The question of whether an agent has the authority to enter into an arbitration agreement is one which will most likely be determined by reference to domestic laws. Accordingly, the arbitral tribunal would need to conduct a conflict of laws determination to ascertain which agency laws apply.[78] This is a question for the arbitral tribunal not a court.[79]
(iv) *Alter Ego/Group of Companies*. This is discussed at Section 4.1.1.
(v) *Estoppel*. This is discussed at Section 4.1.2.

4.1.1 Alter ego and group of companies

The alter ego theory arises where:[80]   4.69

> one party so dominates the affairs of another party, and has sufficiently misused such control, that it is appropriate to disregard the two companies' separate legal forms and to treat them as a single entity.

This question is often said to turn on actual or de facto control, and most likely requires 'unfettered control'.[81] Whether this exists is a matter for determination by the arbitral tribunal.[82]   4.70

---

75 64 F 3d 773, 776 (2d Cir 1995) (US Court of Appeals, 2nd Circuit).
76 For a summary of some of these theories, see also M Saraf, 'Who is a Party to an Arbitration Agreement – Case of the Non-Signatory, Institutional Arbitration in Asia', Collection of Papers Presented at ICC–SIAC Symposium, Singapore, 18–19 February 2005, pp. 1–71; and A Yeo, 'Who is a Party – Case of the Non-Signatory, Institutional Arbitration in Asia', Collection of Papers Presented at ICC–SIAC Symposium, Singapore, 18–19 February 2005, pp. 72–80.
77 See Section 2.3.2.
78 See generally Chapter 3.
79 For example, see the Hong Kong High Court decision of *Private Company Triple V Inc v Star (Universal) Co Ltd, Sky Jade Enterprises Group Ltd* [1995] HKCU 27 which decided that the question of whether an agent could bind a principle to an arbitration agreement was a question for the arbitrator.
80 Born, op. cit. fn 19, p. 1154.
81 See, e.g. in relation to shareholders, Malaysian Court Practice Rules of the High Court, Rule 24.1 states, among other things, 'Accordingly, in *Re Tecnion Investments* [1985] BCLC 434 at 439, the Court of Appeal held that a majority shareholder in a company does not necessarily have power over company documents. Although he is in a dominant position, he does not have "unfettered control" of the company so as to be its "alter ego".
82 *Aloe Vera of America Inc v Asianic Food (S) Pte Ltd* [2006] 3 SLR 174.

4.71　Parties frequently incorporate special purpose vehicles for a particular transaction, for example a local subsidiary may be incorporated by a foreign multinational construction company for a project it is undertaking in the subsidiary's country. It may be this subsidiary that actually signs the contract containing the arbitration agreement. Since it is a separate legal entity, its foreign parent will not be prima facie bound by the contract or its arbitration agreement even if it owns 100% of the subsidiary's shares. Domestic legal systems provide a variety of mechanisms by which this 'corporate veil' can be 'lifted' or 'pierced', for instance where there has been fraud or a deliberate attempt to abuse the corporate system for an illegal purpose such as evading liabilities.[83] Generally, legal systems and courts protect corporate personality and are reluctant to lift or pierce a corporate veil.

4.72　In addition to domestic legal provisions relating to piercing a corporate veil or groups of companies, there are several theories that have developed in arbitration practice pursuant to which related companies, particularly parent companies, are considered parties to arbitration agreements. These theories are closely related to domestic alter ego type theories and can be found in both common and civil law jurisprudence.[84] Here the key question is usually factual participation by the related entity in the negotiations and/or, most importantly, the performance of the underlying transaction. The fact that a party and a non-signatory may be part of the same group of companies is not in and of itself sufficient.[85]

4.73　Use of the group of companies and alter ego doctrines in international arbitration is well-established in certain European jurisdictions[86] and certain US states, but has seen very limited application by courts in this region. A Global Arbitration Review publication 'Getting the Deal Through' surveyed the conduct of international arbitration in over 30 countries.[87] Participating authors were asked specifically about the application of the group of companies doctrine. Relevant to this region, it was said to be unsettled law in Australia, not recognised in India (and perhaps Japan), there were no reported cases in Hong Kong, and it was found only to apply in taxation or insolvency matters in New Zealand. While case law from Singapore indicates that both the alter ego and single economic group of companies theories will be recognised in some matters, Singaporean law

---

[83] See, e.g. Korean Supreme Court, Case no. 2004Da26119 (25 August 2006) and the Hong Kong Court of Appeal decision in *China Ocean Shipping Co v Mitrans Shipping Co Ltd* [1995] HKCA 604. See generally, A Capuano, 'The Realist's Guide to Piercing the Corporate Veil: Lessons from Hong Kong and Singapore', (2009) 23 *Australian Journal of Corporate Law* 1. See also Chapter 10, Section 4.4.
[84] See, e.g. *Smith Stone and Knight v Birmingham Corporation* [1939] 4 All ER 116. For a broad but comprehensive discussion of these issues see J Hosking, 'The Third Party Non-Signatory's Ability to Compel International Commercial Arbitration: Doing Justice Without Destroying Consent', (2003–2004) 4 *Pepperdine Dispute Resolution Law Journal* 469, at p. 469. For an even more comprehensive study, see B Hanotiau, 'Problems Raised by Complex Arbitrations Involving Multiple Contracts – Parties – Issues', (2001) 18(3) *Journal of International Arbitration* 251. See also S Jarvin, 'The Group of Companies Doctrine', (2002) *ASA Special Series* 19 (December) p. 19.
[85] Born, op. cit. fn 19, p. 1171.
[86] However, the group of companies doctrine was expressly rejected as part of English law in *Peterson Farms Inc v C&M Farming Ltd* [2004] EWHC 121 (Comm).
[87] G Wegen and S Wilske (eds), *Getting the Deal Through – Arbitration in 33 Jurisdictions Worldwide*, Global Arbitration Review, Law Business Research Inc, 2007. The information is expressed to be current to February 2007.

remains unsettled.[88] It is likely that national perspectives will be influenced by the respective approaches to piercing the corporate veil found in each country's corporate law regime.

While such theories have not been readily applied by domestic courts in the Asia-Pacific, international arbitral tribunals seated in the region have applied such theories on numerous occasions.[89] Given the strong trend towards recognising alter ego or group of companies theories in continental Europe and the US, it is possible that Asia-Pacific jurisdictions will eventually follow suit. The juridical foundation for this development may be the good faith requirement most prevalent in civil legal jurisdictions but also emerging in some common law jurisprudence. It is also possible, however, that those Asia-Pacific jurisdictions following the Common Law tradition will be influenced by the rather conservative approach taken by English courts.

4.74

4.1.2 Estoppel

Estoppel is basically a legal principle by which a party is prevented from denying representations arising out of words or deeds on which another party has relied to its detriment. Even if there is no detrimental reliance, the party making the representations may also be estopped from denying them where such a denial would be unconscionable. Estoppel is a common law principle, although it has been accepted in other jurisdictions in particular in the context of international arbitration.[90] Furthermore, civil law jurisdictions achieve similar results through principles such as good faith and *venire contra factum proprium*.[91]

4.75

There are two stages of the arbitral proceedings at which estoppel may be raised in relation to the arbitration agreement. The first is in front of a domestic court which has been asked to stay litigation, and so prior to the arbitration commencing a party may be estopped (prevented) by that court from denying the existence of the arbitration agreement. The second occurs after an arbitration has been commenced, or even concluded, and one party asserts that there is no arbitration agreement.[92]

4.76

---

88 *Win Line (UK) Ltd v Masterpart (Singapore) Pte Ltd* [2000] 2 SLR 98. It is interesting to note that the judge in that case was Judith Prakash who is frequently tasked with hearing arbitration cases. In this particular case, Judge Prakash refused to extend the doctrines to encompass two companies with completely different shareholders.
89 See, e.g., the arbitration described in the Singaporean court decision of *Aloe Vera of America, Inc v Asianic Food (S) Pte Ltd* [2006] 3 SLR 174, and commentary on that decision suggesting that it can be taken as the first endorsement of the alter ego doctrine in Singapore arbitration law; L Boo, 'Arbitration Law', (2006) 7 *Singapore Academy of Law Annual Review of Singapore Cases* 51.
90 For example in France, see *Golshani v Islamic Republic of Iran*, (Cour de Cassation) dated 6 July 2005, Case no. 01–15912 and more recently *Merial SAS v Klocke Verpackungs – Service GmbH*, 9 October 2008, Case no. 07–06619.
91 The broad acceptance of estoppel and like theories is demonstrated by their utilisation in international law. See JR Weeramantry, 'Estoppel and the Preclusive Effects of Inconsistent Statements and Conduct: The Practice of the Iran-United States Claims Tribunal' (1996) 27 *Netherlands Yearbook of International Law* 113, at pp. 114–15.
92 The Malaysian case of *Bintulu Development Authority v Pilecon Engineering Bhd* [2007] 2 CLJ 422 is one example. From China the Reply of Supreme People's Court to Request of Enforcement of Arbitral Award made in England by Swiss Bangji Co., Ltd (Civil 3, Miscellaneous), No. 47 (2006), also demonstrates this although in the context of enforcement proceedings.

4.77   Examples of both situations can be found in Malaysian jurisprudence. The case of *Lai Sing Kejuruteraan (M) Sdn Bhd v Ten Engineering Sdn Bhd*[93] is an example of the first situation. It was alleged in that case that the arbitration clause had been incorporated by reference. The judge found that the conduct of the party resisting arbitration had been such that it could not be allowed to deny it had intended to incorporate all terms (including the arbitration agreement) into its relationship with the other party.[94] The Malaysian Court of Appeal decision in *Bintulu Development Authority v Pilecon Engineering Bhd*[95] is an example of the second situation. In this case one party attempted to dispute the existence of an arbitration agreement despite its participation in the arbitration without denying jurisdiction. The estoppel takes effect because during the arbitration the party's acts were inconsistent with its subsequent assertion that no arbitration agreement existed. The court there found in favour of arbitration.[96]

4.1.3 Assignment

4.78   An assignment is a legal term that refers to the transfer of property or rights (such as contractual benefits and obligations) to another party.[97] This other party may be a third party that was previously unrelated to the transaction. As such, where a contract containing an arbitration agreement is assigned, the third party ordinarily will not have signed the contract or the arbitration agreement.

4.79   Born has noted a lack of uniform rules concerning the assignment of arbitration agreements.[98] The question of whether rights and obligations of an arbitration agreement are capable of assignment is sometimes addressed within the arbitration agreement itself.[99] Alternatively, a separate clause in the contract may indicate whether the contract as a whole can be assigned. In such a case or where there is no contractual provision expressing this power, regard will need to be had to a number of laws.

4.80   Redfern and Hunter suggest that the effect of an assignment on an arbitration agreement will be determined primarily by two laws – the law governing the assignment and the law governing the arbitration agreement.[100] With respect to the law governing the assignment, some jurisdictions require specific intent to assign the arbitration clause but others assume such intent when a general

---

93 [1997] MLJU 197.
94 Judicial Commissioner Kamalanathan Ratnam made this finding notwithstanding that estoppel had not been pleaded by the parties. He stated 'so long as evidence has been led from which the Court can perceive estoppel there is no need to actually spell it out as a plea' at para 6 citing *Boustead Trading (1985) Sdn BhD v Arab Malaysia Merchant Bank Bhd* [1995] 3 MLJ 331.
95 [2007] 2 MLJ 610.
96 See the discussion of waiver in Chapter 5, Section 3.5.
97 For a detailed discussion of assignment in Anglo-Australian contract law see, G Tolhurst, *The Assignment of Contractual Rights*, Hart Publishing, 2006.
98 Born, op. cit. fn 19, p. 1192.
99 See, e.g., the arbitration clause extracted in the Kuala Lumpur Supreme Court case of *Perbadanan Kemajuan Negeri Perak v Asean Security Paper Mill Sdn Bhd* [1991] 3 MLJ 309 – the relevant part reads 'All disputes, differences and questions which may at any time arise between the parties hereto or their respective representatives or assigns touching or arising out of or in respect of this agreement or the subject matter thereof shall be referred to a single arbitrator'.
100 Redfern, Hunter et al, op. cit. fn 48, para 3–34.

assignment of rights takes place. In the Philippines, the Manila Court of Appeals has held:[101]

> the assignee will be bound by the [arbitration] agreement because assignment involves a transfer of rights as to vest in the assignee the power to enforce such rights to the same extent as the assignor could have enforced them against the other party to the agreement.

A similar position is found in Australia,[102] as well as in China, following the 2000 decision of *China Henan Import-Export Co v Xinquan Trade Ltd*.[103] The position in China was further clarified in the Supreme People's Court's Interpretation of Several Issues regarding the Application of the Arbitration Law of the PRC.[104] Article 9 of the Interpretation indicates that an assignment will bind the assignee, unless the parties have agreed otherwise, the assignee has clearly objected to the arbitration agreement at the time of the assignment, or the assignee is unaware of the arbitration agreement at the time of the assignment.[105] 4.81

Finally, where the enforcement of an arbitral award involving an assignee is sought, it may also be necessary to consider the validity of the assignment pursuant to the laws of the place of enforcement. Although such considerations are undesirable from a policy perspective, an example of it occurring is found in the Malaysian decision of *Harris Adacom Corporation v Perkom Sdn Bhd*.[106] It is not clear why the judge believed it was necessary to consider whether the assignment was valid under Malaysian law in that instance, after having first found that the parties had agreed that Florida law applied to the assignment. 4.82

4.2 Capacity

A party must have the capacity to enter into an arbitration agreement. In every jurisdiction, rules regulate a legal person's ability (be they an individual or corporate entity) to enter into a binding contract. The issue of a party's capacity to enter into an arbitration agreement should be relatively straightforward. An arbitration agreement is no different from any other contract in this respect.[107] Issues as to capacity may be raised before or during the arbitration and may be submitted as a ground to set aside the award. Capacity to enter into an arbitration agreement can also be relevant at the time of enforcement of an award. Article V1(a) of the New York Convention states that enforcement may be refused if one of the parties was 'under some incapacity'. 4.83

A question of capacity often becomes a point of dispute when one of the parties is a state entity. In some jurisdictions, state entities or statutory bodies 4.84

---

101 *Heritage Park v Construction Industry*, CA-G.R SP No. 86342, 9 February 2005.
102 See *Paxton Enterprises Pty Ltd v Brancote Australia NL* [2000] WASC 273.
103 Supreme People's Court, (Civil, Economic), Final, No. 48 (2000).
104 FaShi [2006] No. 7.
105 Chen Wei-qi, 'Recent developments in the judicial interpretation on Arbitration Law in China' (2007) 4(5) *US–China Law Review* 57, at pp. 59–60.
106 (1993) 3 MLJ 506.
107 Capacity was also considered briefly in Chapter 3, Section 2.

are precluded from entering into arbitration agreements. In other situations, where a state offical or body (such as a ministry) has signed the arbitration agreement, a question may arise as to whether that signature binds the state itself.

4.85 This issue has been considered by Dunham and Greenberg.[108] The authors observe that nation states should not be permitted to rely on their own laws to escape an arbitration agreement:[109]

> This principle is also recognised in international arbitral jurisprudence. One leading example is [ICC Case No 1939] rendered in 1971 in which the tribunal stated: 'international ordre public would vigorously reject the proposition that a state organ, dealing with foreigners, having openly, with knowledge and intent, concluded an arbitration clause that inspires the co-contractant's confidence, could thereafter, whether in the arbitration or in execution proceedings, invoke the nullity of its own promise.' The principle that a state may not rely on its national law to escape its obligation to arbitrate appears as a 'truly international public law provision for international arbitration law' which is independent from the content of the domestic law of the state concerned.

5 Defined legal relationship

4.86 The requirement of a 'defined legal relationship' found in Article 7(1) of both the 1985 and 2006 versions of the Model Law, as well as Article II(1) of the New York Convention, means that a single arbitration agreement cannot purport to cover all disputes that might arise between the parties. The arbitration agreement has to be limited in scope to disputes arising *in respect of a defined legal relationship*. The precise circumstances that would amount to a *defined legal relationship* have not been clarified in legislation and any attempt to do so may be fraught with difficulty. New Zealand Court of Appeal authority suggests that 'a defined legal relationship was a relationship which gave rise to the possibility that one party was entitled to some form of legal remedy against the other'.[110] At an earlier stage of those proceedings, Justice Fisher of the New Zealand High Court had opined:

> The next phrase traversed in argument was 'a defined legal relationship'. Several factors suggest that this phrase has a particularly broad meaning. First, the relationship need not be contractual ('whether contractual or not'). Secondly, s 10(1) [of the *New Zealand Arbitration Act 1996*] appears to envisage that arbitration agreements can embrace any dispute which the parties have agreed to submit to arbitration so long as the arbitration agreement is not contrary to public policy or, under any other law, is not capable of determination by arbitration. Thirdly, the survey of policy considerations and implied legislative intentions conducted earlier suggests that Parliament would not have intended to reduce the range of disputes previously amenable to arbitration.

---

[108] P Dunham and S Greenberg, 'Balancing Sovereignty and the Contractor's Rights in International Construction Arbitrations Involving State Entities', (2006) 23(2) *International Construction Law Review* 130.
[109] Ibid., p. 132 (footnotes omitted). See also Chapter 3, fn 10.
[110] *Methanex Motunui Ltd v Spellman* [2004] 3 NZLR 454, at para 61.

Those considerations support the view that 'defined legal relationship' is neither confined to relationships recorded in documents nor to formal relationships such as contracts, trusts or partnership agreements. Consistent with this view, it has been held that they include relationships between persons in breach of statutory duty and their victims: *Hi-Fert Pty Ltd v Kiukiang Maritime Carriers Inc* (1997) 145 ALR 500 (arbitration clause upheld where dispute under Trade Practices Act 1974 (Aust), the Australian equivalent of the Fair Trading Act 1986 (New Zealand), appeal allowed on another aspect (1998) 149 ALR 142).

There must be some limitation imposed by the expression 'defined legal relationship' if complete redundancy is to be avoided. As a bare minimum, the expression would seem to indicate that the dispute must be of a legal nature as distinct from a merely religious, cultural, academic, or social one.[111]

A similarly broad approach can be seen in Australian case law. In *Hi-Fert Pty Ltd v Kiukiang Marine Carriers Inc*,[112] Justice Tamberlin of the Australian Federal Court found that a statutory relationship between a party alleged to have engaged in misleading conduct and the party who claimed loss was a relevant and sufficiently defined legal relationship.

4.87

Born has noted that in practice, 'the "defined legal relationship" requirement has seldom been tested and has very limited practical importance'.[113] His discussion of the issue suggests that the requirement may have originated from historical distinctions between arbitration agreements and submission agreements.[114] The historical distinctions were directed at whether an arbitration agreement was a valid contract, whereas nowadays the focus appears to be on the intended scope of an arbitration agreement. This shift in focus can be seen in the discussion of this issue by Redfern and Hunter.[115] It is also evident in the deliberations of the UNCITRAL Working Group revising the UNCITRAL Arbitration Rules. The phrase 'defined legal relationship' now appears in Article 1 of the 2010 rules. The Working Group's report on its 46th session stated:[116]

4.88

> The Working Group considered whether the words 'in respect of a defined legal relationship, whether contractual or not,' should be added to paragraph (1). It was suggested that these words should not be added as they might unnecessarily limit the scope of the Rules and could raise difficult interpretative questions. It was also said that the reference to a 'defined legal relationship' might not easily be accommodated in certain legal systems.
>
> In response, it was said that the words 'in respect of a defined legal relationship, whether contractual or not' were well recognized given that they were derived from the New York Convention, and were also included in article 7, paragraph (1) of the UNCITRAL Arbitration Model Law. <u>In favour of their retention, it was said that these words put beyond doubt that a broad range of disputes, whether or not arising out of a contract,</u>

---

111 [2004] 1 NZLR 95, at para 83.
112 *Hi-Fert Pty Ltd v Kiukiang Marine Carriers Inc* (1997) 145 ALR 500.
113 Born, op. cit. fn 19, p. 256.
114 See Section 2.2.
115 Redfern, Hunter et al, op. cit. fn 48, para 3–10.
116 UN Doc A/CN.9/619, paras 22 and 23.

could be submitted to arbitration under the Rules and that their deletion could give rise to ambiguity. It was also suggested that these words would have educational impact on the future developments in the field of international arbitration. (Emphasis added)

6 Consolidation, joinder and third party notices

4.89 Consolidation, joinder and intervention are increasingly associated with procedural aspects of arbitrations arising from disputes involving more than two parties or two parties but more than one contract. In contrast, the use of third party notices in international arbitration appears to be less common. Fundamentally, they are all issues of consent and as such are intimately connected to the arbitration agreement(s).

4.90 Consolidation involves the fusion of two or more separate and independently existing arbitrations into one. Joinder and intervention, on the other hand, concern the introduction of one or more additional parties[117] into a single, existing arbitration. Joinder and intervention are opposite sides of the same coin. The former refers to the situation where an existing party to the arbitration seeks to add a new party. The latter is when an entity that is not a party to the arbitration wishes to become a party. Third party notices are a device more commonly known to domestic court procedure and used when one party (typically the respondent) wants a third party, for instance its supplier, to be present at the arbitration because it may have a subsequent action against the third party.

4.91 The practice of consolidating court cases or joining third parties to court actions is widespread within domestic courts. It may further the interests of justice to combine related cases so as to avoid inconsistent outcomes. Mechanisms accordingly exist for courts to make compulsory orders to this effect when it is procedurally efficient to do so. However, as Born notes 'consolidation, joinder and intervention in international arbitration, as well as domestic arbitration, raise additional or different issues than in national court litigation'.[118] A fundamental difference is that a national court with appropriate jurisdiction has the power to compel a party's participation, whereas arbitrators have authority only over proper parties to the arbitration. Another difference stems from the origin and purpose of a national court. Whereas an arbitral tribunal owes its existence and power to the parties' agreement, a national court is an organ of the state. This means the court must consider its jurisdiction at large rather than simply the mandate to resolve particular disputes between parties. Competent courts can, therefore, both unilaterally invite[119] and even compel the participation of third parties.

---

117 Although it is common to speak of the introduction of 'parties', see the discussion of ICC Case No. 12171 below in section 6.3.
118 Born, op. cit. fn 19, p. 2069.
119 ICSID and NAFTA tribunal decisions also have a public interest aspect and it is therefore not surprising that they are given the power to invite third party submissions. See further C Kessedjian, 'Sir Kenneth Bailey Memorial Lecture: Dispute Resolution in a Complex International Society', (2005) 29 *Melbourne University Law Review* 765 at 784. Rule 37(2) of the ICSID Rules was inserted into those Rules in 2006 and NAFTA Free Trade Commission, *Statement of the Free Trade Commission on Non-disputing Party Participation*, 7 October 2003. It states that 'the Tribunal may allow a person or entity that is not a party to the dispute ... to file a

4.92 Consolidation, joinder and intervention deserve proper consideration given the increased complexity of cross-border commercial relationships and the consequential rise in international arbitrations involving more than two parties. This increase can be seen, by way of example, from ICC statistics on multiparty arbitrations. In 2009, 233 ICC arbitrations (or 28.5% of all ICC arbitrations for that year) involved more than two parties. Out of these 233 cases, 206 (88.4%) involved between three and five parties, 21 (9%) involved between six and 10 parties, and six (2.6%) involved more than 10 parties. One case filed in 2009 had 19 different parties. The existence of multiple parties to an arbitration does not, however, necessarily mean that issues of joinder or consolidation will arise. In the three years from 1 January 2007 to 31 December 2009, the ICC Court dealt with only 24 contested requests for consolidation of cases, eight of which were accepted by the court and the remainder rejected. In the same time period, the court heard twenty one contested requests for joinder of a new party, 13 of which were allowed and the rest rejected.[120]

4.93 There are numerous issues that can arise when consolidation, joinder or intervention is sought. For example, the more parties involved in an arbitration the longer it is likely to take, and thus adding parties may adversely affect the speed and efficiency of resolving the initial dispute. Similarly concern for the maintenance of confidentiality can arise. Confidentiality may be an important factor in a party's decision to choose arbitration over litigation. A perceived problem with allowing consolidation, joinder or intervention is that it potentially increases the number of entities that become aware of both the dispute and the evidence. The decision to consolidate, join or permit intervention must therefore give due consideration to issues of confidentiality.[121]

4.94 Consolidation, joinder and intervention, and third party notices are discussed further in turn below. However, irrespective of which of these is being considered, evidence of consent of all participants avoids any debate about whether it is possible. The solutions offered by arbitral rules differ on whether specific consent is needed at the time of the proposed third party participation or whether this can be given broadly, before the issue arises. Voser suggests that joinder should only be permitted on consideration of all the circumstances and in cases where the

---

written submission with the Tribunal regarding a matter within the scope of the dispute'. It then proceeds to set out relevant criteria for the ICSID tribunal to consider including the assistance that the non–party could provide in determining a factual or legal matter and whether that party has a significant interest in the proceedings. It also adds that '[t]he Tribunal shall ensure that the non-disputing party submission does not disrupt the proceeding or unduly burden or unfairly prejudice either party, and that both parties are given an opportunity to present their observations on the non-disputing party submission'. One of the reasons for including this amendment was the public character of many of the issues that arise in ICSID arbitrations and the impact that these arbitrations may have on the wider community. Nonetheless, the rule does not grant the ICSID tribunal a power to compel the filing of a written submission by third party.

120 These figures only include applications for joinder or consolidation made to the ICC Court. Under the ICC Rules and practice it is only the court, and not arbitral tribunals, that can decide to join a new party or consolidate arbitrations. Parties nonetheless sometimes make (misguided) applications to arbitral tribunals for such relief. These statistics are cited from S Greenberg, J Feris and C Albanesi, 'Consolidation, Joinder, Cross-Claims, Multiparty and Multicontract Arbitrations: Recent ICC Experience', in B Hanotiau and EA Schwartz (eds), *Multiparty Arbitration*, Dossier VII, ICC Institute of World Business Law, ICC Publication No. 701, September 2010.

121 Confidentiality is discussed in Chapter 7, Section 11.

'balancing of interest between the party refusing joinder and the party requesting joinder clearly strikes in favour of the party requesting the joinder'.[122] Any dispute as to whether consent had been given would be for the arbitral tribunal to decide, rather than a matter requiring domestic court intervention.

4.95 Given the rise in multi-party arbitrations,[123] it may be desirable that arbitration rules and laws address the issues of consolidation, joinder and intervention more specifically. It is expected that these matters will form a substantive change in the forthcoming ICC Rules, which are expected to become effective as of January 2011.

6.1 Consolidation

4.96 As noted above, consolidation involves bringing two or more separate arbitrations together and hearing them as one. If all parties to all arbitrations agree, consolidation can easily be effected. Courtesy dictates that the arbitral tribunal's consent is necessary, but it would be difficult to conceive of a situation where the arbitral tribunal (or arbitral tribunals) would refuse consolidation in the face of an agreement of all parties. Problems arise when at least one party to one of the arbitrations does not agree to consolidation.

4.97 The Model Law and the New York Convention are silent on the issue of consolidation. This should not be interpreted as meaning that consolidation is not possible, but rather that it is a matter of party autonomy. Born notes that the drafters of the Model Law 'considered but rejected proposals to address [consolidation, joinder and intervention], both in the original 1985 version of the Law and in the 2006 revisions'[124] as it was a matter for party agreement.

4.98 Several countries in the Asia-Pacific region have incorporated specific consolidation provisions into their international arbitration laws. Those provisions generally require parties expressly to opt in to the consolidation regime. Section 24 (in combination with Section 22) of the Australian International Arbitration Act 1974 is an example. When parties have opted in, the relevant arbitral tribunal is empowered to make a decision on consolidation. In contrast, the legislation of Hong Kong and New Zealand ordinarily grants power to their courts to order consolidation in domestic arbitrations and thus it is not necessary for parties specifically to opt in. In both those jurisdictions, parties to an international arbitration may agree to the application of the relevant legislative provisions, but absent such an agreement those legislative provisions are applicable to domestic arbitrations only.[125] The provisions are therefore of the opt-in variety for international arbitration. The laws of Singapore and Malaysia also consider the

---

[122] N Voser, 'Multi-party Disputes and Joinder of Third Parties', (2008) 14 *ICCA Congress Series* 343, at p. 395.
[123] Referred to above at para 4.92.
[124] Born, op. cit. fn 19, p. 2077 (footnotes omitted).
[125] Hong Kong Arbitration Ordinance, Section 6B. The New Zealand legislation first grants the power to the arbitral tribunal, but in the event the arbitral tribunal refuses to order consolidation, a party can seek the same order from a court, New Zealand Arbitration Act 1996, Second Schedule, Article 2.

possibility of consolidation in domestic arbitration. In both jurisdictions the power may be given to the arbitral tribunal where the parties have agreed to confer such a power.[126] It is possible for parties conducting their international arbitration in Malaysia to opt into the application of its law governing the consolidation of domestic arbitrations.

4.99 The arbitral rules used by some institutions in the Asia-Pacific region also contain specific provisions on consolidation. The Indian Council of Arbitration Rule 39 permits the registrar, with the consent of all parties, to direct that hearings be heard jointly, or refer different applications for arbitration proceedings to the same arbitral tribunal. That rule goes on to state specifically that a separate award must still be given in each arbitration. In effect, this procedure does not amount to consolidation but rather a parallel hearing of separate cases by the same panel of arbitrators in each. Similarly, the Rules of the Bangladesh Council for Arbitration specifically state that an arbitral tribunal does not have the power to consolidate proceedings unless consent is given on agreed terms by the parties.[127] JCAA Rule 44 provides that either the JCAA or any arbitral tribunal may, on its own initiative, consider whether consolidation should occur, but may only consolidate once written consent of all the parties is obtained. If, however, the arbitrations all arise out of the same arbitration agreement, then such consent is not needed.[128] There is no apparent requirement that the parties be identical in the different arbitrations to be consolidated under these rules. Such a requirement exists in Article 4(6) of the ICC Rules, giving it the advantage of predictability, but is sometimes criticised as being unnecessarily restrictive.

4.100 Finally, if parties wish to ensure that related arbitrations can be consolidated, this should be considered at the time the arbitration agreement (or agreements, where there are multiple contracts) is drafted. A properly drafted consolidation clause in the contract (or in each of the related contracts, as the case may be) is the best way to ensure that consolidation takes place as the parties desire.

6.2 Joinder and intervention

4.101 The issues of joinder and intervention are similar. Both deal with the introduction of a third party to an existing arbitral proceeding. In the case of joinder, an existing party to the arbitration attempts to bring a third party into the proceedings, and to have that third party bound by the outcome of the proceedings. In the case of intervention, it is the third party itself that is seeking to participate in the arbitration proceedings. As noted above, these questions relate fundamentally to consent.

---

[126] Singapore Arbitration Act 2001, Section 26; Malaysian Arbitration Act 2005, Section 40(2).
[127] BCA Rules, Rule 23.1.
[128] JCAA Rules, Rule 44(1) provides: 'If the Association or the arbitral tribunal determines that it is necessary to consolidate multiple requests for arbitration that contain claims that are essentially and mutually related, the arbitral tribunal, after obtaining the written consent of all the relevant parties, may examine such cases together in the same proceedings; provided that, if multiple requests for arbitration arise out of the same arbitration agreement, no consent of the parties is necessary.'

4.102   If all of the parties to the existing arbitration as well as the potential new party consent to joinder or intervention, there should be no problem effecting it. As an additional part of its consent, the new party would need to agree to the already constituted arbitral tribunal (if there is one) and to the prior proceedings of the arbitration. As in consolidation, the arbitral tribunal's consent would need to be sought as a matter of courtesy.

4.103   Much like consolidation, problems relating to joinder and intervention arise when at least one party – either an existing party or the new party – does not agree. The arbitral tribunal or arbitral institution must consider whether the parties have previously given their consent, and whether that is sufficient.

4.104   Although most arbitration agreements and arbitral rules are silent on the question of joinder, arbitral tribunals have inherent power to consider whether consent has been given to the type of joinder application that is being sought. This power results from the arbitral tribunal's general power to determine the procedure, and is supported analogously by the doctrine of competence-competence.[129] Where the arbitral rules contain specific reference to joinder, an arbitral tribunal will need to apply the mechanism and elements of these provisions carefully, as they reflect exactly the process to which the parties have consented.

4.105   The SIAC Rules specifically describe the conditions for joinder. SIAC Rule 24(b) states that an arbitral tribunal may 'allow other parties to be joined in the arbitration, provided that such person is a party to the arbitration agreement, with the written consent of such third party...'. This is one of the rules that was specifically amended in the 4th Edition of the SIAC Rules following criticism of the 2007 version.[130] The 2010 UNCITRAL Arbitration Rules also now permit joinder in Article 17(5). Pursuant to the new UNCITRAL rule the arbitral tribunal may at the request of any party join a third party provided that the party to be joined is a party to the arbitration agreement, and only after giving existing parties the opportunity to object on the basis of prejudice.

4.106   Beyond this region, examples of rules which deal with joinder and/or intervention include LCIA Rules Article 21.1(h), and Swiss Rules Article 4(2). The Swiss Rules provision is particularly interesting because it does not refer to consent at all:

> Where a third party requests to participate in arbitral proceedings already pending under these Rules or where a party to arbitral proceedings under these Rules intends to cause a third party to participate in the arbitration, the arbitral tribunal shall decide on such request, after consulting with all parties, taking into account all circumstances it deems relevant and applicable.

4.107   There has been a wide range of commentary on this Swiss provision. Some commentators believe that by virtue of this article the parties give their consent to the participation of third parties at the time they conclude their arbitration

---

[129] Competence-competence is dealt with in Chapter 5.
[130] Voser, op. cit. fn 122, p. 399.

agreement – that is usually long before any dispute arises.[131] Other commentators disagree and argue that it is not reasonable to find implicit consent in this way.[132]

The ICC International Court of Arbitration, while its rules are silent on the question of joinder, developed a practice beginning from 2001 according to which the ICC Court itself decides whether new parties can be joined to an arbitration upon the application of an existing party. Three conditions need to be satisfied: 4.108

(i) no step has been taken towards the constitution of the arbitral tribunal (since the third party should, once included, have the right to participate in constituting the arbitral tribunal);
(ii) the party to be joined signed the arbitration agreement (this shows a clear intention beyond basic participation in the negotiation and performance of the contract); and
(iii) the party requesting the joinder has introduced claims against the party to be joined (merely reserving the right to raise claims later, or raising a conditional claim is generally insufficient, but an unfounded claim might be accepted as it is not for the ICC Court to determine whether a claim is well-founded).[133]

During the initial years of implementing this practice, the ICC Court was strict in relation to the second element, that is requiring that the party to be joined signed the contract containing the arbitration agreement. However, in recent years the ICC Court has relaxed that requirement provided that there is evidence that the new entity to be joined is or could be a party to that arbitration agreement.[134] Some examples are described below.[135] 4.109

The ICC Court allowed joinder of a third party where the third party had signed an MOU amending the initial contract, but had not signed the contract itself. The new party was the claimant's parent company. In addition to the new party's signature of the MOU, which indisputably related to the contract and incorporated provisions of it, the ICC Court took into account many other factors, including that the new party had closely participated in the performance of the contract and had played a key role in settlement negotiations relating to the dispute. 4.110

In another case, the ICC Court joined a third party which was, undisputedly, the legal successor of a party to the contract containing the arbitration clause. The successor had signed a second, related contract which contained an identical arbitration clause. In another succession case, the arbitration was commenced by a claimant under a Joint Venture Agreement ('JVA') which it had not signed. 4.111

---

131 T Zuberbühler, K Müller and P Habegger (eds), *Swiss Rules of International Arbitration: Commentary*, Kluwer Law International, 2005, at p. 41; Lew, Mistelis and Kröll, op. cit. fn 16, para 16–42.
132 A Meier, *Einbezug Dritter vor internationalen Schiedsgerichten*, Schulthess, 2007, p. 152.
133 See A Whitesell and E Silva-Romero, 'Multiparty and Multicontract Arbitration: Recent ICC Experience', *ICC International Court of Arbitration Bulletin*, Special Supplement, 2003, p. 10.
134 L Malintoppi and S Greenberg, 'The Practice of the ICC International Court of Arbitration Concerning Multi-Party Contracts and Scrutiny of Awards', *ICC Young Arbitrators Forum*, Barcelona, 26–29 June 2008, para 23 et seq. For a thorough explanation of all the ICC Court's practices in respect of multiparty and multicontract arbitration, see Greenberg, Feris and Albanesi, op. cit. fn 120.
135 The examples are from Malintoppi and Greenberg, ibid.

178   INTERNATIONAL COMMERCIAL ARBITRATION

The respondent in the proceedings (a signatory to the JVA) sought to join a new party which had signed the JVA. According to the claimant, this third party had assigned to the claimant all of its rights, interests and obligations under the JVA. However, the respondent contended that the third party remained separately bound by non-compete obligations in the JVA, and by its arbitration clause. The ICC Court decided that the third party should be joined, leaving to the arbitral tribunal the decision as to whether it had jurisdiction over the new party and, if so, whether that party owed any substantive obligations to the respondent after the assignment.

4.112   Intervention covers the situation where a third party requests to participate as a party in an existing arbitration. Again, as is the case in joining a party, the focus of the arbitral tribunal should be on the consent of the parties. For example, Rule 43 of the JCAA Rules appears to suggest that general consent to its rules is not sufficient and that specific consent from all parties (excluding the third party attempting to intervene) is required:

> *Rule 43. Participation in Proceedings*
> 1. Any interested person who is not a party to a particular arbitration may, with the consent of all the parties to such arbitration, participate in such arbitration as a claimant or be allowed to participate therein as a respondent.
> 2. If the participation in the arbitration provided for in the preceding paragraph occurs before the establishment of the arbitral tribunal, the arbitrators shall be appointed subject to the provisions of Rule 45 and, if such participation occurs after the establishment of the arbitral tribunal, the composition thereof shall not be affected.

4.113   As we observed at the conclusion of the section on consolidation, the best time for parties to contemplate joinder and intervention is during the drafting of the arbitration agreement.[136] A properly drafted joinder clause in the contract (or contracts) is the best way to ensure that it will work effectively and in the way desired by the parties.

6.3 Third party notices

4.114   There is another capacity in which a non-party to the arbitration might be required to participate in it. Third party notices address the situation where an existing party, typically a respondent party, believes it has a right to pursue a third party for any liability that may be awarded against it in the arbitration. Some domestic laws state that by causing the third party to participate in the proceedings, the third party will lose its right to assert that the respondent did not defend the initial case properly. To accommodate these laws, court systems have mechanisms such as 'third party notices' or 'vouching in'. It is questionable whether similar mechanisms are or should be available in international arbitration. However, an ICC arbitral tribunal seated in Zurich has noted that '[d]espite

---

136 See also E Tong Chun Fai and N Dewan, 'Drafting Arbitration Agreements with 'Consolidation' in Mind?', (2009) 5 *Asian International Arbitration Journal* 70.

the lack of statutory regulations, scholars and courts agree that the participation of third persons to an arbitration procedure... based on third person notice is possible in principle....'.[137]

The arbitral tribunal in that instance drew a distinction between participating in an arbitration as a party and participating as a 'collateral intervener'.[138] This distinction was considered important because it was not necessary for a collateral intervener to be a party to the arbitration agreement. The arbitral tribunal further noted that 'the conclusion of an arbitration agreement reflects the intention of the parties to be subject to private and confidential proceedings that exclude third persons. Therefore, third persons can only be admitted to the arbitration proceedings if all parties to the proceedings agree to this'.

7 Enforcement of arbitration agreements

Most arbitration agreements constitute an exclusive mechanism for resolving disputes. By agreeing to arbitrate, the parties agree to waive their right to submit their dispute to a national court. Notwithstanding such agreement, it is often the case that once a dispute arises one of the parties will see an advantage in commencing court proceedings rather than arbitration or will simply want to delay the matter.

Enforcement of arbitration agreements concerns the extent to which a domestic court will respect the parties' exclusive arbitration agreement by staying its own proceeding when a party alleges that there is an arbitration agreement covering the dispute in question. This issue is addressed in the New York Convention,[139] Article II(1) of which provides:

> Each Contracting State shall recognize an agreement in writing under which the parties undertake to submit to arbitration all or any differences which have arisen or which may arise between them in respect of a defined legal relationship, whether contractual or not, concerning a subject matter capable of settlement by arbitration.

If a court in a New York Convention state is called upon to recognise and enforce an arbitration agreement, and the Convention is applicable, pursuant to Article II(3), it must stay the proceedings in favour of arbitration. That Article provides:

> a court of a Contracting State, when seized of an action in a matter in respect of which the parties have made an agreement within the meaning of this article,[[140]] shall, at

---

137 *ICC Case No. 12171*, Award on Third Person Notice, 7 April 2004, (2005) 23(2) *ASA Bulletin* (references omitted).
138 The arbitral tribunal uses the German expression 'Nebenintervention' which it translates as collateral intervener but might also be translated as 'side intervener' or 'side party'.
139 The New York Convention is better known for its provisions on enforcement of arbitral awards. In fact, its title refers only to the recognition and enforcement of arbitral awards.
140 An agreement within the meaning of New York Convention Article II(3) is defined in Article II(1).

the request of one of the parties, refer the parties to arbitration, unless it finds that the said agreement is null and void, inoperative or incapable of being performed.

4.119 The word 'shall' means that the state court has no discretion to refuse to stay its own proceedings and must refer the parties to arbitration unless it finds that the said agreement is null and void, inoperative or incapable of being performed.[141] Similar wording can be found in Article 8(1) of the Model Law:

> A court before which an action is brought in a matter which is the subject of an arbitration agreement shall, if a party so requests not later than when submitting his first statement on the substance of the dispute, refer the parties to arbitration unless it finds that the agreement is null and void, inoperative or incapable of being performed.

4.120 Not surprisingly, given the obligatory nature of the stay, there have been many attempts to narrow the application of this requirement as it appears in the respective international arbitration laws of the countries in this region.[142]

4.121 Neither the New York Convention nor the Model Law stipulates whether the court should investigate the validity of an arbitration agreement. On one interpretation of these provisions, they appear to conflict with the competence-competence rule. That rule and the potential conflict are discussed in detail in Chapter 5.[143]

7.1 Existence of a dispute

4.122 An interesting issue sometimes raised in attempts to deny the enforcement of an arbitration agreement is the question whether the court must determine if there is in fact a dispute. Malaysian legislation follows the New Zealand position of permitting a court to refuse a stay where it finds that there is no dispute between the parties.[144]

> 10. (1) A court before which proceedings are brought in respect of a matter which is the subject of an arbitration agreement shall, where a party makes an application before taking any other steps in the proceedings, stay those proceedings and refer the parties to arbitration unless it finds –
> (a) that the agreement is null and void, inoperative or incapable of being performed; or
> (b) that there is in fact no dispute between the parties with regard to the matters to be referred.

4.123 Judicial criticism of the New Zealand position was made in *Todd Energy Ltd v Kiwi Power (1995) Ltd*.[145] In other jurisdictions, without the wording found in

---

[141] The extent of a domestic court's ability to investigate or decide whether an arbitration agreement is null and void, inoperative or incapable of being performed is discussed in Chapter 5, see section 4.2.
[142] In addition to the discussion elsewhere in this book, see a discussion of Australian case law on this issue by R Garnett, 'The Current Status of International Arbitration Agreements in Australia', (1999) 15 *Journal of Contract Law* 29.
[143] See Chapter 5, Section 4.2.
[144] The extracted text is from the Malaysian Arbitration Act 2005; see also Article 8, Schedule 1 of the New Zealand Arbitration Act 1996.
[145] High Court, Wellington, CP 46/01, 29 October 2001, per Master Thomson.

the Malaysian and New Zealand legislation, courts have also been called on to determine whether there was in fact a dispute. In the Singaporean High Court case of *Dalian Hualiang Enterprise Group Co Ltd v Louis Dreyfus Asia Pte Ltd* it was observed:[146]

> The existence or non-existence of a dispute or difference as envisaged under the relevant arbitration agreement between the parties is crucial to the granting of a stay. For this purpose, a dispute will exist unless there has been a clear and unequivocal admission not only of liability but also quantum : see *Louis Dreyfus v. Bonarich International (Group) Limited* [1997] 3 HKC 597; *Tai Hing Cotton Mill Limited v. Glencore Grain Rotterdam BV* [1996] 1 HKC 363, at 375A-B. In the absence of admissions as to both these aspects, a mere denial of liability or of the quantum claimed, even in circumstances where no defence exists, will be sufficient to found a dispute for the purposes of section 6 of the Ordinance (and Article 8 UNCITRAL Model Law). Thus, finding out whether a dispute (as defined in this way) exists, is the only exercise that the court carries out in a stay application (apart of course from construing the arbitration agreement to discover its full ambit): it does not involve itself in evaluating the merits of the claim.

7.2 Attaching conditions

In some jurisdictions, such as Singapore and Australia,[147] statutes have clothed courts with additional powers to impose conditions on the parties as part of the process of enforcing the arbitration agreement. For example, Section 6(2) of the Singapore International Arbitration Act 2002 states:

4.124

> The court to which an application has been made in accordance with subsection (1) shall make an order, upon such terms or conditions as it may think fit, staying the proceedings so far as the proceedings relate to the matter, unless it is satisfied that the arbitration agreement is null and void, inoperative or incapable of being performed.

In the case of The 'Duden'[148] Judge Andrew Ang of the Singapore High Court said: 'The discretion of the court to impose terms and conditions upon a stay of court proceedings in favour of arbitration is an unfettered discretion.'[149] He continued:

4.125

> That having been said, discretionary power must, of course, be exercised judiciously. The corollary to a wide discretionary power is the great caution with which it should be exercised. Unfortunately, there is little case law (both local and from Australia) on the court's exercise of its discretion with regard to the imposing of conditions on a stay of court proceedings in favour of arbitration.
>
> The main guiding principle in my view is that courts generally should be slow to interfere in the arbitration process.

---

146 [2005] 4 SLR 646, at 663.
147 Section 7(2) of the Australian International Arbitration Act 1974. See also *Walter Rau Neusser Oel und Fett AG v Cross Pacific Trading Ltd* [2005] FCA 1102; the commentary on that decision in C Kee, 'Australian Conditions Imposed in Stay of Foreign Arbitration Matter', (2006) 44(7) *New South Wales Law Society Journal* 68; *WesTrac Pty Ltd v Eastcoast OTR Tyres Pty Ltd* (2008) 219 FLR 461.
148 [2008] 4 SLR 984.
149 Ibid., at 989 (emphasis in original).

4.126　In that case Judge Ang imposed a condition that the defendant waive the time bar defence that might have otherwise been available to it. Had the defendant not made such a waiver, the matter would not have been allowed to go to arbitration. A similar situation arose in the Victorian Supreme Court decision of *Ansett Australia Ltd (Subject to a Deed of Company Arrangement) v Malaysian Airline System Berhad*.[150] In that decision Justice Hollingworth dealt with the limitation period issue by requiring that the arbitration be treated as if it had been commenced on the same day as the litigation had originally commenced. This approach avoided the need to determine issues that would otherwise be left up to the arbitrator, such as the applicable law, as well as not requiring either party to waive their rights expressly. Justice Hollingworth had been asked to impose a number of other conditions which she declined to do. This approach is consistent with that of the New South Wales Court of Appeal which has observed:[151]

> The 'conditions' which s 7(2) of the [Model Law] contemplates are machinery conditions. They relate to hearing and the like procedures and not to conditions which determine, in effect, the substantive rights of the parties.

4.127　The power to impose conditions on the decision to enforce a stay application is unusual. It can be contrasted with Article 8, Schedule 1 of the New Zealand Arbitration Act 1996, and Article 8 of the Model Law, neither of which refer to the ability to impose conditions.

8 Arbitrability

4.128　At its simplest, the question of 'arbitrability' concerns whether a dispute is capable of determination by arbitration. For a matter to be determined by arbitration the parties must have agreed for it to be determined by arbitration – this is a subjective act; something that is personal to the parties. In addition to party agreement, the applicable law must allow disputes of that kind to be determined by arbitration – this is objective; if resolution of that kind of dispute by arbitration is prohibited, the parties' intentions become irrelevant.

8.1 Subjective arbitrability

4.129　Subjective arbitrability concerns whether the parties have agreed to arbitrate certain claims or issues. Usually this requires interpreting the arbitration agreement, including phrases such as 'in connection with' or 'arising out of' the contract. However, phrases like these are not unique to arbitration law. Often domestic jurisdictions will have specific meanings that have been attributed to these phrases by courts. Perhaps unfortunately, the meaning of these phrases may vary

---

150 (2008) 217 FLR 376.
151 *O'Brien v Tanning Research Laboratories Inc* (1988) 14 NSWLR 601, at 622.

from jurisdiction to jurisdiction. Identifying which law applies to the arbitration agreement, and applying that law to it, may significantly affect the outcome.[152]

Take the phrase 'arising out of this contract'. Do claims for pre-contractual misrepresentation arise out of a contract? It is generally accepted that they do, however some jurisdictions previously applied a temporal limitation.[153] For something to arise out of a contract it was argued that it must have occurred post-contract formation. If such a timing requirement existed then pre-contractual claims would fall outside the scope of that phrase in an arbitration agreement.[154] Such an interpretation of an arbitration agreement would be devoid of common, commercial sense. Where commercial parties agree to arbitrate, their presumed desire is for all of their claims – pre-contractual or post-contractual – arising in any way from that relationship to be decided by arbitration. It is very unlikely that they would want to be engaged in a process where some claims relating to a dispute are resolved by a court and other claims in that dispute are determined by arbitration. Such an inefficient and unduly complex process should be avoided.[155] 4.130

In China the Supreme People's Court's Interpretation of Several Issues regarding the Application of the Arbitration Law of the PRC[156] has addressed the issue of intended scope of an arbitration agreement. It is cited as stating that 'when parties to an agreement agreed generally that contractual disputes shall be submitted to arbitration, then the contractual disputes shall be construed as including disputes arising from the establishment, validity, change, assignment, performance, default, interpretation and termination of a contract'.[157] 4.131

The 2007 Hong Kong decision in *Newmark Capital Corporation Ltd v Coffee Partners Ltd*[158] provides insight into the interpretative process that may be 4.132

---

[152] For further elaboration of the meaning of such phrases and the significance of this see Kee, op. cit. fn 147; and C Kee, 'Set-Off in International Arbitration – What Can the Asian Region Learn?', (2005) 1(2) *Asian International Arbitration Journal* 141.
[153] See, e.g. Comandate Marine Corp v Pan Australia Shipping Pty Ltd [2006] FCAFC 192. But see the Malaysian case of *Jan De Nul NV v Inai Kiara Sdn Bhd* [2006] 3 CLJ 46, where the Court of Appeal found that tort claims were not covered by an arbitration clause that read 'any dispute or difference arising out of and/or in connection with this agreement'. The Malaysian court refers with approval to the Full Federal Court of Australia decision of *Hi-Fert Pty Ltd v Kiukiang Maritime Carriers* (1998) 159 ALR 142. Aspects of the *Hi-Fert* decision closely related to this issue were specifically overruled by the Full Federal Court in *Comandate Marine Corp v Pan Australia Shipping Pty Ltd* [2006] FCAFC 192.
[154] This appeared to be the position in Australia prior to the Full Federal Court Decision of *Comandate Marine Corp v Pan Australia Shipping Pty Ltd* [2006] FCAFC 192. In the leading judgment Justice Allsop makes it quite clear that 'arising out of' definitely now includes pre-contractual claims under Australian law. For a discussion of the meaning of other such phrases in Australian law see *Incitec Ltd v Alkimos Shipping Corp* (2004) 206 ALR 558, at 563–564 per Justice Allsop. Further in an Australian domestic context the Victorian Supreme Court in *Transfield Philippines Inc v Pacific Hydro Ltd* [2006] VSC 175 has noted that 'the words "in connection with", which are used in arbitration agreements, are words of the widest import and should not, in the absence of compelling reason to the contrary, be read down'. In New Zealand see, e.g. *Bowport Ltd v Alloy Yachts International Ltd* [2004] 1 NZLR 361; *Mount Cook (Northland) Ltd v Swedish Motors Ltd* [1986] 1 NZLR 720. In Brunei see *L & M Prestressing Sdn Bhd v Engineering Construction Pte Ltd* [1991] BNHC 39.
[155] In this context, see the speech by Lord Hoffman in the UK House of Lords decision *Premium Nafta Products Ltd v Fili Shipping Company Ltd* [2007] 2 All ER (Comm) 1053, at para 13. This was an appeal from *Fiona Trust & Holding Corporation v Privalov* [2007] 4 All ER 951.
[156] FaShi [2006] No. 7.
[157] Wan Exiang and Yu Xifu, op. cit. fn 46, p. 185.
[158] [2007] HKCU 241 (emphasis in original). For other Hong Kong authority see *Xu Yi Hong v Chen Ming Han* [2006] HKCU 1663; *Tommy Cp Sze & Co v Li & Fung (Trading) Ltd* [2003] 1 HKC 41, at 57; *Getwick Engineers Ltd v Pilecon Engineering Bhd* HCA 558/2002 (unreported).

followed by a common law court in this region when determining the scope of an arbitration agreement:

> But the scope of the arbitration clause still has to be ascertained by reference to applicable principles of law and construction.
>
> ...
>
> The first cause of action is a claim in misrepresentation. It does not concern any of the matters mentioned in the arbitration clause. In particular I do not think that the claim is one 'touching' or 'relating' 'to the affairs of CPL' (... Mr. Bartlett's skeleton arguments... stressed the words 'touching' and 'affairs of the Company' but I do not think that, properly read, the word 'touching' applies to the phrase 'affairs of the Company'; the phrase 'affairs of the Company' is preceded by the word 'to' and the more natural word to apply to the entire phrase 'to the affairs of the Company' must be 'relating' and not 'touching'; be that as it may I shall deal with the word 'touching' as well). In no way can the issue of whether certain representations were made... prior to [the Plaintiffs] even signing the SPAs (and becoming members) be regarded as 'affairs of [CPL]'.
>
> ...
>
> It may be said that the alleged acts of making misrepresentations formed part of the 'affairs'.... Further, some of the alleged misrepresentations related to the way the company would be run and managed, and that in demonstrating the 'falsity' of the representations one had to look at the way in which the 'affairs'... were conducted and hence the claim falls within this part of the clause. But I do not think that the phrase 'touching... relating to the affairs of [CPL]' meant these sorts of disputes. I accept... that the phrase 'affairs of the Company'... is intended to cover a complaint about the administration... such as allegations of unfair prejudicial conduct, fraud on minority and similar claims. Otherwise, the clause will cover any or all disputes with CPL, because all disputes with CPL must necessarily arise out of things done (or not done) by CPL and disputes about any such acts or omissions by CPL would be a dispute on the "affairs" of CPL. Article 21.1 is not and cannot be as broad as that. If it is as broad as that, then much of Article 21.1 would be otiose. It would only need to say "all or any disputes with CPL whatsoever". That, however, is not what Article 21.1 says.

4.133 The first sentence of the extracted passage above raises the important consideration of contract construction. The manner in which contracts are construed in each jurisdiction may vary. A well-drafted arbitration clause should be capable of reflecting the parties' intent accurately in any relevant jurisdiction. Most jurisdictions employ an objective theory of contract interpretation, which has led to statements from the Singapore High Court such as '[t]he defendants contended that their subjective intention was for SIAC Rules to apply given the international dimension of the Contract. But it was well established that the subjective intention of a party should not be considered by the court when construing a written document'.[159] It should be noted, however, that approaches to the objective theory of contract interpretation are not uniform, as different jurisdictions allow different levels of consideration of surrounding circumstances and other relevant materials.

---

[159] *Jurong Engineering Ltd v Black & Veatch Singapore Pte Ltd* [2004] 1 SLR 333, at 345.

In the 2007 decision of *Premium Nafta Products Ltd v Fili Shipping Company Ltd*,[160] the House of Lords took what Lord Hoffmann described as a fresh start to the construction of arbitration clauses pursuant to English law. He considered whether there was a difference between the meaning of 'under' a contract and 'arising out of' a contract. His Lordship noted:[161]

4.134

> In my opinion the construction of an arbitration clause should start from the assumption that the parties, as rational businessmen, are likely to have intended any dispute arising out of the relationship into which they have entered or purported to enter to be decided by the same tribunal. The clause should be construed in accordance with this presumption unless the language makes it clear that certain questions were intended to be excluded from the arbitrator's jurisdiction.

This decision, although not generally binding on courts in this region of the world, should be considered particularly persuasive in common law countries. The fresh start was required in part to bring English law into line with world practice,[162] and the decision is to be commended. During the course of his judgment Lord Hope of Craighead referred with approval to the Australian Full Federal Court of Appeal decision in *Comandate Marine Corp v Pan Australia Shipping Pty Ltd*.[163] In the *Comandate* decision Justice Allsop had similarly observed:[164]

4.135

> This liberal approach is underpinned by the sensible commercial presumption that the parties did not intend the inconvenience of having possible disputes from their transaction being heard in two places. This may be seen to be especially so in circumstances where disputes can be given different labels, or placed into different juridical categories, possibly by reference to the approaches of different legal systems. The benevolent and encouraging approach to consensual alternative non-curial dispute resolution assists in the conclusion that words capable of broad and flexible meaning will be given liberal construction and content. This approach conforms with a common-sense approach to commercial agreements, in particular when the parties are operating in a truly international market and come from different countries and legal systems and it provides appropriate respect for party autonomy.

Unfortunately, a subsequent Australian decision of *Seeley International Pty Ltd v Electra Air Conditioning BV*[165] neither referred to the House of Lords decision nor adopted its robust approach. The dispute resolution clause which the court in *Seeley* was called upon to consider referred the parties first to 'friendly discussions' and, failing resolution by that method, to arbitration. The scope of the arbitration clause was quite broad and included 'a dispute, question or difference of opinion ("Dispute") between the parties concerning or arising out of this

4.136

---

160 [2007] 2 All ER (Comm) 1053, an appeal from *Fiona Trust & Holding Corporation v Privalov* [2007] 4 All ER 951.
161 *Premium Nafta Products Ltd v Fili Shipping Company Ltd* [2007] 2 All ER (Comm) 1053, at para 13.
162 'This approach to the issue of construction is now firmly embedded as part of the law of international commerce' per Lord Hope of Craighead, *Premium Nafta Products Ltd v Fili Shipping Company Ltd* [2007] 2 All ER (Comm) 1053, at para 31.
163 [2006] FCAFC 192.
164 Ibid., at para 165.
165 [2008] FCA 29.

Agreement or its construction, meaning, operation or effect or concerning the rights, duties or liabilities of any party'. It also included a separate subclause which read '[n]othing in this [clause] prevents a party from seeking injunctive or declaratory relief in the case of a material breach or threatened breach of this Agreement'.

4.137 The plaintiff had commenced court proceedings seeking two declarations: the first to confirm a particular obligation of the respondent; and the second to state that the respondent was in breach of that obligation. The respondent sought a stay on the basis of the arbitration agreement. After determining that seeking declarations and injunctions from an arbitral tribunal was possible, Justice Mansfield went on to consider whether the parties had in fact included this within the scope of their arbitration agreement. Justice Mansfield noted that the scope of the clause should be robustly assessed, but then decided that in this case the parties had objectively intended recourse to the courts for injunctive or declaratory relief. Justice Mansfield then made declarations in the form requested by the plaintiff.

4.138 As a consequence, Justice Mansfield necessarily determined issues that were clearly within the ambit of the arbitration clause – *the rights, duties or liabilities of any party*. Although upheld on appeal,[166] this decision appears to be incorrect and out of touch with modern arbitral practice and court decisions in most of the world. The decision seems to find a temporal element in the clause, in effect construing the parties' agreement to mean that what was and was not arbitrable would be determined by the relative urgency of the claim – despite the fact that the urgency or not of the particular declarations sought was not analysed in the decision. We respectfully submit that the better interpretation of a contract that specifically gives the power of injunctive and declaratory relief to a court is that it is intended to maintain the status quo that exists between the parties at the time of the commencement of the arbitration proceedings, such as issuing injunctions to prevent property from being destroyed or removed. Such clauses are not for the purposes of enabling courts to determine finally the substantive rights of the parties, which is the task of the arbitral tribunal.

8.2 Objective arbitrability

4.139 Objective arbitrability concerns matters the law actually permits parties to resolve by arbitration. It is a legal, objective test. If the law prevents a particular kind of dispute from being decided by arbitration, then the consent of all the parties to arbitrate that type of dispute becomes irrelevant.

4.140 It was noted in Chapter 1 that judicial attitudes towards arbitration have not always been positive. Despite a now very positive global acceptance of

---

166 *Electra Air Conditioning BV v Seeley International Pty Ltd* [2008] FCAFC 169.

arbitration, some legal systems (and/or courts) occasionally seek to retain some control over the kinds of disputes that may be arbitrated.[167] That control is the issue at the heart of any discussion on objective arbitrability.

4.141 In his article 'A Plea for a Trans-national Approach to Arbitrability in Arbitrable Practice',[168] Lehmann attempted to justify such an approach through a comparison of French, Swiss, German, English and US law. His comparative analysis 'revealed a trend existing in a number of legal systems, incumbent in countries of different legal cultures and with divergent traditions regarding arbitration toward extending the categories of disputes in which arbitral adjudication is permitted'.[169]

4.142 That trend is reflected in several Asia-Pacific jurisdictions. In Singapore for example 'no specific subjects have been identified by statute as being or as not being arbitrable'.[170] However, '[i]t is generally accepted that issues, which may have public interest elements, may not be arbitrable, for example citizenship or legitimacy of marriage, grants of statutory licences, validity of registration of trade marks or patents, copyrights, winding-up of companies'.[171]

4.143 In Sri Lanka, Section 2 of the Arbitration Act states that only matters of an indictment or criminal proceedings are excluded from reference to arbitration. Similarly, but more explicitly, under the Philippines Alternative Dispute Resolution Act, the following matters are not subject to arbitration, mediation, or any other alternative dispute resolution method: 'labour disputes, civil status of persons, validity of marriage, grounds for legal separation, jurisdiction of courts, future legitime [inheritance expectation], criminal liability, and those which by law cannot be compromised.'[172] China's Arbitration Law is also prescriptive. Article 3(1) excludes the arbitration of disputes concerning marriage, adoption, guardianship, support and succession as well as administrative disputes that must be handled by administrative organs as prescribed by law.[173] The Japanese Arbitration Act on the other hand takes an inclusive approach rather than an exclusive one. That Act states that an arbitration agreement will be valid when its subject matter is a civil dispute that may be resolved by settlement between the parties. It does not separately define civil dispute other than to exclude divorce and separation.[174] Indonesia adopts a similar approach. Article 5 of the Indonesian Arbitration and Dispute Resolution Act 1999 reads:

---

[167] For a recent example, see the Indian Supreme Court decision of *N Radhakrishnan v Maestro Engineers* No. 7019 of 2009 which found that although squarely within the scope of the arbitration agreement, an arbitrator would not be competent to deal with a complex matter involving allegations of fraud.
[168] M Lehmann, 'A plea for a transnational approach to arbitrability in arbitrable practice', (2004) 42 *Columbia Journal of Transnational Law* 753.
[169] Ibid., p. 770.
[170] *Aloe Vera of America Inc v Asianic Food (S) Pte Ltd* [2006] 3 SLR 174, at 205.
[171] Ibid.
[172] Alternative Dispute Resolution Act 2004 (Republic Act No. 9285) Chapter 1, Section 6.
[173] Article 3 must be read in conjunction with Article 2 of the Supreme People's Court's Interpretation of Several Issues regarding the Application of the Arbitration Law of the PRC (FaShi [2006] No. 7). See also Chen Wei-qi, op. cit. fn 105, at pp. 58–59.
[174] Japanese Arbitration Act 2003, Article 13(1).

Article 5
(1) Only disputes of a commercial nature, or those concerning rights which, under the law and regulations, fall within the full legal authority of the disputing parties, may be settled through arbitration.
(2) Disputes which may not be resolved by arbitration are disputes where according to regulations having the force of law no amicable settlement is possible.

Korean legislation is similarly broad, with one commentator noting that since the 1999 amendment to the Korean Arbitration Act, all that is required now is that the dispute be 'private and legal'.[175]

4.144 The Australian courts have also taken a positive attitude towards the objective arbitrability of international disputes and consequently there are few types of commercial disputes where arbitration is prohibited. Matters capable of settlement by arbitration have been interpreted as 'any claim for relief of a kind proper for determination in a court'.[176] The leading Australian decision is *Walter Rau Neusser Oel Und Fett AG v Cross Pacific Trading Ltd*[177] in which Justice Allsop promotes a liberal approach. However, as noted above with reference to the Philippines, there are exceptions. Unlike the Philippines legislation non-arbitrable issues are not specifically identified in Australia's enabling arbitration legislation itself – rather it is necessary to look to other issue specific legislation. For example, Section 11 of Australia's Carriage of Goods by Sea Act 1991 declares void an arbitration agreement in a bill of lading or similar document relating to the international carriage of goods to or from Australia, unless the place of arbitration is in Australia. Similarly, Section 8 of the Australian Insurance Contracts Act 1984 potentially impacts the arbitrability of insurance related disputes.[178]

4.145 This type of legislation is not unique to Australia. Section 8 of the New Zealand Insurance Law Reform Act 1977 stipulates that clauses in insurance policies requiring arbitration are not binding. Similarly, in India the Carriage by Air Act 1972, the Specific Relief Act 1963, the Atomic Energy Act 1962 and the Aircraft Act 1934 all have provisions that affect arbitrability and the operation of the Indian Arbitration and Conciliation Act 1996 generally.[179]

4.146 In many jurisdictions, disputes are not arbitrable if determining them through arbitration would contravene public policy or the public interest. However, these are amorphous concepts that are not precisely defined in most, if indeed any,

---
[175] Seung Wha Chang, 'Article V of the New York Convention and Korea', (2008) 25(6) *Journal of International Arbitration* 865, at p. 866. Chang also suggests that 'arbitrability is not often an issue in Korean court proceedings'.
[176] See, for an early example, *Elders CED Ltd v Dravo Corporation* [1984] 59 ALR 206.
[177] [2005] FCA 1102. For discussions on how this case differs from the previous position espoused in *ACD Tridon Inc v Tridon Australia Pty Ltd* [2002] NSWSC 896, see J Morrison, 'Drawing a Line in the Sand: Defining the Scope of Arbitrable Disputes in Australia', (2005) 22(5) *Journal of International Arbitration* 395; J Morrison, 'Defining the Scope of Arbitrable Disputes in Australia: Towards a "Liberal" Approach?', (2005) 22(6) *Journal of International Arbitration* 596; Kee, op. cit. fn 147, p. 68.
[178] Australian courts have also refused stay applications where the dispute involves bankruptcy or insolvency. However, the courts have not stated that these matters are inherently not capable of settlement by arbitration. See, for further discussion, Garnett, op. cit. fn 142, pp. 29–57, and *Tanning Research Laboratories Inc v O'Brien* [1990] 64 ALJR 211.
[179] For a list of non-arbitrable subjects in India see V Reddy and V Nagaraj, 'Arbitrability: The Indian Perspective', (2002) 19 *Journal of International Arbitration* 117, at p. 117.

jurisdictions. Defining public policy or the public interest depends heavily on the local law.[180] We would add another category of dispute that may not be objectively arbitrable in some jurisdictions – *in rem* rights. *In rem* rights are typically rights that can be exercised directly over property, for example a right of exclusive possession. Such rights may not be enforceable by arbitration, as any arbitral award should be enforceable only against the parties to the arbitration agreement. However, damages claims arising out of the breach of *in rem* rights are usually arbitrable.

9 Drafting arbitration agreements

If a contractual dispute arises, the last thing that parties want is an additional dispute about the dispute resolution agreement itself. It stands to reason that arbitration agreements must therefore be drafted with great care and precision. A multitude of issues could be dealt with in an arbitration agreement, however, this section limits itself to dealing with the essential and most advisable elements. 4.147

9.1 Essential elements to include in an arbitration agreement

There are four certainties required for an effective arbitration agreement: 4.148
   (i) certainty regarding the identity of the parties;
   (ii) certainty that the parties have agreed to submit their disputes exclusively to arbitration (and not another method of dispute resolution);
   (iii) certainty as to the subject matter or scope of arbitrable disputes; and
   (iv) certainty of the seat of arbitration, if designated.

9.1.1 Identity of parties

It is essential to ensure that the arbitration agreement specifies the identities of those who are agreeing to arbitrate. If the arbitration agreement forms part of a substantive contract, the term 'parties' will usually be defined in the contract, or will be assumed to mean all the parties to the contract. However, in complex commercial transactions where there is a series of contracts and some of the parties are different in the different contracts, the arbitration clause should be clear about which parties are bound by it.[181] 4.149

9.1.2 Obligation to arbitrate

Arbitration agreements should provide that the dispute <u>will</u> be referred to arbitration. If an arbitration agreement provides that a dispute <u>may</u> be referred to arbitration, or words to the effect that 'the parties might decide to refer a dispute 4.150

---

180 This must be distinguished from international public policy that is discussed in the context of setting aside and enforcement of awards in Chapter 9.
181 See, e.g. Reply of Supreme People's Court to the Non-enforcement Decision by Yulin Intermediate Court against Dongxun Investment Co., Ltd (Civil 4, Miscellaneous), No. 24 (2006).

to arbitration', there is not a clear obligation to arbitrate. Ambiguity may lead to disputes concerning whether the matter is to be referred to the courts or to arbitration, and could even deny enforceable effect to the arbitration agreement.

4.151 Clauses providing for the settlement of disputes by arbitration but which are silent as to whether the parties may also go to court have sometimes led to arguments that the silence permits parties to litigate in courts. Such arguments should not prevail. As the Hong Kong Court of Appeal stated in *Grandeur Electrical Co Ltd v Cheung Kee Fung Cheung Construction Co Ltd*, 'a clause in a contract providing for disputes to be settled by arbitration should not readily be construed as giving a choice between arbitration and litigation unless that is specifically and clearly spelt out'.[182]

4.152 Uniform practice does not exist in relation to whether arbitration agreements containing an option either to arbitrate or litigate are invalid for lack of certainty. In Australia such optional agreements are valid.[183] Similarly, the High Court of Singapore has observed that 'it is clear that an agreement in which the parties have the option to elect for arbitration which, if made, binds the other parties to submit to arbitration is an arbitration agreement'.[184] These remarks were made when considering an earlier decision of a Sri Lankan court involving the same parties. The defendant in the Singaporean proceedings had commenced proceedings against the plaintiff before the Colombo High Court. The plaintiff had sought a stay on the basis of Section 5 of the Sri Lankan Arbitration Act 1995. Section 5 provides:[185]

> Where a party to an arbitration agreement institutes legal proceedings in a court against another party to such agreement in respect of a matter agreed to be submitted for arbitration under such agreement, the Court shall have no jurisdiction to hear and determine such matter if the other party objects to the court exercising jurisdiction in respect of such matter.

4.153 The arbitration clause that the plaintiff relied on read:

> This Agreement shall be governed by and construed in accordance with the laws of England and Wales. In the event that the parties have a dispute over any term or otherwise relating to this Agreement they shall use their best endeavours to resolve it through good faith negotiations. In the event that they fail to do so after 14 days then either party <u>may elect</u> to submit such matter to arbitration in Singapore in accordance with the Arbitration Rules of the Singapore International Arbitration Centre ('SIAC Rules') for the time being in force which rules are deemed to be incorporated by reference with this clause to the exclusive jurisdiction of which the parties shall be deemed to have consented. Any arbitration shall be referred to three arbitrators, one

---

182 [2006] HKCU 1245, Hong Kong Court of Appeal, citing with approval *Tommy CP Sze and Co v Li & Fung (Trading) Ltd* [2003] 1 HKC 418.
183 *Liverpool City Council v Casbee Pty Ltd* [2005] NSWSC 590, citing with approval *PMT Partners Pty Ltd (in liq) v Australian National Parks & Wildlife Service* (1995) 184 CLR 301, at 310, 323; and *Savcor Pty Ltd v State of New South Wales* (2001) 52 NSWLR 587, at p. 594.
184 *WSG Nimbus Pte Ltd v Board of Control for Cricket in Sri Lanka* [2002] 3 SLR 603, at para 30.
185 Section 5 is unusual because it omits the language allowing a court to refuse the stay if the arbitration agreement is 'void, inoperative or incapable of being performed' (see, e.g. Article 8(1) of the Model Law). See also the discussion of this point in Chapter 5, Section 4.2.

arbitrator being appointed by each party and the other being appointed by the Chairman of the SIAC and shall be conducted in the English language. (Emphasis added)

4.154 As is explained in the Singaporean judgment, the Colombo High Court found that the Sri Lankan Arbitration Act referred to compulsory arbitration agreements – that is agreements where the parties were compelled to arbitrate rather than having litigation as an alternative. In this instance, the words 'may elect' were interpreted by the Sri Lankan court to mean that the parties could choose either arbitration or the courts, and thus the clause was not of the sort contemplated by Section 5. The High Court of Colombo refused the stay application and asserted jurisdiction over the dispute.

4.155 Confirmation that the drafting of optional arbitration clauses should be avoided can also be found in judgments from China and South Korea. In China, the Supreme People's Court 'appears to have declared that such a clause is an invalid arbitration clause, but the other party wishing to rely on this article must raise its objection prior to the first substantive hearing in the arbitration'.[186] In South Korea the courts have ruled:[187]

> An optional arbitration clause such as 'the dispute shall be referred to adjudication/arbitration in accordance with the laws of the Purchaser's country' shall be deemed to become valid as an arbitration agreement if any party to the Goods Supply Contract of the present case opts for a recourse to arbitral proceedings instead of the adjudication by a court against the other party and the other party, without particular objections, submits itself to such arbitral proceedings. Therefore, where the other party clearly objected to a settlement by arbitration by vigorously contending the non-existence of an arbitration agreement in its Answer to the defendant's Request for an arbitration, the arbitration clause cannot be deemed as valid as an arbitration agreement.

4.156 When drafting an arbitration clause it is also very important that it is arbitration that the parties are choosing as their dispute resolution method. To be safe, the word 'arbitration' or something similar (e.g. 'arbitrator', 'arbitral tribunal') must appear in the arbitration agreement.

4.157 There is sometimes confusion about the difference between arbitration and expert determination. Although these two processes share some similarities, there are nevertheless fundamental differences, and different consequences at law. For example, a matter may not at law be capable of resolution by arbitration, whereas expert determination of that same dispute may still be possible.[188] While indicative, simply because parties refer to someone as an 'arbitrator' will not clothe that person with the attributes of one, and that person may in fact be

---

[186] M Lin, 'Supreme People's Court Rules on PRC Arbitration Issues', (2007) 24(6) *Journal of International Arbitration* 597, at p. 601, referring to Article 7 of Fa Shi [2006] No. 7.
[187] Supreme Court Decision 2003 Da318 [2003] KRSC 21 (22 August 2003).
[188] In an Australian domestic context this issue arose in *Age Old Builders Pty Ltd v Swintons Pty Ltd* [2003] VSC 307 (Supreme Court of Victoria). In this case the question was whether an agreement to submit disputes to expert determination was void under Section 14 of the Victorian Domestic Building Contracts Act 1995. Section 14 renders any arbitration agreement in a domestic building contract void.

simply an expert.[189] Arbitration is a process involving a judicial inquiry, whereas expert determination does not involve such an activity.[190]

4.158 The two forms of dispute resolution have been contrasted by the Singapore High Court:[191]

> The crucial difference between expert determination and arbitration laid in the procedure and the absence of remedies for procedural irregularity in expert determination. An expert could adopt an inquisitorial, investigative approach, and need not refer the results to the parties before making the decision while an arbitrator needed the parties' permission to take the initiative, and had to refer the results to the parties before making the award.

4.159 Further guidance can be taken from the Hong Kong decision of Justice Kaplan (as he then was) in *Mayers v Dlugash*.[192] He there stated:

> Arbitration is a tried and tested method of dispute resolution where the parties do not wish to litigate their differences before state courts. Expert determination, although having been used for centuries, is perhaps not so widely known. The classic features of expert determination are:
> 1. The expert makes a final and binding decision.
> 2. The decision can only be challenged in the most exceptional circumstances such as where the expert answers the wrong question (see *Jones v Sherwood Computer Services Inc* [1992] 1 WLR 277, *Campbell v Edwards* [1976] 1 WLR 403 and *Nikko Hotels (UK) Ltd v MEPC* (1991) 28 EG 86).
> 3. The expert can be sued for negligence in the absence of an agreed immunity (*Arenson v Gasson Beckman Rutley* [1997] AC 405).
> 4. The expert's determination cannot be enforced as an arbitral award.

4.160 In the context of international commercial arbitration, point 4 is of significant practical relevance. One of the significant advantages of international arbitration is the international enforceability of the award. Expert determinations are not covered by the New York Convention and there is no other international regime for their enforcement. These determinations can only be enforced as a matter of ordinary contract law. Nevertheless the process does have some popularity in various national construction industries. In most cases, parties seeking to enforce such a determination would need to commence proceedings (probably for breach of contract) in the jurisdiction where enforcement is sought.

4.161 The final observation to make about the obligation to arbitrate is that in many jurisdictions it must be an equally shared obligation between all the parties to

---

[189] *Uttam Wires & Machines P. Ltd v State of Rajasthan* [1990] AIR (Del) 72 (High Court, Delhi) as cited by A Jain, 'Pathological Arbitration Clauses and Indian Courts', (2008) 25 *Journal of International Arbitration* 433, at p. 439. Jain identifies a number of Indian decisions on this particular issue and other issues which may lead to a pathological arbitration clause. For a general discussion of pathological arbitration clauses see Section 9.6 below.
[190] *Age Old Builders Pty Ltd v Swintons Pty Ltd* [2003] VSC 307, at para 59 (Supreme Court of Victoria).
[191] *Evergreat Construction Co Pte Ltd v Presscrete Engineering Pte Ltd* [2006] 1 SLR 634 at 635.
[192] [1994] 1 HKC 755, at 757, cited with approval in *Milibow Assets Ltd v Dooyang Hong Kong Ltd* [2001] HKCU 767.

the agreement.[193] An obligation to arbitrate requires that all parties be bound by the outcome. However, this is not quite the same as stating that each party must have the same rights. For example, must all parties to the arbitration agreement have the right to initiate arbitration? In Australia, the answer appears to be no.[194] The influence of English law may well lead the other common law jurisdictions in this region to the same position.[195] In contrast, Yuen has noted that a one-sided agreement, such as one which only allows the seller to designate an arbitral commission would be invalid under Chinese law.[196]

9.1.3 Subject matter and scope of arbitration

An arbitration agreement must clearly specify which disputes it covers. This is closely linked to subjective arbitrability, addressed above. Parties sometimes seek to limit the disputes that will be resolved by arbitration. Extreme care needs to be exercised if parties wish to do this in advance of a dispute arising in order to avoid future disputes about which claims fall within the scope of the arbitration agreement. In the absence of a real reason to limit the scope of arbitrable disputes, and in order to avoid the possibility of parallel court proceedings, an advisable strategy is to maximise as far as possible the scope of the arbitration agreement. Broad wording should be used, such as 'all disputes arising out of, connected with or in any way related to this contract shall be resolved by arbitration.'

4.162

The scope of arbitration agreements was considered in more detail under the headings of subjective arbitrability[197] and defined legal relationship.[198]

4.163

9.1.4 Certainty of the seat if designated

It is strongly advisable to designate a seat of arbitration in the arbitration agreement.[199] If one is designated, it must be clear and certain.[200] There are two reasons for this. First, an ambiguous reference to the seat of arbitration can in a worst case scenario give rise to doubts about the validity or effectiveness of the arbitration agreement. Even in a best case scenario it is possible that additional jurisdictional disputes will arise in the arbitration proceedings and/or a separate court action will be commenced. Second, the chosen seat may have particular

4.164

---

193 For European perspectives on this issue see A Frignani, 'Drafting Arbitration Agreements', (2008) 24 *Arbitration International* 561, at p. 563.
194 See *PMT Partners Pty Ltd (in liq) v Australian National Parks and Wildlife Service* (1995) 184 CLR 301. While this case concerned a domestic arbitration conducted pursuant to legislation that has now been repealed, the relevant definition of 'arbitration agreement' has not changed. It should also be noted here that in the context of ICSID arbitration, only the investor and not the state has the right to institute an ICSID arbitration.
195 For the English position, see *Law Debenture Trust Corp Plc v Elektrim Finance BV* [2005] 1 All ER 476. For commentary on this case, see S Nesbitt and H Quinlan, 'The Status and Operation of Unilateral or Optional Arbitration Clauses', (2006) 22 *Arbitration International* 133.
196 P Yuen, 'Arbitration Clauses in a Chinese Context', (2007) 24 *Journal of International Arbitration* 581, at p. 591.
197 See Section 8.1.
198 See Section 5.
199 A discussion of how a seat is designated in the absence of party agreement can be found in Chapter 2 at Section 6.1.
200 M Hwang and Fong Lee Cheng, 'Relevant Considerations in Choosing the Place of Arbitration', (2008) 4(2) *Asian International Arbitration Journal* 195, at p. 214.

requirements for an arbitration agreement. For example, if the parties chose a seat located in China, the arbitration agreement would need to comply with Article 16 of the Chinese Arbitration Law. That article states that an agreement must contain: (i) an expression of the intent to arbitrate; (ii) a description of the matters subject to arbitration; and (iii) a designated arbitration commission.[201] If parties fail to designate the seat of arbitration, there are default mechanisms in rules and laws for its determination.[202]

9.2 Advisable elements to include

4.165 In addition to the required elements noted above, it is advisable, but not essential, to include the following selective elements in an arbitration agreement:
  (i) the number of arbitrators;
  (ii) the language of the proceedings;
  (iii) the confidentiality of the arbitration proceedings and the resulting award; and
  (iv) any desired special powers for the arbitral tribunal.

4.166 The number of arbitrators is discussed further in Chapter 6.[203] Whether or not it is necessary or desirable to choose the number of arbitrators in advance may depend on the chosen arbitration rules, and whether they provide a suitable mechanism for determining the number of arbitrators in the absence of party choice. Selecting a language in the arbitration agreement may avoid a dispute prior to the commencement of the arbitration as to what should be the language. In choosing the language, the potentially substantial cost, time and logistical issues relating to document translation and use of interpreters during the hearing must be borne in mind.

4.167 Concerning confidentiality, as discussed in Chapter 7,[204] while arbitrations are private, documents and information disclosed during an arbitration may not necessarily be confidential in the absence of a further contractual obligation. In this region, this is especially important for arbitrations seated in Australia and possibly Singapore.[205] The Australian case of *Esso v Plowman*[206] cast doubt on the extent of confidentiality in arbitration under Australian law. In many jurisdictions an obligation of confidentiality is implied. However, it is prudent to assume that it is not. Most sets of arbitral rules now also include specific confidentiality provisions.[207]

4.168 When parties intend to grant arbitrators particular powers, these should be clearly specified in the arbitration agreement. Such specificity is necessary, for example, where parties wish the arbitrators to act as *amiable compositeur*, or to resolve the dispute on the basis of fairness and equity.[208] Special powers

---
201 For further discussion on the requirement of an arbitral institution, see Section 9.3.
202 See Chapter 2, Section 6.1.
203 See Chapter 6, Section 2.1.
204 See Chapter 7, Section 11.
205 Outside the Asia-Pacific, this is also an important consideration in Sweden and the US.
206 (1995) 183 CLR 10. This case is also discussed in Chapter 7, Section 11 of this book.
207 See, e.g. SIAC Rules, Rule 34; HKIAC Rules Article 39; ACICA Rules Article 18.
208 See Chapter 3, Section 8.

might also be given to affirm the arbitral tribunal's authority to award punitive damages, issue ex parte interim relief, make special costs awards, or award specific performance.

9.3 Ad hoc or institutional arbitration?

4.169 Once parties have decided that arbitration will be their chosen method of dispute resolution, they face the further choice as to whether the arbitration will be ad hoc or institutional.[209] That decision should be specified in the arbitration agreement. In an institutional arbitration, the arbitral institution provides certain support services for the arbitration. In ad hoc arbitrations there is no institution involved. Most international arbitrations are conducted under the auspices of an arbitral institution.[210]

4.170 Although never going so far as to usurp the arbitral tribunal's decision-making power, different institutions administer arbitrations in varying degrees.[211] It is important that parties and their legal representatives appreciate these differences when choosing an institution. The choice of institution and corresponding rules can have a significant influence on the kind of arbitration that will occur.

4.171 The ICC and SIAC Rules, for example, provide for considerable institutional involvement and supervision, whereas the ACICA Rules take a much more hands-off approach. This difference is manifested in a number of ways throughout the arbitration. For instance, an award delivered in an ICC or SIAC arbitration will be reviewed by the ICC Court or SIAC Registrar,[212] while there is no similar provision in the ACICA Rules.

4.172 In terms of costs, under the ACICA Rules arbitrators are paid based on the arbitrators' usual hourly rates. The ICC and SIAC, on the other hand, both administer all of the costs in their arbitrations, each using a comparable system based on the monetary value of the dispute.

4.173 The ICC, SIAC and ACICA Rules all follow a similar procedure with regard to challenges to arbitrators. Challenges are determined by the institution. A different procedure has been adopted by the Vietnam Arbitration Centre. The Arbitration Rules of the Centre refer challenges first to the unchallenged arbitrators. The President of the Centre then effectively acts as an umpire if necessary.

4.174 Aside from technical differences in institutional rules, it is very important to understand that when parties choose a set of institutional rules they are not simply choosing that procedure, but that institution as well. Institutions vary immensely in their level of experience and the quality of the staff.

4.175 Drawing an analogy between choosing a law firm and choosing an arbitration institution serves to illuminate the particularities associated with the latter choice. There are two essential differences. First, the choice of an arbitral institution is usually made in a contractual dispute resolution clause. Such clauses are

---

[209] See also Chapter 7, Section 3.1.2.
[210] See the statistics in Chapter 1, Section 3.4.7.
[211] The basic services provided by arbitral institutions were explained in Chapter 1, Section 3.4.7.
[212] ICC Rules Article 27; SIAC Rules, Rule 27.1.

agreed long before a dispute actually arises and before anyone knows the type or subject matter of the dispute or how much it could be worth to the parties. Conversely, a law firm is usually chosen as and when the need arises: the choice is made with the benefit of knowing the particular dispute or commercial issues. Second, it is generally not possible to change the choice of arbitral institution after signing the contract in which that choice is contained. That choice can only be varied if all of the parties to the arbitration agree. This contrasts with the choice of a law firm, which can usually be changed at any time if the client is not satisfied with the legal services rendered. Consequently, in choosing an arbitration institution, it is advisable to consider carefully the costs, range of services, supervision and support it is able to provide before it is selected and agreed to in a dispute resolution clause.

4.176 Parties sometimes attempt to agree on one institution's rules but with a different institution administering those rules. Mason notes that 'ICC officials have complained that the "mixing and matching" scenario is something they have been faced with quite a bit'.[213] The problem is not one limited to ICC experience as Mason also cites LCIA and ICDR examples. Trying to mix and match institutional rules is a very dangerous and risky strategy. In the case of a highly specialised institution like the ICC, for example, other institutions are not able to provide the services that are contemplated under the ICC Rules. The attempted mix and match is highly likely to lead to costly jurisdictional disputes and to invalidate the award or make it unenforceable.[214]

4.177 As noted above, an 'ad hoc arbitration' is one that is not administered by an institution. Ad hoc is something of a term of art in arbitration. In common parlance, the phrase refers to something established for a singular or sole purpose. In the context of arbitration, the emphasis is instead on the lack of institutional administration of the arbitration. This specific focus is understandable and quite logical – every single arbitration would be ad hoc if the common parlance meaning was applied. In *Bovis Lend Lease Pte Ltd v Jay-Tech Marine & Projects Pte Ltd*,[215] the High Court of Singapore had cause to consider the difference between ad hoc and institutional arbitration. It chose to explain that difference in this way: '... the parties selected an ad hoc arbitration since they did not submit it to the administration of any particular institution....'[216]

4.178 There may be some limited institutional involvement in an ad hoc arbitration, such as performing the role of appointing authority. This should not be considered as an act of administering the arbitration. Parties agree to institutions performing this role because they are usually best placed to do so, particularly because they often possess lists of suitable and competent arbitrators at their disposal. Parties

---

[213] PE Mason, 'Whether Arbitration Rules Should Be Applied by the Issuing Arbitral Institution', (2009) *Lexis Nexis Emerging Issues Analysis* 1149, p. 4. See also *Insigma Technology Co Ltd v Alstom Technology Ltd* [2009] 1 SLR 23 (High Court of Singapore) discussed in Section 9.6.
[214] See further J Kirby, 'Insigma Technology Co Ltd v Alstom Technology Ltd: SIAC Can Administer Cases under the ICC Rules?!?', (2009) 25 *Arbitration International* 319, at p. 326 on the costs involved.
[215] [2005] SGHC 91.
[216] Ibid., para 21.

may nominate anyone (e.g. a private individual, an institution, a judge, etc.) to act as appointing authority.

Ad hoc arbitration agreements often adopt a set of ad hoc rules, the most common being the UNCITRAL Arbitration Rules.[217] The parties can alternatively rely on the local law at the seat of arbitration to provide the relevant rules of arbitration (e.g. the procedure set out in the Model Law for those countries that have adopted it), or can stipulate at length in the contract specifically agreed procedures to be followed. 4.179

Aside from practical issues relating to the everyday conduct of the arbitration, the choice between ad hoc or institutional arbitration can, in rare circumstances, affect the validity of the arbitration agreement, and thus jeopardise the enforceability of the award. An institution must be chosen where China is the seat of arbitration.[218] Furthermore, if the seat is in China, it is unclear whether non-Chinese institutions can administer the arbitration.[219] The issue arose in the *Wuxi Woco-Tongyong Rubber Engineering Co Ltd v Züblin Int'l GmbH*[220] case, in which the Wuxi Intermediate People's Court refused to enforce an award on the basis of Article V(1)(a) of the New York Convention. This article permits enforcement to be denied if the arbitration agreement is not valid under the law of the place where the award was made. The court had reasoned that the arbitration agreement did not specify an institution. It appeared to be making a very literal interpretation of the arbitration agreement, which read 'Arbitration: ICC Rules, Shanghai shall apply'. Since that decision, the Interpretation of Several Issues regarding the Application of the Arbitration Law of the PRC[221] was promulgated by the PRC Supreme People's Court. It indicates in contrast to the *Züblin* decision that an arbitration agreement will be valid if an arbitral institution can be identified from the chosen arbitral rules.[222] 4.180

9.4 Multi-tiered arbitration agreements

A multi-tiered arbitration clause provides for one or more other steps, such as an amicable form of dispute resolution, before arbitration. For example, the clause might first require negotiation, followed by mediation and then arbitration. 4.181

---

217 It is interesting to note that appointing authorities are expected to be given an increased role and greater responsibility under the proposed revisions to these rules.
218 Article 16 of the Chinese Arbitration Law has been interpreted in this way. See the discussion in Section 9.3. See also Wan Exiang and Yu Xifu, op. cit. fn 46, p. 185; Chi Manjiao, 'Is the Chinese Arbitration Act Truly Arbitration-Friendly: Determining the Validity of Arbitration Agreement under Chinese Law', (2008) 4(1) *Asian International Arbitration Journal* 104.
219 Jingzhao Tao and C von Wunschheim, 'Articles 16 and 18 of the PRC Arbitration Law: The Great Wall of China for Foreign Arbitration Institutions', (2007) 23 *Arbitration International* 309.
220 *Wuxi Woco-Tongyong Rubber Engineering Co Ltd v Zueblin Int'l GmbH*, Wuxi Intermediate People's Court, (Civil 3), (Final), No. 1 (2004) – (decision dated July 19, 2006).
221 FaShi [2006] No. 7.
222 For further discussion of this case and the situation regarding institutional arbitration agreements in China generally, see N Darwazeh and F Yeoh, 'Recognition and Enforcement of Awards under the New York Convention China and Hong Kong Perspectives', (2008) 25 *Journal of International Arbitration* 837; and F Yeoh, 'The People's Courts and Arbitration A Snapshot of Recent Judicial Attitudes on Arbitrability and Enforcement', (2007) 24 *Journal of International Arbitration* 635.

According to a 2008 survey these clauses are becoming increasingly popular.[223] A variety of issues need to be considered when drafting these clauses. Do the parties intend that negotiation and then mediation are conditional prerequisites to arbitration, such that there is no consent to arbitrate until mediation has occurred? Or do the parties intend that in the event there is a serious disagreement between the parties, mediation can be overlooked and a party may commence arbitration directly without attempting mediation?[224] Clauses may also permit a choice between arbitration and court litigation but, as previously discussed, this is not advisable.[225]

4.182   Because of the many difficulties that can plague a multi-tiered arbitration clause, it is advisable to use one prepared by an institution and modify it only to the extent absolutely necessary. The sample ACICA clause is:

> Any dispute, controversy or claim arising out of, relating to or in connection with this contract, including any question regarding its existence, validity or termination, shall be resolved by mediation in accordance with the ACICA Mediation Rules. The mediation shall take place in Sydney, Australia [or choose another city] and be administered by the Australian Centre for International Commercial Arbitration (ACICA).
>
> If the dispute has not been settled pursuant to the said Rules within 60 days following the written invitation to mediate or within such other period as the parties may agree in writing, the dispute shall be resolved by arbitration in accordance with the ACICA Arbitration Rules. The seat of arbitration shall be Sydney, Australia [or choose another city]. The language of the arbitration shall be English [or choose another language]. The number of arbitrators shall be one [or three, or delete this sentence and rely on Article 8 of the ACICA Arbitration Rules].

9.5 What *not* to include in an arbitration agreement

4.183   Long and detailed arbitration clauses generally take a long time to draft and in the event of arbitration are not overly helpful. Although at the time of drafting the procedure to be followed may seem clear and certain in a lengthy arbitration clause, it might produce some problems if an unforeseen circumstance eventuates (which is often the case) and the clause lacks the flexibility to deal with this in an appropriate way. Consequently, it is best to keep the clause as simple as possible and carefully adapt a standard form institutional clause to fit any particular

---

[223] *International Arbitration: Corporate Attitudes and Practices 2008*, study conducted by Pricewaterhouse-Coopers and Queen Mary College, p. 11.
[224] An example of the difficulties which might be encountered when using a multi-tiered clause can be seen in the Sichuan PepsiCo arbitrations. In April 2008, the Intermediate People's Court of Chengdu refused enforcement of an arbitral award based on Article V(1)(d) of the New York Convention. The court indicated that the party seeking enforcement could not establish that it had complied with the consultation requirements in the dispute resolution clause. It should be noted that other factors may have influenced this decision, such as the criminal conviction of one of the majority arbitrators. For further discussion of this case, see Darwazeh and Yeoh, op. cit. fn 222. The issue has arisen a number of times in investor-state arbitrations where the investment treaty under which a claim is brought requires a period of consultation or negotiation before an arbitration claim is filed.
[225] Clauses of this kind were discussed above in Section 9.1.2.

requirements. If a complex or detailed clause is desired for any reason, it should be checked by an expert arbitration lawyer.

Parties are sometimes inclined to put time limits in arbitration agreements; for example, time limits for the parties to choose their respective arbitrators for nomination; or time limits for the arbitrator to render the award. Unless drafted particularly carefully, attempts of this kind are dangerous. Potentially, the failure to meet a time limit could invalidate the entire arbitration proceeding. Thus where institutional or ad hoc rules contain time limits, these should be preferred. Such rules contain methods that enable the modification of time limits if necessary.

9.6 Pathological arbitration agreements

Frederic Eisemann, a former Secretary-General of the ICC Court, was the first legal commentator to use the term 'pathological' in the context of arbitration agreements.[226] It has since been used to describe ambiguous or unclear arbitration agreements. Such agreements frequently cause additional problems when a dispute between the parties arises. While in theory a pathological arbitration agreement could be fixed by subsequent agreement of the parties, the reality is that parties often refuse to agree on anything once a dispute has arisen.

The modern trend in international arbitration law is to apply an interpretation that favours arbitration and gives meaning and effect to the clause, even if an arbitration agreement is at first blush potentially pathological.[227] The French phrase for this approach is often used – '*effet utile*' (effective interpretation). As a consequence of this approach to interpretation, the defects in many arbitration clauses are overcome and the arbitration proceeds.

Examples of defects include:
(i) naming the arbitral institution incorrectly or identifying a non-existent institution;
(ii) empowering one institution to administer another institution's rules;[228]
(iii) referring to an arbitral institution by its location rather than by its name;[229]
(iv) failing to indicate clearly that the award is final and binding;[230]
(v) identifying a specific arbitrator who has died or become unable to act thereafter; and

---

[226] F Eisemann, 'La clause d'arbitrage pathologique' in Associazione italiana per l'arbitrato, *Commercial Arbitration Essays in Memoriam Eugenio Minoli*, UTET, 1974.
[227] For example, the Seoul Civil District Court upheld the validity of an arbitration agreement which provided for more than one arbitration institution in the clause. The court found that once one party had elected an institution, the other party was deemed to have waived its rights to object to jurisdiction, 83 Kahap 7051, 12 April 1984 as cited in Seung Wha Chang, op. cit. fn 175. See also *Insigma Technology Co Ltd v Alstom Technology Ltd* [2009] SGCA 24, at para 31.
[228] See also *Insigma Technology Co Ltd v Alstom Technology Ltd* [2009] SGCA 24, at para 31.
[229] See, e.g. Arbitration Court of the German Coffee Association, *Panamanian buyer v Papua New Guinean seller*, 28 September 1992, Rechtsprechung kaufmännischer Schiedsgerichte, vol. 5, Section 3B.
[230] See, e.g. *Undisclosed Plaintiff v Cosmo Futures Co Ltd* (Japan), 16 May 2003 (Sapporo District Court).

(vi) drafting terms that are inherently contradictory to other terms in the arbitration agreement.

4.188 The first of the typical defects noted above has been described by Lawrence Boo, then Deputy Chairman of SIAC, as the most common. In a presentation to the Regional Arbitration Conference organised by the Malaysian Institute of Arbitrators in June 2007, Boo provided a number of examples of problematic clauses received by SIAC. The examples concerning non-existent institutions where SIAC jurisdiction was declined included:

> ... Any dispute will be settled by the rules of arbitration of the **International Chamber of Trade of Singapore** by one or several arbitrators appointed accordingly [sic] to the rules...
>
> ... Such arbitration shall be held under the auspices of **A.A.L.C.C. Regional Centre for Commercial Arbitration at Singapore** in accordance with the UNICTRAL Arbitration Rules as modified by the rules of the centre...

4.189 Yang reports that in several cases in China confusion has arisen over references to CIETAC, stating that '[a]t least one published case has held that the choice of CIETAC could refer to any of the three institutions in the CIETAC group'.[231] Yang indicates that in the case in question the same parties conducted two CIETAC arbitrations simultaneously, one in Shanghai and the other in Beijing, with opposite results.

4.190 The second category referred to above concerns requesting one institution to administer the rules of another. This can be particularly problematic because in general only the institution whose rules it is can properly administer arbitrations conducted under those rules. Clauses that attempt to choose two institutions at once will almost certainly cause greater cost and significantly increase the risk of an unenforceable award.[232]

4.191 An example of this situation was considered by the High Court of Singapore in *Insigma Technology Co Ltd v Alstom Technology Ltd*.[233] The circumstances of this case demonstrate the difficulties associated with clauses of this kind. The arbitration agreement at issue appeared as a clause in the parties' contract. It read in part:

> ... Any and all such disputes shall be finally resolved by arbitration before the Singapore International Arbitration Centre in accordance with the Rules of Arbitration of the International Chamber of Commerce in effect and the proceedings shall take place in Singapore and the official language shall be English...

4.192 When a dispute arose, the defendant began an ICC arbitration. The plaintiff objected on the basis that either the clause was pathological or that it called for SIAC arbitration using the ICC Rules. After both parties nominated their

---
[231] Howard Yinghao Yang, 'CIETAC Arbitration Clause Revisited', (2008) 24 *Arbitration International* 603, at pp. 605, 606.
[232] See Kirby, op. cit. fn 214, at p. 326 on the costs involved.
[233] [2009] 1 SLR 23.

arbitrators but before full constitution of the arbitral tribunal, the proceedings before the ICC Court were withdrawn and referred to SIAC.

As has been noted elsewhere,[234] an arbitral tribunal has the authority to hear arguments about its own jurisdiction. In this case the respondent made submissions to the arbitral tribunal that it lacked jurisdiction, arguing amongst other things that there was not a valid arbitration clause. The arbitral tribunal found that a valid arbitration clause existed. As the parties had clearly intended to arbitrate their disputes, the critical question for the arbitral tribunal was whether the manner agreed to was workable. The arbitral tribunal found that it was workable because the SIAC (in a letter to the arbitral tribunal) had indicated which bodies and individual officers within the SIAC would perform the roles of the functionaries described under the ICC Rules – for example the function of the ICC Court would be performed by the SIAC Board of Directors. The arbitral tribunal also placed significant emphasis on the respondent's assertion in the abandoned ICC arbitration that the clause provided for ICC arbitration administered by SIAC. The arbitral tribunal, applying principles analogous to estoppel, considered that the respondent should not be permitted to go back on its submissions made to the ICC that SIAC had been agreed as the administering body. 4.193

The respondent had also challenged the manner in which the arbitral tribunal had been constituted. It was argued that as the SIAC appointment process had been followed, and not that prescribed in the ICC Rules, the arbitral tribunal was improperly constituted. The arbitral tribunal also found against the respondent on this point since it had not established that different arbitrators would have been appointed under the ICC Rules. 4.194

The respondent challenged the finding of jurisdiction and commenced proceedings in the High Court of Singapore. Judge Prakash upheld the award. While we support the pro-arbitration position adopted in the judgment, we do not believe it can be taken as a precedent. The case certainly should not be understood as inferring that an arbitration agreement which calls on one institution to apply the rules of another will be upheld as valid. The reasoning of the judgment is not without difficulties, in particular the finding that the parties had not bargained for institutional arbitration but for a hybrid ad hoc arbitration. Accordingly the decision should be interpreted as turning on particular actions by the parties involved, in particular the respondent's express position taken during the abandoned ICC arbitration.[235] The decision was appealed unsuccessfully to the Court of Appeal, which agreed with the High Court's reasons.[236] 4.195

---

234 See Section 3.
235 See also Kirby, op. cit. fn 214, at p. 328.
236 *Insigma Technology Co Ltd v Alstom Technology Ltd* [2009] SGCA 24, at para 29.

5

Arbitral jurisdiction

1 Introduction

5.1   The features and requirements of arbitration agreements were examined in Chapter 4. This chapter addresses procedural and other issues that can arise when a party wishes to contest an arbitral tribunal's jurisdiction. It also considers the link between an arbitral tribunal's authority to rule on its own jurisdiction and the control of that authority by domestic courts.

5.2   An arbitral tribunal's jurisdiction is far from automatic. It derives from the disputing parties' free will, i.e. their agreement to arbitrate. The consensual nature of arbitral jurisdiction must be contrasted with the jurisdiction of domestic courts, which is established by the domestic law of the forum and any applicable treaties dealing with international judicial competence.

5.3   The consensual basis of arbitration means that a respondent party can attempt to contest or deny arbitral jurisdiction. The objecting party might never have agreed to arbitrate or, even if it previously agreed, may now prefer to litigate the dispute in a domestic court. In the latter case the objecting party may seek to escape its obligation to arbitrate by denying its previous agreement. Alternatively, that party might raise jurisdictional objections in an attempt to delay and frustrate the resolution of the dispute.

5.4   After introducing and summarising the procedure of jurisdictional objections (Section 2), we examine preliminary issues concerning arbitral jurisdiction (Section 3), before dealing with the competence-competence rule and prima facie jurisdictional decisions by courts (Section 4), prima facie jurisdictional decisions by arbitral institutions (Section 5), and finally the effects of a court, institution or arbitral tribunal's jurisdictional decision (Section 6).

Jurisdiction is handled very differently in arbitrations under the ICSID Convention. This is discussed separately in Chapter 10. The present chapter focuses on jurisdiction in international commercial arbitration.

5.5

2 Overview and summary of jurisdictional objections

Jurisdictional objections are generally raised at the outset of an arbitration. If an arbitration progresses to completion, a party may also deny arbitral jurisdiction at the end, during a procedure to challenge the award or to resist enforcement of the award. However, a party's failure to raise jurisdictional objections promptly may give rise to a finding that the party is deemed to have waived those objections.

5.6

Overall, a party (typically the respondent) wanting to contest jurisdiction has the following options available to it:[1]

5.7

(i) First, the respondent may challenge jurisdiction by making its objections directly with the arbitral tribunal. Arbitral tribunals are empowered to decide on their own jurisdiction by virtue of a principle found in virtually all arbitration laws and rules known as the 'competence-competence' rule.[2]

- An essential feature of the competence-competence rule is that an arbitral tribunal's decision that it possesses jurisdiction is _not_ final – it can be reviewed by a domestic court during proceedings to set aside the decision. Save for exceptional circumstances (and erroneous decisions by some domestic courts), the only domestic court with jurisdiction to set aside an arbitral tribunal's jurisdictional decision is a court at the seat of arbitration.[3]

- However, while a court at the seat of arbitration can always hear an action to set aside an arbitral tribunal's decision that the arbitral tribunal possesses jurisdiction, this is not true when an arbitral tribunal decides that it lacks jurisdiction. As explained further below, only some legal systems expressly empower their courts to review an arbitral tribunal's negative jurisdictional decision.

(ii) Second, the respondent party may refuse to participate in the arbitration, wait for the arbitral tribunal's final award and then (i) seek to have that award set aside (i.e. challenge it) at the seat of arbitration on the basis that the arbitral tribunal did not have jurisdiction to make the award or (ii) wait

---

[1] Most of the issues summarised in this list are dealt with in more detail below in this chapter. For an analysis of the different kinds of uncooperative respondent tactics, see M Hwang, 'Why is There Still Resistance to Arbitration in Asia?', Lunchtime address to The International Arbitration Club, Singapore, Autumn 2007. An earlier version of the paper was published in G Aksen, K-H Bockstiegel, MJ Mustill, PM Patocchi and AM Whitesell (eds), _Global Reflections on International Law, Commerce and Dispute Resolution: Liber Amicorum in Honour of Robert Briner_, ICC Publishing, 2005. See also M Philippe and P Blondeau, 'Comment se manifestent certaines tactiques dilatoires dans l'arbitrage', (1999) 15(7) _Dalloz Affaires_ 169, at p. 1097.
[2] This rule is discussed in Section 4.
[3] Regarding setting aside proceedings see Chapter 9, Section 3.2.

for the claimant to commence proceedings to enforce the award and then resist enforcement for the same reason.
- Either of these strategies raises significant risks for the respondent. The failure to participate in the arbitration will mean that the respondent's views, arguments and position were not heard by the arbitral tribunal. This means that if its jurisdictional plea before the domestic court fails (whether in the seat of arbitration or before the court where the opposing side is trying to enforce the award), it will be faced with and bound by an award made in circumstances where its position was never argued before the arbitral tribunal. Additionally, in some circumstances the respondent's failure to participate will be considered as a waiver of its right to object to the arbitral tribunal's jurisdiction.
- If the respondent participates in the arbitration without raising an objection to the arbitral tribunal's jurisdiction but subsequently contests that jurisdiction before a court, the respondent will almost always be considered by the court to have waived its right to object to arbitral jurisdiction. (The facts on which a waiver is based may also or alternatively be used to support the invocation of other legal doctrines, such as issue estoppel or abandonment[4]).

(iii) Third, the respondent may seek from the arbitration's outset a ruling directly from a domestic court at the seat of arbitration that the arbitral tribunal lacks jurisdiction. Whether or not a court at the seat of arbitration is competent to decide an issue of arbitral jurisdiction before the arbitral tribunal has ruled on its own jurisdiction depends on the local law and practice of the courts. It depends, in particular, on that jurisdiction's interpretation and application of the competence-competence rule.
- A respondent sometimes seeks a similar ruling from a court outside the seat of arbitration – for example a court in its home jurisdiction. As a general rule, a decision from a court outside the seat of arbitration should not affect the arbitral tribunal's jurisdiction because the court concerned would not be competent under the law of the seat of arbitration to make such a decision.

(iv) Fourth, another alternative is for the respondent to commence court litigation proceedings against the claimant on the substance of the dispute. If it does so, the other side could accept – expressly or implicitly – the domestic court's competence, thereby waiving its right to invoke the arbitration agreement in connection with that dispute. For example, if the opposing party proceeds to argue its defence before the domestic court without objecting to that court's jurisdiction on the basis of the parties' arbitration agreement it will usually be considered to have waived the arbitration

---

[4] The concept of waiver is applied differently by domestic courts depending on the jurisdiction concerned. A discussion of the differences between waiver and other doctrines such as issue estoppel or abandonment is beyond the scope of this book, and we use the catch-all term 'waiver' to cover all of those legal concepts even at the risk of over-simplification in some contexts.

agreement for that dispute. If, however, the opposing party contests the court's jurisdiction on the basis of the arbitration agreement then that court will, depending on its law, either rule on the arbitral tribunal's jurisdiction or order the parties to arbitrate their dispute (thus staying or dismissing its own proceedings), including their dispute as to the issue of the arbitral tribunal's jurisdiction.

Most of the issues set out in the above summary are developed in much more detail in the following sections. 5.8

3 Preliminary issues relating to arbitral jurisdiction

3.1 Partial and absolute jurisdictional objections

An objection to an arbitral tribunal's jurisdiction can be absolute (i.e. contesting arbitral jurisdiction *per se*, or over a particular party *per se*) or partial (i.e. only with respect to certain of the claims or issues submitted to arbitration). 5.9

Absolute jurisdictional objections are the most common. They are usually raised on the ground that one of the alleged parties to the arbitration is not a proper party to the arbitration agreement. They may also be raised on grounds, for example, that the respondent did not have capacity to enter into the arbitration agreement, that the arbitration agreement is illegal, void or incapable of being performed, or that the claimant has waived its right to invoke the arbitration agreement.[5] 5.10

Partial jurisdictional objections arise primarily as a consequence of the concept that an arbitral tribunal has jurisdiction to decide only those matters which the parties have agreed that it can decide. Sometimes an arbitration agreement expressly limits arbitral jurisdiction to certain carefully defined issues. Those issues could be listed in the arbitration agreement, or listed in a document created at the outset of the arbitration such as the terms of reference.[6] 5.11

Even if no specific list of issues exists, a partial jurisdictional objection could arise from the plain language of the arbitration agreement. A typical arbitration clause contained in a contract may provide for the resolution of *all disputes relating to this contract* (or words to that effect). The respondent could argue that the parties did not agree to arbitrate non-contractual claims, for example pre-contractual or post-contractual tort claims. That would be a partial jurisdictional objection. In the face of a more broadly drafted clause, for example providing for the resolution of *all disputes arising out of or in connection with this contract*, such an argument would be very difficult to sustain. 5.12

---

5 Various examples of absolute jurisdictional objections are provided in the discussion of Article 6.2 of the ICC Rules below in Section 5.
6 In relation to Terms of Reference see Chapter 7, Section 6.5.

5.13   A partial jurisdictional objection based on the scope of an arbitration clause was raised before the Singapore High Court in the 2004 case *Sabah Shipyard (Pakistan) Ltd v Government of the Islamic Republic of Pakistan*.[7] The parties disputed whether the ICC arbitral tribunal had jurisdiction to decide on a claim for costs which had been incurred during a prior, related ICC arbitration which had been withdrawn. It was argued that the costs claim from the previous arbitration did not fall within the scope of the arbitration agreement providing for arbitration of disputes 'arising out of or in connection with' the contract. The Singapore High Court disagreed. It found that the parties must have intended that the costs of a prior arbitration arising out of the same contract could be settled by a subsequent arbitral tribunal.

5.14   Partial jurisdictional objections can arise in many other ways. A party could argue for example that one of its opponent's claims arises from a different contract. The other contract might contain a different dispute resolution clause, such as an inconsistent arbitration clause or a clause designating a domestic court as competent.[8]

5.15   Partial jurisdictional objections can also arise by virtue of the law governing the arbitration agreement or the law governing the arbitration proceedings. Either of those laws may place limits on the kind of claims that are capable of resolution by arbitration, some subject matters being considered inarbitrable.[9] Accordingly, a partial jurisdictional objection could allege that certain issues are inarbitrable under the relevant law.

5.16   Finally, a distinction needs to be drawn between an arbitral tribunal's *jurisdiction* and the scope of its *powers*. It is sometimes argued that an arbitral tribunal does not possess the power, legally speaking, to make certain orders. For example, there has historically been debate about the extent of arbitrators' powers to order certain preliminary injunctive relief, and in particular interim injunctions that affect a party's ability to deal with immovable property. Such issues concern an arbitral tribunal's powers rather than its jurisdiction over the claims or parties involved and should be clearly distinguished.

3.2 Jurisdictional objections raised by a party

5.17   The most common scenario in which a jurisdictional issue will arise is where the respondent objects to the arbitral tribunal's jurisdiction at the beginning of the arbitration. Arbitration laws and rules usually require a party to raise any jurisdictional objections early, generally prior to that party's first submission on the substance of the dispute.[10] Failure to do so can mean irrevocable waiver of that party's right to raise jurisdictional objections. A comparison of the

---

7 *Sabah Shipyard (Pakistan) Ltd v The Government of the Islamic Republic of Pakistan* [2004] 3 SLR 184; [2004] SGHC 109; [2004] 1 CLC 149.
8 See the examples provided in the discussion of Article 6.2 of the ICC Rules below in Section 5.
9 On arbitrability see Chapter 4, Section 8.
10 But see the discussion of the position in China below.

relevant provisions of the Model Law and the 1976 UNCITRAL Arbitration Rules follows.

Article 16(2) of the Model Law provides: 5.18

> A plea that the arbitral tribunal does not have jurisdiction shall be raised not later than the submission of the statement of defence. A party is not precluded from raising such a plea by the fact that he has appointed, or participated in the appointment of, an arbitrator. A plea that the arbitral tribunal is exceeding the scope of its authority shall be raised as soon as the matter alleged to be beyond the scope of its authority is raised during the arbitral proceedings. The arbitral tribunal may, in either case, admit a later plea if it considers the delay justified.

Article 21(3) of the 1976 UNCITRAL Arbitration Rules is slightly different:[11] 5.19

> A plea that the arbitral tribunal does not have jurisdiction shall be raised not later than in the statement of defence or, with respect to a counter-claim, in the reply to the counter-claim.

Both Articles provide that if a respondent wants to raise jurisdictional objections, it must do so not later than when filing its statement of defence. The Model Law expressly provides, in addition, that mere participation in the constitution of an arbitral tribunal will not preclude the respondent from later objecting to jurisdiction. In contrast to the Model Law, the UNCITRAL Arbitration Rules deal expressly with objections regarding arbitral jurisdiction over counterclaims. However, delay in raising such an objection would be caught by the general wording of Article 16(2) of the Model Law. Thus an objection to the arbitral tribunal's exercise of authority must be brought as soon as the matter is raised in the arbitration. That 'catch all' covers jurisdiction over new claims, including counterclaims. Finally, only the Model Law expressly empowers the arbitral tribunal to admit a later plea if it considers the delay justified. 5.20

Numerous jurisdictions including Hong Kong, Singapore, Malaysia, India, Korea, Australia and New Zealand have adopted Article 16(2) of the Model Law without any substantive modification.[12] Japan has chosen a slightly different approach. Article 23(2) of the 2003 Japanese Arbitration Law states: 5.21

> A plea that the arbitral tribunal does not have jurisdiction shall be raised promptly in the case where the grounds for the assertion arise during the course of arbitral proceedings, or in other cases before the time at which the first written statement on the substance of the dispute is submitted to the arbitral tribunal (including the time at which initial assertions on the substance of the dispute are presented orally at an oral

---

11 For example, in institutional rules see ACICA Rules Article 24.3, CIETAC Rules Article 6, SIAC Rules Article 25.2, HKIAC Rules Article 20.3, and ICSID Rules, Rule 41(1). Article 23(2) of the 2010 UNCITRAL Arbitration Rules is slightly different, referring also to set-offs. Moreover, that Article includes the additional text in Article 16(2) of the Model Law starting from the second sentence of Article 16(2). Therefore, there is no longer much difference between the UNCITRAL Rules and the Model Law except that the latter does not refer to counterclaims.

12 The corresponding section numbers in the Acts may differ but the provision is the same. China is very different, (see the discussion of Article 29 of the Chinese Arbitration Law below at Section 4.2). See also Article 13(2) of the 2006 Chinese Supreme People's Court Interpretations which confirms that a party which has failed to raise an objection to jurisdiction before the first hearing in the arbitration is precluded from requesting the Supreme People's Court to rule on jurisdiction.

hearing). However, the arbitral tribunal may admit a later plea if it considers the delay justified.

5.22 This provision is clearly inspired by the Model Law but its language is stricter. The jurisdictional objections must be raised *before* any written or oral submission on the merits is filed.

5.23 If a party participates in the arbitration but fails to raise a jurisdictional objection within the time limit specified by the applicable law, its silence may amount to entering into an arbitration agreement. Article 7(2) of the Model Law refers to an arbitration agreement being in writing 'if it is contained in ... an exchange of statements of claim and defence in which the existence of an agreement is alleged by one party and not denied by another'. An example of where the respondent's failure to object to jurisdiction worked against it is found in *Bauer (M) Sdn Bhd v Daewoo Corp*.[13] Although the Malaysian Court of Appeal agreed with the trial judge that the parties had not incorporated an arbitration agreement into their contract, it found that the acts of the respondent in participating in the arbitration estopped it from subsequently denying the arbitrator's jurisdiction. Thus its failure to raise its jurisdictional objection in good time extinguished its right to do so at a later stage.

3.3 Arbitral tribunal's ex officio examination of jurisdiction

5.24 Jurisdictional objections can only be raised by an entity named as a party to arbitration proceedings. However, regardless of whether jurisdictional issues are raised by one or more parties, it is prudent for all arbitral tribunals to consider on their own initiative whether they have jurisdiction, both absolute and with respect to each claim on which they have been asked to rule.[14] An arbitral tribunal should always comment on jurisdiction in its award(s), even if it is only to cite the arbitration agreement and confirm that neither party objected to jurisdiction.

5.25 An express decision on jurisdiction must also be made if one or more parties to the arbitration proceedings does not participate at all.[15] Unlike domestic court proceedings, 'default judgments' cannot be issued simply because a party fails to appear in an arbitration. If a party does not participate, the arbitration continues without the defaulting party or parties.[16] In these circumstances, the arbitral tribunal should examine and take an express decision on its own jurisdiction. Before doing so, it should ask the participating party or parties to file submissions on jurisdiction and expressly provide an opportunity for the non-participating parties to do so as well. Each non-participating party should be kept informed of and invited to participate in all steps in the arbitration.

---

13 [1999] 4 MLJ 545. See also for China, Reply of Supreme People's Court to the Request of Enforcement of Arbitral Award made in England by Swiss Bangji Co., Ltd (Civil 4, Miscellaneous), No. 47 (2006).
14 See, e.g. ICSID Rules Rule 41(2).
15 In 2009, there was at least one non-participating party in 6% of ICC arbitration cases at the time the ICC Court was requested to take decisions in connection with constituting the arbitral tribunal and other preliminary matters.
16 See Chapter 7, Section 6.10 on non-participating parties.

It is essential for an arbitral tribunal to examine and rule on jurisdiction where the respondent is not participating because the respondent may subsequently raise its objections in court proceedings challenging the award or resisting its enforcement. As noted above, however, failing to participate in an arbitration in the hope that the award can later be challenged is a high-risk strategy. If the respondent loses on the jurisdictional arguments before the courts, it will find itself bound by the substance of an arbitral award resulting from a procedure in which it did not defend its position.

In addition to an arbitral tribunal's duty to ensure that it has jurisdiction over all of the claims submitted to it, an arbitral tribunal must of its own initiative ensure that it does not decide issues incapable of settlement by arbitration under the law governing the arbitration agreement or the law of the seat of arbitration.[17] Arbitrators must also ensure that parties do not use arbitration to avoid certain mandatory provisions of a domestic law.[18]

3.4 Appropriate time to decide jurisdiction

When an arbitral tribunal is faced with a challenge to its jurisdiction, it has two broad options as to when it will decide that challenge. The first is that it can bifurcate the proceedings, thus hearing arguments on jurisdiction separately and then rendering a decision on jurisdiction before proceeding to examine the merits.[19] The second is that it can decide to join the issue of jurisdiction to the merits and decide both in one single award.

An arbitral tribunal's power to split an arbitration into separate phases arises from its general powers to manage the proceedings.[20] In addition, the Model Law and most arbitration laws expressly reiterate this power in relation to jurisdictional decisions. Article 16(3) of the Model Law provides that 'the arbitral tribunal may rule on a [jurisdictional objection] either as a preliminary question or in an award on the merits'.[21] Article 186 of the Swiss Private International Law Act 1987, which appears to have been inspired by Article 21(4) of the 1976 UNCITRAL Arbitration Rules, is different in that it provides a presumption in favour of deciding jurisdiction as a preliminary matter: 'The arbitral tribunal shall, as a rule, decide on its jurisdiction by preliminary award.' The ACICA Rules,

---

17 Deciding a dispute that is not capable of settlement by arbitration under the law of the seat of arbitration is not always fatal to the award. See Chapter 4, Section 8 on arbitrability.
18 See discussion in Chapter 3, Section 4 regarding mandatory rules.
19 A decision on jurisdiction is sometimes taken in the form of a procedural order and sometimes in the form of an award. However, it is now more common to find such decisions in the form of an award. Awards on jurisdiction are preferable because they permit scrutiny if the competent arbitral institution's rules provide for scrutiny, immediate enforceability and challenge (in some but not all jurisdictions). As discussed further below in Section 6.2, a negative jurisdictional decision cannot technically be an award.
20 An arbitral tribunal can bifurcate, trifurcate or add even more phases to an arbitration. See further Chapter 7, Section 6.9 in this regard. See also Chapter 7, Section 6.1 describing the typical procedural steps in an arbitration.
21 Hong Kong, Singapore, Malaysia, Korea, the Philippines, New Zealand and Australia have not modified the Model Law in this regard. Section 23(4) of the Japanese Arbitration Law is slightly different, but equivalent. Section 16(5) of the Indian Arbitration and Conciliation Act is slightly different again, but it is not clear whether it applies differently. In China this does not apply because there is no competence-competence rule empowering the arbitral tribunal to decide jurisdiction (see Section 4.2 below).

unlike most rules in this region,[22] follow the 1976 UNCITRAL Arbitration Rules and Swiss approach. Article 24.4 of the ACICA Rules is almost identical to Article 21(4) of the UNCITRAL Arbitration Rules: 'In general, the Arbitral Tribunal should rule on a plea concerning its jurisdiction as a preliminary question. However, the Arbitral Tribunal may proceed with the arbitration and rule on such a plea in its final award.'[23] In investment arbitrations, the usual practice is for the arbitral tribunal to make an award on jurisdiction before it proceeds to determine the merits. Rule 41(3) of the ICSID Rules states that when a jurisdictional objection is raised, the proceeding on the merits may be suspended.[24]

5.30 The advantage of deciding jurisdiction separately from the merits is that it saves a long and costly proceeding on the merits when it is uncertain whether or not the arbitral tribunal possesses jurisdiction. Time and costs could have been wasted if the arbitral tribunal later rules that it does not have jurisdiction.

5.31 On the other hand, the advantages of combining jurisdiction and the merits are twofold. First, bifurcating the proceedings will almost always add time and, as a consequence, costs to the overall procedure if the arbitral tribunal finds that it has jurisdiction. Second, if the jurisdictional objections are in any way intertwined with the substantive issues in dispute there may be a degree of overlap. A classic example is where a respondent argues that it is not a proper party to either the contract or the arbitration agreement.[25] The issues may be similar for both decisions. Separating jurisdiction from the merits when they are closely related is not only potentially inefficient, because issues may have to be re-argued, but can create a risk that the arbitral tribunal inadvertently decides something in the jurisdiction phase that will constrain or influence its subsequent decision on the merits. Similarly, the arbitral tribunal would put itself in a difficult position if it decided in favour of jurisdiction and then, subsequently when examining the merits, discovered facts that would have led it to a different conclusion on jurisdiction. Some jurisdictional issues are best decided only after the arbitral tribunal is cognisant of all the relevant facts.

5.32 The factors for an arbitral tribunal to consider when deciding whether to rule on jurisdiction separately from the merits are, therefore: (i) the complexity of the jurisdictional issues (high complexity sometimes leans in favour of bifurcation); (ii) the degree of potential overlap between the jurisdictional and substantive issues (significant potential overlap being a strong factor against bifurcation); and (iii) considerations of economy and efficiency. Without prejudging the issues, international arbitrators may also consider their first

---

[22] The institutional arbitration rules in this region repeat the Model Law approach except for the ACICA Rules (Article 24.4), BANI Rules (Article 18.4) and KCAB International Rules (Article 19.4), which all follow the Swiss approach.
[23] The 2010 UNCITRAL Arbitration Rules use a different construction in Article 23(3), and there is no longer a presumption in favour of ruling on jurisdiction as a preliminary matter.
[24] See also Article 36(1) of the ASEAN Comprehensive Investment Agreement, signed 26 February 2009 ('Where issues relating to jurisdiction or admissibility are raised as preliminary objections, the tribunal shall decide the matter before proceeding to the merits.')
[25] An arbitration clause in a contract is separate and distinct from the substantive contract containing it. This means that a party may have entered into one but not the other. This point is discussed in more detail in Chapter 4, Section 3.

impressions of the likelihood of success of the jurisdictional objections. If the objections appear to be frivolous, which is not uncommon in attempted dilatory tactics, this may lean against bifurcation which would serve only to delay progression to the merits of the case. The reverse also applies: if the jurisdictional objections seem prima facie well founded, it may make sense to deal with them first before time and money is wasted on a proceeding on the merits.

It has been said by a well-known arbitrator that 'the best course for an arbitral tribunal to take is... where possible, it should hear arguments on the issue of jurisdiction as a preliminary matter and render an interim award on the point. This enables the parties to know where they stand at a relatively early stage'.[26] However, for the reasons set out above, we consider that there are often very good reasons not to hear jurisdiction separately. In many cases, bifurcation will only cause delay and additional costs and may pose risks where the issues are intertwined with the merits. 5.33

3.5 Waiver of the right to invoke an arbitration agreement

A party that has waived an arbitration agreement loses its right to rely on the arbitration agreement.[27] Waiver may either be express (e.g. the party expressly states that it waives the arbitration agreement) or implied by a party's conduct. In practice, disputes about express waiver are rare. Implied waiver on the other hand is sometimes alleged by a party contesting arbitral jurisdiction or resisting the stay of a court action.[28] Ultimately, the requirements for establishing that waiver has occurred will depend on the law governing the arbitration agreement. The rest of this section discusses mainly the general principles relevant to implied waiver. 5.34

Poudret and Besson explain:[29] 5.35

> The arbitration agreement is terminated in the case of mutual waiver, which can be explicit or tacit and is not subject to any requirements of form. Such waiver shall be deemed made where the claimant proceeds before a court and the respondent pleads on the merits without invoking the arbitration clause to contest the jurisdiction of the court.

As Poudret and Besson note, the most common form of implied waiver occurs during domestic court proceedings. It will occur where the following conditions are met: 5.36

  (i) one of the parties to the arbitration agreement commences court litigation against another party or parties to the arbitration agreement;

---

26 S Jarvin, 'Objections to Jurisdiction' in W Newman and D Hill, *The Leading Arbitrator's Guide to International Arbitration*, 2nd edn, JurisNet, 2008, p. 102.
27 As noted in the introduction to this chapter, we use 'waiver' as an umbrella term that should be understood to encompass different legal terminology for different circumstances (such as issue estoppel or abandonment).
28 See Chapter 4, Section 7 on the enforcement of arbitration agreements.
29 J-F Poudret and S Besson, *Comparative Law of International Arbitration*, 2nd edn, Sweet & Maxwell, 2007, para 379, p. 322. See also E Gaillard and J Savage (eds), *Fouchard Gaillard Goldman on International Commercial Arbitration*, Kluwer Law International, 1999, p. 441.

(ii) the claim brought in the litigation falls within the scope of, and is capable of settlement under, the arbitration agreement; and

(iii) the defendant party in the litigation responds on the merits but does not challenge the court's jurisdiction on the basis of the parties' arbitration agreement.

5.37 If the above conditions are met, and subject to the exception for provisional relief mentioned below, the arbitration agreement will ordinarily be waived with respect to the claim brought and as between the parties to the litigation proceedings. The waiver should not affect non-parties to the litigation. Nor should it affect claims other than those raised by the plaintiff in the litigation.[30]

5.38 These conditions for waiver are set out to varying degrees in arbitration laws and arbitral case law. An example is Article 28 of the Chinese Arbitration Law:[31]

> If the parties have concluded an arbitration agreement and one party institutes an action in a People's Court without declaring the existence of the agreement and ... the other party does not, prior to the first hearing, raise an objection to the People's Court's acceptance of the case, he shall be deemed to have waived the arbitration agreement and the People's Court shall continue to try the case.

5.39 In *ICC Arbitration No. 4367* of 1984, involving related domestic court proceedings in India, the arbitral tribunal emphasised that for implied waiver to occur the parties to the arbitration agreement must be the same as the parties to the court proceedings:[32]

> The claimant contends that the [Indian] suits ... are separate and independent remedies brought against another party to preserve the security of a guarantee agreement. This we accept. The defendant to the suits is the [Indian] Bank, which is not a party to the 1964 Contract or to the arbitration clause therein, and the claims are brought in respect of a guarantee agreement between the claimant and the Bank dated ... 1965, which is the basis of the dispute to which the Indian Courts have [been seized]. The fact that the respondent unilaterally has made application to be added as defendant to the suits in no way affects our view that the suits before the Indian Courts are independent remedies separate from those before this Tribunal which do not affect our jurisdiction.

5.40 Implied waiver cannot be based on mere assumption – it occurs where the parties' conduct amounts to the expression of a clear intention to relinquish their

---

[30] If, however, the claims not raised in the litigation are closely related to the raised claims, the opposing party might contest arbitral jurisdiction on grounds such as issue estoppel, claim preclusion, merger of claims, bad faith, or similar. For a detailed discussion of Australian case law on the waiver of arbitration agreements see M Pryles, 'The Kaplan Lecture 2009: When is an arbitration agreement waived?', (2010) 27(2) *Journal of International Arbitration* 105, particularly at p. 117 et seq.

[31] For an explanation of this provision in the light of a recent Chinese Supreme Court interpretation, see Wan Exiang and Yu Xifu, 'Latest Evolution in the Judicial Intendance Mechanism over Arbitration in China', (2008) 3(2) *Front Law China* 181, at p. 189. See also JS Mo, 'Legality of the Presumed Waiver in Arbitration Proceedings under Chinese Law', (2001) 29 *International Business Lawyer* 21.

[32] Published in 1986 XI *Yearbook of Commercial Arbitration*, p. 134. See also the partial award in ICC case no. 9787 of 1988, where the arbitral tribunal held that there could be no waiver since the related court proceedings were filed between the parties' counsel and not the parties themselves, published in 2002 XXVII *Yearbook Commercial Arbitration*, p. 181.

contractual rights to arbitrate. The arbitral tribunal in *ICC Case No. 6840* of 1991 considered that implied waiver requires an unequivocal act:[33]

> it is a principle that the waiver of a right should not be presumed and that it must clearly result from the actions of the interested party. In this case, contrary to what A declares, B did not clearly manifest its intention to waive the arbitration clause.

5.41 Singaporean case law confirms that for an act to be considered as waiver or revocation of an arbitration agreement the party must have demonstrated a clear and unambiguous intention to waive that agreement.[34]

5.42 Outside of this region, the French Cour de Cassation has clearly held that a party will be deemed to have implicitly waived its right to arbitrate only if it has performed unequivocal acts establishing a clear intention to abandon such rights:[35]

> the abandonment of the right to take advantage of an arbitration clause may result only from clear and manifest acts expressing without any doubt the intention to abandon such right . . .

5.43 There is an exception to the principle that failing to raise an arbitration agreement can imply a waiver of the right to do so. Commencing an action or entering an unconditional appearance in a state court in relation to proceedings for temporary injunctive relief or provisional or conservative measures cannot amount to a waiver of the arbitration agreement, even if the parties are identical and the subject matter is within the scope of the arbitration agreement. Most arbitration laws and some rules expressly provide that seeking such relief, before or after the arbitral tribunal is constituted, is not inconsistent with an arbitration agreement.[36] The provisional relief exception was explained by the Philippines Supreme Court in *Transfield Philippines Inc v Luzon Hydro Corporation and Australia and New Zealand Banking Group Ltd and Security Bank Corporation*:[37]

> As a fundamental point, the pendency of arbitral proceedings does not foreclose resort to the courts for provisional reliefs (sic). The Rules of the ICC, which governs the parties' arbitral dispute, allows the application of a party to a judicial authority for

---

[33] Authors' translation from original French. ICC arbitration award no. 6840, 1991, *Collection of ICC Arbitral Awards*, vol. III., p. 470. In addition, the Swiss Federal Tribunal acknowledged this principle in the famous Fomento decision in 2001, *Fomento de Construcciones y Contratas SA v Colon Container Terminal SA*, ATF 127 III 279.

[34] *ABC Co v Owners of the Ship or Vessel 'Q'*, decision of SAR Tan in Admiralty in Rem no. 251 of 1995, High Court of Singapore, 9 May 1996, cited in H Alvarez, N Kaplan and D Rivkin, *Model Law Decisions*, Kluwer Law International, 2003, p. 136.

[35] Authors' translations from original French. Cour de Cassation, 18 February 1999, *Igla c/Société Soulier et autres*, (1999) 2 *Revue de l'Arbitrage*, p. 299 et seq.

[36] See, e.g. Article 9 of the Model Law ('It is not incompatible with an arbitration agreement for a party to request, before or during arbitral proceedings, from a court an interim measure of protection and for a court to grant such measure.'). Article 9 of India's Arbitration and Conciliation Act goes further than the Model Law by extending the period during which interim measures can be granted through to the time an award is enforced. See DF Donovan, 'The Allocation of Authority Between Courts and Arbitral Tribunals to Order Interim Measures: A Survey of Jurisdictions, the Work of UNCITRAL and a Model Proposal', (2004) 12 *ICCA Congress Series* 203.

[37] GR no. 146717, 19 May 2006, Supreme Court of the Philippines.

214   INTERNATIONAL COMMERCIAL ARBITRATION

interim or conservatory measures.[38] Likewise, Section 14 of Republic Act (R.A.) No. 876 (The Arbitration Law) recognizes the rights of any party to petition the court to take measures to safeguard and/or conserve any matter which is the subject of the dispute in arbitration. In addition, R.A. 9285, otherwise known as the 'Alternative Dispute Resolution Act of 2004,' allows the filing of provisional or interim measures with the regular courts whenever the arbitral tribunal has no power to act or to act effectively.

5.44   As a general proposition a defendant to a court proceeding who wants the dispute to be determined by arbitration must raise the arbitration agreement (or object to the court's jurisdiction) 'not later than when submitting his first statement on the substance of the dispute'[39] or it will be too late. In Hong Kong, this phrase from the Model Law has been interpreted fairly liberally by courts, in favour of arbitration.[40] The Philippines legislation is slightly different, requiring the objection to be raised 'not later than the pre-trial conference'.[41] The pre-trial conference would usually be later than a party's first statement on the substance of the dispute.

5.45   A party participating in any court proceeding where an arbitration agreement may cover the same dispute should be very cautious about implicitly waiving the arbitration agreement. Whether as plaintiff or defendant, it is prudent expressly to mention in each submission to the court that by making that submission the party does not intend to waive its right to invoke the arbitration agreement.

4 Arbitral tribunal's determination of jurisdiction: Competence-competence rule

5.46   There are various facets to the competence-competence rule.[42] At its simplest, it empowers an arbitral tribunal to decide on any and all objections as to its own jurisdiction. A more thorough consideration of the competence-competence rule reveals close links to the courts, and in particular the circumstances under which a court will allow an arbitral tribunal to rule on its jurisdiction prior to a court

---

38 Article 23(2) of the 1998 ICC Rules provides: 'Before the file is transmitted to the Arbitral Tribunal, and in appropriate circumstances even thereafter, the parties may apply to any competent judicial authority for interim. or conservatory measures. The application of a party to a judicial authority for such measures or for the implementation of any such measures ordered by an Arbitral Tribunal shall not be deemed to be an infringement or a waiver of the arbitration agreement.'
39 Model Law, Article 8(1).
40 See, e.g. *Louis Dreyfus Trading Ltd v Bonarich International (Group) Ltd* [1997] 3 HKC 597 (Hong Kong Supreme Court) noting that the statement on the merits must be a formal and deliberate act.
41 Section 24 of the Philippines Alternative Dispute Resolution Act 2004 provides: 'A court before which an action is brought in a matter which is the subject of an arbitration agreement shall, if at least one party so requests not later than the pre-trial conference, or upon the request of both parties thereafter, refer the parties to arbitration unless it finds that the arbitration agreement is void, inoperative or incapable of being performed'. See also in similar terms Rule 4.2 of the Philippines Supreme Court Special Rules of Court for Alternative Dispute Resolution Proceedings, effective 30 October 2009.
42 Competence-competence is often identified by its German name 'Kompetenz-Kompetenz'. The French sometimes call it 'compétence de la compétence'. In international arbitration, all of the different names and ways of spelling the concept are synonymous. What must be kept in mind though is that the approach of domestic courts to determining the meaning and scope of competence-competence can vary immensely, such that it can be quite different from jurisdiction to jurisdiction.

examining that jurisdiction. It is therefore a rule that affects the temporal priority as between the arbitral tribunal and the courts in decisions relating to the arbitral tribunal's jurisdiction. There is great variation in the approaches by different courts in this respect. Section 4.1 introduces the competence-competence rule and Section 4.2 examines it from the perspective of Asia-Pacific courts.

4.1 Introduction to the competence-competence rule

5.47 The competence-competence rule means that an arbitral tribunal may be authorised to determine its own jurisdiction. This may at first seem illogical given that the arbitral tribunal's decision could be in the negative. How could an arbitral tribunal decide that it does not have jurisdiction if a consequence of that decision is that the arbitral tribunal did not have jurisdiction to make it in the first place? Given the consensual basis for arbitral jurisdiction, one might consider that without an agreement to arbitrate, an arbitral tribunal could not – as a matter of common sense – decide anything, and any decision it does make would be void of any effect. Pursuing that line of reasoning, one may argue that only a competent court could rule on the jurisdiction of arbitral tribunals.

5.48 Arbitral tribunals can, however, decide on their own jurisdiction, and even rule that they do not have jurisdiction. As explained by Fouchard, Gaillard and Goldman, 'the competence-competence principle also allows arbitrators to determine that an arbitration agreement is invalid and to make an award declaring that they lack jurisdiction without contradicting themselves'.[43]

5.49 In order to overcome the apparent contradiction of an arbitral tribunal deciding that it does not have jurisdiction, the competence-competence rule must exist above and beyond the agreement to arbitrate. Arbitration experts therefore tend to agree that the source of an arbitral tribunal's power to determine its own jurisdiction is *not* the agreement to arbitrate but rather the law governing the arbitration proceedings.[44] In other words, an arbitral tribunal has the authority to decide on its own jurisdiction ultimately because an applicable domestic arbitration law authorises it to do so. This was confirmed by a decision of the Supreme Court of British Columbia, Canada. While outside the Asia-Pacific, the decision is of interest because British Columbia's international arbitration law is based on the Model Law. The court in *H&H Marine Engine Services Ltd v Volvo Penta of the Americas Inc*[45] refused to recognise the competence-competence rule as applying automatically, but found that it only applies where the law governing the arbitration proceedings or the arbitral rules enact the principle.

43 Gaillard and Savage, op. cit. fn 29, para 658.
44 P Mayer, 'L'Autonomie de l'Arbitre International dans l'Appréciation de Sa Propre Competence', *Recueil des Cours La Haye V*, Kluwer Law International, 1989, p. 344; Gaillard and Savage, op. cit. fn 29, at para 658 note that the jurisprudential basis of the rule is 'the arbitration laws of the country where the arbitration is held and, more generally, in the laws of all countries liable to recognize an award made by arbitrators concerning their own jurisdiction'. Antonias Dimolitsa explains that 'the competence-competence principle has always been seen as a concession on the part of national legal systems, so that arbitrators might rule on their own jurisdiction, subject to possible review by courts'. A Dimolitsa, 'Separability and Kompetenz-Kompetenz', (1998) 9 *ICCA Congress Series* 217, at p. 228.
45 2009 BCSC 1389.

5.50   The competence-competence rule is almost universally recognised in arbitration laws, but in distinctly varying degrees and in different ways.⁴⁶ Even in laws where it is not expressly recognised, the competence-competence rule is sometimes implied into those laws and applied as a general principle of international arbitration law and/or practice.⁴⁷ However, as shown by the British Columbian case referred to in the previous paragraph, it should not be assumed that the competence-competence rule applies as a matter of course. Some courts will only apply it where the *lex arbitri* (or perhaps arbitration rules) enact it specifically.

5.51   The competence-competence rule is set out in Article 16(1) of the Model Law:⁴⁸

> The arbitral tribunal may rule on its own jurisdiction, including any objections with respect to the existence or validity of the arbitration agreement. For that purpose, an arbitration clause which forms part of a contract shall be treated as an agreement independent of the other terms of the contract. A decision by the arbitral tribunal that the contract is null and void shall not entail ipso jure the invalidity of the arbitration clause.

5.52   The first sentence of this Article enacts the competence-competence rule, while the following sentences concern the related concept of separability of an arbitration clause; that is the concept that for the purposes of an arbitral tribunal ruling on jurisdiction an arbitration clause in a contract is considered as a separate agreement from the contract containing it.⁴⁹

5.53   In addition to its recognition by virtually all legal systems,⁵⁰ the competence-competence rule is reiterated in most arbitration institutional rules. Typical regional examples include Rule 25 of the 2007 SIAC Rules ('The Tribunal shall have the power to rule on its own jurisdiction, including any objections with respect to the existence, termination or validity of the arbitration agreement') and Rule 33 of the JCAA Rules ('The arbitral tribunal may decide challenges made regarding the existence or validity of an arbitration agreement or its own jurisdiction').⁵¹

5.54   It is important to understand that while these institutional rules repeat the competence-competence principle, they are generally not considered to be the ultimate source of its authority, because they apply only by virtue of the parties'

---

⁴⁶ For a very thorough general overview of the competence-competence rule and a comparative analysis of several representative European and North American approaches to it, see WW Park, 'The Arbitrator's Jurisdiction to Determine Jurisdiction', (2006) 13 *ICCA Congress Series* 55.

⁴⁷ See, e.g. the discussion referring to the Partial Award of 1996 in ICC case 7878 (unpublished) in H Grigera Noan, 'Choice of Law Problems in International Commercial Arbitration', (2001) vol. 289 *Recueil des cours*, p. 53.

⁴⁸ This applies unmodified or in a substantively similar way regarding the competence-competence aspect in the following arbitration laws: New Zealand, Malaysia (Section 18(2), which provides a breakdown of the rule's elements), Singapore, Hong Kong, Australia, India and Korea. China is very different and is discussed below.

⁴⁹ On the issue of separability see Chapter 4, Section 3.

⁵⁰ The only notable exception in this region, China, is discussed below at Section 4.2.

⁵¹ CIETAC Rule 6(1) is very different (see discussion at Section 4.2).

agreement. If an arbitral tribunal lacks jurisdiction over a party, then any chosen arbitration rules do not apply with respect to that party either, and the authority supposedly sourced in such rules disappears. As noted above, theoretically, the ultimate authority for the principle of competence-competence must therefore be found in the arbitration law of the seat of arbitration, either by express legislative recognition, judicial acceptance or by virtue of its status as a general principle of international arbitration law. Nonetheless, the British Columbian case of *H&H Marine Engine Services Ltd v Volvo Penta of the Americas Inc*[52] curiously suggests that the source of competence-competence authority can alternatively be arbitral rules.

5.55 While arbitration rules (as opposed to laws) are not ordinarily considered to be the ultimate source of competence-competence powers, there are certain advantages in selecting arbitration rules which reiterate the principle. Redfern and Hunter[53] note that selecting such rules confirms the parties' desire for the competence-competence rule to be applied as set out in the chosen rules. They also explain that in some jurisdictions arbitrators only decide their own jurisdiction to the extent that the parties authorise them to do so. That authorisation may be in the form of the putatively applicable arbitration rules. Finally, reiteration of the principle in arbitration rules specifically chosen by the parties can be used as an additional argument as to why a domestic court seized of a matter covered by an arbitration agreement should take only a prima facie examination of that agreement before referring the parties to arbitration.[54]

5.56 The competence-competence rule is sometimes said to have a negative and a positive effect.[55] The positive effect is that parties gain a right to have their jurisdictional dispute determined by an arbitral tribunal, at least in the first instance. The negative effect is that the parties lose their right to have the jurisdictional dispute determined by a court. An essential component of the competence-competence rule is sometimes overlooked. That component is that an arbitral tribunal's decision that it has jurisdiction is not final. As discussed in Section 6.2 below, such decisions are capable of review by or appeal to courts in the seat of arbitration.[56]

5.57 The competence-competence rule can therefore be considered as a rule of temporal priority, empowering the arbitral tribunal to rule on its jurisdiction in the first instance. As noted above, the extent to which a court will give priority to the arbitral tribunal varies immensely depending on the jurisdiction of the court concerned and on other circumstances. This is the subject of the next section.

---

52 2009 BCSC 1389.
53 A Redfern, M Hunter, N Blackaby and C Partasides, *Law and Practice of International Commercial Arbitration*, 4th edn, Sweet and Maxwell, 2004, para 5.44.
54 This is discussed further in the following section.
55 The terminology known as the 'negative effect' of competence-competence was used in E Gaillard, 'Convention d'arbitrage' (1994) *Juris-Classeur Droit International*, FAAC.586/5, Paris p. 49 and E Gaillard, 'Les manoeuvres dilatoires des parties et des arbitres dans l'arbitrage commercial international', (1990) *Revue de l'arbitrage* 759, at p. 771.
56 Model Law Article 16(3) expressly recognises this in connection with positive jurisdictional rulings. A discussion of the situation in relation to negative jurisdictional rulings can be found below at Section 6.2.

4.2 Competence-competence rule and extent of domestic court intervention

5.58 Domestic courts can be called on to decide, or at least consider, arbitral jurisdiction in several circumstances before an arbitral tribunal has ruled on jurisdiction. The most common is when a party has commenced an action on the merits of the dispute in a domestic court and the opposing side contests the court's jurisdiction on the basis of the arbitration agreement.[57] In these circumstances, the domestic court should refer the parties to arbitration provided that there is a binding arbitration agreement.[58] In so doing, to what extent does that domestic court consider the existence, scope and validity of the arbitration agreement? And to what extent does its decision bind the arbitral tribunal or override the arbitral tribunal's authority to rule on its own jurisdiction under the competence-competence rule?

5.59 There is variation among courts as to the extent to which priority is given to the arbitral tribunal to decide on jurisdiction. Certain courts will scarcely look at an arbitration agreement if an arbitral tribunal has already been constituted.[59] They will wait until a party seeks to challenge the arbitral tribunal's jurisdictional decision and then may exercise their control over jurisdiction. At the other extreme, some courts will in certain circumstances accept to rule definitively on arbitral jurisdiction before an arbitral tribunal does, thus usurping the arbitral tribunal's competence-competence powers.[60] Somewhere in the middle lie the vast majority of courts (including most Asia-Pacific courts) which are a hybrid and will examine only the prima facie existence of an arbitration agreement before staying their own proceedings and referring the parties to arbitration for the resolution of their dispute, including their dispute about whether the arbitral tribunal has jurisdiction.[61] In order to satisfy such a prima facie test, the party seeking to rely on the arbitration agreement generally has to show that there is an arguable case in favour of arbitral jurisdiction. The courts may refuse such an application if it is clear that a challenge to the arbitrator's jurisdiction should succeed.

---

57 Another instance is when a court is requested to provide support to start arbitration proceedings (for example to appoint an arbitrator where a party has defaulted in doing so) and there is doubt as to arbitral jurisdiction (see the discussion of *SPB v Patel Engineering* below in Section 4.2). Another still is when the parties have expressly agreed that a court should decide the jurisdictional dispute as a preliminary matter before commencement of the arbitration such as under the domestic Australian Commercial Arbitration Acts (briefly discussed below in Section 4.2). See also Sections 32 and 72 of the English Arbitration Act 1996 and Article 11 of the Sri Lankan Arbitration Act, which allows an application to the High Court of Sri Lanka to determine arbitral jurisdiction even during an arbitration.
58 See Chapter 4, Section 7 regarding the enforcement of arbitration agreements.
59 No example has been found in the Asia-Pacific, but see Article 1458 of the French New Code of Civil Procedure.
60 For example, Section 11 of the Sri Lankan Arbitration Act allows an application to the High Court of Sri Lanka to determine arbitral jurisdiction at any time, even during an arbitration. This is also the approach under US Federal law, see *Sandvik AB v Advent Int. Corp.* 220 F 3d 99, 3d Circuit, 2000.
61 Various different approaches to this temporal question of when a court can and will examine arbitral jurisdiction under the competence-competence rule are discussed in Park, op. cit. fn 46, p. 55, particularly at p. 62 et seq.

ARBITRAL JURISDICTION 219

As explained in Chapter 4,[62] Article 8 of the Model Law mirrors Article II 5.60
of the New York Convention in relation to stays of domestic court proceedings
when there is an arbitration agreement. Both provisions aim to ensure that when
there is an arbitration agreement and a party objects to the domestic court's
jurisdiction, the court immediately refers the parties to arbitration. Article 8(1)
of the Model Law states:[63]

> A court before which an action is brought in a matter which is the subject of an
> arbitration agreement shall, if a party so requests not later than when submitting his
> first statement on the substance of the dispute, refer the parties to arbitration unless it
> finds that the agreement is null and void, inoperative or incapable of being performed.

The operative language (identical in the New York Convention)[64] is that a court 5.61
must refer the parties to arbitration 'unless it finds that the said agreement is
null and void, inoperative or incapable of being performed'. The language here
could be understood to suggest that the court would need to make a 'finding'
on arbitral jurisdiction before referring the parties to arbitration. If a court were
to do so, however, this would undermine the competence-competence rule by
usurping the arbitral tribunal's authority to rule on its own jurisdiction.[65]

The extent of a court's authority to rule on jurisdiction before an arbitral 5.62
tribunal has had the opportunity to do so is a subject of judicial and academic
debate.[66] Most commentators consider that the court should go no further than
checking prima facie that there is an arbitration agreement, leaving the jurisdictional issues to be decided by the arbitral tribunal.[67] Another alternative though

---

62 See Chapter 4, Section 7.
63 Some Asia-Pacific jurisdictions have additional or differing provisions. New Zealand and Malaysia have added the phrase 'or that there is not in fact any dispute between the parties with regard to the matter agreed to be referred'. See Chapter 4, Section 7.1. Section 10(1) of the Malaysian Arbitration Act also has a potentially shorter time limit for raising the arbitration agreement (i.e. '... before taking any other steps in the proceedings'). Section 7 of the Australian International Arbitration Act 1974 employs different but equivalent language. It also incorporates the Model Law in addition to its Section 7, such that Australia has two provisions (plus Article II(3) of the New York Convention, making the total three) serving the same purpose, albeit sometimes in different scenarios. Singapore (see Section 6 of Singapore's International Arbitration Act) is similar. Japan's Arbitration Law (Article 14) is also slightly different from the Model Law. As described below (Section 4.2), India and Sri Lanka have modified Article 8 of the Model Law to remove 'unless it finds...' and following language.
64 The only substantive difference in Article II(3) of the New York Convention is that there is no requirement that the party contesting the court's jurisdiction has to do so when making its first submission on the substance of the dispute.
65 For the sake of completeness, it should be noted that if a domestic court finds that the arbitration agreement 'is null and void, inoperative or incapable of being performed', then it will not refer the matter to arbitration. In these circumstances the court proceedings will usually continue and the competence-competence rule does not apply, unless the arbitration in question is seated outside the jurisdiction of the state court. If it is a foreign court, the arbitration may well continue despite parallel proceedings in a foreign domestic court.
66 For general discussions see Poudret and Besson, op. cit. fn 29, p. 440, para 489 et seq; JD Lew, LA Mistelis and SM Kröll, *Comparative International Commercial Arbitration*, Kluwer Law International, 2003, p. 349, para 14–60; Gaillard and Savage, op. cit. fn 29, pp. 401 and 406; Park, op. cit. fn 46, pp. 55–153.
67 A well-known supporter of the prima facie approach is Emmanuel Gaillard. See the recent publication, E Gaillard and Y Banifatemi, 'Negative Effect of Competence-Competence: The Rule of Priority in Favour of the Arbitrators' in E Gaillard and D Di Pietro (eds), *Enforcement of Arbitral Agreements and International Arbitral Awards, The New York Convention in Practice*, Cameron May, 2008, p. 259 ('domestic courts should not, in parallel and with the same degree of scrutiny, rule on the same issue [of jurisdiction], at least at the outset of the arbitral process. In other words, the court should limit, at that stage, the review to prima facie determination that the agreement is not 'null and void, inoperative or incapable of being performed.') See also earlier works, e.g. Gaillard, 1990, op. cit. fn 55; E Gaillard, 'L'effet négatif de la compétence-compétence'

220 INTERNATIONAL COMMERCIAL ARBITRATION

would be for a court to make a definitive ruling on jurisdiction so that the matter is out of the way. If so, the only appropriate court to do so would be one at the seat of arbitration. It would not make sense if any court in the world could rule on the validity of an arbitration agreement in respect of arbitration proceedings seated abroad.[68]

5.63 Frédéric Bachand[69] argues strongly in favour of the prima facie approach. After observing that there is conflicting case law,[70] Bachand goes on to consider the drafting history of the Model Law. His analysis leads him to conclude that:[71]

> the Model Law's travaux préparatoires, basic structure and underlying principles reveals that the drafters considered the prevention of dilatory jurisdictional objections to be a more important objective and, consequently, that Article 8(1) ought to be interpreted as requiring courts seized of referral applications to apply a prima facie standard while reviewing the tribunal's jurisdiction.

5.64 Bachand's reasoning is compelling but it is to be contrasted with numerous authors who consider that examining the drafting history of the Model Law would lead to the opposite conclusion.[72]

5.65 The issue has come before various domestic courts around the world, including in the Asia-Pacific. As noted above, most Asia-Pacific jurisdictions give the arbitral tribunal the first opportunity to decide jurisdiction, thus limiting the court's power to a prima facie examination of arbitral jurisdiction. These decisions accordingly lend support to Bachand's interpretation of Article 8(1) of the Model Law.

5.66 Unequivocal support for the prima facie approach can be seen in Hong Kong decisions made subsequent to those cited by Bachand in the above referenced article. In *PCCW Global Ltd v Interactive Communications Service Ltd*, it was noted that:[73]

---

in J Haldy, J-M Rapp and P Ferrari (eds), *Études de procédure et d'arbitrage en l'honneur de Jean-François Poudret*, Stampfli, 1999, p. 387; E Gaillard, 'The Negative Effect of Competence-Competence', (2002) 17(1) *Mealey's International Arbitration Report* 27.
68 It should be noted however that a foreign court might need to rule on whether an arbitration agreement is 'null and void, inoperative or incapable of being performed' in the context of an application under Article II(3) of the New York Convention or Article 8(2) of the Model Law (or its equivalent) to stay a foreign domestic court proceeding (see Chapter 4, Section 7).
69 F Bachand, 'Does Article 8 of the Model Law Call for Full or Prima Facie Review of the Arbitral Tribunal's Jurisdiction?', (2006) 22(3) *Arbitration International* 463.
70 Bachand, ibid. cites numerous cases both for and against the prima facie approach. Bachand draws his examples from Canada, Australia, New Zealand and Hong Kong. However support for the prima facie view can also be found in India. See the discussion of *Shin-Etsu Chemical Co Ltd v Aksh Optifibre Ltd* (2005) 7 SCC 234 below. Numerous other decisions are cited in Alvarez, Kaplan and Rivkin, op. cit. fn 34, p. 55 et seq.
71 Bachand, op. cit. fn 69, p. 476.
72 These include, notably, leading commentators on the Model Law such as HM Holtzmann and JE Neuhaus, *A Guide to the UNCITRAL Model Law on International Commercial Arbitration: Legislative History and Commentary*, Kluwer, 1989. See also comments in Dimolitsa, op. cit. fn 44, p. 217, at p. 234; Mayer, op. cit. fn 44, at p. 344; Park, op. cit. fn 46, pp. 69 and 87.
73 [2007] 1 HKC 327 at para 12. See also *The Incorporated Owners of Sincere House v Sincere Company Ltd* [2005] HKLT 18; [2007] 2 HKC 424 citing with approval *Daily Win Engineering Ltd v The Incorporated Owners of Greenwood Terrace*, HCCT 133/2000 [2001] HKC 1252 that 'The court should do no more than forming a prima facie view on the existence of an arbitration agreement between the parties'.

the proper test to apply... is whether there is a prima facie or plainly arguable case that the parties were bound to arbitrate.... It is only when it is clear that there was no agreement to arbitrate... that the stay should be refused.

5.67 This was endorsed in *Kin Yat Industrial Co Ltd v MGA Entertainment (HK) Ltd*[74] and again in *Ocean Park Corporation v Proud Sky Co Ltd*,[75] which described Hong Kong law as now settled in this respect:

> 42. In terms of the benchmark for the existence of an arbitration agreement, Burrell J[[76]] held that it had to be demonstrated that there was a good prima facie, or a plainly arguable case, that an arbitration agreement existed and bound the parties, and that the onus of so doing lay upon the defendant applicant for the stay, and that in determining whether such a case had been made out, the court should look first at the evidence in support of the defendant's contention, the relevant test being satisfied if the court was of the view that cumulatively the evidence was cogent and arguable and not dubious or fanciful. The learned judge also held that it was for the arbitrator, and not the court itself on a stay application, to make a detailed final determination as to the existence or otherwise of an arbitration agreement, a matter upon which the arbitrator would have the benefit of oral testimony from both sides.
> 43. [This] decision... was approved and followed in the Court of Appeal in *PCCW Limited v. Interactive Communications Service Ltd*, CACV 18 of 2006 (unrep.)...
> 44. The law on this point in this jurisdiction thus appears settled. The question for the court in this application thus boils down to whether, on the evidence read as a whole, and bearing in mind the burden upon the applicant for the desired stay, it can be said to be 'plainly arguable' that an arbitration agreement existed on the basis of the documentation before the court?

5.68 The position has been given less attention in Singapore but nevertheless appears relatively certain. For example, in *Dalian Hualiang Enterprise Group Co Ltd v Louis Dreyfus Asia Pte Ltd*,[77] the Singapore High Court ruled on an appeal from a lower court's decision to stay its proceedings because there was an arbitration agreement. In the course of its judgment the High Court clearly took the view that its examination of jurisdiction was prima facie only:[78]

> it is not for the court on an application for a stay of proceedings to reach any final determination as to the scope of the arbitration agreement or whether a particular party to the legal proceedings is a party to the arbitration agreement because those are matters within the jurisdiction of the arbitral tribunal. Only where it is clear that the dispute is outside the terms of the arbitration agreement or that a party is not a party to the arbitration agreement or that the application is out of time should the court reach any final determination in respect of such matters on an application for a stay of proceedings. Where it is arguable that the dispute falls within the terms of the

---

74 [2007] HKCU 435: 'The proper test is well-established: is there a prima facie or plainly arguable case that the parties were bound by an arbitration clause? The onus is on the defendant to demonstrate that there is.' The court supports this with numerous prior authorities.
75 [2007] HKCU 1974.
76 In *Pacific Crown Engineering Ltd v Hyundai Engineering and Construction Co Ltd* [2003] 3 HKC 659.
77 [2005] 4 SLR 646.
78 *Dalian Hualiang Enterprise Group Co Ltd v Louis Dreyfus Asia Pte Ltd* [2005] 4 SLR 646, at p. 652.

arbitration agreement or where it is arguable that a party to the legal proceedings is a party to the arbitration agreement then, in my view, the stay should be granted and those matters left to be determined by the arbitral tribunal.

5.69 In Sri Lanka, the provision relating to stays of court proceedings does not even mention the exception of the arbitration agreement being null and void, inoperative or incapable of being performed, thus strongly recognising the competence-competence principle.[79] Despite this omission, however, the provision might well be interpreted in a way that the courts could refuse the stay if they find that the arbitration agreement is manifestly void.

5.70 A similar provision to that in Sri Lanka is found in Section 8 of the Indian Conciliation and Arbitration Act. Curiously though, Section 8 has been interpreted as providing even more scope for court interference than the standard Model Law provision. Some conflicting court decisions have left a rather murky state of affairs in India concerning the scope of a court's examination of an arbitration agreement when a party is seeking a stay of court proceedings.

5.71 In order to understand these cases we need briefly to recall a peculiarity of Indian arbitration law. India has adopted the Model Law but with various modifications. Section 8 of the Indian Conciliation and Arbitration Act 1996 modifies Article 8 of the Model Law as follows:

> A judicial authority before which an action is brought in a matter which is the subject of an arbitration agreement shall, if a party so applies not later than when submitting his first statement on the substance of the dispute, refer the parties to arbitration.

5.72 Thus, like in Sri Lanka, the additional text found in Article 8 of the Model Law ('unless it finds that the said agreement is null and void, inoperative or incapable of being performed') is omitted.

5.73 Section 8 deals only with the enforcement of arbitration agreements where the seat of arbitration is in India.[80] This contrasts with the Model Law in which Article 8 also applies where the seat of arbitration is outside the country concerned.[81] In India, a different provision – Section 45 of the same Act – deals with the enforcement of arbitration agreements where the place of arbitration is outside India. Section 45 includes the additional language: 'unless it finds that the said agreement is null and void, inoperative or incapable of being performed.'

5.74 In *Shin-Etsu Chemical Co Ltd v Aksh Optifibre Ltd*,[82] the Supreme Court of India considered its power under Section 45 of the Indian Act to rule on the validity of

---

[79] Article 5 of the 1995 Sri Lankan Arbitration Act provides: 'Where a party to an arbitration agreement institutes legal proceedings in a court against another party to such agreement in respect of a matter agreed to be submitted for arbitration under such agreement, the Court shall have no jurisdiction to hear and determine such matter if the other party objects to the court exercising jurisdiction in respect of such matter.'
[80] Section 2(2) of the Indian Arbitration Act 1996 provides that Part I of the Act (which includes Section 8) applies only where the seat of arbitration is within India.
[81] Article 1(2) of the Model Law provides that 'The provisions of this Law, except articles 8, 9, 35 and 36, apply only if the place of arbitration is in the territory of this State'. In the 2006 version of the Model Law, this is extended to Articles 17H, 17I, and 17J.
[82] (2005) 7 SCC 234.

an arbitration agreement. Section 45 rather than Section 8 was relevant because the seat of arbitration was outside India. The arbitration clause provided for ICC arbitration seated in Tokyo with Japanese substantive law governing the contract. Justice Srikrishna framed the question for determination by the Supreme Court as follows:[83]

> The core issue in this case is: Whether the finding of the court made under Section 45 of the [Act] that the arbitration agreement, falling within the definition of Section 44 of the Act, is or is not 'null and void, inoperative or incapable of being performed' should be a final expression of the view of the court or should it be a prima facie view formed without a full-fledged trial?

The Supreme Court justices in the course of their reasoning referred to Swiss, French, UK, USA, Hong Kong, Canadian and other jurisprudence. They considered what was the most appropriate time for Indian courts to control arbitral jurisdiction (i.e. at the time of hearing a stay application before the arbitration begins or at the time of hearing an objection to enforcement of the award). Ultimately a 2:1 majority held that a challenge to an arbitration agreement under Section 45 on the ground that it is null and void, inoperative or incapable of being performed is to be determined on a prima facie basis only. The majority explained that the proper time for a court to examine jurisdiction fully was at the stage of an action in connection with the enforcement of an award:[84] 5.75

> Even after the court takes a prima facie view that the arbitration agreement is not vitiated on account of factors enumerated in Section 45, and the arbitrator upon a full trial holds that there is no vitiating factor in the arbitration agreement and makes an award, such an award can be challenged under Section 48(1)(a).... The award will be set aside under Section 48(1)(a) if the party against whom it is invoked satisfies the court inter alia that the agreement was not valid.... The two basic requirements, namely, expedition at the pre-reference stage, and a fair opportunity to contest the award after full trial, would be fully satisfied by interpreting Section 45 as enabling the court to act on a prima facie view.

Dissenting Justice Sabharwal felt that the language of Section 45 as compared to Section 8 and the interests of efficiency leaned in favour of a full-scale examination of jurisdiction by the courts. 5.76

The initial application for a stay in *Shin-Etsu Chemical* had erroneously been brought under Section 8 rather than Section 45. The references to Section 8 led the Supreme Court to make *obiter dictum* comments about its meaning. These comments confirm what one would understand from the plain language of Section 8:[85] 5.77

> Unlike Section 45, the judicial authority under Section 8 has not been conferred the power to refuse reference to arbitration on the ground of invalidity of the agreement.

---

[83] (2005) 7 SCC 234, at pp. 263–264.
[84] (2005) 7 SCC 234, at p. 238.
[85] Dissenting Justice Sabharwal's decision at (2005) 7 SCC 234, at p. 244 and p. 251. It should be noted that the majority judges expressly agreed with Justice Sabharwal regarding interpretation of Section 8. They differed regarding Section 45.

It is evident that the object [of Section 8] is to avoid delay and accelerate reference to arbitration leaving the parties to raise objection, if any, to the validity of the arbitration agreement before the arbitral forum and/or post award under Section 34 of the Act.
...

As already noticed, unlike Section 45 the objection as to the validity of the arbitration agreement cannot be raised as a defence to an application filed under Section 8.

5.78 Different judges of the Indian Supreme Court gave a contradictory interpretation of Section 8 in *SBP v Patel Engineering*,[86] a decision handed down just a few months after *Shin-Etsu Chemical*. This time, the seat of arbitration was in India rather than abroad. The question before the Supreme Court was whether the court's appointment of a default arbitrator (because the parties' agreed mechanism for appointing the arbitrator had failed) under Section 11(6) of the Indian Arbitration and Conciliation Act was an exercise of administrative or judicial power. The Supreme Court overruled an earlier five-judge decision and held by majority that it is a judicial function. The majority judges, referring to previous authority, surprisingly interpreted Section 8 of the Act as requiring a fully fledged, final determination of arbitral jurisdiction:[87]

8. ... while functioning under Section 11(6) of the Act, a Chief Justice or the person or institution designated by him, is bound to decide whether he has jurisdiction, whether there is an arbitration agreement, whether the applicant before him is a party, ... Section 11(7) makes his decision on the matters entrusted to him, final.
...

15. We may at this stage notice the complementary nature of Sections 8 and 11. Where there is an arbitration agreement between the parties and one of the parties, ignoring it, files an action before a judicial authority and the other party raises the objection that there is an arbitration clause, the judicial authority has to consider that objection and if the objection is found sustainable to refer the parties to arbitration. The expression used in this Section is 'shall' and this Court in P. Anand Gajapathi Raju v. P.V. G. Raju and in Hindustan Petroleum Corporation Ltd. v. Pink City Midway Petroleum ... has held that the <u>judicial authority is bound to refer the matter to arbitration once the existence of a valid arbitration clause is established. Thus, the judicial authority is entitled to, has to and is bound to decide the jurisdictional issue raised before it, before making or declining to make a reference</u>. (Emphasis added)

5.79 The majority made very clear that the court's determination of arbitral jurisdiction under Section 8 or 11 was final, and not reviewable by an arbitral tribunal. The majority explained that once the court has determined arbitral jurisdiction under Section 8 or 11, Section 16 of the Act (which reflects Article 16 of the Model Law and empowers an arbitral tribunal to rule on its own jurisdiction) would not apply to that arbitration.[88]

---

[86] *SBP & Co v Patel Engineering Ltd* 2005 8 SCC 618; 2005 (9) SCALE 1.
[87] Paragraphs 8 and 15 of Justice Balasubramanyan's judgment in *SBP & Co v Patel Engineering Ltd* 2005 8 SCC 618; 2005 (9) SCALE 1.
[88] Paragraph 19 of Justice Balasubramanyan's judgment notes that 'where the jurisdictional issues are decided under [Section 8 and/or Section 11] ... Section 16 cannot be held to empower the arbitral tribunal to ignore the decision given by the judicial authority or the Chief Justice before the reference to it was made.

Patel Engineering accordingly achieves a result opposite to what the plain language of Section 8 suggests. If *Patel Engineering* is followed,[89] courts in India will undertake a full and final review of the validity of an arbitration agreement before referring parties to arbitration under Section 8. This will eviscerate the effect of the competence-competence rule enshrined in Section 16(3) of the Act. Where, however, the seat of arbitration is outside India, the courts should follow *Shin-Etsu Chemical*, which adopts the much more sensible approach of taking only a prima facie decision on arbitral jurisdiction before referring the parties to arbitration. In such cases, the arbitral tribunal will be left to rule on its own jurisdiction.[90]

5.80

In certain jurisdictions, the law takes a different approach. The parties may agree to derogate from the competence-competence rule and empower the courts with exclusive jurisdiction to decide on arbitral jurisdiction.[91] An example is the uniform Commercial Arbitration Acts (for domestic arbitration) in Australia, which provide parties with the possibility to seek a ruling on a point of law from the competent State Supreme Court.[92] Parties can and do use this provision to seek a ruling on arbitral jurisdiction from the courts, rather than having the arbitral tribunal decide.

5.81

It is very unusual for an arbitration law not to recognise the competence-competence rule at all, but one example is China.[93] The Chinese Arbitration

5.82

The competence to decide does not enable the arbitral tribunal to get over the finality conferred on an order passed prior to its entering upon the reference by the very statute that creates it.... The finality given to the order of the Chief Justice on the matters within his competence under Section 11 of the Act, are incapable of being reopened before the arbitral tribunal'.

89 *Patel* is more authoritative than *Shin-Etsu*. As pointed out in an article discussing the cases, '*Patel Engineering* was decided by a seven judge bench of the Supreme Court while *Shin-etsu* was decided by a three judge bench. Under the rules of precedent in India, *Patel Engineering* carries greater weight than *Shin-etsu* and, insofar as there is a conflict between the decisions, it may well be argued that *Patel Engineering* prevails'. See A Ray and D Sabharwal, 'Competence-Competence: An Indian Trilogy', (2007) *Mealey's International Arbitration Report* 26, at p. 30.

90 A subsequent Supreme Court of India case, *Agri Gold Exims Ltd v Sri Lakshmi Knits and Wovens*, Civil Appeal No. 326 of 2007, 23 January 2007 (2007 (1) *Arb LR* 235), touched on various issues of jurisdiction but did not address the scope of court review of an arbitration agreement because the existence and validity of the arbitration agreement was not contested in that matter. However, it did comment that there was no 'discretion' not to grant a stay under Section 8 of the Indian Arbitration and Conciliation Act. While not addressing the competence-competence issue directly, see also *Bhatia International v Bulk Trading S.A.* (2002) 4 SCC 105, *Venture Global Engineering v Satyam Computer Services* (2008) 4 SCC 190; [2008] INSC 40, which both find that Part I of the Indian Arbitration and Conciliation Act 1996 can apply even to foreign arbitrations if not excluded. The more recent decision of *Max India Ltd v General Binding Corporation*, Delhi High Court, 6 May 2009 is encouraging, however. While not a Supreme Court decision, it takes a more arbitration-friendly approach to the jurisdiction of Indian courts over the conduct of arbitrations seated outside India.

91 It is rare for this possibility to be expressly permitted by arbitration laws whether in the Asia-Pacific or elsewhere, and especially in civil law jurisdictions. Poudret and Besson contend that it is prohibited in Switzerland for parties to agree that a court will decide on jurisdiction because the competence-competence rule is mandatory. (Poudret and Besson, op. cit. fn 29, p. 389, para 462).

92 Section 39 of the Victorian Commercial Arbitration Act provides: 'with the consent of all the other parties – the [Victorian] Supreme Court shall have jurisdiction to determine any question of law arising in the course of the arbitration.' The Commercial Arbitration Acts are principally applicable to domestic arbitrations, but are also applicable where parties to an international arbitration seated in Australia have excluded the Model Law. See also Schedule 2 of Section 5 of the New Zealand Arbitration Act 1996, and Section 72 of the English Arbitration Act 1996.

93 All other Asia-Pacific jurisdictions that are the focus of this book enact the competence-competence rule in some form (see above footnote 91). However, the rule is not recognised in the Pacific Islands (Fiji, Papua New Guinea and the Solomon Islands) or Vanuatu (which has no law on arbitration at all). See S Greenberg, S Fitzgerald and B Gehle, 'International Commercial Arbitration Practice in Australia, New Zealand and

Law does not empower the arbitral tribunal to determine its own jurisdiction. It reserves that power to the administering arbitral institution (usually translated as 'arbitration commission' for Chinese institutions) or to the local court (i.e. the People's Court). Article 20 provides:[94]

> If a party challenges the validity of the arbitration agreement, he may request the arbitration commission to make a decision or the People's Court to give a ruling. If one party requests the arbitration commission to make a decision and the other party requests the People's Court for a ruling, the People's Court shall rule.
>
> A party's challenge of the validity of an arbitration agreement shall be raised prior to the arbitration tribunal's first hearing.

5.83 The scope of an arbitration commission's involvement in China is somewhat unique. Effectively, the arbitration commission's ruling on jurisdiction replaces that of an arbitral tribunal in other jurisdictions.[95]

5.84 Jingzhou Tao explains that there can sometimes be overlapping involvement of domestic courts and the arbitration commission in determining jurisdiction.[96] The arbitration commission ordinarily takes the lead role unless a party has commenced a court action prior to the arbitration proceedings. A court may revise the arbitration commission's decision upon an application to set aside the award or enforce the award. If so, the court should inform the arbitration commission of its decision so that the latter, if it has already taken a decision on jurisdiction, can suspend or even terminate the arbitration.[97]

5.85 Tao also explains that whenever there is a dispute between parties about which arbitration commission has been chosen, the competent Intermediate People's Court decides.[98] An example in point was where the arbitration agreement provided for disputes to be submitted to the 'Beijing arbitration organisation'.[99] The clause was pathological because there are two arbitration commissions in Beijing, CIETAC and the BAC (Beijing Arbitration Commission), neither of which was correctly named in the arbitration agreement. When the claimant filed for arbitration with the BAC, the respondent reacted by seeking a declaration about the validity of the arbitration agreement from the Beijing Intermediate People's Court. The court, applying a 1996 ruling from the Supreme People's Court, held that the clause was valid and that the claimant was at liberty to choose one

---

the Pacific Islands', in HA Grigera Naón & PE Mason (eds), *International Commercial Arbitration Practice: 21st Century Perspectives*, Lexis Nexis, 2010, Chapter 15.

[94] It should be noted that while Article 5 of the Chinese Arbitration Law appears, on its face, similar to Article 8 of the Model Law and Article II of the New York Convention, it is of limited effect given that the competence-competence rule is not recognised in China. See Jingzhou Tao, *Arbitration Law and Practice in China*, 2nd edn, Kluwer, 2008, p. 86, para 241 ('In practice, Article 5 bestows on the Court the authority to decide on the validity of the arbitration agreement instead of giving such power to the arbitration institution or arbitral tribunal in accordance with the doctrine of competence-competence.')

[95] See generally Jingzhou Tao, ibid., pp. 63–73 and 85–89.

[96] Ibid., pp. 70–71.

[97] Ibid., pp. 70–71.

[98] Ibid., p. 64 et seq.

[99] ZhongChen International Engineering Contracting Co Ltd v Beijing Construction Engineering Group Co Ltd, Beijing Second Intermediate People's Court, (Economic & Arbitration) No. 657, (2001) – (decision dated 18 April 2001).

of the arbitration commissions in Beijing. The court also confirmed that it, i.e. the court, was the appropriate forum to determine jurisdiction given the lack of clarity about which arbitration commission was designated.

Under the 2005 CIETAC Rules, where the parties have agreed on CIETAC as the arbitration commission, the position is different. Article 6(1) of those Rules provides that 'CIETAC shall have the power to determine the existence and validity of an arbitration agreement and its jurisdiction over an arbitration case. The CIETAC may, if necessary, delegate such power to the arbitral tribunal'. Thus, in contrast to Article 20 of the Chinese Arbitration Law, CIETAC can now delegate its power to make jurisdictional rulings to the arbitral tribunal. This is a step towards recognition of competence-competence in China. 5.86

As the above analysis demonstrates, the trend in the Asia-Pacific Model Law jurisdictions is, overall, now strongly in favour of a prima facie limitation on the scope of court examination of jurisdiction. This approach is also favoured by most continental European jurisdictions[100] and has rapidly growing support in the US.[101] 5.87

It has been suggested that:[102] 5.88

> in the civil law system, when courts are satisfied that the arbitration agreement exists and is valid, their decision to refer the matter to arbitration is final, whereas in the common law system the decision is more often than not a mere stay in court proceedings, the courts not being deprived of their jurisdiction.

The description of that distinction is not entirely correct, at least in so far as the practical effect on the arbitral tribunal's decision on jurisdiction. When a common law court stays its own proceeding, that stay is in principle permanent (unless and until the arbitral tribunal decides there is no valid arbitration agreement, or the parties agree to waive the arbitration agreement). Both common and civil law courts can – depending on their law and rules of court – place certain conditions on an order to stay (or end) their own proceedings. The nature of such conditions 5.89

---

100 The seminal Swiss case is probably *Foundation M v Bank X*, Swiss Federal Tribunal, 29 April 1996, ATF 122 III 139, 1996, (ASA New Bull 527). The Federal Tribunal confirmed that where the seat of arbitration is in Switzerland the Swiss courts must decline jurisdiction unless a brief examination of the arbitration clause reveals that it is null and void, inoperative or incapable of being performed. The French courts have gone further, also covering the situation where the seat is not in France. See, e.g. *American Bureau of Shipping v Copropriété Maritime Jules Verne*, CASS CACIV 1ère 26 Juin 2001, *Revue de l'arbitrage* 529. The Cour de Cassation confirmed that the only question for the French judge before referring the jurisdictional dispute to arbitration is whether the arbitration clause is 'manifestly null or inapplicable.' These and other cases are discussed in Gaillard and Banifatemi, op. cit. fn 67, p. 264. See also P Fouchard, 'La coopération du Président du Tribunal de Grande Instance à l'arbitrage', (1985) *Revue de l'arbitrage* 5, at p. 27, noting that 'manifestly void' in Article 1458 of the French New Code of Civil Procedure is interpreted strictly; as confirmed in case law commented upon by Jose Rosell in the IBA Arbitration Committee D Newsletter of October 2002. Under French law, the courts are not permitted to examine an arbitration agreement at all once an arbitral tribunal has been constituted and is dealing with the matter. See Article 1458 of the New Code of Civil Procedure.
101 For example, there is strong support for the competence-competence rule in *Buckeye Check Cashing Inc v Cardegna*, 546 US (2006), 21 February 2006. The US Supreme Court confirmed that arbitrators should first decide on their jurisdiction even in the face of an allegation that the underlying contract was void for illegality. The court also confirmed the notion of separability, see the discussion in A Samuel, 'Separability and the US Supreme Court Decision in *Buckeye v Cardegna*', (2006) 22(3) *Arbitration International* 477. Under US Federal law, the courts can, however, order a full examination of the arbitration clause at any time during the arbitration process: *Sandvik AB v Advent Int Corp* 220 F 3d 99 (3d Circuit, 2000).
102 Dimolitsa, op. cit. fn 44, p. 217, at p. 234.

depends on that law or rules, rather than whether the motion is described as a stay or termination of the proceeding.

4.3 Conclusions on competence-competence

5.90 The importance of the competence-competence rule is obvious. Without it, only the courts could decide disputes about arbitral jurisdiction. This would mean that any time a party raises a jurisdictional objection an arbitral tribunal would either have to wait for the courts to decide the matter before proceeding, or proceed without knowing whether it has jurisdiction. The first option could cause delays and inefficiency while the second might be strongly objected to by the party contesting jurisdiction, thus reducing that party's confidence in the process.

5.91 The previous section referred to certain arbitration laws under which the parties may derogate from the competence-competence rule and empower the courts with exclusive jurisdiction to decide on arbitral jurisdiction. The perceived advantage of this approach is said to be efficiency since the courts have the ultimate say on jurisdiction in any event. An efficient court deciding jurisdiction once and for all at the outset would avoid the cost and delay of an arbitration proceeding to the merits if the courts later find that the arbitral tribunal did not have jurisdiction. This approach is also attractive from the perspective of an underlying principle of arbitration: party autonomy.[103] It could be said that if the parties want the courts to decide jurisdiction in certain circumstances then it is arguable that they should be permitted to do so.

5.92 Conversely, perhaps the strongest argument in favour of competence-competence is the need to avoid dilatory tactics, because jurisdiction is often contested by a respondent wanting to cause delay and disruption in the arbitral proceedings. Competence-competence also relieves sometimes over-burdened and disinterested courts from having to deal with arbitration matters which might otherwise disappear because the parties settle or the respondent is eventually satisfied with the outcome of the arbitral process and decides not to contest jurisdiction.

5.93 In addition, the expertise of experienced international arbitrators generally means that they are far better placed than domestic courts to examine most questions of jurisdiction arising in international arbitrations. First, international arbitrators will apply – within the limitations and framework of the law governing the arbitration agreement – concepts of international arbitral practice which are widely accepted by the international legal and business communities. International arbitrators should take an approach that international commerce has come to expect from international arbitration whereas even experienced domestic courts can approach international arbitral jurisdiction from a rather parochial standpoint. Second, in applying this international approach, wise international

---

103 See Chapter 7, Section 2 regarding the issue of party autonomy.

arbitrators may give great weight to the character of the underlying transaction and the broad commercial context leading to the conclusion of the arbitration agreement. This may involve hearing the parties on the factual and commercial aspects of the conclusion of that agreement to establish what was really intended, both in terms of which parties (scope *rationae personae*) were supposed to be bound by the agreement and which disputes (scope *rationae materiae*) were intended to be submitted to arbitration.

Limiting the scope of the competence-competence rule would deny the parties the benefit of having a neutral, experienced, international arbitral tribunal decide what can be a key issue, i.e. jurisdiction. It is nonsense to suspect that international arbitrators have a tendency to find in favour of jurisdiction against all odds. While arbitrators' decisions on jurisdiction often find in favour arbitration, this is because many jurisdictional objections are brought for tactical or dilatory purposes and because experienced arbitrators are likely to make efforts to elicit the parties' real intentions over and above technical or formalistic jurisdictional arguments. 5.94

Furthermore, the competence-competence rule means that a court which is later required to review an arbitral tribunal's decision on jurisdiction will benefit from having the arbitral tribunal rule on jurisdiction in the first instance. Bachand quite rightly points out that:[104] 5.95

> courts will have the opportunity to take into consideration the earlier reasoning and decision of the arbitrators, which will render their task easier, while decreasing the chances that their decision will ignore general principles of international commercial arbitration.

Issues such as which disputes the parties submitted to arbitration and which parties were intended to be bound by the arbitration agreement must, therefore, ideally be left to the greatest extent possible in the arbitral tribunal's hands. Subsequent court review of jurisdiction (i.e. at the time of a setting aside or enforcement action) should ideally be limited to issues of international public policy and objective arbitrability.[105] This maximises the policy in favour of the competence-competence rule; that is, it is better to run a risk of a later contradictory court finding on jurisdiction than let a party utilise a spurious jurisdictional objection to cause delays and inconvenience. 5.96

---

[104] Bachand op. cit. fn 69 p. 463, n 13. Bachand cites Mayer op. cit. fn 44 at p. 350: ('L'examen successif est une garantie de bonne administration de la justice; le juge pourra s'inspirer de la motivation adoptée par l'arbitre; ou y trouver au contraire une faille révélatrice'.) Bachand's translation is: 'The successive examination ensures the sound administration of justice; the judge will have the opportunity to take into consideration reasons provided by the arbitrator; or, on the contrary, to find a revealing flaw.' See also Park, op. cit. fn 46, p. 144.

[105] The differences between subjective and objective arbitrability are explained in Chapter 4, Section 8. Sigvard Jarvin notes that opponents of the full competence-competence rule tend to consider that state courts should at least decide the jurisdictional issue first if it concerns objective arbitrability or public policy, since these are matters that the court must ultimately control anyway. Jarvin refers to allegations of bribery, corruption and violation of good morals as best suited to court determination. Jarvin, op. cit. fn 26, pp. 92–93, 96 and 99–100; see also the 1st edn (2004) of the same book, where he elaborates further. However, we consider that these issues can and should be dealt with by an arbitral tribunal first.

230   INTERNATIONAL COMMERCIAL ARBITRATION

5.97   In sum, we strongly support the competence-competence rule and believe that a court's initial role should be nothing more than a prima facie examination of jurisdiction. If the court considers that there is an arguable case for jurisdiction, it should refer the parties to arbitration.

5 Arbitral institution's examination of jurisdiction

5.98   The rules of some arbitral institutions expressly permit the institution to examine the prima facie existence of an arbitration agreement before the arbitral tribunal does so. If there is clearly no arbitration agreement, the case is dismissed. Conversely, if the institution finds prima facie that jurisdiction exits, then the arbitral tribunal may decide jurisdiction after hearing full argument on the issue.

5.99   The best known example is Article 6(2) of the ICC Rules.[106] This provides:

> If the Respondent does not file an Answer, as provided by Article 5, or if any party raises one or more pleas concerning the existence, validity or scope of the arbitration agreement, the [ICC Court] may decide, without prejudice to the admissibility or merits of the plea or pleas, that the arbitration shall proceed if it is prima facie satisfied that an arbitration agreement under the Rules may exist. In such a case, any decision as to the jurisdiction of the Arbitral Tribunal shall be taken by the Arbitral Tribunal itself. If the [ICC Court] is not so satisfied, the parties shall be notified that the arbitration cannot proceed. In such a case, any party retains the right to ask any court having jurisdiction whether or not there is a binding arbitration agreement.

5.100   As can be seen from its language, the ICC Court does not analyse *sua sponte* whether an arbitration agreement under the ICC Rules exists. Article 6(2) is triggered only when the respondent does not file an answer to the request for arbitration and/or objects to the arbitration clause. In such cases, the ICC Court's analysis is limited to a mere prima facie review of the existence of an arbitration agreement under the ICC Rules. If there is a prima facie basis to start the arbitration the decision on jurisdiction is left to the arbitral tribunal. The main advantage of a provision like Article 6(2) of the ICC Rules is that it saves significant time and cost where there appears to be no way that an arbitral tribunal could accept jurisdiction over the case.

---

[106] In this region, the only example somewhat comparable to Article 6(2) of the ICC Rules is Article 7(2) of the BANI Rules ('The Board of BANI shall review the petition to determine whether or not the arbitration agreement or arbitration clause in the contract is adequate to provide a basis of authority for BANI to examine the dispute.'). Article 18 of the BANI Rules reserves to the arbitral tribunal the power to decide any jurisdictional issues. Article 6(1) of the CIETAC Rules provides that CIETAC has the power to determine the existence and validity of an arbitration agreement and its jurisdiction over a case. That power can be delegated to the arbitral tribunal if necessary. However CIETAC's determination of jurisdiction is not prima facie like the other examples provided because its decision is final (subject only to review by a domestic court), and is not subject to a full decision by the arbitral tribunal (see above Section 4.2). Rule 6(4) of the BAC Rules is equivalent to Article 6(1) of the CIETAC Rules. Article 36(3) of the ICSID Rules provides that the Secretary General of ICSID shall refuse to register a request for arbitration where the dispute described therein is 'manifestly outside the jurisdiction of the Centre'. The 2010 SIAC rules include a procedure for prima facie examination of jurisdiction by SIAC. The rule is very similar to Article 6.2 of the ICC Rules.

The ICSID Secretary-General also plays a role in determining jurisdiction pursuant to Article 36(3) of the ICSID Convention. Under that provision, the Secretary-General 'shall register the request [for arbitration] unless he finds, on the basis of the information contained in the request, that the dispute is manifestly outside the jurisdiction of the Centre'.

We have already explained above (Section 4.2) that it is common for Chinese arbitral institutions to rule on the jurisdiction of arbitral tribunals. This is very different from the prima facie examination of the existence of an arbitration agreement by the ICC Court under Article 6(2) of the ICC Rules. The Chinese institutions actually replace the arbitral tribunal's role in determining jurisdiction, and are empowered to do so by the *lex arbitri*.[107] In contrast, if the ICC Court decides that there is a prima facie agreement to arbitrate, this does not relieve the arbitral tribunal from its duty to decide jurisdiction. Quite to the contrary, the arbitral tribunal must fully examine and rule on jurisdiction in accordance with the competence-competence principle.

5.101

5.102

Some of the ICC Court's most complex decisions under Article 6(2) arise in the context of multi-party and multi-contract arbitrations.[108] Examples of each are provided below. These examples also illustrate the types of jurisdictional issues that can arise in international arbitration generally.

5.103

5.1 Examples in multi-party arbitrations[109]

The ICC Court is often confronted with situations where a claimant has identified in the request for arbitration several respondents, one or all of which have not signed the arbitration agreement. The claimant may seek to include these non-signing entities on the basis of legal theories such as representation, corporate succession, group of companies, agency, assignment, estoppel or alter ego.[110] Normally, the ICC Court is prima facie satisfied that a non-signatory respondent can be included in the arbitration if there is evidence that it has been closely involved with the contract containing the arbitral clause, e.g. if it participated in the negotiations, performance and/or termination of the contract. Two examples may assist to clarify these types of situations.

5.104

---

107 Article 20 of Chinese Arbitration Act.
108 Multi-party arbitrations are becoming increasingly common. In each year from 2001–2009 around 30% of arbitrations submitted to the ICC involved more than two parties. In 2009, 233 ICC arbitrations (or 28.5% of all ICC arbitrations for that year) involved more than two parties. Out of these 233 cases, 206 (88.4%) involved between three and five parties, 21 (9%) involved between six and ten parties, and six (2.6%) involved more than ten parties. One case filed in 2009 had 19 different parties.
109 The examples of 'multi-party' and 'multi-contract' arbitrations below come from L Malintoppi and S Greenberg, 'The Practice of the ICC International Court of Arbitration Concerning Multi-Party Contracts and Scrutiny of Awards', paper provided at the ICC Young Arbitrators Forum, Barcelona, 26–29 June 2008. Case numbers and other details (such as reasons) of these examples cannot be provided for reasons of confidentiality. Issues relating to multi-party arbitration are dealt with in Chapter 4, Section 6.
110 See Chapter 4, Section 4.1 for a full discussion of non-signatory parties and arbitration agreements. For a more recent and thorough explanation of all of the ICC Court's practices, giving numerous examples, in respect of multiparty and multicontract arbitrations, see S Greenberg, J Feris and C Albanesi, 'Consolidation, Joinder, Cross-Claims, Multiparty and Multicontract Arbitrations: Recent ICC Experience', in B Hanotiau & EA Schwartz (eds) *Multiparty Arbitration*, Dossier VII, ICC Institute of World Business Law, ICC Publication No. 701, September 2010.

5.105   In the first example, two claimants introduced a request for arbitration against four respondents, only two of which had signed the contract containing the relevant arbitration agreement. The claimants argued that since all four potential respondents were part of the same group of companies, they should all be parties to the proceedings, even though some of them had not signed the contract. On the basis of the information submitted, the ICC Court decided that the arbitration proceedings could be initiated against all four respondents because the claimants had satisfied the prima facie test by showing that all respondents had participated in the negotiations and performance of the agreement.

5.106   By contrast, in the second example, a request for arbitration was introduced by the claimant against one respondent on the basis of a sales agency contract. The claimant later sought to raise claims against two other companies, arguing that they formed part of the same group of companies. Unlike in the previous example, the claimant contended that the burden was on the respondents to show that they did not share the same duties and responsibilities as the first respondent. The ICC Court decided that the matter could not proceed against the two additional respondents.

5.107   The ICC Court can also be called upon to take an Article 6(2) decision with respect to one or more claimant parties. Article 6(2) is triggered in this scenario when, for example, the respondent admits that it is subject to an arbitration agreement with one of the claimants, but denies that an arbitration agreement exists between it and another claimant.

5.108   An example was a case in which two claimants commenced arbitration against a single respondent. Only the first claimant had signed the contract containing the arbitration agreement and the second claimant was its corporate parent. The ICC Court found that there was a prima facie arbitration agreement between the respondent and the first claimant, but not between the respondent and the second claimant as there was no evidence that it could be a party to the arbitration agreement. Another example involved a case commenced by four claimants against six respondents. Several respondents argued that there was no prima facie arbitration agreement between them and the third and fourth claimants. The ICC Court agreed. The matter went forward with the first two claimants only, the second two being dismissed.

5.109   Of course the ICC Court often finds that a case will proceed with all of the claimants. In one recent example in a construction case, the first claimant was the contractor and a party to the contract with the respondent owner. The second claimant, a party related to the first, had not signed the contract containing the arbitration clause but had provided in a separate document a guarantee to secure the first claimant's performance. The respondent contended that there was no arbitration agreement between it and the second claimant. The ICC Court took into account inter alia that the document containing the guarantee did not have its own dispute resolution clause and decided that the matter would proceed with both claimants. It would be for the arbitral tribunal to determine whether it had jurisdiction over the second claimant.

5.2 Examples in multi-contract arbitrations

Another important type of jurisdictional objection concerns multi-contract arbitrations, i.e. where a request for arbitration is filed based on more than one distinct agreement. The ICC Court has generally allowed such arbitrations to proceed under Article 6(2) of its Rules only when the following conditions have been met: (i) all contracts are signed by the same parties; (ii) all contracts are related to the same economic transaction and (iii) the dispute resolution clauses in the contracts are compatible (e.g. reference to the ICC, choice of the same seat of arbitration, referral to the same domestic court of jurisdiction, and the same method for constituting the arbitral tribunal).[111]

The ICC Court was confronted with a case where two different contracts contained clauses providing for different dispute resolution methods: arbitration under the ICC Rules in one and jurisdiction of the courts of Paris in the other. The ICC Court decided that a single arbitration could not proceed on the basis of these two contracts.

In another case, the only notable differences in the arbitration clauses contained in the two relevant contracts were the place of arbitration (Paris and Geneva) and the language of the arbitration (English and French). Those factors were viewed by the ICC Court as preventing a single arbitration from proceeding on the basis of the different contracts.[112]

6 Effects of jurisdictional decisions

6.1 Effect of a court or arbitral institution's prima facie examination of jurisdiction

If a competent domestic court at the seat of arbitration decides that there is no arbitration agreement (i.e. in most jurisdictions, that the arbitration agreement is 'null and void, inoperative or incapable of being performed'[113]) before the arbitral tribunal has ruled on jurisdiction, then the competence-competence rule does not come into effect. The substantive dispute will most likely go to court and there is nothing left for the arbitral tribunal to decide. However, a ruling by a court that is not competent, which will ordinarily be the case of a foreign court outside the seat of arbitration, that there is no arbitration agreement does not bind an arbitral tribunal sitting abroad. It is not uncommon that arbitration proceedings continue despite a foreign court's ruling that there is no arbitration agreement, and even despite a foreign court's injunction to prevent the arbitration from proceeding.

---
111 AM Whitesell and E Silva-Romero, 'Multiparty and Multicontract Arbitration: Recent ICC Experience', *ICC International Court of Arbitration Bulletin*, Special Supplement, 2003, p. 7, at p. 15. Many more recent examples of multicontract cases are provided in Greenberg, Feris and Albanesi, op. cit. fn 110.
112 Whitesell and Silva-Romero, ibid.
113 This is the language of Article 8(1) of the Model Law and Article II(3) of the New York Convention, explained above at Section 4.2.

5.114 If an arbitral institution, such as the ICC Court, decides that there is no prima facie arbitration agreement, the last sentence of Article 6(2) of its Rules provides that any party retains the right to ask any court having jurisdiction whether or not there is a binding arbitration agreement. It has very occasionally happened that the ICC Court decided that there was no prima facie jurisdiction over a party and a court at the seat of arbitration has ruled otherwise, meaning that the excluded party may be readmitted into the arbitration or into a new arbitration.

5.115 Where a competent court or arbitral institution makes a prima facie ruling that there is an arbitration agreement, the jurisdictional dispute is then transferred to the arbitral tribunal. The previous prima facie decision of the court or arbitral institution has no bearing on the arbitral tribunal's subsequent decision on its jurisdiction. The arbitral tribunal should start over, de novo, and should not be influenced at all by the earlier prima facie ruling.

5.116 That said, without affecting the ultimate outcome, these prima facie determinations are probably sufficient to ensure that an arbitral tribunal will not simply dismiss the case as it might do in circumstances where no such prior ruling had been taken and there was clearly no basis for asserting arbitral jurisdiction.[114] Prima facie determination by a court or institution may also reassure the arbitral tribunal of its competence-competence powers, so that it will be sure to conduct a full examination of jurisdiction before deciding against it. In those senses, therefore, a prima facie ruling could be considered as having some effect on the subsequent arbitration proceedings.

5.117 If the prima facie decision is from a court as opposed to an arbitral institution, the extent that such a court decision is relevant may in turn depend on the extent of that court's initial examination of the jurisdictional issue.[115] If the court has examined nothing more than the prima facie existence of an arbitration agreement, as is the norm, then that decision should make no difference at all to the arbitral tribunal's decision on jurisdiction. If, on the other hand, the court is located at the seat of arbitration and it has probed a little deeper, as some courts do, then there is arguably slightly less work left for the arbitral tribunal on those particular points.

6.2 Recourse against an arbitral tribunal's jurisdictional decision

5.118 As emphasised above, a feature of the competence-competence rule is that an arbitral tribunal's decision on its jurisdiction is *not* final. It is subject to subsequent court review. As will be seen below, implementing this principle is different according to whether the arbitral tribunal finds that it does or does not have jurisdiction.

---

[114] Jarvin, op. cit. fn 26, pp. 102–104.
[115] See discussion at Section 4.2 above.

It should be noted that in investor-state arbitration conducted under the ICSID Convention there is no scope whatsoever for court review of jurisdictional decisions.[116]

5.119

6.2.1 Positive jurisdictional decisions

The Model Law provides two possibilities for court review of an arbitral tribunal's decision that it has jurisdiction. First, it provides a mechanism to seek immediate review under Article 16(3):[117]

5.120

> If the arbitral tribunal rules as a preliminary question that it has jurisdiction, any party may request, within thirty days after having received notice of that ruling, the court specified in article 6 to decide the matter, which decision shall be subject to no appeal; while such a request is pending, the arbitral tribunal may continue the arbitral proceedings and make an award.

Several observations can be made about this Article. First, nothing is said about recourse from negative jurisdictional decisions, an omission which is discussed further below. Second, Article 16(3) creates a different form of recourse for positive jurisdictional decisions than the recourse available against awards in accordance with Article 34 of the Model Law (discussed below). It has been suggested that this may be because preliminary rulings on jurisdiction are not considered to be awards, whether for the purposes of the Model Law or for certain legal systems generally.[118] A second reason for different treatment is that a positive decision on jurisdiction is subject to de novo review by the courts, rather than the limited grounds available to review awards under Article 34 of the Model Law.[119] Another observation from Article 16(3) is that the arbitration proceedings will continue during the domestic court's review of the arbitral tribunal's decision that it has jurisdiction. This ensures that the arbitration is not delayed while a potentially lengthy court proceeding takes place.

5.121

The other Model Law provision indirectly providing for recourse from a positive jurisdictional decision is Article 34, dealing with setting aside proceedings.[120] This states in the relevant part:

5.122

1) Recourse to a court against an arbitral award may be made only by an application for setting aside in accordance with paragraphs (2) and (3) of this article.
2) An arbitral award may be set aside by the court specified in article 6 only if:

---

116 Jurisdictional decisions by ICSID tribunals may be challenged under Article 52 of the ICSID Convention. Article 52(1)(b) provides that if the ICSID tribunal 'manifestly exceeded its powers', this is a ground for annulment. No provision in Article 52 explicitly refers to the Model Law Article 34 grounds of party incapacity or arbitration agreement invalidity. See Chapter 10, Section 8.
117 This applies unmodified or virtually unmodified in most Asia-Pacific jurisdictions. In Singapore, leave of the High Court is needed (Section 10 of the International Arbitration Act). New Zealand and India are different in that they permit recourse from negative jurisdictional decisions (see the discussion below in this section). The very different situation in China was discussed above in Section 4.2.
118 See L Boo, 'Ruling on Arbitral Jurisdiction – Is that an Award?', (2007) 3(2) *Asian International Arbitration Journal* 125, at p. 132 and p. 140.
119 See further Section 6.3 below.
120 On setting aside proceedings, see Chapter 9, Section 3.

(a) the party making the application furnishes proof that:
  (i) a party to the arbitration agreement referred to in article 7 was under some incapacity; or the said agreement is not valid under the law to which the parties have subjected it or, failing any indication thereon, under the law of this State; or
  ...
  (iii) the award deals with a dispute not contemplated by or not falling within the terms of the submission to arbitration, or contains decisions on matters beyond the scope of the submission to arbitration...

5.123 Article 34(2)(a)(i) deals with invalid arbitration agreements while Article 34(2)(a)(iii) deals with issues as to the scope of the submission to arbitration. As noted above there is doubt about whether decisions on jurisdiction are in fact awards.[121] As they are not generally considered to be awards, Article 34 of the Model Law should not be available to set aside a decision dealing exclusively with jurisdiction, but could be used to set aside an award on the merits on the ground that the arbitral tribunal lacked jurisdiction. Similarly, enforcement of an award on the merits could be resisted on the equivalent basis of lack of jurisdiction under Article V of the New York Convention.[122]

5.124 Section 16 of the Indian Arbitration and Conciliation Act differs from Article 16(3) of the Model Law in that it does not provide for immediate court review of an arbitral tribunal's decision on jurisdiction.[123] Subsections 5 and 6 of Section 16 state:

(5) The arbitral tribunal shall decide on a [jurisdictional objection] and, where the arbitral tribunal takes a decision rejecting the plea, continue with the arbitral proceedings and make an award.
(6) A party aggrieved by such an arbitral award may make an application for setting aside such an arbitral award in accordance with section 34.

5.125 The effect of these subsections is that there is no possibility for immediate recourse against an arbitral tribunal's positive jurisdictional decision in India. The aggrieved party has no right to challenge a positive jurisdictional decision until an arbitral award is rendered on the merits. Only thereafter is it entitled to challenge that award under Section 34 of the Indian Arbitration and Conciliation Act (which mirrors Article 34 of the Model Law). This interpretation was confirmed by the Supreme Court of India in 2005. The Supreme Court noted that where an arbitral tribunal takes a positive jurisdictional decision, the aggrieved party: 'has to wait until the award is made to challenge that decision in an appeal against the arbitral award itself in accordance with Section 34 of the Act.'[124]

5.126 Despite these provisions, in practice international arbitrators sitting in India do sometimes render positive decisions on jurisdiction in the form of partial

---
121 Boo, op. cit. fn 118, p. 132 and p. 140.
122 See further Chapter 9, Section 6 in that respect.
123 A proposal was made during the UNCITRAL Model Law Working Group for an approach similar to that adopted by India to be adopted for the Model Law generally. See Holtzmann and Neuhaus, op. cit. fn 72, p. 174 et. seq.
124 *SPB v Patel Engineering* (2005) (8) SCC 618, at para 6 or 2005 (9) SCALE 1 (Supreme Court of India).

awards. Applying Section 16 of the Indian Arbitration and Conciliation Act correctly, recourse from such decisions should not be available until the time a final award is rendered. If an Indian court did purport to hear an action to set aside such a partial award on jurisdiction, this should not prevent the arbitral tribunal from proceeding with the arbitration by virtue of Section 16(5).

Article 16(3) of the Model Law sets a 30-day deadline to apply for court review of a positive jurisdictional decision. Missing the statutory deadline means that a party loses its right to immediate court review of the arbitral tribunal's jurisdictional ruling. 5.127

Regardless of the expiry of any such deadline, jurisdiction may effectively be challenged by using one of the two other mechanisms mentioned above, that is by seeking to set aside or by resisting enforcement of a subsequent award on the merits. However, by missing the deadline, a party might well be considered to have lost its right to challenge jurisdiction even in such later proceedings on the basis that it ought to have challenged the award on jurisdiction as provided for in Article 16(3) of the Model Law or its equivalent. Furthermore, as noted several times above, contesting jurisdiction for the first time during an action to set aside or enforce an award is a very risky strategy. First, if the objecting party participated in the arbitration without raising its jurisdictional objections or reservations, its conduct may have given rise to the establishment of an arbitration agreement under Article 7(2) of the Model Law.[125] Second, even if the objecting party did not participate in the arbitration, courts in developed arbitral jurisdictions are likely to give great weight to any decision of the arbitral tribunal in favour of its jurisdiction. The court might well consider that by failing to participate in the arbitration and challenge the jurisdictional decision under Article 16(3), the challenging party's belated challenge should be treated with suspicion. 5.128

6.2.2 Negative jurisdictional decisions

As noted above, Article 16(3) of the Model Law does not specify whether there is any recourse against a negative jurisdictional decision. Similarly, if jurisdictional decisions are not awards then review would not be available under Article 34 of the Model Law. For reasons that are not entirely clear, neither the Model Law nor most arbitration laws provide for recourse against an arbitral tribunal's decision that it *lacks* jurisdiction.[126] 5.129

There are two exceptions in this region.[127] First, the New Zealand Arbitration Act specifically amends the Model Law in this respect. Article 16(3) of Schedule 1 to that Act provides that 'if the arbitral tribunal rules on [a jurisdictional 5.130

---

[125] See above Section 3.2 and the discussion of this point in Chapter 4, Section 2.1.
[126] The Singapore Court of Appeal has expressly confirmed that reading Articles 16(3), 34 and Article 5 of the Model Law together precludes recourse to the courts from a negative jurisdictional ruling. See *PT Asuransi Jasa Indonesia (Persero) v Dexia Bank SA* [2007] 1 SLR 597 (Singapore Court of Appeal), paras 61–74.
[127] See generally P Sanders, *Quo Vadis Arbitration*, Kluwer Law International, 1999, pp. 180–187. Chinese law may recognise recourse from negative jurisdictional decisions; see Jingzhao Tao, op. cit. fn 94, p. 70, paras 193 et seq. Examples outside this region are also rare, but one is the English Arbitration Act 1996 (see Sections 30(2) and 67(1)).

objection] as a preliminary question, any party may request, within 30 days after having received notice of that ruling, the High Court to decide the matter'. There is accordingly no limitation that the decision on jurisdiction be positive in order for it to be reviewable by the High Court of New Zealand. The second example is India. Section 37 of the Indian Arbitration and Conciliation Act dealing with 'Appealable Orders' includes as appealable an arbitral tribunal's order that it does not have jurisdiction.[128] This means that in India immediate recourse is available from a negative jurisdictional ruling but not from a positive one.

5.131 The omission of express recourse against negative jurisdictional decisions in most arbitration laws is curious. There are several possible reasons for this which are developed below.

5.132 It should first be recalled that while there is debate about whether a positive jurisdictional decision of an arbitral tribunal constitutes an award for the purposes of the Model Law and/or New York Convention, negative jurisdictional decisions certainly do not constitute awards.[129] A negative jurisdictional decision cannot be an award because the arbitral tribunal had no jurisdiction to make it in the first place. Pieter Sanders accordingly points out that to consider a negative jurisdictional decision as an award is 'legally dubious and unworkable'.[130]

5.133 In *PT Asuransi Jasa Idonesia (Persero) v Dexia Bank SA*,[131] a specific issue before the Singapore Court of Appeal was whether or not an arbitral tribunal's negative jurisdictional decision 'constitutes an award for the purposes of [the Singapore International Arbitration Act] such that it may be set aside by the Court if the circumstances of the case justify'.[132] The court held that:[133]

> the definition of an 'award' in s 2 of the Act is clear. It does not include a negative determination on jurisdiction as it is not a decision on the substance of the dispute. On the contrary, it is a decision not to determine the substance of the dispute, and therefore cannot be an award for the purposes of Art 34 of the Model Law.

5.134 Because negative jurisdictional decisions are not awards, they cannot in principle be treated as reviewable under provisions of arbitration laws which deal with recourse against or enforcement of awards, such as Article 34 of the Model Law.

5.135 While negative jurisdictional decisions are not awards, recourse against them could be expressly provided for in the law. Yet the Model Law is silent. During the drafting of the Model Law, it was suggested that a sentence be added to clarify the jurisdiction of a court to review negative jurisdictional decisions. One proposed

---

[128] See Section 37(2)(a) of that Act. The Supreme Court of India has confirmed that this allows recourse from negative jurisdictional decisions: 'an acceptance of the objection to jurisdiction or authority, could be challenged then and there, under Section 37 of the Act.' See *SPB v Patel Engineering* (2005) (8) SCC 618, at para 6 or 2005 (9) SCALE I (Supreme Court of India).
[129] They may nonetheless be treated as awards under the rules of certain arbitral institutions, one example being the ICC International Court of Arbitration, which treats them as awards for the purpose of its award scrutiny process.
[130] Sanders, op. cit. fn 127, pp. 186–187.
[131] [2007] 1 SLR 597 (Singapore Court of Appeal).
[132] Ibid., at para 61.
[133] Ibid., at para 66. See also para 71: 'Accordingly, in both form and substance, the Second Award is a pure negative ruling on jurisdiction and is therefore not an award for the purposes of the Act.'

addition to Article 16(3) was: 'A ruling by the arbitral tribunal that it has no jurisdiction may be contested by any party within 30 days before the Court.'[134] This language was not included in the final draft. The UNCITRAL Working Group commented that it would depend 'on the general law on arbitration or civil procedure of a model law country whether court control of a negative ruling could be sought other than by way of a request in any substantive proceedings as referred to in Art. 8(1)'.[135] However, as noted above, the general law on arbitration rarely deals with recourse from negative jurisdictional rulings, thus leaving a legal vacuum.

5.136 One reason given during the UNCITRAL Working Group debates on this issue was that it would be 'inappropriate' for a court to compel an arbitral tribunal to continue with an arbitration after it had found that it lacked jurisdiction.[136] This does not seem to be a sufficient reason to deny an aggrieved party recourse from a negative jurisdictional ruling. First, it would be open for an arbitrator to resign if he or she felt uncomfortable deciding the case after having ruled against jurisdiction. Second, there is no reason why the same arbitral tribunal would necessarily have to hear the case. The court could simply set aside the arbitral tribunal's decision and leave it to the parties to start a new arbitration.

5.137 In our view, the key underlying reason for different treatment relates to the fundamental difference between the effects of a positive as opposed to negative jurisdictional decision.[137] A positive jurisdictional ruling means a finding that the party objecting to jurisdiction has waived or opted out of its right to go to court. Considering that access to justice is a basic human right, it follows that positive jurisdictional rulings must be reviewable because ultimately the competent state court effectively decides whether that party has truly opted out of its right to a day in court. When an arbitral tribunal decides that it does not have jurisdiction, however, the right to bring the claim to a domestic court is rejuvenated. There is only a denial of a right to access arbitral justice which has traditionally not been considered a fundamental human right. Furthermore, the right to arbitral justice is purely contractual, whereas state court justice is a product of and directly protected by the state itself.

5.138 Another often overlooked reason why state courts are reluctant to review an arbitral tribunal's negative jurisdictional decision relates to the grounds for establishing domestic court jurisdiction in international matters. If an arbitral tribunal rejects arbitral jurisdiction, there may be no reason for a court in the putative seat of arbitration to assert jurisdiction over the matter. As has been noted elsewhere in this book,[138] parties often choose the seat of their arbitration

---

134 UN Doc A/CN.9/WG.II/WP.40, Article XIII(3). See also Holtzmann and Neuhaus, op. cit. fn 72, p. 496.
135 A Broches, *Commentary on the UNCITRAL Model Law on International Commercial Arbitration*, Kluwer Law International, 1990, p. 88.
136 Report of UNCITRAL's 18th Session (June 1985), UN Doc A/40/17, No. 163. See the discussion in Boo, op. cit. fn 118, p. 129.
137 This reason was also discussed during the UNCITRAL Working Group and is touched on in several cases cited in Boo, op. cit. fn 118, p. 125.
138 See Chapter 2, Section 6.2.

because of its neutrality. The seat may have absolutely no connection to the dispute, the contract or the parties. Where an arbitral tribunal has rejected jurisdiction, the putatively agreed seat of arbitration is usually rejected as well. As a consequence, the local court's international jurisdiction rules may not provide it with any ground on which to assert jurisdiction to review a negative jurisdictional ruling short of specific legislative recognition.

5.139   In practice, the absence in most jurisdictions of a means of recourse from negative jurisdictional decisions is very unfortunate and frustrating. An incorrect arbitral tribunal decision that there is no jurisdiction could deny the aggrieved party access to all of the advantages of arbitration that it seeks. That party would have two options for having its substantive dispute resolved, neither of which is satisfactory. First, it could start an action in some domestic court with all of the disadvantages that it sought to avoid by choosing arbitration in the first place; e.g. potentially inflexible and unfamiliar procedure, non-specialist judges, non-neutrality and judgment enforcement difficulties. Alternatively, the aggrieved party could attempt to constitute a new arbitral tribunal.[139] This would raise a question as to whether there is a jurisprudential basis to argue that the initial decision would prevent another arbitral tribunal from reconsidering the jurisdictional issue.[140] Theoretically, it is possible that a party could continue to constitute arbitral tribunals until one decided that it had jurisdiction since negative jurisdictional decisions have no recognised legal authority. In practice, however, an arbitral tribunal would be reluctant to overrule a prior arbitral tribunal's decision on the same jurisdictional question, even if the *res judicata* doctrine were technically inapplicable due to the lack of legal effect of the first decision.

5.140   These practical issues outlined in the preceding paragraphs have prompted strong calls for arbitration laws to address and provide for recourse from negative jurisdictional decisions.[141]

6.3 Scope of court review of arbitral tribunal's jurisdictional decisions

5.141   Because one of the consequences of entering into an arbitration agreement is losing one's right to go to court, the ultimate authority to determine that there is a valid agreement to arbitrate must lie with the competent courts. Therefore, when a court at the seat of arbitration reviews an arbitral tribunal's decision on

---

139 See S Greenberg and M Secomb, 'Terms of Reference and Negative Jurisdictional Decisions: A lesson from Australia', (2002) 18(2) *Arbitration International* 125, at p. 133.
140 It has been suggested that if a matter has been decided in one arbitration, the arbitration agreement between the parties (if there is one) is 'null and void, inoperative or incapable of being performed' with respect to that matter under Article II of the New York Convention. See AJ van den Berg, *The New York Convention of 1958: Towards a Uniform Interpretation*, Kluwer Law, 1981, p. 158.
141 See, e.g. P Fohlin, 'A Case for a Right of Appeal from Negative Jurisdictional Rulings in International Arbitrations Governed by the UNCITRAL Model Law', (2008) October *Asian Dispute Review* 113, at p. 114. The author points out that the 2008 Hong Kong draft Arbitration Bill amends Article 16(2) of the Model Law so that there is clearly no recourse from a negative jurisdictional decision. He convincingly explains that this is unsatisfactory, and even more so in international as opposed to domestic arbitration cases.

jurisdiction, the scope of that review is normally de novo. This is implied in the wording of Article 16(3) of the Model Law which empowers the court simply 'to decide the matter' of jurisdiction when a party contests the arbitral tribunal's positive jurisdictional decision. The possibility for a de novo re-hearing results from the fact that domestic courts have the final say on jurisdiction and may need to hear new arguments and evidence in order to make their determination.

This was well explained by the Singapore High Court in *Insigma Technology Co Ltd v Alsthom Technology Ltd*, referring to relevant academic writing:[142]   5.142

> In the text *Jurisdiction and Arbitration Agreements and their Enforcement* by David Joseph QC (2005, Sweet and Maxwell, London) ('*Jurisdiction and Arbitration Agreements*'), it is stated (at para 13.28) that the power of the court in deciding whether the tribunal had jurisdiction is not limited to reviewing the tribunal's decision for error, but involves a re-hearing, including if necessary the calling of witnesses already heard by the tribunal. This statement was based on the authority of a number of first instance English decisions that considered the meaning and effect of s67 of the English Arbitration Act 1996. Whilst I am not aware of any authority on the point in connection with the Model Law, it is my view that, under this legislation too, the court's jurisdiction to decide on the jurisdiction of an arbitral tribunal is an original jurisdiction and not an appellate one. This is clear from the wording of Article 16(3) of the Model Law. It simply provides for the court 'to decide the matter' of jurisdiction after the tribunal has made a ruling that it has jurisdiction. This is not language implying that the court's powers to act are of an appellate nature. Although the word 'appeal' does appear within the Article, the context in which it is found is the specification that there should be no appeal against the decision of the court on jurisdiction.
>
> There are also good reasons why the court should have the power to hear the matter afresh rather than to take the position of an appellate body. These are enumerated in the same paragraph of *Jurisdiction and Arbitration Agreements* and are as follows. First, if the court was limited to a process of review, it might be reviewing the decision of a tribunal that itself had no jurisdiction to make such a finding. Second, the procedure to determine jurisdiction is available to a party that took no part in the arbitral proceedings; if the court was confined to a review of the tribunal's decision this would greatly undermine the ability of the challenging party to make its case. Third, if there is to be a challenge on an issue of fact, the court should not be in a worse position to make an assessment than the tribunal, and should therefore be able to examine witnesses in the usual way. Accordingly, therefore, a party is entitled to raise an objection to jurisdiction before the judge that it had not raised and argued before the arbitrator. However, 'a failure to raise a specific point before the arbitrator is likely to be relevant as to weight.' (Jurisdiction and Arbitration Agreements at [para 13.5].)

Recent authority from the English court of appeal confirms that, in England,   5.143
de novo review of an arbitral tribunal's jurisdictional decision is alternatively available when resisting the enforcement of an award.[143] The seat of arbitration

---
142 [2008] SGHC 134, paras 21–22. The interesting circumstances of this case are discussed in Chapter 4, Section 9.6. The position in England is much the same. See *Dallah Estate and Tourism Holding Company v The Ministry of Religious Affairs, Government of Pakistan*, English Court of Appeal, 20 July 2009, [2009] EWCA Civ 755, para 21.
143 *Dallah Estate and Tourism Holding Company v The Ministry of Religious Affairs, Government of Pakistan* [2009] EWCA Civ 755, English Court of Appeal, 20 July 2009.

was Paris and the respondent, the Ministry of Religious Affairs of the Government of Pakistan, had challenged the arbitral tribunal's jurisdiction in the course of the arbitration. The arbitral tribunal found in a partial award that it possessed jurisdiction. The Ministry then ceased participating in the arbitration and the arbitral tribunal proceeded to issue a final award ordering damages of US$19 million against the Ministry. Rather than challenging either of the awards in Paris, the Ministry waited until Dallah, the claimant in the arbitration, sought to enforce the award against it in England and resisted enforcement of the award. The Court of Appeal confirmed the lower court's decisions (i) that jurisdiction could be re-examined de novo by the enforcing court and (ii) that the arbitral tribunal had erred in its finding that it had jurisdiction over the Ministry.

5.144   While rarely, if ever, done, in some jurisdictions parties may effectively be able to exclude the ability of courts to review certain jurisdictional issues. After the jurisdictional dispute arises, the parties could enter into a new arbitration agreement, either expressly or implicitly through conduct or a document such as terms of reference,[144] which empowers the arbitral tribunal to decide *finally* a disputed issue of jurisdiction relating to their initial arbitration agreement. By entering into a second arbitration agreement, the scope of which includes the jurisdictional dispute arising from the first, the aspect of the competence-competence rule that allows court review of jurisdictional decisions would apply only to the second arbitration agreement. Only the new arbitration agreement could be challenged and not the first. This would in effect 'raise the stakes'.[145] The party challenging jurisdiction, if successful, would have a more final resolution of the issue. The party that wins on the jurisdictional issue arising from the first arbitration agreement would have a more final resolution of the issue because only the new arbitration agreement could be challenged in the courts.

6.4 Subsidiary orders with negative jurisdictional decisions

5.145   If an arbitral tribunal decides that it does not have jurisdiction over a party, and/or rejects *absolute* jurisdiction,[146] then it ceases from that moment to have any authority with respect to that party. It logically follows that an arbitral tribunal in these circumstances has no power to make a subsidiary order, such as an order for costs.[147]

---

[144] For example, terms of reference could in some circumstances inadvertently include an agreement that the arbitral tribunal finally decide a jurisdictional issue arising from the initial arbitration agreement, see Greenberg and Secomb, op. cit. fn 139, p. 135.
[145] See the example of this given in Park, op. cit. fn 46, pp. 64–65 and his discussion at pp. 72–79 et seq giving examples of US cases which have confirmed this approach. Not all jurisdictions will allow this though as it might be seen as an attempt to oust the jurisdiction of the courts completely. See, e.g. *Czarnikow v Roth Schmidt* [1922] 2 KB 478 concerning the traditional prohibition on ousting court jurisdiction).
[146] See Section 3.1 above.
[147] Other possible subsidiary orders include orders of confidentiality, payment of fees to the arbitrator and interim measures of protection (or more likely, unwinding interim measures of protection).

5.146　　This situation is well-illustrated by the case of *CDC v Montague* in Queensland, Australia.[148] CDC commenced arbitration against Montague and three other parties. The arbitrator ultimately found that he did not have jurisdiction to hear the disputes between CDC and Montague because Montague was not a party to any arbitration agreement with CDC. He made an award of costs against CDC in favour of Montague in order to compensate Montague for being dragged into an arbitration to which Montague was not a proper party. The seat of arbitration was in Auckland, New Zealand, but Montague sought to enforce the costs award in Queensland, Australia under the New York Convention.

5.147　　CDC resisted enforcement of the award for costs, arguing as follows:[149]

> once the Arbitrator determined that he had no jurisdiction to entertain proceedings instituted by the Appellant [CDC] because he was not a party to a written agreement containing an arbitration clause, from that time he lacked power to make any order with respect to the cost of the arbitration proceedings which he initiated in the International Court of Arbitration.

5.148　　As Simon Greenberg and Matthew Secomb explain,[150] at first blush this may seem to be a rather ambitious but technically correct argument. While it may seem somewhat unfair to refuse enforcement where the costs incurred by Montague were incurred as a result of CDC's wrongful allegation of a valid arbitration agreement, arbitration is based upon the consent of the parties. If both parties did not agree to the arbitration agreement, how could they be bound by that arbitration agreement and hence bound by a costs award made on the basis of jurisdiction deriving from it?

5.149　　The District Court of Queensland allowed enforcement of the award and CDC appealed. The Queensland Court of Appeal confirmed that the costs award was enforceable, relying on the fact that CDC had signed the ICC terms of reference[151] which included costs as an issue for the arbitrator to decide. As Justice Ambrose stated:[152]

> In my view, the short answer to this rather unmeritorious contention is that the Terms of Reference signed by Counsel for the Appellant and by Counsel for the Respondent and the other defendants and indeed the Arbitrator himself on 13 September 1996 in clear and explicit terms require the Arbitrator to determine 'what decision should be taken with regard to the cost of arbitration'.
>
> In my view, the Terms of Reference, signed by or on behalf of all parties to it, come directly within sub-article 1 of Article 2 of the Convention as 'an agreement in writing under which the parties undertake to submit to arbitration all or any differences which have arisen or which may arise between them in respect of a defined legal relationship'.

---

[148] *Commonwealth Development Corp (UK) v Montague* [2000] QCA 252 (Supreme Court of Queensland Court of Appeal), Appeal Justice Thomas, Justices Ambrose and Fryberg, 27 June 2000. The case is discussed in Greenberg and Secomb, op. cit. fn 139, p. 125. The following discussion draws from that article.
[149] *Commonwealth Development Corp (UK) v Montague* [2000] QCA 252 (Supreme Court of Queensland Court of Appeal), p. 5.
[150] Greenberg and Secomb, op. cit. fn 139, p. 127.
[151] See Chapter 7, Section 6.5, on terms of reference.
[152] *Commonwealth Development Corp (UK) v Montague* [2000] QCA 252 (Supreme Court of Queensland Court of Appeal), p. 5.

5.150   The Court of Appeal decision accordingly lends strong support for the value of terms of reference, which were initially conceived of by the ICC and are now also required by other arbitration institutions.[153] However, the decision leaves one wondering what would have happened had there been no terms of reference in this matter. Montague could possibly have been left having incurred unrecoverable costs, short of the hazardous option of commencing a court proceeding, somewhere, for damages.

5.151   Provisions in some arbitration laws may implicitly suggest that costs can be awarded with negative jurisdictional rulings,[154] but express language to this effect is not found in Asia-Pacific jurisdictions nor many, if any, in the world.[155] It is hoped that courts enforcing awards in these circumstances will take a pragmatic approach and enforce the subsidiary order, as the Queensland courts did in *CDC v Montague*.

5.152   Finally, as mentioned in the preceding section, recourse against negative jurisdictional decisions should be addressed expressly in arbitration laws. The same is true for the enforceability of subsidiary orders made with negative jurisdictional decisions.

---

[153] SIAC adopted a similar document called the 'Memorandum of Issues' in its 2007 Rules. However, this has been abandoned in its 2010 Rules.

[154] Consider, for example, Articles 23(4)(2) and 49(3) and (4) of the Japanese Arbitration Act. These provisions read together arguably allow costs orders together with a ruling to terminate arbitral proceedings when there is no jurisdiction. See also Section 6(1)(b) of the New Zealand Arbitration Act and the very similar provision at Section 44(1)(c) of the Malaysian Arbitration Act.

[155] Section 37 of the Swedish Arbitration Act provides some protection for respondents who win on jurisdiction by ensuring that they do not have to pay the arbitral tribunal's costs save exceptional circumstances. However, the Act does not deal with party legal costs etc. in the case of a negative jurisdictional ruling.

6

The arbitral tribunal

1 Introduction

High quality arbitrators are an essential ingredient of effective arbitration proceedings. As arbitration specialists have noted, '[t]he reputation and acceptability of international arbitration depends on the quality of the arbitrators themselves'.[1] The composition of the arbitral tribunal can significantly affect a range of important factors including whether the arbitration is conducted efficiently and economically, whether the award is susceptible to challenge, and even an individual party's chances of success or failure. Issues surrounding the constitution of the arbitral tribunal therefore deserve special attention.

6.1

This chapter follows the life cycle of an arbitral tribunal chronologically. Section 2 describes how an arbitral tribunal is constituted, including the number of arbitrators and their appointment in multiparty arbitrations. In Section 3 we discuss the process of choosing an arbitrator, whether as chairperson, sole arbitrator or party-nominated co-arbitrator, as well as the qualities and qualifications that are generally desirable for international arbitrators. The formal appointment process is discussed in Section 4. In Section 5 we examine the obligations of arbitrators, such as diligence, impartiality and independence, and disclosure of potential conflicts of interest. Section 6 deals with challenges to arbitrators. Finally, issues relating to the resignation, removal and replacement of arbitrators are addressed in Section 7.

6.2

---

[1] A Redfern, M Hunter, N Blackaby and C Partasides, *Law and Practice of International Commercial Arbitration*, 4th edn, Sweet & Maxwell, 2004, at para 4–47.

2 Constitution of the arbitral tribunal

6.3 The main principle guiding the appointment of arbitrators is party autonomy. In their contract or even after a dispute arises, parties are free to agree on the number of arbitrators, how they will be appointed, and who they will be. Where there is no agreement or one party refuses or fails to participate in the constitution of the arbitral tribunal, the applicable arbitration rules or procedural law will provide a fallback mechanism to prevent the constitution process from being frustrated.[2]

6.4 An issue that requires determination prior to constitution of the arbitral tribunal is the number of arbitrators to be appointed. Once the number is agreed or decided, the procedural question of how to constitute the arbitral tribunal arises. Disputes involving more than two parties may require special arrangements to be considered when constituting the arbitral tribunal. This section discusses these three issues in turn.

2.1 Number of arbitrators

6.5 For obvious reasons, the number of arbitrators should be odd – usually one or three, but occasionally five. Parties often specify the number of arbitrators in their arbitration agreement, or agree on it once the dispute has arisen.

6.6 There are several factors that may need to be considered when deciding the number of arbitrators.[3] Appointing a sole arbitrator usually produces significant cost savings because only one arbitrator's fees and expenses have to be paid. A sole arbitrator may also be more time effective. For example, coordinating meetings and hearing times should be easier and decisions should be made faster because the sole arbitrator, in contrast to the chairperson of a three-member tribunal, is not required to deliberate or reach consensus with any other arbitrators. Furthermore, the desire to reach consensus among three arbitrators may sometimes lead to compromised solutions as opposed to straightforward outcomes. In extreme cases, co-arbitrators that have been nominated by one of the parties have been suspected of deliberately sabotaging the arbitration process, by causing delay or otherwise, to provide some advantage or benefit to the nominating party.[4] This is rare because most international arbitrators are highly professional[5] but it can occur when a party selects a party-nominated co-arbitrator for the wrong reasons. This will not occur in sole arbitrator tribunals because individual parties have no right to select a member of the panel (unless all parties agree on that person).

---

[2] See generally O Akseli, 'Appointment of Arbitrators as Specified in the Agreement to Arbitrate', (2003) 20 *Journal of International Arbitration* 247.
[3] See generally J Kirby, 'With Arbitrators, Less Can be More: Why the Conventional Wisdom on the Benefits of having Three Arbitrators may be Overrated', (2009) 26(3) *Journal of International Arbitration* 337.
[4] Ibid., at p. 354, citing numerous references.
[5] JD Lew, LA Mistelis and SM Kröll, *Comparative International Commercial Arbitration*, Kluwer Law International, 2003, p. 228, at para 10–19.

6.7 On the other hand, opting for a sole arbitrator means that the outcome of the arbitration will be determined by one person alone. This may increase the risk of misunderstandings and errors. The combined knowledge, skills, expertise, cultural awareness, and perhaps even languages of three arbitrators may prove beneficial to the quality of the decisions and the parties' confidence in the process.[6] Perhaps the most compelling reason for preferring three arbitrators is that each side usually is entitled to nominate one member of the arbitral tribunal.[7] Moses has observed that 'it is generally believed that the award is more likely to be within parties' expectations when considered by three arbitrators and that unusual or inexplicable awards are less likely to occur'.[8] After making a similar observation, Redfern and Hunter suggest that '[i]t follows that the ultimate award is more likely to be acceptable to the parties'.[9]

6.8 ICC statistics show that when the number of arbitrators is determined by party agreement, the number agreed is usually three. In 2008, a three-member tribunal was appointed in 61% of ICC arbitrations. In 93.5% of those cases, the number of three was determined by party agreement rather than by the ICC Court.[10] This is different for sole arbitrator cases. In the ICC arbitrations where there were sole arbitrators in 2008, the parties decided the number in only 69.4% of cases. In the remaining 30.6% of cases, it was the ICC Court which decided that there would be a sole arbitrator.[11]

6.9 Where parties agree on a number of arbitrators, they should be careful to record that agreement clearly. Arbitration agreements occasionally contain apparent inconsistencies where the plural 'arbitrators' is used interchangeably with 'arbitrator,' leaving ambiguity as to what the parties intended. Although party choice as to the number of arbitrators will be respected,[12] that choice must first in fact be exercised. An Indian Supreme Court decision in 2009 found that an arbitration clause which merely referred to 'arbitrator(s)' without specifying a number did not amount to an agreement for a three-person arbitral tribunal.[13]

6.10 Absent party choice, most arbitration laws and rules provide a default number of arbitrators or a mechanism for determining the number. A brief survey of the laws and institutional rules in the Asia-Pacific reveals variation among the approaches.

---

6 Ibid., para 10–18.
7 Redfern, Hunter, et al, op. cit. fn 1, para 4–17.
8 M Moses, *The Principles and Practice of International Commercial Arbitration*, Cambridge University Press, 2008, at p. 117.
9 Redfern, Hunter, et al, op. cit. fn 1, para 4–187.
10 Article 8(2) of the ICC Rules provides: 'Where the parties have not agreed upon the number of arbitrators, the Court shall appoint a sole arbitrator, save where it appears to the Court that the dispute is such as to warrant the appointment of three arbitrators.'
11 J Fry and S Greenberg, 'The Arbitral Tribunal: Applications of Articles 7–12 of the ICC Rules in Recent Cases', (2009) 20(2) *ICC International Court of Arbitration Bulletin* 12, at p. 15.
12 In the Singaporean decision of *NCC International AB v Land Transport Authority of Singapore* [2008] SGHC 186, the Singapore High Court found that Rule 5.1 of the SIAC Rules did not give the SIAC the discretion to alter the number of arbitrators where the parties have already agreed.
13 *Sime Darby Engineering SDN BHD v Engineers India Ltd*, Arbitration Petition 3/2009.

6.11 The Model Law in Article 10 provides for a default of three arbitrators.[14] Many jurisdictions, such as Australia, the Philippines, South Korea, Sri Lanka, and Bangladesh have adopted the Model Law approach without amendment. Malaysia defaults to three arbitrators for international and one arbitrator for domestic arbitration.[15] The position in Japan is slightly different. Although providing a basic default of three arbitrators where there are two parties, if it is a multiparty arbitration the question of the number of arbitrators can be referred to a court.[16] By contrast, Singapore, although adopting the Model Law, altered Article 10 of the Model Law to provide that the default should be one arbitrator.[17] Likewise, a sole arbitrator default has been adopted by India.[18] Hong Kong has specifically vested the power in the HKIAC to determine the number of arbitrators when the parties have failed to do so.[19] Article 30 of the Arbitration Law of China does not specify a default number; it simply stipulates that an arbitral tribunal may be composed of one or three arbitrators.

6.12 Turning to institutional rules, again there is variation as to the fallback number of arbitrators. There are broadly four approaches which can be distilled from rules in this region. The most common is that found in its simplest form in Rule 23 of the JCAA Rules and Article 11 of the KCAB International Rules: the default is one arbitrator, but a party can request the institution to consider whether, given the particulars of the dispute, three arbitrators would be better. A slight variation of this approach is found in Rule 5.1 of the SIAC Rules, where SIAC's Registrar may decide in favour of three, rather than the default of one, where it appears in the light of 'the complexity, the quantum involved or other relevant circumstances of the dispute, that the dispute warrants the appointment of three arbitrators'.

6.13 The second approach does away with the default of one arbitrator. An example is Article 8 of the ACICA Rules, which gives ACICA discretion to choose the number after taking into account all relevant circumstances. The HKIAC Rules provide that the HKIAC Council will decide the number of arbitrators absent a choice by the parties. The HKIAC Rules enumerate a detailed procedure and several factors to be considered in deciding the number of arbitrators:

> *Article 6 – Number of Arbitrators*
> 6.1 If the parties have not agreed upon the number of arbitrators, the HKIAC Council shall at the request of a party decide whether the case shall be referred to a sole arbitrator or to a three-member arbitral tribunal, taking into account the factors set out in Rule 9 of the 'Arbitration (Appointment of Arbitrators and Umpires) Rules' made under the Hong Kong Arbitration Ordinance. These include:

---

14 Model Law Article 10 provides
 (1) The parties are free to determine the number of arbitrators.
 (2) Failing such determination, the number of arbitrators shall be three.
15 Malaysian Arbitration Act 2005 Section 12(2).
16 Japanese Arbitration Act 2003 Article 16.
17 Singapore International Arbitration Act Section 9.
18 Indian Arbitration and Conciliation Act 1996 Section 10.
19 Hong Kong Arbitration Ordinance 1963 Section 34C(5).

(a) the amount in dispute;
(b) the complexity of the claim;
(c) the nationalities of the parties;
(d) any relevant customs of the trade, business or profession involved in the said dispute;
(e) the availability of appropriate arbitrators; and
(f) the urgency of the case.
6.2 Before deciding on the number of arbitrators to be appointed, the HKIAC Council shall allow the other party or parties to the arbitration to serve on the HKIAC Secretariat brief written responses in support of their contention as to the number of arbitrators appropriate for their dispute. Where no such reasons are served on the HKIAC Secretariat within 14 days of the day on which a request for responses has been made by the HKIAC Secretariat, the HKIAC Council may proceed with the decision.

6.14 A third and very unusual approach is seen in Rule 22 of the Indian Council of Arbitration Rules, where the number of arbitrators is determined by the amount in dispute and whether the parties have paid their cost deposit:

Rule 22
The number of arbitrators to hear a dispute shall be determined as under:
(a) Where the claim including determination of interest, if any, being claimed up to the date of commencement of arbitration in terms of Rule 15, does not exceed Rs. One crore and where the arbitration agreement does not specify three arbitrators, the reference shall be deemed to be to a sole arbitrator, unless the parties to the dispute agree to refer the dispute to three arbitrators within thirty days from the date of notification of request for arbitration.
(b) Where the claim including determination of interest, if any, being claimed up to the date of commencement of arbitration in terms of Rule 15 exceeds Rs. One crore, the dispute will be heard and determined by three arbitrators, unless the parties to the dispute agree to refer the dispute to a sole arbitrator within thirty days from the date of the notification of the request for arbitration.
(c) Where three arbitrators have to be appointed as per the above sub-rule and any of the parties to the dispute fails to make the necessary deposit towards the cost and expenses of arbitration, instead of three arbitrators, the Registrar may appoint a sole arbitrator, where the claim is up to One crore. Where the claim is for more than Rs. One crore, the Registrar may appoint arbitrator/s on behalf of the Respondent as well the as Presiding Arbitrator.

6.15 The problem with rules (or agreements) which determine the number of arbitrators based on the value of the dispute is that the value in dispute may not be clear at the outset of a case. For example, the claimant may be seeking unquantified or declaratory relief and/or the respondent may not yet have filed its counterclaims.

6.16 The fourth approach, reflected by way of example in Article 5 of the PDRCI Rules, is simply to state a default of three, like the Model Law.

6.17 It is interesting to see how the UNCITRAL Arbitration Rules have evolved in that respect. The 1976 version provides for a default number of three arbitrators. However, it appears likely that there will be a slight change. The default position under the 1976 Rules has been retained, subject to a new discretion granted to

250   INTERNATIONAL COMMERCIAL ARBITRATION

the Appointing Authority to appoint a sole arbitrator at the request of a party. This discretion is limited to certain circumstances, such as the failure of a respondent to participate in constituting the arbitral tribunal. This approach overcomes the problem in the 1976 rules that where the respondent is not participating the claimant can be left with no option but to proceed with an unnecessarily expensive three-member arbitral tribunal to decide a small case.

2.2 Procedure for constituting the arbitral tribunal

6.18 All institutional arbitration rules recognise the principle of party autonomy by allowing parties to agree on the procedure for constituting the arbitral tribunal and to participate in its constitution. Should party autonomy fail, all rules provide a default process to ensure that the arbitral tribunal is constituted and that the arbitration proceeds. The default rules prevent a recalcitrant party from frustrating the process by, for example, refusing to nominate an arbitrator. By adopting arbitration rules in their arbitration agreement, the parties voluntarily agree to this default process. The appointment of arbitrators by an 'appointing authority' or institution, as specified in the arbitration rules, is therefore entirely consistent with party autonomy.

6.19 Typically, if the parties fail to agree on an arbitrator (in the case of a single arbitrator) or if one party fails to nominate/appoint a co-arbitrator, the arbitral institution will make the appointment. In a three-person arbitral tribunal, each side usually nominates one arbitrator and the party-nominated co-arbitrators may be charged with jointly appointing the chairperson. If the co-arbitrators are unable to agree, that responsibility may again shift to the institution, depending on its rules. Rules 6 and 7 of the 2007 SIAC Rules are an example of this process:

> Rule 6: Sole Arbitrator
> 6.1 If a sole arbitrator is to be appointed, either party may propose to the other the names of one or more persons, one of whom would serve as the sole arbitrator. Where parties have reached an agreement on the nomination of a sole arbitrator, Rule 5.3 shall apply.
> 6.2 If within 21 days after receipt by the Registrar of the Notice of Arbitration made in accordance with Rule 3, the parties have not reached an agreement on the nomination of a sole arbitrator, the Chairman [of SIAC] shall make the appointment as soon as practicable.
> 6.3 A decision of the Chairman [of SIAC] under this Rule shall not be subject to appeal.
>
> Rule 7: Three Arbitrators
> 7.1 If three arbitrators are to be appointed, each party shall nominate one arbitrator.
> 7.2 If a party fails to make a nomination within 21 days after receipt of a party's nomination of an arbitrator, the Chairman [of SIAC] shall proceed to appoint the arbitrator on its behalf.
> 7.3 Unless the parties have agreed upon another procedure for appointing the third arbitrator, the third arbitrator who shall act as the presiding arbitrator shall be appointed by the Chairman [of SIAC]. Any nomination made pursuant to the

procedure agreed to by the parties shall be subject to confirmation pursuant to Rule 5.3.

7.4 A decision of the Chairman [of SIAC] under this Rule shall not be subject to appeal.

6.20 If the parties have opted for ad hoc arbitration, reference will have to be made either to their chosen ad hoc rules or to the applicable procedural law. Article 11 of the Model Law provides the following mechanism for the constitution of the arbitral tribunal:

Article 11. Appointment of arbitrators
(1) No person shall be precluded by reason of his nationality from acting as an arbitrator, unless otherwise agreed by the parties.
(2) The parties are free to agree on a procedure of appointing the arbitrator or arbitrators, subject to the provisions of paragraphs (4) and (5) of this article.
(3) Failing such agreement,
  (a) in an arbitration with three arbitrators, each party shall appoint one arbitrator, and the two arbitrators thus appointed shall appoint the third arbitrator; if a party fails to appoint the arbitrator within thirty days of receipt of a request to do so from the other party, or if the two arbitrators fail to agree on the third arbitrator within thirty days of their appointment, the appointment shall be made, upon request of a party, <u>by the court or other authority specified in article 6</u>;
  (b) in an arbitration with a sole arbitrator, if the parties are unable to agree on the arbitrator, he shall be appointed, upon request of a party, by the court or other authority specified in article 6.
(4) Where, under an appointment procedure agreed upon by the parties,
  (a) a party fails to act as required under such procedure, or
  (b) the parties, or two arbitrators, are unable to reach an agreement expected of them under such procedure, or
  (c) a third party, including an institution, fails to perform any function entrusted to it under such procedure, any party may request the court or other authority specified in article 6 to take the necessary measure, unless the agreement on the appointment procedure provides other means for securing the appointment.
(5) A decision on a matter entrusted by paragraph (3) or (4) of this article to the court or other authority specified in article 6 shall be subject to no appeal. The court or other authority, in appointing an arbitrator, shall have due regard to any qualifications required of the arbitrator by the agreement of the parties and to such considerations as are likely to secure the appointment of an independent and impartial arbitrator and, in the case of a sole or third arbitrator, shall take into account as well the advisability of appointing an arbitrator of a nationality other than those of the parties. (Emphasis added)

6.21 As can be seen in the Model Law extract above, Article 11(3)(a) refers the appointment responsibility to 'the court or other authority specified'. This is an extremely important task and the different jurisdictions in this region have designated a variety of persons and institutions to perform it. In Singapore, the Chairman of SIAC has been designated in the legislation as the person to select default arbitrators.[20] Similarly in Malaysia the Director of the KLRCA is given

---

[20] Singapore International Arbitration Act 2002 Section 8(2).

the responsibility, however should the director be unable or fail to make the appointment, parties can approach the High Court.[21] The Philippines is another jurisdiction in which a specific person is nominated, in this instance the 'National President of the Integrated Bar of the Philippines (IBP) or his duly authorized representative',[22] failing which the parties can turn to a Regional Trial Court.[23] In Hong Kong, the appointing power under the legislation is referred to HKIAC as an institution.[24] The Indian legislation nominates 'the Chief Justice of India or the person or institution designated by him'.[25] Australia,[26] New Zealand[27] and Japan[28] each designate courts.

6.22 Parties sometimes identify a specific individual or individuals as arbitrator(s) in their arbitration clause in a contract.[29] It is not advisable to attempt to select arbitrators before a dispute has arisen. While a perceived advantage is that the arbitral tribunal composition will be faster and more certain, difficulties arise when the named person passes away in the interim period or for some other reason is unable or unwilling to act once a dispute arises. Additionally, that person might, in the course of his or her personal life or professional activities since the arbitration agreement was made, have developed a conflict of interest.

6.23 In *Ace Pipeline Contracts Private Ltd v Bharat Petroleum Corporation Ltd*[30] the parties' arbitration agreement provided that the arbitrator would be the marketing director of one of the parties or another officer of that party designated by the marketing director. It stated that all disputes:

> arising out of or in relation to this agreement shall be referred to the Sole Arbitration of the Director (Marketing) of the Corporation or of some officer of the Corporation who may be nominated by the Director (Marketing). The Vendor will not be entitled to raise any objection to any such Arbitrator on the ground that the Arbitrator is an Officer of the Corporation or that he has dealt with the matters to which the contract relates or that in the course of his duties as an Officer of the Corporation he had expressed views on all or any other matters in dispute or difference.

6.24 This rather draconian clause, at least for the party opposing the corporation, was upheld by the Indian Supreme Court which ruled:

> In the present case, in fact the appellant's demand was to get some retired Judge of the Supreme Court to be appointed as arbitrator on the ground that if any person

---

[21] Malaysian Arbitration Act Section 13.
[22] Philippines Alternative Dispute Resolution Act Section 26.
[23] Philippines Alternative Dispute Resolution Act Section 27.
[24] Hong Kong Arbitration Ordinance Section 12.
[25] Indian Arbitration and Conciliation Act Section 11. With respect to this section, see the Indian Supreme Court decision of *Citation Infowares Ltd v Equinox Corporation*, Arbitration Application No. 8 of 2008, which considered whether the Chief Justice could appoint an arbitrator even where foreign law governed the main contract.
[26] Australian International Arbitration Act 1974 Section 18. However following the introduction of amendments to the Act, provision will be made for the government to designate a prescribed authority (such as ACICA) without requiring further legislative change.
[27] New Zealand Arbitration Act 1996 Article 11, Schedule 1.
[28] Japanese Arbitration Law 2003 Article 17.
[29] See, e.g. the Indian Supreme Court case of *Ace Pipeline Contracts Private Ltd v Bharat Petroleum Corporation Ltd* (2007) 5 SCC 304 discussed below.
[30] (2007) 5 SCC 304 (Indian Supreme Court).

nominated in the arbitration clause is appointed, then it may suffer from bias or the arbitrator may not be impartial or independent in taking decision. Once a party has entered into an agreement with eyes wide open it cannot wriggle out of the situation that if any person of the respondent-BPCL is appointed as arbitrator he will not be impartial or objective. However, if the appellant feels that the arbitrator has not acted independently or impartially, or he has suffered from any bias, it will always be open to the party to make an application under Section 34 of the Act. . . .

Rather than identifying a specific arbitrator in the arbitration agreement, a better practice is to identify in advance an appointing authority (which could even be an individual identified by his or her position) or institution charged with selecting arbitrators if the parties cannot agree – an example may be the chairperson of the Chartered Institute of Arbitrators. However, the most common and effective approach is by reference to a set of arbitration rules as described above. 6.25

Because the constitution of the arbitral tribunal can be used as a tactical instrument, it is not surprising that the appointment of arbitrators can be a source of great controversy. At the heart of this controversy is party involvement in the selection process. The benefits of joint selection of arbitrators by all parties can rarely be doubted. Arbitrator selection by an individual party is, however, a potentially different matter. As noted above, it is common for each side in an arbitration to select one of the co-arbitrators. One key advantage of this approach is that the power to select an arbitrator should give the nominating party confidence in the arbitral tribunal. A perceived disadvantage is that the arbitrator could consciously or subconsciously favour the nominating party. As discussed below,[31] parties may nominate co-arbitrators who they believe will assist their case. Nonetheless, arbitrators have mandatory obligations of impartiality and independence. 6.26

2.3 Multiparty arbitrations

As noted above, where three arbitrators are required it is usual that each party nominates one arbitrator and the third, who will act as chairperson, is chosen by the two nominated co-arbitrators, an arbitral institution or some other agreed process. Uncertainty can arise in arbitrations involving more than two parties, because if each party were to nominate an arbitrator the arbitral tribunal would comprise as many arbitrators as there are parties, plus a chairperson. 6.27

There has been very substantial growth in multi-party international arbitrations over the last 10–20 years. Arbitrations involving more than one party now account for approximately one-third of ICC arbitrations. In 2009, 233 ICC arbitrations (28.5%) involved more than two parties. Out of these 233 cases, 206 (88.4%) involved between three and five parties, 21 (9%) involved between six 6.28

---

[31] See Section 3.2.2 below.

and 10 parties, and six (2.6%) involved more than 10 parties. One case filed with the ICC in 2009 had 19 different parties.

6.29 Prior to 1992, unless there was a contrary agreement by the parties, multiple claimants or respondents were ordinarily required to act as one during the composition of the arbitral tribunal. In other words, if a claimant commenced arbitration against two respondents, those two respondents would jointly be expected to nominate one co-arbitrator, whereas the claimant was entitled to nominate the other co-arbitrator. This would effectively mean that the single claimant could choose any arbitrator it wished whereas the two respondents may have to reach a compromise in order to nominate a mutually agreeable arbitrator. This could be seen as an unfair advantage for the claimant.

6.30 In the now famous French *Dutco* case,[32] two respondents argued that because they had different interests they should each be allowed to appoint an arbitrator. The ICC arbitration agreement in that case provided for two party-nominated arbitrators, one nominated by each side. The third and presiding arbitrator was to be selected by the co-arbitrators. The multiple respondents agreed under protest to appoint one co-arbitrator jointly and then later challenged the award, arguing that the arbitral tribunal had been improperly constituted. The French Cour de Cassation agreed, finding that equality in the appointment process was fundamental to arbitration and, under the particular circumstances, equality was lacking in the disputed appointment process.

6.31 This decision prompted the ICC, the next time it amended its arbitration rules, to modify the appointment procedure in multi-party cases in order to ensure equality. Consequently, Article 10 of the 1998 ICC Rules provides that if the multiple claimants or multiple respondents cannot agree on a candidate for joint nomination, then the ICC Court may appoint all three arbitrators – thus restoring equality because neither side is permitted to choose an arbitrator.[33] This change triggered amendments to other institutional arbitration rules throughout the world. Rules changes were made despite the fact that it appears that only one other court – China's Supreme People's Court – has ever considered a similar issue.[34] The decision of the Chinese court is consistent with the *Dutco* principle that parties cannot waive in advance their right to participate in the constitution of the arbitral tribunal.[35]

---

32 *Siemens AG and BKMI Industrienlagen GmbH v Dutco Consortium Construction Co*, French Cour de Cassation, First Civil Chamber, 7 January 1992.
33 Article 10 of the ICC Rules provides: '(1) Where there are multiple parties, whether as Claimant or as Respondent, and where the dispute is to be referred to three arbitrators, the multiple Claimants, jointly, and the multiple Respondents, jointly, shall nominate an arbitrator for confirmation pursuant to Article 9. (2) In the absence of such a joint nomination and where all parties are unable to agree to a method for the constitution of the Arbitral Tribunal, the Court may appoint each member of the Arbitral Tribunal and shall designate one of them to act *as* chairman. In such case, the Court shall be at liberty to choose any person it regards as suitable to act as arbitrator, applying Article 9 when it considers this appropriate.'
34 This was a point noted by the Supreme People's Court which found an arbitral clause which deprived a party of a right to participate in the appointment process was invalid because it offended equality, as cited in Wang Sheng Chang, 'Formation of the Arbitral Tribunal', (2001) 17(4) *Arbitration International* 401, at Section II(b).
35 On this issue, it is interesting to note that Article 24 of the CIETAC Rules seems to be inconsistent with the *Dutco* decision because the Chairman of CIETAC is only concerned with appointing the arbitrator on behalf of any joint parties that have not been able to agree.

It seems that at least one aspect of the *Dutco* principle does not apply in India. As previously discussed, in *Ace Pipeline Contracts Private Ltd v Bharat Petroleum Corporation Ltd*[36] the Indian Supreme Court upheld an arbitration clause contained in a contract which designated the marketing director of one of the parties as the arbitrator, and expressly denied the opposing party the right to object to the independence of that arbitrator on that ground. This offends the *Dutco* principle in the sense that the Indian courts allowed the parties to preclude, in advance of the arbitration, one side from objecting to the identity of the arbitrator.

6.32

The main concern of the *Dutco* principle is to ensure equality in multi-party arbitrations. Two aspects of equality must be respected. The first is that all parties to the arbitration agreement must agree to and be aware of the appointment process. This may seem a somewhat trite observation. However, this was missing among the *Dutco* participants. The ICC Rules in force at that time did not contain a specific procedure for multiparty arbitrations, so no process had been agreed. Second, all parties should be treated equally meaning that, in certain circumstances, if one party loses the right to nominate an arbitrator so should all. As noted above, that principle was reflected in Article 10 of the 1998 ICC Rules.

6.33

Most major sets of international arbitration rules now have specific provisions on the appointment process for multi-party arbitrations.[37] A typical example is Article 11 of the ACICA Rules:

6.34

> *11 Appointment of Arbitrators in Multi-Party Disputes*
> 11.1 For the purposes of Articles 9 and 10, the acts of multiple parties, whether as multiple Claimants or multiple Respondents, shall have no effect, unless the multiple Claimants or multiple Respondents have acted jointly and provided written evidence of their agreement to ACICA.
> 11.2 If three arbitrators are to be appointed and the multiple Claimants or multiple Respondents do not act jointly in appointing an arbitrator, ACICA shall appoint each member of the Arbitral Tribunal and shall designate one of them to act as Chairperson, unless all parties agree in writing on a different method for the constitution of the Arbitral Tribunal and provide written evidence of their agreement to ACICA.

While Article 11 of the ACICA Rules is similar to Article 10 of the ICC Rules, one difference is the discretion left to the ICC Court not to appoint all three members of the arbitral tribunal, whereas the ACICA Rules leave no such discretion. This is clear from the word 'shall' in Article 11.2 of the ACICA Rules as compared to 'may' in Article 10(2) of the ICC Rules.

6.35

---

36 (2007) 5 SCC 304 (Supreme Court of India). See also the description of aspects of this case above, at Section 2.2.
37 ACICA Rules Article 11; CIETAC Rule 24; HKIAC Rules Article 8.2; KCAB International Rule 4; 2010 SIAC Rules Rule 9; ICC Rules Article 10; and 2010 UNCITRAL Arbitration Rules Article 10. The JCAA Rules do not provide for a specific rule in the case of multiple claimants or respondents, but do expressly state in Rule 10(2) that 'Multiple claimants or respondents shall be deemed to be one party for purposes of the appointment of arbitrators'.

6.36　Interestingly, the CIETAC Rules do not follow this approach. Article 24(2) provides that where the multiple claimants or multiple respondents cannot agree on an arbitrator, CIETAC will appoint only the arbitrator for the side that could not agree on one. It will not appoint all three arbitrators.[38]

3 Choosing an arbitrator

6.37　The autonomy of parties to choose arbitrators is a frequently cited benefit of arbitration.[39] A poor choice will extinguish this benefit, and may even be detrimental to the party that made the choice. It has been suggested, not surprisingly, that 'when selecting arbitrators a party's objective should be, from the beginning, to obtain the majority of arbitrators which it wants'.[40] By implication this includes the choice of the chairperson. As noted above arbitration rules usually refer the selection of the chairperson to either the co-arbitrators or an institution, and as such the choice is often beyond direct party involvement. However, counsel representing clients have developed strategies to influence that choice indirectly.[41]

6.38　When considering what is desired in an arbitrator, it is useful to distinguish between qualifications and qualities. Qualifications should be given its natural meaning, which involves some kind of formal, recognised training. Qualities, on the other hand, are attributes. These may not be tangible or easily definable, as they may be something esoteric such as the manner in which an arbitrator approaches a problem. Qualifications and qualities are discussed in turn.

3.1 Qualifications of an international arbitrator

6.39　As a general rule there are no formal qualifications necessary to become an international arbitrator. Legal knowledge and experience is not required but is highly desirable. This does not necessarily mean experience practising as a lawyer or even the attainment of a law degree. Many arbitral institutions conduct courses for non-legal professionals which include a legal component. Legal knowledge may also be gained by other professionals through experience sitting as an arbitrator. Most arbitration laws and rules do not provide any required qualifications for arbitrators. Certain exceptions are mentioned below.

---

38 Article 24(2) of the CIETAC Rules provides: 'Where the Claimant side and/or the Respondent side fail to jointly appoint or jointly entrust the Chairman of the CIETAC to appoint one arbitrator within fifteen (15) days from the date of receipt of the Notice of Arbitration, the arbitrator shall be appointed by the Chairman of the CIETAC.'
39 See generally D Bishop and L Reed, 'Practical Guidelines for Interviewing, Selecting and Challenging Party-appointed Arbitrators in International Commercial Arbitration', (1998) 14 *Arbitration International* 395, at p. 395.
40 CR Seppälä, 'Recommended Strategy for Getting the Right International Arbitral Tribunal: A Practitioner's View', 6 *Transnational Dispute Management*, Issue 1, March 2009.
41 See the discussion below, and see generally, ibid.

First, it has been suggested that as a result of what may have been a legislative oversight, only licensed Japanese lawyers (bengoshi) can sit as arbitrators in Japan. The problem arises because the Japanese Lawyers Law[42] covers arbitration and the Arbitration Law did not create an exception for arbitrators. Commentary suggests that a lawyer not licenced in Japan who acts as an arbitrator would not violate the Lawyers Law provided it was considered a legitimate business conduct.[43] In practice, it is not uncommon for lawyers who are not qualified in Japan to sit as international arbitrators in arbitrations seated in Japan. We are not aware of any case where this has given rise to a successful challenge against the arbitrator or the award.

6.40

In North Korea, requirements for performing the role of an arbitrator (referred to in the legislation as a judge) are set out in Article 19 of the External Arbitration Law. Article 19(4) is quite broad but the wording 'if needed' suggests this is to be an option of last resort:

6.41

Article 19
The judges can be a person of the following qualifications:
1. A member of the arbitration committee concerned.
2. A lawyer or economic expert who is able to examine and solve a dispute.
3. A person who is experienced as an attorney or a judge.
4. A well-known overseas Korean compatriot or a foreigner experienced in arbitration affairs, if needed.

Indonesia also stipulates particular requirements in its Arbitration and Dispute Resolution Act:[44]

6.42

Article 12
(1) The parties who may be appointed or designated as arbitrators must meet the following requirements:
   a. Being authorised or competent to perform legal actions;
   b. Being at least 35 years of age;
   c. Having no family relationship by blood or marriage, to the third degree, with either of the disputing parties;
   d. Having no financial or other interest in the arbitration award; and
   e. Having at least 15 years experience and active mastery in the field.
(2) Judges, prosecutors, clerks of courts, and other government or court officials may not be appointed or designated as arbitrators.

One may wonder how North Korean courts determine that an overseas compatriot is 'well known' and how Indonesian courts determine that a person has 'active mastery in the field'. Other jurisdictions require particular qualifications of arbitrators in domestic arbitrations but not the same, or at all, in international

6.43

---

42 Article 72 Bengoshi Ho, Law No. 205 of 1949.
43 T Nakamura, 'Commercial Litigation/Arbitration', in L Nottage (ed), *Japan Business Law Guide*, vol. 2, CCH Asia, looseleaf service, paras 83–570.
44 Article 12 of the Indonesia Arbitration and Dispute Resolution Act (Law No. 30 of 1999).

arbitrations.⁴⁵ Taiwanese law requires arbitrators in general to receive certain training subject to various exemptions.⁴⁶

6.44   It has been suggested that it is not possible to appoint a bankrupt person as arbitrator in South Korea.⁴⁷ However, there does not appear to be a clear prohibition on appointing a bankrupt to the role. The rationale for the exclusion may be a legal incapacity to contract. If this is the reason then it should not be taken as a general rule, because a bankrupt's ability to contract may vary from jurisdiction to jurisdiction. It would, however, seem prudent to avoid appointing a bankrupt arbitrator if possible.

6.45   Rather unusually, the Rules of Arbitration of the Bangladesh Council of Arbitration specifically provide for 'disqualifications' (including insolvency):

> *8.6 Disqualifications*
> 8.6.1 An Arbitrator who has attained the age of 75 years or more will automatically cease to be a member of the Panel of Arbitrators. A person who has been appointed as an Arbitrator in a reference before attaining the age of 75 years may continue to serve as an Arbitrator till pronouncement of the final Award in the said reference pending before the Council.
> 8.6.2 An Arbitrator shall also ipso facto be disqualified to serve as an Arbitrator if:
>   a. he is found to be of unsound mind by a court of competent jurisdiction; or
>   b. he is adjudged as insolvent; or
>   c. he is sentenced to a term of imprisonment exceeding six months for any criminal offence involving moral turpitude; or
>   d. by notice in writing to the Council he expresses unwillingness to serve as an Arbitrator; or
>   e. his name is deleted from the list of Panel by the Council under Rule 8.4.

6.46   Despite the various requirements that have been cited in the previous paragraphs, it should be recalled that most arbitration laws in the Asia-Pacific do not require any particular qualifications for arbitrators. The qualifications of arbitrators can, however, sometimes affect the manner in which courts may review any resulting arbitral award. This is true regardless of whether these qualifications were expressly sought by the parties or specified in the law or rules. The New Zealand courts have had cause to make observations on this point. In the 2000 Court of Appeal decision of *Gold and Resource Developments (NZ) Ltd v Doug Hood Ltd*⁴⁸ it was noted:

> Where the arbitrator chosen by the parties is legally qualified, it will be harder to obtain leave to appeal the arbitral decision on a question of law. As Lord Donaldson of Lymington MR stated in *Ipswich Borough Council v Fisons PLC* [1990] at p 724, if the chosen arbitrator is a lawyer and the problem is purely one of law, the parties must be assumed to have had good reason for relying on that lawyer's expertise.

---
45 See, e.g. Article 8 of the Arbitration Law of Taiwan.
46 Ibid.
47 Kyu Wha Lee and Yong Joon Yoon, 'Korea', *The International Comparative Legal Guide to International Arbitration 2006* 258, at p. 260.
48 [2000] 3 NZLR 318, at 334.

In 2004, a further statement was made in another New Zealand case, *Methanex Motunui Ltd v Spellman*.[49] Although lengthy it is worthwhile extracting the relevant passage:

6.47

> It seems clear that as a general principle, and in the absence of agreement to the contrary, lay arbitrators must confine their fact finding to the information provided by the parties. It seems implicit in the authorities that this is subject only to those matters that would have been the subject of judicial notice in Courts of general jurisdiction, there being no reason for requiring arbitrators to be more blinkered than Judges in that respect. But with that qualification, lay arbitrators must draw their facts from evidence provided by the parties.
>
> The position is different where arbitrators have been chosen for their expertise in the subject-matter of the dispute. Even without express agreement on the subject, it is presumed that such arbitrators can draw on their knowledge and experience for general facts, that is to say facts which form part of the general body of knowledge within their area of expertise as distinct from facts that are specific to the particular dispute: *Zermalt Holdings SA v Nu-life Upholstery Repairs Ltd* [1985] 2 EGLR 14. An arbitrator appointed for his or her special knowledge, skill, or expertise, is entitled to draw upon those sources for the purpose of determining the dispute and need not advise the parties that he or she is doing so: *Mediterranean and Eastern Export Co and Checkpoint Ltd v Strathclyde*.
>
> In the absence of agreement to the contrary, not even experts may rely upon their extraneous knowledge of the specific events in question, whether or not derived from independent work or investigations they may have carried out: *F R Waring (UK) Ltd v Administracao Geral Do Acucar E Do Alcool EP* [1983] 1 Lloyd's Rep 45. But otherwise objectionable fact finding by an expert arbitrator may be rendered acceptable if notice and opportunity to respond is given to the parties.

Similarly in 2006 the Supreme Court of Victoria observed:[50]

6.48

> the standard to be applied in considering the sufficiency of an arbitrator's reasons depends upon the circumstances of the case including the facts of the arbitration, the procedures adopted in the arbitration, the conduct of the parties to the arbitration and the qualifications and experience of the arbitrator or arbitrators. For example, in a straightforward trade arbitration before a trade expert, a less exacting standard than would be expected of a judge's reasons should be applied in considering the adequacy of the reasons for the making of an award. On the other hand, in a large-scale commercial arbitration, where the parties engage in the exchange of detailed pleadings and witness statements prior to a formal hearing before a legally qualified arbitrator, a higher standard of reasons is to be expected. This is especially so where the arbitrator is a retired judicial officer.

Although this case concerned a domestic arbitration governed by the Victorian Commercial Arbitration Act, it had various international elements. The Victorian Act specifically requires reasons in arbitral awards,[51] and allows a challenge on

6.49

---

49 [2004] 1 NZLR 95, at 135 (New Zealand High Court).
50 *BHP Billiton Ltd v Oil Basins Ltd* [2006] VSC 402, at 26. See also Chapter 8, Section 3.2.
51 Section 29(1)(c) of the Victorian Commercial Arbitration Act 1984. A similar, though not identical requirement, is found in Article 31 of the Model Law.

260   INTERNATIONAL COMMERCIAL ARBITRATION

the basis of an error of law on the face of the award.[52] When dismissing the subsequent appeal, the Court of Appeal added:[53]

> Furthermore, in the usual course of events, disputants choose their arbitrators on the basis of qualifications, knowledge or a skill which is fitted to the nature of the dispute, and so to preparing the type of determination which is appropriate. Disputants are also likely to adopt a form of arbitral proceeding which is consonant with those requirements.

6.50   The arbitration agreement may require that arbitrators possess specific qualifications (such as an engineering degree or expertise in a particular industry). If the stated qualification is drafted in mandatory terms, an arbitrator who does not possess it could be challenged. Alternatively, the award could be challenged or its enforcement could be refused on the basis that the constitution of the arbitral tribunal or the arbitral procedure was not in accordance with the parties' agreement.[54]

6.51   It is usually preferable not to provide for any strict qualifications of arbitrators in the arbitration clause as this may unduly burden the appointment process once a dispute arises. Unusual qualifications, or combinations of qualifications, may severely limit the number of potential candidates. Furthermore, the specified qualifications may not be necessary or even useful in all cases. For example, the parties to a construction contract might specify that all arbitrators must be engineers with a certain speciality. These engineers might not be suitable if the dispute concerns legal or commercial issues relating to the contract, rather than technical matters. It is better that qualifications specified in arbitration agreements are expressed as being desirable rather than mandatory.[55] Further qualifications, including mandatory qualifications, could be specified by agreement of the parties once the dispute has actually arisen.

3.2 Qualities of an arbitrator

6.52   Qualities of an arbitrator concern the individual's attributes. There are a number of generic attributes relevant to most arbitrators, such as language abilities and experience. Beyond that, a distinction can be drawn between qualities that are desirable in a chairperson or sole arbitrator, compared to those desirable in a party-nominated co-arbitrator. These are addressed below.

6.53   Furthermore, it is important to consider not only the individual members of the arbitral tribunal but also the collective qualities of the arbitral tribunal as a whole[56] to deal with the disputed issues, cultural differences and expectations of the parties. Cultural adaptability is maximised when a three-member

---

52 Section 38 of the Victorian Commercial Arbitration Act 1984.
53 *Oil Basins Ltd v BHP Billiton Ltd* (2007) VSCA 255, at 58. The judgment in this case also usefully demonstrates the importance of knowing the unique characteristics of the *lex arbitri* in any given case. The court distinguishes many of the appellants' arguments on the basis that the English Arbitration Act is different from the Victorian Commercial Arbitration Act.
54 See generally Chapter 9 concerning the challenge and enforcement of arbitral awards.
55 For a discussion of what should and should not be included in arbitration agreements, see Chapter 4.
56 R Goodman-Everard, 'Cultural Diversity in International Arbitration – A Challenge for Decision-makers and Decision-making', (1991) 7(2) *Arbitration International* 155, at p. 155.

arbitral tribunal includes arbitrators of three different nationalities.[57] The diversity of nationalities brings to the panel a richness of legal experience and training, languages and cultures. The combined skills and backgrounds of the three arbitrators increases the prospects that all parties' arguments will be thoroughly understood and that the procedure and outcome will take into account the international character of the arbitration.

3.2.1 Chairpersons and sole arbitrators

6.54 The chairperson must be fair and be seen to be fair so as to inspire and maintain the confidence of the parties and co-arbitrators. He or she must also have an ability to control the parties, manage the co-arbitrators and conduct the proceedings efficiently.[58] The potential for obstructionist behaviour from parties, or even sometimes co-arbitrators, is a real possibility in international commercial arbitration, and a good chairperson should therefore be able to respond to this behaviour. In addition, the chairperson should be particularly capable of understanding and analysing legal issues and problems. This applies to both substantive and procedural legal issues. Chairpersons are frequently chosen because of their experience with the law and practice of international arbitration itself.[59] Overall, the most significant quality a chairperson can have is to inspire confidence in the arbitral process.

6.55 Arbitration rules frequently invest extra powers in the chairperson vis-à-vis the co-arbitrators. For example, Article 17.3 of the ACICA Rules states in part that '[q]uestions of procedure may be decided by the chairperson alone . . . '.[60] A well-organised person with good managerial skills would therefore be a more desirable candidate than a disorganised and curt person. Similarly, but more importantly, the presiding arbitrator is often empowered to deliver the award alone where a majority decision cannot be reached. For example, CIETAC Rule 43.5 states that 'Where the arbitral tribunal cannot reach a majority opinion, the award shall be rendered in accordance with the presiding arbitrator's opinion'.[61]

6.56 In contrast, neither the Model Law nor the UNCITRAL Arbitration Rules give this power to the chairperson, instead requiring a majority decision. The issue of whether the stance of the UNCITRAL Arbitration Rules on this particular point should be changed was keenly debated in the UNCITRAL Working Group II.[62]

---

57 On the issue of nationality of arbitrators, and in particular the nationality of the chairperson, see Ilhyung Lee, 'Practice and Predicament: The Nationality of the International Arbitrator (with Survey Results)', (2008) 31(3) *Fordham International Law Journal* 603.
58 See generally T Webster, 'Selection of Arbitrators in a Nutshell', (2002) 19(3) *Journal of International Arbitration* 261.
59 Kirby, op. cit. fn 3, at p. 354.
60 See also KCAB International Rules Article 30; SIAC Rules, Rule 15.3 and Beijing Arbitration Commission Article 39.2, all of which provide the chair this power subject to prior confirmation by the other members of the arbitral tribunal. Under UNCITRAL Arbitration Rules, Article 31(2) also permits the arbitral tribunal to pre-authorise the presiding arbitrator to make procedural decisions, but such decisions are subject to revision.
61 See also KCAB International Rules Article 30; Beijing Arbitration Commission Article 39.1; ICC Rules Article 25.1; SIAC Rules, Rule 27.
62 47th session, 10–14 September 2007, Vienna. The decision to retain the majority rule provision in the 2010 UNCITRAL Arbitration Rules may have been influenced by the fact that the rules are used in many investment arbitration disputes. See L Nottage and K Mills, '"Back to the Future" for Investor-State Arbitrations: Revising Rules in Australia and Japan to Meet Public Interests', (2009) 26(1) *Journal of International Arbitration* 25, at p. 54.

During the course of that debate it was suggested that a majority rule may force a presiding arbitrator to agree with the least unpalatable opinion of one of the co-arbitrators. Where the rules require a majority, an ideal chairperson should be able to convince a co-arbitrator towards his or her view or be capable of finding a compromised, but still appropriate, solution.

6.57 The qualities desired of sole arbitrators are similar to those of chairpersons, except that sole arbitrators are not required to manage co-arbitrators and the additional powers allocated to chairpersons are obviously not applicable. A good sole arbitrator should, in addition to the qualities required of a chairperson, be exceptionally well organised, self-motivated, able to work alone and meticulously diligent. This is because he or she will have to scrutinise and organise his or her own work, without the comfort of reminders and a sounding board in the form of co-arbitrators.

6.58 As noted above,[63] some practitioners suggest that parties can take steps to influence the appointment of the chairperson or sole arbitrator. There are several ways this may be achieved. In the first instance it is open to parties to choose a method of appointment involving their participation in the nomination of the chairperson. Seppälä suggests that parties should attempt to agree on a profile identifying some of the qualifications or qualities both parties want in the chairperson.[64] The profile is then submitted to the arbitral institution which is asked to provide a list of potential candidates. The parties then try to reach an agreement to appoint someone from that list. The same process can also be utilised when a sole arbitrator is to be appointed. However, where a list procedure cannot be agreed for the chairperson, Seppälä notes that parties can often exercise indirect influence. He notes that arbitration rules, such as the ICC Rules[65] (and laws[66]), often require that consideration be given to the parties' and co-arbitrators' nationalities when appointing a chairperson. While the parties' nationalities are already known, as may be the nationality of the co-arbitrator nominated by the opposing party, one could deliberately pick an arbitrator of a particular nationality to narrow the pool of potential chairpersons.

3.2.2 Party-nominated co-arbitrators

6.59 Particular qualities are sought in party-nominated co-arbitrators. These are often qualities which the appointing party perceives as suggesting that the arbitrator's presence on the arbitral tribunal will increase its chances of success. Of course, arbitrators – regardless of how they are appointed – are duty-bound to act at all

---

63 See Section 3.
64 Seppälä, op. cit. fn 40.
65 ICC Rules Articles 9.1 and 9.5, ACICA Rules Article 9.3, JCAA Rules, Rule 25.3. Article 11.2 of the HKIAC Rules states that the chairperson must have a different nationality to that of the parties, but does not mention the co-arbitrators. Nationality is not specifically mentioned in the SIAC Rules.
66 Article 11(5) Model Law directs that the nominated court or other appointing authority 'in the case of a sole or third arbitrator, shall take into account as well the advisability of appointing an arbitrator of a nationality other than those of the parties'. An equivalent provision is not needed in the Chinese Arbitration Law due to the effective prohibition of ad hoc arbitration in China.

times with impartiality and independence, and must not blindly support the party that nominated them.⁶⁷ That said, an individual arbitrator's views on or approach to particular issues might be known or expected. An aspect of the person's legal, cultural or other background or experience may mean he or she is likely to take a particular approach. This background research or 'due diligence' on the mind and outlook of an arbitrator has become an essential part of preparing for an arbitration.

6.60 This position is well summarised by a comment from Martin Hunter which has since been cited many times. Hunter says that 'when I am representing a client in an arbitration, what I am really looking for in a party nominated arbitrator is someone with the maximum predisposition towards my client but with the minimum appearance of bias'.⁶⁸ Although, in Hunter's own words, this comment 'provoked a lively reaction'⁶⁹ when it was made and was certainly met with some resistance, it can safely be said that it reflects common practice. Pierre Lalive notes that '[Hunter] just said out loud what everyone silently thinks, and one may even wonder if the lawyer acting differently would not betray his client!'⁷⁰ Other commentators have noted that selection of arbitrators predisposed to their clients' case is a 'natural and expected aspect of the party appointment system' and 'need carry no suggestion of disqualifying partiality'.⁷¹

6.61 Hunter describes the ideal appointee as 'someone who is likely to be genuinely persuaded by my argument'.⁷² He gives the example that 'in representing a government who has nationalised an oil company I'm not likely to choose an investment banker from a capitalist country with many years experience of battling for investors in less developed countries or someone who has published a series of articles showing that he has a conservative viewpoint on the interpretation of the phrase "prompt, adequate and effective" compensation'.⁷³ There is thus a considerable element of common sense in choosing the right party-nominated arbitrator.

6.62 Whether the selection of an arbitrator sympathetic to an argument actually helps in the long term is difficult to prove empirically. One can project that if at least one arbitrator understands certain reasoning or sympathises with a line of argument, some of that reasoning or argument should be transposed into the award and into any decisions taken by the arbitral tribunal. On the other hand, if a co-arbitrator's views are markedly different from those of the chairperson this may lead to confrontation or tension, and could thus be counterproductive to the nominating party's interests.

---

67 See further below the discussion of the standards of independence applicable to party-nominated co-arbitrators.
68 M Hunter, 'Ethics of the International Arbitrator', (1987) 53 *Arbitration* 219, p. 223; (then restated in M Hunter, 'The Arbitral Process and the Independence of Arbitrators', (1991) *ICC Publication No. 472*, p. 164.).
69 Hunter, 1987, ibid., at p. 225.
70 P Lalive, 'Conclusions' in 'The Arbitral Process and the Independence of Arbitrators', (1991) *ICC Publication No. 472*, pp. 119 and 122.
71 Bishop and Reed, op. cit. fn 39, at p. 396.
72 Hunter (1987), op. cit. fn 68, p. 225.
73 Ibid.

6.63   In that sense, it is vital for party-nominated arbitrators to act fairly and impartially with regard to arguments submitted by the party that did not appoint them. Selection of an overtly non-neutral arbitrator has unquestionable tactical disadvantages, apart from the possibility of challenge and removal of the arbitrator. Several commentators believe that advocacy in favour of the arguments of the arbitrator's nominating party is unhelpful because a good chairperson is likely to detect such partiality and treat with considerable suspicion and caution any suggestions made by that arbitrator.[74] Such an approach by a co-arbitrator may actually increase the chairperson's willingness to form a majority with the other co-arbitrator. As Hunter says, it is 'entirely counterproductive to a party's interests if the arbitrator [it] has nominated demonstrates (inadvertently or otherwise) at an early stage of the arbitration that he is going to vote for that party regardless of the merits of the case'.[75]

6.64   The service provided by a lawyer to his or her client when presented with an opportunity to participate directly in constituting the arbitral tribunal must include a choice of the best possible co-arbitrator. Choosing an unhelpful co-arbitrator wastes one of the single most proactive steps that can be played by a party's lawyer in constituting the arbitral tribunal. It is worth reiterating that the integrity of the arbitral process is not to be compromised by encouraging conscious appointment of non-neutral arbitrators. To the contrary, nomination of an arbitrator who is actually biased or is perceived to be so is almost inevitably contrary to the nominating party's interests.

6.65   Some debate exists over the appropriateness of appointing young practitioners as co-arbitrators.[76] Current practice shows that parties are sometimes hesitant to appoint someone who does not have a well-established reputation in international arbitration. This is rumoured to have resulted in a perceived 'elite' group of arbitrators who share between themselves appointments in the majority of significant cases. It is understandable that one feels more secure appointing someone who has already proved his excellence. Why take the risk of appointing someone 'new'? Indeed it takes time, patience and effort to build expertise and to be recognised as a competent practitioner worthy of appointment as a co-arbitrator. A prominent practitioner and arbitrator has commented that:[77]

> individual reputations in this field grow only by the slow accretion of evidence of independence and fair mindedness in numerous instances when it really matters. Elitism is no sin; the ambition to work at the highest possible level is surely a healthy one. The building of a reputation in this challenging context is a lengthy process, which offers no assurance of success. However, it creates a depth of confidence which can never be achieved by self-serving declarations.

---

74 Kirby, op. cit. fn 3, at p. 349; K-H Bockstiegel, 'The Arbitral Process and the Independence of Arbitrators', (1991) *ICC Publication No. 472*, p. 23; A Berlinguer. 'Impartiality and Independence of Arbitrators in International Practice', (1995) 6 *American Review of International Arbitration* 339, at p. 346; Redfern, Hunter, et al, op. cit. fn 1; A Lowenfeld, 'The Party-appointed Arbitrator in International Controversies: Some Reflections', (1995) *Texas International Law Journal* 30, at pp. 59–70. Lowenfeld notes that being overly sympathetic turns the chairperson off and often leads to a challenge by the opposing party.
75 Hunter (1987), op. cit. fn 68, p. 26.
76 Kirby, op. cit. fn 3, at p. 354.
77 J Paulsson, 'Ethics, Elitism, Eligibility', (1997) 13 *Journal of International Arbitration* 13, at p. 19.

6.66 This point is certainly true. However, the creation of an exclusive elite can also undermine the provision of quality services to parties. Well-known arbitrators may well accept too many cases, thus becoming too busy fully to involve themselves in every case. This can mean they are less able to study the case thoroughly and may even delegate work to their associates. Criticism is then levelled by parties who feel they are paying for a distinguished arbitrator when it is in fact somebody else carrying out the work.

6.67 On the other hand, a younger arbitrator is more likely to prioritise the arbitration, schedule early hearing dates, have more time to devote to the arbitration, see the appointment as a privilege, and be very diligent, even if he or she does not have the same amount of experience. Several organisations have been established to enhance the training and profile of younger practitioners. Examples in this region include the Australasian Forum for International Arbitration (AFIA); the Asian Chapter of the ICC Young Arbitrators Forum, and the Young Members Group of Charted Institute of Arbitrators (CIArb) East Asia Branch.[78]

3.2.3 Pre-appointment interviews

6.68 It has become common for counsel and even parties to interview prospective arbitrators and in particular co-arbitrators before deciding whether to appoint them. This is another form of the due diligence parties will conduct on arbitrators. Not surprisingly, this practice is sometimes controversial because it can lead to a perception of partiality. However, it is not prohibited and can be beneficial if used wisely and within ethical limits. While it is vital that discussions be kept at a very general level and that the particulars of the case itself are not discussed, it can be beneficial for an arbitrator to learn something about the case so as to evaluate his or her own suitability. Arbitrators might also be questioned on matters such as time availability.

6.69 The IBA Guidelines on Conflicts of Interest in International Arbitration[79] deal with pre-appointment interviews. They provide on the 'green list' (meaning that it does not have to be disclosed) the following rule:[80]

> the arbitrator has had an initial contact with the appointing party or an affiliate of the appointing party (or the respective counsels) prior to the appointment, if this contact is limited to the arbitrator's availability and qualifications to serve or to the names of possible candidates for a chairperson and did not address the merits or the procedural aspects of the dispute.

6.70 There is relatively little institutional guidance on how pre-appointment interviews should be conducted. The Practice Guidelines on the Pre-Appointment Interview of Prospective Arbitrators issued in 2007 by the Chartered Institute of Arbitrators are unique in this regard. The guidelines mainly contain commonsense advice. For example, the interview should take place in a business setting and not in a social environment such as over dinner. The meeting should be

---

[78] These associations and others that are similar are discussed in Chapter 1, Section 4.
[79] See 'IBA Guidelines on Conflicts of Interest in International Arbitration', www.int-bar.org/images/downloads/guidelines%20text.pdf accessed on 3 July 2010, and Section 5.2.2 below.
[80] Ibid., Green List 4.5.1.

planned well in advance with details of exactly how long it will take, who will be present, and how the interview will be conducted. For the benefit of both the party and the arbitrator a precise record of the interview should be made and provided to the opposing side once the arbitrator has been appointed. Interviews of sole or presiding arbitrators should not take place in the presence of one party alone. The guidelines also suggest that unsuccessful interviewees should usually only be compensated for reasonable expenses but not time. Those who are successfully appointed should submit their claims for expenses and time in the usual way – carefully noting that they relate to the interview. In practice, arbitrators rarely charge fees for these pre-appointment interviews.

6.71 Pre-appointment interviews become most controversial when the parties do not limit themselves to interviewing one prospective arbitrator about availability etc., but interview several candidates with the aim of establishing which one is most likely to decide in their favour. This practice has been termed a 'beauty parade',[81] in a similar way to beauty contests between law firms that are pitching to a client for prospective briefs. Whether beauty parades are ethically acceptable depends primarily on the content of the discussions and whether they are disclosed to the opposing party. The recommendations of the above-mentioned Chartered Institute Guidelines are helpful in this respect.

4 Formal appointment of arbitrators

6.72 It is important to distinguish between the nomination and the appointment of an arbitrator. Simply because a person is nominated (or proposed) to act as arbitrator does not impose an obligation on him or her to accept the nomination. Much like an ordinary contract for services, the position hinges on the principles of offer and acceptance. The nomination only binds the arbitrator once accepted. As reviewed below, the arbitrator's acceptance of the nomination may be all that is required to appoint an arbitrator but under certain rules the acceptance may constitute only a pre-condition to appointment.[82]

6.73 The point at which appointment occurs can be of importance as it carries certain effects. It is generally only when an arbitrator has been appointed that he or she may be afforded immunity from civil liability.[83] The point of time from which immunity takes effect may vary under some institutional rules because even if arbitrators accept the nomination there may be further steps to be taken

---

[81] Referred to in French as 'concours de beauté' by VV Veeder, 'L'indépendance et l'impartialité de l'arbitre dans l'arbitrage international', in L Cladiet, T Clay and E Jeuland (eds), *Médiation et Arbitrage*, Litec, 2005, at p. 219.
[82] Some common law practitioners refer to the act of acceptance as 'entering the reference'.
[83] There is a generally accepted view that a contractual (or at least quasi-contractual) relationship exists between the arbitrators and the parties, although it is not without its critics. If such a relationship does exist, then arbitrators may find themselves subject to civil damages claims. Although most claims one might expect would naturally arise after the commencement of the arbitration (and hence after the appointment of the arbitrator), it is conceivable that a claim such as for breach of confidentiality may occur before an arbitrator's appointment. For a discussion of the contractual relationship between arbitrators and parties see K Lionnet, 'The Arbitrator's Contract', (1999) 15(2) *Arbitration International* 161; and Lew, Mistelis and Kröll, op. cit. fn 5, at p. 276, para 12–4.

for them to be officially appointed. For example, under Article 9 of the ICC Rules, party-nominated arbitrators who have accepted nomination must thereafter be confirmed by the ICC Court or Secretary-General. Consequently, under this procedure a party-nominated arbitrator is not appointed until he or she has been confirmed.[84] At the opposite end of the scale are the ACICA Rules, which follow the more common formula (also used, for example, in the UNCITRAL Arbitration Rules). The terminology adopted in the ACICA Rules refers solely to the appointment of arbitrators with no mention as to their nomination. Implicit in this wording is the need first to nominate an arbitrator, who is then required to accept or decline the nomination. Upon acceptance, the arbitrator would be appointed under those Rules.

The 2007 SIAC Rules follow the ICC approach. In a circular released to announce those 2007 Rules, Lawrence Boo, then SIAC's Deputy Chairperson, stated:[85]   6.74

> The unequivocal, institutional nature of SIAC arbitration is embodied in the 2007 Rules...
> (i) SIAC's role as the appointing authority is clarified in Rule 5, whether arbitrators are party-appointed, party nominated, agreed to by parties, or nominated or appointed by any third person. In all cases, an arbitrator is not deemed to be appointed until confirmed by the Chairman of SIAC.

The equivalent provision now appears as Rule 6 in the 2010 SIAC Rules. Indeed, in this edition the Chairman's authority appears to be further emphasised by reference to the finality of his/her decision in Rule 6.4.   6.75

5 Obligations of arbitrators

'International arbitrators should be impartial, independent, competent, diligent and discreet.' Such is the first line of the Introductory Note of the 1987 IBA Rules of Ethics for International Arbitrators.[86] This guideline highlights the fact that being an arbitrator carries certain duties and obligations. However, it has been suggested that there are people who will willingly accept an appointment as an arbitrator without fully appreciating their duties.[87] This could seriously affect the conduct of a specific arbitration, but it will also tarnish the reputation of arbitration generally. The responsibility for ensuring that potential arbitrators are aware of their obligations should be shared by the prospective arbitrators and those who are appointing them.   6.76

This section begins by considering the general obligations of arbitrators and their potential liability. It then moves to a specific discussion of their disclosure   6.77

---

84 For an explanation of the appointment process in ICC arbitration see Fry and Greenberg, op. cit. fn 11.
85 Circular, Release of New SIAC Rules, 3rd edn, 1 July 2007, Schedule of fees and practice notes, 28 May 2007 (www.siac.org.sg/Pdf/WhatnewsRules2007Circular.pdf).
86 Although these rules are not directly binding on either arbitrators or parties (unless specifically adopted by agreement), they are one of the few such guidelines of their kind. They cover not only the duty of disclosure, but issues such as fees, diligence, involvement in settlement discussions and confidentiality of deliberations.
87 Redfern, Hunter, et al, op. cit. fn 1, at para 5–11.

obligation. The special obligations of impartiality and independence are addressed separately in the discussion on challenges to arbitrators in Section 6.

5.1 General obligations and potential liability

6.78   In accepting an appointment, arbitrators agree to the inherent duties of care and diligence attached to their role. These duties may not be spelt out in arbitration rules but are nonetheless implied. As part of these duties, arbitrators should make themselves available and be able to devote the time and effort necessary to read the parties' submissions carefully, examine the evidence produced, attend all meetings and hearings, and work on producing a quality award after a thorough, unbiased analysis of the entire case. Naturally, an arbitrator should refrain from doing anything which would prejudice the arbitration or the parties.

6.79   Born suggests that the obligations of international arbitrators can be summarised as:[88]
- a duty to resolve the parties' dispute in an adjudicatory manner;
- a duty to conduct the arbitration in accordance with the parties' arbitration agreement;
- a duty to maintain the confidentiality of the arbitration;
- in some contexts, a duty to propose a settlement to the parties; and
- a duty to complete the arbitrator's mandate.

6.80   The first duty Born refers to is particularly important. It encompasses a number of more discrete obligations and significantly overlaps with the other duties he lists. Redfern and Hunter describe this as a duty to act judicially,[89] which perhaps better captures the nature of the obligation. Although arbitrators are given wide discretion to determine the parties' disputes, there are expectations about the process which will lead to that determination. This is clearly described in Rule 15(2) of the SIAC Rules, which reads:[90]

> In the absence of procedural rules agreed by the parties or contained in these Rules, the Tribunal shall conduct the arbitration in such manner as it considers appropriate to ensure <u>the fair, expeditious, economical and final determination of the dispute</u>. (Emphasis added)

6.81   We have referred to the fundamental importance of a fair process repeatedly throughout this book. It includes the issues of impartiality and independence which are discussed separately below.[91] The requirements of an expeditious and economical process in part relate to availability. The arbitrator must allocate the time and commitment to see the arbitration through to its prompt completion. Arbitrators should be professional, calm and diligent in this process.

6.82   Some rules expressly refer to an obligation on the arbitrator to make every effort to deliver an enforceable award.[92] Where it is not referred to expressly

---
[88] G Born, *International Commercial Arbitration*, Kluwer, 2009, at p. 1615.
[89] Redfern, Hunter, et al, op. cit. fn 1, at para 5–24.
[90] See the discussion of arbitrators' duties in Chapter 7, Section 4.3. The equivalent provision in the 2010 SIAC Rules is Rule 16.1.
[91] See Section 6.1.1.
[92] ICC Rules Article 35; SIAC Rules, Rule 35.3; LCIA Rules Article 32.2.

such an obligation may be implied generally or in the requirement of final determination.[93] There are nevertheless limits to this obligation. Even the most experienced international arbitrators cannot foresee every single issue (such as a form or process requirement) that every possible enforcement court in the world might raise. Even if arbitrators have this information at their disposal, it may not be practicable to attempt to comply with all such requirements in a single case. Furthermore, theoretically some of these requirements may be contradictory, rendering it impossible to deliver an award simultaneously enforceable in two particular jurisdictions. Therefore, arbitrators should make every effort to ensure that they deliver an award that: (i) complies with the spirit of the New York Convention; (ii) is enforceable at the seat of arbitration; and (iii) is enforceable in any jurisdictions that the arbitral tribunal can reasonably foresee that a party to the arbitration may seek to enforce the award.

If an arbitrator breaches a general obligation during the course of an arbitration, the breach might provide grounds for an application to remove the arbitrator. The resignation, removal and replacement of arbitrators is considered in Section 7 below. In some circumstances, parties may even be able to bring legal action against an arbitrator. 6.83

As briefly referred to above, some international arbitration laws provide arbitrators with protection from civil law suits.[94] Although the precise wording differs slightly between the various legislation, for obvious reasons immunity is not generally given in situations where there has been fraud or some similar intentional dishonesty on the part of the arbitrator. The New Zealand legislation takes a slightly different approach. Rather than providing a blanket statement of immunity from liability and then carving out exceptions, it provides a general immunity from negligence in the course of acting in the capacity of an arbitrator without any other qualification.[95] 6.84

Most international arbitration rules also contain an exclusion of liability provision to protect arbitrators and arbitral institutions from civil liability.[96] In early 2009 a decision of the Paris Court of Appeal caused concern among the arbitration community when it suggested that the ICC Court could not validly exclude liability for acts or omissions in the performance of its essential duties.[97] The reasoning of this decision, while directed at an arbitral institution, could arguably be applied mutatis mutandis to arbitrators. While arbitrators and arbitral institutions should be accountable for their actions or omissions, it is important they 6.85

---

[93] Born, op. cit. fn 88, at p. 1621.
[94] See, e.g. Section 28 of the Australian International Arbitration Act; Section 2GM of the Hong Kong Arbitration Ordinance; Section 47 of the Malaysian Arbitration Act; Section 25 of the Singapore International Arbitration Act. Japan is an exception. There are relatively few cases from this region involving the liability of arbitrators. In a Victorian Supreme Court case concerning a domestic Australian arbitration, the legal costs associated with an annulled award were unsuccessfully sought against the arbitrator in *Mond v Berger* [2004] VSC 150. There is a New Zealand High Court case from 1994, *Pickens v Templeton* [1994] 2 NZLR 718, however this was prior to the introduction of Section 13 of the New Zealand Arbitration Act.
[95] Section 13 of the New Zealand Arbitration Act '[a]n arbitrator is not liable for negligence in respect of anything done or omitted to be done in the capacity of arbitrator'.
[96] See, e.g. ACICA Rules Article 44; HKIAC Rules Article 40; SIAC Rules Article 33.
[97] *SNF (France) v Chambre De Commerce Internationale (France)*, Paris Court of Appeal, First Chamber C, 22 January 2009, 07–19492.

are able to perform their functions without fear of spurious liability claims. Given the considerable sums of money frequently involved in international commercial arbitrations, potential exposure to civil liability claims could have detrimental consequences on the manner in which arbitrators and institutions conduct arbitrations.

6.86   The Japanese Arbitration Law does not expressly address the issue of immunity for an arbitrator against civil liability. Rather unusually it contains criminal sanctions for miscreant arbitrators. Significantly these would apply whenever the seat of arbitration was in Japan, even if the offending conduct took place in a different jurisdiction.[98]

5.2 Disclosure obligations

6.87   Arbitration laws and rules impose a duty of disclosure of all facts or circumstances that may give rise to justifiable doubts as to the arbitrator's impartiality or independence. Impartiality and independence represent core obligations of an arbitrator. They are so widely recognised that they amount to general international principles and are therefore incumbent on any arbitrator in all circumstances. All arbitration laws and rules require arbitrators to be and remain independent, although there is variation in the precise language used. The concepts of impartiality of independence are closely related but not exactly the same.[99]

6.88   Identifying which facts or circumstances an arbitrator should disclose is not always easy. The International Bar Association published in 2004 Guidelines on Conflicts of Interest in International Arbitration to assist arbitrators in deciding what should be disclosed. These Guidelines are discussed below, after reviewing the general principles of disclosure as found in arbitration laws and rules.

5.2.1 General principles of disclosure

6.89   Most laws and rules require prospective and serving arbitrators to disclose to the parties any circumstances that might give rise to a reasonable doubt about their independence or impartiality. When the parties have opted for institutional arbitration, the arbitrator's disclosure obligations may extend to the arbitral institution.

6.90   Article 12(1) of the Model Law is typical of the laws in this region:

> When a person is approached in connection with his possible appointment as an arbitrator, he shall disclose any circumstances likely to give rise to justifiable doubts as to his impartiality or independence. An arbitrator, from the time of his appointment and throughout the arbitral proceedings, shall without delay disclose any such circumstances to the parties unless they have already been informed of them by him.

---

[98] L Nottage, 'Japan's New Arbitration Law: Domestication Reinforcing Internationalisation?', (2004) 7(2) *International Arbitration Law Review* 54, at pp. 57, 59; and T Nakamura, 'Salient Features of the New Japanese Arbitration Law Based Upon the UNCITRAL Model Law on International Commercial Arbitration', (2004) 17 *Japanese Commercial Arbitration Association Newsletter* 1, at p. 5.
[99] See Section 6.1.1.

The second sentence is important because it requires a continuing obligation of disclosure right through until the end of the proceedings.

6.91 Under the CIETAC Rules, the arbitrator's disclosure obligation is only to CIETAC and not the parties.[100] CIETAC then communicates the disclosure to the parties.

6.92 Depending on the arbitration rules, the arbitrator may have to sign a declaration or statement of independence when appointed. Article 7(2) of the ICC Rules provides in this regard:

> Before appointment or confirmation, a prospective arbitrator shall sign a statement of independence and disclose in writing to the Secretariat any facts or circumstances which might be of such a nature as to call into question the arbitrator's independence in the eyes of the parties. The Secretariat shall provide such information to the parties in writing and fix a time limit for any comments from them.

6.93 Once a declaration of this kind has been made, a presumption exists that the arbitrator is impartial and independent as at the date of the declaration. The onus of rebutting that presumption lies with the party bringing the challenge.[101]

6.94 Disclosure duties can be very strict, requiring arbitrators associated with large law firms to check thoroughly whether any offices of their firm have acted or are acting for a party or one of its subsidiaries. A recent decision of the Paris Court of Appeal suggests that an arbitrator's actual knowledge of a potential conflict of interest involving his law firm is not necessary, and that constructive knowledge may be sufficient to disqualify the arbitrator.[102] It should be noted that this case is currently being appealed to the Cour de Cassation, France's highest court.

5.2.2 IBA Guidelines

6.95 The different national tests, as well as cultural attitudes towards impartiality and independence, can create doubts as to what an arbitrator must disclose. The IBA has noted that 'even though laws and arbitration rules provide some standards, there is a lack of detail in their guidance and of uniformity in their application. As a result, members of the arbitration community often apply different standards in making decisions concerning disclosure, objections and challenges'.[103] As noted above, in order to assist its members and the profession generally the IBA has produced Guidelines on Conflicts of Interest in International Arbitration ('IBA Guidelines'), setting out principles and examples of circumstances arbitrators should disclose in connection with impartiality and independence.

---

100 CIETAC Rules Article 25.
101 See, e.g. the US decision *Consolidated Coal v Local 1643 United Mine Workers*, 48F 3d 125 (4th Cir 1995) (US Court of Appeals, Fourth Circuit).
102 Paris Court of Appeal, 12 February 2009 (07/22164).
103 IBA Guidelines (Conflicts), op. cit. fn 79, at p. 3.

6.96   The IBA Guidelines do not have the force of law but are merely guidelines. Nonetheless, they are now widely referred to by parties, arbitrators and courts.[104] The Secretariat of the ICC Court also refers to them in footnotes to memoranda that it prepares to brief the ICC Court on its decisions on challenges and contested arbitrator confirmations. The Guidelines certainly do not bind the ICC Court. Both the current and former Secretaries General of the ICC Court have explained why the ICC Court is not bound.[105]

6.97   The IBA Guidelines consider various scenarios concerning when issues as to impartiality and independence arise and when they do not. For ease of reference, these are then categorised by colour – red, orange, and green. Situations described in the Red List are those which create a conflict of interest. This list is divided into two sub-categories: the 'non-waivable Red List' and the 'waivable Red List'. Situations described in the non-waivable Red List give rise to a conflict of interest which automatically disqualifies arbitrators from accepting or continuing their mandate, regardless of whether a party has challenged the arbitrator. As an example, the non-waivable Red List contains the situation where 'the arbitrator has a significant financial interest in one of the parties or the outcome of the case'.[106] However, a situation where 'the arbitrator has given legal advice or provided an expert opinion on the dispute to a party or an affiliate of one of the parties' falls into the waivable Red List.[107] This means a conflict of interest exists that must be disclosed. The effect of a waivable Red List categorisation is that the arbitrator cannot continue to act unless the parties agree otherwise.

6.98   The Green List covers situations which do not give rise to a conflict of interest and, according to the IBA Guidelines, need not be disclosed. An example of these situations is a pre-appointment interview with a party that is limited to availability etc.[108] or the fact that 'the arbitrator has previously published a general opinion (such as in a law review article or public lecture) concerning an issue which also arises in the arbitration (but the opinion is not focused on the case that is being arbitrated)'.[109]

6.99   In-between situations fall into the tricky Orange List, which is 'a non exhaustive enumeration of situations which (depending on the facts of a given case) in the eyes of the parties may give rise to justifiable doubts as to the arbitrator's impartiality or independence'.[110] The arbitrator is under a duty to disclose those

---

[104] See, e.g. L Trakman, 'The Impartiality and Independence of Arbitrators Reconsidered', (2007) 10 *International Arbitration Law Review* 999, who suggests that the jury is still out on whether the guidelines are the cause of the increase in challenges, but does describe the increase as a 'flood'. Contrary to Trakman's suggestion, the ICC Court has not seen an increase in the number of challenges since the Guidelines were released in 2004. See also Fry and Greenberg, op. cit. fn 11, at p. 17.
[105] See AM Whitesell, 'Independence in ICC Arbitration: ICC Court Practice concerning the Appointment, Confirmation, Challenge and Replacement of Arbitrators', (2007) *ICC International Court of Arbitration Bulletin* 7, Special Supplement, at p. 36; and Fry and Greenberg, op. cit. fn 11, at p. 17.
[106] IBA Guidelines (Conflicts), op. cit. fn 79, Non Waivable Red List, 1.3.
[107] Ibid., Waivable Red List 2.1.1.
[108] Ibid., Green List, 4.5.1.
[109] Ibid., Green List, 4.1.1.
[110] Ibid., Part II, para 3.

situations. If an Orange List disclosure is made and the parties fail to object, then the parties are understood to have accepted the arbitrator. Although it may sound like a clear and simple approach, in practice, it can require a very onerous conflict of interest check. For example, an arbitrator must disclose that 'the arbitrator's law firm has within the past three years acted for one of the parties or an affiliate of one of the parties in an unrelated matter without the involvement of the arbitrator'.[111]

The IBA Guidelines are not without their critics.[112] When reading them it is important to remember the perspective from which they were drafted. Michael Bond has observed that:[113]

6.100

> [o]ne might reasonably question whose interests the [IBA] Working Group served. It consisted of 19 members; of the 13 members for whom information is available from Martindale Hubbell, eight work at firms with more than 275 lawyers. Five of those members work at firms with more than 500 lawyers, including the world's largest law firm....

This might explain what is sometimes considered a relaxed approach by the IBA Guidelines to situations where the arbitrator's law firm has provided services for or against one of the parties to the arbitration.

Finally, numerous gaps in the IBA Guidelines have been identified. One of the gaps – the situation where an arbitrator is concurrently serving as co-counsel with one of the parties' counsel in another matter – is significant because it led to four successful challenges or non-confirmations of arbitrators by the ICC Court between 1 July 2004 and 1 August 2008.[114]

6.101

6 Challenges to arbitrators

After formal appointment of an arbitrator, that arbitrator can be challenged. A successful challenge will result in the impugned arbitrator's removal. Ordinarily, he or she will be replaced but sometimes the remaining arbitrators can proceed without such a replacement. The possibility for parties to challenge arbitrators ensures the integrity of the arbitration process. As explained below, depending on the arbitral rules adopted, challenges to arbitrators may be determined by the authority that appointed the arbitrator, the arbitral institution (or its delegate), the unchallenged members of the tribunal, or even the arbitral tribunal including the challenged arbitrator.

6.102

---

111 Ibid., Orange List, 3.1.4.
112 See, e.g. M Ball, 'Probity Deconstructed: How Helpful, Really, are the New International Bar Association Guidelines on Conflicts of Interest in International Arbitration?', (2005) 21(3) *Arbitration International* 323. Despite expressing some criticisms, Ball does conclude by stating that the guidelines have made an important contribution.
113 M Bond, 'A Geography of International Arbitration', (2005) 21(1) *Arbitration International* 99, at p. 104.
114 Fry and Greenberg, op. cit. fn 11, at p. 17.

6.103   There are two main grounds on which to challenge an arbitrator: partiality or lack of independence, discussed in Section 6.1, and misconduct, discussed in Section 6.2.

6.1 Challenges for partiality or lack of independence

6.104   The underlying purpose of independence or impartiality requirements is to ensure that the parties are treated equally and that the award is not influenced by an arbitrator's bias. What matters most, therefore, is ensuring that the arbitrator is free of any influence on his or her decision-making. It follows that a party should be entitled to challenge an arbitrator who it considers to be lacking impartiality for any reason. Challenges for partiality or lack of independence are by far the most common form of challenge.

6.105   The concepts of impartiality and independence are distinguishable. Section 6.1.1 explains the distinction. Section 6.1.2 focuses on the challenge process. Sections 6.1.3 and 6.1.4 address how allegations of partiality and lack of independence are assessed by arbitral institutions and by courts respectively. An issue raised in the context of the assessment of impartiality and independence is whether the same standard applied to chairpersons or sole arbitrators should apply to party-nominated co-arbitrators. This is addressed in Section 6.1.5. We then discuss how impartiality and independence are treated in 'arb-med' proceedings in Section 6.1.6.

6.1.1 Impartiality and independence distinguished

6.106   Most laws and rules use 'independence' and/or 'impartiality' as the operative language to test arbitrator bias.[115] These terms are considered to be clearer and more precisely definable than the concept of 'neutrality.'[116] Although closely related, independence and impartiality are generally considered to be technically distinguishable terms, but somewhat interchangeable for practical purposes in international arbitration.

6.107   Some practitioners contend that the overall concept that covers both impartiality and independence is clear without the need for individual definition of

---

[115] Article 12(2) of the Model Law provides that 'An arbitrator may be challenged only if circumstances exist that give rise to justifiable doubts as to his impartiality or independence'. The UNCITRAL Arbitration Rules Article 9, and 2010 UNCITRAL Arbitration Rules Article 11, also mention both 'impartiality and independence,' as do the 2010 SIAC Rules, Rule 11; ACICA Rules (Article 13); BCA Rules, Rule 9.12; KCAB International Rules, Article 13; ICA Rules, Rule 26; and LCIA Rules (Articles 5(2), 10(3)). Article 11(1) of the ICC Rules states that an arbitrator may be challenged 'for an alleged lack of independence or otherwise', but does not expressly mention impartiality.

[116] Some consider that 'neutrality' involves mainly the question of nationality. See P Lalive, 'On the Neutrality of the Arbitrator and the Place of Arbitration', (1984) *Swiss Essays on International Arbitration* 23, at p. 24. The term has also been used synonymously with impartiality in particular with respect to the different standards for party-appointed arbitrators in some US arbitration rules. See M Smith, 'Impartiality of the Party-appointed Arbitrator', (1990) 6 *Arbitration International* 320, at p. 323. It is also used synonymously with independence. See G Bernini, 'The Arbitral Process and the Independence of Arbitrators', (1991) *ICC Publication No. 472*, p. 31. For a suggested solution to the labyrinth of opinions regarding the meaning of the term 'neutrality' see Berlinguer. op. cit. fn 74, at 346.

each of these terms,[117] while others have argued that excessive analysis of the definitions in inconsistent ways has led to greater confusion rather than clarity.[118] Despite such commentary, distinct definitions are extractable from scholarly writings.

6.108 A generally accepted definition of independence is the absence of actual, identifiable relationships with a party to proceedings or someone closely connected to the party.[119] The test for independence examines the appearance of bias and not actual bias[120] and is thus entirely objective. It looks only at tangible elements; facts that can be shown or proved. Satisfying a test for independence does not require showing the effect of any relationships on the mind of the arbitrator concerned. Offending relationships could be of a business, social, family or financial nature. Slightly more contentious is the question whether identifiable relationships between a party's legal counsel and an arbitrator affect independence.[121] Generally, such relationships are examined to see whether they are relevant to independence. Relationships with counsel are likely to affect independence if they involve financial dependence, such as regular referrals of work. They will probably affect independence if social relationships go beyond ordinary business encounters (such as membership of the same professional association) to significant social contact outside of business.

6.109 In limited circumstances, the fact that an arbitrator and counsel share barristers' chambers may affect independence. This issue arose in the ICSID case of *Hrvatska Elektroprivreda v Slovenia*.[122] There, however, the claimant's applied to prevent the counsel from acting in the arbitration rather than to challenge the arbitrator. The particularly experienced arbitral tribunal ruled in favour of the claimant and ordered that the counsel could not participate in the case. The arbitral tribunal cited the respondent's late announcement of the involvement of that particular counsel as a critical factor.

6.110 Impartiality, in contrast to independence, is a subjective concept, concerned with the tendency of an arbitrator actually to favour one of the parties' positions. Impartiality is not concerned with the outside appearance of bias. It does not necessarily require tangible relationships that could be the cause of the arbitrator acting unfairly. It examines the likelihood of an arbitrator actually having a state of mind or prejudgment that favours one side in the dispute. A lack of impartiality could be caused by totally immeasurable, psychological motives or prejudices,[123]

---

[117] X De Mello, 'Réflexions sur les règles déontologiques élaborées par l'International Bar Association pour les arbitres internationaux', (1988) *Revue de l'arbitrage* 333, at p. 342.
[118] Berlinguer, op. cit. fn 74, at p. 343.
[119] Ibid., p. 346; MS Donahey, 'The Independence and Neutrality of Arbitrators', (1992) 9 *Journal of International Arbitration* 31, at p. 31; Smith, op. cit. fn 116, at p. 323.
[120] Donahey, ibid., p. 31.
[121] See, e.g. A Hirsch, 'Les Arbitres: peuvent-ils connaitre les advocates des parties?' (1990) *ASA Bulletin* 7 and S Bond, 'The ICC Arbitrator's Statement of Independence: A Response to Prof Alain Hirsch', (1990) *ASA Bulletin* 85.
[122] ICSID Case No. ARB/05/24, Tribunal's Ruling of 6 May 2008.
[123] There are several theories which attempt to explain otherwise unexplainable incidences of bias. See, for example, R Delgado, C Dunn, P Brown, H Lee and D Hubbert, 'Fairness and Formality: Minimising the Risk of Prejudice in Alternative Dispute Resolution', (1985) *Wisconsin Law Review* 1359, at p. 1375.

so it is foreseeable that an arbitrator could act partially without any objectively explainable or provable reason for doing so.[124] It 'is thus a subjective and more abstract concept than independence, in that it involves primarily a state of mind. This presents special difficulties in terms of measurement....'.[125]

6.111 A case against an arbitrator for an alleged lack of impartiality could most easily be made out where the arbitrator blatantly favours one party. Blatant favouritism is very rare and difficult to prove,[126] so statutes referring to impartiality usually reduce the evidentiary burden by allowing for removal of arbitrators where there are justifiable or reasonable doubts as to their impartiality.[127] Unfortunately, whether advances in neurological science will ever enable us realistically to test impartiality remains a question so hypothetical that it can safely be ignored. Rather, in order to prove partiality or lack of independence, we must rely on objective factors that can be proved and tested in front of a court, arbitral tribunal or institution. In practice therefore, much like the way independence is assessed, objective factors (i.e. independence) are the best means to examine impartiality.

6.1.2 Procedure

6.112 The procedural aspects of the challenge process will be determined by any express provisions of the arbitration agreement itself, the parties' choice of arbitration rules or the *lex arbitri*. For example, if the parties have chosen institutional arbitration like ICC or SIAC, a body (or individual) within the relevant institution will rule on the challenge.[128] Other rules vest the power in different bodies, such as the authority that appointed the arbitrator,[129] the unchallenged members of the tribunal,[130] or even the arbitral tribunal including the challenged arbitrator.[131] If a procedure has not been determined by the parties, the *lex arbitri* should provide one. Where the Model Law applies, Article 13 (set out below) provides that the challenge will first be submitted to the arbitral tribunal and, if the challenge is rejected, may be submitted to a designated court.

6.113 There are three possible scenarios once a challenge is filed and before that challenge is determined. First, the opposing party may agree to the challenge. The arbitrator's mandate would then ordinarily terminate, although an arbitrator

---

[124] The situation is explained as being '... where a judge is not a party to a suit and does not have a financial interest in its outcome, but in some other way his conduct or behaviour may give rise to a suspicion that he is not impartial...' *R v Bow Street Metropolitan Stipendiary Magistrate and others, ex parte Pinochet Ugarte (No. 2)*, (1991) 1 All ER 557, 586 (House of Lords).
[125] Redfern, Hunter, et al, op. cit. fn 1, at p. 239, para 4–55.
[126] The Singaporean High Court decision of *Turner v Builders Federal* [1988] 1 SLR 532 could be interpreted in this light. The court inferred that the arbitrator had predetermined the issues and found a clear indication of bias (at para 102): 'there is no doubt in my mind that Mr Smith has approached this arbitration with a prejudiced mind, to the point of being hostile to one of the parties'. Another example commonly referred to by a number of commentators is *Re Catalina (Owners) and Norma M V (Owners)* [1938] 61 Lloyd's Law Reports 360 (King's Bench, Divisional Court), where the arbitrator, during the course of the proceedings, had been heard to express the view that all Portuguese people were liars.
[127] For example, the Model Law, Article 12(2).
[128] ACICA Rules Article 14.4; CIETAC Rules Article 26(6); HKIAC Rules Article 11.7; ICC Rules Article 11; ICA Rules, Rule 26; JCAA Rules, Rule 29(5); KCAB International Rules Article 13(5); SIAC Rules, Rule 12.
[129] UNCITRAL Arbitration Rules Article 12.
[130] VIAC Rules Article 11; ICSID Convention Article 58.
[131] As discussed below this is the procedure set out in the Model Law Article 13(2). See also generally Appendix 1 'Asia-Pacific arbitral institutions at a glance' which includes details on who determines challenges in accordance with each institution's rules.

occasionally purports to remain on the panel despite all parties agreeing to remove him.[132] A second possible scenario is that the arbitrator resigns. The arbitrator may not wish to continue the mandate if one party has lost confidence in him or her. A question arises as to whether such resignations should be accepted. The ICC Court does not always accept an arbitrator's resignation in these circumstances.[133] It is important to note that tendering a resignation after having been challenged should not be seen as an admission that the challenge was justified. Article 11(3) of the UNCITRAL Rules specifically provides in relevant part that:

> When an arbitrator has been challenged by one party, the other party may agree to the challenge. The arbitrator may also, after the challenge, withdraw from his office. <u>In neither case does this imply acceptance of the validity of the grounds for the challenge</u>. (Emphasis added).

6.114 The third scenario is perhaps the most frequent: the arbitrator does not resign and the opposing party contests the challenge. In this scenario a decision on the merits of the challenge will have to be taken.

6.115 The 2010 SIAC Rules 12 and 13 provide a typical example of the procedure for a challenge submitted to an arbitral institution:[134]

> *Notice of Challenge*
> 12.1 A party who intends to challenge an arbitrator shall send a notice of challenge within 14 days after the receipt of the notice of appointment of the arbitrator who is being challenged or, except as provided in Rule 10.6, within 14 days after the circumstances mentioned in Rule 11.1 or 11.2 became known to that party.
> 12.2 The notice of challenge shall be filed with the Registrar and shall be sent simultaneously to the other party, the arbitrator who is being challenged and the other members of the Tribunal. The notice of challenge shall be in writing and shall state the reasons for the challenge. The Registrar may order a suspension of the arbitration until the challenge is resolved.
> 12.3 When an arbitrator is challenged by one party, the other party may agree to the challenge. The challenged arbitrator may also withdraw from his office. In neither case does this imply acceptance of the validity of the grounds for the challenge...
>
> *Decision on Challenge*
> 13.1 If, within 7 days of receipt of the notice of challenge, the other party does not agree to the challenge and the arbitrator who is being challenged does not withdraw voluntarily within 7 days of receipt of the notice of challenge, the Committee of the Board [of SIAC] shall decide on the challenge.
> ...
> 13.5 The Committee of the Board's decision made under this Rule shall be final and not subject to appeal.

6.116 Pursuant to Rule 13.5, the decision of the Committee of the Board of SIAC is expressed to be final, expressly denying any opportunity of appeal to SIAC or

---
[132] Fry and Greenberg, op. cit. fn 11, at p. 27.
[133] Ibid., at p. 28.
[134] See also ACICA Rules Article 14; CIETAC Rules Article 26; HKIAC Challenge Rules; ICC Rules Article 11; JCAA Rules, Rule 29; KCAB International Rules Article 13.

perhaps even a court. If Rule 13.5 is intended to preclude the right of an appeal to the courts, then it appears to conflict with the opportunity provided in Article 13(3) of the Model Law to have a court review a challenge decision. Article 13(3), which is extracted below, provides that a party may, within 30 days, ask a court to review a decision that has rejected a challenge. The language of the Article strongly suggests that this right exists even where the challenge procedure has been agreed by the parties. It is therefore unclear whether Rule 13.5 of the SIAC Rules (or its equivalent in other institutional arbitration rules)[135] would be effective in preventing review by the courts under a provision of law such as Article 13(3) of the Model Law.[136]

6.117 Although it is not a feature of institutional arbitration rules in this region, some rules like those of the German Institution of Arbitration ('DIS Rules') invest the arbitral tribunal with power to rule on the challenge.[137] The challenged arbitrator remains on the arbitral tribunal during this process and participates in the decision. Although this may at first seem unusual, the same approach is used in Article 13(2) of the Model Law, which is set out below. A variation of this procedure is found in the Arbitration Rules of the Vietnam Arbitration Centre, which refer challenges first to the unchallenged arbitrators. The President of the Centre then effectively acts as an umpire if necessary.[138]

6.118 If the parties have chosen ad hoc arbitration, their chosen rules may provide for a challenge procedure. If the chosen arbitration rules are silent, or no rules have been chosen, it is necessary to examine the *lex arbitri*. Article 13 of the Model Law provides:

Article 13 – Challenge procedure
(1) The parties are free to agree on a procedure for challenging an arbitrator, subject to the provisions of paragraph (3) of this article.
(2) Failing such agreement, a party who intends to challenge an arbitrator shall, within fifteen days after becoming aware of the constitution of the arbitral tribunal or after becoming aware of any circumstance referred to in article 12(2), send a written statement of the reasons for the challenge to the arbitral tribunal. Unless the challenged arbitrator withdraws from his office or the other party agrees to the challenge, the arbitral tribunal shall decide on the challenge.
(3) If a challenge under any procedure agreed upon by the parties or under the procedure of paragraph (2) of this article is not successful, the challenging party may request, within thirty days after having received notice of the decision rejecting the challenge, the court or other authority specified in article 6 to decide on the challenge, which decision shall be subject to no appeal; while such a request is pending, the arbitral tribunal, including the challenged arbitrator, may continue the arbitral proceedings and make an award.

---

135 Similar provisions, although not referring expressly to 'appeals' are found for example in the ICC Rules Article 7(4); ACICA Rules Article 43.2; KCAB International Rules Article 10.3.
136 See also *Saipem S.p.A. v Bangladesh*, ICSID Case No. ARB/05/7, Award of 30 June 2009, discussed in Chapter 9, Section 9.2.2. With relevance to the determination of challenges to arbitrators, the ICSID tribunal found (at paras 137–144) that the ICC Court's authority as regards the determination of challenges is not exclusive under Bangladesh law. That ICSID tribunal's reasoning could be applied analogously to other laws.
137 DIS Rules Section 18.3.
138 VIAC Rules Article 11.

A party wishing to challenge an arbitrator should do so as soon as practicable 6.119
after it becomes aware of the facts leading to its concern. There are two primary
reasons to act promptly. First, there are likely to be significant costs involved
if it becomes necessary to remove an arbitrator in an arbitration that has been
proceeding for a long period of time. Second, by failing to take steps against an
arbitrator at the first opportunity, a party may lose its right to make the challenge.
Generally, arbitration rules provide that any challenge has to be brought within
a certain time (usually 15 or 30 days) from when the arbitrator was appointed
or, if later, from when the challenging party became aware of the facts giving
rise to the challenge.[139]

The New Zealand High Court case of *Grey District Council v Banks*[140] pro- 6.120
vides an example of the consequences of failing to challenge an arbitrator within
the required time limits. Although concerning a domestic arbitration, the relevant provisions[141] replicate Articles 12 and 13 of the Model Law in all material
respects. At its simplest, this case involved an arbitrator who had a clear and
undisputed financial interest in the outcome of the arbitration. Justice Panckhurst observed:[142]

> In my view it is beyond argument that Mrs Banks has a personal interest sufficient to
> justify challenge to her impartiality and independence in this case. Article 12 supplies
> the standard, namely 'if circumstances exist that give rise to justifiable doubts as to the
> arbitrator's impartiality or independence . . .'. Where, as here, the appointed arbitrator
> has a direct financial interest in the very question which is the subject matter of the
> arbitration then doubts about their impartiality and independence abound. It is difficult
> to imagine a more obvious case of personal interest.

However, Justice Panckhurst found that any action to remove the arbitrator must 6.121
fail because it had been brought outside the 15 day time limit provided in Article
13(2) (as per the Model Law). This caused him to further observe:[143]

> This Court may only decide on a challenge in terms of Art 13(3) where a challenged
> arbitrator refuses to withdraw from office. The exercise of that limited power is subject
> to compliance with the requisite time limits. There must be both a challenge made by
> a party within the 15 days provided and an appeal to this Court within 30 days. This, it
> seems to me, is an unsatisfactory situation but one from which there is no escape . . .

It should be noted that, although time limits such as these may preclude the 6.122
removal of an arbitrator, there may still be grounds to have an award set aside,
or to resist its enforcement, on the basis that the arbitrator was not independent.

---

139 ACICA Rules Article 14.1 (15 days); CIETAC Rules Article 26.3 (15 days); HKIAC Rules Article 11.5 (15 days); ICC Rules Article 11.2 (30 days); JCAA Rules, Rule 29.3 (two weeks); KCAB International Rules Article 13. 3 (15 days); SIAC Rules, Rule 11.1 (14 days).
140 [2003] NZAR 487. The case was then upheld on appeal.
141 Articles 12 and 13, First Schedule New Zealand Arbitration Act 1996.
142 [2002] NZAR 487 at 496.
143 Ibid., at 495.

6.1.3 Assessment of impartiality and independence by arbitral institutions

6.123   Since arbitration is in principle confidential, the decisions of arbitral institutions on any matters (including challenges) are usually kept confidential and not disclosed. Moreover, the general practice of arbitral institutions is not to provide reasons for their decisions, either to the challenged arbitrator, any other arbitrators or to the parties. Many institutional rules contain provisions like that found in Rule 8 of the HKIAC Challenge Rules:[144]

> The Council's determination in respect of any challenge shall be given to the parties in writing. The Council may in its sole discretion decide whether to support such determination with reasons.

6.124   There is movement within some institutions towards providing some guidance and insight into their thinking when determining challenges alleging partiality or a lack of independence. Institutions have adopted different paths to providing this information. In 2006 the LCIA announced that it would put in place procedures to begin publishing challenge decisions on its website.[145] Taking another approach, the ICC regularly publishes articles describing the ICC Court's practice and citing examples and trends relating to challenge decisions.[146] A number of the examples cited below are drawn from those publications.

6.125   Challenges against international arbitrators must be determined on a case by case basis. Guidance, whether in terms of articles by institutions or the actual publication of decisions, is to be welcomed and encouraged. However, there is a danger, particularly where individual decisions are published, that these may be seen as a body of precedent. A body of precedent could work contrary to the concept of case by case determination and might encourage reducing challenges to a matter of technicalities in precedents, which would be unfortunate. Furthermore, publishing individual challenge decisions might delay and complicate the issuing of those decisions and cause additional costs.[147]

6.126   In the highly supervised form of arbitration practised by the ICC Court, there is a number of stages at which the ICC Court may consider whether an arbitrator is independent. The first occasion is at the time of confirmation. Under the ICC Rules, nominated arbitrators do not formally commence their role until confirmed by the ICC Court or Secretary General (a similar approach is now taken in the SIAC Rules). As part of that confirmation process, the

---

144 Some rules provide that reasons need not be given (e.g. ACICA Rules Article 43.2; CIETAC Rules Article 26.6); while others provide that reasons will not be given (e.g. ICC Rules Article 7(4)). The JCAA Rules, KCAB International Rules and SIAC Rules do not state whether reasons will be provided.
145 As at the time of writing no decisions had been published by the LCIA.
146 See, e.g. Fry and Greenberg, op. cit. fn 11; Whitesell, op. cit. fn 105, at p. 7; D Hascher, 'ICC Practice in relation to the Appointment, Confirmation, Challenge and Replacement of Arbitrators', (1995) 6(2) *ICC International Court of Arbitration Bulletin* 4; S Bond, 'The Experience of the ICC in the Confirmation/Appointment Stage of an Arbitration' in *The Arbitral Process and the Independence of Arbitrators*, (1991) ICC Publication 472, p. 9.
147 For an explanation of the reasons why the ICC Court does not publish challenge decisions see Fry and Greenberg, op. cit. fn 11, at p. 30, and Whitesell, op. cit. fn 105, at p. 39.

nominated arbitrator is required to complete a statement of independence. If the nominated arbitrator discloses any matters, the statement of independence is referred to as a 'qualified statement of independence'. All statements of independence from party-nominated arbitrators (both qualified and unqualified) are sent to the parties prior to the ICC Court deciding whether to confirm the appointment. The parties then have an opportunity to object to the arbitrator's confirmation.

Examples of confirmation of ICC arbitrators despite objection from one of the parties include the following:[148] 6.127

(i) where the opposing party alleged that there had been prior contact between the appointing party and nominated arbitrator. The party and arbitrator explained, and the ICC Court found, that the contact had simply been that necessary to determine whether the arbitrator was available to serve in the case;

(ii) where an arbitrator had served in the same political party and same parliament as counsel for one of the parties; and

(iii) where it was alleged that the arbitrator had failed to disclose that he had co-authored a legal book with one of the parties' counsel. The arbitrator had also worked in the same firm as that counsel. The arbitrator was confirmed, taking into account that more than nine years had elapsed since the arbitrator and counsel had been members of the same firm.

In contrast, the ICC Court has refused to confirm nominations in instances where the matters raised could call into question the independence of the arbitral tribunal. Examples of non-confirmation include:[149] 6.128

(i) where an arbitrator was an acting as a director of a company that had an indirect shareholding in the respondent;

(ii) where an arbitrator's law firm was part of an alliance of law firms to which the firm representing one of the parties also belonged; and

(iii) where an arbitrator was already acting as a co-arbitrator in a related arbitration where he had been nominated by the same party.

The second stage at which the ICC Court considers the independence of arbitrators is when a party files a challenge pursuant to Article 11 of the ICC Rules. This rule is quite wide and also allows for challenges based on the conduct of the arbitration.[150] As the examples below demonstrate, there is a wide variety of grounds on which independence challenges are brought and dismissed by the ICC Court:[151] 6.129

---

[148] ICC International Court of Arbitration, 'Independence of Arbitrators', (2007), *ICC International Court of Arbitration Bulletin*, Special Supplement. See in particular Whitesell, op. cit. fn 105, pp. 7–42. Further and more recent examples are provided in Fry and Greenberg, op. cit. fn 11.
[149] ICC International Court of Arbitration, ibid. See in particular Whitesell, op. cit. fn 105, pp. 7–42. Further and more recent examples are provided in Fry and Greenberg, op. cit. fn 11.
[150] Removal of an arbitrator for technical misconduct is discussed below, see Section 6.2.1.
[151] ICC International Court of Arbitration, op. cit. fn 148. See in particular Whitesell, op. cit. fn 105. Further and more recent examples are provided in Fry and Greenberg, op. cit. fn 11.

(i) The ICC Court rejected a challenge where one party claimed that the chairperson had studied and lived for some years in the country where the other party was incorporated. This, it was alleged, caused doubts about his independence.

(ii) The ICC Court rejected a challenge to a chairperson who was also chairperson of another arbitration in which one of the parties' counsel was sitting as a co-arbitrator. Although the challenge failed, the ICC Court observed that this is the kind of matter that should be disclosed in the statement of independence.

(iii) The ICC Court rejected a challenge to a party-nominated arbitrator alleged to have had direct contact and discussions with the nominating party. The challenged arbitrator acknowledged that he had discussed the names of potential chairpersons of the arbitral tribunal with the party. However, he stated that he came to his own decision on who should take on that role during discussions with the other co-arbitrator and that his direct discussions with the party did not involve the substance of the dispute.

6.130 In the following cases, the ICC Court accepted the challenge:[152]

(i) where a party-nominated arbitrator revealed that he had previously acted for one party in a matter concerning an earlier but related transaction;

(ii) where a sole arbitrator whose law firm and the firm auditing one of the parties were part of the same law firm alliance; and

(iii) where a chairperson was from a law firm which was acting in a claim against the parent company of one of the parties to the arbitration. The challenge was upheld notwithstanding that the law suit was not related to the arbitration and it was a foreign office of the chairperson's firm.

6.131 Because other regional institutions have not so far published information about specific challenges, it is not possible to compare the ICC Court's approach with other institutional practice.

6.1.4 Assessment of impartiality and independence by domestic courts

6.132 An arbitrator's (or a judge's) impartiality and independence is a public policy matter. Therefore, in principle the courts maintain ultimate control over determining whether an arbitrator is independent and impartial. The fact that a challenge to an arbitrator is dismissed by an arbitral institution competent to decide the challenge in accordance with its rules does not in and of itself prevent a court from setting aside an award on the ground that, under its own standard, the challenge should have succeeded. It is therefore crucial to understand how courts assess these issues.

6.133 In reviewing the cases below, it is important to consider the perspective from which an arbitrator's impartiality or independence will be judged. This is not

---

[152] ICC International Court of Arbitration, op. cit. fn 148. See in particular Whitesell, op. cit. fn 105. Further and more recent examples are provided in Fry and Greenberg, op. cit. fn 11.

always clear. For example, English courts have on occasion been criticised for failing to consider properly the appearance of bias from the perspective of the party challenging the arbitrator.[153]

6.1.4.1 *The different tests used by domestic courts*

Courts in this region currently test the impartiality and independence of judges and arbitrators by the same standard. The convincing arguments against applying the same standard to arbitrators and judges are discussed below.[154] The benefit of doing so is that there are more examples of cases dealing with impartiality or independence that can be examined with a view to determining the approach of the relevant court. As the analysis below indicates, there appears to be at least two, and probably three, different tests currently used by courts in this region to determine whether an arbitrator (or judge) should be disqualified. 6.134

The recent history of the issue as it developed in England provides useful guidance as it has subsequently influenced the common law Asia-Pacific jurisdictions.[155] *R v Sussex Justices; Ex Parte McCarthy*[156] introduced what became known as the 'reasonable apprehension' test of bias.[157] Although the dominant test for a considerable period of time, it was never definitively affirmed as settled law. The alternative test had been couched in terms of a 'real likelihood' of bias.[158] Perhaps trying to bring the tests together, Lord Goff famously considered the issue in *R v Gough*.[159] Taking its name from the case, not the judge, the '*Gough* test' enquires 'whether there was any real danger of unconscious bias on the part of the decision maker . . .'.[160] Lord Goff explained that 'I prefer to state the test in terms of real danger rather than real likelihood, to ensure that the court is thinking in terms of possibility rather than probability of bias'.[161] 6.135

This test was followed in *Laker Airways Inc v FLS Aerospace Ltd*[162] and again affirmed in *AT & T Corporation and Lucent Technologies Inc v Saudi Cable Co.*[163] 6.136

---

153 A Merjian, 'Caveat Arbitrator: Laker Airways and the Appointment of Barristers as Arbitrators in Cases Involving Barrister Advocates from the same Chambers', (2000) 17 *Journal of International Arbitration* 31.
154 See Section 6.1.4.3.
155 See also S Luttrell, 'Go Back to Gough: An Argument for the "Real Danger" Test for Arbitrator Bias in the Common Law Seats of the Asia Pacific', (2008) 16 *Asia Pacific Law Review* 2.
156 [1924] 1 KB 356 (King's Bench, High Court).
157 This is sometimes termed the 'reasonable suspicion' test. As Justice Deane of the High Court of Australia noted in *Webb v The Queen* [1993] 181 CLR 41, at 68: 'I have used the word "apprehension" in preference to the word "suspicion" for the reason that the latter word is capable of conveying shades of meaning which are inappropriate in this context. As a practical matter, however, there is little, if any, difference between the content of the two words when prefaced by "reasonable".'
158 See, e.g. *Tracomin SA v Gibbs Nathaniel (Canada) Ltd* [1985] 1 Lloyd's Rep 586.
159 *R v Gough* [1993] AC 646. For a detailed discussion of the Gough test in international arbitration see S Luttrell, *Bias Challenges in International Arbitration – The Need for a 'Real Danger' Test*, Kluwer Law International, 2009.
160 *AT & T Corporation and Lucent Technologies Inc v Saudi Cable Co* [2000] EWCA Civ 154, 128.
161 *R v Gough* [1993] AC 646, at 737.
162 [1999] 2 Lloyd's Rep 45 (Queen's Bench, Commercial Court).
163 [2000] EWCA Civ 154 (Court of Appeal).

The *AT & T* case involved a challenge to the independence of the chairperson of an arbitral tribunal. The factual scenario is a classic example of why, in an increasingly complex global commercial world, the commercial and professional activities of the relatively small group of leading international arbitrators may give rise to challenges to their independence.[164] In 1992, the Saudi Arabian Government invited seven international telecommunications companies to tender for a project. Among the tenders were AT & T and Northern Telecom Ltd. The former was successful. A term of the tender required that certain supplies would be sourced from the Saudi Cable Co. A dispute arose between AT & T and the Saudi Cable Co, and the matter went to ICC arbitration in 1995. During the proceedings, AT & T became aware that the chairperson of the arbitral tribunal was a non-executive director of Northern Telecom Ltd – one of the unsuccessful tenderers. AT & T challenged the chairperson. The challenge was rejected by the English Court of Appeal, applying the *Gough* test.

6.137 The *Gough* test itself was reinterpreted in the House of Lords decision *Porter v Magill*.[165] In that case Lord Hope phrased the test as 'whether the fair-minded and informed observer, having considered the facts, would conclude that there was a real possibility that the arbitral tribunal was biased'.[166] The difference between this test and *Gough* is the perspective from which the alleged bias is to be considered. Under the *Gough* test, the court must determine whether it considers that there is a perception of bias. Applying *Porter*, the determination must be made from the standpoint of a fair-minded and informed but outside observer – in other words not the court itself. In another House of Lords decision, Lord Mance has implicitly noted that this is not an easy task:[167]

> But the fair-minded and informed observer is him or herself in large measure the construct of the court. Individual members of the public, all of whom might claim this description, have widely differing characteristics, experience, attitudes and beliefs which could shape their answers on issues such as those before the court, without their being easily cast as unreasonable. The differences of view in the present case illustrate the difficulties of attributing to the fair-minded and informed observer the appropriate balance between on the one hand complacency and naivety and on the other cynicism and suspicion.

6.138 Turning to the Asia-Pacific region, the leading decision on this issue in New Zealand is *Muir v Commissioner of Inland Revenue*[168] which expressly rejects the *Gough* test by overruling previous authority.[169] One aspect of this judgment could be read to infer that the *Porter v Magill* test and the reasonable apprehension test

---

164 For a similarly classic factual scenario from this region, see *Jung Science Information Technology Co Ltd v ZTE Corporation* HCCT 14/2008 (Hong Kong High Court, Court of First Instance) discussed at Section 6.1.4.2.
165 [2002] 2 AC 357.
166 See also *AWG Group Ltd (formerly Anglian Water Plc) v Morrison* [2006] EWCA Civ 6.
167 *R v Abdroikov, R v Green* and *R v Wilkinson* [2008] 1 All ER 315, at 81.
168 [2007] 3 NZLR 495 (Court of Appeal).
169 *Auckland Casino Ltd v Casino Control Authority* [1995] 1 NZLR 142 (Court of Appeal).

are one and the same.[170] However, the better reading is that the reasonable apprehension test now applies in New Zealand:[171]

> In our view, the correct inquiry is a two-stage one. First, it is necessary to establish the actual circumstances which have a direct bearing on a suggestion that the Judge was or may be seen to be biased. This factual inquiry should be rigorous, in the sense that complainants cannot lightly throw the 'bias' ball in the air. The second inquiry is to then ask whether those circumstances as established might lead a fair-minded lay observer to reasonably apprehend that the Judge might not bring an impartial mind to the resolution of the instant case. This standard emphasises to the challenged Judge that a belief in her own purity will not do; she must consider how others would view her conduct.

6.139 In Australia, the reasonable apprehension test is well established as the test applicable to judges. It is, however, likely that the test applicable to arbitrators will soon be the *Gough* test. In late 2009, a Bill was introduced into the Australian parliament to amend Australia's International Arbitration Act. One aspect specifically requiring amendment in the legislators' view was the test for arbitrator bias. The explanatory memorandum, which accompanied the bill, stated that the amended legislation would 'provide that the test for whether there are justifiable doubts as to the impartiality or independence of an arbitrator is the real danger of bias test set out in *R v Gough*'.[172] The significance of this change is the perspective from which the danger of bias is assessed. As noted above in the *Gough* test it is the perspective of the court and not a generic fair-minded observer.

6.140 The test in Singapore is termed 'reasonable suspicion'. It was noted with approval by the Singapore Court of Appeal in *Re Shankar Alan S/O Anant Kulkarni* that:[173]

> In the [Re Singh Kalpanath] decision, Chan Sek Keong J in fact emphasised that the concern was not whether there is in fact a real likelihood or possibility of bias, but simply whether a reasonable man without any inside knowledge might conclude that there was an appearance of it.

6.141 There is Hong Kong case law which appears either to confuse or merge the *Porter* and reasonable suspicion tests. In the 2007 decision of *Lee Hong Dispensary*

---

170 'We prefer the approach in *Porter v Magill* and *Webb* because of the way in which it confirms the appropriate "window" through which the relevant conduct is to be viewed: that is, it emphasises how something might reasonably be regarded by the public, in the form of the reasonable informed observer.' [2007] 3 NZLR 495, at 35. This comparison can be understood as limited to characterising the test from the perspective of a reasonable person rather than the court.
171 [2007] 3 NZLR 495, at 36 and 37.
172 Australian International Arbitration Amendment Bill 2009, Explanatory Memorandum, para 92. See also the Australian International Arbitration Amendment Bill 2009 Section 14. The amended section is expected to appear as Section 18A in the International Arbitration Act as amended.
173 [2006] SGHC 194, at 110. See also *Turner v Builders Federal* [1988] SLR 532 (High Court); *Jeyaretnam v Lee Kuan Yew* [1992] 2 SLR 310 (Court of Appeal); *Tang Kin Hwa v TCM Practitioners Board* [2005] 4 SLR 604 (High Court).

Superstore Co Ltd v Pharmacy and Poisons Board, a Court of First Instance decision, Justice A Cheung observed:[174]

> the applicable test for apparent bias may be found in *Deacons v White & Case Ltd Liability Partnership* [2004] 1 HKLRD 291. In that case, the Court of Final Appeal endorsed the 'reasonable apprehension test'. In short, the court must ascertain all the circumstances which have a bearing on the suggestion that the judge or tribunal was biased. It must then ask whether those circumstances would lead a fair-minded and informed observer to conclude that there was <u>a real possibility</u> that the judge or tribunal was biased. The material circumstances will include any explanation given by the judge or tribunal under review as to his knowledge or appreciation of those circumstances. Where that explanation is accepted by the applicant for review, it can be treated as accurate. Where it is not accepted, it becomes one further matter to be considered from the viewpoint of the fair-minded observer. The court does not have to rule whether the explanation should be accepted or rejected. Rather it has to decide whether or not the fair-minded observer would consider that there was a real possibility of bias notwithstanding the explanation advanced. (Emphasis added)

6.142 However, higher authority places the *Porter v Magill* version as the test applicable in Hong Kong. In 2005 Chief Justice Li, on behalf of the Court of Final Appeal, noted that '[t]he test for disqualification is whether the circumstances are such as would lead a reasonable, fair-minded and well-informed observer to conclude that there is a real possibility that the judge would be biased in dealing with the matter'.[175] He reaffirmed that position in *Suen Wah Ling t/a Kong Luen Construction Engineering Co v China Harbour Engineering Co (Group)*.[176]

6.143 Malaysian law is perhaps the hardest to identify with certainty. As in England, Malaysian courts have struggled to find a settled position. The Malaysian Federal court has described bias as 'a state of mind that is in some way predisposed to a particular result, or that is closed with regard to a particular issue'.[177] Cases from 2005 and 2006 suggest that the question to be asked is whether there is a 'real danger' of bias – in other words the *Gough* test.[178] However, in the 2007 case of *Seraya Sdn Bhd v Government of Sarawak*,[179] Justice Clement Skinner observed: 'So it can be seen that [. . .] it is necessary to apply the standard of a reasonable and fair minded person knowing all the relevant facts.' It should be noted that this 2007 decision is only High Court authority whereas the earlier 2006 case of *Dato' Tan Heng Chew v Tan Kim Hor*[180] is a Federal Court decision and thus more authoritative.

---

174 [2007] HKCU 379, at para 17.
175 *Ng Yat Chi v Max Share Ltd* [2005] HKCU 69, at para 121.
176 [2008] HKCU 570; see also *Jung Science Information Technology Co Ltd v ZTE Corporation* HCCT 14/2008.
177 *Tan Kim Hor v Tan Chong & Motor Co Sdn Bhd* [2003] 2 MLJ 278, at 285.
178 *Darshan Singh v Farid Kamal Hussain* [2005] 3 MLJ 502; *Majlis Peguam Malaysia v Raja Segaran* [2005] 1 MLJ 15; *Dato' Tan Heng Chew v Tan Kim Hor* [2006] MLJU 11.
179 [2007] MLJU 0595.
180 [2006] MLJU 11. This case explicitly rejects any need to modify the *Gough* test in line with the *Porter v Magill* changes.

The above analysis has shown that there are arguably three different tests currently applied in this region among common law jurisdictions – the *Gough* test, the *Porter v Magill* test and the reasonable apprehension test. One may question whether there are, in fact, three tests because, as noted above, various courts have a tendency to treat *Porter v Magill* and the reasonable apprehension test as the same. In our view, however, there are persuasive arguments that they are different. The reasonable apprehension test has a lower threshold. The *Porter v Magill* test effectively requires a finding that the fair-minded person would, as a matter of fact, consider that there was a real possibility of bias. In contrast, the reasonable apprehension test merely requires that a reasonable suspicion of bias might occur. These tests could conceivably lead to different outcomes. The distinction was carefully considered by Justice Deane in the Australian High Court decision of *Webb v The Queen*.[181] Justice Deane was contrasting the reasonable apprehension test with the *Gough* test, however in this respect *Porter v Magill* does not differ from *Gough*.

6.144

6.1.4.2 *Selected court decisions on partiality and lack of independence*

While the previous section assessed the tests applied by courts, this section provides regional and international court decisions in which parties have called into question (rightly or wrongly) the impartiality and/or independence of an arbitrator.

6.145

The 2008 Hong Kong decision of *Jung Science Information Technology Co Ltd v ZTE Corporation*[182] is an example of an unsubstantiated allegation of bias where there is some form of connection between counsel and an arbitrator. The High Court's Court of First Instance in Hong Kong considered a challenge against a well-known arbitrator from this region. The challenge was dismissed. The party challenging the arbitrator cited as one of its grounds for challenge an alleged friendship between the arbitrator and a partner in one of the law firms acting for the opposing party. To support its allegations the party argued that the arbitrator and the partner were both board members of HKIAC and that they had often both spoken at the same conferences. When dismissing the challenge the court observed:[183]

6.146

> It would not occur to the objective onlooker in possession of the following relevant facts and circumstances to even consider it possible that Mr Yang was influenced to favour ZTE with whom he had no relationship whatsoever merely because ZTE happened to be represented in the opening stage of the Arbitration by a solicitor with whom he had a social and professional relationship in arbitration-related matters:
> (1) The international arbitration circle in Hong Kong is small. Frequent contacts between persons which are active in this area are to be expected. Links and connections can arise without calling into question independence and impartiality between colleagues.

---
181 [1993] 181 CLR 41, at pp. 71–74.
182 HCCT 14/2008.
183 *Jung Science Information Technology Co Ltd v ZTE Corporation*, HCCT 14/2008 at 56.

(2) Both Mr Yang and Mr Moser (whose profile on the internet is adduced in evidence) are senior, highly experienced and well-respected practitioners in international arbitration in Hong Kong and overseas.
(3) Both can be expected to observe high standards of integrity.
(4) Given the time they have respectively been involved and the standing they have respectively attained in international arbitration in Hong Kong and elsewhere, the social and professional interactions described by Mr Yang are not and cannot be said to be out of the ordinary. One would have expected them to know or even be very familiar with each other.
(5) That relationship is open given what JSIT managed to find out about it from the internet and from instructing a local firm of solicitors.
(6) Freshfields and Mr Moser's representation of ZTE has likewise been open at all material times. Correspondence emanating from Freshfields were marked with a file reference which included what anyone more familiar with legal practice in Hong Kong would have realized to be Mr Moser's initials thereby signifying his involvement in the matter.
(7) Mr Yang was in fact nominated and appointed by the HKIAC, not by Freshfields.
(8) In any event, Mr Moser ceased acting for ZTE before the close of pleadings and before the Arbitration became procedurally contentious.
(9) The arbitral tribunal did rule against ZTE in favour of JSIT on whether the Jurisdictional Challenge should be decided as a preliminary issue and on five items of technical documents sought by JSIT from ZTE. (Emphasis added)

6.147 Another ground which might give rise to concerns about impartiality are those instances when an arbitrator has private contact with one party or appears to have received some sort of personal correspondence from that party. In the Singapore case of *Turner (East Asia) Pte Ltd v Builders Federal (Hong Kong) Ltd*, Judicial Commissioner Chan Sek Keong observed that '[w]hile I would agree that there is no absolute rule against an arbitrator corresponding directly with the parties, this, in my view, should only be done in very exceptional circumstances'.[184] At around the same time, the Western Australian Supreme Court found that the mere fact an arbitrator had become aware that one party had rejected a settlement offer did not give rise to a reasonable apprehension of bias.[185]

6.148 The 1997 Victorian Court of Appeal decision in *Gascor v Ellicott*[186] provides an interesting example of a prior relationship challenge. This Australian decision concerned an allegation of apprehended bias against an arbitrator. The arbitrator had previously acted as counsel for one of the parties in a different but not entirely unrelated arbitration. As a consequence, many of the same expert witnesses were expected to appear. When acting as counsel in the earlier arbitration, the arbitrator had had to cross-examine these witnesses apparently in a vigorous manner. A second ground for the challenge was that the arbitrator had failed to disclose this prior relationship. The matter was first raised before the arbitrator, who dismissed the challenge. The challenge was also unsuccessful

---
[184] [1988] 1 SLR 532, at 55 (High Court).
[185] *Pindan Pty Ltd v Uniseal Pty Ltd* [2003] WASC 168.
[186] [1997] 1 VR 332.

in the courts. The Victorian Court of Appeal found that '[a]lthough there were similarities in subject matter ... the circumstances did not show that a fair-minded member of the public might entertain a reasonable apprehension that, because of the arbitrator's participation as arbitrator ..., he might not bring an impartial and unprejudiced mind to the resolution of the issues raised in the present arbitration'.[187] More recently the Victorian Supreme Court rejected a challenge where the arbitrator had previously acted as counsel for a particular type of client.[188] In this case the concern appears to have been that the arbitrator's previous instructions from trade unions implied he held particular views. The challenge was rejected, particularly because none of the parties to the arbitration were trade unions.

Another interesting independence case is the English Court of Appeal decision in *Sumukan Ltd v Commonwealth Secretariat*.[189] Although ultimately turning on a number of different matters including questions of diplomatic immunity, the court did not accept that a clause which allowed only one party to appoint the entire arbitral tribunal was invalid. In that instance Lord Justice Toulson felt that the independent, fair-minded observer would look at all the circumstances including 'the eligibility of the person appointed'.[190] 6.149

The unsuccessful *Gascor* challenge referred to above can be contrasted with a challenge that was successful in fairly similar circumstances in the 2005 English decision *ASM Shipping Ltd v TTMI Ltd*.[191] In that case, the challenged arbitrator had previously been instructed by one of the firms of solicitors acting in the arbitration. The arbitrator's involvement in the earlier case was apparently quite brief. However, as one of the witnesses from the earlier arbitration was also to be a witness in the current arbitration, there was a concern of potential bias. During the earlier arbitration, particularly serious allegations had been made against this witness, and the implication of the challenge was that the arbitrator must have known about these allegations, and would not be able to dismiss them from his mind. The arbitrator could not recall ever previously meeting the witness and denied knowledge of the allegations. Despite this, the court found that a suspicion of bias was possible and removed the arbitrator. The decision has been strongly criticised.[192] 6.150

Another example of this situation comes from the District Court of The Hague.[193] Although a Dutch decision, it does have a strong connection to the Asia-Pacific. A Malaysian company was involved in an arbitration with the Republic of Ghana. The Republic of Ghana's submissions relied in part on an earlier published arbitral award in a completely separate arbitration but one 6.151

---

187 [1997] 1 VR 332, at 333.
188 *Able Demolitions & Excavations v State of Victoria* [2004] VSC 511.
189 [2007] EWCA Civ 1148.
190 [2007] EWCA Civ 1148, at 71.
191 [2005] EWHC 2238 (Comm).
192 H Dundas, 'Conflicts of Interest in International Arbitration – A Wrong Turning', February 2006, IBA Legal Practice Division, *Arbitration Committee Newsletter*, at p. 14.
193 District Court of Hague, pet. No. HA/RK 2004, 778.

which had considered a virtually identical issue. One of the current arbitrators disclosed that he had been engaged as counsel to have the earlier award set aside. The Republic of Ghana then challenged the arbitrator, and the matter ultimately ended up before the District Court of The Hague. The court conditionally upheld the challenge, whereupon the arbitrator resigned as counsel in the other matter. Commentary on this decision notes that in order for a challenge to be upheld on this basis the role of arbitrator and counsel should be concurrent.[194] That is, an arbitrator should not be disqualified simply because he or she has previously acted as counsel on a similar issue. This concurs with the Australian position noted above.[195] However, the IBA Guidelines place this in the waivable Red List.[196]

6.152 It was noted by the Supreme Court of Victoria decision in *Gascor v Ellicott*[197] that the failure of an arbitrator to disclose a matter that might give rise to justifiable doubts would not itself give rise to justifiable doubts. In practice, however, failure of an arbitrator to disclose facts or circumstances relevant to independence or impartiality will be treated with suspicion.

6.153 The issue of disclosure by an arbitrator was considered in early 2009 by the Paris Court of Appeal because the chairman of an ICC arbitral tribunal omitted to disclose, among other things, that the Beijing office of his law firm had advised the parent company of one of the parties on an unrelated project in China.[198] The chairman had disclosed that certain offices of his law firm had advised and represented several companies of the claimant's group. However, the respondent discovered from the program of an international conference that the chairman's law firm was currently acting for the claimant's affiliated companies in China. The respondent challenged the chairman under the procedures in the ICC Rules but the ICC Court rejected the challenge.

6.154 The respondent protested the challenge rejection during the arbitration and later sought to set aside the arbitral tribunal's partial award on the ground that the arbitral tribunal had been improperly constituted. The Paris Court of Appeal found that the chairman had not been exhaustive in his verification of potential conflicts of interest. The court noted, but did not give significant weight to, the fact that the chairman's law firm employs over 2200 lawyers in some 32 countries, and that the chairman probably had no personal knowledge of the Chinese matter in question. The court concluded that 'by reason of the lack of independence of the arbitrator, the arbitral tribunal has been irregularly constituted ... [and] the partial award of 10 December 2007 must be set aside'. The court also emphasised that an arbitrator's duty to disclose facts likely to constitute a conflict of interest exists throughout the arbitration. One cannot simply rely on the declaration of independence provided at the appointment stage. It should be noted

---

194 IBA Legal Practice Division, *Arbitration Committee Newsletter*, March 2005.
195 The case referred to earlier is *Able Demolitions & Excavations v State of Victoria* [2004] VSC 511.
196 See Section 5.2.2.
197 [1997] 1 VR 332.
198 Paris Court of Appeal, 12 February 2009 (07/22164), (authors' translation).

that this decision has been appealed to the Cour de Cassation, France's highest court.

6.1.4.3 *Inappropriateness of using the same bias test for judges and arbitrators*

6.155 It was noted above that courts in this region generally apply the same test for independence and impartiality to both judges and arbitrators.[199] Indeed, courts in most jurisdictions apply the same test whether the person in question is a judge, arbitrator, juror or an administrative official with delegated authority. Despite this trend, there are compelling differences suggesting that arbitrators should be treated somewhat differently.

6.156 Arbitrators are not judges. Judges are generally required to take an oath of office. As the Scottish Court of Session has stated:[200]

> The judicial oath is an important protection, not only against actual bias, but also against apparent bias, because it is not only in many ways definitive of a judge's duty, it also so imbues the judge that it becomes his or her second nature, unconsciously as well as consciously, to abide by it. Obviously, the judicial oath, and all that it carries with it, cannot serve as a complete guarantee of impartiality, but in our opinion the fair-minded and informed observer, taking account of these considerations, would give it great weight. Such an observer would also recognise the desirability of a judge keeping in touch with the world beyond the courts, and that his or her personal interests and experience may lead to membership of or involvement with external organisations.

6.157 The last sentence of the extract is particularly poignant to this discussion. It is certainly true that judges should keep in touch with the world beyond the courts, but they are not expected to maintain an active, financial role in that world as ordinary citizens might do. In contrast, arbitrators are neither tenured adjudicators nor bound by a judicial oath and are often professionally engaged in various spheres of business, finance and industry. Indeed, it may be precisely because of their commercial (and *not* judicial) experience that arbitrators are chosen. This view is echoed in changes to the Australian International Arbitration Act. The explanatory memorandum to the amendment bill stated:[201]

> Equating arbitrators with judges is not consistent with the principles underpinning arbitration. While there is no doubt that an arbitrator should be impartial, arbitrators will be selected by the parties in some instances because of their specific knowledge of an industry or particular arrangements. More typically an arbitrator will be a senior member of an international law firm, barrister, expert in a particular field or an academic. Accordingly, it is appropriate to apply a standard different than that for judges to such persons.

6.158 On the opposite side of the debate are those, such as a respected arbitrator from this region,[202] who have suggested that arbitrators should be held to stricter

---
199 See also Luttrell, 2008, op. cit. fn 155.
200 *Helow v Advocate General* [2007] CSIH 5, at para 35.
201 International Arbitration Amendment Bill 2009 (Australia), Explanatory Memorandum, para 89.
202 FS Nariman, 'Standards of Behaviour of Arbitrators', (1988) 4(4) *Arbitration International* 311.

standards than judges. This line of argument suggests that because arbitrators are part of the commercial world they are more exposed to temptation.

6.159 Both of these positions are considered to be extremes by those who argue that the current approach adopted by, for example, the English courts is the middle and appropriate position.[203]

6.160 Parties who have chosen arbitration should generally be understood to accept and give little, if any, weight to some of the more distant connections that might nevertheless force the recusal of a judge. As previously noted, the pool of highly experienced international arbitrators is relatively small, although rapidly growing. So, on the one hand, the same people often find themselves involved in arbitrations as either arbitrator or counsel; and on the other hand, conflicting out too many arbitrators may result in inexperienced or otherwise inappropriate appointments.

6.1.5 The standard for party-nominated co-arbitrators

6.161 It is not clear whether the standard for deciding whether an arbitrator is independent or impartial should be applied equally to all arbitrators. In some jurisdictions like the US, there is sometimes said to be a greater expectation and therefore perhaps tolerance that party-nominated arbitrators will pursue the interests of the nominating party. In this region the issue has been addressed in New Zealand, where all arbitrators are held to the same standard of impartiality and independence. The following passage from *Banks v Grey District Council* can be interpreted as meaning the same standards apply to the entire tribunal, and may well find favour in other regional courts – certainly those of the common law tradition. The New Zealand Court of Appeal held:[204]

> ... each arbitrator has a fundamental duty to act fairly and impartially. This duty is at the essence of arbitration, and extends to party-appointed arbitrators. The observation of Tompkins J in *Tolmarsh Developments Ltd v Stobbs* [1990] LVC 835 at p 838 is in point:
>
> 'At the stage when the two arbitrators have entered upon the reference and are endeavouring to reach agreement, it is essential that they must be, and must be seen to be, acting impartially, objectively and with an absence of bias.'

6.162 Even when nominated by a party, an arbitrator is under a duty to be and remain impartial and independent. A party-nominated arbitrator does not 'represent' that party within the arbitral tribunal. It was noted above in Section 3.2.2 that it is in fact not in the nominating party's interests to choose a biased arbitrator. Most experienced arbitrators say that they do not feel a particular duty toward the party that nominated them, but tend to pay particular attention to the arguments presented by that party. This is perfectly acceptable and does not mean that the arbitrator will necessarily favour the position of the nominating party or try to influence the other arbitrators in that respect. The same standard for impartiality

---

[203] S Singhal, 'Independence and Impartiality of Arbitrators', (2008) 11(3) *International Arbitration Law Review* 124, at p. 125.
[204] [2004] 2 NZLR 19, at para 27.

and independence can therefore be applied to all arbitrators, regardless of who nominated the arbitrator.

6.1.6 Impartiality and arb-med or med-arb

6.163 Arb-med is a dispute resolution process which combines arbitration and mediation.[205] The mediation, if it occurs, will take place with the parties' consent at an appropriate stage during the arbitration proceedings. A more common variation is med-arb, where arbitration is preceded by mediation. Issues of impartiality will not arise in connection with the arb-med or med-arb processes if the arbitrator and mediator are different people. But it may be the same individual who is asked to wear both hats. In those circumstances the question of impartiality becomes very real.

6.164 In mediation, parties frequently have a private, confidential caucus with the mediator. This is a virtual antithesis of arbitration procedures which require all communications to take place with all parties present (or in copy in the case of written communications). One significant concern is the fear that one party might, in private, give the arbitrator important information that the opposing party is unaware of, and is therefore unable to respond to and clarify. Thus, at first glance it seems unlikely that mediation and arbitration could co-exist with the same individual taking on both roles.

6.165 The standard approach of *lex arbitri* in jurisdictions where arb-med or med-arb is permitted is simply to require that the parties agree in writing to the arbitrator acting also as a mediator. However, among arbitral legislation around the world, two countries in this region stand out for their guidance and regulation on this issue. Those jurisdictions are Hong Kong and Singapore.[206] Both of these jurisdictions provide a mandatory waiver. By entering into an agreement to allow the arbitrator to act as a mediator, the parties have waived their right to challenge the arbitrator on that basis. Both jurisdictions also stipulate that the arbitrator must reveal to all parties any information considered to be relevant to the arbitration prior to recommencing the arbitral process after a mediation attempt. In both pieces of legislation this is a mandatory provision from which the parties cannot derogate.[207]

6.166 Irrespective of whether the *lex arbitri* provides guidance on how the arb-med process should be conducted, the question remains whether it is realistically possible for an arbitrator not to form certain views subsequent to a mediation attempt. Will arbitrators be able to avoid being influenced by information disclosed to them by a party in a private caucus session during a mediation? As a general rule the answer to that question may be yes. As Rosoff has observed:[208]

---

[205] Arb-med is explained and considered in Chapter 7, Section 6.12.
[206] The Hong Kong legislation is extracted in Chapter 7 at para 7.92. Section 16 of the Singapore International Arbitration Act. See generally J Rosoff, 'Hybrid Efficiency in Arbitration: Waiving Potential Conflicts for Dual Role Arbitrators in Med-Arb and Arb-Med Proceedings', (2009) 26(1) *Journal of International Arbitration* 89, at p. 98.
[207] Rosoff, ibid., at p. 100.
[208] Ibid., at p. 97 (references omitted).

294   INTERNATIONAL COMMERCIAL ARBITRATION

Disregarding information is a required skill that arbitrators should possess. Arbitrators may be required to consciously disregard information that is not presented during arbitral proceedings, such as public documents, information in the media and previous experience during the course of 'normal' arbitration proceedings. Additionally, arbitrators may also be required to disregard evidence they deem inadmissible after first reviewing the evidence for admissibility.

6.167 As a practical matter, it would seem highly advisable for arbitrators to seek not only the parties' agreement in writing, but also to have the parties waive challenge rights which may arise from the mediation process. Naturally, such a waiver would not affect the arbitrator's duty to act independently and impartially.[209] Arbitrators might alternatively consider inviting the parties to adopt provisions similar to those found in the Hong Kong and Singaporean legislation.[210]

6.2 Challenges for misconduct

6.168 Most arbitration rules and laws provide a mechanism for removing arbitrators for reasons other than relating to their independence or impartiality. Arbitrators can be removed for misconduct or when they fail to perform their functions, or fail to perform them in good time.

6.169 After examining what constitutes misconduct and the procedure for such challenges, this section provides examples of arbitral institution and court decisions on misconduct.

6.2.1 Definition and procedure

6.170 Misconduct is not a term used in the Model Law or international arbitration statutes generally. However, it remains relatively common in domestic arbitration statutes. Singapore's domestic legislation no longer uses the term misconduct but, when it did, in 2002 the Singapore High Court observed:[211]

> There is no statutory definition of what constitutes 'misconduct' but this term has been discussed in many cases and academic texts and there is a clear understanding of what it means in relation to the behaviour of an arbitrator in respect of himself or the proceedings. It should be noted at once that to find misconduct on the part of the arbitrator does not of itself impute any slur on his character. Misconduct can be found in respect of the technical handling of the arbitration and need not be a matter of bias or prejudice or other disreputable action on the part of the arbitrator.
>
> No actual bias or partiality need be shown as long as the court is satisfied from the conduct of the arbitrator, either by his words, his action or inaction or his handling of the proceedings, that he displayed a real likelihood that he might not be able to act judicially.

---

209 Ibid., p. 96.
210 See generally M Hwang, 'The Role of Arbitrators as Settlement Facilitators – Commentary', (2004) 12 ICCA Congress Series 571.
211 *Koh Bros Building and Civil Engineering Contractor Pte Ltd v Scotts Development (Saraca) Pte Ltd* [2002] 4 SLR 748, at p. 755.

As the above citation suggests, there is occasionally overlap in domestic court case law between decisions dealing with an allegation of partiality or dependence and issues of misconduct. In some legal systems, the courts consider partiality or dependence as a species of misconduct. 6.171

Article 14 of the Model Law provides for removal of an arbitrator who 'becomes de jure or de facto unable to perform his functions or for other reasons fails to act without undue delay'. The mechanism in Article 14 is very different from Article 13 (which deals with challenges as to independence and impartiality) because it provides a direct route to the court and is not time limited. However, it does not give the court a supervisory role as the article is not invoked by technical misconduct – that is, the court cannot assess whether the arbitrator is conducting the proceedings in an appropriate manner. A court is only able to intervene to keep the arbitration moving when it has effectively stopped – albeit by the drastic measure of removing the arbitrator. 6.172

Although the Singapore (domestic) Arbitration Act adopts much of the Model Law, Section 16 follows the English model.[212] In the Singaporean decision of *Yee Hong Pte Ltd v Powen Electrical Engineering Pte Ltd*,[213] the court examined the differences between the former Singaporean legislation governing domestic arbitration and the then new legislation. After noting that the word 'misconduct' had been removed from the legislation it observed that the test was now one of 'substantial injustice':[214] 6.173

> Under s 16(1)(b) of the Act, an applicant has to show that the arbitrator's conduct of the proceedings has caused or will cause him to suffer substantial injustice. Loss of confidence in an arbitrator's ability to come to a fair and balanced conclusion is itself not capable of being substantial injustice. Dyson J in *Conder Structures v Kvaerner Construction Ltd* [1999] ADRLJ 305 said, and I adopt his statement, that loss of confidence in an arbitrator is neither a sufficient nor a necessary condition of substantial injustice. Previously, as long as the court was satisfied that from the conduct of the arbitrator a

---

212 English Arbitration Act 1996 Section 24(1)(d).
Section 16 of the Singapore Arbitration Act states:
16. (1) A party may request the Court to remove an arbitrator –
    (a) who is physically or mentally incapable of conducting the proceedings or where there are justifiable doubts as to his capacity to do so; or
    (b) who has refused or failed –
        (i) to properly conduct the proceedings; or
        (ii) to use all reasonable despatch in conducting the proceedings or making an award, and where substantial injustice has been or will be caused to that party.
    (2) If there is an arbitral or other institution or person vested by the parties with power to remove an arbitrator, the Court shall not exercise its power of removal unless it is satisfied that the applicant has first exhausted any available recourse to that institution or person.
    (3) While an application to the Court under this section is pending, the arbitral tribunal, including the arbitrator concerned may continue the arbitration proceedings and make an award.
    (4) Where the Court removes an arbitrator, the Court may make such order as it thinks fit with respect to his entitlement, if any, to fees or expenses, or the repayment of any fees or expenses already paid.
    (5) The arbitrator concerned is entitled to appear and be heard by the Court before it makes any order under this section.
    (6) No appeal shall lie against the decision of the Court made under subsection (4).
213 [2005] 3 SLR 512.
214 Ibid., at 527.

reasonable person would think that he had displayed real likelihood of not being able to act judicially, that was enough to remove him for misconduct. That is no longer the case. The test now is different.

6.174 Despite this, it may be possible to argue that apparent breaches of natural justice are the result of bias and therefore impartiality.[215] Such an approach would avail the complainant of the procedures in Article 13 of the Model Law. As noted before there is occasional overlap between misconduct and bias.

6.175 An evident policy of the Model Law is to ensure that the arbitration proceeds through to an award. For example, a challenged arbitrator is empowered to proceed and deliver an award notwithstanding a pending challenge against the arbitrator.[216] However, this does not necessarily prevent a party from challenging the award for that reason after it has been delivered. In the New Zealand High Court decision of *Grey District Council v Banks*[217] (the appeal from which was referred to above), Justice Pankhurst specifically stated that he made no comment on whether failing to object in time would affect any later challenge to an award.

6.176 Most arbitration rules also deal with the situation where an arbitrator misconducts the proceedings in some way. Article 15(2) of the ACICA Rules provides a typical example:[218]

> In the event that an arbitrator fails to act or in the event of the de jure or de facto impossibility of him or her performing his or her functions, the procedure in respect of the challenge and replacement of an arbitrator as provided in the preceding Articles shall apply.

6.177 Article 14(2) of the KCAB International Rules vests the same power in the institution. However, it does not indicate exactly how that power is to be exercised:

> The Secretariat may remove any arbitrator who fails to perform his or her duties or unduly delays in the performance of his or her duties, or is legally or actually unable to perform his or her duties.

6.178 Arbitrators are usually only removed on the application of a party to the proceeding. The above provision does not make clear whether a replacement can be on the KCAB's own initiative. Article 27(1) of the CIETAC Rules is similarly unclear. The ICC Court's power to remove an arbitrator on its own initiative is examined in the next section. The Indian Council of Arbitration Rules,[219] the JCAA Rules[220]

---

215 See observations made in *Mitsui Engineering & Shipbuilding Co Ltd v Easton Graham Rush* [2004] 2 SLR 14, at 26.
216 See, e.g. *Mitsui* ibid., where an interim injunction to prevent a challenged arbitrator from proceeding to an award was refused.
217 [2003] NZAR 487.
218 See also for example: PDRCI Rules Article 13(2); SIAC Rules, Rule 13(2); UNCITRAL Rules Article 13(2); 2010 UNCITRAL Arbitration Rules Article 12(3); and ICC Rules Article 12(2). The 2010 SIAC Rules, Rule 14.2 notably also expressly refers to fulfilling functions within prescribed time limits.
219 ICA Rules, Rule 27.
220 JCAA Rules, Rule 30.

and the Rules of Arbitration of the Bangladesh Council of Arbitration[221] include similar provisions.

6.2.2 Arbitral institution decisions on misconduct

As noted above, the fact that arbitration is in principle confidential means that published decisions of arbitral institutions are rare. Nonetheless, some examples of ICC Court decisions on the removal of arbitrators have been made public.

Article 12(2) of the ICC Rules provides that an arbitrator will be replaced 'on the Court's own initiative when it decides that he is prevented de jure or de facto from fulfilling his functions, or that he is not fulfilling his functions in accordance with the Rules or within the prescribed time limits'. According to Fry and Greenberg, 'the most common ground for initiating replacement proceedings is when the arbitrator is causing unacceptable delays, is not responding to correspondence from the Secretariat and/or the parties, or is not conducting the arbitration in accordance with the Rules'.[222] Article 12(2) resulted in the removal of an arbitrator by the ICC Court on 19 occasions between 1998 and 2008. The following represent recent examples:[223]

(i) Due to a series of disagreements among them, the members of the arbitral tribunal were having difficulties working together, and there were serious delays in the completion of a majority award in accordance with the ICC Rules. The ICC Court replaced the chairman of the arbitral tribunal. With a strong, fresh chairman, the case quickly moved back on track.

(ii) In another case, replacement proceedings were initiated on the basis that the arbitrator was not available for a hearing at any of the times requested by the parties. One party pointed out this scheduling difficulty to the Secretariat and the ICC Court decided to initiate replacement proceedings. The sole arbitrator immediately resigned.

(iii) In yet another case, the sole arbitrator had little previous experience acting as an international arbitrator. This showed in the way that he managed (or failed to manage) the file. Doubt existed as to whether the sole arbitrator had verified that his correspondence reached the intended addressees and whether messages left with his assistant reached him. Furthermore, the sole arbitrator's statements on jurisdiction in the draft terms of reference suggested prejudgment of the issue. The sole arbitrator resigned after the replacement proceedings were commenced.

(iv) There was also a case in which the ICC Court decided to initiate replacement proceedings against the co-arbitrator nominated by the respondent after he twice cancelled his participation in the hearing on the merits at the eleventh hour, appearing to prioritise his other professional activities. The situation caused delays and additional costs for the parties and other members of the arbitral tribunal. After the ICC Court had initiated the replacement

---

221 BCA Rules, Rule 9.8.1.
222 Fry and Greenberg, op. cit. fn 11, at p. 29.
223 Ibid.

proceedings, but before all of the parties' comments had been sought for the purposes of the ICC Court's final decision on the removal, the respondent agreed with the claimant's proposal that the arbitrator be replaced by agreement of the parties under Article 12(1) of the ICC Rules.

6.181 Not all of the above-mentioned examples would fall under a typical definition of misconduct, however they illustrate how an institutional arbitrator removal provision can be utilised.

6.2.3 Court decisions on misconduct

6.182 Most allegations of arbitrator misconduct heard before courts tend to involve matters of procedure. A common expression associated with court-based applications of this kind is that a party has 'lost confidence' in the arbitrator's ability to perform his or her duties. This appears to have derived from the notion of misconducting the arbitration.

6.183 During an unsuccessful challenge attempt in *Anwar Siraj v Ting Kang Chung*[224] where incompetence was alleged, it was noted by the Singapore High Court that:

> A subjective lack of confidence in the arbitrator by one party is not a sufficient ground to remove him. The test is an objective one and there must exist real grounds for which a reasonable person would think there is a real likelihood that the arbitrator could not or would not fairly determine the issue on the basis of the evidence and the arguments to be adduced before him (*Hagop Ardahalian v Unifert International SA* (The 'Elissar') [1984] 2 Lloyd's Rep 84 at 89).
>
> The applicant must show that his decision was likely to have been coloured by something which should have no part at all in a fair decision-making process.

6.184 In 2001, in what was also a failed attempt to remove an arbitrator, but this time in the High Court of Hong Kong, Justice Burrell observed:[225]

> [Challenging an arbitrator] is a serious application to make and would only be granted in exceptional circumstances. In this case, it seems to me that the application is made for no better reason than the arbitrator consistently made findings contrary to the applicant's submissions (which they no doubt felt were correct) and they therefore lost confidence. What they lost confidence in was not the arbitrator's ability to discharge his duties properly but in the prospects of him making findings in their favour.

6.185 More recently, in *Gingerbread Investments Ltd v Wing Hong Interior Contracting Ltd*[226] Justice Burrell was called on again to consider an application alleging misconduct. On that occasion it was noted that a 'mere error of law cannot constitute misconduct ... but relying on utterly irrelevant evidence *might* provide evidence of misconduct'.[227]

---

[224] [2003] 2 SLR 287, at 297.
[225] *CCECC (HK) Ltd v Might Foundate Development Ltd* [2001] HKCU 916, at para 62.
[226] HCCT 14/2008 (Hong Kong, High Court).
[227] HCCT 14/2008 at 23, 24 (original emphasis).

6.186   An example of a regional court ordering the removal of arbitrators is *Sea Containers Ltd v ICT Pty Ltd*.[228] The decision was controversial not so much for the legal outcome but rather the New South Wales Court of Appeal's scathing review of the arbitral tribunal's conduct. In that case, the members of the arbitral tribunal put fee proposals to the parties prior to their appointment in the ad hoc arbitration. The parties agreed to these proposals and the arbitral tribunal was constituted. After the arbitration had commenced the arbitral tribunal asked the parties to agree to pay both hearing cancellation fees and security for the arbitrators' costs – neither of which had been contemplated in the original fee agreement. There was disagreement about whether the arbitral tribunal could require the parties to make these payments, and various proposals were put and withdrawn at different stages by each of the parties. Eventually one party agreed to pay extra fees but the other did not. While this was occurring, the parties appeared to be making progress towards settling the case. When the parties sought a stay of the proceedings, the arbitral tribunal refused to make the consent order unless both parties agreed to the payment of cancellation fees. The party that refused to agree challenged the arbitral tribunal, arguing that as a certain level of hostility between that party and the arbitral tribunal had developed, that party was concerned that it might not receive equal treatment.[229] The New South Wales Court of Appeal removed all three members of the arbitral tribunal.

6.187   The arbitral tribunal in *ICT* was comprised of three arbitrators with a significant amount of combined arbitration (both domestic and international) and judicial experience. It is therefore somewhat surprising that the situation was allowed to develop. The issue could have been avoided had the arbitrators addressed premature termination in their initial fee agreements. Such a provision was, and still is, commonplace in ad hoc arbitrator fee arrangements. The New South Wales Court of Appeal in *ICT* cited with approval the following passage from Mustill and Boyd written in 1989:[230]

> These are all cases in which the arbitrator seeks to be paid for work done before the reference came to an end. It is, however, possible that the arbitrator will look for more than this. He may argue that but for the premature termination of the reference he would have been entitled to earn additional fees, and that the loss of fees is something for which he should be compensated. Such an argument may in isolated cases reflect a genuine hardship. The arbitrator may have been asked to set aside several weeks for the hearing. If the dispute is settled immediately beforehand, the arbitrator may not be able to fill the space with sufficiently remunerative work. The Court would no doubt feel sympathy in such a case, but it is unlikely to provide redress. A claim in damages would be hopeless, for even if the relationship could properly be explained in terms of contract, it would be absurd to contend that the parties committed a breach by failing to continue with the reference of a dispute which for practical purposes had ceased to exist: for example, because it was settled or because in the exercise of a statutory

---

228 [2002] NSWCA 84 (Australia).
229 For a further detailed discussion of this case see S Greenberg, 'Latest Developments in International Arbitration Down Under', (2003) 7(2) *Vindobona Journal*, at p. 287.
230 MJ Mustill and SC Boyd, *The Law and Practice of Commercial Arbitration in England*, 2nd edn, Butterworths, 1989, at pp. 243–44.

or common law jurisdiction the court had prevented it from being pursued. Nor is the proposition more attractive if the relationship is one of status, rather than contract. Public policy demands that the arbitrator should be paid for what he has done, but not that he should be paid for what he has not done. Indeed, considerations of policy point the other way, for the Court would not wish to confer on the arbitrator a right to compensation, the existence of which might inhibit the freedom of the parties to settle the dispute as they think best, or to invoke the supervisory jurisdiction of the Court when circumstances so required. Much the better view, we suggest, is to treat the risk of a settlement as an occupational risk of arbitrating. If a dispute is so large and the potential hardship to the arbitrator so great the risk appears unacceptable, there is nothing to prevent the arbitrator from stipulating as a condition for agreeing to accept the appointment that he shall be recompensed for keeping his time available.

6.188 The question of arbitrator fees has also been considered in detail in Switzerland. The Swiss Federal Tribunal found that a challenge to an arbitrator's fees did not constitute reasonable grounds for affecting independence or impartiality.[231] In this case a partially successful claimant was unhappy with the award of damages it received and sought to challenge the arbitral tribunal's independence. The arbitral tribunal had decided in a partial award that the respondents were liable for wrongful contract termination. It subsequently turned to the quantification of damages. During this second stage of the proceedings, the claimant kept increasing the amount in dispute. Concurrently, the arbitral tribunal also requested several advances on its fees and costs. The claimant repeatedly protested against those amounts, and requested the reduction of what it alleged was an excessive hourly rate fixed by the arbitral tribunal. In the final award, the claimant was granted very little compared to what was claimed, and was ordered to bear the entirety of the arbitration costs and the respondents' legal costs.

6.189 The claimant argued, in its challenge before the Swiss Federal Tribunal, that there were reasonable doubts as to the impartiality and independence of the arbitrators. Its argument relied in part on an allegation that the arbitral tribunal applied an excessive hourly rate only after the claimant's request for hours spent on the case. It also alleged a conflict of interest between the claimant and the arbitral tribunal as to the fixing of fees. The Swiss Federal Tribunal dismissed the claim, emphasising that a dispute as to an arbitrator's fees is not, of itself, a ground that would affect independence or impartiality.

6.190 In the 1998 Hong Kong decision of *Charteryard Industrial Ltd v Incorporated Owners of Bo Fung Gardens*,[232] the court removed an arbitrator for misreading the arbitration rules and failing to give reasons for his decision. It was noted that simply misreading the rules would not have been sufficient on its own. In a similar vein, but perhaps more controversially, the arbitrator in the Malaysian case of *Sineo Enterprise Sdn Bhd v Jayarena Construction Sdn Bhd*[233] was removed on the basis that an arbitrator does not have the power to adopt a procedure that involves no oral hearing without the parties' consent. The arbitrator had decided

---

231 4P.263/2002, *A Ltd v B SA*, (unreported Swiss Supreme Court, 10 June 2003).
232 [1998] 4 HKC 171 (Court of First Instance).
233 [2005] MLJU 216 (High Court).

that an interlocutory application did not require an oral hearing, even though one party had repeatedly sought one. Other examples include the Australian state of New South Wales Supreme Court decision in *Reganam Pty Ltd v Crossing*[234] where the court was satisfied that the arbitrator was 'unsuitable' for the particular dispute.[235] In that instance the judge described errors made by the arbitrator in the award as 'manifest and it is not unfair to describe them as fundamental and elementary'.[236]

7 Resignation and replacement of arbitrators

Challenging an arbitrator is not the only circumstance in which a vacancy may occur on an arbitral tribunal. An arbitrator may resign his or her appointment, be subjected to an agreement by the parties to replace him or her, or may pass away during the course of the arbitration. This usually leads to replacement.

6.191

7.1 Resignation of arbitrators

It is always possible for an arbitrator to resign. The decision to resign is significant and should not be taken lightly. An arbitrator should only resign in circumstances where the integrity or efficiency of the arbitral process would be compromised by the arbitrator's continued involvement. For example, this might include situations where a conflict of interest (real or perceived) arises, or the arbitrator is appointed as a judge or to some other public position which will demand significant time commitments. An arbitrator might also resign due to illness or when his or her relationship with the other members of the arbitral tribunal becomes difficult or unprofessional; for example where a chairperson of an arbitral tribunal cannot control or work with his co-arbitrators.

6.192

Two arbitral institutions reserve the power to refuse to accept an arbitrator's tender of resignation. They are the Bangladesh Council of Arbitration[237] and the ICC Court.[238] Fry and Greenberg point out that between 1998 and 2008 the ICC Court received 208 tenders of resignation, five of which were rejected.[239] There was a further rejection in 2009. The rejected resignations tend to be where an arbitrator offers to resign after having been challenged and the ICC Court considers that this is not warranted. Examples of accepted resignations include where a conflict of interest has arisen or where an arbitrator feels that the complexity of the case has exceeded his qualifications. Arbitrators may also

6.193

---

234 [2007] NSWSC 582.
235 Another Australian decision to use the phrase 'suitable' was *Enterra Pty Ltd v ADI Ltd* [2002] NSWSC 700, however in that case it was noted that an arbitrator was not unsuitable simply because of difficulties with available times to conduct the arbitration.
236 *Reganam Pty Ltd v Crossing* [2007] NSWSC 582, at para 68.
237 BCA Rules, Rule 9.8.1.
238 ICC Rules Article 12.1.
239 Fry and Greenberg, op. cit. fn 11, at p. 28.

resign after the ICC Court commences proceedings to remove and replace the arbitrator, as foreseen in Article 12(2) of the ICC Rules. In one ICC case, the entire arbitral tribunal tendered its resignation after its award on jurisdiction was set aside by a court at the seat of arbitration.[240] The ICC Court accepted the resignation of all three arbitrators.

7.2 Agreements to replace arbitrators

6.194 Concerning party agreement to replace an arbitrator, one might expect that where all parties agree on replacement, the arbitrator would step down. This did not happen in one ICC Court case in 2008. The parties there agreed that the co-arbitrator nominated by claimant should be replaced because, despite what was stated on his curriculum vitae, he was not able to work in the language of the arbitration without the assistance of translators and interpreters. The arbitrator, who was from a developed Western European country, refused to recognise the parties' agreement to replace him, arguing that the Secretariat of the ICC Court should be required to provide translations and interpretation services. He also contended that if he were removed, he would be entitled to damages consisting of his fees through until the end of the case. The ICC Court took note of the parties' agreement, in accordance with Article 12(1) of the Rules, and replaced the arbitrator with a new nominee provided by the claimant.[241]

7.3 Replacement of arbitrators

6.195 When an arbitrator resigns or is removed, the question of how to proceed with the arbitration inevitably arises. If the arbitration is institutional, the rules will contain a procedure to appoint a replacement. This is usually the same method adopted for the original appointment. Article 22 of the Japanese Arbitration Law is typical:[242]

> Unless otherwise agreed by the parties, where the mandate of an arbitrator terminates under any of the grounds described in each item of paragraph (1) of the preceding article, a substitute arbitrator shall be appointed according to the rules that were applicable to the appointment of the arbitrator being replaced.

6.196 The other aspect to the question of how to proceed concerns the conduct of the arbitration itself – and in particular whether it is necessary to repeat previous proceedings. In some instances it may be necessary and appropriate to provide the new arbitrator with an opportunity to hear witness testimony and oral submissions made prior to his or her appointment. In other instances, simply reading the transcript and submissions may be sufficient, thus saving considerable time

---

240 Ibid.
241 Ibid.
242 Model Law Article 15; Chinese Arbitration Law 1994 Article 37; Malaysian Arbitration Act 2005 Section 17; New Zealand Arbitration Act 1996 Article 15, Schedule 1; ICC Rules Article 12(5).

and expense. Most arbitral rules empower the arbitral tribunal to order that hearings be repeated, if the arbitral tribunal deems it necessary.[243] For example, Article 15 of the 2010 UNCITRAL Arbitration Rules and Article 13.1 of the HKIAC Rules state:

> If an arbitrator is replaced, the proceedings shall resume at the stage where the arbitrator who was replaced ceased to perform his/her functions, unless the arbitral tribunal decides otherwise.

The UNCITRAL Arbitration Rules,[244] SIAC Rules[245] and PDRCI Rules[246] are slightly different. They state that hearings will be repeated if the chairperson of the arbitral tribunal is the replaced arbitrator, and if the parties have not agreed otherwise.

6.197

---

[243] ACICA Rules Article 16; CIETAC Rule 27(3); ICA Rules, Rule 27; JCAA Rules, Rule 8.2; KCAB International Rules Article 4; ICC Rules Article 12(4).
[244] UNCITRAL Arbitration Rules Article 14.
[245] SIAC Rules, Rule 14.
[246] PDRCI Rules Article 14.

7

Procedure and evidence

1 Introduction

7.1 This chapter concerns the procedure governing the conduct of an arbitration. Its temporal scope commences from the claimant's initiation of the arbitration and extends up to the closure of the arbitral proceedings.

7.2 Parties opting for international commercial arbitration are given considerable freedom to choose and individually tailor the procedure of the arbitration. Arbitral procedure may be conducted in flexible, cost-efficient and innovative ways that are attractive to the business community. Through this free choice of the parties, arbitral procedure has evolved to be significantly distinct from the rigid procedures traditionally adopted by courts. In a study on the views of in-house counsel at leading multinational corporations published in 2006, flexibility of procedure emerged as the most widely recognised advantage of international commercial arbitration.[1] Another relevant finding in that study was that 'active participation of the parties in determining and shaping the procedure inspires confidence in the process'.[2]

7.3 Section 2 of this chapter explores the important role of party autonomy in arbitral procedure. Rules, procedural law and guidelines are discussed in Section 3. Section 4 focuses particularly on core arbitral procedural rights and

---

[1] *International Arbitration: Corporate Attitudes and Practices 2006*, study conducted by Pricewaterhouse-Coopers and Queen Mary College, 2006, p. 6. See also, L Mistelis, 'International Arbitration – Corporate Attitudes and Practices – 12 Perceptions Tested: Myths, Data and Analysis Research Report', (2004) 15 *American Review of International Arbitration* 525, at p. 547 et seq. Similarly, in a subsequent study *International Arbitration: Corporate Attitudes and Practices 2008*, PricewaterhouseCoopers and Queen Mary College, 2008, p. 5, most of the corporate counsel surveyed considered that the flexibility of procedure was a major benefit of arbitration.
[2] PricewaterhouseCoopers and Queen Mary College, 2006, ibid., p. 6.

304

duties. Section 5 deals with the way international arbitration balances traditional differences between the common and civil law systems on matters of procedure. Section 6 considers a number of procedural stages involved in an arbitration. Issues relating to evidence are discussed in Section 7. This is followed by an overview of procedural aspects of arbitration hearings in Section 8. Sections 9 and 10 deal with, respectively, interim measures and security for costs. The chapter concludes with an examination of privacy and confidentiality in Section 11.

2 Party autonomy

2.1 The principle

A foundation stone on which the entire edifice of international commercial arbitration rests is the principle of party autonomy. A major component of this principle involves the parties' freedom to choose the procedure to be applied in their arbitration.[3] During the preparatory work of the Model Law, party autonomy was referred to in the following terms:[4] 7.4

> Probably the most important principle on which the model law should be based is the freedom of the parties in order to facilitate the proper functioning of international commercial arbitration according to their expectations. This would allow them to freely submit their disputes to arbitration and to tailor the 'rules of the game' to their specific needs.

Ultimately, the drafters of the Model Law embodied this principle in Article 19(1), which has since been referred to as 'the Magna Carta for party autonomy in all modern laws on international commercial arbitration'.[5] That bedrock provision declares:[6] 7.5

> Subject to the provisions of this Law, the parties are free to agree on the procedure to be followed by the arbitral tribunal in conducting the proceedings.

Further confirmation of the party autonomy principle is found in Article V(1)(d) of the New York Convention and Article 34(2)(a)(iv) of the Model Law, which 7.6

---

3 Other facets of party autonomy include freedom to choose the seat of arbitration, the applicable law, the number of arbitrators, the procedure for appointing and challenging the arbitrators, etc. See e.g. Model Law Articles 10, 11, 13 and 28.
4 'Report of the [UN] Secretary-General: Possible Features of a Model Law on International Commercial Arbitration', 14 May 1981, UN Doc A/CN.9/207, (1981) XII *UNCITRAL Yearbook*, p. 78, para 17. Similarly, see Justice Prakash's observation in *Bovis Lend Lease Pty Ltd v Jay-Tech Marine and Projects Pte Ltd* [2005] SGHC 91 (Singapore High Court) 6 May 2005, at para 18 ('One of the most important principles in arbitration law is that of party autonomy').
5 VV Veeder, 'Whose Arbitration is it Anyway: The Parties' or the Arbitration Tribunal's: An Interesting Question?', in LW Newman and RD Hill (eds), *The Leading Arbitrators' Guide to International Arbitration*, 2nd edn, Juris Publishing, 2008, p. 337, at p. 341.
6 This provision is found in various forms in almost all international arbitration laws in the region, including the Australian International Arbitration Act (by way of adoption of the Model Law pursuant to Section 16 of that Act and see also Section 21); the Chinese Arbitration Law Article 4; the Hong Kong Arbitration Ordinance Section 2AA(2)(a); the Indian Arbitration and Conciliation Act Section 19(2); the Japanese Arbitration Law Article 26; the Korean Arbitration Act Article 20; the Singapore International Arbitration Act Section 15.

empower a court to refuse enforcement or set aside an award if the party resisting enforcement establishes that 'the arbitral procedure was not in accordance with the agreement of the parties'.

2.2 Limits to party autonomy

7.7 Despite its importance, the autonomy of parties to determine the procedure is not absolute. In a number of circumstances, their freedom is controlled or limited by law.[7] The reason why total freedom is not granted was well articulated during the preparatory work of the Model Law:[8]

> ... To give parties the greatest possible freedom does not mean, however, to leave everything to them by not regulating it in the model law. Apart from the desirability of providing 'supplementary' rules ... what is needed is a positive confirmation or guarantee of their freedom. Thus, the model law should provide a 'constitutional framework' which would recognize the parties' free will and the validity and effect of their agreements based thereon.
>
> ... Yet ... it is not suggested to accord absolute priority to the parties' wishes over any provision of the law. Their freedom should be limited by mandatory provisions designed to prevent or to remedy certain major defects in the procedure, any instance of denial of justice or violation of due process. Such restrictions would not be contrary to the interest of the parties, at least not of the weaker and disadvantaged one in a given case. They would also meet the legitimate interest of the State concerned which could hardly be expected to issue the above guarantee without its fundamental ideas of justice being implemented.

7.8 The main limits or constraints on party autonomy are summarised below:
  (i) *Parties' failure to agree* – Party autonomy is premised on consent. The power of parties to dictate the way the proceedings are conducted dissipates rapidly when they are unable to reach agreement. In such cases, specific default provisions in the chosen set of rules or the *lex arbitri* may be triggered or the arbitral tribunal may be empowered to make the relevant determination.
  (ii) *Fundamental, mandatory due process principles* (also known as natural justice principles) – These principles are discussed in Section 4, and are found in some form in all arbitration legislation. Article 18 of the Model Law encapsulates two of the key due process principles: 'The parties shall be treated with equality and each party shall be given a full opportunity of presenting his case.'[9] The consensus in virtually all systems of law is that these principles are essential requirements akin to basic human rights that

---

7 For a detailed analysis of this subject, see M Pryles, 'Limits to Party Autonomy in Arbitral Procedure', (2007) 24(3) *Journal of International Arbitration* 327.
8 'Report of the [UN] Secretary-General: Possible Features of a Model Law on International Commercial Arbitration', op. cit. fn 4, paras 18–19. See also F Nariman, 'Judicial Supervision and Intervention: Before or During Arbitral Proceedings under the UNCITRAL Model Law of Commercial Arbitration 1985 and under the New Indian Law – the Arbitration and Conciliation Act 1996' in M Pryles and M Moser (eds), *The Asian Leading Arbitrators' Guide to International Arbitration*, JurisNet, 2007, p. 329, at p. 330 ('Modern States, both in the West and in the East, have shown a marked reluctance to universalize the concept of absolute arbitral freedom.').
9 As to the meaning of a 'full' opportunity, see Section 4.1.

cannot be overridden by private agreement. An award might be set aside or be unenforceable if tainted by transgressions of such due process requirements.

(iii) *Other mandatory procedural laws* – If the procedural rules agreed by the parties conflict with any non-derogable provisions of the *lex arbitri*, then the latter will usually prevail.[10] For example, Section 15A of the Singapore International Arbitration Act states explicitly that any rules of arbitration chosen by the parties shall be given effect only to the extent that they are not inconsistent with provisions in the Model Law or Part II of that Act (relating to international arbitration) from which the parties cannot derogate.[11] A noteworthy mandatory law in mainland China is the requirement of institutional arbitration, i.e. parties cannot choose ad hoc arbitration.[12]

(iv) *Institutional requirements* – Although not a major impediment to party autonomy, institutional requirements may occasionally constrain party autonomy. For example, under some institutional rules parties are not free to exclude the supervision that is part of that institution's procedure.[13] At the same time, it is only by virtue of party autonomy that such institutional rules could apply in the first place, because the parties would have chosen them.

(v) *Third parties* – No matter what the parties to the arbitration agree, their agreement by itself cannot legally bind a third party. Further, while procedural rules may enable arbitral tribunals to request a third party to perform a certain act (e.g. under IBA Rules of Evidence Article 8(4)), this request contains no legal force. In such a case, however, assistance may be sought from the national courts of a competent jurisdiction to issue an order that legally obliges a third party to act.

(vi) *Arbitral tribunal discretion* – Subject to the exceptions cited above, where parties agree on the procedure to be adopted, the arbitral tribunal is in principle duty-bound to follow that agreement. Philip Yang has observed that '[i]t is generally accepted that if the parties agree on certain matters in arbitral proceedings, then the arbitral tribunal is duty-bound or has no choice but to follow such wishes of the parties . . . The parties can even terminate the arbitration proceedings by agreement'.[14] If the arbitral tribunal cannot accept the parties' agreement on a matter of procedure, it should ordinarily offer its resignation. However, in practice an experienced arbitral tribunal may effectively require the parties to abide by certain procedural rules

---

10 See, e.g. SIAC Rules, Rule 1.1; ACICA Rules Article 2.2. Mandatory laws are discussed in Chapters 2 and 3; see especially Chapter 2 Section 7.2, and Chapter 3, Section 4.
11 See also the provision for mandatory rules in Article 4(1) and Schedule 1 of the English Arbitration Act 1996.
12 See, e.g. *People's Insurance Company of China, Guangzhou Branch v Guangdong Guanghe Power Co Ltd*, (2003) *Min Si Zhong Zi* No. 29, cited in Chua Eu Jin, 'Arbitration in China', (2005) 1 *Asian International Arbitration Journal*, p. 86. See also Wang Wenying, 'Distinct Features of Arbitration in China: An Historical Perspective', (2006) 23(1) *Journal of International Arbitration* 49, at pp. 53 and 57.
13 See, e.g. ICC Rules Article 27; SIAC Rules, Rule 27; CIETAC Rules Article 45. See also Chapter 8, Section 3.6.
14 P Yang, 'The Organisation of International Arbitration Proceedings', in Pryles and Moser (eds), op. cit. fn 8, p. 165, at p. 217.

and decisions despite a reluctance by both parties. Usually, this is done by gentle persuasion, but sometimes more senior arbitrators possess the confidence, judgment and experience to express strong views on a matter, which the parties effectively have to accept.

(vii) *The role of domestic courts* – Court decisions concerning a given arbitration are often not fully consistent with what the parties originally agreed in relation to that arbitration. A notable example of court interference with party autonomy is found in the Singapore case of *Dermajaya Properties Sdn Bhd v Premium Properties Sdn Bhd*.[15] In that case the parties chose the UNCITRAL Arbitration Rules to apply to their arbitration but the court took the view that because they were not fully compatible with the Model Law, they were completely excluded in favour of the Model Law.[16]

3 Rules, procedural law and guidelines

3.1 Arbitration rules

3.1.1 Choice of arbitration rules

7.9 The parties may, but are not required to, agree on a set of institutional or ad hoc arbitration rules to apply to their arbitration. If they do not agree on a set of arbitration rules, then none will apply. Alternatively, they may simply formulate their own rules or rely on the procedural law at the seat of arbitration.

7.10 If a set of arbitration rules is chosen, the choice may be expressed in the parties' arbitration agreement or made before or during the arbitral proceedings. Parties commonly refer in their arbitration agreement to a set of institutional rules. For instance, parties may agree to an arbitration clause that reads:

> Any dispute, controversy or claim arising out of or relating to this contract, including the validity, invalidity, breach or termination thereof, shall be settled by arbitration in Hong Kong under the Hong Kong International Arbitration Centre Administered Arbitration Rules in force when the Notice of Arbitration is submitted in accordance with these Rules.

7.11 By virtue of this clause, the procedural rules of HKIAC will govern the proceedings if a dispute arising out of that contract is submitted to arbitration. Should the procedural rules chosen by the parties be silent as to any matter, the necessary procedure may be chosen by further agreement between the parties or it may be determined by the arbitral tribunal or the *lex arbitri*.

7.12 If no specific rules are indicated but reference is made to an arbitration institution only, that reference generally implies that the parties have agreed on the

---

15 [2002] 2 SLR 164 (Singapore High Court).
16 Swift legislative action followed to avoid damage to Singapore's reputation as an arbitration-friendly venue. Article 15A was inserted into the Singapore International Arbitration Act, which provides that a provision in the arbitration rules chosen by the parties would be given effect to the extent that it is not inconsistent with mandatory provisions of that Act. See generally, M Pillay, 'The Singapore Arbitration Regime and the UNCITRAL Model Law', (2004) 20 *Arbitration International* 355, at pp. 375–383.

rules of that institution. The reverse also applies. If the parties choose a set of institutional arbitration rules, they are presumed to have chosen that institution to administer the arbitration.

Consistent with the party autonomy principle, parties are free to choose the procedural rules of any arbitral institution. Some of the arbitration institutions in the region that have formulated their own rules include ACICA, CIETAC, JCAA, KCAB, SIAC and HKIAC. The KLRCA, on the other hand, has not drafted its own detailed set of rules but has adopted (with modifications) the UNCITRAL Arbitration Rules to govern arbitrations conducted under its auspices.[17] If an arbitration is ad hoc, the rules typically adopted by the parties are the UNCITRAL Arbitration Rules. However, an arbitration can be entirely ad hoc, with no set of arbitration rules involved. 7.13

A number of arbitration institutions offer two or more sets of rules from which parties may choose. Those rules may be designed specifically for the business sector in which the parties operate or the type or magnitude of dispute that may arise. For example, the HKIAC has adopted 'Short Form Arbitration Rules' that contain very brief periods (e.g. 14 days) within which to submit written submissions; a 'Small Claims Procedure' for disputes involving less than US$50 000; 'Securities Arbitration Rules'; and a 'Semiconductor Intellectual Property Arbitration Procedure'.[18] In addition to offering its own set of arbitration rules, the JCAA has 'Administrative and Procedural Rules for Arbitration under the UNCITRAL Arbitration Rules'.[19] The latter facilitate arbitrations administered by the JCAA but specifically enable those arbitrations to be conducted under the UNCITRAL Arbitration Rules. 7.14

The procedural rules chosen never cover all the procedural issues that may arise. Usually, once an arbitral tribunal has been appointed, it will hold a preliminary meeting with the party representatives in which many points of procedure will be finalised. For example, at this meeting it may be decided when written submissions and documentary evidence should be filed, hearing dates may be fixed and the applicable rules of evidence may be determined. Other questions of procedure are raised and dealt with frequently during an arbitration. 7.15

It is rare that parties do not indicate (through an express choice or by implicitly incorporating institutional rules) what rules will govern their arbitration. But if they do not agree on any rules, the law of the seat of arbitration will govern the arbitral procedure. If the seat of arbitration is in a Model Law country, the Model Law specifically provides a number of fallback procedural provisions. Those relating to the procedure of the arbitration are principally contained in Articles 19–22. In other countries, absent an agreement by the parties, provisions of the domestic law (which may be different from the Model Law) will apply. 7.16

---

[17] See Rule 1 of the KLRCA Rules.
[18] These documents are available at www.hkiac.org/show_content.php?article_id=34. Similarly, SIAC has a range of arbitral rules designed for specific industry sectors, available at www.siac.org.sg/cms/. In addition, many institutions now have separate rules for expedited arbitrations. See Chapter 7, Section 6.11.
[19] As amended and effective on 1 July 2009.

3.1.2 Differences between institutional and ad hoc arbitration procedure

7.17　The degree of supervision or administration offered by arbitral institutions varies. While the policy of most arbitral institutions is to leave the arbitral tribunal as free as possible, some are more proactive in ensuring that the arbitration proceeds smoothly and efficiently and complies with its own rules. The ICC Rules, for example, while being very flexible on procedure generally, require an arbitral tribunal to draw up 'terms of reference' that identify the issues to be determined.[20] The 2007 SIAC Rules also contain a requirement for a 'memorandum of issues' which is a very similar document.[21]

7.18　It follows that ad hoc arbitrations are generally more flexible in the procedure that they may adopt because they are not constrained by the requirements set by arbitral institutions. But the lack of an arbitral institution may in fact be a drawback because such institutions perform important administrative functions and employ counsel with the relevant legal experience, who are available to advise the arbitral tribunal and parties on day-to-day issues. Where a party is recalcitrant or otherwise difficult, the support of a supervisory institution will help to minimise that party's misconduct. Arbitrators also find comfort with the support of an experienced institution that offers a neutral sounding-board for complicated aspects of arbitration practice.[22] Institutional support can also minimise the adverse impact of an arbitrator who is not performing his functions diligently or in due time by requiring the arbitrator to do so or, ultimately, by removing him.

3.1.3 Failure to object to non-compliance with procedural rules

7.19　A party that does not object to a failure to comply with an applicable procedural rule may be deemed to have waived its right to object subsequently. Many institutional rules contain a provision addressing this issue. For example, Article 28 of the HKIAC Rules provides:[23]

> A party who knows or ought reasonably to know that any provision of, or requirement arising under, these Rules (including the agreement to arbitrate) has not been complied with and yet proceeds with the arbitration without promptly stating its objection to such non-compliance, shall be deemed to have waived its right to object.

7.20　This rule is related to the doctrines of waiver and estoppel.[24] It requires that procedural objections be raised not long after the time the non-compliance occurred,

---

20 See ICC Rules Article 18.
21 See SIAC Rules, Rule 17. This requirement is not included in the 2010 SIAC Rules.
22 See, e.g. G Born, *International Commercial Arbitration*, Kluwer Law International, 2009, pp. 150–151; M Moses, *The Principles and Practice of International Commercial Arbitration*, Cambridge University Press, 2008, pp. 9–10; and JDM Lew, LA Mistelis and SM Kröll, *Comparative International Commercial Arbitration*, Kluwer Law International, 2003, paras 3–14 to 3–16 and 3–20 to 3–23.
23 See also, Model Law Article 4; ACICA Rules Article 31; CIETAC Rules Article 8; ICC Rules Article 33; JCAA Rules, Rule 51; KCAB International Rules Article 43; SIAC Rules, Rule 35.1; UNCITRAL Arbitration Rules Article 30.
24 See, e.g. Bin Cheng, *General Principles of Law as Applied by International Courts and Tribunals*, Stevens and Sons, 1953, pp. 141–149 and Y Derains and E Schwartz, *A Guide to the ICC Rules of Arbitration*, 2nd edn, Kluwer Law, 2005, p. 379. See also JR Weeramantry, 'Estoppel and the Iran-United States Claims Tribunal',

otherwise the right to object later may be lost. However, it has been commented that in China, the legality of such presumed waiver provisions in arbitration procedural rules may be questionable because they deprive parties of the legal right to sue, i.e. it may preclude them from bringing a court action to challenge the award.[25]

3.1.4 Applicable version of rules

A question as to the applicable version of any arbitration rules can arise when the rules are revised or otherwise amended between the time the arbitration agreement is concluded and the time the arbitration is commenced.[26] This situation arose in *Black and Veatch Singapore Pte Ltd v Jurong Engineering Ltd*.[27] In that case, the contract at issue contained an agreement to arbitrate under the SIAC arbitration rules. At the time the agreement was entered into, SIAC had only one set of rules. By the time the dispute arose, SIAC had two sets of rules – one for domestic and one for international arbitration. The Singapore High Court found that the parties had agreed on SIAC administered arbitration generally, and that they would be bound to the most appropriate SIAC Rules available at the time of their submission to arbitration. Consequently, because the arbitration was domestic, it was held that the domestic rules of SIAC were applicable even though they did not exist at the time the arbitration agreement was concluded. This decision is consistent with international practice.[28] The Singapore Court of Appeal, confirming the High Court's decision, also noted that the burden of proving an earlier or less appropriate version of arbitration rules applies lies with the party seeking the application of such rules.[29] 7.21

The presumption in favour of the latest or most appropriate set of arbitration rules should be compared with the KCAB's press release in 2007 announcing its new rules, which stated:[30] 7.22

> These newly enacted Rules that go into effect shall be applied to international arbitration cases in which the parties have a written agreement to resolve disputes through arbitration in accordance with these Rules. Therefore, as a general rule, the existing arbitration rules shall be applied to those cases in which the parties have no agreement about these new Rules.

(1996) 27 *Netherlands Yearbook of International Law* 113, at pp. 114–117. See also Chapter 4, Section 4.1.2 of this book.
25 See J Mo, 'Legality of the Presumed Waiver in Arbitration Proceedings under Chinese Law', (2001) 29 *International Business Lawyer* 21, at p. 25 (also noting that in China, the legality of a deemed/presumed act (e.g. a waiver) must be stipulated by law, and that there is no provision in China's 1994 Arbitration Law that deals with a party's waiver of its right to challenge the validity of an arbitral award).
26 See generally S Greenberg and F Mange, 'Institutional and Ad Hoc Perspectives on the Temporal Conflict of Arbitral Rules', (2010) 27(2) *Journal of International Arbitration* 225.
27 [2004] SGCA 30 (Singapore Court of Appeal).
28 See, e.g. ICC Rules Article 6(1) and HKIAC Rules Article 1.4. See generally Greenberg and Mange, op. cit. fn 26.
29 [2004] SGCA 30, at para 15 and paras 19–26.
30 KCAB Notice, 'New International Arbitration Rules' (7 February 2007) www.kcab.or.kr/ (viewed 11 June 2007).

3.2 IBA Rules of Evidence

7.23 Efforts toward greater harmonisation of arbitral procedure have been made through the adoption of guidelines or rules in areas usually left uncharted by the mainstream arbitral rules. We have seen, for example, in Chapter 6 the formulation of guidelines on arbitrators' conflicts of interest. Another prime manifestation of these efforts is the International Bar Association Rules on the Taking of Evidence in International Commercial Arbitration ('IBA Rules of Evidence').[31] These Rules, as indicated in their Preamble, are designed not to supplant but 'to supplement the legal provisions and the international or ad hoc rules according to which the Parties are conducting their arbitration'.

7.24 The IBA Rules of Evidence have in large measure established a generally acceptable synthesis of common law and civil law practice in relation to presenting and obtaining evidence, including the often delicate issue of discovery or production of documents. In David Rivkin's forward to the IBA Rules of Evidence, he notes that the Rules 'reflect procedures in use in many different legal systems, and they may be particularly useful when the parties come from different legal cultures'. However, they have not been immune to the criticism that they are more oriented towards a common law approach.[32] On the other hand, it may be said that the provisions relating to document production are more akin to the civil law approach because they require the requesting party to identify a document or a narrow category of documents. Overall, the IBA Rules of Evidence have gained a wide degree of respect and their use in international arbitration is constantly on the increase.[33]

7.25 The IBA Rules of Evidence could play many roles in an arbitration. As the Preamble to the Rules states, they may be adopted in whole or in part by the parties and the arbitral tribunal or they may be varied or simply used as guidelines in developing procedures for the particular circumstances of an arbitration. Frequently, parties agree that the arbitral tribunal may refer to them for guidance without being bound by them.[34] However, even where parties have not agreed

---

[31] Adopted by a resolution of the IBA Council on 1 June 1999. These 1999 Rules had their genesis in the IBA's *Supplementary Rules Governing the Presentation and Reception of Evidence in International Commercial Arbitration*, adopted on 28 May 1983, (1985) X *Yearbook of Commercial Arbitration* 152. A revised version of the 1999 Rules was adopted by the IBA Council on 29 May 2010. This occurred just prior to publication. As a result, references to the 'IBA Rules of Evidence' in this book are to the 1999 Rules unless otherwise stated. Among other things, the 2010 revisions provide greater guidance on (i) the content of expert reports, (ii) requests for documents or electronic information, and (iii) issues of legal privilege. The 2010 Rules also expand confidentiality protections concerning produced or submitted documents and provide for the use of videoconference technology.
[32] See G Born, *International Commercial Arbitration: Commentary and Materials*, 2nd edn, Kluwer Law International, 2001, p. 485; and Born, 2009, op. cit. fn 22, vol. II, p. 1793.
[33] See, e.g. Yang, op. cit. fn 14, pp. 184–185.
[34] In a survey conducted by the IBA Rules of Evidence Subcommittee, 18% of participants indicated they chose the IBA Rules of Evidence in an arbitration agreement in every case or most cases. Thirty-one percent replied that they were chosen in some instances. When asked how often the IBA Rules are adopted later (i.e. if not in the arbitration agreement), for example, in the terms of reference or in arbitral tribunal directions, 43% said in every or most cases and 42% said in some cases. These figures were kindly provided to the authors by one of the members of the IBA Rules of Evidence Subcommittee, which revised those Rules. See also TC Thye and J Choong, 'Disclosure of Documents in Singapore International Arbitrations: Time for a Reassessment', (2005) 1 *Asian Journal of International Arbitration* 49, at p. 59 ('the IBA Rules can be (and

on their use, it is not uncommon for arbitral tribunals to refer to them.[35] Some arbitrators consider themselves to be 'inspired though not bound' by the IBA Rules of Evidence while others prefer to adopt them as binding.[36]

The broad acceptance of the IBA Rules of Evidence is also manifested in the fact that institutional rules are starting to refer to them explicitly. Article 27(2) of the ACICA Rules states that in relation to evidence and the hearing, the arbitral tribunal 'shall have regard to, but is not bound to apply' the IBA Rules of Evidence. However, Article 27(3) adds that '[a]n agreement of the parties and the Rules (in that order) shall at all times prevail over an inconsistent provision in the [IBA Rules of Evidence]'.

7.26

4 Core procedural rights and duties

State courts exercise supervisory jurisdiction over arbitrations that are seated in that state. A major aim of this supervisory function is to ensure that the fundamental procedural rights of parties are protected. The core procedural rights of parties and duties of arbitral tribunals are discussed in this section.

7.27

4.1 Right to present case

A fundamental right accorded to all parties to an arbitration is that each party be given a reasonable opportunity to present its case.[37] It is a procedural right based on the Latin maxim *audi alteram partem* (hear the other side). This right includes the entitlement to be notified as to the commencement of arbitration proceedings, as well as hearings and other steps in the arbitration, and the right to answer the assertions made by the opposing party.

7.28

To enable the presentation of each party's case, all documents or information supplied to the arbitral tribunal by one party should at the same time be communicated to the other parties.[38] The 1976 version of the UNCITRAL

7.29

---

are) used as persuasive guidelines of accepted international arbitral practice. As such, they provide a useful starting point on, inter alia, how to approach the contentious issue of disclosure of documents. The IBA Rules themselves have some degree of built in flexibility, allowing the arbitral tribunal to exercise its discretion as best suits the individual case.').

35 See, e.g. P Yuen and J Choong, 'Is Arbitration Value for Money? Assessing Some Common Complaints about the Costs of International Arbitration', 2008 *Asian Dispute Review* 76 (commenting that the IBA Rules of Evidence 'have been increasingly widely accepted in Asia, even where parties have not agreed in advance that they should apply.'). See also Seung Wha Chang, 'Document Production under the Asian Civil Law System', in Pryles and Moser, op. cit. fn 8, p. 267, at p. 268; B Hanotiau, 'The Conduct of the Hearings', in Newman and Hill (eds), op. cit. fn 5, at p. 359, at p. 364.

36 See, e.g. Moses, op. cit. fn 22, p. 165.

37 See Model Law Article 18; UNCITRAL Arbitration Rules Article 15(1); HKIAC Rules Article 14(1); ICC Rules Articles 15(2) and 22(1); KCAB International Rules Article 20(3); Hong Kong Arbitration Ordinance Section 2GA(1)(a). See also ICSID Convention Article 45(2). In Thailand, Section 17(2) of the Arbitration Act 1987 provided that '[u]nless otherwise agreed by the arbitration agreement or law, an arbitrator shall have the power to conduct any procedure as he deems appropriate taking the principle of natural justice as a prime consideration' but now more fidelity toward Article 18 of the Model Law is found in Section 25 of Thailand's Arbitration Act 2002.

38 Model Law Article 24(3); UNCITRAL Arbitration Rules Article 15(3).

Arbitration Rules frames this as obligatory. However, this obligation was a matter of minor controversy during the revision of the UNICTRAL Arbitration Rules. The Working Group considered that while this contemporaneous communication generally reflected an important principle, there would be circumstances where it would be inappropriate and have the potential to create procedural inequality. It occasionally occurs that one party is given a short extension of the time in which it must communicate submissions. If the rule is rigidly enforced and the procedure calls for a simultaneous exchange of briefs, the late-filing side would arguably have an unfair advantage because it would see the opposing side's submissions that were filed on time – thus impinging on another fundamental right – to be treated equally. The Working Group therefore recommended giving the arbitral tribunal a discretion to vary the rule.[39] The issue was further discussed by the Commission with the result that the 2010 UNCITRAL Rules give the arbitral tribunal discretion only where it is permitted by applicable law. A related requirement is that any expert report or evidentiary document relied on by the arbitral tribunal must be communicated to the parties.[40]

7.30   Certain rules and laws, such as Article 2GA of the Hong Kong Arbitration Ordinance, expressly provide for the giving of a 'reasonable' opportunity to each party to present its case.[41] The term 'reasonable' avoids reference to a 'full' opportunity to present a party's case, as is the terminology used in Article 18 of the Model Law.[42] The high standard inherent in the word 'full' has led some to comment that the phrasing may enable parties to make the arbitration unmanageable, for example, by demanding that an excessively high number of witnesses be called or by requesting the presentation of legal argument in an unreasonably lengthy fashion.[43] Responding to these arguments, the 2010 UNCITRAL Arbitration Rules now use the word 'reasonable'.[44]

7.31   There is very little case law on expansive claims to a 'full' opportunity to present a case, perhaps indicating how spurious such a claim would be. Chamber Three of the Iran-US Claims Tribunal squarely rejected any misuse of the word 'full' when it stated:[45]

---

39 Working Group Report, UN Doc A/CN.9/665, para 127.
40 Model Law Article 24(3).
41 Similar wording is contained in CIETAC Rules Article 29(2); HKIAC Rules Article 14; ICC Rules Articles 15(2) and 22. See also JCAA Rules, Rule 32 (referring to a 'sufficient opportunity'); KCAB International Rules Article 22 (referring to a 'fair opportunity') and Section 20 of the Malaysian Arbitration Act 2005 (referring to a 'fair and reasonable opportunity').
42 See, also UNCITRAL Arbitration Rules Article 15; Japanese Arbitration Law Article 25(2); Section 25 of Thailand's Arbitration Act 2002. Interestingly, Article 17(1) of the ACICA Rules employs the words 'full opportunity', whereas Article 13(1) of the ACICA Expedited Rules refers to a 'reasonable opportunity'.
43 See T Sawada, 'Conduct of the Hearings', in Pryles and Moser, op. cit. fn 8, p. 289, at p. 291. However, parties now have the choice of selecting expedited procedures such as those provided by a number of arbitral institutions. See Section 6.11.
44 Report of the Working Group on Arbitration and Conciliation on the work of its forty-fifth session, (Vienna, 11–15 September 2006), UN Doc A/CN 9/614, para 77.
45 *Dadras International v Islamic Republic of Iran*, (1995) 31 Iran-US CTR 127, at 144. Similarly, see Bin Cheng, op. cit. fn 24, p. 296. Additionally, Redfern and Hunter suggest the word 'full' must be interpreted from an objective (rather than subjective) standpoint. A Redfern, M Hunter, N Blackaby and C Partasides, *Law and Practice of International Commercial Arbitration*, 4th edn, Sweet & Maxwell, 2004, para 6–07. See also the 1999 IBA Rules of Evidence Article 8(1) (and Article 8(2) of the 2010 version of those Rules) and Lew, Mistelis and Kröll, op. cit. fn 22, paras 22–61 and 22–71.

the Tribunal is unpersuaded that any Party can credibly claim that it has been denied a 'full opportunity of presenting [its] case' given the procedural history of these Cases. The key word is 'opportunity': the Tribunal is obliged to provide the framework within which the parties may present their cases, but is by no means obliged to acquiesce in a party's desire for a particular sequence of proceedings or to permit repetitious proceedings.

Finally, it should be noted that a party's right to present its case does not necessarily include the right to an oral hearing. Although it is not a common practice, an arbitral tribunal may decide within the discretion granted to it to determine the facts or legal points at issue on the documents alone. However, some arbitral rules do require the arbitral tribunal to hold a hearing if a party so requests.

4.2 Right to equal treatment

The rights to present one's case and to be treated equally overlap significantly.[46] However, it is helpful to keep the two separate as each also possesses distinctive features.

The requirement that parties be treated with equality is well established and constitutes a cardinal principle of arbitral procedure.[47] This right is enshrined in virtually all international commercial arbitration instruments, and is frequently found in the same provision that deals with the opportunity to present one's case.[48]

However, there is no precise formula to determine how parties are to be treated equally. An apposite institutional rule is Article 15(2) of the ICC Rules, which provides that 'the Arbitral Tribunal shall act fairly and impartially and ensure that each party has a reasonable opportunity to present its case'.[49] The reason for referring to 'fairly and impartially' rather than 'equal treatment' has been said to be that 'in some cases, treating the parties in precisely the same manner may lead to unfair results'.[50] It would be injudicious for an arbitrator to apply an equal treatment provision too rigidly. As one experienced arbitrator from the region has said, the arbitral tribunal's obligation 'to treat parties equally [at a hearing] does not require allowing an equal number of witnesses or an equal amount of time'.[51]

In this regard, the drafting history of the UNCITRAL Arbitration Rules also provides valuable insight because an earlier draft that formed the basis for those rules

---

46 See, e.g. D Caron, L Caplan, and M Pellonpää, *The UNCITRAL Arbitration Rules: A Commentary*, Oxford University Press, 2006, p. 29 ('the issue of equality has mainly arisen as a question concerning the right to present one's case').
47 See, e.g. Bin Cheng, op. cit. fn 24, p. 290.
48 See, e.g. KCAB International Rules Article 20(3); CIETAC Rules Article 19; Model Law Article 18; UNCITRAL Arbitration Rules Article 15(1); Japanese Arbitration Law 2003 Article 25(1); Hong Kong Arbitration Ordinance Section 2GA(1)(a); Malaysian Arbitration Act 2005 Section 20; Indian Arbitration and Conciliation Act 1996 Section 18.
49 Section 2GA(1)(a) of the Hong Kong Arbitration Ordinance also uses the 'fair and impartial' wording in preference to 'equality of treatment'.
50 Derains and Schwartz, op. cit. fn 24, p. 229.
51 Sawada, op. cit. fn 43, p. 297.

required parties to be treated with 'absolute equality'.[52] The modifier 'absolute' was subsequently deleted. Some commentators have observed that this deletion 'indicates that the provision aims to guarantee not so much formal equality as equality in the sense of justice and fairness'.[53]

4.3 Arbitrators' duty to avoid delay and expense

7.37 Related to arbitral procedure and to some extent procedural rights is an emerging duty on arbitrators to avoid unnecessary costs and delay.[54] As an example, Section 2GA(1)(b) of the Hong Kong Arbitration Ordinance requires arbitrators 'to use procedures that are appropriate to the particular case, avoiding unnecessary delay and expense, so as to provide a fair means for resolving the dispute to which the proceedings relate'.[55] Similar considerations are echoed in Rule 15(2) of the SIAC Rules, which provides that '[i]n the absence of procedural rules agreed by the parties or contained in these Rules, the arbitral tribunal shall conduct the arbitration in such manner as it considers appropriate to ensure the fair, expeditious, economical and final determination of the dispute'.[56] Where the Model Law applies, in extreme circumstances parties may apply to the court under Article 14(1) to terminate the mandate of an arbitrator if he 'fails to act without undue delay'.[57]

7.38 A number of institutional rules, such as Article 33 of the KCAB International Rules, impose a time limit within which the arbitral tribunal should render its award.[58] This time period is extendable. Under the ICC Rules, the failure of the

---

52 Preliminary Draft Set of Arbitration Rules for Optional Use in Ad Hoc Arbitration Relating to International Trade, 'Report of the Secretary-General on the Preliminary Draft Set of Arbitration Rules', UN Doc A/CN.9/97 (1974), reprinted in (1975) VI *UNCITRAL Yearbook* 163, at pp. 172–173.
53 Caron, Caplan and Pellonpää, op. cit. fn 46, p. 28.
54 See, e.g. Yang, op. cit. fn 14, pp. 173–176. Some rules also require the *parties* to act in a manner that makes the arbitration efficient. For example, the HKIAC Rules Article 14(7) provides that the 'parties shall do everything necessary to ensure the fair and efficient conduct of the proceedings.' See also the ICA Rules Annexure 1: 'Guidelines for Arbitrators and the Parties for Expeditious Conduct of Arbitration Proceedings'.
55 See also Hong Kong Arbitration Ordinance Section 2AA (declaring that '[t]he object of this Ordinance is to facilitate the fair and speedy resolution of disputes by arbitration without unnecessary expense') and Section 15(3) of that Ordinance (giving courts, upon application by a party, the power 'to remove an arbitrator . . . who fails to use all reasonable dispatch in entering on and proceeding with the reference and making an award . . . ').
56 See also JCAA Rules, Rule 32(4) ('The arbitral tribunal shall make efforts towards the expedited resolution of the dispute.'); and ICA Rules, Rule 63 ('The arbitral tribunal shall make the award as expeditiously as possible . . . '). The need 'to avoid unnecessary delay or expenses' has also been included in the HKIAC Rules Article 14(1). Similar provisions are found in Section 33(1)(b) of the English Arbitration Act 1996; and the LCIA Rules Article 14(2).
57 Delay is also a common ground for arbitrators to be removed under the ICC Rules Article 12(2), which allows the ICC Court to remove an arbitrator 'on the Court's own initiative when it decides that he is prevented de jure or de facto from fulfilling his functions, or that he is not fulfilling his functions in accordance with the Rules or within the prescribed time limits'. See also J Fry and S Greenberg, 'The Arbitral Tribunal: Applications of Articles 7–12 of the ICC Rules in Recent Cases', (2009) 20(2) *ICC International Court of Arbitration Bulletin* 12, at para 108, p. 29 ('The most common reason for initiating replacement proceedings is when the arbitrator is causing unacceptable delays, is not responding to correspondence from the Secretariat and/or parties, or is not conducting the arbitration in accordance with the Rules.'). Similarly, see Rule 14 of the 2010 SIAC Rules, which potentially also permits a party to challenge an arbitrator for undue delays.
58 See also CIETAC Rules Article 42; IAC Rules, Rule 63; ICC Rules Article 24; JCAA Rules, Rule 53(1). This issue is dealt with in more detail in Chapter 8, Section 3.4.

arbitral tribunal to complete the arbitration in a timely manner may lead to a reduction in its fees, which are fixed by the ICC Court, or in an extreme case one or more members of the arbitral tribunal may be replaced.[59] In certain jurisdictions, domestic courts may hold arbitrators personally liable if they have not rendered an award within the time period agreed by the parties.[60]

7.39 Other rules such as the 1976 UNCITRAL Arbitration Rules do not make specific reference to delay and expense avoidance. They simply provide the arbitral tribunal with the discretion to conduct the proceedings 'in such manner as it considers appropriate'.[61] Even where the rules are silent, however, arbitral tribunals have an inherent duty to avoid unnecessary delays and expense.

7.40 Should parties choose expedited arbitral procedures, extra pressure is applied on arbitrators (as well as the parties) to complete the arbitration within a short time-frame. Article 3(1) of the ACICA Expedited Arbitration Rules, for example, states that its 'overriding objective ... is to provide arbitration that is quick, cost effective and fair, considering especially the amounts in dispute and complexity of issues or facts involved ...'. Article 3(2) adds that '[b]y invoking these Rules the parties agree to accept the overriding objective and its application by the Arbitrator'.

7.41 Matthew Gearing has drawn attention to the growing perception that international arbitration is a slower and more expensive dispute resolution process when compared with litigation. He has taken the view that a more pro-active approach by arbitrators is needed to improve efficiency in arbitration. In his opinion, a major reason behind this problem is the conflict between an arbitrator's duty to implement more efficient procedures and the duty to abide by the parties' wishes.[62]

7.42 A growing concern about time and costs in arbitration prompted the ICC Commission on Arbitration to set up a special Task Force in 2004 dedicated to the issue. As a result of its research the ICC published in 2007 a guide called *Techniques for Controlling Time and Costs in Arbitration*.[63] It is a practical tool designed to stimulate the conscious choice of arbitral procedures with a view

---

59 See Fry and Greenberg, op.cit. fn 57, at p. 28 et seq for examples of the application of Article 12(2) of the ICC Rules in these circumstances. See also Derains and Schwartz, op. cit. fn 24, p. 303.
60 See, e.g. *Jiliet v Castagnet*, Case 1660 FS-P+B (French Cour de Cassation), 6 December 2005, reported and reviewed in (2006) 1 *Stockholm International Arbitration Review* 149.
61 UNCITRAL Arbitration Rules Article 15(1). But see Article 17(1) of the 2010 UNCITRAL Arbitration Rules.
62 Matthew Gearing, address at 'ADR in Asia Conference 2008: Arbitration and Mediation – Global Platforms for Dispute Resolution', Hong Kong, 12 September 2008. Similar concerns about the speed and costs of international commercial arbitration were expressed by the former Chief Justice of India, Justice Lahoti, in a paper entitled 'International Commercial Arbitration Challenges and Possibilities in Asian Countries (with Special Reference to India)', delivered at a SIAC arbitration seminar in Singapore on 'Arbitration in India and Singapore: Sharing Perspectives', 27 June 2008. With specific regard to concerns of in-house counsel in corporations about the cost of arbitration, see PricewaterhouseCoopers and Queen Mary College, 2006, op. cit. fn 1, pp. 19–20.
63 Available at www.iccwbo.org/uploadedFiles/TimeCost_E.pdf. See also the approaches to delays in arbitration addressed in D Rivkin, 'Towards a New Paradigm in International Arbitration: The Town Elder Model Revisited', Instituto Universitario de Estudios Europeos, Universidad San Pablo, Madrid, *Serie Arbitraje Internacional y Resolución Alternativa de Controversias*, Número 1/2007; and BS Vasani and KD Tallent, 'Proportional Autonomy: Addressing Delay in International Arbitration through a Deadline for the Rendering of Final Awards', (2008) 2 *Dispute Resolution International* 255.

to organising an arbitration that is efficient and appropriately tailor-made. It is intended to encourage arbitrators and parties to create a new dynamic at the outset of an arbitration whereby the parties can review the suggested techniques and agree on appropriate procedures and, if they fail to agree, the arbitral tribunal can decide on such procedures. While this document was conceived with the ICC Rules of Arbitration in mind, the vast majority of the techniques suggested by the document can be used in virtually any arbitration.

5 Balancing common law and civil law procedure

7.43 International commercial arbitration frequently involves two or more parties based in jurisdictions whose legal traditions are different. Striking an appropriate balance between these traditions in terms of the arbitral procedure is one of international arbitration's key advantages. Often one party is from a common law jurisdiction and the other from a civil law jurisdiction. A traditional characterisation of these two legal systems is that the common law is said to be adversarial (i.e. the judge largely leaves the presentation of the case to the parties), whereas civil law procedure is described as inquisitorial (i.e. the judge tends to play a more active role in ascertaining the truth and is less dependent on the arguments put forward by the parties).[64]

7.44 In the Asia-Pacific, while many jurisdictions have their roots in the common law,[65] the laws of a significant number of others are based on the civil law tradition.[66] This difference between various Asia-Pacific legal systems is sometimes overlooked by practitioners trained solely in common law jurisdictions.

7.45 An arbitral tribunal composed of lawyers from civil law jurisdictions may be more inclined to follow rules of procedure applied by civil law courts. A corresponding preference for common law procedure may be observed in respect

---

[64] Added caution must be exercised in assuming that procedure from either common or civil law is relatively homogenous. For example, US document production is significantly different from that in the UK. As regards the differences in civil law jurisdictions, it has been said that 'there is possibly as much difference between the outlook and practice of a French avocat and of a German Rechtsanwalt as between those of an English and of an Italian lawyer'. C Reymond, 'To What Extent is Civil Law Procedure Inquisitional?', (1989) 8 *Arbitration* 159. There are also enormous differences among Asia-Pacific jurisdictions in this regard. For a general comparison of common law and civil law, including procedural issues, see, e.g. C Pejovic, 'Civil Law and Common Law: Two Different Paths Leading to the Same Goal', [2001] *Victoria University of Wellington Law Review* 42.
[65] These countries include Australia, Brunei, Hong Kong, India, Pakistan, the Philippines, Malaysia, New Zealand, Sri Lanka and Singapore.
[66] These countries include Japan, South Korea, Indonesia, Taiwan, Thailand and Vietnam. To group these countries as having similar systems of law is far from wise, and far from a reality. The variety of different legal traditions found in Asia may be gleaned from the historical origins of the laws of each country. For example, Japanese civil procedure was based on the German model. See T Nakamura, 'Commercial Litigation/ Arbitration', in L Nottage (ed), *Japan Business Law Guide*, vol. 2, CCH Asia Pte Ltd, looseleaf service, paras 80–140. South Korea's legal system was modelled on the systems found in Germany, France and Japan in the 1960s. See Seung Wha Chang, 'Republic of Korea' in M Pryles (ed), *Dispute Resolution in Asia*, 3rd edn, Kluwer Law International, 2006, p. 237, at p. 237. Indonesia's was based on the Dutch system of civil law. See K Mills, 'Indonesia', in Pryles, ibid., p. 165, at p. 166. Additionally, Seung Wha Chang has commented that although East Asia (i.e. China, Japan and Korea) have civil law traditions, there is a general misperception that they are deeply rooted in the legal systems of that region. Seung Wha Chang, op. cit. fn 35, p. 269. The background to Asia-Pacific legal cultures is discussed in Chapter 1.

of arbitral tribunals that are composed of arbitrators trained in common law jurisdictions.[67] When arbitrators from both the civil law and the common law sit together, cross-cultural influences may lead to the adoption of the better aspects from each tradition and the avoidance of weaker aspects. It is instructive to examine briefly the general features of both common law and civil law approaches to litigation. From this comparison, it is easier to identify the hybrid practices that are common in international arbitration.

The following table, at the risk of oversimplification, is an attempt to provide a general comparison of common law, civil law and international arbitration procedure for resolving private, contractual commercial disputes. What emerges from the international arbitration column is a mixed process that cannot be categorised as having a distinctly common law or civil law foundation.[68]

7.46

Comparative Table

	Civil Law[69]	Common Law[70]	International Arbitration[71]
Written Submissions or Pleadings	Contain legal and factual arguments that are to be proved by the documents or witness statements and authorities attached to the pleadings. Generally a consecutive filing of statement of claim, a defence and a reply.	Contain summary statements of the material facts, with no evidence and very little law. Generally, a consecutive filing of statement of claim (by plaintiff), a defence (by defendant) and a reply (by plaintiff).	Contain facts, law, documentary evidence, witness statements, and expert reports on which the parties rely. Typically two rounds of a consecutive exchange of such submissions. Simultaneous exchanges are also sometimes made.
Witness Statements or Affidavits	Factual witness statements are of limited probative value, and are usually brief. In France, for example, there are generally few witness testimonies in civil and commercial cases. When witnesses give testimony they ordinarily submit an 'attestation' as to facts witnessed, which under Article 202 of the French Code of Civil Procedure must contain their name, their relationship with	Affidavits written in the name of a person (called a deponent) and sworn by them to be true constitute prominent documents that are filed with the court and provided to the other party. In an affidavit, the deponents – usually key witnesses – make a statement as to their knowledge or belief in relation to relevant facts or in relation to the meaning and context of key documents.	Witness statements are often attached to written briefs (see above). Where the international arbitration involves predominantly common law lawyers and arbitrators, witness statements may be exchanged at a later stage rather than with the briefs. Article 4(5)(c) of the IBA Rules of Evidence requires witnesses to affirm the truth of the statement.

(cont.)

---

67 Hanotiau, op. cit. fn 35, pp. 359–360.
68 See, e.g. Peter Caldwell's observation that '[m]any international arbitrations are conducted in a manner that can be said to be neither inquisitorial nor adversarial, but an amalgam of the two.' P Caldwell, 'Must Arbitration be a Bloodbath?', (2006) *Asian Dispute Review* 86, at p. 87.
69 The information in the civil law column is based on Hanotiau, op. cit. fn 35, pp. 360–361 and the helpful comments provided by Maître Romain Dupeyré.
70 This column is more reflective of English court procedure rather than US procedure.
71 This column shows a common approach in international arbitration but it is certainly not the only approach because international arbitration procedures vary immensely.

Comparative Table (cont.)

	Civil Law	Common Law	International Arbitration
	the parties and must be handwritten. There is, however, no specific sanction when these requirements are not satisfied. Under Article 202, witnesses must also state they are aware that any false statement is punishable by criminal sanctions.	Affidavits of witnesses are typically filed at a later stage of the written process, after both sides have exchanged pleadings setting out their claims and the facts alleged to support the claims.	
Documentary Evidence	Contemporaneous documentary evidence is usually attached to written pleadings and is considered as the most important evidence. Documents do not need to be confirmed by a witness. However, the court must be convinced of the document's probity. If in doubt, it might ask for a document to be confirmed by a witness or expert.	Documents are tendered as evidence through witnesses. This is done mainly through affidavits in which the deponent exhibits the document and states from his or her knowledge how the document came into existence, e.g. the deponent drafted it. Documents may also be tendered as evidence through witnesses giving oral evidence.	Documents are attached to the written briefs of the parties or to witness statements or both. Documentary evidence (particularly if contemporaneous with the events in dispute) is given considerable weight, and may be considered as the most important evidence.
Document Requests	A party's obligation is to produce only documents on which that party relies. If a party requires documents held by the other party, it may ask the court to order the other party to produce it (see, e.g. Article 11 of the French Code of Civil Procedure). Requests for specific documents are regularly ordered, but general discovery requests are not. A party can, for example, request a court, before initiating a court action, to order the other parties to produce certain documents on which the outcome of a potential dispute might depend (see, e.g. Article 145 of the French Code of Civil Procedure).	Requests for broad and voluminous categories of documents may be granted. Frequently, if one party requests, the court will order the other party to set out in an affidavit a list of relevant documents which it has in its possession – whether or not they support or weaken the disclosing party's case. The requesting party may then inspect and take copies of those documents. This process is often referred to as document discovery.	Orders to produce documents are increasingly being granted, most often in the limited manner prescribed in Article 3 of the IBA Rules of Evidence (i.e. the requesting party must identify the document or narrow category of documents and explain why it is relevant). Broad requests are usually refused.
Hearings	A hearing may take place without witness testimony but this depends on the evidence submitted by the parties. If there is insufficient documentary evidence, the judge may call a witness. Or if a party has a strong desire to bring a witness, the court may	A hearing (also called a trial) would normally consist of opening statements, witness testimony (and cross-examination) and closing arguments. Oral evidence is considered highly important. In most cases, witnesses appear	Unless the case is relatively simple or the amount at issue does not justify the expense, a hearing is usually held. Arbitral institutions may have special rules for documents only or expedited arbitrations. See, e.g. HKIAC and ACICA.

Comparative Table (*cont.*)

	Civil Law	Common Law	International Arbitration
	agree. The parties restate the arguments developed in their written submissions. Oral testimony is considered secondary to documentary evidence.[72] The oral hearing would rarely exceed one or two days. Hearings are not always necessary and parties may agree that the court will decide on the basis of the parties' documents and written submissions. If this is the case in France, the lawyers file their 'dossier de plaidoirie' with the court but make no oral statement.[73]	at hearings and give evidence.[74] The hearing is of critical importance because this is where the main legal arguments are submitted (and often won or lost) and where the witness evidence on the facts could make or break a case (usually depending on the judge's assessment as to the credibility of the witness and his testimony). It is not uncommon for hearings to take several weeks, months and occasionally even years in a complex case.	Documentary evidence is generally given more weight than the oral evidence from witnesses. The length of a hearing depends on the case but hearings are generally much shorter in duration in comparison with common law courts. A hearing of more than a week or two is considered long. Witnesses are usually cross-examined.
Post-hearing	For post-hearing activity by the court, see the section on expert witnesses below. Post-hearing briefs are possible only at the request of the court for additional information if needed to take a decision. This practice is known as 'note en délibéré' under French law and is subject to Article 445 of the French Code of Civil Procedure. Post-hearing briefs may not be permitted simply because the parties want to file them.	Once the hearing is over, ordinarily no more exchanges with the judge take place until the judgment is delivered.	It is quite common for the arbitral tribunal to accept post hearing written briefs that comment on the evidence or issues that were raised at the hearing. These briefs may also recapitulate a party's arguments generally.
Expert Witnesses	The court may (on its own motion or at the request of one of the parties) request the advice of one or more technical experts	Courts do not appoint experts. It is up to a party to retain its own expert witness to give an opinion as to, for example, a medical,	The parties are free to appoint their own expert witnesses. Experts are usually required to file written statements, give

(*cont.*)

---

[72] In this regard, Hanotiau remarks that '[i]f the claims are supported by contracts or exchanges of [correspondence], judges will generally not go further. If a contract is still contradicted by testimony, it is not unusual for the contract to prevail. There has traditionally been a distrust of witnesses in the civil law system. The evidence is predominantly documentary.' Hanotiau, op. cit. fn 35, p. 360.

[73] See L Cadiet and E Jeuland, *Droit judiciaire privé*, 5th edn, Litec, 2006, para 899.

[74] Of course, in cases that involve solely a dispute as to a point of law, witnesses may not be required.

Comparative Table (cont.)		
Civil Law	**Common Law**	**International Arbitration**
appointed by the court during or after the hearing (see, e.g. Article 232 of the French Code of Civil Procedure). Court appointment of experts is frequent in practice. A court would draft the terms of reference of the experts. Courts are not bound by the expert's report. Parties may hire their own expert to dispute the findings of the court-appointed expert. Experts must respect the due process rights of the parties.	scientific or technical issue that might be in dispute. Expert witnesses appear at the oral hearing to give evidence, are cross-examined by representatives of the opposing side and questioned by the judge.	testimony at a hearing and be subjected to cross-examination. The arbitral tribunal sometimes appoints one or more independent experts to report to the arbitral tribunal. If so, any such report will normally be provided to the parties who may also request an opportunity to cross-examine the expert. See, e.g. Article 6 of the IBA Rules of Evidence.

6 Arbitral proceedings

6.1 Overview of typical procedural steps

7.47 Again, at the risk of oversimplification, the following list sets out in sequential order many of the most typical procedural steps from the commencement to the closure of an international arbitration:

(i) notice of arbitration;
(ii) response to the notice of arbitration;
(iii) appointment of arbitrators;
(iv) preliminary meeting between the arbitral tribunal and the parties at which procedural timetables and documents such as terms of reference might be prepared (this meeting may be in person, by telephone, video-link, or dispensed with altogether);
(v) exchange of written submissions (witness statements may instead be attached to pre-hearing briefs);
(vi) disclosure of documentary evidence (requests to produce);
(vii) oral hearing (with witnesses of fact and expert witnesses);
(viii) post-hearing submissions;
(ix) deliberations of the arbitrators;
(x) issuance of the award; and
(xi) setting aside or enforcement of the award in domestic courts.

7.48 As a consequence of the flexible character of arbitral procedure and party autonomy, all these steps may not feature in an arbitration and other steps not mentioned may also be adopted. In addition to the above sequence, it should be borne in mind that the arbitration procedure may sometimes be split into different phases. There may, for example, be separate phases dealing with jurisdiction, liability and quantum.

The flexibility of arbitral procedure is further enhanced by the wide discretion granted to the arbitral tribunal in its conduct of the proceedings. A typical example of this type of discretion is contained in Article 20(2) of the KCAB International Rules, which provides:[75]

7.49

> Subject to the Rules, the Tribunal may conduct the arbitration in whatever manner it considers appropriate, provided that the parties are treated with equality and that each party has the right to be heard and is given a fair opportunity to present its case.

However, vesting the arbitral tribunal with an overly wide discretion may have a negative side effect. As Philip Yang has observed, it may lead to unpredictability or uncertainty, particularly 'if the parties and their legal representatives are going before an unfamiliar international tribunal (which often happens), as it can render every application in arbitration proceedings a guessing game'.[76]

7.50

6.2 Initiating the arbitration

The notice of arbitration (or request for arbitration) initiates the arbitration process. This document demands that a certain dispute be referred to arbitration. It typically includes details of the parties, the arbitration clause or agreement invoked, the nature of the claim and remedy sought, and proposals for the appointment of arbitrators.[77] Institutional arbitration rules often require that the respondent submit an answer (or response) to the notice or request, which is a brief document responding to the notice of arbitration.[78] Later provisions of those rules may require parties to file more detailed written submissions, such as a statement of claim (or case) or a statement of defence.

7.51

The approach of the CIETAC Rules is different in that Article 10 requires a statement of facts and grounds of claim with supporting evidence to be included in the request for arbitration. Thereafter, the respondent is required under Article 11 to submit a 'Statement of Defence' in which the respondent must set forth

7.52

---

[75] This rule is based on Article 19(2) of the Model Law and Article 15(1) of the UNCITRAL Arbitration Rules. A similar provision is found in ACICA Rules Article 17.1. Additionally, HKIAC Rules Article 14.1 instructs the arbitral tribunal to 'adopt suitable procedures for the conduct of the arbitration, in order to avoid unnecessary delay or expenses'; and SIAC Rules, Rule 15.2 states 'the Tribunal shall conduct the arbitration in such manner as it considers appropriate to ensure the fair, expeditious, economical and final determination of the dispute.' A similar additional sentence is now found in Article 17(1) of the 2010 UNCITRAL Arbitration Rules: 'The arbitral tribunal, in exercising its discretion, shall conduct the proceedings so as to avoid unnecessary delay and expense and to provide a fair and efficient process for resolving the parties' dispute.' ICC Rules Article 20(1) empowers the arbitral tribunal 'to establish the facts of the case by all appropriate means'.
[76] Yang, op. cit. fn 14, p. 165.
[77] See, e.g. ACICA Rules Article 4; HKIAC Rules Article 4; ICC Rules Article 4; JCAA Rules, Rule 14; KCAB International Rules Article 8; SIAC Rules, Rule 3. See also Model Law Article 23.
[78] See, e.g. ACICA Rules Article 5; HKIAC Rules Article 5; ICC Rules Article 5; JCAA Rules, Rule 18; KCAB International Rules Article 9; SIAC Rules, Rule 4. The ACICA Rules have adopted a relatively innovative step in this respect, which permits the parties to include the written statements of claim or defence (described below) in their notice of arbitration and answer. This procedure, if adopted by the parties, has the time-saving advantage of enabling work to be carried out on the statements of claim and defence at the same time as the arbitrators are being appointed. See S Greenberg, 'ACICA's New International Arbitration Rules', (2006) 23(2) *Journal of International Arbitration* 193. The Swiss Rules Articles 4(c) and 8 (c) have similar provisions. SIAC Rules, Rule 3.2 provides an option for the claimant to submit its statement of case with the notice of arbitration but is silent as to whether the respondent can submit its statement of defence with its response.

'the facts and grounds on which the defense is based' and include 'the relevant evidence supporting the defense'.[79]

7.53 In arbitrations conducted under the 1976 UNCITRAL Arbitration Rules, after the notice of arbitration (which may also contain a statement of claim) is received by the respondent, there is no requirement for an answer – the parties proceed directly to appointing the arbitrator(s).[80] Following a recommendation from the Working Group, the requirement of a 'response' to the notice of arbitration has been included in Article 4 of the 2010 UNCITRAL Arbitration Rules.[81]

6.3 Representation

7.54 Arbitration rules and laws generally do not require that a person representing a party in an arbitration be a lawyer. Article 6 of the ACICA Rules, for example, provides that 'parties may be represented or assisted [in the arbitration] by persons of their choice'.[82] In practice, however, lawyers virtually always represent the parties in large international commercial arbitrations. In this regard, arbitration legislation tends to provide that lawyers need not be qualified in the jurisdiction in which the arbitration takes place in order to be permitted to represent clients in that arbitration.[83] And, typically, no restriction is placed on the nationality of the representatives.[84]

7.55 In 1988, the Singapore High Court in *Builders Federal (Hong Kong) Ltd and Joseph Gartner & Co v Turner (East Asia) Pte Ltd*[85] interpreted Singapore's Legal Profession Act as not permitting foreign lawyers to represent clients in arbitrations seated in Singapore. However, the Singapore legislature subsequently amended that Act to eliminate any restrictions on the ability of foreign lawyers to act for clients in arbitrations seated in Singapore.[86]

7.56 In the arbitration at issue in *Government of Malaysia v Zublin Muhibbah Joint Venture*,[87] Zublin required the assistance of an American attorney. Malaysia objected on the ground that the attorney retained was not an advocate and solicitor under the Malaysian Legal Profession Act 1976. In response, Zublin applied to the High Court of Kuala Lumpur arguing that the Act did not prevent

---
79 A similar procedure is found in ICA Rules 15 and 18.
80 See, e.g. UNCITRAL Arbitration Rules Articles 3–8.
81 Report of Working Group II (Arbitration and Conciliation) on the work of its forty-ninth session, (Vienna, 15–19 September 2008), UN Doc A/CN.9/665, para 40.
82 ACICA Rules Article 6. Similar types of freedom as to representation are provided in other institutional rules in the region, e.g. CIETAC Rules Article 16; HKIAC Rules Article 5(8); SIAC Rule 20. But see ICA Rule 45 ('where the dispute is purely of a commercial nature, the parties shall have no right to be represented by lawyers except where, having regard to the nature or complexity of the dispute, the arbitral tribunal considers it necessary in the interests of justice . . . '). See also Australian International Arbitration Act Section 29(2); and Hong Kong Arbitration Ordinance Section 2F.
83 See Greenberg, op. cit. fn 78, p. 193; and M Polkinghorne, 'More Changes in Singapore: Appearance Rights of Foreign Counsel', (2005) 22 *Journal of International Arbitration* 75.
84 See, e.g. CIETAC Rules Article 16(2).
85 Singapore High Court, 30 March 1988, reported in (1988) 2 *Malaysian Law Journal* 280; and (1988) 5(3) *Journal of International Arbitration* 139.
86 See Polkinghorne, op. cit. fn 83.
87 [1990] 3 MLJ 125 (High Court, Kuala Lumpur). The Government of Malaysia filed an appeal to the Malaysian Supreme Court, which dismissed the appeal without comment. (1991) XVI *Yearbook of Commercial Arbitration* 166.

foreign lawyers from representing parties to arbitration proceedings. The High Court agreed with Zublin and dismissed Malaysia's objection. It considered that an arbitral tribunal was not a court of law and, accordingly, the Act was not applicable.

One exception in the region is found in Indonesia's BANI Rules, Article 5(2) of which provides: 7.57

> if a party is represented by a foreign advisor or a foreign legal advisor in an arbitration case relating to a dispute that abides by the Indonesian law, the foreign advisor or the foreign legal advisor may attend only if he is accompanied by an Indonesian advisor or legal advisor.

The situation in China also requires specific note. The position of the Chinese Ministry of Justice has been said to be that 'Foreign law firms are not prohibited from representing clients in arbitration cases in China; however, when Chinese law is applied or Chinese law issues are concerned, they should refrain from providing legal advice or comments, but assist clients in engaging local lawyers to do so'.[88] The practical impact of this is restrictive. It has been observed that on its face this appears to permit 'foreign law firms to practice arbitration in China; however, since Chinese law is applied or otherwise implicated in almost every arbitration case in China, the prohibition on providing advice or commenting on relevant China law issues constitutes a restriction'.[89] 7.58

The cross-border freedom to provide legal services and the continuing rise in recourse to international arbitration raises a problem that will need to be addressed by the international arbitration community in the future. If the bar association in the jurisdiction where a lawyer obtains his authorisation to practise legitimately suspends or cancels that lawyer's right to practise, he may still be permitted to represent a client in an international arbitration that takes place in another jurisdiction. A standard may one day need to be established to measure and control the professional conduct of lawyers practising in international arbitration. Institutional rules and domestic laws may also need to empower arbitral tribunals to refuse a party's chosen representative in appropriate cases.[90] 7.59

6.4 Preliminary meeting

Once an arbitral tribunal has been appointed, the arbitrators may confer by teleconference or email and discuss issues relating to the organisation and conduct of the proceedings. Thereafter, the arbitral tribunal might hold a preliminary meeting with the parties. At this preliminary meeting the arbitral tribunal, in 7.60

---

[88] Letter from Ministry of Justice quoted in Jingzhou Tao, 'Challenges and Trends of Arbitration in China', (2004) 12 *ICCA Congress Series* 84. See also Articles 15 and 32 of the Chinese State Council's Regulations on Representative Offices of Foreign Law Firms in China, 22 December 2001. Nonetheless, Article 16 of the CIETAC Rules places no such restriction on lawyers and states that either Chinese or foreign citizens may be authorised by a party to act as its representative.
[89] Jingzhou Tao, ibid.
[90] See Greenberg, op. cit. fn 78, pp. 193–194. The IBA formulated a code of ethics for lawyers in 1956 and revised it in 1988. References to these rules are not frequent and they do not cover the situation from the perspective of an arbitral tribunal, i.e. whether there are circumstances in which the arbitral tribunal may refuse to hear a party's chosen representative.

consultation with the parties, will decide a number of procedural issues such as: the method of communication between the arbitral tribunal and the parties; how document production will take place; how oral evidence will be heard; and a timetable for service or exchange of written submissions.[91]

6.5 Terms of reference

7.61 The ICC is well known for requiring 'terms of reference' to be drawn up by the arbitral tribunal as soon as it receives the arbitration file from the ICC Secretariat. Aside from certain administrative details, Article 18(1) of the ICC Rules requires that those terms include a summary of the parties' claims and the particulars of the applicable procedural rules. They may also include a list of issues to be determined. The terms of reference must be signed by the arbitral tribunal as well as the parties.[92] In some instances, where an original arbitration agreement is defective, the terms of reference – because they are signed by the parties – may be considered as a substitute arbitration agreement.[93] A default procedure is provided in Article 18(3) in case a party refuses to sign the terms of reference.

7.62 A similar procedure for a 'memorandum of issues' is found in Rule 17 of the 2007 SIAC Rules. This procedure has been omitted from SIAC's 2010 Rules.

7.63 The terms of reference or equivalent will often be prepared or finalised at the preliminary meeting referred to above.

6.6 Written submissions

7.64 Like virtually all aspects of arbitration procedure, the type, number and sequence of written submissions is flexible and varies greatly.

7.65 Detailed written submissions are ordinarily served or submitted after the notice of arbitration and answer, but may be done away with in a small arbitration. It is common for the exchange of written submissions to take place consecutively rather than simultaneously.[94] Accordingly, the claimant is normally the first party to file a written submission on substantive issues (a respondent may be required to submit his objections first if there is an initial jurisdictional phase). This document usually takes the form of a statement of claim,[95] attached to which would be the documentary evidence and witness statements relied on by

---

[91] Some institutional rules specify precise times within which certain procedural steps must be made. See, for example, ICC Rules Articles 5(1), 18(2) and 24; and SIAC Rules, Rules 16.3, 16.4 and 27.1. Other types of matters that might be discussed are conveniently listed in a document prepared by UNCITRAL entitled Notes on Organizing Arbitral Proceedings (1996), available at http://www.uncitral.org/pdf/english/texts/arbitration/arb-notes/arb-notes-e.pdf.
[92] See ICC Rules Articles 18(1). See also *Commonwealth Development Corp (UK) v Montague* [2000] QCA 252 (Supreme Court of Queensland Court of Appeal), discussed in S Greenberg and M Secomb, 'Terms of Reference and Negative Jurisdictional Decisions: A Lesson from Australia', (2002) 18(2) *Arbitration International* 125.
[93] See Greenberg and Secomb, ibid.
[94] See, e.g. ACICA Rules Articles 21 and 22; HKIAC Rules Articles 17 and 18; SIAC Rules, Rule 16; UNCITRAL Arbitration Rules Articles 18 and 19.
[95] Other names used to denote this pleading include 'statement of case', 'memorial', 'claim submissions' or 'points of claim'. Philip Yang observes that the first three terms indicate informal pleadings (which would include the factual and legal arguments, as well as documentary evidence) whereas the latter suggests a briefer style of pleading. Yang, op. cit. fn 14, p. 187.

the claimant.[96] After a statement of claim is served or submitted,[97] the respondent is required to serve or submit a statement of defence,[98] to which would ordinarily be attached supportive documentary evidence and witness statements. If there is a counterclaim, this would usually be filed with the statement of defence.[99] There may be a second round or even further rounds of pre-hearing exchanges of submissions.[100]

7.66 Certain international commercial arbitration rules specifically provide the option for arbitrations to be determined only on the submitted documents, including the written submissions, witness statements and documentary evidence.[101] As a consequence, there may be no hearing at all. In this regard, Article 24(1) of the Model Law provides:[102]

> Subject to any contrary agreement by the parties, the arbitral tribunal shall decide whether to hold oral hearings for the presentation of evidence or for oral argument, or whether the proceedings shall be conducted on the basis of documents and other materials. However, unless the parties have agreed that no hearings shall be held, the arbitral tribunal shall hold such hearings at an appropriate stage of the proceedings, if so requested by a party.

7.67 Although in practice it is relatively rare for arbitral proceedings to be based solely on documents, this may result in very fast and economical arbitrations.[103]

7.68 Documentary evidence is often attached to pre-hearing written submissions. However, in rare cases, a party might wish to withhold a document for a later stage of the proceedings. This might be part of a strategy used to withhold the document until the cross-examination of a witness. Caution should be applied in adopting such a technique because (1) that document may be required to be disclosed in a document production request and (2) it is highly probable that the other party will object to the document's later inclusion on the grounds that

---

96 Certain rules may require that if the documents are especially voluminous, lists of them should be submitted in lieu of the documents. See, e.g. LCIA Rules Article 15(6).
97 Exactly how this is done may be agreed at a preliminary meeting between the arbitral tribunal and the parties. Institutional rules often deal with the statement of claim specifically, see, e.g. ACICA Rules Article 21; HKIAC Rules Article 17; SIAC Rules, Rule 16; 1976 UNCITRAL Arbitration Rules Article 18; 2010 UNCITRAL Arbitration Rules Article 20.
98 Other names used to denote this pleading include, 'counter-defence submissions', 'rebuttal', or 'points of defence'. Institutional rules often deal with the statement of defence specifically, see, e.g. ACICA Rules Article 22; HKIAC Rules Article 18; SIAC Rules, Rule 16; 1976 UNCITRAL Arbitration Rules Article 19; and 2010 UNCITRAL Arbitration Rules Article 21.
99 See, e.g. ACICA Rules Article 22.2; HKIAC Rules Article 18.3; SIAC Rules, Rule 16.5; 1976 UNCITRAL Arbitration Rules Article 19(3); and 2010 UNCITRAL Arbitration Rules Article 21(3).
100 See, e.g. 2010 UNCITRAL Arbitration Rules Article 24; 1976 UNCITRAL Arbitration Rules Article 22; Rule 31 of the ICSID Rules. Even in fast track arbitrations the discretion to allow further rounds is granted to the arbitral tribunal. See, e.g. the HKIAC Short Form Arbitration Rules Article 7; and the ACICA Expedited Rules Article 21.
101 See, e.g. HKIAC Short Form Arbitration Rules Article 12; ACICA Rules Article 17.2; HKIAC Rules Article 38; CIETAC Article 29(2) and 54; SIAC Rules, Rule 21.1; 1976 UNCITRAL Arbitration Rules Article 15(2); 2010 UNCITRAL Arbitration Rules Article 17(3); ICC Rules Article 20(6); LCIA Rules Article 19(1). See also Article 24(1) of the Model Law. One Asian arbitrator has remarked that the tendency in international arbitration is to hold hearings in all but very simple cases. Sawada, op. cit. fn 43, p. 290.
102 See also ICC Rules Article 20(2) and 20(6). An inversion of this rule is found in Article 36 of Indonesia's Arbitration and Dispute Resolution Act 1999, which requires that the dispute be heard and decided first on the basis of written documents, but that oral hearings may take place with the approval of the parties or if the arbitrators deem it necessary.
103 See, e.g. Yang, op. cit. fn 14, pp. 171–172. Article 13.2 of the ACICA Expedited Arbitration Rules is notable here because its starting position is that no hearings should be held. However, this is subject to exceptions.

(i) it has been submitted out of time; (ii) it is unfair to surprise the opposing party with such a document; and/or (iii) extra time is needed to respond to it, with the costs of any adjournment to be paid by the late-submitting party.[104]

7.69 As regards the filing or service of the written submissions, deadlines are usually set by the arbitral tribunal in consultation with the parties. The amount of time may vary according to the complexity of the circumstances and legal issues in dispute. In the absence of agreement by the parties and subject to the arbitral tribunal's (or arbitral institution's) discretion, some institutional rules fix time periods for submission.[105]

7.70 Post-hearing written submissions are common in larger cases. In these submissions, parties are typically permitted to comment on the evidence that was given during the hearing or they may be permitted to summarise in one final document all factual and legal arguments presented during the proceedings. All parties are normally required to submit these briefs simultaneously at a set date subsequent to the final hearing.[106]

7.71 If an exhibited document is not in the language of the arbitration, the submitting party may be required to translate it. Sometimes, to save costs, it might be agreed that certain documents or documents in certain languages do not need translation. It might be felt that the time and cost of translation outweighs the benefit of translating them.

6.7 Amendment of claims

7.72 Many institutional rules and laws in the region provide for the amendment of the claim or defence. For example, Article 23 of the ACICA Rules provides that:[107]

> During the course of the arbitral proceedings either party may amend or supplement its claim or defence unless the Arbitral Tribunal considers it inappropriate to allow such amendment having regard to the delay in making it or prejudice to the other party or any other circumstances it considers relevant. However, a claim may not be amended in such a manner that the amended claim falls outside the scope of the arbitration clause or separate arbitration agreement.

7.73 The ICC Rules are different in this respect. They are silent as to 'amendments' to claims but prohibit the introduction of 'new claims' falling outside the scope

---

104 See, e.g. Article 36(2) of the 2005 CIETAC Rules, which provides that the arbitral tribunal may disallow evidence filed out of time.
105 See, e.g. CIETAC Rules Article 12; KCAB International Rules Article 9; LCIA Rules Article 15; SIAC Rule 16.7. It is to be noted that JCAA Rule 12 expressly prevents the parties (not the arbitral tribunal) from agreeing on an extension of the time to submit an answer to the request for arbitration or a counterclaim.
106 See Hanotiau, op. cit. fn 35, p. 388.
107 This provision is very similar to HKIAC Rules Article 19, UNCITRAL Arbitration Rules Article 20 and 2010 UNCITRAL Arbitration Rules Article 22. Article 19.2 of the HKIAC Rules adds that the administrative and arbitrators' fees may be adjusted if an amendment is made. See also CIETAC Rules Article 14; SIAC Rules, Rule 24(c); JCAA Rules, Rule 20; KCAB International Rules Article 17; Model Law Article 23(2) and Vietnam's Ordinance on Commercial Arbitration 2003 Article 28. Concerning the factors that might be considered in applying Article 20 of the UNCITRAL Arbitration Rules, see *Rockwell International Systems Inc v Government of the Islamic Republic of Iran* (1989) 23 Iran-US CTR 150, para 73; G Aldrich, *The Jurisprudence of the Iran-United States Claims Tribunal*, Clarendon Press, 1996, pp. 420–433; and Caron, Caplan and Pellonpää, op. cit. fn 46, pp. 466–475.

of the terms of reference without the arbitral tribunal's permission.[108] No definition of a 'new claim' is provided. A mere amendment to, say, the quantum of the claim, or refining the language of a claim will not normally be considered as a new claim. More complex amendments may give rise to arguments that they effectively constitute new claims. However, even if certain claims are considered to be new they may fall within the scope of the claims as set out in the terms of reference. Even if they do not, the arbitral tribunal has discretion to authorise them after considering 'the nature of such new claims... the stage of the arbitration and other relevant circumstances'.[109] Eric Schwartz observes that 'there should... not normally be an issue about whether a party's articulation of new *legal arguments* gives rise to a "new claim" within the meaning of Article 19' (Emphasis added).[110] Furthermore, if a new claim is not admitted, that does not amount to rejection of the claim. A claim not admitted, subject to jurisdictional requirements, may be reintroduced in a later proceeding.

6.8 On-site inspections

Colloquially, an on-site inspection may be referred to as a 'see, touch and smell' exercise. It gives the arbitral tribunal an important impression of a place or object that is relevant to the arbitration and may provide the arbitrators with a deeper understanding of the factual issues in dispute. The power to conduct on-site inspections is given to most courts and arbitral tribunals.[111]   7.74

The IBA Rules of Evidence cover this issue in Article 7. An inspection under those Rules may be requested by one of the parties or may be initiated by the arbitral tribunal itself. The arbitral tribunal may also require parties to allow inspection by the arbitral tribunal-appointed expert. The Rules cover the inspection of 'any site, property, machinery, or any other goods or process, or documents'. No real criteria have been provided to guide the arbitral tribunal as to why, when and how an on-site inspection should be conducted. It thus remains a largely discretionary power. In conformity with due process requirements, parties or their representatives should have the right to attend any on-site inspection.   7.75

Article 57 of the UNCITRAL Notes on Organizing Arbitral Proceedings warns against communications at on-site inspections between arbitrators and a party concerning points at issue without the presence of the other party. Otherwise this would offend the principles of equal treatment and the opportunity to present one's case. Article 58 of the Notes also cautions that statements made by   7.76

---

108 See Article 19 of the ICC Rules ('no party shall make new claims or counterclaims which fall outside the limits of the Terms of Reference unless it has been authorized to do so by the Arbitral Tribunal...').
109 ICC Rules Article 19. See generally Derains and Schwartz, op. cit. fn 24, pp. 266–270.
110 E Schwartz, '"New Claims" in ICC Arbitration: Navigating Article 19 of the ICC Rules', (2006) 17(2) *ICC International Court of Arbitration Bulletin* 55, at p. 58.
111 See, e.g. Model Law Article 24; HKIAC Rules Article 15.3; ICSID Rules, Rule 37; JCAA Rules, Rule 37(3); KCAB International Rules Article 22(1)(b); SIAC Rules, Rule 24(f); UNCITRAL Arbitration Rules Article 16(3). The 2010 UNCITRAL Rules appear to now include this power in Article 18(2) although the provision is worded differently. It is now based on the wording in the LCIA Rules. As to national courts in Asian common law countries, see C Lau, 'The Process of Obtaining Evidence and Discovery in Asia' in Pryles and Moser, op. cit. fn 8, p. 259, at p. 265.

representatives of a party present at an on-site inspection should not be treated as evidence in the proceedings.

7.77   Finally, Article 24(2) of the Model Law provides that for any meeting of the arbitral tribunal at which inspection of property is to take place, the parties should be given sufficient advance notice. Again, this is simply an application of due process principles.[112]

6.9 Bifurcation and trifurcation

7.78   A procedural device that may increase efficiency in arbitration involves splitting the procedure into several phases. Bifurcation and trifurcation, respectively, divide the proceedings into two or three phases, for example, one dealing with jurisdictional issues,[113] one dealing with liability and a final one with quantum or costs.[114] Partial arbitral awards may be issued for each phase before the following one begins. This division can save costs and time. For example, if the arbitral tribunal determines that it lacks jurisdiction over the matter, the division dispenses with the parties' need to expend time, effort and legal fees to produce detailed written pleadings on the merits.[115] And if the case fails on liability grounds, pleadings and expert opinions as to the quantification of the damages will be rendered unnecessary. The proceedings may also be broken down into further phases, such as to enable the arbitral tribunal to dispose of different arguments separately. A decision or partial award by an arbitral tribunal on a distinct issue may also prompt parties to settle the dispute.[116]

6.10 Party default and non-participating parties

7.79   Some international arbitrations involve a respondent that decides not to participate in the arbitration. Less often, a claimant may file a notice of arbitration but thereafter it may fail to submit a statement of claim. The arbitration's procedural laws and rules usually stipulate the consequences in these situations of party default.

7.80   In the context of ICC arbitration, in 2009 there was at least one non-participating party in 6.4% of ICC arbitration cases.[117] Non-participation raises

---

112 See also, Article 20(2) of the Model Law.
113 Section 3.4 of Chapter 5 addresses situations where it might not be suitable to split the proceedings.
114 Institutional rules of procedure do not usually make specific reference to bifurcation or trifurcation. But it is well accepted that the power to bifurcate or trifurcate lies within the arbitral tribunal's discretion to conduct the proceedings in a manner it considers appropriate. A rare instance of a set of rules that makes specific reference to bifurcation is KCAB International Rules Article 20(3).
115 See the discussion on whether to decide jurisdiction separately at Section 3.4 of Chapter 5.
116 See H Heilbron, 'Assessing Damages in International Arbitration: Practical Considerations', in Newman and Hill, op. cit. fn 5, p. 445.
117 This figure is based on failure to participate, not necessarily from the very outset of the arbitration but from the time the ICC Court took its initial decisions in connection with constituting the arbitral tribunal and other preliminary matters, i.e. the Secretariat's 'first submission' of the case to the ICC Court.

the question whether the arbitration should proceed ex parte (i.e. without the respondent's participation).[118] In a domestic court in both civil law and common law systems, non-participation by the defendant will normally invest the plaintiff with a right to a default judgment against the defendant. In arbitration, however, refusal by the respondent to participate does not override the arbitral tribunal's duty to examine and question the claimant's position. Importantly, the claimant is still required to prove its case. According to Article 25(b) of the Model Law, if:

> the respondent fails to communicate his statement of defence... the arbitral tribunal shall continue the proceedings without treating such failure in itself as an admission of the claimant's allegations.

Once an arbitral tribunal is satisfied that a well-founded case is made out, it must issue an award that is accompanied by reasons for its decisions and detailing the circumstances of the respondent's failure to participate. To ensure that the respondent has been given an opportunity to present its case, the arbitral tribunal usually allocates periods of time for the respondent to file a defence, etc. When a hearing is called, time is allocated to hear the respondent and the respondent is given due notice.[119] It is essential that all communications between the arbitral tribunal and the participating parties are sent to any non-participating party.[120]

7.81

Most institutional arbitral rules expressly address the situation where a respondent has failed to file written submissions or appear at the hearing.[121] They empower the arbitral tribunal to proceed with the arbitration as outlined above. The non-participating respondent may seek to set aside or resist enforcement of the resulting award. In considering such applications, a domestic court seized of the matter should not, absent exceptional circumstances, hold that a party's refusal to participate equated to an inability to present its case.[122]

7.82

Hainan Machinery Import & Export Corporation v Donald & McArthy Pte Ltd[123] illustrates this point. Hainan initiated CIETAC arbitration proceedings but some of the documents it relied on were in Chinese. Donald wrote twice to CIETAC requesting a translation of those documents and stating that it did not agree

7.83

---

118 See, generally, Redfern, Hunter, et al., op. cit. fn 45, paras 6–119 to 6–122; and B Beaumont, 'Ex Parte or Default Proceedings in International Arbitration', (2004) *Asian Dispute Review* 76.

119 Under Article 44 of Indonesia's Arbitration and Dispute Resolution Act 1999, if a respondent does not appear at a hearing, the arbitral tribunal is required to call a second hearing. It is only if the respondent fails to attend this second hearing that the arbitral tribunal may determine the claim in favour of the claimant 'unless the claim is unfounded or contrary to law.'

120 See, e.g. Beaumont, op. cit. fn 118, p. 77 (commenting that in a case where the respondent fails to participate in the arbitral proceedings, the arbitral tribunal has a duty 'to require the claimant to fill the gaps, all the while adhering to the rules of natural justice, by copying all such requests, or demands, to the defaulting party.... the defaulting party must be kept supplied with copies of all correspondence, pleadings, evidence and submissions up to and including the issuance of the award'.).

121 See, e.g. ACICA Rules Article 29; CIETAC Rules Article 34; HKIAC Rules Article 26; ICA Rules, Rules 46 and 54(ii); ICC Rules Article 25; JCAA Rules, Rule 35; KCAB International Rules Article 29; SIAC Rules, Rule 21.3; and UNCITRAL Arbitration Rules Article 28. See also the Model Law Articles 25 and 28; and the Japanese Arbitration Law 2003 Article 33.

122 In this regard, Redfern, Hunter et al., identify two situations in which a 'refusal' to participate is not altogether clear: where the party creates a delay so unreasonable that it amounts to abandoning its right to present its case; and where the party disrupts the hearing to such an extent that it is impossible to conduct it and as such the party's conduct is equivalent to a refusal to participate. Redfern, Hunter, et al., op. cit. fn 45, para 6–120.

123 [1996] 1 SLR 34 (Singapore High Court).

to the institution of arbitration proceedings. Although informed of the hearing Donald did not attend. After the hearing, Donald was informed that it had taken place and was given an opportunity to submit materials. Donald simply replied stating that it did not agree to the arbitration. An award was rendered in favour of Hainan. Enforcement of the award was sought and granted in Singapore. The decision of the Singapore High Court in granting enforcement noted that there were no errors of procedure made in the arbitration.[124]

7.84 Not all laws or rules address a claimant's failure to submit a statement of claim after it has made a request for arbitration. The procedural laws or the arbitral rules that deal with such a circumstance generally require termination of the arbitral proceedings.[125] If the claimant fails to appear at the hearing without sufficient cause, institutional rules ordinarily provide the arbitral tribunal with the discretion to continue with the proceedings.[126]

6.11 Expedited arbitration procedures

7.85 In certain circumstances, the parties to arbitration may desire a swift resolution of their dispute. The principle of party autonomy allows them to agree on an expedited or fast-track procedure.[127] Parties may prefer faster dispute resolution at the possible sacrifice of a better quality decision. A more cost effective process is an important feature of expedited arbitration, particularly where the amount in dispute is relatively small.[128] The rapid determination of legal rights has also been considered positive in the sense that it reduces prolonged uncertainty.[129]

7.86 Expedited rules may be contained within the standard arbitration rules of an institution,[130] they may take the form of a separate body of self-contained rules on expedited procedure,[131] or they might be specifically formulated by the parties themselves. Fast-track rules may include:

---

[124] *Hainan Machinery Import & Export Corporation v Donald & McArthy Pte Ltd*, [1996] 1 SLR 34 at para 15. See also *Texaco Overseas Tankship Ltd v Okada Kaiun KK* (1985) 10 *Yearbook of Commercial Arbitration* 483, (Osaka District Court), 22 April 1983.
[125] See, e.g. Model Law Article 25(b); ACICA Rules Article 29.1; HKIAC Rules Article 26; UNCITRAL Arbitration Rules Article 28.
[126] See, e.g. ACICA Rules Article 29.2; ICA Rules, Rules 46 and 54(i); JCAA Rules, Rule 35; KCAB International Rules Article 29; SIAC Rules, Rule 21.3; UNCITRAL Arbitration Rules Article 28(2); and 2010 UNCITRAL Arbitration Rules Article 30(2). The CIETAC Rules Article 34(1) states that this conduct may be deemed as a withdrawal of the claimant's request for arbitration.
[127] See generally, M Silverman, 'The Fast-Track Arbitration of the International Chamber of Commerce – The User's Point of View', (1993) 10(4) *Journal of International Arbitration* 113; B Davis, O Lagacé Glain and M Volkovitsch, 'When Doctrines Meet – Fast-Track Arbitration and the ICC Experience', (1993) 10(4) *Journal of International Arbitration* 69; S Smid, 'The Expedited Procedure in Maritime and Commodity Arbitrations', (1993) 10(4) *Journal of International Arbitration* 59; PY Tschanz, 'The Chamber of Commerce and Industry of Geneva's Arbitration Rules and their Expedited Procedure', (1993) 10(4) *Journal of International Arbitration* 51.
[128] See, e.g. M Mustill, 'Comments on Fast-Track Arbitration', (1993) 10(4) *Journal of International Arbitration* 121, at p. 123.
[129] See B Davis, 'Fast Track Arbitration and Fast-Tracking Your Arbitration', (1992) 9(4) *Journal of International Arbitration* 43, at p. 43.
[130] See, e.g. CIETAC Rules Articles 50–58; JCAA Rules, Rules 59–67; HKIAC Rules Article 38; 2010 SIAC Rules, Rule 5.
[131] See, e.g. ACICA Expedited Arbitration Rules (2008); HKIAC Documents-only Procedure (2000); HKIAC Small Claims Procedure (2003); WIPO Expedited Arbitration Rules (2002).

(i) expedited constitution of the arbitral tribunal;[132]
(ii) a requirement that the proceedings be conducted by a sole arbitrator;[133]
(iii) shortened time limits for submission of briefs;[134]
(iv) 'documents-only' determinations without oral hearings;[135] and/or
(v) a relatively short period within which the award must be issued.[136]

Some arbitration rules specifically provide for expedited proceedings in cases involving less than a specified disputed amount.[137]

7.87

6.12 Arb-med

As its name suggests, arb-med is a fusion of arbitration and mediation. Under this process, arbitrating parties agree that their arbitrator may act as a mediator in the same dispute at some point during the arbitral proceedings.[138] The essential difference between arbitration and mediation is that the latter is facilitative. It involves an impartial third party mediator who assists the parties to arrive at a settlement.[139] Unlike an arbitrator, a mediator lacks the power to impose a decision on the parties. Conciliation is a term that is commonly used to denote mediation,[140] although to some the two terms have distinct meanings.[141] Unless otherwise indicated, we use conciliation as a synonym for mediation.

7.88

While the Model Law does not address whether an arbitrator may become a mediator in the same dispute, many of this region's Model Law countries have

7.89

---

132 See, e.g. ACICA Expedited Arbitration Rules Article 8(2); HKIAC Rules Article 38.2(a); LCIA Rules Article 9.
133 See, e.g. CIETAC Rules Article 52; HKIAC Rules Article 38.1(b).
134 See, e.g. ACICA Expedited Arbitration Rules Article 22; CIETAC Rules Article 53.
135 See, e.g. ACICA Expedited Arbitration Rules Article 13.2; HKIAC Rules Article 38.2(c).
136 See, e.g. ACICA Expedited Arbitration Rules Article 27; CIETAC Rules Article 56; HKIAC Rules Article 38.2(d). Rule 5.2(e) of the 2010 SIAC Rules adds that the arbitral tribunal shall state its reasons in summary form, unless parties agree no reasons are to be given.
137 See, e.g. CIETAC Rules Article 50; HKIAC Rules Article 38; the 2010 SIAC Rules, Rule 5.1(a).
138 For a wide variety of interesting views on arb-med, including from some Asia-Pacific arbitrators, see (2004) 12 *ICCA Congress Series* 531 et seq. See also L Nottage and R Garnett, 'The Top Twenty Things to Change In or Around Australia's International Arbitration Act' in L Nottage and R Garnett (eds), *International Arbitration in Australia*, Federation Press, forthcoming 2010, ch. 8, pt. IV.E.
139 In relation to the particularly long tradition of mediation in China, see Xiaobing Xu and G Wilson, 'One Country, Two-International Commercial Arbitration-Systems', (2000) 17(6) *Journal of International Arbitration* 47, at p. 64 et seq (section VIII(D)); G Kaufmann-Kohler and Fan Kun, 'Integrating Mediation into Arbitration: Why It Works in China', (2008) 25(4) *Journal of International Arbitration* 479, at pp. 480–486; S Hilmer, *Mediation in the People's Republic of China and Hong Kong (SAR)*, Eleven International Publishing, 2009, pp. 8–11 and 69–74; and generally (2009) 17 *Asia Pacific Law Review*, Special Issue on Mediation. See also China's Supreme People's Court opinion entitled 'Several Opinions on Establishing and Improving of a Dispute Resolution System and the Linking of Litigation and Alternative Dispute Resolution Mechanism' (2009) No. 45, issued on 24 July 2009. Prior to this, agreements reached through mediation were enforceable only through mediation conducted under CIETAC auspices or through judges using Chinese civil procedure. Now, according to para 10 of the opinion, such agreements are enforceable if the mediation is carried out by other mediation organisations. See FP Phillips, 'Important Development in Chinese Business Mediation', 8 September 2009, at http://businessconflictmanagement.com. In Hong Kong, the High Court's Practice Direction 31, effective from 1 January 2010, requires that parties must consider mediation before they litigate. Some predict that this will increase the use of mediation prior to arbitration.
140 See, e.g. CIETAC Rules Article 40.
141 Used in its strict sense, conciliation refers to a process whereby a conciliator hears the parties' positions and then proposes terms of settlement that the conciliator believes are a fair compromise which the parties are free to accept or reject. See K Tashiro, 'Conciliation or Mediation during the Arbitral Process: A Japanese View', (1995) 12 *Journal of International Arbitration* 2, at p. 119, n. 1; Hilmer, op. cit. fn 139, pp. 5–6 and Moses, op. cit. fn 22, p. 14.

enacted domestic legislative provisions enabling arb-med procedures.[142] Often, it is observed that there is a preference for non-confrontational dispute settlement methods in the Asia-Pacific.[143] Whether or not this is correct for the region as a whole, the fact remains that arb-med, in various manifestations, is recognised in many countries in the region.[144]

7.90 In relation to China in particular, it has been observed by Michael Moser that '[o]ne of the unique characteristics of arbitration in China is that proceedings before the international arbitration bodies frequently involve conciliation'.[145] From a Chinese perspective, the advantages of arb-med have been summarised as follows:[146]

> Chinese scholars strongly believe that the combination of the two procedures has more advantages than does keeping them apart. First, separate procedures can be avoided and substantial time and money can be saved; second, the Chinese experience shows that more of the successful conciliation cases are conducted by arbitrators during arbitration proceedings than by conciliators in the process of stand-alone conciliation; third the combination of arbitration with conciliation can make good use of the advantages of both. An arbitral award based on a settlement agreement may not only satisfy both parties' needs and thus transform antagonists into friends but may also be enforced in court.

7.91 The CIETAC Rules provide for arb-med in Article 40:

> 2. Where both parties have the desire for conciliation or one party so desires and the other party agrees when approached by the arbitral tribunal, the arbitral tribunal may conciliate the case during the course of the arbitration proceedings.
> 3. The arbitral tribunal may conciliate the case in the manner it considers appropriate.
> 4. The arbitral tribunal shall terminate the conciliation and continue the arbitration proceedings if one of the parties requests a termination of the conciliation or if the arbitral tribunal believes that further efforts to conciliate will be futile.
> ...

---

[142] See, e.g. Section 30(1) of the Indian Arbitration and Conciliation Act 1996; and Article 38(4) of the Japanese Arbitration Law 2003. See generally S Harpole, 'The Role of the Third Party Neutral when Arbitration and Conciliation Procedures are Combined: A Comparative Survey of Asian Jurisdictions', in Pryles and Moser, op. cit. fn 8, p. 526.
[143] See, Chapter 1, Section 4.2.2, particularly fn 163.
[144] A good illustration of the diversity in practice in the region is provided in Harpole, op. cit. fn 142, pp. 525–532. In relation to Singapore, see LS Yang and L Chew, 'Arbitration in Singapore', in PJ McConnaughay and TB Ginsburg (eds), *International Commercial Arbitration in Asia*, 2nd edn, JurisNet, 2006, p. 355 (observing in relation to arbitration in Singapore that 'arbitrators see themselves as having a role in helping the parties to reach a settlement without having to go through an arbitration ... It is fair to say that many arbitrators attempt to mediate a settlement before the arbitration begins, although there are no records as to how often this occurs.'); and concerning Japan, Professor Taniguchi has stated in his guest lecture at AFIA's 19th Symposium in Sydney, 7 August 2009, that arb-med is frequently used in JCAA arbitrations, which occurs against a cultural background where judges often mediate in proceedings before them, see report by L Hui and A Lees in (2009) 4 *AFIA News*, September 2009, at p. 7.
[145] M Moser, 'People's Republic of China', in M Pryles, *Dispute Resolution in Asia*, 3rd edn, Kluwer Law International, 2006, p. 85, at p. 93.
[146] Xiaobing Xu and Wilson, op. cit. fn 139, p. 66–67 (footnotes omitted). See also Kaufmann-Kohler and Fan Kun, op. cit. fn 139, pp. 490–491. It has been reported that before 1983, most CIETAC cases were settled through a process that combined arbitration and mediation and the settlement rate of CIETAC cases by arbitrators using conciliation during the periods 1983–1988 and since 1989 have been, respectively, 50% and 20–30%. See Hilmer, op. cit. fn 139, pp. 104–105, citing Seung Wha Chang, *Resolving Disputes in the PRC: A Practical Guide to Arbitration and Conciliation in China*, China Law Handbook, 1996, p. 52.

7. Where conciliation fails, the arbitral tribunal shall proceed with the arbitration and render an arbitral award.
8. Where conciliation fails, any opinion, view or statement and any proposal or proposition expressing acceptance or opposition by either party or by the arbitral tribunal in the process of conciliation shall not be invoked as grounds for any claim, defence or counterclaim in the subsequent arbitration proceedings, judicial proceedings or any other proceedings.

One of the important features evident from the above provisions is that parties must consent to the conciliation process. However, there is no requirement that the agreement to conciliate be in writing. In contrast, a writing requirement is found in a number of domestic laws in the region.[147] As an example of such laws, Section 2B of the Hong Kong Arbitration Ordinance provides:[148] 7.92

(1) If all parties to a reference consent in writing, and for so long as no party withdraws in writing his consent, an arbitrator or umpire may act as a conciliator.
(2) An arbitrator or umpire acting as conciliator
   (a) may communicate with the parties to the reference collectively or separately;
   (b) shall treat information obtained by him from a party to the reference as confidential, unless that party otherwise agrees or unless subsection (3) applies.
(3) Where confidential information is obtained by an arbitrator or umpire from a party to the reference during conciliation proceedings and those proceedings terminate without the parties reaching agreement in settlement of their dispute, the arbitrator or umpire shall, before resuming the arbitration proceedings, disclose to all other parties to the reference as much of that information as he considers is material to the arbitration proceedings.
(4) No objection shall be taken to the conduct of arbitration proceedings by an arbitrator or umpire solely on the ground that he had acted previously as a conciliator in accordance with this section.

Section 30(1) of India's Arbitration and Conciliation Act 1996 is more compact:[149] 7.93

It is not incompatible with an arbitration agreement for an arbitral tribunal to encourage settlement of the dispute and, with the agreement of the parties, the arbitral tribunal may use mediation, conciliation or other procedures at any time during the arbitral proceedings to encourage settlement.

---

147 See, e.g. Singapore International Arbitration Act Section 17(1) and the Philippines Alternative Dispute Resolution Act 2004 Section 36.
148 See similarly the Singapore International Arbitration Act Article 17.
149 Likewise, Article 38(4) of the Japanese Arbitration Law 2003 provides that '[a]n arbitral tribunal or one or more arbitrators designated by it may attempt to settle the civil dispute subject to the arbitral proceedings, if consented to by the parties'. Similar provisions are found in China's Arbitration Law Article 51 and Sri Lanka's Arbitration Act No. 11 of 1995 Section 14(1). In relation to the Japanese Arbitration Law Article 38(4), it has been commented that if the settlement is unsuccessful and the arbitration is resumed, there is no provision on how to avoid challenges against the arbitrator who has served as the mediator. See D Roughton, 'A Brief Review of the Japanese Arbitration Law', (2005) 1 *Asian International Arbitration Journal* 127, at pp. 133–134.

7.94 In Australia, the International Arbitration Act does not provide for arb-med but the process is contemplated for domestic arbitration in the state Commercial Arbitration Acts.[150]

7.95 General Standard 4(d) of the IBA Guidelines on Conflicts of Interest in International Arbitration provides that an 'arbitrator may assist parties in reaching a settlement of the dispute at any stage of the proceedings'. However, the arbitrator must obtain 'an express agreement by the parties that acting in such a manner shall not disqualify the arbitrator from continuing to serve as arbitrator'. The General Standard concludes that:

> notwithstanding such an agreement, the arbitrator shall resign if, as a consequence of his or her involvement in the settlement process, the arbitrator develops doubts as to his or her ability to remain impartial or independent in the future course of the arbitration proceedings.

7.96 It has been observed that '[m]any cases show that the party's frank confidential chats with the arbitrator acting as a mediator [do] not make resumption of the arbitrator's work as an adjudicator difficult'.[151] However, this may not always reflect the reality of the situation.

7.97 Some of the attractive features of arb-med are reported to be that (1) it provides a 'gentler solution' to arbitration, (2) it facilitates a continuation of commercial relations, and (3) arbitrators have the power to make binding decisions if the mediation attempted during the arbitration fails. As regards the latter feature, it is considered that the decision-making power of arbitrators tends to increase the chances that the parties resolve their differences in the mediation because a failure to settle will result in a binding arbitral award that may not be satisfactory to one or even all of them.[152]

7.98 However, arb-med has to contend with concerns as to certain practical realities. Redfern and Hunter highlight some of the more salient issues, particularly when an arbitrator becomes a mediator but is required to shift back to his role as an arbitrator if the conciliation fails:[153]

> how open are the parties likely to be with the mediator . . . if they know that he might be called upon to act as arbitrator in the same dispute? And how can the arbitrator satisfy or appear to satisfy the requirements of 'impartiality' and 'a fair hearing' if he has previously held private discussions with the parties separately and indicated his views to them?

7.99 Enforcement of an award may be jeopardised or the award may be set aside if such requirements are not present. Given the potential risks, caution should be exercised before utilising arb-med procedures if the arbitrator may be expected to resume his or her arbitral role failing successful mediation. Arb-med may, however, be an effective and value-added procedure if an arbitrator changes his

---

150 See Section 27 of Australia's uniform Commercial Arbitration Act, which applies in all Australian states.
151 Sawada, op. cit. fn 43, p. 309.
152 T Sawada, 'Hybrid Arb-Med: Will West and East Never Meet?', (2003) 14(2) *ICC International Court of Arbitration Bulletin* 29, at pp. 32–33.
153 Redfern, Hunter, et al., op. cit. fn 45, at para 1–82.

or her role to that of a mediator and, as a result, facilitates a voluntary settlement of the dispute.

6.13 Termination of the proceedings

Under Article 32(1) of the Model Law a final award terminates the arbitral proceedings.[154] Other circumstances in which proceedings may be terminated include:

(i) the claimant's withdrawal or discontinuance of a claim, which is not objected to by the respondent;[155]
(ii) an agreement by the parties to terminate or discontinue the proceedings;[156]
(iii) a finding by the arbitral tribunal that continuation of the proceedings has become unnecessary or impossible;[157] or
(iv) the failure of the parties to act.[158]

Once the arbitral tribunal issues an award that leaves no more disputed issues between the parties to be determined, the arbitral proceedings are brought to a close and the arbitral tribunal becomes *functus officio*, i.e. it has discharged its duty.[159] However, this may not terminate the matter between the parties because they may be entitled to challenge the award before domestic courts.

Notwithstanding the above, the mandate of the arbitral tribunal may revive if there is a request by a party (or decision by the arbitral tribunal on its own initiative) to correct or interpret the award,[160] or if a court hearing a setting aside application determines that the arbitral tribunal shall 'resume the arbitral proceedings or to take such other action as in the arbitral tribunal's opinion will eliminate the grounds for setting aside'.[161]

7 Evidence

More than half a century ago, Bin Cheng observed that the 'conviction of the Tribunal as to the truth of the assertions of the parties is secured by means of evidence'.[162] The validity of this elegant statement has not diminished. It has equal relevance today.

---

154 See also JCAA Rules, Rule 50(1).
155 See, e.g. Model Law Article 32(2)(a); ICSID Rules, Rule 44. Under the former provision, the arbitral tribunal must not issue an order for the termination of the proceedings if the respondent objects and the arbitral tribunal recognises that the respondent has 'a legitimate interest . . . in obtaining a final settlement of the dispute'.
156 Model Law Article 32(2)(b); JCAA Rules, Rule 50(1); ICSID Rules, Rule 43.
157 Model Law Article 32(2)(c).
158 See, e.g. ICSID Rules, Rule 45 (parties are deemed to have discontinued with the proceedings if they fail to take any steps during six consecutive months or any other period as may be agreed by the parties and approved by the tribunal).
159 See, e.g. JCAA Rules, Rule 50(3).
160 See Chapter 8, Section 7.
161 Model Law Article 34(4).
162 Bin Cheng, op. cit. fn 24, p. 307.

7.104   Evidence is largely unregulated in international arbitration. Party autonomy dictates matters of evidence. Failing an agreement between the parties, the arbitral tribunal is usually empowered to decide on the admissibility, relevance, materiality and weight of evidence.[163] In this regard, the Supreme Court of India in *Municipal Corporation of Delhi v Jagan Nath Ashok Kumar*[164] observed:

> Appraisement of evidence by the arbitrator is ordinarily never a matter which the Court questions and considers. The arbitrator in our opinion is the sole judge of the quality as well as the quantity of evidence and it will not be for the Court to take upon itself the task of being a judge of the evidence before the arbitrator.

7.105   The three general categories of evidence in international commercial arbitration are: (1) documentary evidence; (2) factual evidence given by witnesses; and (3) expert evidence. These are discussed in turn after a short examination of the burden and standard of proof.

7.1 Burden and standard of proof

7.106   Concerning the burden of proof in international commercial arbitration, each party must prove the facts on which it relies.[165] However, the standard or degree of proof required is a matter for the arbitral tribunal to determine. Many broad and flexible formulae are used to address this issue in arbitration rules. For example, Article 23(10) of the HKIAC Rules provides that the 'arbitral tribunal shall determine the admissibility, relevance, materiality and weight of any matter presented by a party, including as to whether or not to apply strict rules of evidence'.[166] The discretion thus vested in an arbitral tribunal under this provision is broad and unconstrained.[167]

7.107   Redfern and Hunter, while acknowledging that the standard of proof in international arbitration is not precise, appear to distil generally from arbitral practice a 'balance of probability' standard.[168] In *Dadras International v Islamic Republic of Iran*, the Iran-US Claims Tribunal adopted a stricter standard of proof for allegations of forgery, requiring 'clear and convincing' evidence.[169] Similarly, a high standard of proof may be required to sustain allegations of serious misfeasance,

---

[163] See, e.g. HKIAC Rules Article 23(10); UNCITRAL Arbitration Rules Article 25(6); 2010 UNCITRAL Arbitration Rules Article 27(4); both the 1999 and 2010 IBA Rules of Evidence Article 9(1).
[164] (1987) 4 SCC 497.
[165] See, e.g. ACICA Rules Article 27.1; CIETAC Rules Article 36(1); HKIAC Rules Article 23(1); JCAA Rules, Rule 37(1); KCAB International Rules, Rule 22(3); UNCITRAL Arbitration Rules Article 24(1); the 2010 UNCITRAL Arbitration Rules Article 27(1).
[166] See, e.g. Model Law Article 19(2); the Indian Arbitration and Conciliation Act 1996 Section 19(4); SIAC Rules, Rule 24(p).
[167] See, e.g. Caron, Caplan and Pellonpää, op. cit. fn 46, p. 621 et seq.
[168] See Redfern, Hunter, et al., op. cit. fn 45, para 6–67. See also *Saipem S.p.A. v Bangladesh*, ICSID Case No. ARB/05/7, Award of 30 June 2009, at para 114.
[169] (1995) 31 Iran-US CTR 127, at 162, para 124. See also the adoption of a 'clear and convincing' proof standard by the Eritrea-Ethiopia Claims Commission due to the gravity of the claims asserted. *Central Front, Eritrea's Claims 2, 4, 6, 7, 8 and 22 (Eritrea v Ethiopia)*, Partial Award (Eritrea Ethiopia Claims Commission, 28 April 2004), para 6, available at www.pca-cpa.org.

such as bribery, fraud or corruption.[170] These standards may be contrasted with the 'beyond reasonable doubt' and 'prima facie' standards used in some domestic legal systems. Lew, Mistelis and Kröll observe that the standard of proof may be a matter of substantive law and may depend on the subjective views of the arbitrators in each case.[171]

7.108 There may also be exceptional cases, for example, when a claimant produces prima facie evidence in a situation where proof of a fact is extremely difficult and there is an absence of rebuttal by the respondent. In such cases, the arbitral tribunal might shift the burden of proof on relatively little evidence or it may not insist on very rigorous standards of proof.[172]

7.109 Proof would not usually be required in the event the fact or proposition is uncontroversial, common knowledge or obvious.[173] This practice is in harmony with the principle of judicial notice.[174]

7.2 Documentary evidence

7.110 A particular feature of international arbitration that distinguishes it from proceedings in common law courts is its emphasis on evidence in the form of contemporaneous documents created around the time the transaction or the events giving rise to the dispute took place.[175] This is often considered to be the best evidence because it represents one of the most accurate records of the events that took place. The following passage by Bin Cheng explains this:[176]

> 'Testimonial evidence', it has been said, 'due to the frailty of human contingencies is most liable to arouse distrust.' On the other hand, documentary evidence stating, recording, or sometimes even incorporating the facts at issue, written or executed either contemporaneously or shortly after the events in question by persons having direct knowledge thereof, and for purposes other than the presentation of a claim or the support of a contention in a suit, is ordinarily free from this distrust and considered of higher probative value.

7.111 A party to common law court proceedings is generally required to introduce documents through a witness. By contrast, in international arbitration a party relying on a document might well introduce it by exhibiting it to its pleadings or

---

170 See Lau, op. cit. fn 111, p. 259, at p. 261; A Crivellaro, 'Arbitration Case Law on Bribery: Issues of Arbitrability, Contract Validity, Merits and Evidence' in K Karsten and A Berkeley (eds), *Arbitration: Money Laundering, Corruption and Fraud*, ICC Publishing, 2003, p. 109, at p. 118.
171 Lew, Mistelis and Kröll, op. cit. fn 22, para 22–26.
172 See, e.g. *W Jack Buckamier v Islamic Republic of Iran*, (1992) 28 Iran-US CTR 53, at 74–76; Aldrich, op. cit. fn 107, p. 334; and Bin Cheng, op. cit. fn 24, p. 323 et seq.
173 See Lew, Mistelis and Kröll, op. cit. fn 22, at para 22–25.
174 As to judicial notice constituting a general principle of law, see Bin Cheng, op. cit. fn 24, p. 303.
175 See, e.g. CN Brower, 'Evidence Before International Tribunals: The Need for Some Standard Rules', (1994) 28 *The International Lawyer* 47, at p. 54. See also the comparative table in Section 5 above.
176 Bin Cheng, op. cit. fn 24, pp. 318–319, quoting the *Naomi Russell* case (1931), Mexico-US Special Claims Commission, Opinions of Commissioners under the 10 September 1923 Convention between the US and Mexico, as extended by the Convention concluded on 17 August 1929, Washington, 1931, p. 184.

memorials. The consequence is that in international arbitration, documents are readily admitted without arguments as to whether they are admissible.[177]

7.2.1 Document production – Domestic court practice

7.112 Domestic court practice as to document production helps understand approaches to document production in international arbitration. Domestic practice varies considerably.[178] At one end of the spectrum must be placed the US document discovery procedure, which is broad and extensive.[179] Next in line are the more temperate discovery procedures of English courts and former British colonies, which view discovery as integral but require or order document disclosure on a less extensive scale than in the US. And on the other end of the spectrum, one finds many civil law jurisdictions.[180] At this end of the spectrum, one may also find some Asia-Pacific countries with civil law systems, such as Korea, which has very limited discovery procedures in its courts.[181] This disparity in practice has led Giorgio Bernini to conclude:[182]

> the taking of evidence in international arbitrations is likely to present itself as the occasion in which the different approaches characterising the contribution of civil and common law attorneys and arbitrators may give rise to a serious cultural clash. Discovery, in particular, is bound to remain a very controversial issue in arbitration. Nonetheless, the actual practice of arbitration shows signs of adjustment, and, despite theoretical differences, a workable *modus vivendi* has emerged in the reality of arbitration practice at [the] international level.

7.113 One comparison between US, other common law jurisdictions and civil law discovery practice, puts it this way:[183]

> Broadly speaking, in civil law jurisdictions, parties are relatively immune from orders to produce documents. Instead, disputes are adjudicated on the basis of documents

---

177 Admissibility may, however, become an issue when the document's authenticity is challenged. See Lau, op. cit. fn 111, p. 262. Unlawfully obtained documents might not be introduced into evidence. See, e.g. *Methanex Corp v United States of America*, NAFTA Chapter 11 Arbitration, 3 August 2005, at para 54.
178 See, e.g. G Kaufmann-Kohler, 'Globalization of Arbitral Procedure', (2003) 36 *Vanderbilt Journal of Transnational Law* 1313, p. 1325 et seq; and Lew, Mistelis and Kröll, op. cit. fn 22, at para 22–49.
179 The legal term 'discovery' as is used in the US is not simply limited to the process of document production. It also refers to the wider process of finding facts and evidence through devices such as interrogatories and witness out-of-court testimony (depositions). See generally Seung Wha Chang, op. cit. fn 35, p. 267. It has been said that discovery in the US 'may be had of facts incidentally relevant to the issues in the pleadings even if the facts do not directly prove or disprove the facts in question', GC Hazard and M Taruffo, *American Civil Procedure: An Introduction*, Yale University Press, 1993, p. 113.
180 See, e.g. G Bernini, 'The Civil Law Approach to Discovery: A Comparative Overview of the Taking of Evidence in the Anglo-American and Continental Arbitration Systems', in Newman and Hill (eds), op. cit. fn 5, pp. 270–273. Two important principles that influence the civil law approach to document discovery are: (1) the maxim *onus probandi incumbit ei qui affirmat*, meaning 'the burden of proof rests on he who affirms' – put another way, it is not for the respondent to produce evidence that will help the claimant; and (2) the right to privacy. See, e.g. C Reymond, 'Civil Law and Common Law Procedures: Which is the More Inquisitorial? A Civil Lawyer's Response', (1989) 5(4) *Arbitration International* 360.
181 See, e.g. G Kim, 'Eastern Asian Cultural Influences', in Pryles and Moser, op. cit. fn 8, pp. 43–44. He notes that in Korea the judge has powers to request evidence and generally a party has no right to demand production of evidence.
182 Bernini, op. cit. fn 180, p. 302.
183 JL Frank and J Bédard, 'Electronic Discovery in International Arbitration: Where Neither the IBA Rules of Evidence Nor US Litigation Principles are Enough', (Nov 2007–Jan 2008) *Dispute Resolution Journal* 62, at p. 67 (footnotes omitted).

voluntarily submitted by the parties. Thus, civil law attorneys and arbitrators tend to dislike U.S. discovery practices, which they believe can be abusive and wasteful. As a result, they are not easily swayed by arguments that discovery, even less extensive discovery, is vital or indispensable to the proper adjudication in international arbitration. Furthermore, even attorneys and arbitrators from common law jurisdictions such as England and Canada will often distance themselves from U.S.-style discovery.

It is noteworthy that in some common law jurisdictions, there appears to be a developing trend away from extensive document discovery.[184]   7.114

7.2.2 Document production – Arbitral practice

Arbitration rules sometimes contain specific provisions that empower arbitral tribunals to order document production. Article 22(1) of the KCAB International Rules provides, for example, that '[u]nless the parties otherwise agree in writing, the Tribunal may at any time during the proceeding order the parties: (a) to produce documents, exhibits or other evidence it deems necessary or appropriate...'.[185]   7.115

Although it is impossible to generalise about the type of document discovery usually permitted by international commercial arbitral tribunals, one thing is clear: extensive US style court discovery is rarely, if ever, practised. In this regard, Seung Wha Chang has examined 15 ICC arbitration cases involving at least one Korean party. Although it is a relatively small sample of cases, the results are revealing and reflect anecdotal evidence. The analysis indicated that 14 of the cases followed more or less the limited document production regime of the IBA Rules of Evidence, even though in most cases these rules were not explicitly relied on by the arbitrators. The one exception in which extensive discovery was permitted involved a Korean party and a US party, two arbitrators who were US judges, representation of both parties by US law firms, California as the place of arbitration, and Californian governing law.[186]   7.116

It is also clear that there is great variation in the extent of discovery or document production that is permitted in international arbitration. It depends on the procedure agreed by the parties, the circumstances surrounding the request and on the preferences of the arbitrator(s), which might in turn depend on their legal background and experience. Lawyers trained in common law systems should not assume that the practice of obtaining evidence through discovery that may be familiar to them will be appropriate or acceptable in an international commercial arbitration. On the other hand, lawyers trained in civil law systems should be ready to accept at least some form of document production.   7.117

---

184 See, e.g. Thye and Choong, op. cit. fn 34.
185 While no details of the document production process is provided, it would seem to give broad enough discretion to adopt the procedures in the IBA Rules of Evidence. See Seung Wha Chang, op. cit. fn 35, p. 277. See also JCAA Rules, Rule 37(4) and (5); CIETAC Article 37; Beijing Arbitration Commission Rules Articles 30 and 32; SIAC Rules, Rule 24(h); UNCITRAL Arbitration Rules Article 24; China's Arbitration Law Article 43.
186 Seung Wha Chang, op. cit. fn 35, p. 285. Similarly, Gary Born has remarked that 'when parties from common law jurisdictions arbitrate before a common law arbitrator in a common law state, discovery along common law lines is a very distinct possibility.' Born, 2001, op cit. fn 32, p. 485.

7.2.3 Court assistance in document production

7.118 The Hong Kong Arbitration Ordinance serves as a good example of a domestic law that allows courts to assist arbitral tribunals in requesting the production of documents. Under Section 2GB, an arbitral tribunal is empowered to make orders or give directions in respect of the discovery of documents. However, the arbitral tribunal cannot compel a party to act. If a party refuses to so act, the assistance of the court may be sought.[187] In such a case, Section 2GG(1) becomes relevant:

> An award, order or direction made or given in relation to arbitration proceedings by an arbitral tribunal is enforceable in the same way as a judgment, order or direction of the Court that has the same effect, but only with the leave of the Court or a judge of the Court. If that leave is given, the Court or judge may enter judgment in terms of the award, order or direction.

7.119 Section 2GG(2) adds that the above provision may also apply to an award, order or direction made or given whether in or outside Hong Kong. This means that an arbitral tribunal seated in Singapore may make a document production order which may be enforced in Hong Kong. However, section 2GG would not be helpful if an arbitral tribunal in Hong Kong issued an order against a person outside of Hong Kong. That would depend on the laws in force in the state having jurisdiction over that person.

7.120 Courts in the region are also empowered to compel the production of documents from a non-party on application by a party or an arbitral tribunal.[188]

7.121 As regards civil law systems, it has been noted that although the means to compel production exists, its use in litigation is limited.[189] In some Asian jurisdictions based on the civil law tradition, this situation is changing and there is a trend in court civil procedure toward widening the scope of document production. These changes are bringing those systems closer to the IBA Rules of Evidence document production regime.[190] For example, in South Korea the old Korean Civil Procedure Law limited the scope of document production to certain types of documents, whereas its new Civil Procedure Law has, under Article 344(2), expanded its scope to all documents, with certain exceptions for confidentiality or privilege.[191] A similar change has taken place in the Japanese Code of Civil Procedure.[192]

---

187 See also the Indian Arbitration and Conciliation Act 1996 Section 27.
188 See, e.g. P Megens, P Starr and P Chow, 'Compulsion of Evidence in International Commercial Arbitration: An Asia-Pacific Perspective', (2006) 2(1) *Asian International Arbitration Journal* 32, p. 47 et seq (providing an analysis of the positions under the laws of Australia, Hong Kong, China, Singapore and Malaysia).
189 See, e.g. Lew, Mistelis and Kröll, op. cit. fn 22 at para 22–49.
190 See, generally, Seung Wha Chang, op. cit. fn 35, pp. 279 and 281.
191 Seung Wha Chang comments on these new Korean civil procedure rules that '[a]pparently, the scope of document production is more limited, and requirements for a request are stricter than ones under the IBA Rules of Evidence. Nevertheless, it is important to note that document production under the new KCPA is more liberal than traditional approaches to document production under the civil law system.... Overall, it is stated that the gap between the KCPA and the IBA Rules of Evidence is not too wide to be reconciled with each other.' Seung Wha Chang, op. cit. fn 35, p. 279.
192 See generally Nakamura, op. cit. fn 66, para 80–150 and Article 220 of the Japanese Code of Civil Procedure.

PROCEDURE AND EVIDENCE   343

While South Korea does not have a provision specifically on court powers to make document production orders, Article 28 of its Arbitration Law (as amended in 1999) provides at a general level for a request from a party or arbitral tribunal for court assistance in taking evidence. It is unclear from that provision what the exact parameters of such assistance may be but under Article 28(1) the arbitral tribunal is expressly permitted to specify the matters to be recorded by the court and other particulars necessary for investigation. Some illumination is also provided in Article 28(3), which refers to examination of witnesses and inspection of property. Article 35(1) of the new Japanese Arbitration Law states that, subject to party agreement, a party or an arbitral tribunal may apply: 7.122

> to a court for assistance in taking evidence by any means that the arbitral tribunal considers necessary such as entrustment of investigation, examination of witnesses, expert testimony, investigation of documentary evidence... or inspection... prescribed in the Code of Civil Procedure.

However, in practice Japanese courts are reported to be generally disinclined to grant document production requests.[193] 7.123

7.2.4 IBA Rules of Evidence and document production

The IBA Rules of Evidence have attempted to reconcile differences between common law and civil law practices in respect of document production.[194] They are developing a reputation for taking a well-balanced approach to document production, and are frequently used as a guide or are adopted by the parties.[195] 7.124

A study of Chinese, Japanese and South Korean national civil procedure law and national arbitration law, as well as the arbitration rules of CIETAC, JCAA and KCAB, concluded that these laws and rules should not be an impediment to the application of the IBA Rules of Evidence.[196] 7.125

The starting point for the IBA Rules of Evidence in respect of document production is Article 3(1): a party must submit all documents on which it relies and which are available to it (except for documents already submitted by another party).[197] In the event a party needs to request another party to the arbitration to produce documents, it must submit a request to the arbitral 7.126

---

[193] See K Sadaka and N Sawasaki, 'Japan', in *The International Comparative Legal Guide to: Litigation and Dispute Resolution 2008*, Global Legal Group, p. 164, para 7.1, available at www.iclg.co.uk/khadmin/Publications/pdf/1661.pdf.
[194] See the introduction to the IBA Rules of Evidence in Section 3.2 above. Unless indicated otherwise, the current Section is based on the 1999 IBA Rules of Evidence. At the time of writing in 2010, these Rules were revised.
[195] See B Hanotiau, 'Document Production in International Arbitration: A Tentative Definition of "Best Practices"', (2006) *ICC International Court of Arbitration Bulletin*, Special Supplement, p. 113; and Seung Wha Chang, op. cit. fn 35, p. 268. One exception appears to be China: it has been observed that Chinese arbitrators normally follow domestic court procedures rather than methods such as those contained in the IBA Rules of Evidence. Seung Wha Chang, ibid., p. 283, citing an interview with Michael Moser, then Chairman of the Hong Kong International Arbitration Centre.
[196] Seung Wha Chang, op. cit. fn 35, p. 270.
[197] It is worth noting that the 2010 IBA Rules of Evidence have adopted in an extensive definition of a 'Document':

> a writing, communication, picture, drawing, program or data of any kind, whether recorded or maintained on paper or by electronic, audio, visual or any other means...

tribunal (Article 3(2)).[198] That request must identify each document requested or a 'narrow and specific' category of documents reasonably believed to exist (Article 3(3)(a)). Additionally, the request must state (1) how the documents are relevant and material to the outcome of the case, (2) that the documents are not in the possession, custody or control of the requesting party, and (3) why the requesting party assumes the other party has possession, custody or control of the documents (Article 3(3)(b) and (c)).

7.127   Pursuant to Article 3(5), the party to whom the request is made may object on the basis of the reasons set forth in Article 9(2). These reasons are:

a) lack of sufficient relevance or materiality;
b) legal impediment or privilege under the legal or ethical rules determined by the Arbitral Tribunal to be applicable;
c) unreasonable burden to produce the requested evidence;
d) loss or destruction of the document that has been reasonably shown to have occurred;
e) grounds of commercial or technical confidentiality that the Arbitral Tribunal determines to be compelling;[199]
f) grounds of special political or institutional sensitivity (including evidence that has been classified as secret by a government or a public international institution) that the Arbitral Tribunal determines to be compelling; or
g) considerations of fairness or equality of the Parties that the Arbitral Tribunal determines to be compelling.

7.128   The arbitral tribunal must, in consultation with the parties, consider the request and the objections, if any. Under Article 3(6), if the arbitral tribunal considers that the issues the requesting party seeks to prove are relevant and material and none of the Article 9(2) exceptions applies, the arbitral tribunal may order production of the requested documents. Note here that even if all the conditions in the Rules as to production are satisfied by the requesting party, the presence of the word 'may' in Article 3(6) still gives the arbitral tribunal a discretion to deny the production request.

7.129   One difficulty that has been encountered in practice in the application of the IBA Rules of Evidence relates to the failure of Article 9(2) to refer to the criteria contained in Article 3(3)(a).[200] This omission may be interpreted to imply that in cases where the requesting party fails to describe the requested documents in sufficient detail or makes an overly broad request, a basis for denying the request

---

198 In practice, parties and arbitral tribunals often agree to modify this rule so that requests for production are submitted directly to the opposing party, and only disputed requests are submitted to the arbitral tribunal for decision. Article 2 of the 2010 IBA Rules of Evidence requires the arbitral tribunal to invite the parties to consult each other with a view to agreeing on an efficient, economical and fair process for the taking of evidence.
199 A claim that the requested documents are confidential (e.g. they contain commercially sensitive information or trade secrets) is not a ground that would always exempt a party from disclosing. The arbitral tribunal might permit the deletion of confidential information before documents are disclosed or limit access to specified persons such as lawyers or experts but not the parties and their in-house counsel. An additional level of comfort may be provided by the parties' lawyers entering into a confidentiality agreement or the issuance of a protective order by the arbitral tribunal. See generally Yang, op. cit. fn 14, p. 193.
200 Article 3(3)(a) of the IBA Rules of Evidence requires that the Request to Produce contain: '(i) a description of a requested document sufficient to identify it, or (ii) a description in sufficient detail (including subject matter) of a narrow and specific requested category of documents that are reasonably believed to exist.'

under Article 9(2) may not exist. We do not consider that this interpretation of the IBA Rules of Evidence comports with one of the objectives of the Rules, which is to provide more specificity in document requests. In our experience, the objecting party could simply rely on Article 3(3)(a) and argue that the document request does not comply with that Article.

Based on the foregoing paragraphs, it may be seen that the IBA Rules of Evidence do not allow an automatic right to document production, and much less an entitlement to a full-blown discovery procedure as practised in the US. They have created a hybrid system that attempts to combine the divergent document discovery practices found in the civil law and common law systems. 7.130

If a request to produce is made and a requested party fails without satisfactory explanation to produce any document in contravention of an order to produce, the arbitral tribunal may infer that this document would be adverse to the interests of that party (Article 9(4)).[201] However, this may be a relatively weak sanction in the event that a critical document is not disclosed, especially given that in practice arbitral tribunals (as discussed below) are generally reticent to rely on adverse inferences. 7.131

In certain jurisdictions, the *lex arbitri* may assist the arbitral tribunal. For example, Section 2GG of the Hong Kong Arbitration Ordinance, discussed above, makes an arbitral tribunal's discovery order enforceable in the same way as a court order. However, while this might be effective against a party situated within the jurisdiction of the courts of the *lex arbitri*, it is unlikely to have any effect on a foreign party situated outside that jurisdiction. In the latter situation, Philip Yang comments that:[202] 7.132

> If a foreign party irrevocably says that it has no such document to disclose, it is usually the end of the matter in an international arbitration. There is no point in further pursuing the matter as it ultimately will be a waste of time. If the arbitrator does not accept the reason for non-disclosure and is confident of its existence, he or she can of course and should always forewarn the foreign party that an adverse inference may be drawn against him or her.

While arbitral tribunals are empowered to draw an adverse inference, rarely are such inferences made, even if the refusal to produce concerns a document of high relevance.[203] One of the factors that may affect the apparent reticence of arbitral tribunals to draw an adverse inference is doubt that (i) the document exists, (ii) is in the possession of the requested party and (iii) is essential for the disposition of the case. It has been suggested that if an adverse inference is 7.133

---

[201] Similar provisions for domestic courts to draw adverse inferences in cases of non-compliance with a document disclosure order are found in Asia-Pacific civil procedure laws. See, e.g. the Japanese Civil Procedure Law Article 224(1); the South Korean Civil Procedure Law Article 349. Adverse inferences were drawn in a number of Iran-US Claims Tribunal awards. See Aldrich, op. cit. fn 107, pp. 339–341. In *William J Levitt v Islamic Republic of Iran*, 27 Iran-US CTR 164, for example, the arbitral tribunal noted that it was an accepted principle that adverse inferences may be drawn if a party fails to submit evidence that was likely to be at its disposal. It added that this failure did not relieve the other party of its 'obligation to muster all the evidentiary support at its disposal.' See also E Gaillard and J Savage (eds), *Fouchard, Gaillard, and Goldman on International Commercial Arbitration*, Kluwer, 1999, at para 2075.
[202] Yang, op. cit. fn 14, p. 192.
[203] See, e.g. Brower, op. cit. fn 175, at p. 56.

incorrectly made, the award may be challenged or difficulties in its enforcement may be encountered.[204]

7.134   Other significant document production features of the IBA Rules of Evidence include the appointment of an impartial expert to review documents and report on objections made to their production (Article 3(7)); the production of documents from persons or organisations not a party to the arbitration (Article 3(8)); a request to produce that is initiated by the arbitral tribunal itself (Article 3(9)); and the submission of documents that become relevant and material as a consequence of the documents previously submitted to the arbitral tribunal (Article 3(10)).

7.135   The IBA Rules of Evidence are gaining a widespread reputation as 'the' standard for document production in international commercial arbitration in the Asia-Pacific region, if not the world. It appears that the international arbitration community is coming to grips with the divergent approaches to document production. Harmonisation in practice, with the assistance of the IBA Rules of Evidence, is gradually starting to emerge. As noted earlier, the IBA Rules of Evidence were revised and updated at the time of writing in 2010 and it is hoped that in this new form they will now even better serve the international arbitration community.[205]

7.136   A future challenge which has been dealt with in the IBA Rules revision relates to discovery of electronic documents, such as emails and, more importantly, purely electronic information such as metadata. This kind of discovery is now possible in the US, at an enormous cost to businesses who might be faced with such an order. It is yet to make its way into the mainstream of international arbitration but attempts will no doubt be made when the stakes are high enough. Concern about the consequences of 'e-discovery' on international arbitration has prompted the ICC Commission on Arbitration, the Chartered Institute of Arbitrators and the ICDR to examine 'e-discovery' issues.[206]

7.3 Witness evidence

7.3.1 Witness evidence generally

7.137   As stated previously, documentation contemporaneous to the time when the relevant events took place is usually the most favoured type of evidence in

---

[204] See Caron, Caplan and Pellonpää, op. cit. fn 46, pp. 578–579. However, regional case law characterises an arbitral tribunal's error in relation to the drawing of adverse inferences as one in the assessment of evidence and therefore an error of law or fact that is not a ground for setting aside an award. See, e.g., *Dongwoo Mann and Hummel Co Ltd v Mann and Hummel GmbH* [2008] SGHC 67, especially at para 70 (Singapore High Court).

[205] See Section 3.2 above.

[206] The ICC Commission on Arbitration set up in 2008 a special Task Force to study the potential impact of 'e-disclosure'. The Chartered Institute of Arbitrators issued on 2 October 2008 a 'Protocol for E-disclosure in Arbitration'. See www.ciarb.org. A significant topic of the IBA's review of its 1999 Rules of Evidence was 'e-disclosure'. ICDR has issued 'Guidelines for Information Disclosure and Exchange in International Arbitration Proceedings'. On the need for international arbitration to keep pace with domestic litigation trends in electronic production, see RD Hill, 'The New Reality of Electronic Document Production in International Arbitration: A Catalyst for Convergence?', (2009) 25 *Arbitration International* 87. See also CS Devey, 'Electronic Discovery/Disclosure: From Litigation to International Commercial Arbitration', (2008) 74 *Arbitration* 369; and N Tse and N Peter, 'Confronting the Matrix: Do the IBA Rules Require Amendment to Deal with the Challenges Posed by Electronically Stored Information?', (2008) 74 *Arbitration* 28.

international commercial arbitration. This does not mean that witnesses cannot provide important evidence in an arbitration, which evidence may take the form of statements or affidavits written specifically for the purpose of the arbitration, or of oral testimony at the hearing (or a combination of the two). An important point about witness evidence is that its content relates to what the witness observed, did or knew. In other words, witnesses are called to give factual evidence. Their role is generally not to give evidence about their opinions, especially when they are not qualified to do so. That is the role assigned to expert witnesses (addressed in the next section), who are selected on the basis of their qualifications and experience to provide opinions. Arbitral tribunals usually have the discretion to allow, refuse or limit the appearance of witnesses.[207]

7.138 Domestic laws vary considerably as to witness evidence. There is no consistent practice among jurisdictions as to whether a party to the dispute, or one of its employees or officers, may be a witness or whether witnesses may be interviewed and prepared for testimony. In some jurisdictions, it may even be unethical for witnesses to be contacted by a party or its counsel prior to giving testimony.[208] Notwithstanding all these differences, it is important to bear in mind that most of these national rules do not apply to international arbitrations. Nonetheless, these differences often mean that different individuals (party representatives, lawyers and arbitrators) involved in an arbitration bring different expectations as to the approach toward witnesses.

7.139 The ideal goal in international arbitration is to establish a level playing field for legal representatives. This implies dispensing with local bar or law society rules as to, for example, contact with witnesses. In the absence of common rules of conduct, it is possible that one side's lawyers might want to meet at length with its witnesses to rehearse their answers to questions likely to be asked at the hearing, whereas the other side's lawyers may consider this an ethical violation and may be reluctant to conduct such a rehearsal with their own witnesses.[209] The IBA Rules of Evidence, which are discussed below, fill this gap by attempting to provide a neutral standard of universal application.

7.140 Whether witnesses may stay in the hearing room before and after their testimony varies considerably depending on the particular case, and the parties' and the arbitral tribunal's preferences. There is generally less concern where experts are involved, it being felt that it is valuable to have each side's expert hear the other's evidence to facilitate better responses to it. However, the situation in relation to witnesses of fact is more difficult. If no consensus can be reached between

---

207 See, e.g. SIAC Rules, Rule 22.2; and IBA Rules of Evidence Article 8(1).
208 See generally IBA (Committee D) Working Party, 'Commentary on the New [1999] IBA Rules of Evidence', (2000) *Business Law International* 16, pp. 26–27; UNCITRAL Notes on Organizing Arbitral Proceedings, op. cit. fn 91, paras 67 and 68; and Hanotiau, op. cit. fn 35, pp. 375–376.
209 See, e.g. Gaillard and Savage, op. cit. fn 201, pp. 701–2, para 1285. See also UNCITRAL Notes on Organizing Arbitral Proceedings, op. cit. fn 91, para 67. Bernard Hanotiau has commented that 'it is uncommon and in many countries even unethical or illegal to meet a witness in domestic proceedings to prepare with him his statement and to prepare the witness before his examination. What the witness will say must be pure surprise, the exact opposite of what an American lawyer would expect'. B Hanotiau, 'Civil Law and Common Law Procedural Traditions in International Arbitration: Who has Crossed the Bridge?', in *Arbitral Procedure at the Dawn of the New Millenium*, Reports of the International Colloquium of CEPANI, 15 October 2004, Bruylant, 2005, p. 86.

the parties, such witnesses may be required to wait outside the hearing room before and after their testimony.[210] Numerous issues are raised concerning their presence in the hearing room. For example, if they are present their testimony may be influenced by what they hear other witnesses say;[211] yet the presence of another witness who has knowledge of the relevant facts may deter a testifying witness from making untrue statements. A compromise often adopted is that witnesses are allowed to remain in the hearing room only after they have given evidence.[212]

7.141 A witness who refuses to give evidence may be compelled to do so by the courts at the seat of arbitration. For example, Section 13(2) of the Singapore International Arbitration Act provides that the 'court may order that a subpoena to testify . . . shall be issued to compel the attendance before an arbitral tribunal of a witness wherever he may be within Singapore'.[213] The Indian Arbitration and Conciliation Act expressly states that persons failing to attend or refusing to give evidence shall be subject to the same penalties incurred for like offences in suits before courts.[214] In Japan, if a witness declines to appear before the arbitral tribunal, courts may examine the witness for the arbitral tribunal.[215]

7.3.2 IBA Rules of Evidence and witnesses

7.142 The means by which witnesses provide written evidence under the 1999 IBA Rules of Evidence is by witness statements that contain an affirmation by the witness of its truth. Witness statements may be contrasted with affidavits. The latter is a more formal statement that is sworn and often used in common law litigation.[216] Article 4(5) of the IBA Rules sets out the written statement's required contents. One of the more important Article 4(5) requirements is the need to identify the source of the witness's information as to the facts described. Article 4(1) expresses the common practice that, prior to the hearing, parties give notice as to the identity of the witnesses on whose testimony they will rely and a summary of the subject matter of their testimony.[217]

7.143 Under the IBA Rules of Evidence, any person is permitted to present evidence, including a party, a party's officer, employee or other representative (Article 4(2)). This rule recognises the reality that parties will need to call as

---

[210] Article 23(7) of the HKIAC Rules provides that the 'arbitral tribunal may require the retirement of any witness or witnesses or expert witnesses during the testimony of other witnesses or expert witnesses'.
[211] See Hanotiau, op. cit. fn 35, p. 385.
[212] See UNCITRAL Notes on Organizing Arbitral Proceedings, op. cit. fn 91 para 65.
[213] See also Section 14(1) of the Singapore International Arbitration Act. See generally, Megens, Starr and Chow, op. cit. fn 188.
[214] Indian Arbitration and Conciliation Act Article 27(5). See also the Singapore International Arbitration Act Article 14(1).
[215] Nakamura, op. cit. fn 66, para 83–720.
[216] Even if parties to an arbitration agree that written evidence of witnesses should take the form of affidavits, it has been suggested that the IBA Rules of Evidence provide a useful guide as to the form an affidavit should take. Lau, op. cit. fn 111, p. 264.
[217] See, e.g. Article 4(1) IBA Rules of Evidence; Article 25(2) UNCITRAL Arbitration Rules.

witnesses the individuals who were involved in the relevant project or the dispute. These people are usually current or former employees of the party.

The Rules also enable a party, its officers, employees, legal advisors or other representatives to 'interview' witnesses (Article 4(3)). The meaning of 'interview' is not defined.[218] The Commentary to the IBA Rules of Evidence notes that the arbitral tribunal 'may consider the scope of any such interview and the effect, if any, on the credibility of the witness'.[219] It is now generally understood within the field of international commercial arbitration (contrary to the practice in certain domestic jurisdictions) that witnesses may be prepared by counsel or other persons before giving their oral evidence. In this regard, one Asian arbitrator has remarked that '[l]awyers' contact could be beneficial if witnesses receive welcome help to make their statements simple and clear'.[220] But, of course, there are limits. For example, under no circumstances should counsel coach the witness to tell a version of events that both the counsel and witness know to be untrue. Bernard Hanotiau provides some prudent advice in this regard:[221] 7.144

> Witness preparation should not become witness manipulation. The starting point for any witness preparation is to remind the witness to tell the truth. Moreover, a witness who has been 'over-prepared' may quickly lose credibility in the eyes of the arbitral tribunal.

Witnesses who have submitted witness statements are required to testify at a hearing unless the parties agree otherwise (Article 4(7)). In many cases, the parties agree that some witnesses are not required to give testimony at the oral hearing. On this point, the IBA Rules of Evidence provide that such an agreement is not to be considered as acceptance of the correctness of the witness statement (Article 4(9)). 7.145

Concerning witnesses required to attend the hearing, the parties frequently agree that a witnesses' evidence in chief (also known as 'direct evidence') is limited to a witness statement submitted prior to the hearing. At the hearing, those witnesses would affirm the content of their statement and thereafter be subject to cross-examination by opposing counsel. This practice helps to reduce the hearing time required. The alternative is known as 'direct examination', where the counsel for the party that has called the witness asks questions intended to draw out the evidence in chief. After direct examination and cross-examination, counsel calling the witness usually conduct a re-examination (also known as 7.146

---

[218] The same term, without definition, is also used in SIAC Rules, Rule 22.5; HKIAC Rules Article 23(9) and Article 20(6) of the LCIA Rules.
[219] IBA (Committee D) Working Party, op. cit. fn 208, p. 12.
[220] Sawada, op. cit. fn 43, p. 300.
[221] Hanotiau, op. cit. fn 35, p. 366. A cautionary anecdote told to pupil barristers is one where a seasoned barrister cross-examines a witness, who keeps repeating a certain version of events. The barrister finally asks: 'And who told you to say this?' Oblivious to the consequences, the witness responds 'He did', simultaneously pointing to the barrister who called the witness.

're-direct examination') as to points raised in the cross-examination.[222] A re-cross examination may be allowed after that.

7.147   As indicated above, a party may insist that a witness who has submitted a witness statement be present for cross-examination at a hearing. Should that witness fail to appear without a valid reason, the arbitral tribunal may be required to disregard that witness statement, unless the circumstances are exceptional (Article 4(8)). Parties wishing to present evidence from a person who refuses to appear voluntarily have the option of requesting the arbitral tribunal 'to take whatever steps are legally available to obtain the testimony of that person' if that person's testimony would seem to be relevant and material (Article 4(10)). This could mean that the arbitral tribunal requests a domestic court to order that person to give testimony. Additionally, the arbitral tribunal by its own motion may order that any person testify (Article 4(11)).

7.148   In addition to written witness statements, Article 8 of the IBA Rules of Evidence addresses oral witness testimony at hearings. This provision gives the arbitral tribunal 'complete control' at all times over evidentiary hearings. Article 8(1) also empowers the arbitral tribunals to

> limit or exclude any question to, answer by or appearance of a witness (which term includes, for the purposes of this Article, witnesses of fact and any Experts), if it considers such question, answer or appearance to be irrelevant, immaterial, burdensome, duplicative or covered by a reason for objection set forth in Article 9.2.

7.4 Expert evidence

7.149   Arbitrations often require expert evidence to explain on the basis of any discipline, for example engineering, chemistry, accounting or science, why or how certain events took place. Experts are expected to possess specialised professional experience and/or academic credentials in the subject area in which they testify. Expert evidence may be given by party-appointed experts or tribunal-appointed experts. One point to bear in mind about experts is that no matter how grandly qualified or experienced an expert may be, no guarantee exists that his or her opinion will be accepted by the arbitral tribunal.

7.4.1 Party-appointed experts

7.150   Article 5 of the 1999 IBA Rules of Evidence deals with party-appointed experts. They are required to submit an expert report containing, inter alia, the expert's 'opinions and conclusions, including a description of the method, evidence and information used in arriving at the conclusions' (Article 5(2)). Unless otherwise agreed by the parties, the experts must appear for testimony (Article 5(4)), failing which and absent exceptional circumstances, the arbitral tribunal must disregard that expert's testimony (Article 5(5)). If the parties agree that the

---

[222] For a practical example of an order stipulating the procedure for the examination of witnesses, see *Saipem SpA v Bangladesh*, ICSID Case No. ARB/05/7, Award of 30 June 2009, at para 75.

expert need not appear for testimony, such an agreement is not to be considered as reflecting acceptance of the expert report's correctness (Article 5(6)). The arbitral tribunal also has the discretion to order any party-appointed experts who have submitted reports on the same or related issues to meet and attempt to reach agreement on those issues in respect of which they expressed differences of opinion (Article 5(3)).[223]

One practice in China is of note here. Some CIETAC arbitrators view testimony of a party-appointed expert as inherently biased (because they consider that such testimony almost invariably favours the party that retained the expert) and may refuse to admit the testimony without any regard to the weight or substance of the evidence.[224] While party-appointed experts may sometimes be treated with suspicion, rejecting their evidence altogether is unnecessary and inappropriate. As Michael Moser and Peter Yuen have commented, an amendment to the CIETAC Rules expressly acknowledging the rights of parties to appoint their own experts and the need for arbitral tribunals to give them due consideration would be welcome.[225]

7.151

7.4.2 Tribunal-appointed experts

An arbitral tribunal may appoint its own expert or experts.[226] But, in practice, party-appointed experts are far more common than arbitral tribunal-appointed experts.[227] If an expert is appointed by the arbitral tribunal, it is prudent for the arbitral tribunal to draft terms of reference for the expert.[228] The appointed expert must be independent. In this regard, the 1999 IBA Rules of Evidence require that, before acceptance, the expert must submit a statement of independence from the arbitral tribunal and the parties (Article 6(2)). Those Rules also authorise arbitral tribunal-appointed experts to request from any party information or access to documents, goods, samples, property or a site for inspection (Article 6(3)). Where a disagreement between the arbitral tribunal-appointed expert and a party arises as to the relevance, materiality or appropriateness of the expert's request, the Rules provide a safeguard: the arbitral tribunal must

7.152

---

223 See Section 7.4.3 below.
224 M Moser and P Yuen, 'The New CIETAC Arbitration Rules', (2005) 21 (3) *Arbitration International* 391, at 399.
225 Ibid.
226 See, e.g. Model Law Article 26; Japanese Arbitration Law 2003 Article 34; SIAC Rules, Rule 23; CIETAC Rules Article 38; HKIAC Rules Article 25; UNCITRAL Arbitration Rules Article 27; and 2010 UNCITRAL Arbitration Rules Article 29.
227 See Hanotiau, op. cit. fn 35, p. 386, who suggests experts are appointed by arbitral tribunals only if they are 'absolutely indispensable'. In *CMS Gas Transmission Co v Argentine Republic*, Award, 12 May 2005, (2005) 44 ILM 1205, at para 50, the arbitral tribunal stated that it had retained independent experts 'so as to better understand the underlying assumptions and methodology relied upon in the valuation reports offered by the parties' experts'. At the Iran-US Claims Tribunal, it was initially thought that technical experts would be appointed in a number of cases to analyse complex or voluminous technical or financial evidence. However, in practice, only a small number of experts was appointed. See Aldrich, op. cit. fn 107, pp. 343–347. In contrast, the United Nations Compensation Commission – a body set up by the UN Security Council to resolve claims by individuals, corporations and states against Iraq resulting from its invasion and occupation of Kuwait – relied heavily on the work of expert consultants to value and verify compensable damages. This reliance was in large measure due to the enormous numbers of claims required to be determined by the Commission.
228 For suggestions as to the content of the terms of reference, see UNCITRAL Notes on Organizing Arbitral Proceedings, op. cit. fn 91, at para 71.

make a decision in regard to that disagreement (Article 6(3)). Non-compliance by a party with an appropriate request by the expert or decision by the arbitral tribunal is to be recorded in the expert's report, which is required to describe the effects of the non-compliance on the determination of the specific issue (Article 6(3)). The report must describe the method, evidence and information used in arriving at its conclusion (Article 6(4)). Parties have a right to see that report, the correspondence between the arbitral tribunal's appointed expert and the arbitral tribunal, and may examine any other document the expert examined (Article 6(5)). Parties may also respond to the report through a separate report prepared by a party-appointed expert (Article 6(5)).[229] The presence of the arbitral tribunal-appointed expert at the hearing may be requested by a party or the arbitral tribunal. At that hearing, the arbitral tribunal-appointed expert may be questioned by the arbitral tribunal, the parties or by party-appointed experts (Article 6(6)). Finally, the report of the arbitral tribunal's expert does not bind the arbitral tribunal,[230] which must assess the expert's conclusions 'with due regard to all the circumstances of the case' (Article 6(7)).

7.153   In *Luzon Hydro Corp v Transfield Philippines*,[231] the applicant challenged an arbitral award on the basis that the tribunal-appointed expert retained to assist it went much further than was agreed by the parties – allegedly the expert was actively involved in assessing the evidence. Additionally, the applicant alleged a breach of natural justice on the basis that the expert's report to the arbitral tribunal was not provided to the parties for comments. The Singapore High Court rejected the application on a number of grounds, which included a finding that the arbitral tribunal adequately set out the expert's tasks in a letter to the parties; that the expert communicated to the parties in his invoices descriptions of his activities; no compelling evidence indicated that the expert exceeded his role; what the expert said to the arbitral tribunal was confidential; and no party objected to the role of the expert until the award was issued.[232]

7.154   This decision differs from the rule in Article 6(5) of the IBA Rules of Evidence, which states that the parties may examine 'any correspondence between the Arbitral Tribunal and the Tribunal-Appointed Expert'. This serves as a reminder that the IBA Rules of Evidence are certainly not used in every case, and even where they are used they are generally utilised only as guidelines rather than binding rules. The decision also underscores the wide degree of discretion arbitral tribunals are granted in determining the procedure in relation to experts.

7.4.3 Witness conferencing

7.155   Arbitral tribunals may create procedures for the assessment of evidence that are conducive to smoother and more efficient arbitrations. One of these is witness

---

229 See also UNCITRAL Notes on Organizing Arbitral Proceedings, op. cit. fn 91, at para 72.
230 See, e.g. IBA Working Party, 'Commentary on the New [1999] IBA Rules of Evidence in International Commercial Arbitration', (2000) *Business Law International* 16, p. 32; and Hanotiau, op. cit. fn 35, p. 386.
231 [2004] 4 SLR 705 (Singapore High Court).
232 Ibid., at pp. 711–713.

conferencing. A founding father of this technique, Wolfgang Peter, has defined it in the following terms:[233]

> Witness conferencing consists of the simultaneous joint hearing of all fact witnesses, expert witnesses, and other experts involved in the arbitration. It is not an occasional confrontation of two fact witnesses or expert witnesses, but involves all witnesses and experts appearing simultaneously throughout the entire hearing. Witness conferencing is therefore not a 'witness-by-witness' hearing, but a team-versus-team hearing.

There are many different approaches to witness conferencing. Bernard Hanotiau has described it as a debate that 'takes place among informed and specialized witnesses; it is expert knowledge versus expert knowledge and no longer the lawyer's questioning technique versus the witnesses' expert knowledge'.[234]

Every expert need not be present in the conferencing room at the same time. It does not serve much purpose to bring together all these professionals if their evidence is not relevant to each other. For example, the conferencing may be done issue by issue whereby all the electrical experts gather together to discuss the issues relating to their discipline, and thereafter the mechanical experts gather to go through the same process in relation to their sphere of expertise.

Witness conferencing is said to reduce with relative speed many of the divergences among experts and leaves only a few specific points of disagreement for the arbitral tribunal to determine. Further, Wolfgang Peter concludes from his use of the technique that parties who have adopted it will generally settle during or at the end of the hearings, particularly because the conferencing tends to bring to light the respective strengths and weaknesses of the parties' positions.[235] However, from the perspective of professionals acquainted with traditional arbitral procedure, it might prove a bit disorienting. The lawyers, particularly, may feel that they lose control over 'their' party-appointed expert.[236] It was also observed during a recent AFIA Symposium in Seoul that witness conferencing may be problematic for witnesses of fact where there is a power relationship between two opposing witnesses or a cultural divide. Such circumstances may make witnesses uncomfortable about contradicting the other expert's testimony in his or her presence.[237]

In support of witness conferencing, Michael Hwang has asserted that a selling point to sceptical counsel is that[238]

> [i]t gives them the benefit of using their own witnesses to rebut the testimony of the other side's witnesses at the time when the other witnesses are making assertions which require instant contradiction for maximum impact on the tribunal.

---

233 W Peter, 'Witness 'Conferencing'', (2002) 18 *Arbitration International* 47, at p. 48. See also M Hwang, 'Witness Conferencing', in J McKay (ed), *The 2008 Legal Media Group Guide to the World's Leading Experts in Commercial Arbitration*, 2008, p. 3; and IBA Rules of Evidence Article 5(3).
234 Hanotiau, op. cit. fn 35, p. 376.
235 Peter, op. cit. fn 233, p. 47.
236 Hanotiau, op. cit. fn 35, p. 387.
237 See S Davis, '18th AFIA Symposium, Seoul 24 June 2009', (2009) 4 *AFIA News*, September, p. 9.
238 M Hwang, 'Witness Conferencing and Party Autonomy', (2009) October *Transnational Dispute Management* 20.

7.160 Article 5(3) of the 1999 IBA Rules of Evidence (Article 5(4) of the 2010 Rules) invests the arbitral tribunal with the discretion to order the party experts to meet and 'attempt to reach agreement on those issues as to which they had differences of opinion in their Expert Reports, and they shall record in writing any such issues on which they reach agreement' (Article 5(3)). Recognising its potential benefits, domestic courts are now also starting to permit the use of witness conferencing.[239]

8 Hearings

7.161 A hearing typically refers to a meeting at which counsel and the arbitrators are physically present for purposes such as the presentation of each party's oral arguments, examination of witnesses, and for the arbitrators to question the parties' counsel and/or their witnesses. A general feature of arbitration hearings is that they take place in private.

7.162 Hearings in international commercial arbitration usually take place once the written submissions, documentary evidence, witness statements and expert reports have been exchanged. There may well be more than one hearing, and it is not uncommon to have one hearing for each phase in an arbitration (e.g. on jurisdiction, liability, quantum).

7.163 As discussed previously, due process rules demand that parties are given adequate advance notice of the hearing.[240] In the event that a party duly notified of the hearing fails to appear without showing sufficient cause for the failure, the arbitral tribunal may proceed to hear the party that appears, and ultimately issue a default award.[241]

7.164 The power to manage hearings rests with the arbitral tribunal and not the parties. The 1999 IBA Rules of Evidence provide in Article 8(1):[242]

> The Arbitral Tribunal shall at all times have complete control over the Evidentiary Hearing. The Arbitral Tribunal may limit or exclude any question to, answer by or appearance of a witness (which term includes, for the purposes of this Article, witnesses of fact and any Experts), if it considers such question, answer or appearance to be irrelevant, immaterial, burdensome, duplicative or covered by a reason for objection set forth in Article 9.2. . . .

7.165 The IBA Working Party commentary on this provision sheds more light on the rationale of giving such discretion to the arbitral tribunal: 'These provisions are all designed to give the arbitral tribunal the ability to focus the hearing on issues material to the outcome of the case and thereby make the hearing more efficient.'[243]

---

239 See, e.g. Order 44.06 of the Rules of the Supreme Court of Victoria, Australia.
240 See Section 4.1 above.
241 See Section 6.10 above.
242 See also ICC Rules Article 21(3).
243 IBA Working Party, op. cit. fn 230; (2000) *Business Law International* 16, at p. 33.

An example of the procedure that may be followed during an evidentiary 7.166
hearing in an international arbitration is:[244]

(i) *Opening of the hearing* – The sole arbitrator or chair of the arbitral tribunal will open the hearing. The parties and their representatives will be introduced and organisational matters will be explained. Usually, many of the administrative matters relating to the hearing and the order of proceedings will have been agreed or addressed in a procedural order issued prior to the hearing.

(ii) *Opening statements* (sometimes omitted) – A summary presentation of each party's case, highlighting the respective merits and strengths and indicating how this is corroborated by the documentary evidence already filed and the oral evidence that is to follow.[245]

(iii) *Hearing of witnesses of fact* – Not all witnesses who have provided written statements are called to give oral evidence. If a party disputes the content of a witness' written statement, then that witness should normally be called for cross-examination. If he or she does not appear, the witness statement may be disregarded, save exceptional circumstances.[246] Witnesses in international arbitrations rarely testify under oath unless that is mandatory under the law of the seat. However, the witnesses would be expected to affirm that they are telling the truth.[247] The three main phases of taking evidence are the examination in chief (or direct examination), the cross-examination and re-examination (or redirect examination).[248] Examination in chief often does not take place – for the sake of efficiency, counsel for the parties frequently agree that the witness's written statement constitutes the evidence in chief. The arbitral tribunal is usually free to question a witness at any time during these phases.[249] As to the order of appearance of the witnesses, one possibility is for the claimant to have all its witnesses testify first, followed by the respondent's witnesses and thereafter the claimant's rebuttal witnesses, if any.[250] However the

---

[244] For a more detailed discussion of the practical issues involved in a hearing, e.g. expenses, order of presentation, whether an oath is administered, etc., see Hanotiau, op. cit. fn 35, pp. 381–388.
[245] The length of time to make these statements may vary – one arbitrator has indicated a maximum of approximately 2–3 hours. See Hanotiau, op. cit. fn 35, p. 381. Another has shown a preference for half an hour. See Sawada, op. cit. fn 43, p. 303.
[246] See, e.g. IBA Rules of Evidence Article 4(8).
[247] See, e.g. IBA Rules of Evidence Article 8(3). In this regard, the ICSID Rules, Rule 35 are more specific than most – they require each witness of fact to declare: 'I solemnly declare upon my honour and conscience that I speak the truth, the whole truth and nothing but the truth.' Those Rules require expert witnesses to declare: 'I solemnly declare upon my honour and conscience that my statement will be in accordance with my sincere belief.' In some jurisdictions, it is illegal for an arbitrator to administer an oath. That power may be reserved for state organs. See, e.g. the Swedish Arbitration Act 1999 Section 25.
[248] See Section 7.3 above. Article 8(2) of the IBA Rules of Evidence states in part that '[f]ollowing direct testimony, any other Party may question such witness, in an order to be determined by the Arbitral Tribunal. The Party who initially presented the witness shall subsequently have the opportunity to ask additional questions on the matters raised in the other Parties' questioning'. Sometimes, a fourth phase, called re-cross examination is allowed, which enables the respondent to ask questions on additional questions that may have been raised during the re-examination. See Hanotiau, op. cit. fn 35, p. 384.
[249] See, e.g. IBA Rules of Evidence Article 8(2).
[250] Ibid.

arbitral tribunal may prefer to deal with factual witnesses issue by issue.[251] The order of witnesses may also be affected by each individual witness's availability to be present at the hearing.

(iv) *Hearing of expert witnesses* – The presence of expert witnesses will ordinarily be required at the hearing to be examined and cross-examined much like witnesses of fact. Ordinarily, witnesses of fact give their evidence before the expert witnesses, although this is always subject to the particular case and to the arbitral tribunal's preferences.

(v) *Closing arguments* – This stage is reserved for the parties' lawyers to sum up their case on the basis of all the evidence presented to the arbitral tribunal, usually with a focus on the evidence adduced during the hearing. The approach to closing arguments by common lawyers and civil law lawyers may diverge; the style of the former tends to be short and fact-based and the latter tends to concentrate on legal issues and are generally longer. Oral closing submissions are often dispensed with if written post-hearing briefs are to be filed.

(vi) *Closing of the hearing* – Before formally closing the hearing, the sole arbitrator or chairperson may address outstanding and/or future procedural issues such as the date when the full transcript of the hearing will be available and when the post-hearing briefs, if any, should be submitted.[252] Sometimes, in order to satisfy itself that the parties feel they have been treated fairly, and in an attempt to protect the award, parties may be asked by the arbitral tribunal whether they have been given a reasonable opportunity to be heard.[253]

7.167 The closing of the hearing should not be confused with the closing of the proceedings. Written submissions (e.g. post-hearing submissions) may follow after the hearing is closed. Even if no post-hearing briefs are required the arbitral tribunal may raise further questions in writing after the hearing. Once the entire proceedings themselves are closed, it is usually the practice that no further submission or evidence can be made thereafter, unless requested or authorised by the arbitral tribunal.[254] Most institutional rules have a provision that enables the hearing or proceedings to be reopened before the award is issued.[255]

7.168 Like all aspects of arbitration procedure, the venue and nature of a hearing depends on the preferences of the parties and the arbitral tribunal. As mentioned in Chapter 2, the hearing generally need not be held at the seat of arbitration. Hearings usually take place in the conference room of a hotel or in special

---

[251] See, e.g. M Hwang, 'Trial by Issues', paper presented at the APRAG Seoul Conference, 22 June 2009, reprinted in 7 *Transnational Dispute Management*, Issue 1, April 2010.
[252] See also UNCITRAL Arbitration Rules Article 29(1).
[253] See, e.g. ACICA Rules Article 30.1.
[254] See, e.g. HKIAC Rules Article 27.1; ICC Rules Article 22; SIAC Rules, Rule 21.5.
[255] Some rules expressly indicate that this is done only in exceptional circumstances, e.g. HKIAC Rules Article 27.2, but others simply state that the decision to reopen lies at the discretion of the arbitral tribunal, e.g. KCAB International Rules Article 27(2). In all cases, the efficiency of the arbitral process must be taken into account. See also ACICA Rules Article 30.2; JCAA Rules, Rule 49(2); SIAC Rules, Rule 21.5.

arbitration hearing room facilities. Sometimes hearings are held in the facilities of one of the law firms involved in the case.

Modern communications technology may be utilised to assist the conduct of the hearing. The parties might agree that there is no point in incurring the expense of flying a witness to the place where the hearing is held. Such witnesses may attend via telephone or video-link. The HKIAC Electronic Transaction Arbitration Rules, for example, provide that '[h]earings may, without limitation, be conducted in person, by video-link, by telephone or on-line (by email or by other electronic or computer communication)'.[256] Many international arbitration institutions now provide video-conferencing services. However, some practitioners question whether an effective cross-examination can be conducted via video-link.

7.169

9 Interim measures

Interim measures are court or arbitral tribunal orders designed to protect assets or maintain the status quo pending the outcome of legal proceedings.[257] These measures are temporary and usually have effect only up to the time the final award is issued.[258] The importance of this topic is increasing due to a discernible rise in the number of arbitrations in which requests for interim measures are made.[259] Issues relating to interim measures can arise before an arbitral tribunal or before a competent domestic court. These are discussed in turn in Sections 9.1 and 9.2.

7.170

9.1 Tribunal-ordered interim measures

An international arbitral tribunal's power to order interim measures is derived from the parties' agreement, the applicable procedural rules, the law of the seat, and perhaps even from the arbitral tribunal's inherent power to conduct the proceedings as it sees fit.

7.171

Where an arbitral tribunal is empowered to grant interim measures, careful consideration should be given before exercising that power. Key reasons for this caution were articulated by David Williams as follows:[260]

7.172

> In considering whether it is appropriate to grant interim relief an arbitral tribunal must remain acutely aware of the situation in which it is placed. It may be being asked to take immediate action, without full knowledge of the facts and at the risk of pre-judging or even rendering irrelevant its final Award in the arbitration.

---

256 Article 9(1). See also Article 8(1) of the 2010 IBA Rules of Evidence.
257 Interim measures are also known as provisional or conservatory measures. For a detailed examination of the subject (albeit prior to the 2006 Model Law amendments), see A Yeşilirmak, *Provisional Measures in International Commercial Arbitration*, Kluwer Law International, 2005.
258 On the temporary nature of interim measures, see *Firm Ashok Traders v Gurumukh Das Saluja* (2004) 3 SCC 155 (Indian Supreme Ct), at para 17.
259 See, e.g., Report of the UN Secretary General, 'Settlement of Commercial Disputes', UNCITRAL 32nd Session, UN Doc. A/CN. 9/WGII/WP.108 (2000), p. 5.
260 D Williams, 'Interim Measures', in Pryles and Moser, op. cit. fn 8, p. 246 (footnotes omitted).

7.173 In many cases, parties comply voluntarily with interim measures ordered by the arbitral tribunal. The arbitral tribunal's ruling ends the matter and no further steps on its part are necessary. A party that defies an interim measures order may face a range of negative consequences:[261]
   (i) it may expose itself to an action for breach of the arbitration agreement;
   (ii) the arbitral tribunal may draw an adverse inference against it;
   (iii) an award of costs may be made against it; and/or
   (iv) if national courts are called on to assist in the enforcement process and the defiant party still fails to comply, state-backed sanctions involving contempt proceedings, fines and, perhaps in extreme cases, imprisonment could follow.

7.174 The relevant provisions of national laws and of arbitral rules are discussed in turn below, before discussing the controversial issue of applications to arbitral tribunals for *ex parte* interim measures.

9.1.1 National laws

7.175 Before discussing some of the region's national laws in relation to interim measures, it is useful to explain some fundamental changes that were made to the Model Law in 2006. Article 17 of the 1985 Model Law provides:

> Unless otherwise agreed by the parties, the arbitral tribunal may, at the request of a party, order any party to take such interim measure of protection as the arbitral tribunal may consider necessary in respect of the subject-matter of the dispute. The arbitral tribunal may require any party to provide appropriate security in connection with such measure.

7.176 This is a very general instruction that provides no guidance as to the scope and effect of interim measures and the conditions that are required for such measures to be granted. The lack of detail in the 1985 version of the Model Law led to the formulation of major amendments by UNCITRAL in 2006.[262] The new 2006 Model Law Article 17 elaborates significantly on the meaning of interim measures. It provides:[263]

> (1) Unless otherwise agreed by the parties, the arbitral tribunal may, at the request of a party, grant interim measures.
> (2) An interim measure is any temporary measure, whether in the form of an award or in another form, by which, at any time prior to the issuance of the award by which the dispute is finally decided, the arbitral tribunal orders a party to:

---

[261] On these points, see generally, Williams, ibid., pp. 242–254 and Yang, op. cit. fn 14, pp. 214–215.

[262] A very similar provision, but very deliberately omitting references to preliminary orders, now appears in the 2010 UNCITRAL Arbitration Rules as Article 26.

[263] The following footnoted examples of circumstances in which the interim measures may be invoked are largely derived from Williams, op. cit. fn 260, pp. 228–230.

(a) Maintain or restore the status quo pending determination of the dispute;[264]
(b) Take action that would prevent, or refrain from taking action that is likely to cause, current or imminent harm or prejudice to the arbitral process itself;[265]
(c) Provide a means of preserving assets out of which a subsequent award may be satisfied;[266] or
(d) Preserve evidence that may be relevant and material to the resolution of the dispute.[267]

The conditions necessary for interim measures to be granted are set out in Article 17A of the 2006 Model Law. Its first paragraph reads:

7.177

The party requesting an interim measure under article 17(2)(a), (b) and (c) shall satisfy the arbitral tribunal that:
(a) Harm not adequately reparable by an award of damages is likely to result if the measure is not ordered, and such harm substantially outweighs the harm that is likely to result to the party against whom the measure is directed if the measure is granted; and
(b) There is a reasonable possibility that the requesting party will succeed on the merits of the claim. The determination on this possibility shall not affect the discretion of the arbitral tribunal in making any subsequent determination.

Different treatment is accorded to an interim measure to preserve evidence under Article 17(2)(d): the requirements under Article 17A(1)(a) and (b) need only be applied 'to the extent the arbitral tribunal considers appropriate'. As a consequence, a less onerous burden of proof may be required by the requesting party for invoking this sub-paragraph.[268] A requirement that the measure must be urgent was included in earlier drafts of the Model Law amendments. However, the UNCITRAL Working Group decided that the requirement of urgency was not a general condition for the grant of interim relief under Article 17A.[269]

7.178

The 2006 Model Law amendments also contain safeguards to prevent abuse of the interim measures regime: the arbitral tribunal may modify, suspend or terminate the interim measure at any time (Article 17D); it may require appropriate security to be provided (Article 17E); it may require the requesting party to make prompt disclosure of any material change in the basis on which the measure was requested or granted (Article 17F); and the party requesting the

7.179

---

264 For example, a party may be required to keep performing certain contractual obligations or permit access rights to or use of property that was granted before the dispute arose.
265 For example, the arbitral tribunal may issue an anti-suit injunction or order a party to make available for inspection property that is material to the case.
266 For example, the arbitral tribunal may issue what are described in common law litigation as 'Mareva injunctions' or 'freezing orders' to prevent the dissipation of assets that may be used to satisfy an award.
267 This is necessary because arbitral tribunals must have access to relevant and material evidence, which, if not preserved, could be deleted from computers, destroyed or could significantly deteriorate during the period of the arbitration proceedings.
268 The UNCITRAL Working Group generally felt that the very high threshold was not appropriate for all types of interim measures, such as the preservation of evidence. See Report of the Working Group on Arbitration and Conciliation on the work of its forty-third session (Vienna, 3–7 October 2005), UN Doc. A/CN.9/589, para 32. See also S Menon and E Chao, 'Reforming the Model Law Provisions on Interim Measures of Protection', (2006) 2 *Asian International Arbitration Journal* 1, at pp. 8–9.
269 Report of the Working Group II (Arbitration and Conciliation) on the work of its thirty-seventh session (Vienna, 7–11 October 2002), UN Doc. A/CN.9/523, para 29. See Williams, op. cit. fn 260, p. 248.

measure is to be liable for any costs or damages caused by the interim measure if the arbitral tribunal determines that the measure should not have been granted (Article 17G).

7.180　The Singapore International Arbitration Act is a good example of national legislation that grants an arbitral tribunal detailed interim measures powers.[270] Section 12(1) of that Act was amended in 2001 to read:

> Without prejudice to the powers set out in any other provision of this Act and in the Model Law, an arbitral tribunal shall have powers to make orders or give directions to any party for –
> (a) security for costs;
> (b) discovery of documents and interrogatories;
> (c) giving of evidence by affidavit;
> (d) the preservation, interim custody or sale of any property which is or forms part of the subject-matter of the dispute;
> (e) samples to be taken from, or any observation to be made of or experiment conducted upon, any property which is or forms part of the subject-matter of the dispute;
> (f) the preservation and interim custody of any evidence for the purposes of the proceedings;
> (g) securing the amount in dispute;
> (h) ensuring that any award which may be made in the arbitral proceedings is not rendered ineffectual by the dissipation of assets by a party; and
> (i) an interim injunction or any other interim measure.

7.181　Certain domestic laws are more constrained in the powers they grant to arbitral tribunals. For example, unless the parties agree otherwise, Article 19 of the Malaysian Arbitration Act 2005 confines an arbitral tribunal's power to make interim orders in relation to (1) security for costs; (2) document discovery and interrogatories; (3) giving of evidence by affidavit; and (4) preservation, interim custody or sale of any property that is the subject matter of the dispute. In contrast, the Malaysian courts are accorded wider powers under Article 11 of that Act, which enables the Malaysian High Court, in addition to the above four categories, (1) to appoint a receiver; (2) to secure the amount in dispute; (3) to ensure that any award made in the proceedings is not made ineffectual by the dissipation of assets; and (4) to grant an interim injunction or other interim measure.

7.182　The Singaporean and Malaysian laws may be compared with the corresponding legislation in China, Thailand and Vietnam, which contains far more restrictive provisions. The laws of China, Thailand and Vietnam grant no express power to arbitral tribunals to order interim measures. That power is reserved for their domestic courts.[271] Moreover, in China parties cannot apply directly to

---

[270] See also Hong Kong Arbitration Ordinance Section 2GB.
[271] See, e.g. Article 33 of Vietnam's Ordinance on Commercial Arbitration 2003; Article 258 of China's Civil Procedure Law; Articles 28 and 68 of China's Arbitration Law 1995; Section 16 of Thai Arbitration Act 2002. See also MLJ Winckless, 'The History and Current Status of Arbitration in Thailand', (2004) *Asian Dispute Review*, p. 12.

the court for interim measures; the application must be made through an arbitral institution.[272]

9.1.2 Arbitral rules

Arbitration procedural rules have adopted three basic approaches to an arbitral tribunal's power to order interim measures. Some have modelled their provisions on Article 17 of the 1985 Model Law and contain a very general description of the arbitral tribunal's powers to order interim measures. Rule 48(1) of the JCAA Rules, for example, provides that '[t]he arbitral tribunal may, at the request of a party, order any party to take such interim measures of protection as the arbitral tribunal may consider necessary in respect of the subject matter of the dispute'.[273] 7.183

Other arbitration rules include detailed provisions. For example, SIAC Rule 24 and ACICA Rules Article 28 are formulated more along the lines of Article 17 of the 2006 Model Law. The ACICA Rules have made a number of notable modifications or additions to the Model Law. These are set out in Article 28 of those Rules and include:[274] 7.184

(i) a requirement that the arbitral tribunal give reasons if an interim measure is granted as an order rather than an award;
(ii) the inclusion of security for legal and other costs in the definition of interim measures;
(iii) where interim measures are granted and subsequently the arbitral tribunal decides they should not have been, the ability of the arbitral tribunal to decide that the party that requested the measure is liable for the resulting costs or damages;
(iv) the omission of a power pursuant to which arbitral tribunals may order ex parte interim measures as contained in Article 17B of the 2006 Model Law; and
(v) an obligation on the part of the arbitral tribunal to endeavour to ensure that its interim measures are enforceable.

A third (minority) approach adopted by arbitral rules is not to empower the arbitral tribunal to order interim measures. Articles 17 and 18 of the CIETAC Rules, for example, provide that where a party requests measures to protect property or evidence, CIETAC will forward that request to the competent court. This is consistent with Chinese law, referred to in the previous section. 7.185

9.1.3 Ex parte preliminary orders

One of the most contentious subjects in the Model Law 2006 amendments (discussed above) concerned ex parte 'preliminary orders', which an arbitral tribunal is entitled to grant under Article 17B: 7.186

---
272 See, e.g. CIETAC Rules Articles 17 and 18. See also Ge Liu, 'UNCITRAL Model Law v Chinese Law and Practice – A Discussion on Interim Measures of Protection', (2004) 12 *ICCA Congress Series* 278, at p. 280.
273 See also KCAB International Rules Article 28(1).
274 See generally, Greenberg, op. cit. fn 78, p. 197.

(1) Unless otherwise agreed by the parties, a party may, without notice to any other party, make a request for an interim measure together with an application for a preliminary order directing a party not to frustrate the purpose of the interim measure requested.
(2) The arbitral tribunal may grant a preliminary order provided it considers that prior disclosure of the request for the interim measure to the party against whom it is directed risks frustrating the purpose of the measure.
(3) The conditions defined under article 17A apply to any preliminary order, provided that the harm to be assessed under article 17A(1)(a), is the harm likely to result from the order being granted or not.

7.187 The procedure to be adopted subsequent to the granting of a preliminary order is set out in Article 17C. Its main features include providing notice of the order and related information to all parties immediately after the order is made (Article 17C(1)); granting the party against whom the preliminary order is made the opportunity to present its case (Article 17C(2)); and deciding promptly any objection to the order (Article 17C(3)). The order has a life span of 20 days but this may be varied after hearing the party subject to the order (Article 17C(4)). These provisions are an attempt to soften the fact that the order is issued without notifying or hearing submissions from the party against whom it is sought. Further safeguards have been provided for in Articles 17D–G; and unlike interim measures, a preliminary order, while binding on the parties, is not enforceable by a court (Article 17C(5)). This last provision appeared to be essential to maintain the consensus of the UNCITRAL Working Group that formulated the 2006 amendments.[275]

7.188 There are many arguments for and against the Model Law preliminary orders regime. Advocates in favour of it have said that an arbitral tribunal's power to grant ex parte measures enhances the usefulness and efficiency of international arbitration by increasing its independence from state courts and that the element of surprise may be essential for certain interim measures to be effective. They also assert that because state courts regularly grant ex parte measures, there is no reason for arbitration to be any different.[276] Those opposing the regime contend that the granting of ex parte relief by an arbitral tribunal violates fundamental due process principles of international arbitration and it is inconsistent with the consensual nature of arbitration; that the practice may lead arbitrators to prejudge the merits of the dispute without hearing the other party; and that parties always have the option to obtain ex parte interim relief from a court.[277] On balance, we consider that the preliminary orders regime in the Model Law, if used very cautiously, will contribute to the effectiveness of international commercial

---

275 See Menon and Chao, op. cit. fn 268, pp. 14–17 (commenting that if the 'sticking point [as to enforcement] was not resolved, the chances of forging consensus on the entire preliminary orders regime would be jeopardised'.). See also Williams, op. cit. fn 260, p. 252.
276 See K Hobér, 'The Trailblazers v. the Conservative Crusaders, or Why Arbitrators Should Have the Power to Order Ex Parte Interim Relief', (2004) 12 *ICCA Congress Series* 272.
277 See H van Houtte, 'Ten Reasons against a Proposal for *Ex Parte* Interim Measures of Protection in Arbitration', (2004) 20 *Arbitration International* 20.

arbitration. The regime has already been adopted by New Zealand[278] and is likely to be enacted in Hong Kong.[279] Singapore amended its International Arbitration Act in 2009 but did not adopt the preliminary orders provisions in Article 17 of the 2006 Model Law.

9.2 Court assistance

There are a number of reasons why an arbitral tribunal might need the assistance of courts in issuing interim measures. Redfern and Hunter usefully identify five situations:[280]

(i) The arbitral tribunal may not have the powers, particularly if the national law limits powers of arbitrators to order interim measures.[281]
(ii) A need for interim measures might arise (often urgently) before the arbitral tribunal is constituted.[282]
(iii) An arbitral tribunal's powers extend only to the parties involved in the arbitration whereas court orders may be enforced against third parties.
(iv) An interim measure may not be enforceable internationally under the New York Convention[283] and therefore an interim measure may need to be requested directly from a court at the place of execution.
(v) Arbitrators by and large are not given powers to grant ex parte applications to restrain the conduct of another party and therefore the ex parte application will usually need to be determined by a court.[284]

7.189

Although the 1985 Model Law addresses the power of arbitral tribunals to order interim measures, it contains no provision that deals with a court's power to do so. In contrast Article 17J of the Model Law 2006 amendments provides:[285]

7.190

> A court shall have the same power of issuing an interim measure in relation to arbitration proceedings, irrespective of whether their place is in the territory of this State, as

---

278 See Sections 17C-G of the New Zealand Arbitration Act.
279 See Sections 37 and 38 of the Hong Kong Arbitration Bill, which is expected to be passed in early 2011.
280 See Redfern, Hunter, et al., op. cit. fn 45, pp. 332–336, paras 7–11 to 7–17. See also DF Donovan, 'The Allocation of Authority between Courts and Arbitral Tribunals to Order Interim Measures: A Survey of Jurisdictions, the Work of UNCITRAL and a Model Proposal', (2004) 12 *ICCA Congress Series* 203, at pp. 238–239.
281 See, e.g. CIETAC Rules Article 23; Arbitration Law of China 1995 Articles 28 and 45; Thai Arbitration Act 2002 Section 16; Vietnam Ordinance on Commercial Arbitration 2003 Article 33.
282 See, e.g. Indian Arbitration and Conciliation Act Section 9 and Model Law Article 9. See also *Sunderam Finance Ltd v NEPC India Ltd* (1999) XXIV *Yearbook of Commercial Arbitration*, pp. 309–316, 13 January 1999 (Supreme Court of India). Some arbitral institutions have attempted to address this problem by enabling the appointment of a pre-arbitral or emergency arbitrator. See, e.g. the 1990 ICC Rules for a Pre-Arbitral Referee Procedure and Rule 26.2 of the 2010 SIAC Rules.
283 See, e.g. *Resort Condominiums Inc v Bolwell* (1993) 118 ALR 655; (1995) XX *Yearbook of Commercial Arbitration* 628, 29 October 1993, (Queensland Supreme Court, Australia). In contrast, Article 17K of Schedule 1 of New Zealand's Arbitration Act 1996 (as amended), adopting the 2006 version of the Model Law, prescribes that interim measures are binding and enforceable in courts.
284 See, however, the new section in the 2006 Model Law, particularly Article 17B and C, entitling arbitral tribunals to make ex parte preliminary orders, but these are not enforceable. This is discussed in Section 9.1.3 above. In ICC arbitrations, ex parte orders have on rare occasions been made by the arbitral tribunal similar to that which has been contemplated by the 2006 Model Law despite the absence of an express power to do so under the applicable law or in the ICC Rules.
285 This provision of the Model Law amendment should be read in combination with Article 1(2).

it has in relation to proceedings in courts. The court shall exercise such power in accordance with its own procedures in consideration of the specific features of international arbitration.

7.191 A key feature of the Model Law 2006 amendments is its provisions on the enforcement of interim measures. Article 17H provides:

> 17H (1) An interim measure issued by an arbitral tribunal shall be recognized as binding and, unless otherwise provided by the arbitral tribunal, enforced upon application to the competent court, irrespective of the country in which it was issued, subject to the provisions of article 17I.
> (2) The party who is seeking or has obtained recognition or enforcement of an interim measure shall promptly inform the court of any termination, suspension or modification of that interim measure.
> (3) The court of the State where recognition or enforcement is sought may, if it considers it proper, order the requesting party to provide appropriate security if the arbitral tribunal has not already made a determination with respect to security or where such a decision is necessary to protect the rights of third parties.

7.192 As is made clear by Article 17H(1), a court may enforce interim measures made by arbitral tribunals sitting within the enforcing state or elsewhere. This provision also contains certain safeguards such as imposing an obligation on the requesting party to inform the enforcing court of any changes to the interim measure and empowers the enforcing court to order appropriate security from the requesting party. The grounds on which a court may refuse to recognise or enforce an interim measure are dealt with in Article 17I, which provides:

> 17I (1) Recognition or enforcement of an interim measure may be refused only:
>   (a) At the request of the party against whom it is invoked if the court is satisfied that:
>   (i) Such refusal is warranted on the grounds set forth in article 36(1)(a)(i), (ii), (iii) or (iv); or
>   (ii) The arbitral tribunal's decision with respect to the provision of security in connection with the interim measure issued by the arbitral tribunal has not been complied with; or
>   (iii) The interim measure has been terminated or suspended by the arbitral tribunal or, where so empowered, by the court of the State in which the arbitration takes place or under the law of which that interim measure was granted; or
>   (b) If the court finds that:
>   (i) The interim measure is incompatible with the powers conferred upon the court unless the court decides to reformulate the interim measure to the extent necessary to adapt it to its own powers and procedures for the purposes of enforcing that interim measure and without modifying its substance; or
>   (ii) Any of the grounds set forth in article 36(1)(b)(i) or (ii), apply to the recognition and enforcement of the interim measure.
> (2) Any determination made by the court on any ground in paragraph (1) of this article shall be effective only for the purposes of the application to recognize

and enforce the interim measure. The court where recognition or enforcement is sought shall not, in making that determination, undertake a review of the substance of the interim measure.

7.193 The refusal grounds contained in Article 17I explicitly follow some of those contained in Article 36 of the Model Law and in Article V of the New York Convention. Case law on the enforcement refusal provisions in the Model Law or the New York Convention may therefore be of some guidance in determining whether a refusal will be justified. The Article 17I(1) phrase 'may be refused only' indicates that the refusal grounds are exhaustive and that the court maintains the discretion to order recognition or enforcement even if one of the Article 17I grounds is present.

7.194 While the above provisions are new and have so far been enacted in few countries, a number of domestic laws already provide for court enforcement of interim measures ordered by an arbitral tribunal. Section 12(6) of Singapore's International Arbitration Act, for example, provides:[286]

> All orders or directions made or given by an arbitral tribunal in the course of an arbitration shall, by leave of the High Court or a Judge thereof, be enforceable in the same manner as if they were orders made by a court and, where leave is so given, judgment may be entered in terms of the order or direction.

7.195 The laws of some other Model Law countries simply enable their award enforcement laws to apply equally to interim measures ordered by an arbitral tribunal.[287]

7.196 Some laws may specifically allow courts to determine interim measures without the need first to apply to an arbitral tribunal.[288] In some jurisdictions, an application may be made to a court even before arbitral proceedings are commenced.[289] Article 9(ii) of India's Arbitration and Conciliation Act is an example of a domestic law that provides detailed rules as to when courts may order interim measures in an arbitration:[290]

---

[286] A similar provision is found in Section 2GG(1) of Hong Kong's Arbitration Ordinance. In the proposed reform to the Hong Kong legislation this provision is retained but the contemplated new provision further adds that an order or direction in the relevant provisions includes an interim measure. See Section 61(5) of Hong Kong's current Arbitration Bill, which is expected to be passed in early 2011.

[287] See, e.g. Section 23 of the Australian International Arbitration Act 1974 (a provision that requires specific opting in by the parties); and Section 19(3) of the Malaysian Arbitration Act 2005. See also ACICA Rules Article 28(1) ('The Arbitral Tribunal may order [interim measures of protection] in the form of an award . . .'); and Williams, op. cit. fn 260, p. 243. Additionally, see the discussion in Chapter 8, Section 5.3, as to whether an arbitral tribunal's order for interim measures constitutes an 'award' within the meaning of the New York Convention.

[288] See, e.g. Hong Kong's Arbitration Ordinance Section 2GC.

[289] See, e.g. *Sundaram Finance Ltd v NEPC India Ltd* (1999) 2 SCC 479, at para 20, in which the Supreme Court of India (in a domestic arbitration) held that under Article 9 of India's Arbitration and Conciliation Act an application may be made to a national court for interim measures *prior* to the commencement of arbitral proceedings. It added that there must be a 'manifest intention' on the part of the applicant to proceed to arbitration. See also *Firm Ashok Traders v Gurumukh Das Saluja* (2004) 3 SCC 155; and P Nair, 'Surveying the Decade of the "New" Law of Arbitration in India', (2007) 23 *Arbitration International* 699, at pp. 714–715.

[290] An interesting point of comparison is Article 17 of the Indian Arbitration and Conciliation Act, which gives arbitral tribunals the power to order interim measures but provides no detailed enumeration as is the case in Article 9.

A party may, before or during arbitral proceedings or at any time after the making of the arbitral award but before it is enforced in accordance with section 36, apply to a court:

...

(ii) For an interim measure of protection in respect of any of the following matters, namely: –
  (a) The preservation, interim custody or sale of any goods, which are the subject matter of the arbitration agreement;
  (b) Securing the amount in dispute in the arbitration;
  (c) The detention, preservation or inspection of any property or thing which is the subject-matter of the dispute in arbitration, or as to which any question may arise therein and authorising for any of the aforesaid purposes any person to enter upon any land or building in the possession of any party, or authorising any samples to be taken or any observation to be made, or experiment to be tried, which may be necessary or expedient for the purpose of obtaining full information or evidence;
  (d) Interim injunction or the appointment of a receiver;
  (e) Such other interim measure of protection as may appear to the court to be just and convenient,

And the Court shall have the same power for making orders as it has for the purpose of, and in relation to, any proceedings before it.

7.197 Interim court orders may be made by courts located outside the seat of arbitration as is indicated by Article 17J of the 2006 Model Law (quoted above). Such orders are particularly important where assets outside the seat need to be protected. In *Bhatia International v Bulk Trading SA*,[291] even though France was the seat of arbitration, the Indian Supreme Court upheld a lower court's interim order to preserve the subject matter of an ICC arbitration by preventing a party to the foreign arbitration from alienating or otherwise disposing of its business assets located in India. In this case, the Supreme Court controversially used the interim measures provision located in Part I of India's Arbitration and Conciliation Act. Whether Part I actually applies to arbitrations seated outside India is open to some debate because, pursuant to Section 2(2) of the Act, that Part applies 'where the place of arbitration is in India'.[292]

7.198 The Delhi High Court more recently has denied an interim measures request relating to a proposed arbitration in Singapore in *Max India Ltd v General Binding Corporation*.[293] A single judge of the court held that by agreeing in their dispute resolution clause to Singapore law, to SIAC arbitration and to Singapore court

---

291 (2002) 4 SCC 105 (Indian Supreme Court).
292 See, e.g. the critique in Nair, op. cit. fn 289, pp. 717–720. See also N Dewan, 'Arbitration in India: An Unenjoyable Litigating Jamboree!', (2007) 3 *Asian International Arbitration Journal* 113; R Sharma, 'Bhatia International v Bulk Trading SA: Ambushing International Commercial Arbitration Outside India?', (2009) 26(3) *Journal of International Arbitration* 357; and Nariman, op. cit. fn 8, pp. 337–338. The reasoning in *Bhatia* was relied on heavily in the highly controversial case of *Venture Global Engineering v Satyam Computer Services* (2008) 4 SCC 190 (Indian Supreme Court), which is discussed in Chapter 9, Section 3.2.2. See also the Hong Kong Court of Appeal case *The Lady Muriel* [1995] 2 HKC 320.
293 Order of Justice Shiv Narayan Dhingra, 14 May 2009, (High Court of Delhi at New Delhi) OMP No. 136/2009.

jurisdiction, the parties specifically excluded the jurisdiction of Indian courts and Part I of the Indian Arbitration and Conciliation Act. In upholding this decision on appeal, the Division Bench of the Delhi High Court indicated that adequate relief could be provided under the SIAC Rules as well as the Singapore International Arbitration Act.[294]

7.199 In *Swift-Fortune Ltd v Magnifica Marine SA*, the Singapore Court of Appeal upheld a first instance decision by Justice Judith Prakash that Singapore courts have no jurisdiction under Section 12(7) of its International Arbitration Act to grant injunctions in aid of a foreign arbitration and that this provision applied only to an arbitration seated in Singapore.[295] The court left open the question whether Section 4(10) of the Singapore Civil Law Act could be applicable. That provision states that 'an injunction may be granted ... in all cases in which it appears to the court to be just or convenient that such order should be made'.[296] The International Arbitration Act was amended in 2009 to give Singapore courts the power to issue interim measures in respect of foreign arbitrations.[297] The Malaysian Court of Appeal in *Aras Jalinan Sdn Bhd v TIPCO Asphalt Company Ltd* has also ruled that Malaysian courts have no jurisdiction to grant injunctions to assist a foreign seated arbitration.[298]

7.200 Australian courts have displayed a willingness to grant an interim injunction in support of a foreign seated arbitration. For example, in a series of Federal Court of Australia decisions in *Clough Engineering Ltd v Oil & Natural Gas Corporation Ltd*,[299] the contract was governed by Indian law and included an arbitration clause designating India as the seat of arbitration. Before arbitration was commenced, Clough sought an interim injunction from the Australian Federal Court to prevent certain Australian banks from paying out on an unconditional performance bond valued at 10% of the contract price. From Clough's point of view, the injunction would assist in securing payment for an eventual award issued in its favour by the arbitral tribunal seated in India. Justice Gilmour granted an ex

---

[294] *Max India Ltd v General Binding Corporation*, Division Bench, Delhi High Court, 16 July 2009, (FAO (OS) No.193/2009), at para 40. The decision has been commended for not intervening in the arbitral process and for confirming that it is more appropriate for a party seeking relief to approach the court chosen in their contract, see T Karia, 'Appeal Court Upholds Decision on Jurisdiction to Grant Interim Relief', *ILO Newsletter*, 25 August 2009.
[295] See *Swift-Fortune Ltd v Magnifica Marine SA*, [2006] SGCA 42 (Court of Appeal); *Swift-Fortune Ltd v Magnifica Marine SA*, [2006] 2 SLR 323 (High Court). A short time after the High Court judgment in *Swift-Fortune* was handed down, Justice Belinda Ang in *Front Carriers Ltd v Atlantic & Orient Shipping Corp* [2006] 3 SLR 854 (High Court) held that the court had jurisdiction to grant an injunction in Singapore in respect of an arbitration taking place in London and that Section 12(7) could apply to arbitrations seated outside Singapore. An appeal in this case was withdrawn after the Court of Appeal issued its judgment in *Swift-Fortune*. See Leng Sun Chan, 'Injunctions in Aid of Foreign Arbitration: The Singapore Experience', (2007) 3 *Asian International Arbitration Journal* 142, at p. 148.
[296] See Leng Sun Chan, ibid., pp. 148–149 and 154–159.
[297] See Section 12A of the International Arbitration Act, which authorises court-ordered interim measures 'irrespective of whether the place of arbitration is in the territory of Singapore'.
[298] [2008] 4 AMR 533; ILO Case 15609. See K Shanti Mogan, 'High Court Claims No Inherent Jurisdiction', *ILO Newsletter*, 17 April 2008. Also see *Innotec Asia Pacific Sdn Bhd v Innotec GMBH* [2007] 8 CLJ 304; [2007] 8 AMR 67.
[299] [2007] FCA 881 (7 June 2007); [No. 2] [2007] FCA 927 (19 June 2007); [No. 4] [2007] FCA 2110 (21 December 2007); [2008] FCA 191 (29 February 2008); and [2008] FCAFC 136 (22 July 2008).

parte interim injunction in favour of Clough. Subsequently, the injunction was set aside on the basis that the applicant had no arguable case on the merits.[300]

7.201 In relation to overlapping interim measures powers of arbitral tribunals and courts, no settled international practice has developed as to how they should coexist.[301] The Article 17 Model Law amendments of 2006 are silent as to the order of priority when similar interim measures issues are to be decided in respect of the same parties by both a court and an arbitral tribunal. A few national laws in the region have addressed (at least partially) this issue. In Hong Kong, Section 2GB(6) of its Arbitration Ordinance provides that an interim measure may be declined by a court or a judge on the ground that the matter is currently the subject of arbitration proceedings and the court or judge considers it more appropriate for the matter to be dealt with by the relevant arbitral tribunal. In interpreting this provision, the Hong Kong Court of First Instance in *Leviathan Shipping Co v Sky Sailing Overseas Co* showed considerable deference to the arbitral process when it held '[t]he legislature has provided for the intervention of the courts, but... this jurisdiction should be exercised sparingly, and only where there are special reasons to utilize it'.[302]

7.202 Section 11(2) of Malaysia's Arbitration Act 2005 states:

> Where a party applies to the High Court for any interim measure and an arbitral tribunal has already ruled on any matter which is relevant to the application, the High Court shall treat any findings of fact made in the course of such ruling by the arbitral tribunal as conclusive for the purposes of the application.

7.203 Article 9(3) of the First Schedule of the New Zealand Arbitration Act 1996 appears to go further than its Malaysian counterpart. It requires that the New Zealand court treat as conclusive any prior 'ruling or any finding of fact' made by the arbitral tribunal. It would thus seem that from a literal reading the Malaysian Act does not apply to rulings that involve issues other than fact finding.

7.204 It may be concluded from the jurisprudence referred to above that courts and arbitral tribunals are no longer jurisdictional competitors in connection with interim measures. This position is supported by Justice Baragwanath's view of a court's role in an interim measures application arising out of a dispute subject to arbitration:[303]

> the purpose of interim measures is to complement and facilitate the arbitration, not to forestall or to substitute for it. The Court's role is ancillary, to be exercised only to the extent that it is possible or practicable for the arbitrator to deal with the issue.

---
300 *Clough Engineering Ltd v Oil and Natural Gas Corporation Ltd* [2008] FCAFC 136 (22 July 2008).
301 See generally Donovan, op. cit. fn 280, p. 203.
302 [1998] 4 HKC 347. See also Donovan, op. cit. fn 280, p. 220.
303 See also *Sensation Yachts Ltd v Darby Maritime Ltd*, Auckland High Court, 16 May 2005 in which a New Zealand court granted interim measures in support of an arbitration in London. This decision referred to a frequently cited observation by Lord Mustill in *Channel Tunnel Group Ltd v Balfour Beatty Construction Ltd* [1993] AC 334, at 365 (observing that the purpose of court-ordered interim measures is 'not to encroach on the procedural powers of the arbitrators but to reinforce them, and to render more effective the decision at which the arbitrators will ultimately arrive on the substance of the dispute' and that there exists a 'duty of the court to respect the choice of the tribunal which both parties have made, and not to take out of the hands of the arbitrators... a power of decision which the parties have entrusted to them alone').

10 Security for costs

A well-formulated definition of 'security for costs' describes them as orders that:[304]

7.205

> make the right of a claimant or counter-claimant to proceed on his claim conditional on the raising of a bank guarantee or other forms of surety to guarantee, in the case of an unsuccessful claim, any eventual award of legal fees assessed against the claimant or counter-claimant by the arbitral tribunal.

Without security for costs, a respondent to a spurious arbitration claim filed against it by a claimant that has little or no assets finds itself in an undesirable situation. If it does not defend the claim, an adverse award may be issued that is enforceable against it. If it succeeds in defending the claim, it is likely to be left without a remedy for the costs of mounting a defence due to the impecuniosity of the claimant. Security for costs may be granted to cover, for example, fees and expenses of its lawyers, experts, interpreters, the institutional costs etc.

7.206

A number of recent arbitration rules specifically empower an arbitral tribunal to order security for costs.[305] While other sets of arbitral rules do not expressly grant this power, it may be implied into their provisions dealing with interim measures.[306] The grant of power to the arbitral tribunal to order security for costs in arbitral rules is helpful because the power is non-existent or at least uncertain in many arbitration laws, including the 1985 version of the Model Law.[307]

7.207

It is unlikely that Article 17 of the 1985 Model Law on the power of arbitral tribunals to award interim measures (quoted above in Section 9.1.1) could be construed as granting an arbitral tribunal a general power to order security for costs. Of particular significance is the Article 17 phrase 'in respect of the subject-matter of the dispute'. As has been noted elsewhere:[308]

7.208

> Article 17 therefore empowers the arbitral tribunal to order interim measures as long as those interim measures relate to the merits of the substantive dispute. There is a distinction between substantive and procedural matters. Disputes about costs are procedural rather than substantive because they are subsidiary to, and not part of, the 'subject matter of the dispute.'
> ...

---

304 Gu Wexia, 'Security for Costs in International Commercial Arbitration', (2005) *Journal of International Arbitration* 167, at p. 167.
305 ACICA Rules Article 28(2)(e); SIAC Rules, Rule 24(m). Unlike the 1976 UNCITRAL Arbitration Rules, the 2010 version provides for the ordering of security for costs in Article 26(2)(c).
306 For example, it is well known that ICC arbitral tribunals are empowered to order security for costs despite the absence of an express reference thereto in Article 23 of the ICC Rules.
307 See, e.g. the absence of any reference to security for costs in Article 17 of the Model Law. S Greenberg and C Kee, 'Can You Seek Security for Costs in International Arbitration in Australia?', (2005) 26 *Australian Bar Review* 89, at p. 91 et seq; C Kee, 'International Arbitration and Security for Costs – A Brief Report on Two Developments', (2007) 17 *American Review of International Arbitration* 273, at p. 274.
308 Greenberg and Kee, ibid., p. 95.

Further, the phrase 'appropriate security in connection with such measure' in Article 17 is referring to security for the taking of the interim measure itself, and not security in relation to the cost of defending the substantive dispute.

7.209 The above interpretation is supported by the New Zealand case of *Lindow v Barton McGill Marine Ltd*[309] which held that security for costs was not covered by the words 'the subject-matter of the dispute' in the 1985 version of Article 17.

7.210 The 2006 Model Law amendments have revised the relevant parts of Article 17.[310] But this provision still does not necessarily clarify whether an arbitral tribunal can order security for costs.[311] Schedule 1 of New Zealand's Arbitration Act 1996 has been revised to make it abundantly clear that an arbitral tribunal has the power to order security for costs. In its amended form, Article 17 of Schedule 1 defines an interim measure, in relevant part, as follows:[312]

> **interim measure** means a temporary measure (whether or not in the form of an award) by which a party is required, at any time before an award is made in relation to a dispute, to do all or any of the following ... (e) give security for costs ...

7.211 Nonetheless, the New Zealand amendment should not be relied on as a general indication that security for costs is not already encompassed by Article 17(2)(c) of the 2006 Model Law.[313] When UNCITRAL Working Group II came to consider an identical provision in the context of the revision of the UNCITRAL Arbitration Rules it noted:[314]

> A proposal was made that paragraph [17](2)(c) should be amended expressly to refer to security for costs through an addition of the words 'or securing funds' after the word 'assets'. Opposition was expressed to that proposal as it could connote that the corresponding provision in the UNCITRAL Arbitration Model Law was insufficient to provide for security for costs. The Working Group agreed that security for costs was encompassed by the words 'preserving assets out of which a subsequent award may be satisfied.'

7.212 An arbitral tribunal has an effective sanction for non-compliance with security for costs orders: it may simply stay the arbitration until compliance occurs. Section 2GB of the Hong Kong Arbitration Ordinance expressly provides that an arbitral tribunal may strike out a claim if the claiming party fails to provide security for costs.

---

309 (2002) 16 PRNZ 796 (New Zealand High Court).
310 This provision is quoted in Section 9.1 above.
311 See generally Kee, op. cit. fn 307, pp. 273–280.
312 See also the Singapore International Arbitration Act Section 12(1)(a); and Williams, op. cit. fn 260, p. 227, n. 6.
313 Under this provision, an arbitral tribunal is empowered to order a party to '[p]rovide a means of preserving assets out of which a subsequent award may be satisfied'.
314 Report of Working Group II (Arbitration and Conciliation) on the work of its forty-seventh session (Vienna, 10–14 September 2007), UN Doc. A/CN.9/641, para 48.

11 Privacy and confidentiality

Arbitration has developed a reputation as offering a higher level of privacy and confidentiality than that afforded by domestic courts. Privacy has not proved an overly controversial concept. On the other hand, considerable debate has taken place as to the precise scope of confidentiality in international commercial arbitration.[315] The difference between privacy and confidentiality was neatly summed up by Julian Lew:[316]

7.213

> Privacy is concerned with the right of persons other than the arbitrators, parties and their necessary representatives and witnesses, to attend the arbitration hearing and to know about the arbitration. Confidentiality, by contrast, is concerned with the obligation on the arbitrators and the parties not to divulge or give out information relating to the content of the proceedings, evidence and documents, addresses, transcripts of the hearings or the award.

Privacy and confidentiality in arbitration contrast with the public nature of domestic court proceedings. In most jurisdictions, any person may attend court hearings and documents filed with courts are available for inspection by the public. Of course, in certain cases where confidentiality is required, courts may restrict public rights to attend hearings and view documents.

7.214

On the whole, privacy in international commercial arbitration is not the subject of debate. Arbitration rules and laws frequently contain specific provisions stating that hearings are to take place in private.[317] In *Esso Australia Resources Ltd v Plowman* ('*Esso*') Chief Justice Mason observed:[318]

7.215

> Subject to any manifestation of a contrary intention arising from the provisions or the nature of an agreement to submit a dispute to arbitration, the arbitration held pursuant to the agreement is private in the sense that it is not open to the public.... The arbitrator will exclude strangers from the hearing unless the parties consent to attendance by a stranger. Persons whose presence is necessary for the proper conduct of the arbitration are not strangers in the relevant sense. Thus, persons claiming through or attending on behalf of the parties, those assisting a party in the presentation of the case, and a shorthand writer to take notes may appear.

One of the objectives of privacy in arbitration has long ago been described as keeping 'quarrels from the public eyes'.[319] A more recent rationale justifying privacy has been that the agreement to arbitrate is 'between [the parties] and

7.216

---
[315] A well-written comparative study of confidentiality in several regions, including Singapore, Australia and New Zealand, is contained in Q Loh and E Lee, *Confidentiality in Arbitration: How Far Does It Extend?*, Academy Publishing, 2007.
[316] Expert Report of Dr Julian Lew in *Esso v Plowman*, reprinted in (1995) 11 *Arbitration International* 283, p. 285, para 16.
[317] See, e.g. ACICA Rules Article 18(1); SIAC Rules, Rule 21(4); JCAA Rules, Rule 40; CIETAC Rule Article 33(1); HKIAC Rules Article 23(7); China's Arbitration Law Article 40.
[318] (1995) 183 *Commonwealth Law Reports* 10, at p. 26 (High Court of Australia), reprinted in (1995) 11(3) *Arbitration International* 235.
[319] *Russell v Russell* (1880) 14 Ch D 471, at p. 474.

only between them'.[320] As to the benefits of privacy, it has been said that '[t]he informality attaching to a hearing held in private and the candour to which it may give rise is an essential ingredient of arbitration'.[321]

7.217 In contrast, the duty of confidentiality in arbitration finds no generally accepted approach.[322] The absence of uniformity has led Yves Fortier to comment that 'with respect to confidentiality in international commercial arbitrations, nothing should be taken for granted'.[323] Confidentiality issues often arise in parallel arbitrations (but with different parties) where one arbitration may be relevant to and possibly determine the outcome of another. The question therefore arises whether the transcripts, pleadings, witness evidence, submitted documents and award in the first arbitration may be disclosed in the second. The same situation arises between an arbitration and related court proceedings with different parties.

7.218 The English courts on the one hand take the view that there is an implicit duty to maintain confidentiality in arbitration proceedings. Lord Justice Lawrence Collins in *Emmott v Michael Wilson & Partners Ltd* summarised the English position as follows:[324]

> there is an obligation, implied by law and arising out of the nature of arbitration, on both parties not to disclose or use for any other purpose any documents prepared for and used in the arbitration, or disclosed or produced in the course of the arbitration, or transcripts or notes of the evidence in the arbitration or the award, and not to disclose in any other way what evidence has been given by any witness in the arbitration. The obligation is not limited to commercially confidential information in the traditional sense.
>
> ... this is in reality a substantive rule of arbitration law reached through the device of an implied term.

7.219 Nonetheless, while under English case law the obligation is imposed as a matter of law, English courts still need to determine whether a given case falls within established exceptions.[325] In the earlier English High Court case of *Hassneh Insurance Co of Israel v Mew* it was considered that this duty of confidentiality is derived from the privacy of hearings:[326]

---

320 *The Eastern Saga* [1984] 2 Lloyd's Rep 373, at p. 379.
321 *Hassneh Insurance Co of Israel v Mew* [1982] 2 Lloyd's Rep 243, pp. 246–247.
322 For a detailed examination of this issue see M Pryles, 'Confidentiality', in Newman and Hill, op. cit. fn 5, pp. 501–552. As to the secrecy of court proceedings that are ancillary to a confidential arbitration or confidential award, see VV Veeder, 'Transparency of International Arbitration: Process and Substance', in LA Mistelis and JDM Lew (eds), *Pervasive Problems in International Arbitration*, Kluwer Law International, 2006, p. 89.
323 LY Fortier, 'The Occasionally Unwarranted Assumption of Confidentiality', (1999) 15(2) *Arbitration International* 131, at p. 138. See also AH Raymond, 'Confidentiality in a Forum of Last Resort: Is the Use of Confidential Arbitration a Good Idea for Business and Society?', (2005) 16 *American Review of International Arbitration* 479, at p. 497 et seq.
324 [2008] EWCA Civ 184 at para 105. See also *Dolling-Baker v Merrett*, [1991] 2 All ER 890; *Ali Shipping Corporation v Shipyard Trogir* [1998] 2 All ER 136; and *Department of Economics, Policy & Development of the City of Moscow v Bankers Trust Company and International Industrial Bank* [2003] EWHC 1377.
325 See, e.g. *Ali Shipping Corporation v Shipyard Trogir* [1998] 2 All ER 136 (English Court of Appeal), pp. 147–148.
326 [1982] 2 Lloyd's Rep 243, at p. 247.

If it be correct that there is at least an implied term in every agreement to arbitrate that the hearing shall be held in private, the requirement of privacy must in principle extend to documents which are created for the purpose of that hearing. The most obvious example is a note or transcript of the evidence. The disclosure to a third party of such documents would be almost equivalent to opening the door of the arbitration room to that third party. Similarly witness statements, being so closely related to the hearing, must be within the obligation of confidentiality. So also must outline submissions tendered to the arbitrator. If outline submissions, then so must pleadings be included.

7.220 Other jurisdictions such as France, Germany and Switzerland also imply a duty of confidentiality of arbitral proceedings and documents submitted during them.[327]

7.221 In this region, the Singapore High court in *Myanma Yaung Chi Oo Co Ltd v Win Win Nu* has followed the English line of authority.[328] Justice Kan Ting Chiu stated that it is 'more in keeping with the parties' expectations to take the position that proceedings are confidential' with the possibility of disclosure in certain circumstances.[329]

7.222 In New Zealand, legislation has gone as far as stating that the parties to an arbitration agreement are deemed to have agreed that the parties shall not publish, disclose, or communicate any information relating to arbitral proceedings or to an award made in those proceedings.[330] The New Zealand legislation is quoted below.

7.223 On the other hand, the Australian High Court has famously declined to imply a general duty of confidentiality. In *Esso*,[331] Chief Justice Mason's majority judgment discussed the relevant law and concluded that complete confidentiality in arbitration could be achieved only by agreement of the parties. In support of this position, he indicated that (1) no implied obligation of confidence attached to witnesses, who were not bound by the arbitration agreement and could disclose their knowledge of the proceedings to third parties; (2) parties could legitimately disclose the arbitral proceedings or the award in certain court proceedings (e.g. applications to challenge the arbitrator or the award), which proceedings could be published; and (3) parties may in certain circumstances be entitled to disclose to a third party the existence and details of the proceedings and the award (e.g. under an insurance policy or stock exchange disclosure requirements). He concluded on this basis that he did not consider 'that confidentiality is an essential attribute of a private arbitration imposing an obligation on each party not to disclose the proceedings or documents and information provided in and for the purposes of the arbitration'.[332] For the same reasons, he rejected the argument

---

[327] See Gu Wexia, 'Confidentiality Revisited: Blessing or Curse in International Commercial Arbitration?', (2004) 15 *American Review of International Arbitration* 607, at p. 610.
[328] [2003] SGHC 124.
[329] Ibid., at para 17.
[330] See Section 14A(1) of the New Zealand Arbitration Act 1996. This provision was introduced into the Act through the New Zealand Arbitration Amendment Act 2007.
[331] (1995) 183 *Commonwealth Law Reports* 10, reprinted in (1995) 11(3) *Arbitration International* 235.
[332] *Esso v Plowman* (1995) 11 *Arbitration International* 235, at p. 246.

that as a matter of law all agreements to arbitrate contained an implied term that each party will not disclose information provided in and for the purposes of the arbitration.[333] However, the Chief Justice distinguished between documents voluntarily produced by a party and documents that a party is compelled to produce, for example under a document production order. The latter were held to be subject to an implied obligation of confidentiality. Even though *Esso* concerned a domestic arbitration, it has had a substantial effect in the world of international commercial arbitration.

7.224   As Michael Pryles has put it, *Esso* 'is not an antipodean aberration'.[334] Courts from the US[335] and Sweden[336] have also indicated that no general implied obligation of confidentiality exists. Similarly, investment arbitration tribunals have denied that confidentiality automatically applies to arbitral proceedings.[337]

7.225   If a document or other material is considered to be confidential (implicitly or by agreement), common law courts have formulated numerous exceptions. Michael Hwang has observed that defining these exceptions is impossible by statute or by judicial formulae and consequently common law courts have introduced exceptions in incremental steps, which he has summarised as follows:[338]

(i) where there is a public interest, e.g. where the public has a legitimate interest to know about health or environmental issues;[339]

(ii) where a court is required to determine matters relating to the arbitration, which means details of the arbitration may be heard in an open court;[340]

(iii) where the parties have consented to disclosure – this may be implied, e.g. from an application to court asking for the removal of an arbitrator, which implicitly gives consent to the arbitrator to reveal matters concerning the arbitration to the court;

---

333 Ibid., pp. 246–247. See also *Associated Electric and Gas Insurance Services Ltd v European Reinsurance Co of Zurich* [2000] UKPC 11, at para 20, (Privy Council), which displayed reservations about characterising confidentiality as an implied term.
334 Pryles, op. cit. fn 322, p. 501 at p. 552.
335 See *United States v Panhandle Eastern Corporation*, 118 FRD 346 (D Del 1988).
336 See *Bulgarian Foreign Trade Bank Ltd v AI Trade Finance Inc*, 27 October 2000 (Swedish Supreme Court), reprinted in (2000) 15 *Int'l Arb Rep* B-1.
337 See, e.g. *Metalclad Corp v United Mexican States*, Award of 20 August 2000, 5 ICSID Reports 209, at para 113 ('unless the agreement between the parties incorporates such a limitation [i.e. the obligation of confidentiality], each of them is still free to speak publicly of the arbitration'); and *Loewen Group v United States*, Decision on Hearing of Respondent's Objection to Competence and Jurisdiction, 5 January 2001, at para 26. It is of interest to note that Chief Justice Mason, who wrote the main judgment in the *Esso v Plowman* case referred to above, was one of the arbitrators in *Loewen*. See also *Amco Asia v Indonesia*, 24 *International Legal Materials* 365 (1985). See generally J Misra and R Jordans, 'Confidentiality in Arbitration: An Introspection of the Public Interest Exception', (2006) 23 *Journal of International Arbitration* 39; and L Mistelis, 'Confidentiality and Third Party Participation: *UPS v Canada* and *Methanex Corporation v United States*', (2005) 21 *Arbitration International* 205.
338 M Hwang, 'Defining the Indefinable – Practical Problems of Confidentiality in Arbitration', Kaplan Lecture 2008, 17 November 2008, The Hong Kong Club, Hong Kong. See also *Improving the Arbitration Act 1996*, New Zealand Law Commission Report No. 83 (2003), at para 5 ('it is arguable that no statutory implied term [of confidentiality] can ever set out exhaustively all of the exceptions that may arise; these need to be determined on a case-by-case basis.').
339 See, e.g. *Commonwealth of Australia v Cockatoo Dockyard Pty Ltd* [1995] 36 NSWLR 662 (NSW Court of Appeal), at 680. See also *TV New Zealand v Langley Productions Ltd* [2000] 2 NZLR 250 (New Zealand Court of Appeal) (holding that the public had a right to know how much a TV personality was paid).
340 See generally Veeder, op. cit. fn 5, p. 89.

(iv) by compulsion of law, e.g. pursuant to anti-money laundering legislation or a public authority's statutory power to demand information;
(v) with the leave of court if one party to the arbitration does not consent to disclosure to a third party;
(vi) to protect the legitimate interests of an arbitrating party, e.g. to enforce rights established by an earlier arbitration award or to evidence a position taken in an earlier arbitration in support of an issue estoppel argument;[341]
(vii) where the interests of justice require it, e.g. where inconsistent evidence has been given by a party in two separate arbitrations;[342]
(viii) where there is an obligation to disclose, e.g. by corporations to shareholders, during a takeover due diligence, to an insurance company or by listed companies to a stock exchange;
(ix) everyday situations, e.g. accidentally leaving a document in a public place; and
(x) where disclosure has been made to professional or other advisers and persons assisting in the conduct of the arbitration, e.g. lawyers, in-house counsel and executives, potential witnesses, investigators, secretaries, transcribers, copy personnel, or interpreters.

At the time of the decision in *Esso*, most national legislation did not address the issue of confidentiality at all.[343] The Model Law does not expressly refer to confidentiality. However, more states are starting to include confidentiality provisions in their arbitration laws.[344] New Zealand has extensive legislative provisions on confidentiality.[345] In 2007, it introduced the following sections into its Arbitration Act 1996:

7.226

14A An arbitral tribunal must conduct the arbitral proceedings in private.
14B (1) Every arbitration agreement to which this section applies is deemed to provide that the parties and the arbitral tribunal must not disclose confidential information.
    (2) Subsection (1) is subject to section 14C.
14C A party or an arbitral tribunal may disclose confidential information–
    (a) to a professional or other adviser of any of the parties;
    or
    (b) if both of the following matters apply:
        (i) the disclosure is necessary–
            (A) to ensure that a party has a full opportunity to present the party's case, as required under article 18 of Schedule 1; or
            (B) for the establishment or protection of a party's legal rights in relation to a third party; or

---

341 See, e.g. *Associated Electric and Gas Insurance Services Ltd v European Reinsurance Co of Zurich*, [2000] UKPC 11.
342 See, e.g. *London & Leeds Estates Ltd v Paribas Ltd* (No. 2) [1995] EGLR 102.
343 See J Paulsson and N Rawding, 'The Trouble with Confidentiality', (1995) 11 *Arbitration International* 303.
344 See, e.g. Section 23 of Philippines Alternative Dispute Resolution Act 2004.
345 See Sections 14A to 14I of the New Zealand Arbitration Act 1996. Hong Kong is likely to enact detailed provisions on confidentiality. Sections 16–18 of its Arbitration Bill (due to be passed in early 2011) are modelled on the New Zealand legislation.

(C) for the making and prosecution of an application to a court under this Act; and
  (ii) the disclosure is no more than what is reasonably required to serve any of the purposes referred to in subparagraph (i)(A) to (C); or
(c) if the disclosure is in accordance with an order made, or a subpoena issued, by a court; or
(d) if both of the following matters apply:
  (i) the disclosure is authorised or required by law (except this Act) or required by a competent regulatory body (including New Zealand Exchange Limited); and
  (ii) the party who, or the arbitral tribunal that, makes the disclosure provides to the other party and the arbitral tribunal or, as the case may be, the parties, written details of the disclosure (including an explanation of the reasons for the disclosure); or
(e) if the disclosure is in accordance with an order made by–
  (i) an arbitral tribunal under section 14D; or
  (ii) the High Court under section 14E.

7.227 A number of other provisions of this Act, namely Articles 14D–14I, deal with disclosure of confidential information and privacy in arbitration-related court proceedings.

7.228 Arbitration procedural rules, much like arbitration laws, are not uniform in their provisions on confidentiality. One of the most detailed in the region is SIAC Rule 34, which provides:[346]

> 34.1 The parties and the Tribunal shall at all times treat all matters relating to the proceedings, and the award as confidential.
> 34.2 A party or any arbitrator shall not, without the prior written consent of all the parties, disclose to a third party any such matter except:
>   (a) for the purpose of making an application to any competent court of any State under the applicable law governing the arbitration;
>   (b) for the purpose of making an application to the courts of any State to enforce or challenge the award;
>   (c) pursuant to the order of or a subpoena issued by a court of competent jurisdiction;
>   (d) to a party's legal or other professional advisor for the purpose of pursuing or enforcing a legal right or claim;
>   (e) in compliance with the provisions of the laws of any State which is binding on the party making the disclosure; or
>   (f) in compliance with the request or requirement of any regulatory body or other authority.
> 34.3 In this Rule, 'matters relating to the proceedings' means the existence of the proceedings, and the pleadings, evidence and other materials in the arbitration proceeding created for the purpose of the arbitration and all other documents produced by another party in the proceedings or the award arising from the proceedings but excludes any matter that is otherwise in the public domain.

---

[346] For other detailed provisions on confidentiality, see ACICA Rules Article 18 and HKIAC Rules Article 39.

As was noted by Chief Justice Mason in *Esso*, no obligation of confidentiality attaches to witnesses. Consequently, special provisions are included in arbitral rules that address witness confidentiality. Article 18(4) of the ACICA Rules provides: 7.229

> To the extent that a witness is given access to evidence or other information obtained in the arbitration, the party calling such witness is responsible for the maintenance by the witness of the same degree of confidentiality as that required of the party.

One way to do this is to require each witness to sign a confidentiality agreement. Article 18(4) of the ACICA Rules should be compared with CIETAC Rule Article 33(2): 7.230

> For cases heard in camera, the parties, their representatives, witnesses, interpreters, arbitrators, experts consulted by the arbitral tribunal and appraisers appointed by the arbitral tribunal and the relevant staff members of the Secretariat of CIETAC shall not disclose to any outsiders any substantive or procedural matters of the case.

The following table provides a snapshot of the confidentiality provisions in Rules relevant to the region.[347] 7.231

Institution	Confidentiality of existence of arbitration	Confidentiality of documents used/generated	Arbitrator bound by confidentiality	Witness bound by confidentiality	Confidentiality of award
ACICA	Yes	Yes	Yes	Yes	Yes
BANI	? ('all matters related to the arbitral reference')	Yes	Yes		Yes
CIETAC			Yes	Yes	
HKIAC	Yes	Yes	Yes		Yes
ICC	Not automatic but arbitral tribunal has the power to so order	Not automatic but arbitral tribunal has the power to so order	ICC Court and Secretariat bound	Not automatic but arbitral tribunal has the power to so order	Not automatic but arbitral tribunal has the power to so order
ICSID			Yes		Yes
JCAA		Yes	Yes		
KCAB		Yes	Yes		
KLRCA	? ('all matters related to the arbitration proceedings')		Yes		Yes
SIAC	Yes	Yes	Yes		Yes
WIPO	Yes	Yes	Yes	Yes	Yes

Some general observations may be made from this table. The ACICA, HKIAC and SIAC Rules offer significant protection in terms of confidentiality. Wide protections of confidentiality are also granted by the WIPO Rules particularly because of the sensitivity associated with the intellectual property disputes WIPO is called on to decide. On the other end of the spectrum is ICSID, which requires the publication of excerpts from ICSID awards. 7.232

---

347 The format of this table and much of its information has been based on Michael Hwang's PowerPoint slides used during his Kaplan Lecture. Hwang, op. cit. fn 338.

7.233   In contrast, the ICC Rules do not explicitly address the issue of confidentiality. They grant, however, the right to privacy in hearings, enable the arbitral tribunal to take measures to protect trade secrets and confidential information, and to make any other orders as to confidentiality.[348] In addition, the Statutes and Internal Rules of the ICC International Court of Arbitration ensure that its work remains confidential.[349]

7.234   By way of conclusion to this section, the UNCITRAL Notes on Organizing Arbitral Proceedings provide sound advice regarding confidentiality:[350]

> It is widely viewed that confidentiality is one of the advantageous and helpful features of arbitration. Nevertheless, there is no uniform answer in national laws as to the extent to which the participants in an arbitration are under the duty to observe the confidentiality of information relating to the case. Moreover, parties that have agreed on arbitration rules or other provisions that do not expressly address the issues of confidentiality cannot assume that all jurisdictions would recognise an implied commitment to confidentiality. Furthermore, the participants in an arbitration might not have the same understanding as regards the extent of confidentiality that is expected. Therefore, the arbitral tribunal might wish to discuss that with the parties and, if considered appropriate, record any agreed principles on the duty of confidentiality.

---

[348] ICC Rules Articles 20(7) and 21(3).
[349] ICC Rules Appendix I Article 6 and Appendix II Articles 1 and 3.
[350] UNCITRAL Notes on Organizing Arbitral Proceedings, op. cit. fn 91, at para 31.

8

The award
Content and form

1 Introduction

An arbitral tribunal's core function is to make decisions that resolve the dispute submitted to it. These determinations are expressed in written documents called awards.[1]

This chapter concerns aspects of the award that are internal to the arbitration. These aspects are to be contrasted with matters pertaining to the award that are external or outside the control of the arbitral tribunal, such as court litigation relating to setting aside awards or their enforcement. Those external aspects are dealt with in Chapter 9.

A logical starting point for this chapter is the deliberation process arbitrators engage in to make their decisions (Section 2). We then proceed to discuss the content, form and effect of an award (Section 3), the definition of an award (Section 4), the various categories of awards (Section 5), costs awards (Section 6), and the correction and interpretation of awards (Section 7).

8.1

8.2

8.3

2 Deliberations and decision-making

Once the arbitral tribunal considers that the parties have been given a reasonable opportunity to present their cases, e.g. through the presentation of oral and/or

8.4

---

[1] The arbitral tribunal may also make written decisions in the form of orders. Such decisions usually relate to procedural matters and ordinarily cannot be challenged or enforced in the same way as awards. If the arbitral tribunal issues an order in respect of interim measures, the question arises whether this may be classified as an award that is enforceable. This issue is discussed in Section 5.3.

written evidence and submissions on the law and facts, the proceedings will be declared closed.[2] From this point on, the arbitral tribunal must complete its determination of the issues of law and fact in respect of which a decision is required. However, partial deliberations should have begun and been held right through the arbitration. If the arbitral tribunal is composed of a sole arbitrator, obviously the decisions are arrived at by that arbitrator alone and no deliberations with any other persons take place. The situation is different if the arbitral tribunal is composed of more than one arbitrator. In this case, deliberations take place in private among all the arbitrators. Typically, they discuss their viewpoints and try to reach a consensus.

8.5 A useful starting point for this discussion on deliberations is the following description by Vinayak Pradhan:[3]

> It is sometimes thought that the members of an arbitral tribunal only start their deliberations when long shadows are cast at the end of the last day and counsel pack their bags and wearily waft away from the dubious joys of legal battle.
>
> This is a misconception. The arbitrators' discussions on the final submissions and the crystallisation of their appreciation of the dispute and their views on it are the culmination of a series of deliberations which could commence very soon after the arbitration has started.
>
> There is no universal approach to a tribunal's deliberations. The manner in which any given tribunal will approach its task is driven by factors which include personality, competence, experience and commitment of the arbitrators and the legal and cultural systems that they come from.

8.6 A cardinal principle of deliberations is that the views expressed by each arbitrator during this process remain confidential and are not communicated to the parties. Otherwise arbitrators might be less inclined to be candid when they deliberate. The confidentiality of deliberations is not explicitly addressed in many arbitration rules. Article 39(2) of the HKIAC Rules is an exception, providing that the 'deliberations of the arbitral tribunal are confidential'.[4] Rule 9 of the International Bar Association's Rules of Ethics for International Arbitrators states that an arbitrator may disclose deliberations in exceptional cases where 'he considers it his duty to disclose any material misconduct or fraud on the

---

[2] See, e.g. ACICA Rules Article 30 (relating to 'closure of hearings'); HKIAC Rules Article 27; ICC Rules Article 22; JCAA Rules, Rule 53; KCAB International Rules Article 33; UNCITRAL Arbitration Rules Article 29; and 2010 UNCITRAL Arbitration Rules Article 31 (relating to 'closure of hearings').
[3] V Pradhan, 'The Tribunal's Deliberations', in M Pryles and M Moser (eds), *The Asian Leading Arbitrators' Guide to International Arbitration*, JurisNet, 2007, p. 357, at p. 357. See also LY Fortier, 'The Tribunal's Deliberations', in LW Newman and RD Hill (eds), *The Leading Arbitrators' Guide to International Arbitration*, 2nd edn, Juris Publishing, 2008, p. 477.
[4] See also Taiwan Arbitration Law Article 32 ('The deliberations of an arbitral tribunal shall not be made public.'); and Rule 15 of the ICSID Arbitration Rules, which provides:
  1. The deliberations of the Tribunal shall take place in private and remain secret.
  2. Only members of the Tribunal shall take part in its deliberations. No other person shall be admitted unless the tribunal decides otherwise.

part of his fellow arbitrators'. Such an exception may assist in maintaining the integrity of the arbitral process but in practice would rarely, if ever, require application.[5]

In challenges to awards or arbitrators, parties occasionally attempt to rely on evidence as to events or discussions that took place during deliberations. In *Noble China Inc v Lei Kat Chong*,[6] Mr Lei applied to the Canadian courts to set aside two awards made against him. The application was supported by an affidavit by Mr Gao Zongze (one of the arbitrators), who alleged that the other two arbitral tribunal members had been racially biased against both Mr Lei and his witnesses in the case, and had excluded Mr Gao from the decision-making process. The Ontario Supreme Court struck out Mr Gao's affidavit for offending the principle of deliberative confidentiality and it expressed strong concern that the affidavit was unfair to the personal reputations of the other two arbitrators. In that court's view:[7]

8.7

> the motion to strike the Gao affidavit is not about the suppression of evidence. The affidavit is proffered on behalf of an unsuccessful litigant by an individual who was appointed to be an impartial adjudicator, but who has made himself an advocate and witness. Its purpose is to compromise and disturb an award that is adverse to Mr. Lei. The affidavit offends the rule on deliberative secrecy...

In the 2008 Hong Kong case of *Jung Science Information Technology Co Ltd v ZTE Corporation*,[8] an unsuccessful challenge was made against the chairperson of the arbitral tribunal. The challenging party alleged that the chairperson was biased when determining various interlocutory applications. The chairperson was given leave to file evidence.[9] In response, the chairperson wrote two letters discussing the interlocutory decision-making process followed by the arbitral tribunal.[10] No objection appears to have been raised by the parties in regard to these letters. From the court's description of them, the letters described in general terms the deliberation procedure adopted by the arbitral tribunal; they did not reveal the views of each individual arbitrator as to each decision made.

8.8

---

5 See also H Smit, 'Dissenting Opinions in Arbitration', (2004) 15(1) *ICC International Court of Arbitration Bulletin* 37, at p. 40 ('disclosure of deliberations could serve a purpose if the arbitrators misbehaved and their misconduct would remain secret unless disclosed').
6 1998 CanLII 14708 (Ontario Supreme Court), 4 November 1998.
7 Ibid., at p. 86. Earlier in the judgment, at p. 81, the court noted that the purpose of the rule on deliberative secrecy was 'to preserve adjudicative independence so that adjudication occurs with circumspection, reflection and in freedom'. See also R Ellis and P Aterman, 'Deliberative Secrecy and Adjudicative Independence: The *Glengarry* Precipice', (1994) 7 *Canadian Journal of Administrative Law and Practice* 171, at p. 179 ('This freedom from scrutiny – this principle of sanctuary for the decision-making process – enables judges to reflect on the evidence without restriction, to draw conclusions untrammelled by any subsequent disclosure of their thought processes, and, where they are so inclined, to change these conclusions on further reflection without fear of subsequent criticism or of the need for subsequent explanation.').
8 [2008] HKCU 1127, 22 July 2008 (Hong Kong High Court, Court of First Instance). See discussion in Chapter 6, Section 6.1.4.2.
9 *Jung Science Information Technology Co, Ltd v ZTE Corporation*, [2008] HKCU 1127, at para 41.
10 Ibid., at paras 47–48.

8.9   Another case in which an arbitral tribunal's deliberations became the subject of a court proceeding was *Czech Republic v CME Czech Republic BV*.[11] The Svea Court of Appeal admitted testimony by arbitrators as to their deliberations because under Swedish law deliberative confidentiality applied only to judges, not to arbitrators.

3 Content, form and effect of arbitral awards

3.1 Formalities

8.10   The form requirements of an award vary according to the procedural rules adopted or the *lex arbitri*.[12] The Model Law form requirements are set out in Article 31, which provides:

> (1) The award shall be made in writing and shall be signed by the arbitrator or arbitrators. In arbitral proceedings with more than one arbitrator, the signatures of the majority of all members of the arbitral tribunal shall suffice, provided that the reason for any omitted signature is stated.
> (2) The award shall state the reasons upon which it is based, unless the parties have agreed that no reasons are to be given or the award is an award on agreed terms under article 30.
> (3) The award shall state its date and the place of arbitration as determined in accordance with article 20(1). The award shall be deemed to have been made at that place.
> (4) After the award is made, a copy signed by the arbitrators in accordance with paragraph (1) of this article shall be delivered to each party.

8.11   Institutional rules usually contain most of these basic requirements, for example, the need for an award to be in writing,[13] to be signed by the arbitrator(s), to contain the reasons on which it is based[14] and to state the date and place (i.e. the seat of arbitration) where the award was made.[15] But many go further and require extra details including:

---

11 Svea Court of Appeal, Sweden, Case No. T 8735–01, 5 ICSID Reports 439.
12 For examples of arbitration rules of procedure that specify in detail the required contents of an award, see CIETAC Rules Article 43(2); ICSID Rules, Rule 47; and JCAA Rules, Rule 54(1).
13 ACICA Rules Article 33.2; HKIAC Rules Article 30(2); KCAB International Rules Article 31(1); UNCITRAL Arbitration Rules Article 32(2); 2010 UNCITRAL Arbitration Rules Article 34(2). Some Rules do not stipulate in express terms that the award is required to be in writing, but it may be implied that this is the case. See, e.g. CIETAC Rules Article 43(3) ('CIETAC's stamp shall be affixed to the award'); JCAA Rules, Rule 54 and SIAC Rules, Rule 27.
14 ACICA Rules Article 33.3; CIETAC Rules Article 43(2); HKIAC Rules Article 30.3; ICA Rules, Rule 64; KCAB International Rules Article 31(1); JCAA Rules, Rule 54(1)(4); UNCITRAL Arbitration Rules Article 32(3); and 2010 UNCITRAL Arbitration Rules Article 34(3). Most of these rules are subject to the freedom of the parties to agree that no reasons are to be given. In the absence of such an agreement, all arbitral awards should contain reasons. Note also that Article 31(2) of the Model Law allows parties to agree that no reasons are to be given in the award.
15 ACICA Rules Article 33.4; CIETAC Rules Article 43(2); HKIAC Rules Article 30.4; ICA Rules, Rule 65; JCAA Rules, Rule 54(1); KCAB International Rules Article 31(2); UNCITRAL Arbitration Rules Article 32(4); 2010 UNCITRAL Arbitration Rules Article 34(4). This will in most instances establish the seat of arbitration and the date serves to calculate time limits within which any challenge to the award must be brought. See B Cremades, 'The Arbitral Award', in Newman and Hill, op. cit. fn 3, at p. 487. See also Model Law Article 31(3).

(i) the names of the parties and their representatives (if the party is represented);[16]
(ii) the names of the arbitrators;[17]
(iii) the claims made;[18]
(iv) the facts of the dispute;[19] and
(v) the allocation of arbitration costs.[20]

In addition to the above requirements, which are quite standard, the law of the seat should be checked for local particularities. For example, Article 54(1)(a) of Indonesia's Arbitration and Alternative Dispute Resolution Law 1999 requires that the award be headed with the words 'For the sake of Justice based on belief in the Almighty God'. Also, Article 54(4) of that law requires the award to state 'a time limitation within which the award must be implemented'. 8.12

3.2 Reasons for the award

Three different approaches exist in institutional arbitration rules as to the giving of reasons: 8.13
(i) Reasons are required and there is no provision stating that parties may agree to dispense with reasons.[21]
(ii) Reasons are required and there is a provision stating that parties may agree to dispense with reasons.[22]
(iii) No provision requiring reasons is included in the rules.[23]

Points one and two above (and the corresponding footnotes) support Born's view that '[i]t is now a nearly universal principle that international arbitral awards must set forth the reasons for the tribunal's decision, as well as containing a 8.14

---

[16] JCAA Rules, Rule 54(1)(2). Most other institutional rules do not contain this requirement but the names of the parties and their representatives should always be included in an award.
[17] ICSID Rules, Rule 47(1)(c). Other institutional rules generally do not state this requirement expressly but the names of the arbitrators should be included and are in any event usually evident as a result of the signature requirement.
[18] CIETAC Rules Article 43(2); ICSID Rules, Rule 47(1)(h). This is not a requirement that is common to many rules but should always be included in an award.
[19] CIETAC Rules Article 43(2); ICSID Rules, Rule 47(1)(c). This requirement is not often expressed in arbitral rules but should always be included in an award.
[20] ACICA Rules Article 41(3); CIETAC Rules Article 43(2); HKIAC Rules Article 36; ICSID Rules, Rule 47(1)(j); KCAB International Rules Articles 40 and 41; and SIAC Rules, Rule 29.1.
[21] See, e.g. CIETAC Rules Article 43(2); HKIAC Rules Article 30(3); ICC Rules Article 25(2). ICSID Rules, Rule 47(1)(i) is more elaborate, requiring 'the decision of the Tribunal on every question submitted to it, together with the reasons upon which the decision is based'. This provision must be viewed in the context of Article 52 of the ICSID Convention, which provides that the failure to state the reasons on which the award was based may be a ground for its annulment. For national law mandatory requirements of reasons, despite the agreement of the parties, see the Belgian Judicial Code Article 1701; Brazilian Arbitration Law Article 26; French New Code of Civil Procedure Article 1471 (for domestic awards only); and Russian Federation Law on International Commercial Arbitration Article 31(2). See generally G Born, *International Commercial Arbitration*, Kluwer Law International, 2009, pp. 2452–2453. In relation to ICC practice, it has been suggested that in exceptional circumstances, derogation from the reasons requirement may be permitted. See Y Derains and E Schwartz, *A Guide to the ICC Rules of Arbitration*, 2nd edn, Kluwer, 2005, p. 309.
[22] See, e.g. ACICA Rules Article 33(3); ICA Rules, Rule 64; JCAA Rules, Rule 54(1); KCAB International Rules Article 31(1); and UNCITRAL Arbitration Rules Article 32(3); 2010 UNCITRAL Arbitration Rules Article 34(3). See also Model Law Article 31(2).
[23] See, e.g. the SIAC Rules.

dispositive section specifying the relief ordered by the tribunal'.[24] That view is not controversial. Even if the arbitration rules are silent on the issue of reasons, as is the case with the SIAC Rules, the *lex arbitri* may require that reasons be given. Thus if a SIAC arbitration is seated in Singapore, as most are, Article 31(2) of the Model Law, as the *lex arbitri*, would still require reasons.

8.15 A question arises as to the requisite standard of reasoning. In *BHP Billiton Ltd v Oil Basins Ltd*,[25] which involved judicial review of an Australian domestic award, Justice Hargrave of the Victorian Supreme Court held that in a large-scale commercial arbitration the standard of reasoning to be given by an arbitral tribunal is the same as that required by a judge in a comparable court case. He held:[26]

> the standard to be applied in considering the sufficiency of an arbitrator's reasons depends upon the circumstances of the case including the facts of the arbitration, the procedures adopted in the arbitration, the conduct of the parties to the arbitration and the qualifications and experience of the arbitrator or arbitrators. For example, in a straightforward trade arbitration before a trade expert, a less exacting standard than would be expected of a judge's reasons should be applied in considering the adequacy of the reasons for the making of an award. On the other hand, in a large-scale commercial arbitration, where the parties engage in the exchange of detailed pleadings and witness statements prior to a formal hearing before a legally qualified arbitrator, a higher standard of reasons is to be expected. This is especially so where the arbitrator is a retired judicial officer.
>
> ...
>
> My review of the authorities and the facts of this case leads me to conclude that the <u>arbitrators were under a duty to give reasons of a standard which was equivalent to the reasons to be expected from a judge deciding a commercial case</u>. The arbitration is a large commercial arbitration involving many millions of dollars. It was attended with many of the formalities of a legal proceeding, including the exchange of points of claim and defence and of substantial witness statements. The hearing occupied 15 sitting days. In addition to oral argument, substantial written submissions were made by the parties. The arbitrators were obviously chosen for their legal experience and were retired judges of superior courts. Both sides were represented by large commercial firms of solicitors and very experienced Queens Counsel. (Emphasis added)

8.16 The Victorian Court of Appeal affirmed this decision but clarified that 'it is the nature of a dispute which sets the standard for reasons, not the nature of the arbitrator'.[27] It also held:[28]

> As with reasons which a judge is required to give, the extent to which an arbitrator needs to go in explaining his or her decision depends on the nature of the decision.... the judicial obligation to give reasons is not based solely on rights of appeal. Ultimately, it is grounded in the notion that justice should not only be done but be seen to be done. And in point of principle, there is not a great deal of difference between that

---

24 Born, op. cit. fn 21, at pp. 2450–2451. See also the European Convention on International Commercial Arbitration (1961) Article VIII (reasons are required unless the parties agree otherwise).
25 [2006] VSC 402.
26 Ibid., at paras 21 and 23.
27 *Oil Basins Ltd v BHP Billiton Ltd* [2007] VSCA 255, at para 59.
28 Ibid., at paras 54 and 56.

idea and the imperative that those who make binding decisions affecting the rights and obligations of others should explain their reasons. Each derives from the fundamental conception of fairness that a party should not be bound by a determination without being apprised of the basis on which it is made. So, in arbitration, the requirement is that parties not be left in doubt as to the basis on which an award has been given. To that extent, the scope of an arbitrator's obligation to give reasons is logically the same as that of a judge.

There are, however, compelling arguments in support of the proposition that the standard of reasons required of an arbitrator is less onerous than that required of a judge. As is discussed in Chapter 7, there is an emerging duty on arbitrators to resolve disputes expeditiously and efficiently.[29] A commercial arbitrator's role is not that of a national judge who might be making decisions that need to accord with notions of fairness applicable to the community at large or that will set a precedent for future disputes between other parties. As Sir Thomas Bingham (as he then was) has remarked, arbitrators are not required to make a detailed analysis of the law, they need only summarise the arguments and express their conclusion in an intelligible manner.[30] An appropriate standard for arbitration was well formulated by the English Court of Appeal in *Bremer Handelsgesellschaft v Westzucker*:[31]

8.17

> All that is necessary is that the arbitrators should set out what, on their view of the evidence, did or did not happen and should explain succinctly why, in the light of what happened, they have reached their decision and what that decision is. This is all that is meant by a 'reasoned award'.

This decision is to be preferred to the *BHP Billiton Ltd v Oil Basins Ltd* judgments. If extensive reasoning is required, arbitration will 'increasingly mimic litigation, with comparable costs and delays'.[32] Additionally, if the *Oil Basins* approach is adopted in a Model Law state in relation to an international arbitration, it would effectively be augmenting the exhaustive setting aside grounds listed in Article 34(2), i.e. adding a requirement for 'adequate reasons'. Moreover, endless debate could ensue as to whether this standard was met in a given case. This could ultimately weaken the finality of arbitral awards and/or reduce the efficiency of international arbitration because arbitrators would be required to develop extensive reasoning.[33]

8.18

---

29 See Chapter 7, Section 4.3.
30 T Bingham, 'Differences between a Judgement and a Reasoned Award', (1997) 16 *The Arbitrator* 19, at p. 30 et seq.
31 [1981] 2 Lloyd's Rep 130. See also D Caron, L Caplan and M Pellonpää, *The UNCITRAL Arbitration Rules: A Commentary*, Oxford University Press, 2006, p. 880 ('Among the most important obligations that an arbitral tribunal owes the parties is the rendering of a coherent, accurate and complete award.'); and H Lloyd, M Darmon, J-P Ancel, Lord Dervaird, C Liebscher and H Verbist, 'Drafting Awards in ICC Arbitrations', (2005) 16(2) *ICC International Court of Arbitration Bulletin* 19, at para 5.2.2 ('If a national court has ever to examine an award, for example for the purposes of recognition or setting aside, it will naturally be less likely to be critical if the reasoning adopts a pattern with which it is familiar. However, an award cannot be drafted merely to please some national court and on the assumption that it, or its recognition or enforcement, will be challenged.').
32 P Gillies and N Selvadurai, 'Reasoned Awards: How Extensive Must the Reasoning Be?', (2008) 74 *Arbitration* 125, at p. 131.
33 We are only able to note briefly here that just prior to publication, another court in Australia, the New South Wales Court of Appeal in *Gordian Runoff Limited v Westport Insurance Corporation* [2010] NSWCA 57,

3.3 Signature, place and date

8.19 In an arbitral tribunal comprised of three members, all three arbitrators may not be able to sign the award at the same time or place. This is due to a number of factors: the arbitrators frequently reside in three separate countries; final deliberations do not necessarily take place in person (e.g. they can be done by telephone or by email); and it would add unnecessary costs to require arbitrators to travel and be in one place or at the arbitration's seat simply to sign the award. Awards may therefore be circulated to the arbitrators for signature wherever they are. Once signed, the award will typically be couriered back to the relevant arbitral institution, the chairperson or the secretary of the arbitral tribunal. In a three-member tribunal, the date of the award is usually deemed to be the date of its final signature.

8.20 Most modern arbitration laws and arbitral rules state that an award is made or deemed to be made at the seat of arbitration, no matter where it is actually signed.[34] If there is no such provision that deems a signature to be made at the seat, a problem could arise where arbitrators sign the award in a place different to the seat.[35] It could open the door to an argument that the seat of arbitration is the place where the award was signed, which may not be the seat agreed by the parties.

8.21 In England, the House of Lords in *Hiscox v Outhwaite*[36] decided that an award was made at the place where it was signed (Paris), and not at the seat of arbitration (London). Consequently, the English courts held that the award fell within the scope of the New York Convention. The English parliament subsequently amended the Arbitration Act 1996 to ensure that an award was treated as being made at the seat of arbitration 'regardless of where it was signed, dispatched or delivered to any of the parties.'[37]

3.4 Time limits

8.22 Arbitration laws governing international commercial arbitration usually do not prescribe time limits for rendering an award.[38] In contrast, arbitral rules often

---

rejected the reasons standard in *Oil Basins*. See also the judgment by Justice Croft of the Victorian Supreme Court in *Thoroughvision Pty Ltd v Sky Channel Pty Ltd & Anor* [2010] VSC 139. Although he does not reject *Oil Basins*, he still takes a more arbitration-friendly approach to the standard of reasons required in an award.
34 See Indian Arbitration and Conciliation Act Section 31(4); Japanese Arbitration Law Article 39(4); Korean Arbitration Act Article 32(3); Malaysian Arbitration Act Section 33(4); New Zealand Arbitration Act 1996, Article 31(3) of Schedule 1; Model Law Article 31(3); ACICA Rules Article 19.4; CIETAC Rules Article 31(3); HKIAC Rules Article 15(4); and ICA Rules, Rule 65. See generally Chapter 2, Section 3 of this book.
35 In this regard, China's Arbitration Law Article 33 and Indonesia's Arbitration and Dispute Resolution Act Article 54 do not contain such a deeming provision.
36 [1992] 1 AC 562.
37 See Sections 53 and 100(2)(b) of the English Arbitration Act 1996.
38 For example, no time limit is stated in the Model Law. See generally, Born, op. cit. fn 21, at p. 2471; and JDM Lew, LA Mistelis and SM Kröll, *Comparative International Commercial Arbitration*, Kluwer Law International, 2003, at para 24–38. An exception is Section 37(2) of the Spanish Arbitration Act 2003, based on the Model Law, which sets a six-month time limit for awards. The arbitral tribunal may extend the time limit for a period not exceeding two months.

specify a period of time within which the arbitral award should be issued, usually coupled with a means of extending this period. Article 33 of the KCAB International Rules provides an example of such a rule:[39]

1. Unless all parties agree otherwise, the Arbitral Tribunal shall make its Award within forty-five (45) days from the date on which final submissions are made or the hearings are closed whichever comes later.
2. The Secretariat may extend this time limit pursuant to a reasoned request from the Arbitral Tribunal or on its own initiative if it decides it is necessary to do so.

Unsurprisingly, the time limits for rendering an award are relatively shorter in expedited arbitration procedures.[40] For example, under the CIETAC Rules, the period for rendering an award under its summary procedure is an extendable three months from the date the arbitral tribunal is formed (Article 56), whereas an extendable six-month period is adopted under the normal arbitral procedure (Article 42). In the HKIAC Rules, no time limit is specified under the standard procedure, whereas six months is set, with provision for extension, under its expedited procedure (Article 38(2)(d)). 8.23

In some jurisdictions it is vital that the arbitral tribunal comply with time requirements for rendering an award or risk invalidating the award.[41] Once the time limit expires without extension, the view might be taken that this brings to an end the arbitral tribunal's mandate regardless of whether certain issues remain undecided.[42] However, in some cases it has been held that violations of the time limit to render an award will not be a ground for its annulment if no prejudice was caused or if such a harsh penalty is unjustified in the circumstances.[43] Moreover, if the time limit is short, there must be a balance struck between meeting that deadline and ensuring that the parties have been given a reasonable opportunity to present their cases and that the arbitral tribunal has been afforded a reasonable time to deliberate and decide. 8.24

---

[39] See also CIETAC Rules Article 42(1) (six months from formation of arbitral tribunal); ICA Rules, Rule 63 ('preferably' six months from the date of reference to arbitration, with a maximum of two years); ICC Rules Article 24 (six months from signature of terms of reference – while the plain language of this provision suggests that only the ICC Court is empowered to extend the time limit for the final award, in practice the court will always recognise an agreement of all parties to extend the time limit); and JCAA Rules, Rule 53(1) (five weeks from the 'conclusion' of the arbitral tribunal's 'examination' of the case). Rule 27.1 of the SIAC Rules requires that a draft award be submitted to the Registrar within 45 days from the date the proceedings are declared closed. No time is prescribed for issuing an award under the ACICA Rules, HKIAC Rules or either of the UNCITRAL Arbitration Rules.
[40] See Chapter 7, Section 6.11.
[41] See, e.g. *SM Bloch et fils v SM Delatrae Mockfjaerd*, 1984 *Revue de l'arbitrage* 498, 17 January 1984 (Paris Court of Appeal). Additionally, the French Cour de Cassation has held that 'the time-limit fixed by the parties, either directly or by reference to arbitration rules, cannot be extended by the arbitrators themselves ...' *Communauté urbaine de Casablanca v Degrémont*, 1995 *Revue de l'arbitrage* 88, 15 June 1994 (French Cour de Cassation).
[42] Cremades, op. cit. fn 15, p. 492.
[43] See, e.g. *Hasbro Inc v Catalyst USA Inc*, 367 F 3d 689, 10 May 2004 (US Fed 7th Circuit Court of Appeals), at p. 694, paras 18 and 19 ('time was not of the essence under this arbitration agreement. Therefore, the arbitrators did not exceed their authority by issuing an untimely award to the extent that the harsh penalty of forfeiture or rescission was warranted. . . . This is not to say, obviously, that arbitrators may indefinitely delay issuance of an award, in open violation of the AAA rules, without the parties' consent.').

3.5 Drafting an arbitral award

8.25 The award is usually drafted by the sole arbitrator or the chairperson of a three-member tribunal. In the latter circumstance, the chairman may allocate the drafting of different sections to other members of the arbitral tribunal. Any drafts of an award are circulated to all other arbitrators for comment. By signing an award, unless stated otherwise, arbitrators are confirming that the award is an accurate reflection of their views. In terms of the substantive portions of an award, it is the arbitrators alone who must make all the decisions.

8.26 In *Luzon Hydro Corp v Transfield Philippines Inc*,[44] a Singapore High Court case, it was alleged that an expert provided a considerable amount of assistance to the arbitral tribunal. The applicant attempted to set aside the arbitral award on the grounds, among others, that the rules of natural justice had been breached because the expert's involvement was substantially beyond what was agreed by the parties and the expert took over the arbitral tribunal's function of reviewing and determining the relevance of the evidence. The application was dismissed by Justice Prakash for a number of reasons, which included her finding that the applicant had not established that the expert had overstepped his function; that given the complexity of the case, the amount of time spent by the expert was not surprising; and that 'strong and unambiguous evidence of irregularity' was lacking.[45]

8.27 The CIETAC Rules are one of the few sets of procedural rules that include a provision specifically on the duties of arbitrators in making their award. Article 43(1) provides that:

> The arbitral tribunal shall independently and impartially make its arbitral award on the basis of the facts, in accordance with the law and the terms of the contracts, with references to international practices and in compliance with the principle of fairness and reasonableness.

This appears to be an attempt by CIETAC to ensure the quality of its awards. However, the consequences of a failure to comply with these criteria are not clear. For example, what happens where an award makes no reference to 'international practices' or if it is alleged that the award was made unfairly or unreasonably? Might that render an award susceptible to challenge on the basis that it was not in conformity with the chosen rules, which are part of the parties' arbitration agreement?

8.28 International arbitrators should draft an award in a manner that minimises the chance that it will be set aside at the seat of arbitration, or that it will be refused recognition or enforcement under the New York Convention. This concern is reflected in arbitration rules such as Article 35.3 of the SIAC Rules, which provides that SIAC's Chairman, the Registrar and the arbitral tribunal 'shall make every reasonable effort to ensure . . . the enforceability of the award'.

---

[44] [2004] 4 SLR 705 (High Court). See the Experts – OGEMID Discussion on this case by H Dundas and M Hwang, (2005) 2(3) *Transnational Dispute Management*.
[45] *Luzon Hydro Corp v Transfield Philippines Inc* [2004] 4 SLR 705 (High Court), paras 16–19.

To avoid unnecessary problems at the seat of the arbitration, the arbitral tribunal should request the parties to provide information as to the legal requirements for an award in the *lex arbitri* or make its own inquiries.

3.6 Scrutiny of the draft award

CIETAC, the ICC and SIAC have a scrutiny procedure that is not found in most other arbitral institutional rules and is not a feature of ad hoc arbitrations. Before the award is finalised in CIETAC, ICC and SIAC arbitrations, the arbitral tribunal must send a draft for scrutiny, respectively, to CIETAC, the ICC Court or SIAC's Registrar.[46] The relevant 2007 SIAC Rule is Article 27(1), which provides:

8.29

> Before issuing any award, the Tribunal shall submit it in draft form to the Registrar. Unless the Registrar extends time or the parties agree otherwise, the Tribunal shall submit the draft award to the Registrar within 45 days from the date on which the Tribunal declares the proceedings closed. The Registrar may suggest modifications as to the form of the award and, without affecting the Tribunal's liberty of decision, may also draw its attention to points of substance. No award shall be issued by the Tribunal until it has been approved by the Registrar as to its form.

Article 27(1) of the SIAC Rules appears to have been closely modelled on the equivalent provision in the ICC Rules, which is Article 27. A difference between the two sets of rules on this point is that the SIAC draft award must be submitted 45 days from the date on which proceedings are declared closed by the arbitral tribunal, whereas a similar time limit is not stipulated in the ICC Rules. However, ICC awards are to be rendered within six months from the date of the last signature of the Terms of Reference, and ICC arbitrators are required to indicate to the parties and the ICC Secretariat at the time they declare the proceedings closed when they expect to submit their award.[47]

8.30

Scrutiny of awards is one of the cornerstone features of the ICC system. Each award is firstly reviewed by the ICC Secretariat's Counsel in charge of administering the case. He or she occasionally spots an obvious discrepancy which can be brought to the arbitral tribunal's attention even before the award goes to the ICC Court. The award is then reviewed by the Deputy Secretary General and/or the Secretary General or General Counsel. It is then submitted to the ICC Court and reviewed by several ICC Court members.[48] If the award goes to a Plenary Session, an ICC Court member is assigned the task of reporting to the rest of the ICC Court on the award. In 2009, the ICC Court received and scrutinised 415 draft awards, 382 of which were returned to the arbitral tribunal with comments, suggesting modifications of form and/or drawing the tribunal's attention to a point of substance. While this process is thorough, involving more

8.31

---

46 See CIETAC Rules Article 45; SIAC Rules, Rule 27(1); 2010 SIAC Rules, Rule 28.2; ICC Rules Article 27.
47 See Articles 22 and 24 of the ICC Rules.
48 Article 6 of the Internal Rules of the International Court of Arbitration (Appendix II to the ICC Rules) provides that '[w]hen the Court scrutinizes draft Awards in accordance with Article 27 of the Rules, it considers, to the extent practicable, the requirements of mandatory law at the place of arbitration'.

than five or six arbitration specialists reviewing every award, of course there can be no guarantee that all potential problems in an award will be picked up.

8.32 The types of substantive matters that ICC scrutiny may draw attention to is wide-ranging. The ICC Court may question whether all issues have been decided, draw attention to applicable statutes of limitation or point out flaws in the award's analysis.[49] However, it has been said in relation to Article 27 of the ICC Rules that it:[50]

> makes clear that the [ICC] Court's scrutiny process cannot require the arbitral tribunal to change the substance of its award, nor does it involve a review of the facts or a re-examination of questions of law. The tribunal's 'liberty of decision' remains untouched and – while the arbitrators' attention can be drawn to matters of substance – it is not the Court's role to interfere with the tribunal's discretion to decide the case as it sees fit.

8.33 Article 45 of the CIETAC Rules requires that the arbitral tribunal submit the award to CIETAC for scrutiny before it is signed. In response, 'CIETAC may remind the arbitral tribunal of issues in the award on the condition that the arbitral tribunal's independence in rendering the award is not affected'.

3.7 Finality

8.34 Once an arbitral award is issued, it is usually said to be 'final and binding on the parties'.[51] The decisions in awards are not mere recommendations to the parties. They are decisions that the parties are obliged to follow and usually compel the performance of certain acts, such as paying compensation, performing a contractual obligation or surrendering property. Article 33.2 of the ACICA Rules requires that '[t]he parties undertake to carry out the award without delay'. Some rules, such as the CIETAC Rules, go further. Article 43(8) states:

> The arbitral award is final and binding upon both parties. Neither party may bring a suit before a law court or make a request to any other organisation for revising the award.

8.35 Article 35 of the Korean Arbitration Act equates awards issued in arbitrations seated in Korea with court decisions:

> The arbitral award shall have the same effect on the parties as the final and conclusive judgment of the court.

8.36 In Singapore, Justice Prakash stressed the finality of awards in her judgment in *Luzon Hydro Corp v Transfield Philippines Inc*:[52]

---

49 L Malintoppi and S Greenberg, 'The Practice of the ICC International Court of Arbitration Concerning Multi-Party Contracts and Scrutiny of Awards', conference paper delivered at the ICC Young Arbitrators Forum, Barcelona, 26–29 June 2008, para 64.
50 Ibid., paras 70–72.
51 See, e.g. SIAC Rules, Rule 27(8).
52 [2004] 4 SLR 705 (High Court), at para 20.

Whatever its grounds for dissatisfaction and however well founded that may be (a matter that was not, and could not be, argued before me) Luzon had to accept the tribunal's decision, as under the Act there was no avenue for appeal. I could not permit it to mount what appeared to be a 'back-door' appeal ...

In *Tang Boon Jek Jeffrey v Tan Poh Leng Stanley*,[53] the arbitrator delivered an award on 10 January 2000 that was described as 'final save as to costs' and which dismissed Jeffrey Tang's counterclaim. In an additional award on 17 January 2000, the arbitrator acknowledged that he had not dealt with particular issues raised in the counterclaim. Nonetheless, he reaffirmed his 10 January decision and dismissed Mr Tang's counterclaim. On the request of Mr Tang, the arbitrator thereafter permitted both parties to make further submissions on 31 January 2000 in which Mr Tang argued, among other things, that the arbitrator rejected the counterclaim on the basis of a point not argued before him. The arbitrator then delivered an award on 6 March 2000 on costs and reversed his decision on the counterclaim (the '6 March award'). Stanley Tan successfully applied to the Singapore High Court, which set aside the 6 March award on the basis that it was a nullity because the arbitrator was at the time of its making *functus officio* having already dismissed the counterclaim in the 10 January award. Jeffrey Tang appealed this decision to the Court of Appeal. In its reasoning, the Court of Appeal contrasted the Model Law with the English Arbitration Acts of 1950 and 1996 and found that whereas the provisions of the English Acts may render an arbitrator *functus officio* on an issue by issue basis, the Model Law does not.[54] The Court of Appeal effectively found that Article 32 of the Model Law enabled an arbitral tribunal to continue to change its decision up until it had determined all the issues between the parties (including costs) and delivered the final award in the arbitration:[55] 8.37

> It is true that in the 10 January award, as well as the 17 January award, the arbitrator had described the award as 'final'. But the label which the arbitrator gave to the award could not be conclusive if the facts were that there was still the claim on costs which had yet to be adjudicated upon. Accordingly, as the mandate of the arbitrator had not yet been terminated, he was entitled to reconsider his decision and if he thought fit, as he did here, to reverse himself.

Legislative action was taken to reverse the effect of the Court of Appeal's unexpected decision. Sections 19A and 19B were consequently introduced into the Singapore International Arbitration Act, which provide: 8.38

> (1) An award made by the arbitral tribunal pursuant to an arbitration agreement is final and binding on the parties and on any persons claiming through or under them and may be relied upon by any of the parties by way of defence, set-off or otherwise in any proceedings in any court of competent jurisdiction.

---
[53] [2001] 3 SLR 237 (Singapore Court of Appeal).
[54] Ibid., at para 39.
[55] Ibid., at para 38.

(2) Except as provided in Articles 33 and 34 (4) of the Model Law, upon an award being made, including an award made in accordance with section 19A, the arbitral tribunal shall not vary, amend, correct, review, add to or revoke the award.

8.39 These sections confirm what is well known in international arbitration practice: once delivered, all awards are final and have *res judicata* effect. A partial award cannot be revised by the arbitral tribunal in a later award. The *Jeffrey Tang* decision should not in any event be considered as a correct interpretation of the Model Law.[56]

3.8 Notification or deposit of award

8.40 In institutional arbitrations, originals of the final, signed award are usually delivered by the arbitral tribunal to the relevant institution. Depending on the institution, originals or certified copies of the award are then sent to each party once all costs of the arbitration have been paid.[57] In some jurisdictions, notification may not be the final act by an arbitral tribunal. Under Article 32(4) of the Korean Arbitration Act, for example, an original of the award must be deposited with the competent court.

8.41 When an award is completed and before the parties have paid the arbitrators' outstanding fees and expenses, it is not unusual for either the relevant institution or the arbitral tribunal to exercise a lien on the award to secure payment (i.e. it will not release the award before the fees and costs are fully paid). For example, Rule 9 of the HKIAC Schedule of Fees and Costs of Arbitration provides as follows:[58]

> The HKIAC and the arbitral tribunal shall have a lien over any awards issued by a tribunal to secure the payment of the costs referred to in Article 36.1, paragraphs (a), (b), (c) and (f), and may accordingly refuse to release any such awards to the parties until all such costs have been paid in full.

8.42 As regards ad hoc arbitrations, the UNCITRAL Arbitration Rules do not contain a provision that deals with this issue. However, it is well-established practice that ad hoc arbitral tribunals may exercise a lien over an award until all its fees and expenses are paid.

4 Definition of an arbitral award

8.43 Whether or not a decision is characterised as an arbitral award gives rise to significant legal consequences. First and foremost, only those decisions that are

---

[56] For a different view, see Tan Kay Kheng, 'Of Interim Awards: Their Effect Prior to and After the International Arbitration (Amendment) Act 2001', (2002) 14 *Singapore Academy of Law Journal* 143.
[57] See SIAC Rules, Rule 27(5); ICC Rules Article 28(1); JCAA Rules, Rule 55. See also Model Law Article 31(4). Article 33(5) of the ACICA Rules requires the arbitral tribunal to communicate copies of the award to the parties and ACICA.
[58] See also ACICA Rules Article 33.6; ICA Rules, Rule 68; ICC Rules Article 28(1); JCAA Rules, Rule 55(3); KCAB International Rules Article 35(1); and SIAC Rules, Rule 27.5.

'awards' can be the subject of setting aside proceedings (e.g. under Article 34 of the Model Law) and can be recognised or enforced under the New York Convention. It is therefore important to understand what types of decisions constitute arbitral awards.

An arbitral tribunal makes numerous decisions during the term of its mandate. Some of these decisions constitute awards but others do not. Obviously, an arbitral tribunal's 'mere titling of a document as an award does not make it an award'.[59] The difference between awards and decisions has been elaborated by Lew, Mistelis and Kröll in the following terms:[60]

8.44

> While all awards are decisions of the tribunal not all decisions are awards. The term 'decision' is generic and refers to the result of any conclusion or resolution reached after consideration while an 'award' is a decision affecting the rights between the parties and which is generally capable of being enforced, for instance, under the New York Convention.

Types of decisions unlikely to be classified as arbitral awards include:[61]

8.45

(i) negative decisions on jurisdiction;[62]
(ii) procedural rulings or orders made by the arbitral tribunal in respect of routine procedural questions such as the sequence in which witnesses are to be examined at the hearing, document production, or the date on which the oral hearing will commence; and
(iii) decisions pertaining to the arbitration proceedings made by an arbitral institution in the exercise of its administrative functions.

Agreement on a precise, internationally accepted definition of an 'arbitral award' has been elusive.[63] The New York Convention, for example, avoids a specific definition of the term. It states simply that '"arbitral awards" shall include not only awards made by arbitrators appointed for each case but also those made by permanent arbitral bodies to which the parties have submitted'. A definition of an award was proposed for inclusion in the Model Law but it was not adopted.[64]

8.46

---

59 *PT Asuransi Jasa Indonesia (Persero) v Dexia Bank SA* [2006] SGCA 41, (Singapore Court of Appeal) 1 December 2006, at para 70. See also *Resort Condominiums International Inc v Bolwell* (Queensland Supreme Court) 29 October 1993, (Qld SC) (1995) XX *Yearbook of Commercial Arbitration* 628, at para 40 (concluding 'that the 'Interim Arbitration Order and Award' made by the arbitrator on 16 July 1993 is not an 'arbitral award' within the meaning of the Convention nor a 'foreign award' within the meaning of the Act. It does not take on that character simply because it is said to be so.'); and *Tang Boon Jek Jeffrey v Tan Poh Leng Stanley* [2001] 3 SLR 237 (Singapore Court of Appeal), para 38. Similarly, the US Seventh Circuit Court of Appeals held in *Publicis Communication and Publicis SA v True North Communications Inc*, 206 F 3d 725 (7th Cir 2000), at 729, that an arbitral tribunal's decision issued under the name of an 'order' was in fact a final award because it was more than a mere procedural matter and concerned 'the very issue True North wanted arbitrated'. On this issue, see Section 5.3.
60 Lew, Mistelis and Kröll, op. cit. fn 38, at para 24–3 (footnotes omitted).
61 These points reflect the view of Cremades, op. cit. fn 15, p. 484.
62 There is also doubt as to whether a positive decision on jurisdiction constitutes an award for purposes of the Model Law. See Chapter 5, Section 6.
63 See Cremades, op. cit. fn 15, p. 483.
64 See H Holtzmann and J Neuhaus, *A Guide to the UNCITRAL Model Law on International Commercial Arbitration: Legislative History and Commentary*, Kluwer, 1989, pp. 153–154 (commenting that the drafters of the Model Law encountered 'considerable difficulty... in finding an acceptable general definition that would have the effect of properly regulating court control of arbitral decisions'). See also L Boo, 'Ruling on Arbitral Jurisdiction – Is that an Award?', (2007) 3 *Asian International Arbitration Journal* 125, at pp. 131–133.

The failure to agree on a detailed definition in those two seminal international arbitration instruments is reflective of the difficulties encountered in defining an award.

8.47 Nonetheless, definitions of awards are found in the domestic legislation of Malaysia, New Zealand, the Philippines and Singapore (all Model Law countries). Except for the Philippines,[65] they define an award as 'a decision of the arbitral tribunal on the substance of the dispute and includes any interim, interlocutory or partial award'.[66] The Singaporean and Malaysian laws expressly exclude 'orders or directions'. The focus in these jurisdictions is thus the 'substance of the dispute' rather than the title of the document containing the decisions. The substance of the dispute is also emphasised in the description of an award in the ICC Commission on Arbitration's report on drafting arbitral awards:[67]

> An award is generally a decision about the rights and obligations of the parties in the relationship, normally contractual, that gave rise to the dispute and to the arbitration. It is not about the rights and obligations of the parties under the procedure resulting from the arbitration agreement which will be the subject of procedural orders.

8.48 Arbitral rules ordinarily do not define an award but may state that it includes an interim or partial award.[68] The SIAC Rules are an exception because they add that an award is a decision on the 'substance of the dispute'.[69]

8.49 There is doubt as to whether decisions on jurisdiction will constitute an award or whether awards are confined to decisions on the merits of the dispute. The Model Law appears to draw a distinction between these two types of decision. Lawrence Boo argues that its drafters intended to differentiate between a preliminary ruling on jurisdiction and an award on the merits when they provided in Article 16(3) for immediate judicial review upon an arbitral tribunal's preliminary ruling that it has jurisdiction rather than enabling that decision to be contested as an award under Article 34.[70] In relation to a preliminary ruling that the arbitral tribunal lacks jurisdiction (i.e. a negative ruling), he states:[71]

> A decision on the preliminary question of jurisdiction (as opposed to an 'award on the merits') remains only a decision on a preliminary question of jurisdiction and does not morph into an 'award' even if, by virtue of the negative ruling [i.e. that the tribunal lacks jurisdiction] the arbitration comes to an end. This is because such a ruling leaves

---

65 Section 3(f) of the Philippines Alternative Dispute Resolution Act 2004 defines an award as 'any partial or final decision by an arbitrator in resolving the issue in controversy'.
66 See Singapore's International Arbitration Act Section 2(1); Malaysian Arbitration Act 2005; New Zealand Arbitration Act Section 2(1). See also Boo, op. cit. fn 64, at p. 134.
67 Lloyd, et al., op. cit. fn 31, at p. 25.
68 See, e.g. ICA Rules, Rule 2; KCAB International Rules Article 2; and ICC Rules Article 2.
69 See, e.g. SIAC Rules, Rule 1(2) (an 'award' is defined as 'a decision of the Tribunal on the substance of the dispute and includes an interim, interlocutory, partial or final award').
70 Boo, op. cit. fn 64, at p. 133. Compare the Model Law approach with Section 31(4)(a) of the English Arbitration Act 1996, which states that the arbitral tribunal has the power to rule on its own jurisdiction 'in an award as to jurisdiction, or deal with the objection in its award on the merits'. (Emphasis added)
71 Boo, op. cit. fn 64, at p. 135. The review of jurisdictional decisions and the question of whether a decision on jurisdiction can constitute an award are dealt with in Chapter 5, Section 6.

unresolved all the substantive claims, counterclaims and issues that would have been resolved if the tribunal had jurisdiction.

8.50 This view was accepted by the Singapore Court of Appeal in *PT Asuransi Jasa Indonesia (Persero) v Dexia Bank SA*.[72] The court in that case appointed Lawrence Boo as amicus curiae and agreed with his opinion. The Court of Appeal held that a negative determination on jurisdiction:[73]

> is not a decision on the substance of the dispute. On the contrary, it is a decision not to determine the substance of the dispute, and therefore cannot be an award for the purposes of Art 34 of the Model Law.

5 Types of awards

8.51 During the course of an arbitration, a number of different awards may be issued. This is stated, for example, in Section 19A(1) of Singapore's International Arbitration Act, which provides:

> Unless otherwise agreed by the parties, the arbitral tribunal may make more than one award at different points in time during the arbitration proceedings on different aspects of the matters to be determined.

8.52 The main types of arbitral awards are final awards, partial awards, interim or provisional awards, and consent awards. These are discussed in turn below, in addition to default awards and other matters.

5.1 Final awards

8.53 Article 32(1) of the Model Law states that the 'arbitral proceedings are terminated by the final award ... '. However, the term 'final award' is not defined in the Model Law. A final award generally signifies that the arbitral tribunal has determined all issues (or all remaining issues) submitted by the parties and within the jurisdiction of the arbitral tribunal. Nothing more should be left for the arbitral tribunal to decide, not even, for example, costs.

8.54 Awards made at different stages of the arbitration (e.g. partial awards as discussed below) may be 'final' in the sense that the issues determined in them are final and binding on the parties. As mentioned previously, Article 19B of Singapore's International Arbitration Act emphasises this aspect of award finality by providing that, subject to exceptions, 'upon an award being made ... the arbitral tribunal shall not vary, amend, correct, review, add to or revoke the award'.

---

[72] [2006] SGCA 41 (1 December 2006).
[73] *PT Asuransi Jasa Indonesia (Persero) v Dexia Bank SA* [2006] SGCA 41 (1 December 2006), at para 66.

5.2 Partial awards

8.55 A partial award finally decides some but not every remaining disputed issue in the arbitration. Once it is delivered, other issues in the arbitration still remain to be determined. For example, a partial award may state that the claimant is liable for breach of contract but may leave the assessment of the resulting damage and costs to be dealt with at another phase of the proceedings. This assessment will be determined in one or more subsequent awards.

5.3 Interim or provisional awards, orders or measures

8.56 An 'interim' or 'provisional' award is a designation sometimes incorrectly used interchangeably with the term 'partial' award. Interim or provisional awards more correctly denote a determination by the arbitral tribunal that is not final, i.e. one that does not settle a matter permanently.[74] An example of an interim award would be one that orders interim measures of protection, for example, restraining a party from disposing of property that is the subject of the dispute pending the final award.[75]

8.57 Whether an arbitral tribunal's decision ordering interim or provisional measures constitutes an 'award' that may be set aside or enforced, particularly under the New York Convention, is not altogether settled. It is hoped that the answer should depend on the substance of the order rather than its title or form.

8.58 The view that procedural directions or orders for the production of documents do not constitute awards is reasonably uncontroversial. For example, a well-regarded commentary states that:[76]

> Measures taken by arbitrators which do not decide the dispute either wholly or in part are not awards. This is true of orders for the hearing of witnesses and document production, for example, which are only procedural steps and as such are incapable of being the subject of an action to set aside.

8.59 A case on point is *Gingerbread Investments Ltd v Wing Hong Interior Contracting Ltd*.[77] Justice Burrell of Hong Kong's High Court was there required to determine whether a document issued by the arbitrator entitled 'Order for Directions No 6 – Reasons' was an award. If so, it could be set aside. Gingerbread submitted that because detailed and lengthy reasons were provided, it should be treated as an award. Justice Burrell considered that the presence of reasons was not determinative. He held that the document was not an award because '[t]he arbitrator headed his reasons "Order for Directions"; it concerned discovery of documents;

---

[74] See Lew, Mistelis and Kröll, op. cit. fn 38, at para 24–24; and Born, op. cit. fn 21, at p. 2434.
[75] See, e.g. Article 24(2) of the HKIAC Rules ('interim measures may be established in the form of an interim award'). Interim measures are dealt with in detail in Chapter 7.
[76] E Gaillard and J Savage (eds), *Fouchard, Gaillard, and Goldman on International Commercial Arbitration*, Kluwer, 1999, at para 1355. See also the numerous materials cited by Born, op. cit. fn 21, at p. 2020, fn 368; and Lew, Mistelis and Kröll, op. cit. fn 38, at para 23–94.
[77] Judgment of 14 March 2008 (Hong Kong High Court).

it was a pre-hearing application; it was not a determination of a substantive issue'.[78]

8.60 Uncertainty is more prevalent where an order or measure is more than a mere procedural direction. Some courts examine whether it finally resolves a part of the dispute submitted to arbitration. This was the approach taken by the Supreme Court of Queensland, Australia, in *Resort Condominiums International Inc v Bolwell*. In that case, the arbitral tribunal issued an 'Interim Arbitration Order and Award' that was essentially an injunction restraining the respondent from carrying out certain activities that would be contrary to a licence agreement. The court held that:[79]

> [w]hilst it is true that a valid interlocutory order is in one sense 'binding' on the parties to the arbitration agreement at least until it is varied or discharged by the tribunal which made it, Sect. 8(1) when read with Sect. 8(2) of the [Australian International Arbitration Act[80]] makes it clear that the award which may be enforced must be an award which is final and binding on the parties. An interlocutory order which may be rescinded, suspended, varied or reopened by the tribunal which pronounced it, is not 'final' and binding on the parties as referred to earlier in these reasons.

8.61 Because the 'Interim Order and Award' did not finally determine issues submitted to arbitration, it was held not to be enforceable under Australia's International Arbitration Act, which implements the New York Convention. Nonetheless, there is a growing body of authority indicating that an order for provisional measures of protection qualifies as an enforceable award. Born cites a number of authorities in support of the view. He considers that:[81]

> provisional measures should be and are enforceable as arbitral awards under generally-applicable provisions for the recognition and enforcement of awards. Provisional measures are 'final' in the sense that they dispose of a request for relief pending the conclusion of the arbitration. Orders granting provisional relief are meant to be complied with, and to be enforceable, in the parties' conduct outside the arbitral process; they are in this respect different from interlocutory arbitral decisions that merely decide certain subsidiary legal issues (e.g. choice of law, liability) or establish procedural timetables. It is also highly important to the efficacy of the arbitral process for national courts to be able to enforce provisional measures. If this possibility does not exist, then parties will be able and significantly more willing to refuse to comply with provisional relief, resulting in precisely the serious harm that provisional measures were meant to foreclose.

78 Ibid., at para 9.
79 *Resort Condominiums International Inc v Bolwell*, 29 October 1993, (Queensland Supreme Court) (1995) XX *Yearbook of Commercial Arbitration* 628, at para 39. See also *Inforica Inc. v CGI Information Systems and Management Consultants Inc.*, [2009] ONCA 642 (CanLII), in which the Ontario Court of Appeal, albeit in a domestic arbitration case, held that a procedural order for security for costs was not an award.
80 Sections 8(1) and (2) of the Australian International Arbitration Act provide as follows:

> Subject to this Part, a foreign award is binding by virtue of this Act for all purposes on the parties to the arbitration agreement in pursuance of which it is made.

> Subject to this Part, a foreign award may been enforced in a court of a State or Territory as if the award had been made in that State or Territory in accordance with the law of that State or Territory.

81 Born, op. cit. fn 21, at p. 2023 (footnote omitted). See the numerous authorities he cites at pp. 2021–2023. However, a vast proportion of these authorities are from the US.

He subsequently adds:[82]

> The principal risk of treating decisions on disclosure, provisional measures, stays and similar issues as awards is that the arbitral process will be disrupted or delayed by piecemeal interlocutory judicial appeals. That is a serious risk, but it is not appreciably altered by treating these interlocutory arbitral decisions as awards. Rather, doing so provides a mechanism for enforcing a tribunal's interlocutory rulings, which should not delay the arbitral process (and the availability of which may instead expedite that process).

8.62 Born's position is confirmed, for example, in *Southern Seas Nav Ltd v Petroleos Mexicanos of Mexico City*, where the US District Court for the Southern District of New York confirmed an order for interim measures on the basis that:[83]

> such an award is not 'interim' in the sense of being an 'intermediate' step toward a further end. Rather it is an end in itself, for its very purpose is to clarify the parties' rights in the 'interim' period pending a final decision on the merits ... if an arbitral award of equitable relief based upon a finding of irreparable harm is to have any meaning at all, the parties must be capable of enforcing or vacating it at the time it is made.

8.63 Support for this growing trend is found in the introduction of Article 17H in the 2006 amendments to the Model Law providing for the enforcement of interim measures[84] and the inclusion of provisions in institutional rules that interim measures may be ordered in the form of an award. These new developments are to be welcomed.[85]

5.4 Consent awards

8.64 A consent award is also frequently referred to as an 'award on agreed terms' or 'settlement award'. Where the parties settle their dispute during the arbitration, they may request the arbitral tribunal to record their settlement in the form of a consent award. This is provided for under Article 30 of the Model Law:[86]

> (1) If, during arbitral proceedings, the parties settle the dispute, the arbitral tribunal shall terminate the proceedings and, if requested by the parties and not objected to by the arbitral tribunal, record the settlement in the form of an arbitral award on agreed terms.

---

[82] Born, op. cit. fn 21, at p. 2358 (footnote omitted).
[83] 606 F Supp 695 (1985).
[84] This provision is discussed in Chapter 7, Section 9. New Zealand is the only state in the region so far to have adopted Article 17H, see Article 17H of Schedule 1 to the New Zealand Arbitration Act 1996. It should not be forgotten that even if the new Model Law provisions apply, they will be restricted to enforcement of provisional measures at the seat of the arbitration.
[85] Article 28(1) of the ACICA Rules, for example, provides:

> Unless the parties agree otherwise in writing, the Arbitral Tribunal may, on the request of any party, order interim measures of protection. The Arbitral Tribunal may order such measures in the form of an award, or in any other form (such as an order) provided reasons are given, and on such terms as it deems appropriate.

See also Article 24.2 of the HKIAC Rules; and Born, op. cit. fn 21 at pp. 2357–2358.
[86] See also Indian Arbitration and Conciliation Act Section 30; Japanese Arbitration Law (2003) Article 38; Singapore International Arbitration Act, Section 18; ICSID Rules, Rule 43; KCAB International Rules Article 34; SIAC Rules, Rule 27(7); ICC Rules Article 26.

(2) An award on agreed terms shall be made in accordance with the provisions of article 31 and shall state that it is an award. Such an award has the same status and effect as any other award on the merits of the case.

The phrase 'not objected to by the arbitral tribunal' indicates that the arbitral tribunal is not obliged to 'rubber stamp' any settlement agreement. For example, an arbitral tribunal may object to terms it considers to contravene international public policy.[87] Rule 62 of the ICA Rules is more specific in that it prescribes two criteria that arbitrators need to take into account. It states:

> Should the Parties arrive at a settlement of the dispute by common agreement before the Arbitral Tribunal and the Arbitral Tribunal is satisfied that such agreement is genuine and not to defeat the purpose of any law, the arbitral tribunal shall render an award as per the agreement of the Parties.

The advantage for the parties of having their settlement recorded in the form of a consent award is that the award can then be enforced, if necessary, under the New York Convention. A mere contractual settlement agreement would not fall within the scope of the New York Convention, and would have to be enforced like any contract. For this reason, an arbitral tribunal requested to issue a consent award should ensure that the award complies with the various form requirements for arbitral awards, regardless of the form of the parties' settlement agreement. Thus the issuance of a consent award is not a mere rubber stamp, but requires the arbitral tribunal to draft an award, incorporating in some way the parties' settlement.

5.5 Default awards

As discussed in Chapter 7, if a party refuses to participate in an arbitration, the arbitral tribunal may proceed with the arbitration in the absence of that party. Provided that all parties, including the absent party, are given an opportunity to present their cases, the arbitral tribunal may issue an award despite one or more parties' non-participation. Most arbitral rules provide for such default awards.[88]

It is important to distinguish between a default award and the notion of a summary judgment, usually available in domestic courts. A summary judgment may be issued almost automatically in favour of the plaintiff if the respondent does not appear and contest the plaintiff's case. In arbitration, however, where a party does not participate, the arbitral tribunal must still test the evidence, reason its decisions, and cannot blindly accept the submissions of the participating party. It is not uncommon that a default award rejects some of the claimant's claims for want of sufficient evidence despite the fact that the claimant's case was not opposed.

---

[87] A similar discretion to deny the issuance of an award on agreed terms is found in ACICA Rules Article 35.1; HKICA Rules Article 32.1; ICC Rules Article 26. Other rules such as JCAA Rules, Rule 54(2) and KCAB International Rules Article 34 do not provide this type of express discretion.

[88] See, e.g. ACICA Rules Article 29; CIETAC Rules Article 34; HKIAC Rules Article 26; ICA Rules, Rule 53; KCAB International Rules Article 29; SIAC Rules, Rule 21.3; and ICC Rules Articles 6(3) and 21(2). See Chapter 7, Section 6.10.

5.6 Domestic, non-domestic, foreign and international awards

8.69 Awards are also categorised from the perspective of the place where they are made. Although practice varies from state to state, for illustrative purposes the following four descriptions are noted:
  (i) 'domestic' awards – courts in state A would consider an award 'domestic' if it is made in state A, arises out of an arbitration between parties from state A and the dispute in question has little or no connection with another state;
  (ii) 'foreign' awards – courts in state A would consider an award 'foreign' if it is made in a foreign state;[89]
  (iii) 'international' awards – even if the seat of arbitration was in state A, courts in that state may consider that it is an 'international' award where (i) the parties have places of business in different states; (ii) the location of at least one of the party's places of business is in a foreign state; (iii) at least one of the party's countries of business is different to the place where a substantial part of the commercial relationship's obligations was performed; (iv) at least one of the party's countries of business is different to the place most closely connected to the dispute; or (v) the parties agree that the subject matter of the arbitration agreement relates to more than one country;[90] and
  (iv) awards 'not considered as domestic awards', otherwise referred to as 'non-domestic' awards.[91]

8.70 Hwang and Lee provide a concrete example that helps to understand the difference among domestic, foreign and international awards.[92] They indicate that by way of a drafting mistake in the Malaysian International Arbitration Act 2005, an international award issued by an arbitral tribunal seated in Malaysia is not covered by that Act, Article 38(1) of which provides:

---

[89] Section 3 of Australia's International Arbitration Act, for example, speaks of a 'foreign' award as 'an arbitral award made, in pursuance of an arbitration agreement, in a country other than Australia'. In Article 1 of the Ordinance on Recognition and Enforcement of Foreign Awards 1995 (Vietnam) (now repealed), one of the definitions of a 'foreign arbitral award' was an award made within Vietnamese territory by a foreign arbitrator. This definition does not comport with the generally accepted definition of a foreign award. See R Garnett and KC Nguyen, 'Enforcement of Arbitration Awards in Vietnam', (2006) 2 *Asian International Arbitration Journal* 137, at pp. 139 and 149.
[90] These criteria are based on Model Law Article 1(3).
[91] The meaning of non-domestic awards is discussed in Chapter 9, Section 5.2. The second sentence in Article I(1) of the New York Convention speaks of 'arbitral awards not considered as domestic awards in the State where their recognition and enforcement are sought'. In Australia, this part of Article I(1) has not been enacted in its domestic law. See R Garnett and M Pryles, 'Recognition and Enforcement of Foreign Awards under the New York Convention in Australia and New Zealand', (2008) 25 *Journal of International Arbitration* 899, at p. 900. Hong Kong and mainland China also do not have domestic provisions that enable the New York Convention to be applicable to Article I(1) non-domestic awards.

As regards 'a-national awards', see J Rubenstein and G Fabian, 'The Territorial Scope of the New York Convention and Its Implementation in Common and Civil Law Countries', in E Gaillard and D Di Pietro (eds), *Enforcement of Arbitration Agreements and International Arbitration Awards: The New York Convention in Practice*, Cameron May, 2008, at pp. 101–132; and Lew, Mistelis and Kröll, op. cit. fn 38, at paras 25–18 and 25–19.
[92] M Hwang and S Lee, 'Survey of South East Asian Nations on the Application of the New York Convention', (2008) 25(6) *Journal of International Arbitration* 873.

On an application in writing to the High Court, an award made in respect of a domestic arbitration or an award from a foreign State shall, subject to this section and section 39, be recognized as binding and be enforced by entry as a judgment in terms of the award or by action.

The gap arises because an award, for example, issued by a SIAC arbitral tribunal seated in Kuala Lumpur between a Malaysian and Japanese party is neither an award made in a 'domestic arbitration' (which is defined in Section 2(1) of the Malaysian Act as all arbitrations which are not international) nor a 'foreign' award. It is rather an award made in an international arbitration seated in Malaysia, in other words, an 'international award'. 8.71

The above definitions are not universally accepted and may not necessarily be valid in all jurisdictions. For example, the definition of an 'international' award may not apply in Indonesia (as the following case shows) and many other countries. The Indonesian Supreme Court in *Ascom Electro AG v PT Manggala Mandiri Sentosa*[93] held that 'international arbitration awards' referred only to awards made outside of Indonesia. In so finding, it dismissed an application to enforce as an international award an award issued in an arbitration seated in Indonesia between a local party and a foreign party. 8.72

5.7 Majority decisions, separate and dissenting opinions

One or more dissenting opinions may be issued whenever all of the arbitrators cannot agree on something. In that situation the award will be based on the views of the majority, if there is one.[94] In the rare event that there is no majority, for example if all three arbitrators have different views, procedural rules usually prescribe that the award is to be made by the chairperson alone.[95] The UNCITRAL Arbitration Rules are a notable exception to this practice; they require a majority decision. Obviously, the question of a majority decisions does not arise in arbitrations that involve a sole arbitrator. 8.73

Separate opinions are given by arbitrators who agree with the dispositive part of the award but disagree with the reasoning adopted in the award. In international commercial arbitrations between private parties, separate opinions are very rare. They are more common in arbitrations involving states. In this regard, the ICSID Rules provide specifically for separate opinions in Rule 47(3). Similarly, separate opinions accompanied Iran-US Claims Tribunal awards on a number of occasions. 8.74

Dissenting opinions can potentially be more problematic. Most institutional rules are silent as to whether dissenting opinions are permitted.[96] But in practice arbitral institutions accept them as a part of the arbitral process.[97] A dissent may 8.75

---
[93] Decision of 22 September 1993, cited in Hwang and Lee, ibid., at p. 876.
[94] See, e.g. ACICA Rules Article 32; CIETAC Rules Article 43(4); HKIAC Rules Article 29(1); ICA Rules, Rule 61; KCAB International Rules Article 30; SIAC Rules, Rule 27(4).
[95] See, e.g. ACICA Rules Article 32; CIETAC Rules Article 43(5); HKIAC Rules Article 29(1); ICA Rules, Rule 61; KCAB International Rules Article 30; SIAC Rules, Rule 27(4); and ICC Rules Article 25(1).
[96] See exceptionally, CIETAC Rules Article 43(4). As to dissenting opinions generally, see M Rubino-Sammartano, *International Arbitration Law and Practice*, 2nd edn, Kluwer, 2001, at p. 766 et seq.
[97] See Smit, op. cit. fn 5.

be indicated by an arbitrator's refusal to sign the award. If this happens, the other members of the arbitral tribunal should record this fact in the award, a practice which some jurisdictions consider mandatory.[98] The dissent might also take the form of a written opinion stating the reasons why the arbitrator disagreed with the majority's conclusions. A dissenting opinion may be attached to the award but does not form part of the award.[99]

8.76 Although judges frequently dissent in the common law system, dissenting opinions are generally not part of the legal tradition in the civil law system.[100] Following more of a civil law approach, dissenting opinions in international commercial arbitrations between private parties are not common, but are certainly not as rare as separate opinions. A good indication can be obtained from ICC statistics in this respect. In the five years from 2004 to 2008, the ICC Court scrutinised and approved a total of 1719 arbitral awards (including awards of sole arbitrators and three-member arbitral tribunals), 142 of which were rendered by a majority of the arbitral tribunal. A further two awards over that period were rendered by the chairman of the arbitral tribunal alone, in accordance with Article 25(1) of the ICC Rules, because no majority could be formed. Taking a closer look at the 2008 statistics, in that year the ICC Court scrutinised and approved 407 awards, of which 229 were rendered in arbitrations with three-member arbitral tribunals. Of those 229 awards, 31 were made by a majority of the arbitral tribunal. It is also interesting to consider the form of the dissenting opinions. In 2008, of the 31 ICC awards made by a majority, 23 dissenting arbitrators issued a separate dissenting opinion; five dissenting arbitrators put their dissent into the body of the majority award; and three dissenting arbitrators did not write a dissenting opinion. It is also interesting to note that in five of these 31 cases, the dissenting arbitrator preferred to remain anonymous, not identifying him or herself at all.

8.77 On the one hand, dissenting opinions should be discouraged because they may affect the efficacy and the integrity of the arbitration.[101] It has been observed that

---

[98] In most institutional rules, and generally in practice, where one of the arbitrators refuses to sign, the signatures of the majority will be sufficient provided the reason for the omitted signature is stated. See ACICA Rules Article 33.4; HKIAC Rules Article 30(4); JCAA Rules, Rule 54(5); KCAB International Rules Article 31(2); SIAC Rules, Rule 27(4); UNCITRAL Arbitration Rules Article 32(4); 2010 UNCITRAL Arbitration Rules 34(4); Model Law Article 31(1). In the Netherlands, Article 1057 of the Code of Civil Procedure requires that if a dissenting arbitrator refuses to sign, the majority arbitrators should mention this 'beneath the award signed by them'. The Netherlands Supreme Court in *Bursa Büyüksehir Belediyesi v Güris Insaat VE Mühendislik AS*, 5 December 2008, Netherlands Court Reports [NJ 2009, 6], agreed with the findings of lower courts that an award should be set aside for failure to comply with this Article 1057 requirement. See A Hoogveld and M Van Leeuwen, 'Dissenting Opinions and Non-compliance: Grounds for Setting Aside an Award?', International Law Office, Newsletter, 19 March 2009. This court decision appears to be a very strict application of Article 1057. It gives precedence to form over substance. In effect, a majority opinion in that case had been established and the courts should in such circumstances make concerted efforts to give effect to the majority view rather than focus on formalistic requirements. Nonetheless, this case illustrates the importance of complying with all local laws relating to the form of an award.
[99] See, e.g. CIETAC Rules Article 43(4). See also *Bursa Büyüksehir Belediyesi v Güris Insaat VE Mühendislik AS*, (Netherlands Supreme Court), 5 December 2008, Netherlands Court Reports [NJ 2009, 6].
[100] See Smit, op. cit. fn 5, at p. 37; and L Levy, 'Dissenting Opinions in International Arbitrations in Switzerland', (1989) 5 *Arbitration International* 35, at 39.
[101] As to the importance placed in some jurisdictions on the collegial process by which arbitral tribunals reach a decision, see *Bursa Büyüksehir Belediyesi v Güris Insaat VE Mühendislik AS*, Netherlands Supreme Court, 5 December 2008, Netherlands Court Reports [NJ 2009, 6].

dissents may be used (abusively) to provide a basis for an attack on the award in court.[102] On the other hand, however, an arbitrator who has formed a view should not be forced to look for compromises to please his fellow arbitrators. The individual arbitrators should endeavour to convince each other of their respective views, but if they cannot then a dissent may be necessary.[103]

6 Costs

It has been observed that costs are sometimes more fiercely contested than the substantive issues in dispute.[104] Costs are particularly relevant in the resolution of commercial disputes because some degree of proportionality might be expected between the value of the dispute and the cost of resolving it. In larger arbitrations costs might amount to several million or even tens of millions of US dollars.[105] The power to award costs lies with the arbitral tribunal but may be subject to the arbitration clause, the applicable procedural rules or the *lex arbtri*. The rationale underlying the ordering of costs is that they are considered to have been necessarily incurred in the course of making a valid claim or defending an unfounded claim. As a result, an arbitrator may consider that they are properly due to the prevailing party.[106]

8.78

Three primary options are open to the arbitral tribunal in awarding costs:

8.79

(i) All reasonable costs are to be borne by the overall losing party.
(ii) The reasonable costs are to be allocated on some kind of proportional basis, depending on the success of each party, and possibly taking into account other factors like the procedural conduct of the parties.
(iii) Each party is to bear its own costs.

The details contained in the ACICA Rules illustrate the types of costs that may be incurred in arbitration proceedings. Article 39 of those Rules reads:

8.80

> The Arbitral Tribunal shall fix the costs of arbitration in its award. The term 'costs of arbitration' includes only:
> (a) the fees of the Arbitral Tribunal, to be stated separately as to each arbitrator, and to be fixed in accordance with Article 40;

---

[102] Smit, op. cit. fn 5, at p. 40. See also Cremades, op. cit. fn 15, p. 491 (commenting that one view of dissenting opinions is that they demonstrate to the party that appointed the dissenting arbitrator that he has defended their interests correctly).
[103] See, e.g. Smit, op. cit. fn 5, at p. 38 ('the dissenting opinion represents the prevalence of individual integrity over collegial solidarity'). A rather unique dissent took place in *Tokios Tokelės v Ukraine*, ICSID Case No. ARB/02/18, Decision on Jurisdiction (29 April 2004), in which the president of the ICSID arbitral tribunal dissented and the majority was formed by the two party-nominated arbitrators.
[104] P Yang, 'The Organisation of International Arbitral Proceedings' in M Pryles and M Moser (eds), *The Asian Leading Arbitrators' Guide to International Arbitration*, JurisNet, 2007, p. 217, at p. 221.
[105] See, e.g. Derains and Schwartz, op. cit. fn 21, p. 370; and the very interesting figures as to the total fees of arbitrators and counsel in K Sachs, 'Time and Money: Cost Control and Effective Case Management', in L Mistelis and J Lew (eds), *Pervasive Problems in International Arbitration*, Kluwer Law International, 2006, p. 111.
[106] See P Karrer and M Desax, 'Security for Costs in International Arbitration: Why, When, and What If . . . ', in R Briner, LY Fortier, KP Berger and J Bredow (eds), *Law of International Business and Dispute Settlement in the 21st Century: Liber Amicorum Karl-Heinz Böckstiegel*, Carl Heymanns Verlag, 2001, p. 339.

(b) the travel (business class airfares) and other reasonable expenses incurred by the arbitrators;
(c) the costs of expert advice and of other assistance required by the Arbitral Tribunal;
(d) the travel (business class airfares) and other reasonable expenses of witnesses to the extent such expenses are approved by the Arbitral Tribunal;
(e) the legal and other costs directly incurred by the successful party if such costs were claimed during the arbitral proceedings, and only to the extent that the Arbitral Tribunal determines that the amount of such costs is reasonable;
(f) ACICA's registration fee and administration fee; and
(g) fees for facilities and assistance provided by ACICA in accordance with Articles 7 and 42.5.

It is of interest to note that in New Zealand, the Supreme Court has held that a failure to deal with costs in an award renders it incomplete, even if an order for costs was not sought by either of the parties.[107]

6.1 Costs of the arbitration v parties' costs

8.81 Costs fall into two basic categories: (1) costs of the arbitration; and (2) the parties' costs. The former includes the fees and expenses of the arbitrators, the institution administering the arbitration, experts appointed by the arbitral tribunal and costs arising from the hearing (such as hiring a venue, translation and transcription services). The latter includes fees and expenses of a party's lawyers, its witnesses, party-engaged expert witnesses, and the party itself. However, the parties' legal costs are sometimes subsumed under 'costs of the arbitration'.[108]

8.82 It has been estimated from an analysis of ICC cases that the parties' costs amount to 82% of the overall costs. Arbitrator's fees and expenses and institutional administrative expenses amount to 16% and 2%, respectively.[109]

6.2 Payment of costs: By which party and in what proportion?

8.83 National laws vary in the manner in which they address the awarding of costs. Usually, they permit the parties to agree on how costs will be awarded but also provide a default rule if no agreement is reached. Section 27(1) of Australia's International Arbitration Act (which is an opt-in provision) provides, for example, that '[u]nless the parties to an arbitration agreement have . . . otherwise agreed, the costs of an arbitration . . . shall be in the discretion of the arbitral tribunal'.[110]

---

[107] See *Casata Ltd v General Distributors Ltd*, [2006] 2 NZLR 721. On decisions on costs in New Zealand, see generally T Kennedy-Grant, 'The New Zealand Experience of the UNCITRAL Model Law: A Review of the Position as at 31 December 2007', (2008) 4 *Asian International Arbitration Journal* 1, at pp. 50–53.

[108] See, e.g. Article 6 of Schedule 2 of the New Zealand Arbitration Act 1996 (describing the 'costs and expenses of an arbitration' as 'the legal and other expenses of the parties, the fees and expenses of the arbitral tribunal, and any other expenses related to the arbitration'). See also ACICA Rules Article 39; and HKIAC Rules Article 36.1.

[109] Report of ICC Commission on Arbitration, *Techniques for Controlling Time and Costs in Arbitration*, ICC Publication, 2007, p. 11. That report also sets out some helpful points on reducing the costs of the parties' presentation of their cases.

[110] Similarly, see Malaysia's Arbitration Act Section 44(1); and India's Arbitration and Conciliation Act Section 31(8).

However, the Hong Kong Arbitration Ordinance limits the parties' ability to agree to pay their own costs.[111] Different still is Article 22(4) of the 2003 Vietnam Ordinance on Commercial Arbitration, which prescribes that the losing party must bear the costs of the arbitration. The Model Law contains no provision that deals with the awarding of costs.

In the US, in domestic arbitration it is usual for each party to bear its own costs.[112] But this practice is not common in international commercial arbitration.[113] Many arbitral rules provide that in principle the <u>costs of the arbitration</u> be borne by the unsuccessful party.[114] Such procedural rules, however, treat the <u>parties' legal costs</u> differently in the sense that they give discretion to the arbitral tribunal to award the successful party its reasonable legal costs.[115] Accordingly, the amount of legal costs ordered is often less than the actual legal costs incurred and claimed by the successful party.[116]

8.84

A case in which the reasonableness of a party's costs became a significant point of dispute was *VV v VW*.[117] In the arbitration VV's principal claims against VW amounted to S$927 000. In response, VW raised counterclaims of S$20 million against VV. The arbitrator dismissed VV's claims and determined that he had no jurisdiction over the counterclaims. He also ordered VV to pay VW's costs in the amount of S$2.25 million for legal fees, disbursements and witnesses' expenditures. VV applied to the Singapore courts to set aside the costs award because it was, among other things, so disproportional it was against public policy. This public policy argument was rejected by Justice Prakash of the Singapore High Court. She determined that if parties have contracted to settle disputes by arbitration, no matter how unreasonable the resulting award could be, it could not be injurious to the public good or shocking to the conscience. She added that it was not part of the public policy of Singapore to ensure that arbitration costs were to be assessed on proportionality principles. The application to set aside the award was dismissed.

8.85

---

111 Hong Kong's Arbitration Ordinance Section 2GJ(2) provides that a 'provision of an arbitration agreement to the effect that the parties, or any of the parties, to the agreement must pay their own costs in respect of the arbitration proceedings arising under the agreement is void. However, such a provision is not void if it is part of an agreement to submit to arbitration a dispute that had arisen before the agreement was made'.
112 See, e.g. the AAA Commercial Arbitration Rules Article 50.
113 Chamber Two of the Iran-US Claims Tribunal is an exception in that it consistently left each of the parties to bear its own costs. Chambers One and Three, in contrast, frequently awarded costs but not in amounts sufficient to cover the actual costs of the successful party. See G Aldrich, *The Jurisprudence of the Iran-United States Claims Tribunal*, Clarendon Press, 1996, at p. 480.
114 See ACICA Rules Article 41(1); CIETAC Rules Article 46; HKIAC Rules Article 36.4; KCAB International Rules Article 40; PDRCI Rules Article 40; UNCITRAL Arbitration Rules Article 40(1); 2010 UNCITRAL Arbitration Rules Article 42(1). See also SIAC Rules, Rule 29.
115 See ACICA Rules Article 41(2); CIETAC Rules Article 46(2); KCAB International Rules Article 41; SIAC Rules, Rule 31(1) and UNCITRAL Arbitration Rules Article 40(2). But compare the 2010 UNCITRAL Arbitration Rules which make the apportionment of the costs of representation and assistance subject to the same principles as other costs (see UN Doc. A/CN.9/646, para 28). Nevertheless the reasonableness requirement is still found in 2010 UNCITRAL Arbitration Rules Article 40(2)(e).
116 See A Redfern, M Hunter, N Blackaby and C Partasides, *Law and Practice of International Commercial Arbitration*, 4th edn, Sweet & Maxwell, 2004, at para 8–95. That paragraph neatly sets out some of the multidimensional problems that may explain why a less than full amount is awarded.
117 [2008] SGHC 11 (High Court Singapore).

8.86 'Costs follow the event' is a term that refers to the practice whereby the overall loser in the arbitration is required to pay the costs of the proceeding and the reasonable legal and other costs of the overall winner. While having its origins in English litigation and domestic arbitration, this practice is also sometimes adopted in international arbitration. The practice, however, may sometimes be highly disadvantageous to a party that is the overall loser because it applies even where that party has succeeded in a number of its arguments and has persuaded the arbitral tribunal to reduce substantially the amount claimed. Consequently, a respondent that persuades an arbitral tribunal to reduce an award made against it to a fraction of the sum claimed may still be required to pay the bulk of the costs, including the claimant's legal costs.[118]

8.87 In some jurisdictions, the 'costs follow the event' principle may not be recognised. As an example, the Philippines Court of Appeals in *Luzon Hydro Corporation v Baybay and Transfield Philippines Inc* held that the principle was not accepted under Philippines law and that the arbitral tribunal in the case at issue 'gravely abused its discretion' in applying the principle.[119] Accordingly, the award at issue was set aside in respect of its decision on costs. The relevant rationale of the Philippines law is that a litigant cannot be penalised for exercising its right to litigate.[120]

6.3 Sealed offers

8.88 To counteract the potentially harsh outcome of the 'costs follow the event' principle as described above, the practice of using a 'sealed offer' has evolved in domestic common law jurisdictions and is occasionally used in international arbitrations.[121] This essentially involves a written offer by one party to settle the dispute made 'without prejudice save as to costs'. As Poupak Anjomshoaa explains:[122]

> The offer is 'sealed' and 'without prejudice' because it is not to be brought to the attention of the arbitral tribunal before the determination of the substantive dispute, in case it influences the decision of the tribunal with regard to the merits of the substantive case.[[123]] However, in order that the offer can be taken into account in assessing liability for costs, it must be brought to the attention of the arbitral tribunal before the tribunal makes a determination on costs, hence the wording 'save as to costs'.

8.89 If the overall winner of the arbitration refuses to accept a 'sealed offer', and the amount of this offer is more than the amount awarded to it by the arbitral

---

118 See P Anjomshoaa, 'The Costs of International Arbitration and the Use of Sealed Offers', (2007) *Asian Dispute Review* 19, at p. 20.
119 (2007) XXXII *Yearbook of Commercial Arbitration* 456, at p. 472, para 40.
120 Ibid. But see Rule 21 of the Philippines Supreme Court Special Rules of Court on Alternative Dispute Resolution, effective October 2009.
121 Sometimes this is known as a 'Calderbank letter', the name being derived from the case of *Calderbank v Calderbank* [1975] 3 All ER 333.
122 Anjomshoaa, op. cit. fn 118, p. 20.
123 For example, the offer may give the tribunal the impression that the respondent has admitted liability and is offering to settle.

tribunal, then such offer is said to displace the 'costs follow the event' principle. Consequently, an overall winner who rejects a sealed offer and who is awarded less than the amount of that offer will be required to pay the costs that the loser incurred subsequent to the time the offer could have been accepted.[124] Sealed offers are rare in international commercial arbitration, but are known to have occasionally been used. Whether they will be accepted wholeheartedly into the mainstream of international arbitration is yet to be seen. It merits noting that Article 44(2) of the Malaysian Arbitration Act 2005, applicable to domestic arbitrations, contains a provision that resembles the 'sealed offer' practice:

> Unless otherwise agreed by the parties, where a party makes an offer to the other party to settle the dispute or part of the dispute and the offer is not accepted and the award of the arbitral tribunal is no more favourable to the other party than was the offer, the arbitral tribunal, in fixing and allocating the costs and expenses of the arbitration, may take the fact of the offer into account in awarding costs and expenses in respect of the period from the making of the offer to the making of the award.

Article 44(3) prevents an offer made under subs (2) from being communicated to the arbitral tribunal 'until it has made a final determination of all aspects of the dispute other than the fixing and allocation of costs and expenses'.[125]

8.90 On the other hand, an LCIA arbitral tribunal has held that an offer sent from the respondent's English law firm to the claimant's American law firm 'without prejudice save as to costs' was an offer not to be taken into account by the arbitrators in determining costs.[126] In the arbitral tribunal's view, the offer did not inform the claimant and its US attorney sufficiently about the serious consequence of rejecting it and that it would be unfair to adopt this English practice against lawyers from other jurisdictions. The decision thus turned on a lack of notice and does not appear to reject the practice of sealed offers.

6.4 Arbitrators' fees

8.91 In determining the fees of arbitrators, the two most common approaches are by hourly rate, either agreed with the parties or fixed by the institution, or by a fee calculated as a regressive percentage of the amount in dispute. Both these types of fees vary and, in institutional arbitration, depend on the approach adopted by each institution. Fees calculated on the amount in dispute have the advantage of predictability and proportionality. These fees can be estimated with reasonable certainty at the outset of the arbitration and will be proportionate to the value of the dispute. On the other hand, hourly rates have the advantage of certainty for the arbitrators since the value of a dispute does not necessarily provide a reliable

---

124 Anjomshoaa, op. cit. fn 118.
125 A similar provision is found in Article 6(2) of Schedule 2 of the New Zealand Arbitration Act 1996.
126 See J Wood, 'Protection Against Adverse Costs Awards in International Arbitration', (2008) 74(5) *Arbitration* 139, at pp. 142–146. See also, P Yang, 'Costs in International Administered Arbitration', (2009) *Asian Dispute Review* 87, at p. 89.

indication of the amount of time required by the arbitrators to dispose of a case. In addition, parties choosing an institution which applies a fee scale based on the amount in dispute should ensure that the institution applies the scale with some degree of flexibility so that the arbitrators are neither grossly overpaid nor grossly underpaid for the work they have actually done. Parties choosing an institution applying an hourly rate should ensure that someone (either the institution or the parties) carefully checks the reasonableness of the hours claimed, as one would always do when engaging a service based on an hourly rate.

8.92 Parties should be very wary of fee structures which appear to provide low remuneration for arbitrators. Good international arbitrators are usually senior professionals accustomed to receiving fees at least equivalent to the upper end of the fees charged for their profession in their home jurisdictions. If the fee structure is too low, the parties are unlikely to be able to retain appropriately qualified arbitrators, or, if they do, those arbitrators may not be willing to dedicate the amount of time required to deal with the case properly.

6.5 Taxation of costs

8.93 Generally, in international arbitration there is no taxation process as is practised in the common law system. Taxation of costs is the process that may take place in domestic litigation if costs are ordered to be paid by one side but parties cannot agree on the reasonableness of the amount of those costs. In that event, the amount may be determined by a third person authorised by the court, sometimes known as a taxing master.

8.94 One exception to the general position that taxing of costs does not apply in international arbitration is found in Rule 31(2) of the 2007 SIAC Rules. This provides that a party's legal costs are to be taxed by SIAC's Registrar.[127] In the event an arbitral tribunal allows costs to be determined by a taxing master of a national court, care must be exercised. That taxing master would typically issue a final costs certificate. Should there be a need for foreign enforcement, an arbitral tribunal's award on costs would be the better option because it would be covered by the New York Convention. A taxing master's certificate would not. Accordingly, an award of costs by the arbitral tribunal would be preferable.[128] Also, arbitrators – having presided over the case – are familiar with the professional work required for the particular arbitration in question and are thus in a better position than a taxing master to determine the reasonableness of the costs sought.[129]

---

[127] A similar provision is found in the Singapore International Arbitration Act Article 21.
[128] A case related to the enforcement of a costs award is *Commonwealth Development Corp (UK) Ltd v Montague* [2000] QCA 252 (Supreme Court of Queensland Court of Appeal). This case is discussed in Chapter 5, Section 6.4, and also in S Greenberg and M Secomb, 'Terms of Reference and Negative Jurisdictional Decisions: A Lesson from Australia', (2002) 18(2) *Arbitration International* 125.
[129] Yang, op. cit. fn 104, at pp. 220–224.

7 Correction and interpretation of awards

Virtually all arbitration rules contain provisions that enable ambiguities, mistakes or minor errors in an award to be interpreted or corrected after it has been issued by the arbitral tribunal, or for an additional award to be made as to claims not dealt with in the original award.[130] In regard to legislation, Article 33 of the Model Law enables parties to make within 30 days of receipt of the award or another agreed period a request for the arbitral tribunal to:[131]

(i) correct any computational, clerical, or typographical errors in the award;
(ii) interpret a specific point or part of the award; or
(iii) make an additional award as to claims presented but omitted from the award.

8.95

Applications to correct or interpret awards are not all that rare. For example, in 2009, 415 awards were rendered by ICC arbitral tribunals and there were 59 applications under Article 29 of the ICC Rules for the correction or interpretation of an award. Of these 59 applications, 31 were rejected entirely and 28 were accepted, either partially or fully.

8.96

National courts have tended to view the power of an arbitral tribunal to correct or interpret an award restrictively.[132] Likewise, arbitral tribunals have also taken a narrow approach. In *Sedco Inc v National Iranian Oil Co*, the Iran-US Claims Tribunal rejected requests by the respondents to correct, interpret or make an additional award under the equivalent of Articles 35–37 of the 1976 UNCITRAL Arbitration Rules. It took the view that '[t]he Tribunal is without power to entertain the Requests... which amount in effect to a request for an appeal or review of the Award by the Tribunal'.[133] In a SIAC arbitration, it was held that the SIAC rules in force at that time on correction of errors in computation covered miscalculations, use of wrong data in calculations and omission of data from calculations. In the same case, it was also observed that Model Law Article 33 did not empower the arbitral tribunal to correct errors of judgment.[134] As to requests for interpretation, it has been commented that they will be appropriate

8.97

---

[130] See, e.g. ACICA Rules Articles 36–38; CIETAC Rules Articles 47–48; HKIAC Rules Articles 33–35; ICC Rules Article 29; JCAA Rules, Rules 56–58; KCAB International Rules Articles 36–37; SIAC Rules, Rule 28; UNCITRAL Arbitration Rules Articles 35–37; 2010 UNCITRAL Arbitration Rules Articles 37–39. See generally, B Daly, 'Correction and Interpretation of Arbitral Awards under the ICC Rules of Arbitration', (2002) 13(1) *ICC International Court of Arbitration Bulletin* 61.

[131] As to the correction of a clerical error or misnaming of a party in an award by a court hearing an application to enforce the award, see *LKT Industrial Berhad (Malaysia) v Chun* [2004] NSWSC 820 at para 27 (Supreme Court, NSW). See also the ICSID Convention Article 51, which permits an ICSID award to be revised upon discovery of a new fact. Section 11 of the US Federal Arbitration Act gives courts the power to order a modification or correction of an award for various miscalculations of figures, mistakes in description or if the award is 'imperfect in matter of form not affecting the merits of the controversy'.

[132] See, e.g. Judgment of 12 January 2005, DFT 131 III 164 (Swiss Federal Tribunal) (finding that an application for a correction cannot be used as a means to challenge the award). See generally, Born, op. cit. fn 21, p. 2524.

[133] *Sedco Inc v National Iranian Oil Co*, Decision No. DEC 64–129–3 (22 September 1987), 16 Iran-US CTR 282, at para 6.

[134] SIAC Award (parties unidentified), 6 February 1998, CLOUT Case 207, noted in H Alvarez, N Kaplan and D Rivkin, *Model Law Decisions*, Kluwer, 2003, p. 206.

where 'the terms of an award are so vague or confusing that a party has a genuine doubt about how the award should be executed'.[135]

8.98 Some arbitral rules expressly stipulate that no additional fees can be charged by the arbitral tribunal for interpreting, correcting or completing an award as a result of an application by a party.[136] This practice is sensible as long as the application is based on a real oversight of some kind on the part of the arbitral tribunal.

---

[135] Daly, op. cit. fn 130, at pp. 63–64.
[136] See, e.g. ACICA Rules Article 41(4); HKIAC Rules 36(7); UNCITRAL Arbitration Rules Article 40(4). The position under the 2010 UNCITRAL Arbitration Rules has however changed slightly. Article 40(3) of those 2010 Rules permits the arbitral tribunal to charge certain expenses set out in Article 40(2)(b) to (f). The ICC is also reluctant to require parties to pay for post-award interpretations or corrections, despite Article 2(7) of Appendix III to the ICC Rules, which permits the ICC Court to fix an advance to cover fees and expenses resulting from an application for correction or interpretation of an award. See Daly, op. cit. fn 130, at p. 66.

9

The award

Challenge and enforcement

1 Introduction

The two principal subjects dealt with in this chapter are the setting aside of arbitral awards and their enforcement. Once an arbitral tribunal has rendered its final award, the arbitral tribunal usually becomes *functus officio*. But this does not necessarily end the legal process between the parties in respect of that dispute. Post-arbitration litigation may follow. On the one hand, a party dissatisfied with the award may challenge it by attempting to set it aside in a domestic court. On the other, if the award is not honoured voluntarily,[1] a successful party may require court assistance to enforce the award against an uncooperative losing party.

9.1

The challenge and enforcement of awards highlight the delicate balance between the autonomy of the arbitral process and the control of national courts. As Michael Riesman has observed in relation to the enforcement of awards:[2]

9.2

> Too much autonomy for the arbitrators creates a situation of moral hazard – and the theory of moral hazard holds that they are more likely to occur in the absence of controls – national courts will become increasingly reluctant to grant what amounts to preferred and fast-track enforcement of awards. But too much national judicial review will transfer real decision power from the arbitral tribunal, selected by the parties in order to be non-national and neutral, to a national court whose neutrality as between the parties may prove to be considerably less than that of an international arbitral tribunal.

---

1 According to a 2008 arbitration survey, 49% of international arbitral awards are honoured voluntarily. A further 8% result in a settlement agreement after the award. Only 11% were found to end in enforcement proceedings. PricewaterhouseCoopers and Queen Mary College, *International Arbitration: Corporate Attitudes and Practices 2008*.
2 Preface of M Reisman in E Gaillard and D Di Pietro (eds), *Enforcement of Arbitration Agreements and International Arbitration Awards: The New York Convention in Practice*, Cameron May, 2008, p. 1.

9.3 Viewed from a general perspective, the legal framework designed to steer a safe passage between these competing interests emphasises minimal judicial interference. Accordingly, domestic courts are given very limited scope to set aside awards. Similarly, courts that are requested to enforce an award are given very narrow grounds on which to refuse such a request.

9.4 This chapter commences with a general discussion as to the finality of arbitral awards (Section 2). It then proceeds to examine the setting aside of awards (Section 3), recognition of awards (Section 4), award enforcement under the New York Convention (Section 5), and the New York Convention grounds upon which recognition or enforcement of an award may be refused (Section 6), enforcement of awards in non-New York Convention states (Section 7), and the execution of awards (Section 8). The chapter concludes with an examination of some other pertinent issues relating to award enforcement (Section 9).

2 Finality of awards

9.5 As discussed in Chapter 8, arbitral awards are final and binding on the parties.[3] The decision of the Singapore Court of Appeal in *PT Asuransi Jasa Indonesia (Persero) v Dexia Bank SA* reflects the generally accepted position on the finality of arbitral awards in international commercial arbitration. The Court of Appeal held that '[e]rrors of law or fact made in an arbitral decision, per se, are final and binding on the parties and may not be appealed against or set aside by a court'.[4] In the same spirit, the US Supreme Court has ruled that even if the parties expressly agree that an award may be appealed to a court, this will not be permitted.[5] Finality is a very important feature of international arbitration, but three exceptions to this general position may be available to an unsuccessful party:

(i) to appeal on a question of fact or law if permitted under the law of the seat of arbitration or, in rare instances, the arbitral procedural rules;
(ii) to apply to the courts at the seat of arbitration to set aside the award; or
(iii) to wait until a court enforcement action is commenced and then object to enforcement.[6]

9.6 As to the first point, it is rare to find provisions under the *lex arbitri* or a set of arbitral rules that permit international arbitral awards to be appealed. This is due in large measure to the importance placed on finality. One frequently cited exception is the US Grain and Feed Trade Association arbitration rules, which have a self-contained right of appeal to an Arbitration Appeals Committee.[7]

---

3 See Chapter 8, Section 3.7.
4 [2007] 1 SLR 597, para. 57.
5 See Section 3.2.3 below.
6 In relation to the strategy of resisting enforcement rather than challenging the award, see *Dallah Estate and Tourism Holding Company v The Ministry of Religious Affairs, Government of Pakistan*, 20 July 2009, [2009] EWCA Civ 755 (English Court of Appeal), which is discussed in Chapter 5, Section 6.3. Applications to correct or interpret awards also affect finality. See Chapter 8, Section 7.
7 See the US Arbitration Rules of the National Grain and Feed Association Section 9, as amended on 31 March 2009.

One of the most notable domestic laws that permits appeals in international arbitrations is the English Arbitration Act 1996. Pursuant to Section 69(3) of this Act, unless parties otherwise agree,[8] leave to appeal to a court on a question of law will be granted if the court is satisfied:

(a) that the determination of the question will substantially affect the rights of one or more of the parties,
(b) that the question is one which the tribunal was asked to determine,
(c) that, on the basis of the findings of fact in the award –
   (i) the decision of the tribunal on the question is obviously wrong, or
   (ii) the question is one of general public importance and the decision of the tribunal is at least open to serious doubt, and
(d) that, despite the agreement of the parties to resolve the matter by arbitration, it is just and proper in all the circumstances for the court to determine the question.

As is evident from the various provisos quoted above, the English Arbitration Act provides limited avenues of appeal. Appeal provisions of this kind are more prevalent in laws applicable to domestic arbitrations.[9] But some laws designed primarily for domestic arbitration allow parties to an international arbitration to opt into the domestic procedure which may permit court appeals on questions of law.[10]

In investor-state arbitration, a good deal of debate has taken place as to whether an appeals mechanism should be established.[11] No groundswell of

9.7

9.8

---

 8 Section 69(1) permits the parties to agree that there will be no appeals. This agreement is frequently made by adopting a set of arbitral rules that contains a waiver of all rights of recourse (e.g. Article 28(6) of the ICC Rules). A recent English High Court case has held that in an award made under the UNCITRAL Arbitration Rules (which contains no provision that excludes appeal rights), an arbitration clause providing that 'the decision of the majority of the arbitrators . . . shall be final, conclusive and binding on the parties', still did not exclude the parties' right to appeal on a question of law under Section 69 of the English Arbitration Act 1996. It added that to exclude the court's jurisdiction, clearer words were required. See *Shell Egypt West Manzala GmbH and Shell Egypt West Qantara GmbH v Dana Gas Egypt Ltd (Formerly Centurion Petroleum Corporation)* [2009] EWHC 2097 (Comm), para 36.
 9 See Australia's uniform domestic Commercial Arbitration Acts Sections 38–41; Hong Kong's Arbitration Ordinance Section 23; Malaysia's Arbitration Act Section 42; New Zealand's Arbitration Act 1996 Section 6(1)(b) combined with Article 5 of the Second Schedule; and Singapore's Arbitration Act (Cap 10) Section 49.
 10 See, e.g. Article 5 of the Second Schedule to New Zealand's Arbitration Act 1996. This provision applies to all domestic arbitration without the need to opt in. Article 5(10) of Schedule 2 of the New Zealand Act is noteworthy for its detailed definition of a 'question of law':
   (a) includes an error of law that involves an incorrect interpretation of the applicable law (whether or not the error appears on the record of the decision); but
   (b) does not include any question as to whether –
      (i) the award or any part of the award was supported by any evidence or any sufficient or substantial evidence; and
      (ii) the arbitral tribunal drew the correct factual inferences from the relevant primary facts.
See also Section 3(3)(b) (combined with Section 42) of Malaysia's Arbitration Act. But see the view taken by the Singapore Court of Appeal in *Northern Elevator Manufacturing Sdn Bhd v United Engineers (Singapore) Pte Ltd (No. 2)* [2004] 2 SLR 494, [2004] SGCA 11, at para 19 ('a "question of law" must necessarily be a finding of law which the parties dispute, that requires the guidance of the court to resolve. When an arbitrator does not apply a principle of law correctly, that failure is a mere "error of law" (but more explicitly, an erroneous application of law) which does not entitle an aggrieved party to appeal').
 11 See generally, K Sauvant (ed), *Appeals Mechanism in International Investment Disputes*, Oxford University Press, 2008; and F Ortino, A Sheppard and H Warner (eds), *Investment Treaty Law: Current Issues*, British Institute of International and Comparative Law, 2006. As to a review mechanism for the enforcement of international arbitral awards see HM Holtzmann, 'A Task for the 21st Century: Creating a New International Court for Resolving Disputes on the Enforceability of Arbitral Awards' in M Hunter, A Marriott and VV Veeder (eds), *The Internationalisation of International Arbitration: The LCIA Centenary Conference*, Graham and Trotman, 1995, pp. 109–114. This proposal has not been well embraced by the international commercial arbitration community.

unified opinion has yet formed as to the establishment or the eventual parameters of such an appeals mechanism. The debate will likely continue given the increased number of investment arbitration awards and the regular need to interpret and apply provisions of investment treaties that are very similar or identical to those dealt with by other investment arbitral tribunals. In Chapter 10, we discuss an investor-state arbitration internal challenge process – the ICSID annulment mechanism – but this is far from an appeals process.

9.9 As to the second and third options of an unsuccessful party noted above, the Singapore High Court in *Newspeed International Ltd v Citus Trading Pte Ltd*[12] held that these options 'were alternatives and not cumulative'. This position is incorrect. That case concerned a CIETAC award rendered in China in favour of Newspeed. Citus unsuccessfully challenged the award in China's Intermediate People's Court. Subsequently, when Newspeed sought to enforce the award in Singapore, Citus resisted enforcement. The Singapore High Court held that Citus was entitled either to seek to set aside the award before a Chinese court or resist enforcement at the place of enforcement. Because it had exercised the former option, the High Court held it was not permitted to resist enforcement. This decision eviscerates the fundamental rights accorded by the New York Convention to the party opposing enforcement. Nothing in the Model Law or the New York Convention states that a failed setting aside application prevents a party from resisting enforcement of the award in another jurisdiction. And it is doubtful whether *res judicata* would have any application as between a setting aside application and an enforcement proceeding because the causes of action are not the same.[13]

9.10 Moreover, while the Singapore High Court in *Newspeed* referred to Justice Kaplan's Hong Kong High Court decision in *Paklito Investment Ltd v Klockner East Asia Ltd*[14] to support its decision, it did not refer to the Hong Kong Court of Final Appeal's decision in *Hebei Import & Export Corp v Polytek Engineering Co Ltd*.[15] The judgment of Sir Anthony Mason in that latter case also referred to *Paklito* but took a different position:[16]

> In [Paklito] Kaplan J expressed the view that a party faced with a Convention award against him has two options. He can apply to the court of supervisory jurisdiction to set aside the award or he can wait to establish a [New York Convention] ground of opposition... such a party is not bound to elect between the two remedies... (Emphasis added)

9.11 The policy reasons that support the finding in *Newspeed* are understandable. International arbitral awards should as far as possible be final. International

---

12 [2003] 3 SLR 1.
13 See, e.g. M Hwang and S Lee, 'Survey of South East Asian Nations on the Application of the New York Convention', (2008) 25(6) *Journal of International Arbitration* 873, at p. 885.
14 [1993] 2 HKLR 39 at 48.
15 [1999] 2 HKC 205; (1999) XXIVa *Yearbook Commercial Arbitration* 652.
16 Ibid., para 45. He observed at para 46 that 'a failure to raise the public policy ground in proceedings to set aside an award cannot operate to preclude a party from resisting on that ground the enforcement of the award in the enforcing court in another jurisdiction'. See also G Smith, 'Resisting Enforcement of a New York Convention Arbitration Award', (2003) *Asian Dispute Review* 32.

judicial comity requires courts to respect decisions made by foreign courts and re-litigation of issues in different courts should be discouraged. However, these are not inflexible rules. *Newspeed* is too rigid a decision.[17]

3 Challenging awards

The typical mode of challenging an award is to apply to have it set aside by the competent court at the seat of arbitration. Most countries in the Asia-Pacific employ the phrase 'setting aside' of an award, which is also part of the Model Law nomenclature. In the US, however, vacate is the generally used term rather than setting aside.[18] The ICSID annulment procedure should not be fully equated with the setting aside procedures commonly found in domestic laws. The annulment process under the ICSID Convention is discussed in Chapter 10, Section 8.

The discussion in this section will first deal with the issue of state control over awards at the seat of arbitration. It will then consider setting aside at the seat of arbitration, examine the problematic issue of courts setting aside awards made outside their territory, touch upon the period of time within which a setting aside application can be made, and examine briefly the consequences of challenging an award. The section will focus on the Model Law's setting aside provisions because most of the countries in the region have used this as the basis for their international arbitration legislation.[19]

3.1 State control over awards at the seat of arbitration

At the seat of the arbitration, a state effectively offers the support of its judicial system to ensure that the parties' agreement to arbitrate is carried out. Nonetheless, state courts retain an important supervisory role that is intended to prevent the arbitration from deviating from fundamental principles of justice, such as due process. Related to this function of judicial supervision is the power of domestic courts to set aside an international arbitral award issued by an arbitral tribunal seated within its jurisdiction. The power of courts to set aside an award on grounds such as those contained in Article 34 of the Model Law is generally considered of such importance that it cannot be excluded by contract.[20] For

---

17 Even in the Singapore courts, the *Newspeed* principle does not appear to be fully embraced. Justice Prakash in *Aloe Vera of America Inc v Asianic Food Pte Ltd* [2006] 3 SLR 174 narrowed the effect of *Newspeed* by noting that a setting aside application and an application to resist enforcement are usually neither identical nor based on similar grounds.
18 See, e.g. the US Federal Arbitration Act, 9 USC §§ 9–10.
19 Laws that diverge from the Model Law setting aside provisions include Article 70 of Indonesia's Arbitration and Dispute Resolution Act 1999; and Articles 58 and 70 of China's Arbitration Law.
20 Swiss law, which is not based on the Model Law, takes a different approach, see the Swiss Private International Law Act, Article 192. See also the decision of the Swiss Federal Supreme Court in *Cañas v ATP Tour* (ATF 133 III 235, 240/241/242) (2007).

example, New Zealand's Court of Appeal in *Methanex Motunui Ltd v Spellman* took the following approach:[21]

> We conclude later in this judgment that Methanex contracted to exclude review. There would be no unfairness in holding Methanex to that bargain. There can be no suggestion of inequality of bargaining position. Further, there were good commercial reasons for the exclusion of review – that is the anticipated inconvenience and expense of post-award litigation. The agreement by Methanex not to resort to the Court was plainly part of the quid pro quo for the rights that it obtained to participate (albeit in a limited way) in the arbitration. It is scarcely just for Methanex to have participated in the arbitration to the extent provided for in the agreement, and then to be permitted to seek (in defiance of what it agreed) to review the award which that arbitration produced.
>
> Despite the considerations referred to above, we have concluded that the law does not permit the parties to exclude review based on the grounds specified in Article 34.

9.15 The degree of control that should be exercised by the state in which an award is made remains a sometimes controversial question. A fine balance exists between the desire of private parties for flexibility, finality and confidentiality of arbitral awards and the public interest requirements of fair, competent and consistent determinations. However, three strong and decisive arguments offered by Redfern and Hunter tilt the balance in favour of limiting state court control:[22]

> Experience shows . . . that there are serious disadvantages in having a system of arbitration that gives an unrestricted right of appeal from arbitral awards. First, the decisions of national judges may be substituted for the decisions of an arbitral tribunal specifically selected by or on behalf of the parties. Secondly, a party that agreed to arbitration as a private method of resolving disputes may find itself brought unwillingly before national courts that hold their hearings in public. Thirdly, the appeal process may be used simply to postpone the day on which payment is due, so that one of the main purposes of international commercial arbitration – the speedy resolution of disputes – is defeated.

9.16 Other reasons for circumscribing the role of state courts include a domestic judge's possible lack of knowledge or understanding of international commercial arbitration or the potential for perceived local bias.

9.17 The extent of control through state courts of international commercial arbitration is determined by the *lex arbitri*. The narrow setting aside grounds listed in Article 34 of the Model Law provide a good model. Some countries, such as France[23] and Switzerland,[24] have even narrower grounds for setting aside. Other

---

21 *Methanex Motunui Ltd v Spellman* [2004] 3 NZLR 454 (New Zealand Court of Appeal), at paras 107–108. The reference to Article 34 in the quotation is to Article 34 of Schedule 1 of New Zealand's Arbitration Act 1996, which closely corresponds to the identically numbered Model Law provision. See also the New York Convention's recognition of the supervisory authority of a state over arbitral awards rendered in its territory under Article V(1)(e).
22 A Redfern, M Hunter, N Blackaby and C Partasides, *Law and Practice of International Commercial Arbitration*, 4th edn, Sweet & Maxwell, 2004, at para 9–36.
23 See Article 1502 of the French Code of Civil Procedure.
24 See Article 190 of the Swiss Private International Law Act 1987.

countries, including England, have wider setting aside grounds, as well as rights of appeal on points of law to national courts.[25]

The procedure established for challenges to ICSID awards is very different. One major difference is that ICSID awards cannot be challenged in domestic courts. The challenge, in the form of an application for annulment, must be submitted to an ad hoc committee which is an ICSID arbitral tribunal formed specifically to determine that particular challenge.[26] This process is discussed in Chapter 10.

9.18

3.2 Setting aside awards

3.2.1 Setting aside at seat of arbitration

Assuming that country Y has adopted the Model Law, an award rendered by an arbitral tribunal seated in Y may be challenged in Y's courts pursuant to Article 34. (An equivalent procedure exists in all non-Model Law countries). However, successful setting aside actions are relatively rare.[27] Paragraph 1 of Article 34 of the Model Law provides:

9.19

> Recourse to a court against an arbitral award may be made only by an application for setting aside in accordance with paragraphs (2) and (3) of this article.

The thrust of this provision is clear: (i) setting aside is the only recourse that a dissatisfied party can have against an award and (ii) the setting aside application must comply with Article 34(2) and (3). Additionally, the provision needs to be read in conjunction with Model Law Articles 1(2) and 6:

9.20

> [Article 1(2)] The provisions of this Law, except articles 8, 9, 35 and 36,[[28]] apply only if the place of arbitration is in the territory of this State.
>
> [Article 6] The functions referred to in articles 11(3), 11(4), 13(3), 14, 16(3) and 34(2) shall be performed by... [Each State enacting this model law specifies the court, courts or, where referred to therein, other authority competent to perform these functions.]

Supposing the seat of an arbitration is Singapore, then Article 1(2) prescribes that an Article 34 setting aside application in relation to an award rendered in that arbitration must take place in Singapore and it must be made before the Singapore High Court, the court specified for the purposes of Model Law Article 6.[29] This fundamental position relating to the setting aside of awards is reflected in most national arbitration laws.

9.21

---

[25] See Sections 68 and 69 of the English Arbitration Act 1996. As mentioned previously, Section 69 contains a right of appeal. Nevertheless, parties are free to agree not to have such an appeal right. The right of appeal in international arbitration is discussed in Section 2 above.
[26] See Rules 50 and 52 of the ICSID Rules.
[27] See, e.g. AJ van den Berg, 'The New York Convention of 1958: An Overview', in Gaillard and Di Pietro, op. cit. fn 2, p. 39, at p. 62.
[28] The 2006 version of the Model Law has added Articles 17 H, 17 I and 17 J to this list of provisions.
[29] See Section 8 of the Singapore International Arbitration Act. In very rare cases, the arbitration may be governed by the procedural law of a state in which the arbitration is not seated and it may be arguable (as indicated in Article V(1)(e) of the New York Convention) that an award obtained in that arbitration may be set aside not at its seat but in the courts located in the state whose procedural law is applicable.

3.2.2 Setting aside foreign awards

9.22 The vast majority of setting aside applications are filed – as they should be – with the courts at the seat of arbitration. As is evident from Section 3.2.1, that is the correct procedure. Nonetheless, a few courts in the region have deviated from it.

9.23 In *Karaha Bodas Co LLC v Perusahaan Pertambangan Minyak Dan Gas Bumi Negara (Pertimina) (No. 2)*,[30] a Cayman Islands company obtained a US$270 million arbitral award against the Indonesian respondents. Notwithstanding that the seat of arbitration was in Geneva, Switzerland, the Indonesian courts set aside the award. Subsequently, enforcement of the Swiss arbitral award was sought in Hong Kong against one of the respondents, Pertamina, which resisted enforcement inter alia on the ground that the award had been set aside by an Indonesian court. The Hong Kong Court of First Instance held (correctly) that the seat of arbitration was in Switzerland and considered 'the fact that the court in Indonesia has now annulled the award under its own law is . . . a matter which has no effect on this court's task'.[31]

9.24 In *Hitachi Ltd v Mitsui & Co and Rupali Polyester*,[32] the Supreme Court of Pakistan assumed jurisdiction in a challenge to an ICC award resulting from an arbitration seated in England on the basis that the proper law of the contract was Pakistani law. Similarly, the Philippines Court of Appeal in *Luzon Hydro Corporation v Baybay and Transfield Philippines*[33] set aside an award on the basis that it was in breach of Philippines public policy even though the arbitration was seated in Singapore.

9.25 Another decision of concern is that of the Indian Supreme Court in *Venture Global Engineering v Satyam Computer Services*.[34] Although India's Arbitration and Conciliation Act 1996 is based on the Model Law, its Supreme Court held that an award made in an LCIA arbitration seated in London between Indian and US parties, though a foreign award, could be set aside under Section 34 of the Arbitration and Conciliation Act 1996, a provision based on Article 34 of the Model Law. This decision applied Section 34 despite its location in Part I of that Act, which Part applies (pursuant to Section 2(2)) 'where the place of arbitration is in India'. The judgment in *Venture Global* has rightly been criticised for creating new law not found in the Indian Arbitration and Conciliation Act.[35]

Article V(1)(e) refers to the setting aside of an award 'by a competent authority of the country . . . under the law of which . . . that award was made'. See also Chapter 2, Section 4.1 of this book.
30 [2003] 4 HKC 488; [2003] HKCFI 288 (Hong Kong). See generally S Luttrell, 'The Enforcement of Foreign Arbitral Awards in Indonesia: A Comment on *Karaha Bodas Company LLC v Perusahaan Pertambangan Minyak Dan Gas Bumi Negara*', (2008) 74 *Arbitration* 101.
31 [2003] 4 HKC 488; [2003] HKCFI 288, at para 16(h).
32 (2000) XXV *Yearbook of Commercial Arbitration* 486, 10 June 1998.
33 (2007) XXXII *Yearbook of Commercial Arbitration* 456. But see Rule 13.4 of the Philippines Supreme Court Special Rules of Court on Alternative Dispute Resolution, effective October 2009, which states, in part, 'A Philippine court shall not set aside a foreign arbitral award'.
34 (2008) 4 SCC 190; [2008] INSC 40, at para 17. This decision drew heavily from an earlier Indian Supreme Court decision *Bhatia International v Bulk Trading SA* (2002) 4 SCC 105, [2002] INSC 132. This case is discussed in Chapter 7, Section 9.2.
35 See S Kachwaha, 'Enforcement of Arbitration Awards in India', (2008) 4 *Asian International Arbitration Journal* 64, at pp. 77–78. See also S Zaiwalla, 'Commentary on the Indian Supreme Court Judgment in *Venture Global Engineering v. Satyam Computer Services Ltd.*', (2008) 25(4) *Journal of International Arbitration* 507; P Ghosal, 'The Butterfly Effect – Expanding Domain of Public Policy Crippling Arbitration in India', (2008) *Asian Dispute Review* 104; and F Nariman, 'Application of the New York Convention in India', (2008) 25 *Journal of International Arbitration* 893, at p. 898. An encouraging sign is the issuance in April 2010 of a Indian Ministry

The above cases in which awards have been set aside by courts outside the seat of the arbitration do not represent correct international arbitral practice. Fortunately, these types of decisions are rare.

3.2.3 Model Law setting aside grounds and their exclusivity

Article 34(2) of the Model Law lists the six grounds upon which a setting aside action may be based. It provides:

> An arbitral award may be set aside by the court specified in article 6 only if:
> (a) the party making the application furnishes proof that:
>   (i) a party to the arbitration agreement referred to in article 7 was under some incapacity; or the said agreement is not valid under the law to which the parties have subjected it or, failing any indication thereon, under the law of this State; or
>   (ii) the party making the application was not given proper notice of the appointment of an arbitrator or of the arbitral proceedings or was otherwise unable to present his case; or
>   (iii) the award deals with a dispute not contemplated by or not falling within the terms of the submission to arbitration, or contains decisions on matters beyond the scope of the submission to arbitration, provided that, if the decisions on matters submitted to arbitration can be separated from those not so submitted, only that part of the award which contains decisions on matters not submitted to arbitration may be set aside; or
>   (iv) the composition of the arbitral tribunal or the arbitral procedure was not in accordance with the agreement of the parties, unless such agreement was in conflict with a provision of this Law from which the parties cannot derogate, or, failing such agreement, was not in accordance with this Law; or
> (b) the court finds that:
>   (i) the subject-matter of the dispute is not capable of settlement by arbitration under the law of this State; or
>   (ii) the award is in conflict with the public policy of this State.

There are three important aspects to this provision:
(i) Paragraph 2 states that the court <u>may</u> set aside the award if any of the grounds is satisfied. In other words, the court retains a discretion <u>not</u> to set aside an award even if one of the grounds has been established.
(ii) The word 'only' is employed to exclude any ground other than those enumerated.
(iii) The two grounds stipulated in sub-paragraph (b) are grounds that the court of its own initiative may raise, even if not raised by the party challenging the award.

Because all the Article 34 grounds are replicated in Article V of the New York Convention and those Article V grounds are discussed in Section 6 below, they will not be discussed here unless there are cases or issues that require special discussion.

---

of Law & Justice consultation paper, which proposes to amend the Arbitration and Conciliation Act 1996 in a manner that would reverse the *Venture Global* decision.

9.30   Article 34, particularly by reason of the exclusive nature of the setting aside grounds, does not permit a court to entertain a challenge application that concerns the merits (such as findings of fact and law) of the award. This was clearly articulated by the Singapore High Court in *Government of the Republic of the Philippines v Philippine International Air Terminals Co Inc*:[36]

> [A]n arbitral award is not liable to be struck down on application in the courts because of allegations that it was premised on incorrect grounds whether of fact or of law. An application to set aside an award made in an international arbitration is not an appeal on the merits and cannot be considered in the same way as the court would consider the findings of a body over whom it had appellate jurisdiction.

9.31   This position is to be contrasted with the well-known finding in the US Supreme Court decision of *Wilko v Swan* (relating to a domestic arbitral award), holding that an award may be set aside for 'manifest disregard of the law'.[37] However, *Wilko v Swan* appears difficult to reconcile with the strong opinion of the US Supreme Court in the more recent case of *Hall Street Associates, LLC v Mattel Inc*.[38] The Supreme Court in this latter case took the view that the setting aside grounds under the US Federal Arbitration Act are exclusive. This ruling suggests that the 'manifest disregard' doctrine, which is not found in the Federal Arbitration Act, may no longer have a valid place in US law.[39] Moreover, other US courts have refused to apply the 'manifest disregard' ground in foreign award enforcement proceedings.[40]

9.32   On one reading of China's Arbitration Law, courts in China have the power to review the procedure as well as the merits of the award in determining whether to set aside awards issued in Chinese domestic arbitrations.[41] On the other hand, 'foreign-related' awards (i.e. those issued inside China with a foreign element) may only be set aside in China on certain procedural grounds.[42]

---

36 [2007] 1 SLR 278, at para 38. The Singapore Court of Appeal confirmed this position in *PT Asuransi Jasa Indonesia (Persero) v Dexia Bank SA* [2007] 1 SLR 597, at para 57: '[e]rrors of law or fact made in an arbitral decision, per se, are final and binding on the parties and may not be appealed against or set aside by a court except in the situations prescribed under s. 24 of the Act and Article 34 of the Model Law . . . .' See also *ABC Co v XYZ Co Ltd*, [2003] SGHC 107, in which the Singapore High Court affirmed that a setting aside application is not a process for reassessing facts already established in the arbitration; and *Dongwoo Mann and Hummel Co Ltd v Mann and Hummel GmbH*, [2008] SGHC 67, at para 70 (Singapore High Court).
37 346 US 427 (1953) (US Supreme Court) at 436. See also the Indian case of *Oil and Natural Gas v Saw Pipes*, discussed in Section 3.2.4 below.
38 128 S Ct 1396, 2008 (US Supreme Court).
39 See, generally, G Born, *International Commercial Arbitration*, Kluwer, 2009, pp. 2639–2646.
40 See, e.g. *M & C Corp v Erwin Behr GMBH & Co KG*, 87 F 3d 844, p. 851 (6th Cir. 1996) (US Ct of Appeals) ('Article V of the Convention lists the exclusive grounds justifying refusal to recognize an arbitral award. Those grounds . . . do not include . . . manifest disregard of the law'); and *Brandeis Intsel Ltd v Calabrian Chemicals Corp*, 656 Fed Sup 160 (Southern District of New York 1987). Nonetheless, *Wilko v Swan* has been relied on as authority in respect of international arbitration in the Philippines. See *Luzon Hydro Corporation v Baybay and Transfield Philippines*, (2007) XXXII *Yearbook of Commercial Arbitration* 456, at pp. 468–469, paras 29–30. See also *Oil and Natural Gas Corporation v Saw Pipes Ltd* (2003) 5 SCC 705, discussed in Section 3.2.4 below.
41 See particularly, provision 5 of first paragraph of the Chinese Arbitration Law Article 58, which permits a court to consider withheld evidence, and the third paragraph of that Law, which permits a court to set aside an award contrary to the public interest.
42 Article 70 of the Chinese Arbitration Law permits foreign-related awards to be set aside if it involves any of the circumstances in paragraph one of Article 260 of the 1991 Chinese Civil Procedure Law (the equivalent is now Article 258 of the 2008 Revised Civil Procedure Law). That first paragraph does not permit public interest or withheld evidence to be considered, as is permitted for setting aside domestic awards. Additionally, a lower court may not set aside a foreign-related award before its decision is confirmed by China's Supreme People's

9.33 Furthermore, there is strong US Supreme Court authority holding that parties cannot extend by agreement the narrow setting aside grounds in the Federal Arbitration Act, for example to create a right of appeal. In the *Hall Street* case,[43] the US Supreme Court held that parties were not free to expand the limited statutory grounds for setting aside awards by private agreement. The case hinged on the interpretation of Sections 9–11 of the US Federal Arbitration Act, which regulate court confirmation, modification or vacation (setting aside) of arbitral awards. Those provisions permit the setting aside of an award on very narrow grounds, such as corruption, fraud or excess of power. However, the parties' arbitration agreement in this case provided that if either party were dissatisfied with the outcome of the arbitral award, it could appeal to a designated US court. The relevant arbitration clause provided:

> [t]he United States District Court for the District of Oregon may enter judgment upon any award, either by confirming the award or by vacating, modifying or correcting the award. The Court shall vacate, modify or correct any award: (i) where the arbitrator's findings of facts are not supported by substantial evidence, or (ii) where the arbitrator's conclusions of law are erroneous.

9.34 The Supreme Court held that the parties could not by contract widen the Federal Arbitration Act and agree to their own procedure under which courts may vacate (i.e. set aside) an arbitral award on the basis of an arbitrator's legal error.

9.35 Even though *Hall Street* related to a domestic arbitration, its reasoning fits well with the underlying philosophy of international commercial arbitration and is likely to be followed in relation to international arbitrations both in the US and in other jurisdictions.[44] A similar approach was taken by the New Zealand Court of Appeal in *Methanex Motunui Ltd v Spellman*[45] when it held that Article 34 of Schedule 1 of New Zealand's Arbitration Act (which corresponds broadly to the identically numbered Model Law provision):

> is expressed in exclusionary terms: it specifies the only grounds upon which a Court may interfere with an award in review proceedings. Accordingly, it is not open to the parties to a submission to arbitration to confer, by contract, a more extensive jurisdiction on the Court, for instance to review for factual error. On this (perhaps literal) approach, a contractual stipulation which further limits the grounds upon which review is available merely supplements Article 34 and does not derogate from it.

9.36 The Tokyo District Court has also espoused this view in *KK Descente v Adidas-Salomon AG*.[46]

Court under its Notice of Issues concerning Setting Aside Foreign-related Arbitral Awards by the People's Court, 23 April 1998. See generally Lanfang Fei, 'Setting Aside Foreign-Related Arbitral Awards under Chinese Law: A Study in Perspective of Judicial Practice', (2009) 26(2) *Journal of International Arbitration* 237; and Li Hu, 'Introduction to the CIETAC Arbitration Rules 2000', (2003) *Asian Dispute Review* 189, at p. 191.
43 128 S Ct 1396, 2008 (US Supreme Court).
44 But see Born, op. cit. fn 39, p. 2669 ('It is difficult to see why parties should not be permitted to contract for 'ordinary' judicial review, of the sort that would apply if the arbitral award was a first instance judgment.').
45 [2004] 3 NZLR 454, at para 105.
46 Tokyo District Court judgment of 26 January 2004, 1847 Hanrei Jiho 123.

3.2.4 Elaboration or qualification of Article 34 grounds

9.37 As mentioned earlier, the setting aside grounds in Article 34 of the Model Law are exclusive. Nonetheless, some domestic laws elaborate on the Article 34 grounds. For example, Section 24 of Singapore's International Arbitration Act provides:[47]

> Notwithstanding Article 34(1) of the Model Law, the High Court may, in addition to the grounds set out in Article 34(2) of the Model Law, set aside the award of the arbitral tribunal if –
> (a) the making of the award was induced or affected by fraud or corruption; or
> (b) a breach of the rules of natural justice occurred in connection with the making of the award by which the rights of any party have been prejudiced.

9.38 In relation to the breach of the rules of natural justice, such breach should be of a serious nature. The integrity of the setting aside procedure would be undermined if trivial breaches were sufficient.

9.39 The notion of public policy often finds more elaboration in national legislation than the reference to it in Article 34 of the Model Law.[48] For example Section 34 of India's Arbitration and Conciliation Act 1996 contains an 'Explanation', which reads:

> it is hereby declared, for the avoidance of any doubt, that an award is in conflict with the public policy of India if the making of the award is induced or affected by fraud or corruption or was in violation of Section 75[[49]] or Section 81.[[50]]

9.40 Controversy surfaced in the international arbitration community after India's Supreme Court in *Oil and Natural Gas Corporation v Saw Pipes Ltd*[51] held in a setting aside application that an award would be contrary to public policy if it was 'patently illegal'. In the Supreme Court's words 'if the award is contrary to the substantive provisions of law or the provisions of the Act or against the terms of the contract, it would be patently illegal, which could be interfered under Section 34 [of the Indian Arbitration and Conciliation Act]', which closely follows Article 34 of the Model Law.[52] The decision has been the subject of much criticism, particularly because it opens the door for Indian courts to examine the merits of

---

47 For similar qualifications or elaborations of Model Law Article 34, see the Australian International Arbitration Act Section 19; Malaysian Arbitration Act Section 37(2); New Zealand Arbitration Act 1996 Article 34(6) of Schedule 1.
48 See Section 6.3 below.
49 Section 75 of the Indian Arbitration and Conciliation Act requires that a conciliator and parties keep all matters relating to conciliation proceedings confidential, including any settlement agreement that is reached.
50 Section 81 precludes the introduction of evidence in arbitral or judicial proceedings regarding any views made by the other party in respect of settlement or admissions made by the other party during conciliation proceedings or proposals by the conciliator.
51 (2003) 5 SCC 705. Although this case concerned a challenge to an award made in a domestic arbitration, it applied the Model Law setting aside provisions. Under Section 2(2) of the Indian Arbitration and Conciliation Act, the Model Law grounds for setting aside (as replicated in Article 34 of the Indian Act) apply 'where the place of the arbitration is in India'. This provision does not distinguish between arbitrations seated in India which are purely domestic or international.
52 (2003) 5 SCC 705.

an award and because (if accepted) the decision effectively adds another setting aside ground to Article 34.[53]

Fortunately decisions like *Saw Pipes* do not appear in other Asia-Pacific jurisdictions. Although it has been observed that a number of Indian courts have relied heavily on *Saw Pipes*,[54] some lower courts have tried to interpret the decision narrowly.[55] The Indian Supreme Court itself in *McDermott International Inc v Burn Standard Co Ltd*, although considering itself bound by *Saw Pipes*, indicated that it was not questioning the correctness of that decision but at the same time observed:[56]

9.41

> The 1996 Act makes provision for the supervisory role of courts, for the review of the arbitral award only to ensure fairness. Intervention of the court is envisaged in few circumstances only, like, in case of fraud or bias by the arbitrators.
>
> ...
>
> ...patent illegality, however, must go to the root of the matter. The public policy violation, indisputably, should be so unfair and unreasonable as to shock the conscience of the court. Where the Arbitrator, however, has gone contrary to or beyond the expressed law of the contract or granted relief in the matter not in dispute would come within the purview of Section 34 of the Act.

Finally, Indonesia's Arbitration and Dispute Resolution Act 1999 does not refer to any of the Model Law grounds. Instead, Article 70 of that Act states that:

9.42

> An application to annul an arbitration award may be made if any of the following are alleged to exist:
> (a) letters or documents submitted in the hearings are acknowledged to be false or forged or are declared to be forgeries after the award has been rendered;
> (b) after the award has been rendered documents are found which are decisive in nature and which were deliberately concealed by the opposing party; or

---

53 See, e.g. Kachwaha, op. cit. fn 35, p. 68; P Nair, 'Surveying the Decade of the "New" Law of Arbitration in India', (2007) 23(4) *Arbitration International* 699, at pp. 730–734; F Nariman, 'Judicial Supervision and Intervention: Before or during Arbitral Proceedings under the UNCITRAL Model Law of Commercial Arbitration 1985 and under the New Indian Law – the Arbitration and Conciliation Act 1996' in M Pryles and M Moser (eds), *The Asian Leading Arbitrators' Guide to International Arbitration*, JurisNet, 2007, p. 353; Justice AM Ahmadi, 'International Arbitration in India: Issues and Pit-Falls', speech delivered in Malaysia (30 March–1 April 2006), quoted in N Dewan, 'Arbitration in India: An Unenjoyable Litigating Jamboree!', (2007) 3 *Asian International Arbitration Journal* 99, at p. 121; Justice Lahoti, 'International Commercial Arbitration Challenges and Possibilities in Asian Countries (with special reference to India)', paper delivered at seminar on 'Arbitration in India and Singapore: Sharing Perspectives', 27 July 2008, Singapore, pp. 3–4; M Saraf, 'Who is a Party to an Arbitration Agreement – Case of the Non-Signatory', in *ICC-SIAC Symposium: Institutional Arbitration in Asia*, SIAC, 2005, p. 1, at pp. 31–33; N Darwazeh and R Linnane, 'The Saw Pipes Decision: Two Steps Back for Indian Arbitration?', (2004) 19(3) *Mealey's International Arbitration Report* 34; N Darwazeh and R Heinemann, 'Error of Law as a Valid Basis for Setting Aside Awards in India?', (2006) July *Transnational Dispute Management* 1; J Gaya, 'Judicial Ambush of Arbitration in India', (2004) 120 *Law Quarterly Review* 571. But see S Sharma, 'Public Policy under the Indian Arbitration Act: In Defence of the Indian Supreme Court's Judgment in ONGC v Saw Pipes', (2009) 26(1) *Journal of International Arbitration* 133. A positive development is the publication in April 2010 of an Indian Ministry of Law & Justice consultation paper, which proposes to narrow the scope of public policy in the Arbitration and Conciliation Act 1996.
54 See the list of case mentioned in N Darwazeh and R Heinemann, ibid.
55 See, e.g. *Indian Oil Corp Ltd v Langkawi Shipping Ltd* (2004) Arb LR 568, High Court of Bombay; and *Daelim Industrial Co v Numaligarh Refinery Ltd*, High Court of Gauhati, Arbitration Appeal No. 1 of 2002 (24 August 2006). Both cases are cited in Kachwaha, op. cit. fn 35, pp. 68–69.
56 (2006) 11 SCC 181. But see the Indian Supreme Court's judgment in *Venture Global Engineering v Satyam Computer Services* (2008) 4 SCC 190; [2008] INSC 40, at paras 19 and 21, which confirms the *Saw Pipes* 'patently illegal' criteria. *Venture Global* has also been heavily criticised. See Section 3.2.2 above.

(c) the award was rendered as a result of fraud committed by one of the parties to the dispute.

9.43 This provision cannot be compared with any other provision on setting aside an arbitral award in the region. It is curious that fundamental grounds such as party incapacity, due process violations, excess of jurisdiction, irregularity of arbitral tribunal composition and the like do not feature in this Article.

3.2.5 Failure to make a timely objection

9.44 Under Article 34(2)(a)(iv) of the Model Law, a party may apply to set aside an award if 'the arbitral procedure was not in accordance with the agreement of the parties'. However, Article 4 of the Model Law may deprive a party of the benefit of Article 34(2)(a)(iv) if it failed to make a timely objection to an irregularity in the application of the agreed procedure. Article 4 states:

> A party who knows that any provision of this Law from which the parties may derogate or any requirement under the arbitration agreement has not been complied with and yet proceeds with the arbitration without stating his objection to such non-compliance without undue delay or, if a time-limit is provided therefor, within such period of time, shall be deemed to have waived his right to object.

9.45 The procedural rules of arbitral institutions contain similar provisions.[57] Some important features of Article 4 of the Model Law are:[58]
   (i) A deemed waiver cannot apply to a non-derogable provision.
   (ii) The Model Law provision covers only parties who 'know' about a failure to comply with a Model Law provision. Contrast this with Article 8 of the CIETAC Rules which also covers parties who 'should have known' or HKIAC Rules Article 28 that speaks of a party 'who ought reasonably to know'.
   (iii) No writing requirement is contained in Article 4 of the Model Law. Article 8 of the CIETAC Rules, again in contrast, requires the objection to be in written form.

3.2.6 Setting aside jurisdictional decisions

9.46 Article 34(1) of the Model Law requires that a setting aside application be made against an 'arbitral award'. A vexing issue in international commercial arbitration is whether an arbitral tribunal's decision on jurisdiction is an 'arbitral award' subject to a setting aside application.

9.47 Where an arbitral tribunal determines that it possesses jurisdiction (i.e. an affirmative jurisdictional ruling), a means of challenge is explicitly provided in Article 16(3) of the Model Law. Under this provision, a party has immediate recourse to the courts to challenge such rulings. On the other hand, no recourse is prescribed in the Model Law if an arbitral tribunal decides that it lacks jurisdiction (i.e. a negative jurisdictional ruling).[59]

---

[57] See, e.g. CIETAC Rules Article 8; HKIAC Rules Article 28; SIAC Rules, Rule 35(1); ICC Rules Article 33.
[58] Most of the points noted here have been made in J Mo, 'Legality of the Presumed Waiver in Arbitration Proceedings under Chinese Law', (2001) 29 *International Business Lawyer* 21, at pp. 23–24.
[59] Whether or not positive and negative jurisdictional rulings are awards is discussed in Chapter 5, Section 6.2.

3.3 Time limits

The time limit within which to bring a setting aside action varies from country to country. The Model Law has adopted a three-month time period in Article 34(3): 9.48

> An application for setting aside may not be made after three months have elapsed from the date on which the party making that application had received the award or, if a request had been made under article 33,[60] from the date on which that request had been disposed of by the arbitral tribunal.

This time period has been adopted in many of the region's domestic laws.[61] On the other hand, under Article 59 of China's Arbitration Law 1994, an application for setting aside must be made within six months from receipt of the award. 9.49

Some distinctive temporal issues relating to setting aside proceedings are: 9.50

(i) In the Singapore High Court case of *ABC Co v XYZ Co Ltd*, Justice Prakash held that 'the court would not be able to entertain any application lodged after the expiry of the three month period as Article 34 has been drafted as the all-encompassing, and only, basis for challenging an award in court. It does not provide for any extension of the time period and, as the court derives its jurisdiction to hear the application from the Article alone, the absence of such a provision means the court has not been conferred with the power to extend time'.[62] The case involved an application to set aside an award made within three months but several months later the applicants sought to add new grounds to the application. The High Court held that only grounds that arose out of the same facts or substantially the same facts as the originally submitted grounds could be added.[63]

(ii) Under Section 34(3) of the Indian Arbitration and Conciliation Act 1996, the application must be made within three months from the receipt of the award, with an extension of 30 days subject to the showing of sufficient cause. The Supreme Court of India held in *Union of India v Popular Construction Company* that this 30-day period cannot be further extended.[64] That court also held in *Union of India v Tecco Trichy Engineers & Contractors*[65] that in the case of government departments, the time period does not run until the 'person concerned' with the arbitration, and not simply the government department, has received a copy of the award. This decision appears to make possible time extensions beyond the three month plus 30 day legislative period in cases involving government departments. Uncertainty has therefore been injected into the Indian Act.

(iii) Section 36(4) of the Korean Arbitration Act explicitly prohibits an application for the setting aside of an award subsequent to its enforcement by

---

60 Article 33 of the Model Law relates to the correction or interpretation of an award or issuance of an additional award.
61 See, e.g. Indian Arbitration and Conciliation Act Section 34(3); Korean Arbitration Act Section 36(3); Malaysian Arbitration Act Section 37(4); New Zealand Arbitration Act Section 34(3) and also Acts which give the Model Law the force of law, such as the Australian International Arbitration Act.
62 [2003] SGHC 107, at para 9.
63 Ibid., at para 21.
64 (2001) 8 SCC 470.
65 (2005) 4 SCC 239.

a Korean court. This provision was enacted to override a provision in an earlier version of that Act which enabled a party to apply to set aside an award after its enforcement was ordered.[66] Theoretically, at least, the new law does not prohibit the setting aside of an award that has been enforced by a court outside of Korea.

3.4 Consequences of challenge

9.51 Depending on the applicable law, a court hearing a challenge to an award may (i) rule in favour of the challenge and set aside the award in whole or in part; (ii) vary parts of the award; (iii) remit the award to the arbitral tribunal for reconsideration; or (iv) refuse to set aside the award despite the applicant having established one or more grounds. An unsuccessful challenge obviously leaves the court no other option but to refuse to set aside the award. However, should a setting aside action be unsuccessful at the seat of the arbitration, this does not preclude the unsuccessful applicant from subsequently resisting enforcement of that same award.[67]

9.52 As mentioned previously, the award annulment procedure under the ICSID Convention is to be contrasted with the diverse options afforded to courts in resolving a setting aside action. A challenge to an ICSID award is not heard by a court but by an arbitral tribunal known as an ad hoc committee. As the name of the process suggests, the powers of the ad hoc committee are limited to annulling all or part of an award. The ad hoc committee cannot vary parts of the award or resubmit it to the original arbitral tribunal. If an annulment application succeeds, the matter must be resubmitted not to the original arbitral tribunal but rather to a newly constituted arbitral tribunal.[68]

9.53 From the perspective of an enforcement action, if the courts at the seat of arbitration have set aside or suspended an award, the enforcing court may refuse to enforce the award pursuant to Article V(1)(e) of the New York Convention.[69] On a number of occasions, particularly in the US and France, courts have enforced awards that have been previously annulled at the seat of the arbitration.[70] Additionally, if an action to set aside an award is pending and, at the same time, an application for enforcement of that award is made in another country, Article VI of the New York Convention gives the court determining the enforcement application the discretion to adjourn its proceedings.[71]

9.54 It must not be forgotten that even if an award is set aside by a court, many jurisdictions provide for the possibility of appealing that court decision to a higher court. Under Section 37 of the Indian Arbitration and Conciliation Act, for example, an appeal is available from a court's decision either to set aside or refuse to set aside an award.[72]

---

66 J-H Choe and K Dharmananda, 'The Enforcement of Arbitral Awards in Korea: Procedure and Potential Challenges', (2006) 2 *Asian International Arbitration Journal* 60, at p. 72.
67 *Hebei Import & Export Corp v Polytek Engineering Co Ltd*, [1999] 1 HKLRD 665.
68 See Article 52(6) of the ICSID Convention and Rule 55 of the ICSID Rules.
69 See Section 6.2.5 below.
70 See Chapter 2, Section 5.2.1.
71 See Section 6.4 below.
72 See also Philippine Alternative Dispute Resolution Act 2004 Section 46.

4 Recognition of awards

Although the New York Convention deals with both recognition and enforcement of awards, the former receives considerably less attention than the latter. Nonetheless, the importance of the recognition of awards should not be underestimated. An enforcement action, for example, cannot take place without recognition (often implicit) of the award by the enforcing court.[73] Moreover, a need to recognise an award without enforcement may arise when a court action is filed involving the same parties to the arbitration and in respect of the same subject matter or dispute determined in the arbitration. In that instance, the party that succeeded in the arbitration may ask the court for formal recognition that the award binds the parties. It may also seek to invoke the award as a set-off or a counterclaim. The approach of the court will depend on its applicable domestic law and persuading the court to recognise the facts or points of law as determined by the arbitral tribunal may prove difficult.[74]

9.55

Article III of the New York Convention requires that '[e]ach Contracting State shall recognise arbitral awards as binding . . .'.[75] Along similar lines, some domestic laws deal with recognition specifically. Section 29(2) of the Singapore Arbitration Act, for example, provides:

9.56

> Any foreign award which is enforceable under subsection (1) shall be recognised as binding for all purposes upon the persons between whom it was made and may accordingly be relied upon by any of those parties by way of defence, set-off or otherwise in any legal proceedings in Singapore.

A notable omission in the Agreement on Mutual Enforcement of Arbitral Awards between Hong Kong and mainland China is any reference to recognition of awards. Accordingly, uncertainty exists as to the ability to make a 'recognition only' application in Chinese courts of an award obtained in Hong Kong and vice versa.[76]

9.57

5 Enforcement of New York Convention awards

The enforcement of awards is one of the main advantages of international commercial arbitration over international litigation. There would be little point in arbitration if the eventual award could not be enforced against the losing party.

9.58

In domestic legal systems, legislation usually provides for the enforcement of arbitral awards made within that state against property or other assets. By and large, that system is not problematic because a state's governmental

9.59

---

[73] See, e.g. Singapore International Arbitration Act Section 27(2) ('[i]n this Part, where the context so admits, 'enforcement' . . . includes the recognition of the award as binding for any purpose').
[74] See AJ van den Berg, *The New York Convention of 1958: Towards a Uniform Interpretation*, Kluwer Law, 1981, p. 244.
[75] Recognition is also mentioned in Article I(1) and (3), Article IV(1) and (2), Article V(1) and (2), Article VII(1) and Article XIII(3) of the New York Convention.
[76] J Lee, 'A Review of the Enforcement of Hong Kong Awards in Mainland China', (2006) *Asian Dispute Review* 52, at p. 55.

control – legal and physical – ordinarily extends to assets within its territory. Problems arise, however, where an award is obtained in one state but its enforcement is sought in another. Sensitive and complex issues of state sovereignty and the extraterritorial effect of decisions arise. The primary solution to these enforcement issues in international commercial arbitration is embodied in the New York Convention. The background and history of this Convention are set out in Chapter 1.

9.60 The effectiveness of the New York Convention is central to the popularity of international arbitration as a dispute resolution method.[77] A frequent point of comparison is the extraterritorial enforcement of domestic court judgments. The 2005 Hague Convention on Choice of Court Agreements adopts a similar mechanism for the recognition and enforcement of civil and commercial court judgments as does the New York Convention for arbitral awards.[78] However, this Convention is not yet in force. Mexico so far is the only state to have acceded to it.[79] Until it is ratified by numerous countries, arbitral awards will have in their transnational enforceability a considerable advantage over domestic court judgments. At the time of writing, 144 states had become parties to the New York Convention.[80]

9.61 The essence of award enforcement under the New York Convention is encapsulated in Article III, pursuant to which state signatories have undertaken to:

---

[77] See, e.g. R Briner and V Hamilton, 'The History and General Purpose of the Convention: The Creation of an International Standard to Ensure the Effectiveness of Arbitration Agreements and Foreign Arbitral Awards', in Gaillard and Di Pietro, op. cit. fn 2, p. 21 ('Thanks to the extent of the support won by the Convention, there now exists a system guaranteeing the effectiveness of arbitration in most countries and certainly in all major trading nations'); M Blessing, 'The New York Convention: Major Problem Areas', in M Blessing (ed), *The New York Convention of 1958*, ASA Special Series No. 9, 1996, p. 17, at p. 18 ('the Convention is truly a centre piece/corner stone for international business and trade and, at the same time, its safety-net and life-vest' (emphasis omitted)); K-H Böckstiegel, 'Future Perspectives', in Gaillard and Di Pietro, op. cit. fn 2, p. 865 ('It is obvious that the Convention on one hand contributed to and on the other hand has become part of the success story of international arbitration in general within the framework of international trade and investment and of international law.').

[78] See, e.g. Articles 8 and 9 of Hague Convention on Choice of Court Agreements, which deal with the recognition and enforcement of court judgments, or refusal thereof. See Chapter 1, fn 43. Of interest for the Asia-Pacific region is the Agreement between the Government of Australia and the Government of New Zealand on Trans-Tasman Court Proceedings and Regulatory Enforcement that was signed on 24 July 2008 but at the time of writing was not yet in force.

[79] The US and European Community have signed the Convention. Both are expected to ratify it soon.

[80] A list of contracting states is set out in Appendix 4 of this book. Almost every major trading nation in the Asia-Pacific region has signed the New York Convention. One major exception is Taiwan (Republic of China). But still Taiwan has implemented provisions similar to the New York Convention in its 1998 Arbitration Law. See for instance Articles 49 and 50 of that Arbitration Law, which are similar to the New York Convention Article V grounds. A specific law (Article 74 of Taiwan's Act Governing Relations between Peoples of the Taiwan Area and the Mainland Area) governs Taiwan's recognition of arbitral awards obtained in mainland China (People's Republic of China). In respect of recognition and enforcement of Taiwanese awards in mainland China, in 1998 the PRC Supreme People's Court promulgated the 'Regulation Regarding the People's Court Recognizing Civil Judgments of a Court of Taiwan'. Under Article 19 of that Regulation, it applies also to arbitral awards rendered in Taiwan. See generally M Chao and JC Huang, 'Arbitration in Taiwan', in Hon Mr Justice Ma and N Kaplan (eds), *Arbitration in Hong Kong: A Practical Guide*, Sweet & Maxwell, 2003, pp. 538–542; and N Kaiser, 'Recognition and Enforcement of Foreign Arbitral Awards in Taiwan', (2009) 4 *AFIA News*, September, p. 4. A number of Pacific Island states are also not parties to the New York Convention. For the position in the Pacific Islands, see S Greenberg, S Fitzgerald and B Gehle, 'International Commercial Arbitration Practice in Australia, New Zealand and the Pacific Islands' in HA Grigera Naón and PE Mason (eds), *International Commercial Arbitration Practice: 21st Century Perspectives*, Lexis Nexis, 2010, Ch 15.

recognise arbitral awards as binding and enforce them in accordance with the rules of procedure of the territory where the award is relied upon, under the conditions laid down in the [Convention's] articles.

9.62 The attractiveness of the New York Convention is rooted in the simplicity of its procedures and the limited grounds afforded to national courts to refuse award enforcement. The revolutionary nature of the Convention is neatly articulated by Michael Reisman:[81]

> The genius of the United Nations Convention on the Recognition and Enforcement of Foreign Arbitral Awards is to be found in the way in which it mobilises national courts as enforcement agencies while simultaneously restricting their scope of national judicial supervision over international arbitration awards.

9.63 In addition to its genius, the success of the New York Convention may also be attributed to its genesis. Robert Briner and Virginia Hamilton have written that the Convention:[82]

> owes its success to several factors. One of these was undoubtedly the conditions in which it was born. As the product of concerted efforts by governments, jurists and the business community, it reflected the aspirations of all those most directly concerned. The text itself was drawn up by specialists and was adjusted and refined through informed discussion amongst plenipotentiaries and practitioners with expert knowledge in the field and with the input of interested consultative bodies. It is perhaps this unique combination of interests that gave to the New York Conference a sense of realism. Rather than attempting the impossible, the Conference sensibly sought to address the most pressing practical problems experienced by the post war-business world. In so doing, it took the path of moderation and pragmatism by producing an exhaustive list of basic requirements for the recognition and enforcement of awards. It gave effect to the will of the parties without asking States to renounce their legal systems. This approach may have been modest and cautious, but it was above all judicious, for not only did it ensure the effectiveness and acceptability of the Convention but also gave it a far-reaching legacy.

9.64 The respect that the New York Convention commands among arbitration practitioners and arbitrators is reflected in Lord Mustill's oft-quoted observation (made two decades ago) that it 'perhaps could lay claim to be the most effective instance of international commercial legislation in the entire history of commercial law'.[83] Since Lord Mustill wrote those words, more than 50 additional states have become parties to the Convention. After being in force for almost half a century, the respect for and effectiveness of this treaty show no signs of abatement.

9.65 A paradox of the New York Convention is that although so many cases and volumes of academic literature exist on the Convention, recourse to it is relatively rare for a number of reasons. Many international arbitrations, for instance, settle well before a final award is made. As an example, between 44–48% of all ICC

---

81 Preface of M Reisman in Gaillard and Di Pietro, op. cit. fn 2, p. 1.
82 Briner and Hamilton, op. cit. fn 77, pp. 19–20.
83 M Mustill, 'Arbitration: History and Background', (1989) 6(2) *Journal of International Arbitration* 43.

arbitrations were withdrawn before a final award was made over the three-year period ending in December 2009.[84]

9.66 And even where an award is issued, most awards are complied with voluntarily. One recent survey of major companies involved in arbitration ('Pricewaterhouse Survey') reported that:[85]

> 84% of respondents indicated that the opposing party had honoured the award in full in more than 76% of cases. Only 3% reported that an award debtor had failed to comply with the award. During the interviews, corporate counsel reported that more than 90% of the awards were honoured by the non-prevailing party.

9.67 The preservation of a business relationship was the principal reason given during that survey for voluntary award compliance. As to non-compliance, only in 11% of cases did the interviewed participants proceed to enforce an award and only 19% of the corporations surveyed encountered difficulties with the enforcement of arbitral awards.[86] Out of that 19%, 70% encountered difficulties due to the lack of debtor assets or an inability to identify such assets and 6% ran into difficulties because the country of enforcement was not a party to the New York Convention.[87]

9.68 Notwithstanding these positive findings, there is room for New York Convention enforcement to improve. At the forefront of the calls for change to the New York Convention is Albert Jan van den Berg, possibly the world's leading expert on the subject. He has argued that the Convention requires many modifications, including additions and the revision of existing provisions, some of which he considers unclear or outdated.[88] His solution to the problem is to establish a new 'Convention on International Enforcement of Arbitration Agreements and Awards' that aims to build on the structure and concepts of the New York Convention.[89] Some have responded to his proposal by drawing attention to

---

[84] Details on ICC statistics can be found in the ICC's Published Statistical Reports for each year. See for example ICC, '2009 Statistical Report', (2010) 21 *ICC International Court of Arbitration Bulletin* 1. A different figure was obtained for settlements in arbitrations generally (25%) in the 2008 PricewaterhouseCoopers and Queen Mary College survey, op. cit. fn 1, p. 2.

[85] PricewaterhouseCoopers and Queen Mary College, op. cit. fn 1, p. 8. For other surveys and commentary on enforcement rates in the region, see R Peerenboom, 'Seek Truth from Facts: An Empirical Study of Enforcement of Arbitral Awards in the PRC', (2001) 49 *American Journal of Comparative Law* 249, at p. 254 (on China); Remarks by Justice Wan E'Xian, Vice President of China's Supreme People's Court, at Academic Conference Celebrating the 50th Anniversary of the New York Convention, Beijing, 6 June 2008, cited in N Darwazeh and F Yeoh, 'Recognition and Enforcement of Awards under the New York Convention – China and Hong Kong Perspectives', (2008) 25 *Journal of International Arbitration* 837, at pp. 839–840, n. 15 (on China); Kachwaha, op. cit. fn 35, p. 81 (on India); and Darwazeh and Yeoh, ibid., pp. 850–851 (on Hong Kong).

[86] PricewaterhouseCoopers and Queen Mary College, op. cit. fn 1, p. 10.

[87] Ibid.

[88] See 'A Closer Look at the "New New York Convention"', (2008) 3(3) *Global Arbitration Review* 14. AJ van den Berg unveiled his 'Hypothetical Draft Convention on the International Enforcement of Arbitration Agreements and Awards' in his keynote speech at the Plenary Session of the 2008 Dublin ICCA Congress. Related documents drafted by him, including 'An Explanation of the Proposed Changes', 'A Comparison of the New York Convention 1958 and What is Proposed' and 'What the 'New' New York Convention Could Look Like . . .' are available at www.arbitration-icca.org/articles.html.

[89] This hypothetical convention has been referred to as the 'Dublin Convention' as it was first proposed by Albert Jan van den Berg at the 2008 ICCA Congress in Dublin.

the practical difficulties associated with states amending the New York Convention or concluding a new treaty. Others consider that the present problems may be solved by better education of the judiciary as to the terms of the current Convention.[90] It remains to be seen whether states will act on any of van den Berg's proposals.

In regard to the application of the Convention in the Asia-Pacific, the Pricewaterhouse Survey noted that respondents cited China most often as the country where difficulties were likely to be encountered in enforcement and execution proceedings. India was also specifically cited as potentially problematic.[91] Additionally, Bose, Yap and Jaliwala have observed:[92]

9.69

> the mere ratification by a country of the New York Convention does not guarantee its effective and expedient implementation. Despite the pro-enforcement language of the New York Convention, the reality is that enforcement of arbitration awards remains problematic in many countries in the world including several Asian jurisdictions. Corruption, local protectionism, faulty regulation, ignorance and systemic inefficiency make enforcement proceedings difficult, time-consuming and sometimes impossible.

Bose, Yap and Jaliwala identify a number of significant problems enforcing arbitral awards under the New York Convention in China, India, Indonesia, Thailand and Vietnam but they also point to reform efforts in these countries to overcome some of the identified problems.[93]

9.70

Australia also has a somewhat unique award enforcement problem if enforcement under the Convention is required in two or more of its internal states or territories. In such a situation, it may be necessary to file multiple parallel enforcement proceedings in the Supreme Courts of the relevant internal states or territories. To overcome this inconvenience, Australia is expected to amend its International Arbitration Act, which will empower its Federal Court to grant Australia-wide enforcement in one centralised order.[94]

9.71

5.1 Implementation of the New York Convention

In most national legal systems, for treaty provisions to have effect in domestic law, they must be implemented by the signatory state through domestic legislation

9.72

---

90 See 'Q&A with Albert Jan van den Berg', (2008) 3(3) *Global Arbitration Review* 21.
91 PricewaterhouseCoopers and Queen Mary College, op. cit. fn 1, p. 11.
92 R Bose, N Yap and A Jaliwala, 'Enforcement of International Arbitral Awards in Asia – Paying Lip Service to the New York Convention', International Congress of Maritime Arbitrators, XVI Congress Papers, Singapore, 2007.
93 Ibid. In relation to China, see Jingzhou Tao, *Arbitration Law and Practice in China*, 2nd edn, Kluwer Law International, 2008, p. 193, para 541 (quoting a CIETAC report which stated '[a]mong the awards refused enforcement and or set-aside by the People's Courts, some did have mistakes, while some were rejected or set aside only because the People's Courts did not fully understand arbitration, or the Courts interpreted the laws too strictly, or even because the Courts were influenced by local protectionism.').
94 See the Australian Federal Justice System Amendment (Efficiency Measures) Bill (No. 1) 2008.

or regulations. An action commenced in a domestic court in respect of rights afforded by a treaty is thus usually possible only by invoking domestic laws and regulations that implement the treaty.

9.73   *Navigation Maritime Bulgare v PT Nizwar*[95] illustrates the point. The New York Convention had been ratified by Indonesia and it had entered into force for that country in January 1982. Nonetheless, the Indonesian Supreme Court held in *Navigation Maritime* that at the time of the enforcement proceedings (1984) foreign arbitral awards were not enforceable under the New York Convention regime because Indonesia had not yet implemented that treaty in its territory through domestic regulations. Similarly, in *Bangladesh Air Service (Pvt) Ltd v British Airways PLC*,[96] it was noted that although Bangladesh had acceded to the New York Convention, it had not passed legislation incorporating the Convention into national law. As a result, the New York Convention could not be relied upon to enforce a foreign award in Bangladesh.[97]

9.74   While the consequence of a state's failure to implement the New York Convention may be that it is inapplicable in that state as a matter of national law, a state party to the New York Convention may still be responsible under international law if an arbitral agreement or award is not recognised or enforced as required by the Convention.[98]

9.75   The method of implementing treaty obligations varies from country to country. In Australia, for example, the text of the New York Convention has not been adopted verbatim. A rephrased version of that text is contained in Sections 3–9 of its International Arbitration Act, although the Convention is annexed to the legislation. In contrast, Article 39(1) of the Korean Arbitration Act simply provides without any further elaboration that '[r]ecognition or enforcement of a foreign arbitral award to which the [New York Convention] applies shall be granted in accordance with the Convention'. China's Arbitration Law includes no reference to the New York Convention. Instead, China's Supreme People's Court has issued a 'Notice Regarding the Implementation of the Convention on the Recognition and Enforcement of Foreign Arbitral Awards Acceded to by China'[99] (China's New York Convention Implementation Notice), which requires that:[100]

---

95 (1986) XI *Yearbook of Commercial Arbitration* 508.
96 (1998) XXIII *Yearbook of Commercial Arbitration* 624, at p. 625 (Bangladesh Appellate Division).
97 Ibid.
98 In *Saipem SpA v Bangladesh*, ICSID Case No. ARB/05/7, Award of 30 June 2009, at paras 163–169 the ICSID arbitral tribunal held that Bangladesh breached international law because its national courts violated Article II of the New York Convention by unlawfully revoking the authority of arbitrators in an ICC arbitration. This was a bilateral investment treaty claim (in other words, it was a claim based on international law) instituted by an Italian company. The case is discussed in Section 9.2 below.
99 Issued by the Supreme People's Court on 10 April 1987 and effective on the same date. Fa Jing Fa (1987) No. 5.
100 One reason why the New York Convention is not contained in a law is that in China treaties may have effect without the need for their implementation through domestic law. See Wang Sheng Chang, 'The Practical Application of Multilateral Conventions Experience with Bilateral Treaties Enforcement of Foreign Arbitral Awards in the People's Republic of China', (1998) 9 *ICCA Congress Series* 461, p. 468.

The Higher People's Courts and the Intermediate People's Courts shall promptly arrange economic and civil judges, enforcement personnel and other related personnel to carefully learn this important Convention and enforce in accordance with the Convention.

While the great majority of Asia-Pacific countries have ratified the New York Convention and properly implemented it, the following are examples of some occasional implementation problems that have arisen in the region: 9.76

(i) Prolonged delays in the implementation of the New York Convention through domestic legislation – in Indonesia, it took nine years;[101] in The Philippines, the Senate ratified the New York Convention in 1965 but specific implementing legislation was enacted only in 2004, under its Alternative Dispute Resolution Act.[102]

(ii) Excessive formal requirements in addition to the documentary requirements of New York Convention Article IV – in Indonesia 'a certification from the diplomatic representative of the Republic of Indonesia in the country in which the International Arbitration Award was rendered' is required and this certification must state 'that such country and the Republic of Indonesia are both bound by a bilateral or multilateral treaty on the recognition and implementation of International Arbitration Awards'.[103]

(iii) Defects in drafting the implementing legislation – in India, the implementing legislation, the Indian Foreign Awards (Recognition and Enforcement) Act 1961, was said to be a 'dead letter' because it contained a drafting defect, cured only after amending legislation was enacted in 1973.[104]

(iv) Substantive differences between New York Convention provisions and the laws or notices implementing them – China's New York Convention Implementation Notice states that if any Article V(1) criteria of the Convention is satisfied, 'the application for recognition and enforcement of award shall be refused' (Emphasis added). This departs from the wording of the New York Convention, which provides that a court may refuse enforcement if any of the Article V refusal grounds are satisfied.[105] In Australia, the legislation implementing the New York Convention has omitted the word 'only' in its provision that corresponds to Article V(1) of that treaty.[106]

(v) Excessive complexity in the implementing laws – in Pakistan the New York Convention has been implemented by a Presidential Ordinance that

---

[101] M Hwang and Yeo Chuan Tat, 'Recognition and Enforcement of Arbitral Awards' in Pryles and Moser, op. cit. fn 53, p. 415.
[102] Ibid., p. 421.
[103] Article 67(2)(c) of the Indonesian Arbitration and Dispute Resolution Act. The authors are aware of a case in which it took one year to obtain and register these formal documents with an Indonesian court whereas the actual arbitral proceedings had taken only six months. See also Hwang and Yeo Chuan Tat, ibid., p. 415.
[104] See FS Nariman, 'Finality in India: the Impossible Dream', (1994) 10 *Arbitration International* 373, at pp. 377–378.
[105] See Jingzhou Tao, op. cit. fn 93, p. 373; Wang Sheng Chang, op. cit. fn 100, p. 470. See also Bose, Yap and Jaliwala, op. cit. fn 92, pp. 1–2. This issue is discussed further in Section 6 below.
[106] See the Australian International Arbitration Act Section 8(5). See also Hwang and Yeo Chuan Tat, op. cit. fn 101, p. 410.

automatically lapses after four months. Consequently, it must be re-enacted every four months, resulting in repeated enactments of this Ordinance. There is a risk under this confusing system that an enforcement application may be brought under the wrong Ordinance and dismissed on merely technical grounds.[107]

9.77 Official gazette notification of a country's New York Convention ratification may also prove problematic, if not fatal, to an enforcement application. This problem arose in *Sri Lanka Cricket v World Sports Nimbus Pte Ltd*,[108] which concerned an enforcement application in Malaysia in respect of an award obtained in an arbitration seated in Singapore. The Malaysian Court of Appeal decision was based on the 1985 Malaysian New York Convention on the Recognition and Enforcement of Foreign Arbitral Awards Act (this Act has since been repealed by Malaysia's Arbitration Act 2005). Section 2(2) of the Act required that:

> the Yang di-Pertuan Agong [the constitutional King and Malaysian head of state] may, by order in the Gazette, declare that any State specified in the order is a party to the New York Convention, and that order shall, while in force, be conclusive evidence that that State is a party to the said Convention.

9.78 The Court of Appeal held that because Malaysia had made a reciprocity reservation under the New York Convention and because Singapore was not gazetted in the manner prescribed by Section 2(2) – even though Singapore was a New York Convention party – the Convention could not be applied and enforcement of the award was refused.

9.79 During an appeal from that decision, the Malaysian Attorney-General's department obtained leave to intervene. But the matter was settled out of court. It appears that the Attorney-General would have argued that the Singapore award should have been recognised.[109] The problem has now been addressed by Section 38 of the Malaysian Arbitration Act 2005, which has dispensed with the gazetting requirement.[110]

9.80 China has encountered a unique problem implementing the New York Convention. Prior to the United Kingdom's handover of Hong Kong to China in 1997, awards made in Hong Kong and enforced in China were subject to the

---

107 See Hwang and Yeo Chuan Tat, op. cit. fn 101, p. 422. The Ordinance is the Recognition and Enforcement (Arbitration Agreements and Foreign Arbitral Awards) Ordinance 2005 (No. VIII of 2005).
108 [2006] 3 MLJ 117 (Malaysia, Court of Appeal). See generally, A Nasruddin, 'Singapore Awards not Enforceable in Malaysia?', (2006) *Asian Dispute Review* 134.
109 Hwang and Yeo Chuan Tat, op. cit. fn 101, p. 420.
110 But see the view of Hwang and Lee, op. cit. fn 13, p. 882. Singapore's gazetting requirement (former Section 32 of its International Arbitration Act) was repealed on 1 January 2010 by its International Arbitration (Amendment) Act 2009. Part II of India's Arbitration and Conciliation Act 1996, which concerns the enforcement of foreign awards, applies only to foreign awards obtained in countries that have been declared by India's central government Official Gazette to be countries to which the New York Convention applies. It has been said recently that less than 50 countries have been Gazetted in this way. See Justice AK Sikri, 'Recognition and Enforcement of Awards in India', paper delivered at arbitration seminar on 'Arbitration in India and Singapore: Sharing Perspectives', 27 July 2008, Singapore, p. 5, n. 18. See also Kachwaha, op. cit. fn 35, p. 75. Article 10 of the Australian International Arbitration Act states that 'a certificate purporting to be signed by the Secretary to the Department of Foreign Affairs and stating that a country specified in the certificate is, or was at a time so specified, a Convention country, is, upon mere production, receivable in any proceedings as prima facie evidence of that fact'.

New York Convention. However, problems arose when Hong Kong became a Special Administrative Region of China. As a consequence, the New York Convention, which applies between two contracting states, no longer remained applicable between them. It took almost two years to fill the legal vacuum that was created. The solution took the form of the Arrangement Concerning Mutual Enforcement of Arbitral Awards between the Mainland [China] and the Hong Kong Special Administrative Region ('MOU').[111] The MOU created a regime whereby arbitral awards rendered in Hong Kong and enforced in China, or vice versa, would be treated as New York Convention awards.[112] Prior to the MOU taking effect, there was a period during which Mainland Chinese courts and Hong Kong courts refused to enforce each other's awards.[113]

9.81 *Hong Kong Heung Chun Cereal & Oil Food Co Ltd v Anhui Cereal & Oil Food Import & Export Co*[114] is an illustrative case. The award at issue was obtained in an arbitration seated in Hong Kong. Enforcement was sought in October 1998 and the matter ended up in the Chinese Supreme People's Court. That court held that because Hong Kong had become a special administrative region on 1 July 1997, the New York Convention did not apply to the enforcement of Hong Kong awards in China after that date. Further proceedings were stalled as no legislative provisions were promulgated to enable awards obtained in Hong Kong to be enforced in mainland China. The case resumed only in 2000 subsequent to the conclusion of the MOU.[115]

9.82 Even with the MOU, it was still uncertain whether ad hoc or non-Chinese arbitral institution awards obtained in Hong Kong could be enforced in the Mainland. This unresolved issue was finally laid to rest at the end of 2009 through a Supreme People's Court notification, which states that the MOU applies to enforcement of ad hoc and foreign arbitral institution awards.[116]

9.83 The above examples demonstrate that it may not be sufficient to check simply whether a country has ratified the New York Convention when planning enforcement strategies. Other factors such as a country's implementation of the New York Convention or its administrative procedures may prove extremely important in assessing the prospects of enforcement.

---

111 The MOU was signed on 21 June 1999. For a detailed analysis of the MOU, see Xian Chu Zhang, 'The Agreement between Mainland China and the Hong Kong SAR on Mutual Enforcement of Arbitral Awards: Problems and Prospects', (1999) 29 *Hong Kong Law Journal* 463; and for an examination of court rulings relating to it see Fei Lanfang, 'Enforcement of Arbitral Awards between Hong Kong and Mainland China: A Successful Model?', (2009) 8(3) *Chinese Journal of International Law* 621.
112 A similar arrangement was negotiated between Macau and mainland China: Arrangement between the Mainland and Macau SAR on Reciprocal Recognition and Enforcement of Arbitral Awards, signed 30 October 2007, entered into force on 1 January 2008. See a discussion of this arrangement in R Pé and M Polkinghorne, 'Two Steps Forward, One Step . . . Sideways – Recent Developments in Arbitration in China', (2008) 25 *Journal of International Arbitration* 407.
113 See Xiaobing Xu and G Wilson, 'One Country, Two-International Commercial Arbitration-Systems', (2000) 17(6) *Journal of International Arbitration* 47.
114 Supreme People's Court (2003) Civil 4 Miscellaneous No. 9, cited in Hwang and Yeo Chuan Tat, op. cit. fn 101, p. 417.
115 Hwang and Yeo Chuan Tat, op. cit. fn 101, p. 417.
116 China's Supreme People's Court Notification regarding the enforcement of Hong Kong arbitral awards in mainland China, 30 December 2009.

5.2 Enforcement at the seat of arbitration

9.84 Two options are possible for the enforcement of an arbitral award within the jurisdiction of the seat of arbitration. First, for enforcement purposes, courts at the seat may not consider the award as falling within the scope of the first sentence of Article I(1) of the New York Convention because it is not a 'foreign award' but rather may treat it as an 'international award' issued within its territory.[117] For example, in Australia, Section 3 of the International Arbitration Act defines a 'foreign award' as 'an arbitral award made, in pursuance of an arbitral agreement, in a country other than Australia, being an arbitral award in relation to which the [New York Convention] applies'. According to that Australian Act, an award obtained in an arbitration in New South Wales involving a claimant from Singapore and a respondent from Hong Kong would not constitute a 'foreign award' under the New York Convention. If enforcement of this award were required in Australia, Articles 35 and 36 of the Model Law could be invoked because the award would have been obtained in an 'international arbitration' within the Article 1(3) Model Law definition.[118]

9.85 In some countries the above type of 'international' award may arguably also be enforced under the New York Convention regime if the enforcing court considers that this award is one that is 'not considered as domestic' pursuant to the second sentence in Article I(1) of that Convention.[119] This enforcement option is not available in Australian courts because Australia has not implemented the second sentence of Article I(1) of the New York Convention in its legislation. Under Chinese law, awards issued inside China are either 'foreign-related awards' (these involve a foreign element) or purely 'domestic awards'. Despite some Chinese judgments to the contrary, 'foreign-related awards' are generally considered not to be 'foreign awards' subject to enforcement in China under the New York Convention.

5.3 Bilateral and multilateral enforcement agreements

9.86 In addition to the New York Convention, there are a number of bilateral and regional agreements between states that aim to facilitate the enforcement of foreign arbitral awards. Article VII(1) of the New York Convention[120] provides, in part, that the Convention:

> shall not affect the validity of multilateral or bilateral agreements concerning the recognition and enforcement of arbitral awards entered into by the Contracting States...

---

117 See, e.g. S Barrett-White and C Kee, 'Enforcement of Arbitral Awards where the Seat of the Arbitration is Australia: How the Eisenwerk Decision might still be a Sleeping Assassin', (2007) 24 *Journal of International Arbitration* 515, at p. 516.
118 See ibid. at pp. 516–517; and van den Berg, 2008, op. cit. fn 27, pp. 41–42.
119 See, e.g. *Bergesen v Joseph Muller Corp* 710 F.2d 928 (2d Cir. 1983), at 932 (US Court of Appeals) (an award issued in New York under New York law in an arbitration between two foreign parties was held to be non-domestic). See also *Jacada (Europe) Ltd v International Marketing Strategies Inc*, 401 F. 3d 701 (6th Cir. 2005), at 708 (US Court of Appeals).
120 On this provision, see generally E Gaillard, 'The Relationship of the New York Convention with Other Treaties and with Domestic Law', in Gaillard and Di Pietro, op. cit. fn 2, pp. 69–87.

Two prominent multilateral treaties dealing with enforcement of arbitral awards are the 1975 Panama Convention[121] and the 1961 European Convention on International Commercial Arbitration.[122] Bilateral treaties that include provisions on award enforcement usually concern other matters as well, such as trade, commerce or investment protection.[123]   9.87

The second part of Article VII(1) of the Convention, often referred to as the 'more-favourable-right' provision, states that it: 9.88

> shall not . . . deprive any interested party of any right he may have to avail himself of an arbitral award in the manner and to the extent allowed by the law or the treaties of the country where such award is sought to be relied upon.

This means that if a conflict arises between the New York Convention and the domestic law of the enforcing state or another international convention signed by that state, the more favourable right to enforce an award will prevail. The Okayama District Court applied this more-favourable-right provision to give preference to the 1974 Japan-China Trade Agreement over the New York Convention in a case involving the recognition and enforcement of an arbitral award.[124]   9.89

5.4 Application of the New York Convention

5.4.1 Scope

The New York Convention facilitates the enforcement of a wide range of awards, including those which assess and order damages, make declaratory statements as to the rights of the parties and require specific performance.[125] Article I(1) of the Convention sets out its scope of application in respect of enforcement. It states: 9.90

> This Convention shall apply to the recognition and enforcement of arbitral awards made in the territory of a State other than the State where the recognition and enforcement of such awards are sought, and arising out of differences between persons, whether physical or legal. It shall also apply to arbitral awards not considered as domestic awards in the State where their recognition and enforcement are sought.

---

[121] The Inter-American Convention on International Commercial Arbitration, reprinted in (1975) 14 ILM 336, signed 30 January 1975, entered into force 16 June 1976. See also D Hascher, 'Enforcement of Arbitral Awards – the New York, Panama and Montevideo Conventions', in 'International Commercial Arbitration in Latin America', *ICC International Court of Arbitration Bulletin*, Special Supplement, December 1996; and AJ van den Berg, 'The New York Convention 1958 and the Panama Convention 1975: Redundancy or Compatibility', (1989) 5 *Arbitration International* 214; van den Berg, (1981) op. cit. fn 74, pp. 101–105.

[122] (1963–1964) 484 *United Nations Treaty Series* 364, signed 21 April 1961, entered into force 7 January 1964. See generally, van den Berg, (1981) op. cit. fn 74, pp. 92–98.

[123] See, e.g. Article IV of the US-Japan Treaty of Friendship, Commerce and Navigation, signed on 2 April 1953 and entered into force on 30 October 1953. See generally van den Berg, (1981) op. cit. fn 74, pp. 105–113.

[124] *Zhe-jiang Provincial Light Industrial Products Import & Export Corp v Takeyari KK*, (1997) XXII *Yearbook of Commercial Arbitration* 744, at p. 746, para 8, District Court, Okayama, 14 July 1993. See generally Gaillard, op. cit. fn 120, pp. 69–87.

[125] The features of an 'award' are discussed in Chapter 8. See generally D Di Pietro, 'What Constitutes an Arbitral Award Under the New York Convention?', in Gaillard and Di Pietro, op. cit. fn 2, pp. 139–160. As to the enforcement of investment treaty arbitral awards under the New York Convention, see T Nakamura, 'The Application of the New York Convention to Investment Arbitration', (2009) 24(3) *Mealey's International Arbitration Report* 25.

9.91 Aside from the description contained in Article I(1), no further definition of 'arbitral awards' is included in the Convention, except that Article I(2) provides:

> The term 'arbitral awards' shall include not only awards made by arbitrators appointed for each case but also those made by permanent arbitral bodies to which the parties have submitted.

9.92 Unlike the title of the New York Convention, which refers to 'foreign' awards, no express reference is made to that term in the text of the Convention. Nonetheless, it is beyond doubt that 'arbitral awards' referred to in the first sentence of Article I(1) means 'foreign awards' because they must have been made in a state other than the enforcing state. Except for the other criteria stipulated in that sentence and, if applicable, the reciprocity or commercial reservation requirements (discussed below), no other requirement is necessary for an award to fall within the scope of the first sentence of Article I(1) and therefore be covered by the New York Convention regime.

9.93 A different view of Article I(1) was (incorrectly) taken by the Indian Supreme Court in *National Thermal Power Corporation v The Singer Company*.[126] In that case, the Supreme Court held that an ICC award made in England was not a foreign award but a domestic Indian award that fell outside the scope of the New York Convention. The court reasoned as follows:[127]

> An award is 'foreign' not merely because it is made in the territory of a foreign State, but because it is made in such a territory on an arbitration agreement not governed by the law of India. An award made on an arbitration agreement governed by the law of India, though rendered outside India, is attracted by the saving clause in Sect. 9 of the Foreign Awards Act and is, therefore, not treated in India as a 'foreign award'.

9.94 This interpretation does not correspond with the plain language of Article I(1) of the New York Convention. Effectively, the Indian Supreme Court's interpretation adds an extra criterion to that provision, i.e. in addition to the territorial requirement, the arbitration agreement also needs to be governed by a foreign law.

9.95 The second sentence of Article I(1) of the New York Convention provides that in addition to foreign awards, the Convention 'shall also apply to arbitral awards not considered as domestic awards in the State where their recognition and enforcement are sought'.[128] These awards are referred to as 'non-domestic' awards. What constitutes such awards is a difficult question. Born has neatly summarised the types of possible 'non-domestic' awards as follows:[129]

---

126 (1993) XVIII *Yearbook of Commercial Arbitration* 403.
127 Ibid., at p. 409, para 18. The Foreign Awards Act referred to in this quotation was subsequently repealed.
128 See *Wuxi Woco-Tongyong Rubber Engineering Co Ltd v Zueblin Int'l GmbH* discussed in Section 6.2.1 below. In that case the Wuxi Intermediate People's Court determined that an award made in an ICC arbitration seated in China fell within the meaning of the second sentence in Article V(1) as it was non-domestic. But under Chinese law, it would have more logically been a 'foreign-related' award issued inside China, the enforcement of which was governed by China's Civil Procedure Law.
129 Born, op. cit. fn 39, p. 2380.

(i) an award made in the State where enforcement is sought under the procedural law of another State; and/or (ii) an award made in the State where enforcement is sought under the arbitration law of that State but regarding a dispute involving an international element; and/or (iii) an award that is regarded as 'a-national' in that it is not governed by any arbitration law.

But the overwhelming approach of national jurisdictions is that 'non-domestic' awards are those made in a territory outside of the enforcing court's national territory. In effect, these jurisdictions consider that little difference exists between 'non-domestic' and 'foreign' awards.[130] A contrasting approach is found in the US. In *Bergesen v Joseph Muller Corp*, for example, an award issued in New York under New York law concerning an arbitration between two foreign parties was held to be non-domestic under the New York Convention because it involved parties domiciled outside the enforcing jurisdiction.[131] However, as Born has noted, the result of this case may have been influenced by the terms of the US implementing legislation of the New York Convention.[132]   9.96

In comparison with the New York Convention, the scope of enforceable decisions under the ICSID Convention is more limited. Article 54(1) of the ICSID Convention imposes on signatory states a duty to enforce only the 'pecuniary obligations' imposed by the award subject to enforcement. No such limitation is found in the New York Convention.   9.97

Despite the relatively wide scope of the New York Convention, types of decision not generally considered to fall within its scope are procedural orders. These may include, for example, orders for document production, hearing of witnesses or other interim orders.[133] An oft-cited case from the region on this point is *Re Resort Condominiums International Inc v Bolwell*[134] in which the Queensland Supreme Court in Australia held that an interlocutory or interim order – described by the arbitral tribunal in that case as an 'Interim Arbitration Order and Award' – did not constitute an 'award.'[135] The basis of the court's decision was that as the so-called award did not finally dispose of any disputed matters between the parties that were agreed to be resolved by arbitration, it was not in fact an award. If the decision had included a final decision on an aspect of the merits of the dispute, it would have been enforceable under the New York Convention.[136] However, it has been commented in relation to this case that there is no reference   9.98

---

130 Ibid., p. 2381.
131 710 F 2d 928 (2d Cir. 1983), at 932 (US Court of Appeals). See also *Jacada (Europe) Ltd v International Marketing Strategies Inc*, 401 F 3d 701 (6th Cir. 2005), at 708 (US Court of Appeals).
132 Born, op. cit. fn 39, p. 2381. Under Section 202 of the US Federal Arbitration Act, an award is non-domestic if the award's relationship with a foreign state 'involves property located abroad, envisages performance or enforcement abroad, or has some other reasonable relation with one or more foreign states.' 9 USC, Section 202. For a practical summary as to the enforcement of an Asian award in the US generally, see J-H Yeum, 'What an Asian Company Needs to Know about Enforcing Arbitral Awards in the United States', (2005) *Asian Dispute Review* 90.
133 See also Chapter 8, Section 5.3.
134 (1993) 118 ALR 655, 29 October 1993, (Qld Supreme Court). See also (1995) XX *Yearbook of Commercial Arbitration* 628, at p. 641.
135 The Interim Arbitration Order and Award, inter alia, restrained the respondents from carrying out certain activities until a final award was issued. (1995) XX *Yearbook of Commercial Arbitration* 628, at pp. 629–630.
136 See R Garnett and M Pryles, 'Recognition and Enforcement of Foreign Awards under the New York Convention in Australia and New Zealand', (2008) 25(6) *Journal of International Arbitration* 899, at p. 909.

440   INTERNATIONAL COMMERCIAL ARBITRATION

in the New York Convention to finality as an enforcement condition. Rather, the New York Convention refers to awards that are 'binding'.[137] It should also be noted that there are cases in which courts have considered orders or interim measures to be enforceable under the New York Convention because of their content, despite their name.[138] An arbitral tribunal's order may be enforceable at the seat of arbitration under domestic legislation as if the order had been made by a court.[139]

9.99   For the sake of completeness it should be mentioned that the New York Convention facilitates the enforcement of awards. It cannot be used to set aside an award.[140] Only a court at the seat of arbitration can set aside an award. Moreover, even if a court refuses enforcement pursuant to the Convention, that decision affects only the enforceability of the award in that state and has no effect on the validity of the award itself. The determination of an award's validity should be left to the courts at the seat of arbitration. Therefore, an Indonesian court's refusal to enforce an award issued in an arbitration seated in Thailand on the basis that due process violations had occurred during the arbitration does not per se prevent the enforcement of that award in Singapore. If, however, that award is set aside by the courts of Thailand, the Singapore courts may refuse enforcement.

5.4.2 Reciprocity reservation

9.100   By virtue of Article I(3) of the New York Convention, a contracting state may limit the Convention's scope by declaring that it will apply the Convention 'to the recognition and enforcement of awards made only in the territory of another Contracting State' (the 'reciprocity reservation').

9.101   Making this reservation limits the application of the New York Convention to awards issued in other states that are parties to that Convention. However, given the current number of states that have signed the Convention, the reciprocity reservation does not create a major barrier. Numerous countries in the region have made a reciprocity reservation, including India, Indonesia, Japan, Korea, China, Malaysia, New Zealand, Pakistan, the Philippines, Singapore and Vietnam.

---

[137] See D Howell, 'Interim Measures of Protection in International Arbitration Proceedings: Towards a New Paradigm?', (2006) *Asian Dispute Review* 18, at p. 20.
[138] See, e.g. *Publicis Communications & Publicis SA v True North Communications Inc.*, 203 F 3d 725 (7th Cir 2000); and *Braspetro Oil Services Co v Management and Implementation of the Great Man-Made River Project*, (Paris Court of Appeal) (1999) XXIVa *Yearbook of Commercial Arbitration* 296; *Southern Seas Navigation Ltd v Petroleos Mexicanos of Mexico City*, 606 F Supp 492 (SDNY 1985). See also T Kojović, 'Court Enforcement of Arbitral Decisions on Provisional Relief: How Final is Provisional?', (2001) 18 *Journal of International Arbitration* 511.
[139] See, e.g. Singapore International Arbitration Act Section 12(6).
[140] See *Compagnie de Saint-Gobain – Pont à Mousson v Fertilizer Corporation of India Ltd*, 28 August 1970, (High Court of Delhi), (1977) II *Yearbook of Commercial Arbitration* 245, discussed in van den Berg, 1981, op. cit. fn 74, pp. 20–22. In *Gulf Petro Trading Co. v Nigerian National Petroleum Corp.*, 512 F.3d 742 (5th Cir. 2008) (US Court of Appeals) the court held that it was 'undisputed that the [New York] Convention precludes a court of secondary jurisdiction [i.e. the enforcing court] from vacating, setting aside, or modifying a foreign arbitral award'.

It is worth noting that the Model Law enforcement provision requires no reciprocity. Article 35 states:

> An arbitral award, <u>irrespective of the country in which it was made</u>, shall be recognised as binding and, upon application in writing to the competent court, shall be enforced subject to the provisions of this article and of article 36. (Emphasis added.)

9.102

Australia did not make a reciprocity reservation under Article I(3). However, the approach of its implementing legislation is effectively one of reciprocity. Thus Section 8 of the Australian International Arbitration Act states that a foreign award will be recognised and enforced in Australia only if it is made in a Convention country or if the party invoking the award is either domiciled or ordinarily resident in Australia or another Convention country. Richard Garnett and Michael Pryles rightly assert that this inconsistency between its treaty obligations and domestic law potentially exposes Australia to liability under public international law in the event a party seeks to enforce an award in Australia but is refused because neither the award nor party has a connection with a Convention country.[141]

9.103

Japan, on the other hand, has made a reciprocity reservation but its Arbitration Law states that its enforcement provisions shall apply to an arbitral award 'irrespective of whether or not the place of arbitration is in the territory of Japan'.[142] Nowhere in this Act is a limitation that reflects Japan's reciprocity reservation.

9.104

Trying to enforce an award made in an arbitration seated in Taiwan in a New York Convention contracting state that has made the reciprocity reservation may be problematic. That other state cannot enforce Taiwanese awards under the New York Convention regime because Taiwan is not a New York Convention state. Many nations, such as Australia, have additional problems because they do not recognise Taiwan as a sovereign state. This lack of recognition raises the interesting question as to whether it is contrary to public policy to enforce an award obtained in a state not recognised by the enforcing state. From the Australian perspective, Michael Pryles has argued persuasively that an award issued in Taiwan may be enforced in Australia and is not contrary to its public policy.[143]

9.105

5.4.3 Commercial reservation

By virtue of Article I(3) of the New York Convention, contracting states may also limit the Convention's scope of application 'to differences arising out of legal relationships, whether contractual or not, which are considered as commercial under the national law of the State making such declaration' (the 'commercial reservation'). Fewer states have made this reservation in comparison with those that have made a reciprocity reservation. Countries in this region having

9.106

---

[141] Garnett and Pryles, op. cit. fn 136, p. 901.
[142] See Japanese Arbitration Law Article 45.
[143] M Pryles, 'The Recognition and Enforcement of Taiwan Arbitral Awards in Australia', (2007) 11 *Vindobona Journal* 25.

made the commercial reservation include India, Indonesia, China, Malaysia, the Philippines and Vietnam.

9.107 A good example of the generally accepted interpretation of the meaning of 'commercial' in Article I(3) of the New York Convention is provided by the Indian Supreme Court:[144]

> The term 'commercial' should be given a wide interpretation so as to cover matters arising from all relationships of a commercial nature, whether contractual or not ...

9.108 This interpretation mirrors the definition of 'commercial' in the second footnote of the Model Law. The Indian Supreme Court added that this interpretation is consistent with the purpose of the New York Convention and with the promotion of international trade and commercial relations. In China's Notice of the Supreme People's Court on the Implementation of the New York Convention, 'commercial relations' comprise 'relationships arising out of contracts, torts or relevant provisions of law'.[145]

9.109 Under the 1995 Vietnamese Ordinance on Recognition and Enforcement of Foreign Awards (now repealed), an enforceable award was required to involve 'a dispute relating to commercial law relations under the law of Vietnam'. Difficulties arose as to the meaning of this phrase in *Tyco Services Singapore Pty Ltd v Leighton Contractors (VN) Ltd*.[146] The case related to an arbitration seated in Australia concerning a contract to construct a hotel in Vietnam. Two awards were made in favour of Tyco. It sought enforcement in Vietnam, which was granted by the trial court but this decision was reversed by Vietnam's Court of Appeal of the Supreme People's Court. One of the issues before the Court of Appeal concerned whether a construction contract constituted a 'commercial law relation' within the meaning of the 1995 Ordinance. The Court of Appeal interpreted this phrase narrowly, basing its interpretation on two Vietnamese commercial regulations. As a consequence, the court concluded that the awards fell outside the scope of the 1995 Ordinance and therefore were not enforceable.[147] It has been said that there were other Vietnamese laws that also could have been consulted (but were not) and that these would have provided a broader meaning of 'commercial', keeping the interpretation consistent with the international practice described above.[148]

9.110 Conversely, the new Vietnamese legislation on enforcement of foreign awards includes a definition of 'commercial' that has been criticised as being too broad.[149]

---

[144] *RM Investments Trading Co Pty Ltd v Boeing Co*, (1994) 4 SCC 541.
[145] Promulgated on and effective on 10 April 1987.
[146] Judgment No. 02/PTDS, 21 January 2003 (Court of Appeal of the Supreme People's Court of Vietnam, Ho Chi Minh City).
[147] Vietnamese legislation was amended by the Ordinance on Commercial Arbitration of 2003, which now defines 'commercial activity' as including, among other things, construction. On the Vietnamese reforms, see generally, Bose, Yap and Jaliwala, op. cit. fn 92, p. 6.
[148] R Garnett and K Nguyen, 'Enforcement of Arbitration Awards in Vietnam', (2006) 2 *Asian International Arbitration Journal* 137, at pp. 141–142. See also Quang Chuc Tran, 'Recognition and Enforcement of Foreign Awards in Vietnam – Shortcomings and Suggested Remedies', (2005) 22 *Journal of International Arbitration* 487.
[149] The Civil Procedure Code (Law on Civil Proceedings (National Assembly)), 15 June 2004. See Garnett and Nguyen, ibid., p. 150.

Under Article 342(2) of that law, the meaning of commercial may extend to labour or employment contracts. It has been suggested that under international arbitration standards this is unlikely to comport with the meaning of 'commercial' in the New York Convention.[150]

5.4.4 Documents required for enforcement

The beauty of the New York Convention enforcement process lies in its simplicity. The role of national courts is trimmed back to an almost administrative function of ordering the award to be enforced. According to Article IV(1), only two items must be furnished by the party seeking enforcement:[151]

9.111

(a) The duly authenticated original award or a duly certified copy thereof;
(b) The original agreement referred to in article II or a duly certified copy thereof.

States are free to make their procedures even less onerous if they wish. Japan is an example. Article 46 of the Japanese Arbitration Law does not require the submission of the arbitration agreement.

9.112

In contrast, some jurisdictions require additional documents. As mentioned previously, Article 67(2)(c) of the Indonesian Arbitration and Dispute Resolution Act requires a third document – a certificate from an Indonesian diplomatic representative in the country where the award was made. In implementing the New York Convention, China has also adopted an application process more complex than the Article IV requirements. In China, in addition to the two items required by Article IV(1), the Regulations of the Supreme People's Court concerning Issues in Relation to Enforcement by the People's Court[152] require applicants:

9.113

(i) to submit a written explanation of the reasons for the application;
(ii) to identify the object against which the award is to be enforced;
(iii) to submit information as to the status of the property belonging to the party against whom enforcement is sought;
(iv) to submit proof of the applicant's identity or proof that the applicant is the successor or assignee of the judgment creditor;
(v) to submit a power of attorney where there is legal representation; and
(vi) to submit any other documents or identification as required by the court.

In connection with the last point, the court is given a wider discretion to request documents than is normally granted to a court in determining a New York Convention enforcement application. It has been said that this discretion may enable a Chinese court to request evidentiary documents relied on by the arbitral

9.114

---

[150] Garnett and Nguyen, ibid., p. 150. They add that the drafting history of the UNCITRAL Model Law and judicial commentary indicate that labour or employment contracts are not commercial. They also note, however, that the US Federal Arbitration Act takes the opposite position.
[151] This provision is replicated in many domestic statutes: see, e.g. Article 37(2) of the Korean Arbitration Act. For an extensive guide to requirements under national laws for enforcement under the New York Convention, see ICC Commission on Arbitration, 'Guide to National Rules of Procedure for Recognition and Enforcement of New York Convention Awards', (2009) *ICC International Court of Arbitration Bulletin*, Special Supplement.
[152] Fa Shi (1998) No. 15, promulgated by the Supreme Court on 8 June 1998. See F Yeoh, 'Enforcement of Dispute Outcomes' in M Moser (ed), *Managing Business Disputes in Today's China: Duelling with Dragons*, Kluwer, 2007, p. 259, at pp. 265–266; and Jingzhou Tao, op. cit. fn 93, p. 163, para 459 and p. 189, para 533.

tribunal in making its award.¹⁵³ This goes well beyond the simple enforcement procedure contemplated under the New York Convention.

9.115   Although not as problematic as China's additional requirements, India also has a requirement in addition to the two in Article IV(1) of the New York Convention. Article 47(1)(c) of the Indian Arbitration and Conciliation Act requires production not only of the original award and the arbitration agreement but also 'such evidence as may be necessary to prove that the award is a foreign award'.

9.116   Additionally, if the documents required in Article IV(1) are not in an official language of the country in which the enforcement application is made, Article IV(2) of the New York Convention prescribes:

> the party applying for recognition and enforcement of the award shall produce a translation of these documents into such language. The translation shall be certified by an official or sworn translator or by a diplomatic or consular agent.

5.5 Temporal issues

5.5.1 Retroactivity of New York Convention

9.117   The general rule in treaty law is that treaties do not have retroactive effect unless a different intention appears from the treaty or is otherwise indicated.¹⁵⁴ The New York Convention is silent as to this issue. The preparatory work of the Convention is inconclusive as to whether its drafters intended the New York Convention to be applied retroactively.¹⁵⁵

9.118   Different approaches have been adopted by different states. Section 14 of the Australian International Arbitration Act expands the scope of the Convention to all awards made before it entered into force in Australia. In contrast, Section 28(2) of Singapore's International Arbitration Act expressly excludes the application of the New York Convention to awards made before the date of its entry into force for Singapore.¹⁵⁶

5.5.2 Time limits

9.119   Domestic laws often specify a time limit within which an enforcement application must be made. Under Thailand's Arbitration Act 2002, for example, the time limit for enforcing a foreign award is three years from the date of receipt of the award. In Hong Kong, it is six years from the date on which the award was

---

[153] Yeoh, ibid., p. 266. Article 30 of the Chinese Supreme People's Court's 'Judicial Interpretation on Relevant Issues Concerning the Application of the PRC Arbitration Law', dated 23 August 2006, Fa shi [2006] No. 7, authorises courts to require arbitral institutions to explain or produce documents in relation to applications to set aside or enforce arbitration awards. See, generally, G Johnston and S Kou, 'The Latest Incremental Reform of Chinese Arbitration Law', (2007) *Asian Dispute Review* 13.
[154] See Article 28 of the Vienna Convention on the Law of Treaties, adopted on 22 May 1969, entered into force on 27 January 1980, 1155 *United Nations Treaty Series* 331.
[155] van den Berg, 1981, op. cit. fn 74, p. 73.
[156] See generally M Pryles, 'Reservations Available to Member States: The Reciprocal and Commercial Reservations' in Gaillard and Di Pietro, op. cit. fn 2, pp. 170–172; and van den Berg, 1981, op. cit. fn 74, pp. 72–80.

dishonoured.[157] In Australia, the applicable law is the Limitation Act applicable in the relevant Australian state, which is generally the same in each state. In New South Wales for example, the limitation period is 12 years for an arbitration agreement made by deed, or otherwise six years.[158]

Japan is unusual in that it does not have a specific limitation period for the enforcement of arbitral awards. In countries where no such period is specifically prescribed, the applicable time limit may be controlled by a general law dealing with limitation periods. The Indian Arbitration and Conciliation Act, for instance, contains no period within which to bring an enforcement application. In the absence of such a provision, courts in India have held that the limitation period is governed by the residual provision prescribed in India's Limitation Act 1963, according to which a three-year period is applicable.[159]

Issues may arise as to when the limitation period starts to run. The court in the Australian case of *Antclizo Shipping Corp v Food Corp of India* held that a reasonable period should be allowed for the losing party to make voluntary payment, after which time begins to run for the award to be enforced.[160] In that case, three months was considered a reasonable period for voluntary payment.

5.5.3 Delays in enforcement

In the Pricewaterhouse Survey, 57% of respondents indicated that enforcement and execution of their arbitral awards had taken less than one year and 14% successfully completed the enforcement process in less than six months. On the other hand, in 5% of cases the enforcement process took between two and four years.[161] Short proceedings were principally credited to the success of the New York Convention whereas lengthy proceedings were usually blamed on local bureaucracy.[162]

An exceptional case in terms of delays in enforcement is *Revpower Ltd v Shanghai Far East Aerial Technology Import and Export Corporation*.[163] It took the successful party in that case two years to register a Stockholm Chamber of Commerce award with the Shanghai Intermediate People's Court. Only after pressure from the Supreme People's Court did the Shanghai Intermediate People's Court

---

157 Section 4(1)(c) of the Limitations Ordinance (Cap 347). See also D Brock, 'Recognition and Enforcement of the Arbitral Award' in Hon Mr Justice Ma and N Kaplan (eds), *Arbitration in Hong Kong: A Practical Guide*, Sweet & Maxwell, 2003, p. 439, at p. 458, para 15–42. In China, it is two years, see Article 215 of the PRC Civil Procedure Law, as amended on 1 April 2008. See Jingzhou Tao, op. cit. fn 93, p. 163, para 557.
158 Australian state of New South Wales' Limitation Act 1969 Section 20.
159 Kachwaha, op. cit. fn 35, pp. 79–80.
160 Supreme Court of Western Australia, M Bredmeyer, 6 November 1998 (unreported), cited in Garnett and Pryles, op. cit. fn 136, p. 902. The case follows *International Bulk Shipping & Service v Minerals Trading Corp* [1996] 1 All ER 1017 (English Court of Appeal).
161 PricewaterhouseCoopers and Queen Mary College, op. cit. fn 1, p. 12.
162 Ibid.
163 The case is unreported but summarised in Wang Sheng Chang, op. cit. fn 100, p. 496. See also Wang Guiguo, 'One Country, Two Arbitration Systems: Recognition and Enforcement of Arbitral Awards in Hong Kong and China', (1997) 14 *Journal of International Arbitration* 5, at pp. 27–28.

accept the case. Even after registration, the Shanghai court is said to have used delay tactics and ultimately dismissed the enforcement application on the ground that the award debtor had filed for bankruptcy and lacked any assets against which enforcement could be sought. It has been suggested that during the period of the delay, the Chinese party transferred its assets to other companies.[164] In response to this case, the Supreme People's Court decreed that local courts must order enforcement within two months from the date enforcement is sought, and that the enforcement process should be completed within six months from the date of that order.[165]

9.124 In the Chinese case of *Hong Kong Heung Chun Cereal & Oil Food Co Ltd v Anhui Cereal & Oil Food Import & Export Co*,[166] the time between the initial application for enforcement and the final decision, which denied enforcement, appears to have been around five years.[167] However, this case is somewhat exceptional as there were delays resulting from the British handover of Hong Kong to mainland China without an agreement on how Hong Kong awards would be enforced in mainland China.[168]

9.125 Bose, Yap and Jaliwala, in their commentary on problematic enforcement processes in Asia, have reported the following award enforcement periods as being of concern in the Asian region: Vietnam – more than one year; India – six to 12 months for uncontested applications and up to two years for contested applications; and Thailand – eight to 18 months at first instance and even longer where an appeal is made to the Supreme Court.[169]

9.126 Some jurisdictions permit appeals for court decisions in relation to the enforcement of arbitral awards, which may also prolong the enforcement process. In certain jurisdictions an appeal is allowed only if a court refuses enforcement.[170] In others, an appeal may be made regardless of whether enforcement was granted or not.[171] In other jurisdictions, third parties may have rights to object to enforcement.[172] This latter practice is to be discouraged; it not only imports uncertainty into the enforcement regime but it may unnecessarily delay the enforcement process.

---

164 Peerenboom, op. cit. fn 85, p. 250, n. 5.
165 Article 4 of Regulation of the Supreme People's Court concerning the Charges and Time-Limits for Review of Recognition and Enforcement of Foreign Arbitral Awards (No. 28, issued on 21 November 1998). See also Wang Sheng Chang, 'CIETAC's Perspective on Arbitration and Conciliation Concerning China', (2004) 12 *ICCA Congress Series* 27, at p. 32–33; and Xiaobing Xu and Wilson, op. cit. fn 113.
166 Supreme People's Court (2003) Civil 4 Miscellaneous No. 9.
167 See Lee, op. cit. fn 76, at p. 53.
168 See also Section 5.1 above.
169 Bose, Yap and Jaliwala, op. cit. fn 92, p. 3.
170 See, e.g. Indonesian Arbitration and Dispute Resolution Act Article 68; and Section 50 of the Indian Arbitration and Conciliation Act. In India an appeal may be possible if enforcement is granted under the Indian Constitution in cases of fundamental importance. See S Kachwaha, 'The Arbitration Law of India: A Critical Analysis', (2005) 12 *Asian International Arbitration Journal* 105, at p. 126; and Kachwaha, 2008, op. cit. fn 35, p. 80. See also China's Supreme People's Court Notice on Prior Reporting System of 28 August 1995.
171 See, e.g. the Vietnam Civil Procedure Code Articles 372–373.
172 See the rights of the People's General Inspectorate in Vietnam to object to an enforcement decision as discussed in Bose, Yap and Jaliwala, op. cit. fn 92, p. 3 (citing Vietnam's Civil Procedure Code, Part XI Procedures for Recognition and Enforcement in Vietnam of Civil Judgments and Decisions of Foreign Courts and Foreign Arbitration).

6 Enforcement refusal grounds

Once a party applying for enforcement (the 'award creditor') has satisfied the Article IV requirements of the New York Convention, the burden shifts to the party against whom enforcement is sought (the 'award debtor') if it wants to resist enforcement. The award debtor must establish one of the grounds set out in Article V. These Article V grounds are exhaustive. As Justice Prakash stated in *Aloe Vera of America Inc v Asianic Food Pte Ltd*, in determining an application to resist enforcement of a foreign award:[173]

9.127

> I can only permit Mr Chiew to resist enforcement if he is able to establish one of the grounds set out in s. 31(2) of the Act [corresponding to New York Convention Article V(1)]. Except to the extent permitted by those grounds, I cannot look into the merits of the Award and allow Mr Chiew to re-litigate issues that he could have brought up either before the Arbitrator or the supervisory court.

This statement reflects not only the plain language and intent of the New York Convention but also well-established practice. Moreover, one of the classic studies on the New York Convention has observed that:[174]

9.128

> As far as the grounds for refusal of enforcement of the award as enumerated in Article V are concerned, [the pro-enforcement bias of the New York Convention] means that they have to be construed narrowly. (Original emphasis)

Article V of the New York Convention permits a court only to enforce or refuse the enforcement of an award. As has been stated already in this chapter, it does not allow a court considering an enforcement application to set aside the award. An anomaly is found in Section 42 of the Philippines Alternative Dispute Resolution Act, which provides: 'If the application for rejection or suspension of enforcement of [a foreign] award has been made, the regional trial court may, if it considers it proper, vacate its decision . . . .' However, effective from October 2009, Rule 13.4 of the Philippines Supreme Court Special Rules of Court on Alternative Dispute Resolution prescribes that 'A Philippine court shall not set aside a foreign arbitral award'.

9.129

Article V(1) of the New York Convention provides:

9.130

> Recognition and enforcement of the award may be refused, at the request of the party against whom it is invoked, only if that party furnishes to the competent authority where the recognition and enforcement is sought, proof that:
> (a) The parties to the agreement referred to in article II were, under the law applicable to them, under some incapacity, or the said agreement is not valid under the law to which the parties have subjected it or, failing any indication thereon, under the law of the country where the award was made; or

---

173 [2006] 3 SLR 174, at para 56. See also *Coutinho Caro & Co USA Inc v Marcus Trading Inc* 2000 WL 435566, at 10 (D Conn, 4 March 2000) (US, District Court), where the court rejected an argument that enforcement of a CIETAC award should be refused because the argument was not based on a New York Convention Article V ground. It has also been commented in van den Berg, 1981, op. cit. fn 74, p. 269 that because the exhaustive list of refusal grounds in Article V does not refer to a mistake in fact or in law '[i]t is a generally accepted interpretation of the Convention that the court before which the enforcement of the foreign award is sought may not review the merits of the award'.
174 van den Berg, 1981, op. cit. fn 74, pp. 267–268.

(b) The party against whom the award is invoked was not given proper notice of the appointment of the arbitrator or of the arbitration proceedings or was otherwise unable to present his case; or
(c) The award deals with a difference not contemplated by or not falling within the terms of the submission to arbitration, or it contains decisions on matters beyond the scope of the submission to arbitration, provided that, if the decisions on matters submitted to arbitration can be separated from those not so submitted, that part of the award which contains decisions on matters submitted to arbitration may be recognized and enforced; or
(d) The composition of the arbitral authority or the arbitral procedure was not in accordance with the agreement of the parties, or, failing such agreement, was not in accordance with the law of the country where the arbitration took place; or
(e) The award has not yet become binding on the parties or has been set aside or suspended by a competent authority of the country in which, or under the law of which, that award was made.

9.131 The phrase 'only if' in the introductory paragraph to Article V(1) indicates that the five grounds are exhaustive (in addition to the Article V(2) grounds). Philippine legislation confirms this by prescribing that 'Any other ground raised shall be disregarded by the regional trial court'.[175]

9.132 The decision in *Re Resort Condominiums International Inc v Bolwell*[176] raised eyebrows in the international arbitration community. The Queensland Supreme Court took the view that Australian courts have a general discretion that extends beyond the Article V grounds to refuse enforcement under the New York Convention. The decision was based on the omission in Section 8(5) of Australia's International Arbitration Act of the 'only if' phrase in Article V(1) of the New York Convention.[177] In the light of the unambiguous wording of the New York Convention, its pro-enforcement objectives, the decisions on this issue by courts in other countries and Australia's international obligations under that treaty, the interpretation of Australia's implementing legislation by the court in *Resort Condominiums* is incorrect. Much clearer words in the Australian legislation would be required to show that the drafters intended to give courts a discretion beyond the Article V refusal grounds.[178]

9.133 Another vital phrase in the Article V(1) introductory paragraph is 'may be refused'. The ordinary meaning[179] of the word 'may' demonstrates without doubt

---

175 Section 45 of the Philippine Alternative Dispute Resolution Act 2004.
176 (1993) 118 ALR 655, 29 October 1993, (Qld Supreme Court). See also (1995) XX *Yearbook of Commercial Arbitration* 628, at p. 641.
177 The relevant part of Section 8(5) of Australia's International Arbitration Act states: 'in any proceedings in which the enforcement of a foreign award by virtue of this Part is sought, the court may, at the request of the party against whom it is invoked, refuse to enforce the award if that party proves to the satisfaction of the court that ... '
178 See M Pryles, 'Interlocutory Orders and Convention Awards: The Case of Resort Condominiums v Bolwell', (1994) 10 *Arbitration International* 385, at p. 393; and Garnett and Pryles, op. cit. fn 136, p. 905. Further concern has arisen because subsequent Australian cases appear not to have disagreed with the finding in *Resort Condominiums*. See, e.g. *International Movie Group Inc (IMG) v Palace Entertainment Corp Pty Ltd* (1995) 128 FLR 458 (Supreme Court of Victoria); and *ACN 006 397 413 Pty Ltd v International Movie Group (Canada) Inc* [1997] 2 VR 31 (Victorian Court of Appeal) where 'uncertainty' of an award appears to have been accepted as a ground for refusal. See the comment on this case in Garnett and Pryles, op. cit. fn 136, pp. 905–906.
179 The term 'ordinary meaning' is used here because it belongs to part of the rules of treaty interpretation as expressed in Articles 31 and 32 of the 1969 Vienna Convention on the Law of Treaties. Consequently, those

that refusal is discretionary. Thus even if one of the five refusal grounds is established, the court can still order enforcement. This comports with the pro-enforcement object and purpose of the Convention. In *China Nanhai Oil Joint Service Corp v Gee Tai Holdings Co Ltd*,[180] Justice Kaplan of the High Court of Hong Kong (as he then was), referring to Article V of the New York Convention, said:

> even if a ground of opposition is proved, there is still a residual discretion left in the enforcing court to enforce nonetheless. This shows that the grounds of opposition are not to be inflexibly applied. The residual discretion enables the enforcing court to achieve a just result in all the circumstances.

The position in Hong Kong is a good model. The party resisting enforcement must establish a real risk of injustice and that its rights have been violated in a material way.[181]

In China, the Supreme People's Court's Notice on the Implementation of China's Accession to the Convention on the Recognition and Enforcement of Foreign Arbitral Awards of 1987[182] appears to be inconsistent with the flexible approach prescribed by the New York Convention. It states that enforcement 'shall' be rejected if the party opposing the application can establish one of the refusal grounds.[183]

China also has a very distinctive process if its lower courts consider that enforcement should be refused. The Supreme People's Court has issued a notice requiring any Intermediate People's Court that intends to refuse recognition or enforcement of a foreign arbitral award issued in a New York Convention state to report its tentative finding to the Higher People's Court.[184] If the Higher People's Court agrees that recognition or enforcement should be refused, it must in turn ask the Supreme People's Court for confirmation that recognition or enforcement can be refused. The overall effect is that no lower Chinese Court can refuse recognition or enforcement unless the Supreme Court approves it. An underlying rationale for this notice appears to be that the Higher People's Court and Supreme People's Court are considered to be less influenced by local protectionism and therefore more objective.[185] A statistic reported in 1999 was

---

articles are applicable to a treaty such as the New York Convention. Other important Article 31 interpretation criteria are the context of the terms and the object and purpose of the treaty. These rules are commonly used in investor-state arbitrations to interpret bilateral investment treaties but less so by domestic courts in interpreting the New York Convention.
180 (1995) XX *Yearbook of Commercial Arbitration* 671.
181 See Brock, op. cit. fn 157, p. 451, para 15–25.
182 Effective as of 10 April 2007.
183 See Hwang and Yeo Chuan Tat, op. cit. fn 101, at 417; and Wang Sheng Chang, op. cit. fn 100, at p. 470.
184 Notice of the Supreme People's Court on the Issues concerning the Treatment of Foreign-Related Arbitration and Foreign Arbitration by the People's Courts, 28 August 1995; and Notice of the Supreme People's Court on the Issues concerning the Invalidation of Foreign-Related Arbitral Awards, 23 April 1998. See also Wang Sheng Chang, 2004, op. cit. fn 165, at p. 32.
185 See, e.g. Jingzhou Tao, op. cit. fn 93, p. 174, para 493 and p. 188, para 528 ('there is considerable concern that the local Intermediate People's Court takes into consideration the public interest, i.e. the adverse effects that recognition and enforcement could wreak upon the local economy'); F Yeoh, 'Enforcement and Dispute Outcomes', in M Moser, op. cit. fn 152, p. 259, at p. 268 (commenting that in local courts '[s]ometimes, judges are motivated by local protectionism and are reluctant to enforce an award against a local Chinese entity, particularly where that local entity enjoys good *guanxi* (or connections) with the local courts or enforcing judges,'); Kam Hung Ho, *The Enforceability of Foreign Related Arbitral Awards in China*, M.A. Thesis, City

that 80% of cases in which the Intermediate and Higher People's Courts contemplated refusing enforcement of an award were resolved in favour of enforcement when sent to the Supreme People's Court.[186] More recently, Judge Wan, the Vice President of the Supreme People's Court, has reported that from 2000 to the end of 2007 only 12 foreign awards were refused recognition or enforcement in China.[187]

9.137 Finally, as a point of comparison, it is worth noting that the internal annulment mechanism of the ICSID Convention also contains limited grounds which, if satisfied, may give rise to the award's annulment. These grounds provide a good comparative contrast to the New York Convention and Model Law grounds. For example, there is a requirement in Article 52 of the ICSID Convention for an award to be reasoned. This requirement is not in the New York Convention.[188]

6.1 Overlap of the New York Convention with Articles 34, 35 and 36 of the Model Law

9.138 As mentioned in Section 3.2.3 above, Article V of the New York Convention (except Article V(1)(e)) has been substantially reproduced in Article 34 of the Model Law, which concerns the setting aside of awards. Additionally, Article 36 of the Model Law, which addresses the recognition and enforcement of awards irrespective of the seat of arbitration, replicates all the New York Convention Article V refusal grounds. Consequently, much of the ensuing discussion on Article V will be relevant mutatis mutandis to understanding the meaning and application of Articles 34 and 36 of the Model Law. In this regard, a Canadian court has observed:[189]

> The grounds for challenging an award under the Model Law are derived from Article V of the New York Convention... Accordingly, authorities relating to Article V of the New York Convention are applicable to the corresponding provisions in Articles 34 and 36 of the Model Law. These authorities accept that the general rule of interpretation of Article V is that the grounds for refusal of enforcement are to be construed narrowly...

9.139 Model Law countries that have also signed or acceded to the New York Convention have to address the overlap between Articles IV to VI of the New York Convention and Articles 35 and 36 of the Model Law. For example, Section 20 of Australia's International Arbitration Act provides that where the Model Law and

---

University of Hong Kong, 2005 (on file with the authors), pp. 23 et seq; and Bose, Yap and Jaliwala, op. cit. fn 92, pp. 5–6.
[186] Wang Sheng Chang, 'Enforcement of Foreign Arbitral Awards in the People's Republic of China', (1998) 9 *ICCA Congress Series* 461, pp. 475–476.
[187] Judge Wan's speech at a symposium in China in June 2008 to celebrate 50 years of the New York Convention, available (in Chinese) at www.civillaw.com.cn/article/default.asp?id=39787. Anecdotal evidence, however, suggests that the Supreme People's Court takes an extremely long time to hand down its decision, if its decision is that the award will not be recognised or enforced.
[188] Those ICSID Convention annulment grounds are discussed in Chapter 10, Section 8.
[189] *Corporacion Transnacional de Inversiones SA de CV v STET Int'l SpA*, 45 O.R. (3d) 183 (1999), at para 21 (Ontario Superior Court of Justice).

the New York Convention overlap, the latter shall prevail. In Singapore (a New York Convention state), Section 3 of its International Arbitration Act provides that the Model Law has force of law in Singapore but Articles 35 and 36 of the Model Law are expressly excluded.

6.2 Article V(1) of the New York Convention

The discussion on the five Article V refusal grounds below is not intended to be exhaustive. Only a selection of cases is presented to illustrate the grounds. A number of the issues raised in Article V(1) are dealt with in more detail elsewhere in this book.   9.140

6.2.1 Party incapacity or agreement invalidity

Article V(1)(a) of the New York Convention refers to three situations in which the consent to arbitrate is defective:[190]   9.141

(i) A party did not have the legal capacity under the law applicable to it to enter into the arbitration agreement.
(ii) The arbitration agreement was not valid under the law chosen by the parties to govern that agreement.
(iii) If the parties did not choose a law to govern that agreement, it was not valid under the law 'where the award was made'.

As to the incapacity of a party, many cases concern whether the parties had the proper authority to sign or otherwise enter into the arbitration agreement. In *Hong Kong Heung Chun Cereal & Oil Food Co Ltd v Anhui Cereal & Oil Food Import & Export Co*,[191] the respondent in the arbitration did not sign the contract pursuant to which the arbitration was initiated. In fact, a third party fabricated documents and purported to enter into the contract under the name of the respondent. Notwithstanding these events, the matter went to arbitration, the respondent failed to persuade the arbitral tribunal that it was not a party to the contract and the subsequent award determined that the respondent was liable for breach of that contract. In an enforcement action, the Supreme People's Court in Beijing found, among other things, that the award was not enforceable on the ground that the party that actually signed the contract lacked capacity.[192]   9.142

A major international arbitration issue in China is that arbitration agreements may be invalid if they fail to include an express designation of an 'arbitration commission', which term has been said to be limited to Chinese arbitration   9.143

---

190 See generally CI Suarez Anzorena, 'The Incapacity Defence under the New York Convention' in Gaillard and Di Pietro, op. cit. fn 2, pp. 615–637; and van den Berg, 1981, op. cit. fn 74, pp. 275–295.
191 Chinese Supreme People's Court (2003) Civil 4 Miscellaneous No. 9. See also *Aloe Vera of America Inc v Asianic Food Pte Ltd*, [2006] 3 SLR 174, at paras 64–69; and *Hebei Peak Harvest Battery Co Ltd v Polytek Engineering Co Ltd*, [1998] 1 HKC 676.
192 See Lee, op. cit. fn 76, at p. 53.

institutions. In *Wuxi Woco-Tongyong Rubber Engineering Co Ltd v Zueblin Int'l GmbH*,[193] an arbitration clause stating 'Arbitration: ICC Rules, Shanghai shall apply' was held to be invalid because it did not explicitly specify an administering arbitral institution. Consequently, an award issued by an arbitral tribunal seated in Shanghai on the basis of this arbitration clause was not enforced by the Wuxi Intermediate People's Court (this judgment was also approved by the Supreme People's Court). The clause was held to be invalid and fell within the scope of the Article V(1)(a) New York Convention refusal ground.[194] The decision in *Zueblin* is not representative of international practice.

9.144 In a more recent case, *Duferco SA v Ningbo Arts & Crafts Import and Export Co Ltd*, the Ningbo Intermediate People's Court enforced an ICC award issued by an arbitral tribunal seated in Beijing.[195] In that case, the court held that the respondent failed to make a timely objection to the arbitration agreement's designation of a non-Chinese arbitral institution – the ICC. Given this fact, the court took the view that under Article 13 of the Chinese Supreme People's Court Interpretations on Certain Issues Relating to the Application of the PRC Arbitration Law[196] ('Notice on Interpretation'), the application to challenge the validity of the arbitration agreement must be dismissed. Notwithstanding this decision, commentators have remarked that because the *Duferco* decision deals largely with the loss of the right to object, it does not clarify or show a change in the approach taken in *Zueblin*.[197]

9.145 Some flexibility appears to have been injected into the Chinese enforcement regime by Articles 3 and 4 of the Notice on Interpretation, pursuant to which a choice of arbitration rules may be acceptable if it sufficiently indicates (without having to be explicit) that a particular arbitral commission was chosen by the choice of those rules. Accordingly, an arbitration clause that states 'All disputes shall be settled under the CIETAC Rules by three arbitrators' now appears to be explicit enough to indicate that CIETAC was the designated arbitral institution (or 'commission', to use the usual translation from Chinese).

9.146 Also relevant to the invalidity of arbitration agreements is Article 27 of the Chinese Supreme People's Court Notice on Interpretation, which appears to prevent a party from mounting an argument <u>after</u> issuance of the award that the arbitration agreement was invalid. Similarly, in the enforcement proceedings in the case of *Xinan Co of China Technology Export-Import Co v Kyoei Boeki KK*, the District Court of Tokyo held that a party was precluded from relying on

---

[193] (2003) Min Si Ta Zi No. 23 (Supreme People's Court, 8 July 2004), cited in Darwazeh and Yeoh, op. cit. fn 85, pp. 841–842; and Mai Tai and P Zheng, 'The Status of ICC Awards in China', (2010) *Asian Dispute Review* 29.
[194] This award's enforcement ought to have been governed by China's Civil Procedure Law because that was the applicable procedural law. Nonetheless, the Wuxi Intermediate People's Court (the court of first instance) took the view that the award was an arbitral award not considered as domestic in the state where enforcement was sought. As such, the court held that the award fell within the meaning of the second sentence of Article I(1) of the New York Convention. See Darwazeh and Yeoh, op. cit. fn 85, p. 840.
[195] Decision of 22 April 2009, ICC award 14006/MS/JB/JEM.
[196] Promulgated by the Judicial Committee of the Supreme People's Court on 26 December 2005, and effective as of 8 September 2006.
[197] Mai Tai and Zheng, op. cit. fn 193, at p. 31.

New York Convention Article V(1)(a) to argue that the arbitral agreement was invalid because the party had not challenged that agreement during the proceedings.[198]

The validity of an arbitration agreement may be challenged in Korea if it is selective, i.e. it leaves open the option to go to domestic courts. The reasoning behind this is that arbitration is defined under Article 3(1) of the Korean Arbitration Act as a dispute settlement procedure that precludes adjudication by courts. If no such preclusion is indicated, then there is no arbitration agreement in the strict sense.[199] However, there is more recent authority from the Korean Supreme Court that it is prepared to consider as valid a selective arbitration clause.[200]

Other issues relating to the validity of arbitration agreements and the capacity to enter into them are discussed in Chapter 4.

6.2.2 Violation of due process

Article V(1)(b) of the New York Convention identifies three violations of due process rights on which a court may rely to refuse enforcement:[201]
(i) No proper notice of appointment of the arbitrator.
(ii) No proper notice of the arbitration proceedings.
(iii) The inability of a party to present its case.

Defences to enforcement based on the failure to give notification of the arbitrator's appointment or of the arbitral proceedings are relatively rare in comparison to the occasions where a party asserts it has been unable to present its case. A restraint on the ability to present one's case is sometimes described as constituting a breach of natural justice rules or a denial of due process. As to the content of this principle, the exposition by the Singapore Court of Appeal in *Soh Beng Tee v Fairmount* as to due process rights in arbitration is highly instructive:[202]

> (1) Parties to arbitration had, in general, a right to be heard effectively on every issue that might be relevant to the resolution of a dispute. The overriding concern was fairness.
>
> (2) Fairness, however, was a multidimensional concept and it would also be unfair to the successful party if it were deprived of the fruits of its labour as a result of a dissatisfied party raising a multitude of arid technical challenges after an arbitral award had been made. The courts were not a stage where a dissatisfied party could have a second bite of the cherry.

---

198 853 Hanrei Taimuzu 266, 27 January 1994, (1995) XX *Yearbook of Commercial Arbitration* 742, cited in Y Taniguchi and T Nakamura, 'Japanese Court Decisions on Article V of the New York Convention', (2008) 25 *Journal of International Arbitration* 857, at pp. 858–860.
199 See, e.g. Seoul District Court Case No. 2000 Ga Hap 37949, 19 September 2000, cited in Choe and Dharmananda, op. cit. fn 66, p. 67.
200 Supreme Court of Korea Case No. 2003 Da 318, 22 August 2003, cited in Choe and Dharmananda, op. cit. fn 66, p. 67.
201 See generally H Verbist, 'Challenges on Grounds of Due Process Pursuant to Article V(1)(b) of the New York Convention' in Gaillard and Di Pietro, op. cit. fn 2, pp. 679–728; and van den Berg, 1981, op. cit. fn 74, pp. 296–310.
202 [2007] SGCA 28, at para 64.

(3) The latter conception of fairness justified a policy of minimal curial intervention, which had become common as a matter of international practice.
(4) The delicate balance between ensuring the integrity of the arbitral process and ensuring that the rules of natural justice were complied with in the arbitral process was preserved by strictly adhering to only the narrow scope and basis for challenging an arbitral award that had been expressly acknowledged under the Act.
(5) It was almost invariably the case that parties proposed diametrically opposite solutions to resolve a dispute. The arbitrator, however, was not bound to adopt an either/or approach.
(6) Each case should be decided within its own factual matrix. It had always to be borne in mind that it was not the function of the court to assiduously comb an arbitral award microscopically in an attempt to determine if there was any blame or fault in the arbitral process; rather, an award should be read generously such that only meaningful breaches of the rules of natural justice that have actually caused prejudice are ultimately remedied.

9.151 *Soh Beng Tee* related to a domestic arbitration but the Court of Appeal indicated that the principles were equally applicable to international arbitrations. It also indicated that for Article V(1)(b) purposes the breach of natural justice should be connected to the making of the award.[203]

9.152 The passage from *Soh Beng Tee* just quoted indicates a high threshold for proving a denial of due process. This is also evident in the *GKN* case decided by the Supreme Court of Korea in which the notice requirement in Article V(1)(b) was at issue.[204] The defendant in that case closed its London office before the notice of LCIA arbitration proceedings was served on its London address. The defendant did not participate in the arbitration and an award was issued in its absence. When an application to enforce the award was made in Korea, the defendant objected. The Korean Supreme Court found that the defendant's right to make a defence was not severely impaired. In its view, the notice was served according to the procedures stipulated under the contract, the wholly owned subsidiary of the defendant in fact received the notice (it used the same office of the defendant) and the principal of the defendant was actually aware (by oral notification) of the notice.[205] The court took a very narrow view of Article V(1)(b):[206]

> the underlying rationale of this provision is not intended to cover all the situations where a party's defense right is infringed. Rather, it is limited to a situation where the level of defense right infringement is too severe to tolerate, and... it shall be determined in accordance with the law of a country where an arbitral award is enforced.

---

[203] Ibid., at para 26.
[204] Korean Supreme Court decision, 10 April 1990, 89 Daka 20252.
[205] This summary is based on the facts as set out in GL Kim and E-Y Park, 'Enforcement of Arbitral Awards in Korea', (2002) *Asian Dispute Review* 161, at p. 161; and Seung Wha Chang, 'Article V of the New York Convention and Korea', (2008) 25 *Journal of International Arbitration* 865, at pp. 867–868.
[206] This quote of the court's decision is taken from Seung Wha Chang, ibid., p. 867.

Paklito Investment Ltd v Klockner East Asia Ltd[207] is a rare instance in which Hong Kong courts have refused to enforce an award. In that case, a dispute under a sale and purchase contract was submitted to a CIETAC arbitral tribunal. The arbitral tribunal decided to appoint an expert to provide an opinion on the goods at issue. The defendant objected to this appointment. On receipt of the expert's report, the defendant notified CIETAC that it intended to comment on the report. Before receiving these comments, an award was rendered in favour of the plaintiff. Enforcement of this award in Hong Kong was resisted on the basis that the defendant was unable to present its case. In his judgment, Justice Kaplan (as he then was) agreed, taking the view that the denial of the opportunity to be heard was a serious irregularity. In his view, the defendant was denied the opportunity to make its case, raise objections, refute evidence or provide its own responsive evidence. He also added: 'I have seen the evidence which the Defendants would like to adduce and it raises serious questions as to the methodology of the Tribunal appointed experts'.[208]

9.153

In another Hong Kong case, *Apex Tech Investment Ltd v Chuang's Development (China) Ltd*,[209] the Court of Appeal applied a two-pronged test in regard to the due process ground. First, the court required that the defendant demonstrate it was unable to present its case. If it succeeded on this point, it was required also to show that the result of the arbitration 'could' have been different had the defendant been given the opportunity to present its case. This sound reasoning is consistent with the discretion given to courts to order enforcement even if an Article V(1) ground is made out.[210] Due process rights are also discussed in Chapter 7, Section 4.

9.154

6.2.3 Excess of jurisdiction

The Article V(1)(c) refusal ground refers to three instances in which the arbitral tribunal has exceeded its jurisdiction:[211]

9.155

(i) The award dealt with a difference not contemplated by the submission to arbitration.
(ii) The award dealt with a difference not falling within the terms of the submission to arbitration.
(iii) The award decided matters beyond the scope of the submission to arbitration.

A saving provision is also contained in Article V(1)(c) which allows those parts of the award that are within the jurisdiction of the arbitral tribunal to be enforced at

9.156

---
207 [1993] 2 HKLR 39 (High Court, Hong Kong).
208 Ibid., p. 47 Articles 37 and 38 of the 2005 CIETAC Rules should now prevent this type of situation from occurring.
209 [1996] 2 HKLR 155.
210 For references to a number of other Hong Kong cases relating to the denial of a right to be heard in the context of award enforcement, see Brock, op. cit. fn 157, p. 450, n. 48.
211 See generally M Azeredo da Silveira and L Lévy, 'Transgression of the Arbitrators' Authority: Article V(1)(c) of the New York Convention' in Gaillard and Di Pietro, op. cit. fn 2, pp. 639–678; and van den Berg, 1981, op. cit. fn 74, pp. 311–321.

the same time as refusing enforcement of those parts that fall outside the arbitral tribunal's jurisdiction.

9.157   The actual text of Article V(1)(c) has justifiably been criticised by Albert Jan van den Berg as being 'somewhat obscure and repetitive'.[212] When dealing with this provision, a distinction is to be drawn between the scope of the arbitration clause and the matters submitted by the parties to the arbitral tribunal for resolution (i.e. its mandate). The arbitral tribunal's mandate is usually narrower than the arbitration agreement's scope. In this context, it is important to note that Article V(1)(c) specifically refers to the 'submission to arbitration' and not to the scope of the arbitration agreement.

9.158   By deciding or dealing with a matter outside its mandate, the arbitral tribunal is acting *ultra petita*, i.e. beyond the authority that was provided to it by the parties. As just discussed, this situation is covered by Article V(1)(c). However, that provision does not cover an arbitral tribunal's *infra petita* acts, i.e. a failure to address what was submitted to it. As van den Berg comments:[213]

> Ground (c) (or any other ground for refusal of enforcement listed in Article V of the Convention) does not mention an arbitral award in which not all (counter) claims submitted to the arbitral tribunal have been disposed of . . . Considering that one of the main features of Article V is that it lists the grounds for refusal exhaustively, an award *infra petita* does not qualify for refusal of enforcement.

9.159   A failure to apply Article V(1)(c) properly is evident in *Hemofarm DD v Jinan Yongning Pharmaceutical Co Ltd*.[214] In that case, Hemofarm and others entered into a joint venture contract (JVC) with Jinan Yongning Pharmaceutical (Jinan Yongning) to establish C, a joint venture company. The JVC provided that disputes connected with it were to be resolved by ICC arbitration in Paris. Jinan Yongning commenced litigation in China against C in the People's Court to recover rent for land and machinery leased to C. C objected to the jurisdiction of the People's Court, pointing to the JVC arbitration clause. The court rejected this argument, holding that C was not a party to the JVC. The court found in favour of Jinan Yongning and effectively froze C's assets. Thereafter, Hemofarm commenced ICC arbitration proceedings in Paris against Jinan Yongning alleging, inter alia, that it was unable to continue with the JVC because of the Chinese litigation. The ICC arbitral tribunal ruled in favour of Hemofarm et al. It found that the Chinese litigation proceedings instituted by Jinan Yongning and the measures the People's Court consequently ordered against C prejudiced Hemofarm's rights and benefits arising out of the JVC, and that by its conduct Jinan Yongning breached the JVC. The arbitral tribunal ordered USD 8 million against Jinan Yongning for damages and costs.

---

212 van den Berg, 2008, op. cit. fn 27.
213 Ibid. But see Born, op. cit. fn 39, pp. 2798–2799.
214 This case is cited in Darwazeh and Yeoh, op. cit. fn 85, pp. 847–849. The facts summarised here are taken from that article.

Hemofarm attempted to enforce the ICC award in China and the matter ulti- 9.160
mately reached the Supreme People's Court. That court determined that disputes between C and a joint venture party could only be litigated before the People's Courts and that the arbitral tribunal had exceeded the scope of the arbitration agreement by 're-adjudicating' and issuing an award in relation to a dispute heard by a People's Court. Accordingly, in addition to other grounds, it refused enforcement pursuant to Article V(1)(c) of the New York Convention. The matter obviously should not have fallen under Article V(1)(c) because the arbitral tribunal was dealing with a dispute between Jinan Yongning and Hemofarm as was contemplated under the JVC. Moreover, it was not attempting to 're-adjudicate' the matter between Jinan Yongning and C. In effect, Jinan Yongning circumvented its arbitration commitments under the JVC by filing its claim against C, and bringing the matter before domestic courts.[215]

The Korean Supreme Court has held that an arbitral tribunal, in interpreting 9.161
an arbitration agreement submitting to arbitration 'legal disputes regarding this contract', was permitted to determine a tort claim and was not surpassing its authority in so doing.[216]

An allegation that an arbitral tribunal is exceeding its jurisdiction must be 9.162
made in a timely fashion. In *Sam Ming City Forestry Economic Co v Lam Pun Hung Trading as Henry Company*,[217] an application to set aside a court enforcement order was made on the ground that the arbitral tribunal lacked jurisdiction to make the award. The court held that the parties had submitted to the arbitral tribunal's jurisdiction by arguing the matter before it and were estopped from raising the jurisdictional objection subsequently.[218] An arbitral tribunal's excess of jurisdiction is also discussed in Chapter 5.

6.2.4 Irregularity in procedure or composition of arbitral tribunal

Article V(1)(d) of the New York Convention refers to two procedural defects:[219] 9.163
(i) The method of composing the arbitral tribunal was not in accordance with the parties' agreement, or failing such agreement, was in violation of the *lex arbitri*.
(ii) The arbitral procedure adopted was not in accordance with the parties' agreement, or failing such agreement, was in violation of the *lex arbitri*.

Article V(1)(d) deals generally with the procedure chosen by the parties and 9.164
confirms the importance international arbitration places on the principle of party

---

215 See Darwazeh and Yeoh, op. cit. fn 85, p. 849.
216 91 Da 17146, 14 April 1992, cited in Seung Wha Chang, op. cit. fn 205, p. 868.
217 Unreported decision, Hong Kong Court of Appeal, 27 June 2001, CLOUT Case 448.
218 See also Article 75 of the Chinese Supreme People's Court Notice of 29 December 2005, Fafa [2005] No. 26, precluding an application for setting aside an award on the basis of lack of jurisdiction if a jurisdictional objection was not raised during the arbitral process. This Notice circulated the Minutes of the Second National Convention on Judiciary Business in connection with Foreign-related Commercial and Shipping Cases. It is not an interpretation of law but represents a judicial consensus on relevant issues that are likely to be followed by Chinese courts. See generally M Lin and T Wong, 'Arbitration in the People's Republic of China: A Recent Notice from the Supreme People's Court', (2006) *Asian Dispute Review* 109, at p. 110.
219 See generally S Jarvin, 'Irregularity in the Composition of the Arbitral Tribunal and the Procedure' in Gaillard and Di Pietro, op. cit. fn 2, pp. 729–756; and van den Berg, 1981, op. cit. fn 74, pp. 322–330.

autonomy.[220] However, the failure to make a timely objection to a procedural irregularity may be fatal to any subsequent attempt to object to enforcement of an award based on that irregularity.[221] In addition, even if significant irregularity is proved and the refusal ground is satisfied, an enforcing court may well use its residual discretion to allow enforcement if it considers that the irregularity is unlikely to have affected the outcome of the case, as has been discussed in Section 6.2.2.

9.165   In a case before the Supreme Court of Korea, the arbitration clause authorised each party to appoint one arbitrator. Nevertheless, the KCAB followed its own appointment procedure and appointed arbitrators not chosen by the parties. Neither party objected during the presentation of their cases at the first hearing. In the Supreme Court of Korea's view, while the appointment process was clearly not in accordance with the parties' original agreement, the conduct of both parties at the hearing constituted a new implicit agreement as to the arbitral tribunal's composition. It consequently rejected the respondent's contention that the composition of the arbitral tribunal was contrary to the parties' agreement.[222]

9.166   Likewise, in the Hong Kong case *China Nanhai Oil Joint Service Corp v Gee Tai Holdings Co Ltd*,[223] the arbitration agreement required disputes to be submitted to CIETAC in Beijing. The plaintiff, however, submitted its claim to CIETAC in Shenzhen. The composition of the arbitral tribunal according to the arbitration agreement should have been based on the Beijing list of arbitrators. This was not the case and the Shenzhen list was used. The defendant therefore attempted to thwart enforcement on the ground that the method of appointing the arbitrators was not made in accordance with the parties' agreement. The court decided that although the arbitrators were not selected in conformity with the arbitration agreement, the defendant was estopped from raising this point because it failed to object to the composition during the proceedings. Justice Kaplan (as he then was) stated:[224]

> It strikes me as quite unfair for a party to appreciate that there might be something wrong with the composition of the tribunal yet not make any formal submission whatsoever to the tribunal about its own jurisdiction, or to the arbitration commission which constituted the tribunal and then to proceed to fight the case on the merits and then 2 years after the award attempt to nullify the whole proceedings on the grounds that the arbitrators were chosen from the wrong CIETAC list.

9.167   Another reason for denying an objection to enforcement despite the satisfaction of an Article V(1)(d) ground is that no prejudice has been caused to the party resisting enforcement. In *Werner A Bock KG v N's Co Ltd*,[225] the Hong Kong Court of Appeal held that the irregularity in the composition of the arbitral tribunal was of such a nature that it would be unjust to refuse enforcement and allow the defendant to benefit from this irregularity because it had not been prejudiced.

---

220 This is discussed in detail in Chapter 7, Section 2.
221 See Chapter 7, Section 3.1.3.
222 2000Da29264, 27 November 2001, cited in Seung Wha Chang, op. cit. fn 205, at pp. 868–869.
223 (1995) XX *Yearbook of Commercial Arbitration* 671.
224 Ibid., p. 677, para 18.
225 [1978] HKLR 281.

9.168 In a rather rigid application of Article V(1)(d), the Chinese Supreme People's Court allowed the Chengdu Intermediate Court to refuse enforcement of two Stockholm Chamber of Commerce awards in *PepsiCo v Sichuan PepsiCo* and *PepsiCo (China) v Sichuan Yunlv Industrial Co Ltd*.[226] The arbitration clauses required specific negotiation periods before a party could commence arbitration. Enforcement was refused because the claimant could not prove compliance with these negotiation periods. In other words, the courts took the view that the procedures followed were not in accordance with the arbitration agreements.

9.169 The composition of arbitral tribunals and arbitral procedure are discussed respectively in Chapters 6 and 7.

6.2.5 Award not yet binding or set aside

9.170 Article V(1)(e) of the New York Convention deals with refusal grounds relating to the award's status at the time of enforcement:[227]
(i) The award has not yet become binding on the parties.
(ii) The award has been set aside or suspended by a competent authority of the country in which that 'award was made'.
(iii) The award has been set aside or suspended under the law of which that 'award was made'.

9.171 To invoke the first point it may be argued that an award has not become binding because it still requires confirmation by the courts of the seat. This argument should be rejected on the ground that 'an award is considered binding on the parties even though an additional formal requirement must be complied with before the award is enforceable in the country where it was made'.[228] It is well accepted that for an award to become binding on a party, leave to enforce the award is not required from the courts of the country in which it was made.[229] In order to avoid the need to seek confirmation of the award from courts in both the jurisdiction where enforcement is sought and the seat of arbitration, i.e. a double *exequatur*, the drafters of the New York Convention used the word 'binding' in Article V(1)(e) rather than 'final'. The latter was the word used in the 1927 Geneva Convention.[230]

9.172 The process for setting aside awards is explained in Section 3 above. It is relatively rare that state courts will enforce awards set aside in other states.[231]

---

226 Judgments dated 30 April 2008, ref. no. 2005 Cheng Min Chu Zi No. 912 and ref. no. 2006 Cheng Min Chu Zi No. 36, cited in Fulbright & Jaworski LLP, *2009 International Arbitration Report*, at p. 7.
227 See generally D Freyer, 'The Enforcement of Awards Affected by Judicial Orders of Annulment at the Place of Arbitration' in Gaillard and Di Pietro, op. cit. fn 2, pp.757–786; and van den Berg, 1981, op. cit. fn 74, pp. 331–358.
228 Garnett and Pryles, op. cit. fn 136, p. 910, citing *Union Nationale des Cooperatives Agricoles de Céréales v Robert Catteral & Co Ltd* [1959] 2 QB 44.
229 See van den Berg, 1981, op. cit. fn 74, p. 337.
230 See van den Berg, 2008, op. cit. fn 27, p. 61. The double *exequatur* requirement under the 1927 Geneva Convention is discussed in Chapter 1, Section 2.3.1.
231 See, e.g. van den Berg, 2008, op. cit. fn 27, p. 62 ('the vast majority of courts in the other Contracting States [i.e. not France and the US] do not enforce arbitral awards that have been set aside in the country of origin'); J Paulsson, 'Delocalisation of International Commercial Arbitration: When and Why It Matters', (1983) 32 *International and Comparative Law Quarterly* 53; and J Paulsson, 'May or Must under the New York Convention: An Exercise in Syntax and Linguistics', (1998) 14 *Arbitration International* 227. Also to be noted here is the provision in Article 36(4) of the Korean Arbitration Act, which states that an award that has been enforced should not be set aside.

Notwithstanding this general position, a number of awards set aside at the seat of arbitration have been enforced in a different country, particularly in France and the US.[232] Two cases that have gained notoriety in this regard are *Hilmarton*[233] and *Chromalloy*.[234] In the first, a French court enforced an award set aside in Switzerland and, in the second, a US court enforced an award set aside in Egypt. In Hong Kong, obiter dicta by Justice Burrell in *Karaha Bodas Co LLC v Perusahaan Pertambangan Minyak Dan Gas Bumi Negara (Pertimina)*[235] suggests that Hong Kong courts may in certain circumstances enforce an award annulled at the seat.[236]

9.173 Concerning suspension, the law at the seat may provide that the enforcement of an award is automatically suspended as a result of, for example, the commencement of a setting aside action. But this is not enough to satisfy Article V(1)(e). Otherwise, a mere application to set aside could defeat an enforcement action. Albert Jan van den Berg has observed[237]

> [i]n order for the suspension to be a ground for refusal of enforcement of the award, the respondent must prove that the suspension of the award has been effectively ordered [i.e. considered and then ordered] by a court in the country of origin.

9.174 The Hong Kong case of *Société Nationale d'Operations Petrolières de la Cote d'Ivoire Holding v Keen Lloyd Resources Ltd*[238] is instructive. The relevant arbitration was seated in France and an application to set aside the award had been made in France. Under French law, this application triggered a six-month stay of execution. During that six-month period, the award creditor sought to enforce the award in Hong Kong. Enforcement was resisted on the ground that the award had 'not yet become binding on the parties' because the award had been challenged and a French stay of execution was in place. The Hong Kong court held that the award was binding until set aside.

9.175 If an application to set aside is made but not yet determined, one option may be to invoke Article VI to have the enforcement proceedings adjourned. This is discussed in Section 6.4 below.

---

232 See generally C Koch, 'The Enforcement of Awards Annulled in their Place of Origin: The French and US Experience', (2009) 26 *Journal of International Arbitration* 267; Born, op. cit. fn 39, pp. 2677–2691; and M Haravon, 'Enforcement of Annulled Foreign Arbitral Awards: The French Supreme Court Confirms the *Hilmarton* Trend', (2007) 22(9) *Mealey's International Arbitration Report* 1.
233 *Hilmarton Ltd v Omnium de traitement et de valorisation (OVT)*, 1994 *Revue de l'Arbitrage* 327; (1995) XX *Yearbook of Commercial Arbitration* 663 (English excerpts). See also *PT Putrabali Adyamulia v Rena Holding et Société Mnogutia Est Epices*, 2007 *Revue de l'Arbitrage* 507 (French Cour de cassation), which involved an Indonesian company. The Cour de Cassation there followed the *Hilmarton* reasoning.
234 *Chromalloy Aeroservices, a Division of Chromalloy Gas Turbine Corp. v Egypt*, 939 F. Supp 907 (D.D.C. 1996).
235 [2003] 380 HKCU 1.
236 *Hilmarton*, *Chromalloy* and *Karaha Bodas* are dealt with in more detail in Chapter 2, Section 5.2.1 generally. At the time of writing another important decision on enforcement of annulled awards was made by the Court of Appeal of Amsterdam in *Yukos Capital v Rosneft*, 28 April 2009 [LJN BI2451]. This decision is analysed in AJ van den Berg, 'Enforcement of Arbitral Awards Annulled in Russia', (2010) 27(2) *Journal of International Arbitration* 179.
237 See van den Berg, 2008, op. cit. fn 27, p. 63; and van den Berg, 1981, op. cit. fn 74, p. 352.
238 [2004] 3 HKC 452 (Hong Kong Court of First Instance).

6.3 Article V(2) of the New York Convention

Article V(2) differs from Article V(1) not simply because of the content of its refusal grounds but because a court may apply Article V(2) ex officio, on its own initiative. It provides that:

> Recognition and enforcement of an arbitral award may also be refused if the competent authority in the country where recognition and enforcement is sought finds that:
> (a) The subject matter of the difference is not capable of settlement by arbitration under the law of that country; or
> (b) The recognition or enforcement of the award would be contrary to the public policy of that country.

9.176

The competent authority, almost invariably a court, may thus raise these two grounds even if the party resisting enforcement has not raised them. In practice, however, it is rare that a court will raise these matters on its own initiative.

9.177

6.3.1 Arbitrability

Article V(2)(a) of the New York Convention deals with objective arbitrability.[239] This concept covers situations where, even if a valid arbitration agreement exists, an arbitral tribunal is not permitted to decide the dispute because of the nature of the subject matter or claims involved. It is to be contrasted with subjective arbitrability, which focuses on the scope of the arbitration agreement. An argument that a particular claim is not subjectively arbitrable would be considered under Article V(1)(c) of the New York Convention, which is discussed above.

9.178

An important aspect of Article V(2)(a) is that it concerns whether the matter is objectively arbitrable under the law of the country where enforcement is sought. Assume an award is issued in an arbitration seated in Thailand and the subject matter is objectively arbitrable under Thai law. If enforcement proceedings are brought in Australia, the Australian court may still determine that the matter is not capable of settlement by arbitration under Australian law and refuse enforcement under Article V(2)(a).[240] Arbitrability is discussed in detail in Chapter 4.

9.179

6.3.2 Public policy

The reference to public policy in Article V(2)(b) of the New York Convention is associated with international rather than domestic standards of public policy.[241] On the international plane, the meaning of public policy has evolved to the extent that the general contours of an internationally accepted standard have

9.180

---

[239] Objective arbitrability is discussed in detail in Chapter 4, Section 8.2. See generally Gaillard and Di Pietro, op. cit. fn 2, pp. 503–594; and van den Berg, 1981, op. cit. fn 74, pp. 359–375.
[240] See Hwang and Lee, op. cit. fn 13, p. 879, referring to the Singapore High Court case of *Aloe Vera of America Inc v Asianic Food Pte Ltd* [2006] 3 SLR 174.
[241] See generally B Hanotiau and O Caprasse, 'Public Policy in International Commercial Arbitration' in Gaillard and Di Pietro, op. cit. fn 2, pp. 787–828; and van den Berg, 1981, op. cit. fn 74, pp. 359–382.

emerged.[242] Fouchard, Gaillard and Goldman's observation on Article V(2)(b) is insightful:[243]

> The provision certainly refers to international public policy, and not domestic public policy. Not every breach of a mandatory rule of the host country could justify refusing recognition or enforcement of a foreign award. Such refusal is only justified where the award contravenes principles which are considered in the host country as reflecting its fundamental convictions, or as having an absolute, universal value.

9.181 Under this standard, the meaning of public policy is narrow. The Singapore Court of Appeal captured the essence of this point in *PT Asuransi Jasa Indonesia (Persero) v Dexia Bank SA*:[244]

> Although the concept of public policy of the State is not defined in the [Singapore International Arbitration] Act or the Model Law, the general consensus of judicial and expert opinion is that public policy under the act encompasses a narrow scope. In our view, it should only operate in instances where the upholding of an arbitral award would 'shock the conscience'... or is 'clearly injurious to the public good or... wholly offensive to the ordinary, reasonable and fully informed member of the public'... or where it violates the forum's most basic notion of morality and justice... (Original emphasis)

9.182 A number of other Asia-Pacific court decisions have also taken a narrow view of public policy in applying Article V(2)(b).[245] Given the high threshold for establishing a breach of public policy, rarely does this ground prevent recognition or enforcement of an award.

9.183 The Indian Supreme Court in *Renusagar Power Co Ltd v General Electric Corp* held that in order to fall within the ground of public policy:[246]

---

242 It is to be noted here that the ICSID Convention does not have a public policy ground for annulment of an award.
243 E Gaillard and J Savage (eds), *Fouchard, Gaillard, Goldman On International Commercial Arbitration*, Kluwer, 1999, at pp. 996–997, paras 1711 and 1712.
244 [2006] 1 SLR 507, at para 59 (citations omitted). The last phrase on morality and justice was taken from the famous judicial pronouncement on this issue in the US case of *Parsons & Whittemore Overseas Co Inc v Societe General de l'Industrie du Papier*, 508 F 2d 969, at 974 (2nd Cir. 1974) (US Court of Appeals). See also International Law Association Committee on International Commercial Arbitration, 'Final Report on Public Policy as Bar to Enforcement of International Arbitral Awards', New Delhi Conference, 2002, pp. 2–7.
245 Hong Kong – *Hebei Import & Export Corp v Polytek Engineering Co Ltd (No. 2)* [1998] 1 HKC 192; and *A v R* [2009] HKCU 632 (High Court), 30 April 2009, at para 23, per Justice Reyes (observing that '[i]f the public policy ground is to be raised, there must be something more, that is, a substantial injustice arising out of an award which is so shocking to the Court's conscience as to render enforcement repugnant.').
Japan – the District Court of Yokohama has held that the contravention of Japanese public policy 'should be such that it falls foul of basic principles or rules of the Japanese judicial order'. *Zhong Guo Hua Gong Jian Sh Quig Dao Gong v Color Chemical Industry KK*, (Dist. Court Yokohama), 25 August 1999, (2002) XXVII *Yearbook of Commercial Arbitration* 515; also cited in Taniguchi and Nakamura, op. cit. fn 198, at pp. 861–862.
Korea – *Adviso NV v Korea Overseas Construction Corporation*, 14 February 1995 (Supreme Court), (1996) XXI *Yearbook of Commercial Arbitration* 612 (holding that '[a]s due regard should be paid to the stability of international commercial order, as well as domestic concerns, [Article V(2)(b)] should be interpreted narrowly'). See also Choe and Dharmananda, op. cit. fn 66, p. 69; and Seung Wha Chang, op. cit. fn 205, at pp. 869–871.
New Zealand – see Tómas Kennedy-Grant's summary of New Zealand cases in T Kennedy-Grant, 'The New Zealand Experience of the UNCITRAL Model Law: A Review of the Position as at 31 December 2007', (2008) 4 *Asian International Arbitration Journal* 1, at p. 26 et seq.
246 *Renusagar Power Co Ltd v General Electric Corp*, 1994 AIR 860 (1995) XX *Yearbook of Commercial Arbitration* 681. See also *Smita Conductors, Ltd v Euro Alloys Ltd* (Indian Supreme Court), 31 August 2001, (2002) XXVII *Yearbook of Commercial Arbitration* 482.

enforcement of the award must invoke something more than the violation of the law of India... Applying the said criteria it must be held that the enforcement of a foreign award would be refused on the ground that it is contrary to public policy if such enforcement would be contrary to (i) fundamental policy of Indian law; or (ii) the interests of India; or (iii) justice and morality.

It is well established, as noted in *Renusagar*, that violating the law of the enforcing country is not an enforcement refusal ground.[247] However, it may be questioned whether the Supreme Court's reference to 'interests of India' comports with the accepted meaning of public policy. Rather, it appears to grant Indian courts wide discretion to refuse enforcement. 9.184

What then are violations that would contravene generally accepted notions of 'international public policy'? An award tainted by fraud, or having some fundamentally illegal purpose (for example illicit drug importation), is an obvious example. As Article 36(3)(a) of Schedule 1 to the New Zealand Arbitration Act 1996 provides, 'an award is in conflict with the public policy of New Zealand if... [t]he making of the award was induced or affected by fraud or corruption'.[248] Another obvious transgression of international public policy is found in the case of *Agro Industries (P) Ltd v Texuna International Ltd*.[249] The Hong Kong High Court there indicated that if the allegation before it were true – that the arbitrator relied on an affidavit in favour of the respondent made by a witness kidnapped by the respondent and obtained through distress – it would be contrary to the public policy of Hong Kong to enforce the award.[250] 9.185

The award having been made by a biased arbitral tribunal is another possible public policy violation (although this may also give rise to a refusal of enforcement under Article V(1)(b)). In this regard, the Hong Kong High Court in *Hebei Import & Export Corp v Polytek Engineering Co Ltd*[251] held that a party resisting enforcement on the basis of public policy must show actual bias rather than apparent bias. Notions of public policy may also be violated where the arbitral 9.186

---

[247] See *Adviso NV v Korea Overseas Construction Corporation*, 14 February 1995 (Supreme Court of Korea), (1996) XXI *Yearbook of Commercial Arbitration* 612 (observing '[w]hen foreign legal rules applied in an arbitral award are in violation of mandatory provisions of Korean law, such a violation does not necessarily constitute a reason for refusal'); and Reply of the PRC Supreme People's Court Regarding the Request of Haikou Intermediary Court for Refusal to Recognise and Enforce the Arbitral Award of the Arbitration Inst. of Stockholm Chamber of Commerce (13 July 2005) [2001] Min Si Ta Zi No. 12 ('violation of compulsory provisions in the administrative regulations and departmental regulations will not naturally constitute a violation of the public policy of China'), quoted in H (Litong) Chen and BT Howes, 'The Enforcement of Foreign Arbitration Awards in China', (2009) 2(6) *Bloomberg Law Reports – Asia Pacific*. See also *Reeves v One World Challenge*, [2006] 2 NZLR 184 (New Zealand Court of Appeal) (holding in a case concerning the enforcement of a foreign judgment that 'simply because a case would be decided differently under New Zealand law was not a weighty enough factor to invoke [the doctrine of public policy]'); and *Amaltal Corp Ltd v Maruha (M3) Corp Ltd* [2004] 2 NZLR 614.
[248] A very similar provision is found in the 'Explanation' to Section 48(2)(b) of the Indian Arbitration and Conciliation Act 1996 and in Section 19 of Australia's International Arbitration Act. The Malaysian Arbitration Act 2005 and the Singapore International Arbitration Act are particular because their setting aside provisions expressly include fraud and corruption as forming part of public policy but no such elaboration of public policy is contained in their enforcement provisions.
[249] (1993) XVIII *Yearbook of Commercial Arbitration* 396.
[250] Ibid., at p. 398, para 6, referring to its ruling made on 29 May 1992.
[251] [1999] 1 HKLRD 665 at 667.

tribunal relies on inadmissible evidence in a manner that is 'repugnant to fairness and justice'.[252]

9.187 A number of courts in the region have from time to time made rather unfortunate interpretations of the meaning of public policy in Article V(2)(b). One example is the Supreme Court of Queensland's decision in *Re Resort Condominiums International Inc v Bolwell*.[253] The court indicated that for an arbitral tribunal's decision to be in conformity with the enforcing state's public policy it must comply with the enforcing state's laws. As previously mentioned, the decision sought to be enforced in that case was entitled 'Interim Arbitration Order and Award'. The court found that this 'Order and Award' was not a foreign award within the meaning of the New York Convention, but added that even if it were such an award, it would still refuse enforcement on Article V(2)(b) public policy grounds. The court adopted a very low threshold to determine whether the terms of the 'Order and Award' were contrary to public policy:[254]

> Many of the orders of the present kind are contrary to the public policy of Queensland not only in the sense that many of them as drafted would not be made in Queensland, particularly without undertakings as to damages and appropriate security and in certain other respects, but also because of possible double vexation and practical difficulties in interpretation and enforcement ...

9.188 It has been said that this approach in *Resort Condominiums* 'is both extremely parochial as well as inconsistent with the traditionally narrow scope of the public policy exception and the pro-enforcement policy underlying the Convention itself'.[255] Additionally, it has been commented that the approach would reduce the number of awards that are enforceable under the Convention and is impractical because the arbitral tribunal generally will not know in what jurisdictions the award will be enforced and, in turn, will not know what legal rules need to be followed.[256]

9.189 The New Zealand case of *Downer-Hill Joint Venture v Government of Fiji*[257] (a case concerning a setting aside application) demonstrates how an alleged denial of natural justice, as a species of public policy, may lead to a re-examination of the merits of a claim. Downer applied to set aside the award on the ground that a breach of natural justice had occurred because the arbitral tribunal made findings of fact that were unsupported by evidence. The High Court held, contrary to ordinary international arbitration principles, that an arbitral tribunal's

---

[252] *Government of India v Cairn Energy India Pty Ltd* [2003] 1 MLJ 348 at pp. 366–367 (Malaysian High Court).
[253] (1993) 118 ALR 655, at p. 680, 29 October 1993, (Qld Supreme Court). See also (1995) XX *Yearbook of Commercial Arbitration* 628, at p. 641.
[254] (1995) XX *Yearbook of Commercial Arbitration* 628, at p. 649.
[255] Garnett and Pryles, op. cit. fn 136, p. 911. A better application of the public policy exception was made by another Australian court in *Corvetina Technology Ltd v Clough Engineering Ltd* [2004] NSWSC 700, at para 18.
[256] O Chukwumerije, 'Enforcement of Foreign Awards in Australia: The Implications of Resort Condominiums', (1994) 5 *Australian Dispute Resolution Journal* 237, at p. 246.
[257] [2005] 1 NZLR 554 (New Zealand High Court).

error of law or fact could constitute a breach of natural justice and therefore could contravene public policy. It added, however, that a high threshold was required and mere mistake was not sufficient. The court took the view that a breach of natural justice must result from the making of a factual finding without any logically probative evidence and also a fundamental miscarriage of justice would have occurred if the erroneous factual finding remained unchanged.[258]

In China, courts may refuse to enforce an award if it 'violates the public interest of the society'.[259] Similarly, the Arrangement Concerning Mutual Enforcement of Arbitral Awards between the Mainland [China] and the Hong Kong Special Administrative Region states that a Mainland court may refuse enforcement if it would be contrary to the 'public interests of the Mainland'. Robert Pé and Michael Polkinghorne, rightly in our view, have described this concept as 'broad and ill–defined, and could, for example, be used to refuse enforcement of an award because of social or economic consequences that would follow if a company that was a significant employer were to be placed under financial strain'.[260] Fortunately, Chinese courts have generally taken a narrow view of Article V(2)(b).[261]

9.190

Another potentially problematic country in the region when dealing with the public policy refusal ground is Vietnam. Article 370(2)(b) of Vietnam's Civil Procedure Code,[262] provides that enforcement may be refused if it is 'contrary to the basic principles of the laws of Vietnam'. In *Tyco Services Singapore Pty Ltd v Leighton Contractors (VN) Ltd*,[263] the Vietnamese Court of Appeal held that 'basic principles' of the local law had been breached because Tyco, a Singapore company, did not possess a foreign construction contractor's licence under Vietnamese regulations and that the contract provided that Tyco was not subject to the tax law of Vietnam. This broad interpretation has been criticised in the following terms:[264]

9.191

---

258 For a similar approach, see also the Indian Supreme Court decision in *Oil and Natural Gas Corporation v Saw Pipes Ltd*, (2003) 5 SCC 705.
259 China's Arbitration Law Article 71 and the 1991 Civil Procedure Law Article 260 (now Article 258 of the 2008 Revised Civil Procedure Law).
260 Pé and Polkinghorne, op. cit. fn 112, p. 407, at p. 411 (footnote omitted). See also Lee, op. cit. fn 76, at p. 53.
261 See, e.g. the *Raw Sugar* case, (2003) Min Si Ta Zi No. 3, (China's Supreme People's Court), 1 July 2003; and *Mitsui & Co (Japan) v Hainan Province Textile Industry Corporation* (2001) Min Si Ta Zi No. 12, (China's Supreme People's Court), 13 July 2005. Both cases are cited in Darwazeh and Yeoh, op. cit. fn 85, pp. 846–847. But see the earlier *Heavy Metal* case [1997] Jing Ta No. 35. This concerned a CIETAC arbitral award finding that a contract for a US heavy metal rock group to perform in China had been breached. Nonetheless, the Supreme People's Court refused to enforce the award taking the view that the finding of contractual breach was in 'manifest disregard' of the 'underlying facts' that the band's performance was against China's 'national sentiments' and was contrary to the 'social and public interest' of the country. This case is summarised in Yeoh, op. cit. fn 152, p. 259, at p. 273.
262 Law on Civil Proceedings (Vietnamese National Assembly), 15 June 2004.
263 Judgment No. 02/PTDS, 21 January 2003 (Court of Appeal of the Supreme People's Court of Vietnam, Ho Chi Minh City), cited in Garnett and Nguyen, op. cit. fn 148.
264 Garnett and Nguyen, op. cit. fn 148, p. 147. The authors make a number of other criticisms of the decision at pp. 145–147. See also the Indonesian case of *ED & F Man (Sugar) Ltd v Yani Haryanto*, in which the violation of a domestic law requiring governmental authorisation to import sugar was held to be a violation of public policy, cited in K Mills, 'Judicial Attitudes to Enforcement of Arbitral Awards and Other Judicial Involvement in Arbitration in Indonesia', (2002) 68 *Arbitration* 106.

The result in the case was also likely to be inconsistent with that country's obligations under the New York Convention, given its excessively wide interpretation of 'basic principles of the law of Vietnam'. The approach effectively requires a foreign award to comply with every provision of Vietnamese law which directly conflicts with the Convention drafters' intention that an award cannot be refused enforcement because of non-compliance with local law.

9.192 An overly broad approach to public policy in the context of setting aside an award has also been taken in the Philippines. Its Court of Appeals in *Luzon Hydro Corp v Hon Rommel O Baybay & Transfield Philippines Inc* held that an award issued by an arbitral tribunal seated in Singapore, which found that costs followed the event, was not consistent with Philippines law.[265] The court found that Philippines public policy prevents a litigant from bearing the other side's costs if its position was bona fide. On this basis, it held that the arbitral tribunal's approach to costs violated Philippines public policy and the award was set aside – despite Singapore being the seat of arbitration.

9.193 Another decision of concern is *Harris Adacom Corp v Perkom Sdn Bhd*,[266] in which the Malaysian High Court indicated that to recognise an award issued in an arbitration between a Malaysian party and an Israeli party would be contrary to public policy.

9.194 It is also worth noting that in Singapore's International Arbitration Act, Section 24 defines the public policy ground for setting aside an award as including fraud, corruption or breach of natural justice. This is to be compared with Section 31(4)(b) of that Act, in which the public policy ground for refusing enforcement of a foreign award contains no such qualification.

9.195 A famous English judgment on public policy in international commercial arbitration is *Westacre Investments Inc v Jugoimport-SPDR Holding Co Ltd*.[267] Westacre and Jugoimport entered into a contract governed by Swiss law under which Westacre endeavoured to procure sales of Jugoimport's military equipment by Kuwait. Jugoimport repudiated the contract and Westacre instituted arbitration proceedings in Switzerland. As part of its defence, Jugoimport alleged that the contract involved bribing Kuwaiti officials and was in violation of Kuwaiti law and public policy. The arbitral tribunal decided in favour of Westacre, finding that there was no corruption and that 'lobbying' to procure public contracts was not illegal under the contract's governing law. An unsuccessful attempt to set aside the award was made before the Swiss Federal Tribunal. In attempting to resist enforcement of the award before the English courts, Jugoimport filed new affidavit evidence to support its corruption allegations. However, the Court of Appeal rejected the challenge to enforcement, taking into account that although the contract would have been contrary to Kuwaiti public policy, it was not contrary to Swiss public policy. Since the parties chose Swiss substantive law and

---

[265] *Luzon Hydro Corporation v Baybay and Transfield Philippines*, (2007) XXXII *Yearbook of Commercial Arbitration* 456, at pp. 468–469, paras 29–30. But see Rule 21 of the Philippines Supreme Court Special Rules of Court on Alternative Dispute Resolution, effective October 2009.
[266] [1994] 3 MLJ 504.
[267] [1999] 3 All ER 864 (English Court of Appeal).

the arbitration took place in Switzerland, objections on grounds of international public policy could not be made before English courts to resist enforcement.[268] One commentator has observed that:[269]

> The Court [of Appeal] held that the public policy of sustaining international arbitration awards on the facts of this case outweighed the public policy of discouraging international corruption. In this context, lest it be thought that the [C]ourt was condoning corruption, the issue of illegality by reason of corruption had been considered and rejected by high calibre ICC arbitrators.

Finally, the case of *VV v VW*[270] merits reference. There the Singapore High Court held that a disproportionate costs award in an arbitration did not constitute a violation of public policy. 9.196

6.4 Adjournment of enforcement proceedings (New York Convention Article VI)

Simultaneous applications are often made (i) by the losing party to set aside the award at the seat of the arbitration and (ii) by the winning party to enforce the award in another country. In such a case, Article VI of the New York Convention gives a domestic court hearing the enforcement application discretion 'if it considers it proper' to adjourn the enforcement proceedings. 9.197

One study has found that the trend in case law under this New York Convention provision is to adjourn enforcement proceedings if the court hearing the enforcement application considers that there is a probability of success in the proceedings to set aside.[271] For example, in *Hebei Import & Export Corp v Polytek Engineering Co Ltd*, the High Court of Hong Kong held that the party seeking the adjournment must demonstrate that the application to set aside the award in the foreign court has 'some reasonably arguable grounds which afford some prospects of success'.[272] Despite this trend in case law, a suspension should not be automatic on showing a likelihood of success in the setting aside proceedings.[273] There may be factors, viewed in their totality, that are more compelling than a 'probable success' approach. Some of these other factors, as noted in *Europcar Italia SpA v Maeillano Tours Inc*,[274] include: 9.198

---

268 For a rare instance of denial of award enforcement on the ground of public policy by the English courts, see *Soleimany v Soleimany* [1999] 3 All ER 847, English Court of Appeal. The award at issue in that case was rendered in a domestic arbitration (the parties were English residents, the contract was made in England, and the arbitration was seated in London). The Court of Appeal held that it was contrary to public policy to enforce an English award ordering payment pursuant to an illegal contract and that it would not enforce 'a contract governed by the law of a foreign and friendly state, or which requires performance in such country, if performance is illegal by the law of that country'. [1999] 3 All ER 847, at p. 861.
269 J Cohen, 'Practical Issues to consider in relation to Enforcing and Resisting Enforcement of International Arbitration Awards', (2006) *Asian Dispute Review* 22, at p. 26.
270 [2008] SGHC 11. See Chapter 8, Section 6.2.
271 R Rico, 'Searching for Standards: Suspension of Enforcement Proceedings under Article VI of the New York Convention', (2005) 1 *Asian International Arbitration Journal* 69.
272 (1999, No. 2) 14 *Mealey's International Arbitration Report*, at pp. G-1–G-15.
273 Rico, op. cit. fn 271, p. 81.
274 156 F 3d. 310 (2d Cir. 1998) (US Court of Appeals), pp. 317–318. See also M Secomb, 'Suspension of the Enforcement of Awards under Article VI of the New York Convention – Proof and LSAS', (2002)

(i) the general objective of arbitration to resolve disputes expeditiously;
(ii) the estimated time for the setting aside proceedings;
(iii) the standard of review to be applied in the setting aside proceedings;
(iv) whether the setting aside application was made before the enforcement application;
(v) whether the setting aside proceedings were brought in circumstances indicating intent to delay resolution of the dispute; and
(vi) a balance of the possible hardships to each party, keeping in mind that the party seeking the suspension could be required to provide suitable security if the enforcement is adjourned.

9.199 The *Europcar* approach appears to have been followed in *Toyo Engineering Corp v John Holland Pty Ltd*.[275] There, the Victorian Supreme Court in Australia granted a stay of enforcement after taking into account factors including the prompt filing of a setting aside application in Singapore and the absence of prejudice to the plaintiff because the adjournment would be relatively short – the Singapore setting aside proceedings were to be held within two months.

7 Non-New York Convention enforcement

9.200 The enforcement of an award in a state that has not ratified the New York Convention, or where the Convention does not apply for some reason, will largely depend on that state's law and practice, which is likely to be far more complex than the New York Convention enforcement procedure. If the enforcing state has adopted the Model Law, it might be possible to enforce the award under Article 36 of the Model Law. If the Model Law is not applicable either, then the party seeking enforcement will be subject to whatever the local law requires in this regard.[276]

9.201 One option that may be available is to sue on the award as evidence of a debt and assert that an implied contractual obligation to perform the award exists by virtue of the arbitration agreement.[277] A pitfall in this approach is that the issues already determined by the arbitral tribunal, even those relating to the merits, may be reopened by the court. In some jurisdictions, the applicant will bear the burden of proof. For example, in Hong Kong it will have to prove that the contract containing the arbitration agreement was properly formed, the arbitral tribunal was properly constituted and that the amount awarded has not been paid.[278]

International Arbitration Law Review 1 (commenting on the situation where an award is set aside due to a 'local particularity' (also known as 'local standard annulments') rather than due to the international standards contained in Article 34(2) of the Model Law).
275 [2000] VSC 553.
276 See, e.g. *Weizmann Institute of Science v Neschis*, 229 F Supp 2d 234 (SDNY 2002) (US District Court), (2003) XXVIII *Yearbook of Commercial Arbitration*, p. 1042.
277 See, e.g. *Stargas SPA v Petredec Ltd (The Sargasso)*, [1994] 1 Lloyds Rep 412; and *Brali v Hyundai Corp* (1988) 84 ALR 176, at p. 183 (Supreme Court of Tasmania, Australia).
278 See Brock, op. cit. fn 157, p. 447, paras 15–18. See also *Christopher Brown v Genossenschaft Oesterreichischer Waldbesitzer Holzwirtschaftsbetriebe Registrierte GmbH*, [1954] 1 QB 8, at p. 9; [1953] 2 All ER 1039, at p. 1040; and *Falkingham v Victorian Railways Commissioner*, [1900] AC 452 (Privy Council).

The action will fail if any one of these points is not established. Additionally, the defendant may have a wide range of defences available to it.[279]

A contractual obligation to perform the award may arise from the chosen arbitration rules. For example, Article 27(8) of the SIAC Rules provides: 9.202

> By agreeing to arbitration under these Rules, the parties undertake to carry out the award without delay. An award shall be final and binding on the parties from the date it is made.

This provision may be construed as part of the parties' contract and the non-compliant party may be liable for non-performance. 9.203

Under Indian law, enforcement proceedings may be brought under the common law ground of justice, equity and good conscience.[280] In respect of such proceedings, it must be shown that:[281] 9.204

(i) there was a contract under which the parties agreed to refer disputes to an arbitral tribunal in a foreign country;
(ii) the award was made in accordance with this agreement;
(iii) the award is valid according to the *lex arbitri*; and
(iv) the award is a subsisting award at the time of the court suit.

In Korea, Article 39(2) of its Arbitration Act specifically addresses awards issued in a country that is not a party to the New York Convention. It provides that such awards are to be governed mutatis mutandis by the same procedures applicable to enforcement of foreign court judgments under Article 217 of the Korean Civil Procedure Act[282] and Article 27 of the Civil Enforcement Act.[283] The former provision requires that:[284] 9.205

(i) the jurisdiction of the arbitral tribunal is recognised under Korean law or a treaty to which Korea is a party;
(ii) the respondent has been properly served with notice of the proceeding;
(iii) the award does not violate good morals or other social orders of Korea; and
(iv) there exists a reciprocal enforcement mechanism.

Article 267 of China's Civil Procedure Law provides that non-New York Convention awards are enforceable in China in accordance with 'the principle of reciprocity'. Based on this wording, if the country in which the award was issued would enforce awards rendered in China, then Chinese courts should grant enforcement. However, it has been observed that reciprocity in China requires that the other state's courts have in fact already enforced a Chinese award. Moreover, even though no Article V(1) New York Convention grounds for refusing to 9.206

---

[279] See, e.g. Brock, op. cit. fn 157, p. 447, paras 15–19.
[280] See, e.g. *Badat & Co Bombay v East India Trading Co*, AIR 1964 SC 538 (Indian Supreme Court).
[281] Justice AK Sikri, op. cit. fn 110, p. 10.
[282] Law No. 547 of 4 April 1960, as amended.
[283] Law No. 6627 of 26 January 2002.
[284] See Choe and Dharmananda, op. cit. fn 66, at p. 65 et seq; and Kim and Park, op. cit. fn 205 at p. 162. See also the recognition given to non-New York Convention awards under Section 43 of Philippine Alternative Dispute Resolution Act 9285 of 2004 and Section 46(3) of Singapore's Arbitration Act of 2001 (Cap 10).

enforce are apparent in Article 267, enforcement of an award seriously in breach of public policy may be refused.[285]

8 Execution of awards

9.207 Obtaining a court order that permits an award creditor to enforce the award is not the end of the process. That order must be executed against assets in order to achieve the ultimate goal: obtaining cash or other assets to satisfy the award. Most discussions of enforcement give scant, if any, attention to execution. Execution must be requested against specified assets. Usually, no separate application for execution is required and it is dealt with in the enforcement proceedings. For example, in *Fuerst Day Lawson v Jindal Exports Ltd*, the Indian Supreme Court held:[286]

> for enforcement of foreign awards there is no need to take separate proceedings, one for deciding the enforceability of the award... and the other to take up execution thereafter. In one proceeding... the Court enforcing a foreign award can deal with the entire matter.

9.208 There is a paucity of empirical evidence as to the ultimate success of enforcement actions in international arbitration and most information derives from anecdotes. Mainland China has been identified as a place where there is a significant gap between enforcement orders and the conversion of this into cash.[287] Also with respect to China, it has been reported that political issues and relationships with the local police and bailiffs have played a role in the chances of success in obtaining cash from an enforcement order.[288] China appears to be aware of this problem and is taking responsive measures. For example, new criminal sanctions have been enacted for the evasion of awards and court judgments. Pursuant to Article 313 of China's Criminal Law, a maximum sentence of three years may be imposed where a party, against whom enforcement is sought, either conceals, transfers or destroys property to avoid satisfying the award. Sanctions are also available against guarantors, parties who have a 'duty to assist' the enforcement but fail to do so and state officials who abuse their official capacity.[289]

9.209 In Hong Kong, the problem with enforcement is said to be the difficulty in identifying company assets against which execution may be made.[290] In practice, if assets are difficult to locate, parties often engage lawyers and/or private investigators to find them.

---

[285] See Yeoh, op. cit. fn 152, p. 259, at pp. 271 and 284.
[286] See, e.g. *Fuerst Day Lawson v Jindal Exports Ltd* (2001) 6 SCC 356, at 371 (Indian Supreme Court).
[287] Cohen, op. cit. fn 269, p. 24.
[288] Ibid.
[289] Wang Sheng Chang, op. cit. fn 165, at p. 33.
[290] Cohen, op. cit. fn 269, p. 24.

9 Other enforcement issues

9.1 *Forum non conveniens*

There have been some US cases in which a party resisting enforcement has asserted that another court is better placed to deal with enforcing the award and has urged the enforcing court to decline enforcement on the basis of *forum non conveniens*. The doctrine has been applied by the US 2nd Circuit Court of Appeal in *Monegasque de Reassurances SAM v Nak Naftogaz of Ukraine* to dismiss a petition seeking confirmation of an arbitral award under the New York Convention.[291] The Court of Appeal considered (incorrectly) that it could apply the *forum non conveniens* doctrine because Article III of the New York Convention permitted it to take into account 'the rules of procedure of the territory where the award is relied upon'. In the court's view, it was easier, more expeditious and less expensive to conduct the enforcement proceeding in the Ukraine and the Ukrainian court was better suited to resolve the legal questions raised. 9.210

Born contends that *forum non conveniens* is not a rule of procedure but:[292] 9.211

> reflects substantive policies and discretionary judgments, not questions of filing fees, time requirements, or similar matters that were contemplated by Article III. Extending Article III's provisions requiring recognition of awards in accordance with domestic 'rules of procedure' to permit non-recognition of awards based on a court's assessment of substantive comity interests, U.S. and foreign regulatory policies, and similar matters distorts the Convention's objectives and would grant national courts excessive discretion to avoid or reformulate a Contracting States['] obligations in particular cases in the guise of forum non conveniens analysis; that is inconsistent with the Convention's objectives and very far from what Article III was meant to accomplish.

Moreover, the US Court of Appeal's decision in the *Nak Naftogaz* case was incorrect because it did not give due consideration to the additional words in Article III of the New York Convention, which states that local rules of procedure are to be taken into account 'under the conditions laid down in the following Articles'. In applying this phrase, attention must be drawn to the absence of *forum non conveniens* as an enforcement refusal ground in Article V of the New York Convention. The doctrine of *forum non conveniens* has no place at all in the context of refusing to enforce awards in New York Convention countries. 9.212

9.2 State responsibility for illegal court interference with award

The responsibility of a state under public international law for its court's interference with an international arbitration or unlawful setting aside of an arbitral 9.213

---

[291] See *Monegasque de Reassurances SAM v Nak Naftogaz of Ukraine*, 311 F 3d 488, at 498 (2d Cir 2002). See the detailed analysis of this case in C Croft, 'The Application of the Doctrine of *Forum Non Conveniens* to Enforcement Proceedings', paper delivered at the conference on 'Institutional Arbitration in Infrastructure and Construction', New Delhi, 17–18 October 2008.
[292] Born, op. cit. fn 39, p. 2402 (footnote omitted).

9.214 award is an intriguing question that became highly contentious in the groundbreaking case of *Saipem SpA v Bangladesh*.[293]

9.214 The dispute in *Saipem* arose out of a 1990 agreement to build a pipeline in Bangladesh between Saipem and Petrobangla, a Bangladesh state entity. The agreement contained an ICC arbitration clause stipulating Dhaka as the seat of arbitration. Disputes arose as to the completion of the project and final payment. Saipem commenced ICC arbitration in 1993. During the arbitration, the arbitral tribunal made a number of adverse findings against Petrobangla. As a result, Petrobangla applied to different courts in Bangladesh to revoke the arbitral tribunal's authority. It asserted that the arbitral tribunal had committed or would commit a substantial miscarriage of justice and it had a reasonable apprehension that it would not get a fair trial. Various Bangladeshi courts stayed the arbitral proceedings and revoked the arbitral tribunal's authority. In particular, the First Court of the Subordinate Judge of Dhaka decided:[294]

> the Arbitral Tribunal has conducted the arbitration proceedings improperly by refusing to determine the question of the admissibility of evidence and the exclusion of certain documents from the record as well as by its failure to direct that information regarding insurance be provided. Moreover, the Tribunal has manifestly been in disregard of [Bangladesh] law and as such the Tribunal committed misconduct.
>
> Therefore, in the above circumstances, it appears to me that there is a likelihood of miscarriage of justice.

9.215 The judge revoked the arbitral tribunal's authority. Saipem chose not to appeal because its chances of success in the circumstances appeared low. The arbitral tribunal resumed the proceedings on 'the ground that the challenge or replacement of the arbitrators in an ICC arbitration falls within the exclusive jurisdiction of the ICC Court and not of the courts of Bangladesh' and that 'the revocation of the authority of the ICC Arbitral Tribunal by the Bangladeshi courts was [thus] contrary to the general principles governing international arbitration'.[295] Petrobangla thereafter obtained an injunction from a Bangladeshi court to restrain Saipem from continuing with the arbitration. But the arbitral tribunal proceeded with its work and rendered an award against Petrobangla for breach of its contractual obligation to pay Saipem.

9.216 Pertrobangla then applied to the High Court Division of the Supreme Court of Bangladesh to set aside the award. In April 2004, the court denied the request on the ground that the award was:[296]

> a nullity in the eye of law and this Award can not be treated as an Award in the eye of law as it is clearly illegal and without jurisdiction inasmuch as the authority of the Tribunal was revoked as [far] back as on 5.4.2000 by a competent Court of Bangladesh.
>
> A non-existent award can neither be set aside nor can it be enforced.

---

293 ICSID Case No. ARB/05/7, Award of 30 June 2009.
294 Quoted in *Saipem SpA v Bangladesh*, ICSID Case No. ARB/05/7, Award of 30 June 2009, para 40.
295 Ibid., para 45.
296 Ibid., para 50.

In October 2004, Saipem instituted an ICSID arbitration against the state of Bangladesh under the 1990 Bangladesh-Italy BIT. In assuming jurisdiction over the matter, the ICSID tribunal emphasised that it was not enforcing the arbitral tribunal's award or converting that award into an enforceable ICSID award, as the respondent asserted.[297] The ICSID tribunal found that the acts of the Bangladesh courts (which were attributable to the state of Bangladesh) amounted to an indirect expropriation because they substantially deprived Saipem of the benefit of the award. In the ICSID tribunal's view, the Bangladesh Supreme Court decision that the award was a 'nullity' was 'tantamount to a taking of the residual contractual rights arising from the investments as crystallised in the ICC Award'.[298]

The ICSID tribunal added, importantly, that the act of any court to set aside an award cannot give rise to an indirect expropriation. It amounts to an expropriation only where the act is also illegal. In the present case, the ICSID tribunal held that illegality was present for two main reasons:
(i) The Bangladesh courts abused their supervisory jurisdiction over the arbitral process – this jurisdiction was exercised to revoke the arbitrators' authority 'for an end which was different from that for which it was instituted and thus violated the internationally accepted principle of prohibition of abuse of rights'.[299]
(ii) The Bangladesh court's revocation of the arbitrators' authority was a breach of Article II of the New York Convention because it prevented the arbitration proceedings that were implementing the arbitration agreement and completely frustrated, if not the words, at least the spirit of the Convention.[300]

When considering this case, it must not be forgotten that the ICSID proceeding was not a backdoor mode of enforcing the ICC award. It was directed at providing redress for illegal court interference with an arbitration. This requirement of illegality indicates that the conduct of a court must be a serious breach of internationally accepted standards if similar types of ICSID claims are to be successful. Arbitration under bilateral investment treaties are examined in Chapter 10.

9.3 State immunity

State immunity, also known as sovereign immunity, may constitute a defence in a court action to enforce an award against (1) a state or state entity or (2) a private corporation (i) wholly owned by a state or (ii) in which the state is a majority shareholder. The New York Convention is silent about state immunity. The principle may enable a state that is a party to an international arbitration to claim immunity from the enforcement powers of another state's courts.

The essence of the rationale underpinning state immunity was identified by Lord Browne-Wilkinson in *Ex Parte Pinochet (No 3)*: '[i]t is a basic principle of international law that one sovereign state (the forum state) does not adjudicate

---
[297] Ibid., para 110.
[298] Ibid., para 129.
[299] Ibid., para 161.
[300] Ibid., para 167.

on the conduct of a foreign state'.[301] Two forms of state immunity are relevant to international arbitration: jurisdictional immunity and immunity from execution. Immunity does not apply to arbitration proceedings per se because that is a private process in which the arbitral tribunal is not exercising a state's powers (as judges do) and the respondent state is deemed to have waived its immunity by agreeing to arbitrate.[302] Issues relating to immunity apply when courts become involved in the arbitral process.

9.222   Historically, a state enjoyed absolute immunity from the exercise of jurisdiction by foreign courts in all matters. But the broadening of state activities, particularly in the domain of commerce, has resulted in restrictions on the immunities afforded to states.[303] Most domestic laws now include a number of exceptions to the general principle of immunity.[304] There is a wide-ranging consensus that state immunity from suit does not apply to commercial activities (i.e. acts *jure gestionis*), as opposed to purely governmental activities (i.e. acts *jure imperii*), to which immunity applies.[305]

9.223   In international arbitration, a waiver of a state's immunity from the supervisory jurisdiction of the courts at the seat of arbitration may be implied from the state's agreement to arbitrate.[306] Some domestic laws expressly endorse this implication. For example, Section 11(1) of Singapore's State Immunity Act 1979 provides:[307]

> Where a State has agreed in writing to submit a dispute which has arisen, or may arise, to arbitration, the State is not immune as respects proceedings in the courts in Singapore which relate to the arbitration.

9.224   The above paragraph is concerned with jurisdictional immunity. It is distinct from the concept of immunity from execution, which involves actually enforcing

---

[301] *R v Bow Street Metropolitan Stipendiary Magistrate, ex parte Pinochet Ugarte*, [2000] 1 AC 147 (England House of Lords). See also Article 5 of the 2004 UN Convention on Jurisdictional Immunities of States and Their Property which provides that a 'State enjoys immunity, in respect of itself and its property, from the jurisdiction of the courts of another State . . .'. UN Doc. A/RES/59/38, 16 December 2004. This Convention is not yet in force but is gaining recognition as an authoritative statement in this field of international law. See, e.g. *AIG Capital Partners, Inc v Kazakhstan* [2005] EWHC 2239 (Com), [2006] All ER (Comm) 11 (English High Court) at para 45, per Justice Aikens; and *Jones v Ministry of Interior al Mamlaka Al Arabiya AS Saudiya (Kingdom of Saudi Arabia)* [2006] UKHL 26, [2007] 1 AC 270 (English House of Lords).
[302] See generally P Dunham and S Greenberg, 'Balancing Sovereignty and the Contractor's Rights in International Construction Arbitrations Involving State Entities', (2006) 23(2) *International Construction Law Review* 130.
[303] See H Fox, *The Law of State Immunity*, 2nd edn, Oxford University Press, 2008, p. 201 et seq.
[304] See, e.g. Part III of the 2004 UN Convention on Jurisdictional Immunities of States and Their Property; Australia's Foreign States Immunities Act 1985 Section 11; Pakistan's State Immunity Ordinance 1981 Section 5; Singapore's State Immunity Act 1979 Sections 5 and 12; and US Foreign Sovereign Immunities Act 1976 Section 1605.
[305] This position is reflected in Article 10 and the definition of 'commercial transaction' in Article 2 of the 2004 UN Convention on Jurisdictional Immunities of States and Their Property. See also M Shaw, *International Law*, 6th edn, Cambridge University Press, 2008, p. 707; and H Fox, 'State Immunity and the New York Convention', in Gaillard and Di Pietro, op. cit. fn 2, p. 829, at pp. 834–835. The issue has emerged recently in Hong Kong in *FG Hemisphere Associates v Democratic Republic of Congo* [2010] 2 HKC 487 (10 February 2010) (Court of Appeal). In that case the court held that Hong Kong followed the restrictive theory on immunity, despite a letter tendered from China's Commissioner of the Ministry of Foreign Affairs Hong Kong Office during the case which stated that China followed the absolute theory of immunity. Congo has been granted leave to appeal.
[306] See generally Fox, op. cit. fn 303, p. 495 et seq.
[307] See also Australia's Foreign States Immunities Act 1985 Section 17; and Article 17 of the 2004 UN Convention on Jurisdictional Immunities of States and Their Property.

the award against the state's assets. On this point, Dunham and Greenberg have observed:[308]

> even if 'a State's consent to commercial arbitration implies consent to all natural and logical consequences of the commercial arbitration', this does not necessarily include enforcement of the award. Immunity from execution is a separate issue from immunity from jurisdiction. While an arbitration might result in an award that is recognisable under the New York Convention, immunity from execution can reduce the chances of actual recovery. A waiver of immunity from execution cannot be implied on the basis of the arbitration agreement.

As discussed in Chapter 10, even the robust enforcement mechanism applicable to awards issued under the ICSID Convention is subject to domestic law concerning state immunity from execution.[309] Some domestic laws specifically address immunity from execution. For example, Sections 30 and 31 of the Australian Foreign States Immunities Act 1985 provide in relevant part as follows: 9.225

30 Immunity from execution

Except as provided by this Part, [[310]] the property of a foreign State is not subject to any process or order (whether interim or final) of the courts of Australia for the satisfaction or enforcement of a judgment, order or arbitration award or, in Admiralty proceedings, for the arrest, detention or sale of the property.

31 Waiver of immunity from execution

(1) A foreign State may at any time by agreement waive the application of section 30 in relation to property, but it shall not be taken to have done so by reason only that it has submitted to the jurisdiction. . . .

In France, the Cour de Cassation in *Creighton v Qatar*[311] held that a state's acceptance of arbitral rules that stipulate something similar to Article 28(6) of the ICC Rules is sufficient to waive both immunity from jurisdiction and immunity from execution.[312] A leading commentator on state immunity has observed that:[313] 9.226

---

308 Dunham and Greenberg, op. cit. fn 302, at p. 147, quoting C Annacker and RT Creig, 'State Immunity and Arbitration', (2004) 15(2) *ICC International Court of Arbitration Bulletin* 70, at p. 71. See also the discussion of the separate consents required for exercise of jurisdiction and of enforcement in Fox, op. cit. fn 303, p. 486 et seq. Recently in Hong Kong, in *FG Hemisphere Associates v Democratic Republic of Congo* [2010] 2 HKC 487 (10 February 2010) the Court of Appeal held at paras 229–234 that Congo's agreement to arbitrate under the ICC Rules (including the obligation to carry out an arbitral award) was not in itself a waiver of a state's immunity from execution.
309 See Chapter 10, Section 9.
310 For example, Article 32 of the Australian Foreign States Immunities Act 1985, subject to exceptions, provides that 'section 30 does not apply in relation to commercial property'.
311 *Creighton Ltd (Cayman Islands) v Minister of Finance and Minister of Internal Affairs and Agriculture of the Government of the State of Qatar*, 6 July 2000, 127(4) JDI (Clunet) 1054 (2000), Cour de Cassation, 1ère Ch Civ; (2000) XXV *Yearbook of Commercial Arbitration* 458. See also E Gaillard, 'Effectiveness of Arbitral Awards, State Immunity from Execution and Autonomy of State Entities – Three Incompatible Principles', in E. Gaillard (ed), *State Entities in International Arbitration*, IAI Series on International Arbitration No. 4, Juris Publishing, 2008, at 179.
312 Article 28(6) of the ICC Rules provides: 'Every Award shall be binding on the parties. By submitting the dispute to arbitration under these Rules, the parties undertake to carry out any Award without delay and shall be deemed to have waived their right to any form of recourse insofar as such waiver can validly be made.'
313 Fox, op. cit. fn 303, p. 496.

[w]here the State has in addition [to consenting to arbitration] committed itself under the [New York Convention or Model Law], all of which instruments impose obligations on the party to honour any arbitral award rendered, an even stronger case of implied waiver of immunity from execution of the award can be argued.

9.227 Justice Aikens' treatment of Section 14(4) of the UK State Immunity Act 1978 in *AIG Capital Partners Inc v Kazakhstan*[314] is also noteworthy. That provision states that the property of a foreign state's central bank is immune from enforcement in English courts. Justice Aikens took the view that this provision 'impinge[s] on the rights of access of parties to the enforcement jurisdiction of the UK courts'.[315] Immediately thereafter he indicated that 'if severe', a restriction on the court remedies available to parties could amount to a limitation of a party's access to court in contravention of Article 6(1) of the European Convention on Human Rights.[316] But in the case before him, Justice Aikens held that the Section 14(4) restriction on enforcement against the property of a foreign state bank was legitimate and proportionate.[317] There is no equivalent multilateral human rights treaty that is in force among states in the Asia-Pacific.

9.228 To be absolutely sure that a state is not immune from the enforcement or execution of an arbitral award, an express waiver of a state's immunity from execution should be included in the arbitration agreement. Another method would be to agree with the state that it will earmark property that can be used to satisfy sums due under an award issued against a state.[318]

---

[314] *AIG Capital Partners, Inc v Kazakhstan* [2005] EWHC 2239; [2006] All ER (Comm) 11 (English High Court).
[315] Ibid. at para 78, per Justice Aikens.
[316] Ibid.
[317] Ibid., at para 79, per Justice Aikens.
[318] See, e.g. Articles 18 and 19 of the 2004 UN Convention on Jurisdictional Immunities of States and Their Property. See also the recommendations for parties contracting with states in Dunham and Greenberg, op. cit. fn 302, at pp. 148–149.

10

Investment treaty arbitration

1 Introduction

In the last decade, investment treaty arbitrations have rapidly increased in number and in significance.[1] As its name suggests, this area of arbitration is based on treaties that enable a foreign investor to claim for loss or damage relating to its investment against a state in which that investment has been made. The three most distinctive features of this form of arbitration in comparison with international commercial arbitration are that:

(i) There is at least one state (or state entity) that is a party to the proceedings, whereas international commercial arbitration does not necessarily involve a state party.[2]

10.1

---

[1] Investment treaty arbitration is referred to synonymously as international investment arbitration, foreign investment arbitration, investor-state arbitration or, simply, investment arbitration. Specific texts in this discipline of arbitration include K Yannaca-Small (ed.), *Arbitration under International Investment Agreements: A Guide to the Key Issues*, Oxford University Press, 2010; Z Douglas, *The International Law of Investment Claims*, Cambridge University Press, 2009; C Dugan, D Wallace, N Rubins and B Sabahi, *Investor-State Arbitration*, Oxford University Press, 2008; P Muchlinski, F Ortino and C Schreuer, *The Oxford Handbook of International Investment Law*, Oxford University Press, 2008; R Dolzer and C Schreuer, *Principles of International Investment Law*, Oxford University Press, 2008; M Dimsey, *The Resolution of International Investment Disputes: Challenges and Practical Solutions*, Eleven International Publishing, 2008; C McLachlan, L Shore and M Weiniger, *International Investment Arbitration: Substantive Principles*, Oxford University Press, 2007; RD Bishop, J Crawford and WM Reisman, *Foreign Investment Disputes: Cases, Materials, and Commentary*, Kluwer Law International, 2005; N Rubins and NS Kinsella, *International Investment, Political Risk, and Dispute Resolution: A Practitioner's Guide*, Oceana Publications, 2005; and M Sornarajah, *The International Law on Foreign Investment*, 2nd edn, Cambridge University Press, 2004. For collections of relevant awards, reviews or summaries see *ICSID Review – Foreign Investment Law Journal*; *The International Lawyer*; *Journal du Droit International, Clunet*; www.iareporter.com; www.investmentclaims.com; www.investmenttreatynews.org; http://ita.law.uvic.ca; and www.kluwerarbitration.com.

[2] However, a large number of arbitrations involving state parties are not, in fact, investment arbitrations. For example, in 2009 78 of the ICC International Court of Arbitration's 817 new cases involved a state or state entity. Moreover, arbitrations involving states are often entirely ad hoc, for example using the UNCITRAL Arbitration Rules, and/or partially administered by the Permanent Court of Arbitration in The Hague. By

478　INTERNATIONAL COMMERCIAL ARBITRATION

(ii) The legal rights invoked generally arise out of treaties and public international law, rather than from domestic law or contracts.
(iii) In the case of ICSID arbitrations, the arbitral process is almost completely delocalised.[3]

10.2　A dedicated chapter on investment treaty arbitration is included in this book not only because of its growing importance and frequency of use but also because it provides a wealth of comparative material for international commercial arbitration.

10.3　This chapter proceeds with an overview of international investment law in Section 2. Investment treaties and their dispute settlement clauses are discussed in Section 3. Various features of ICSID and its jurisdictional requirements are examined in Section 4. The chapter then deals with the advantages, disadvantages and innovative features of the ICSID Convention in Section 5. Substantive aspects of international investment law are briefly surveyed in Section 6. Section 7 outlines the remedies available under investment treaties. This chapter concludes with a discussion of the annulment and enforcement of ICSID awards, respectively, in Sections 8 and 9.

2 International investment law

10.4　The legal framework of modern international investment law has been established primarily through treaties. They take the form of BITs[4] or multilateral treaties.[5] These treaties aim to protect and promote foreign investments as well as to develop the economy of the state in which the investment is made (the host state). The framework strives to increase inflows of foreign direct investment into countries (particularly developing nations) by:
(i) requiring that the host state treat investors in accordance with international standards; and
(ii) granting foreign investors the right to institute an international arbitration against the host state if these standards are not met.

10.5　Increasingly, international commercial lawyers need to understand these rights and protections, whether or not their clients engage directly with the host state or its organs. In other words, if host state action negatively affects a foreign investor or its investment, rights to commence an arbitration against that state

comparison, ICSID's total number of new cases for 2009 was 25, i.e. less than half of the ICC's 2009 case load for states. It should also be noted that, although rare, arbitrations under investment treaties may involve a state claiming against another state.
3　Delocalisation is explained in Chapter 2, Section 5.
4　See, e.g. the Agreement between the People's Republic of China and the Federal Republic of Germany on the Encouragement and Reciprocal Protection of Investments, signed on 1 December 2003 and entered into force 11 December 2005.
5　See, e.g. North American Free Trade Agreement, signed 12 December 1992, entered into force 1 January 1994, 32 *International Legal Materials* 296 and 605; and the Energy Charter Treaty (Annex I to the Final Act of the European Energy Charter Conference), signed 17 December 1991, 34 *International Legal Materials* 373.

may be granted to the investor under an investment treaty even in the absence of a directly negotiated arbitration agreement between them.

The Asia-Pacific region has been associated with a number of significant developments in this area of law.[6] Pakistan was a party to the first bilateral investment treaty (BIT) to be signed.[7] One of the earliest and longest running ICSID cases involved an Asian state.[8] A number of jurisprudentially important investment treaty awards relate to investments made in this region. And China, having concluded upwards of 120 BITs, is second only to Germany in the number of BITs any single country has concluded.[9] Notwithstanding this strong connection with international investment treaties, the Asia-Pacific has not yet seen as many investment treaty arbitrations as would have been expected when compared with other regions of the world.[10]

3 Investment treaties

BITs are treaties signed between two states pursuant to which each offers substantive standards of treatment to private investors that originate from the other state. A vast proportion of BITs also contain dispute settlement clauses (discussed below) to resolve disputes between the investor and the host state. In terms of numbers, upwards of 2700 BITs now exist.[11] UNCTAD has reported that by the end of 2008, states from Asia and Oceania had signed 41% of all BITs, i.e. a total of 1112.[12]

---

6 For other Asia-Pacific perspectives on investment arbitration, see John Savage's following publications: J Savage, 'Investment Treaty Arbitration', in M Pryles and M Moser (eds), *The Asian Leading Arbitrators' Guide to International Arbitration*, JurisNet, 2007, p. 465; J Savage, 'Investment Treaty Arbitration and Asia: Review of Developments in 2005 and 2006', (2007) 3 *Asian International Arbitration Journal* 1; J Savage, 'Investment Treaty Arbitration and Asia: Survey and Comment', (2005) 1 *Asian International Arbitration Journal* 3. See also MJ Moser (ed), *Investor-State Arbitration – Lessons for Asia*, Juris Publishing, 2008 and PJ Turner, M Mangan and A Baykitch, 'Investment Treaty Arbitration – An Australian Perspective', (2007) 24 *Journal of International Arbitration* 103.
7 Treaty for the Promotion and Protection of Investments (with Protocol and exchange of notes) between Pakistan and the Federal Republic of Germany, 457 UNTS 23, signed at Bonn on 25 November 1959 and entered into force on 28 April 1962.
8 *Amco Asia Corp v Republic of Indonesia*, ICSID Case No. ARB/81/1. The case was registered in 1981 and a final decision in that case (a second annulment decision) was issued in 1992.
9 See *International Investment Rule Making: Stocktaking, Challenges and the Way Forward*, UNCTAD Series on International Investment Policies for Development (2008), UN Doc. UNCTAD/ITE/IIT/2007/3, at p. 24.
10 See L Nottage and R Weeramantry, 'Investment Arbitration for Japan and Asia: Five Perspectives on Law and Practice', Sydney Centre for International Law, Working Paper No. 21, March 2009, at www.law.usyd.edu.au/scil/WorkingPapers.html. Investment claims have been brought against several states from the Asia-Pacific region, including Bangladesh, India, Indonesia, Malaysia, Myanmar, Mongolia, New Zealand, Pakistan, the Philippines, Sri Lanka, Thailand and Vietnam. These claims include those instituted under the ICSID Convention as well as non-ICSID arbitrations. For a list of most of these cases, see Savage, 'Investment Treaty Arbitration' op. cit. fn 6, at p. 477. For a list of cases in which the claimants are from the Asia-Pacific region, see Nottage and Weeramantry, ibid., at Appendix D.
11 See UNCTAD, *Recent Developments in International Investment Agreements*, International Investment Agreement Monitor No. 3 (2009), UN Doc UNCTAD/WEB/DIAE/IA/2009/8, at p. 2. See also JW Salacuse, 'BIT by BIT: The Growth of Bilateral Investment Treaties and their Impact on Foreign Investment in Developing Countries', (1990) 24 *International Lawyer* 655; KJ Vandevelde, 'A Brief History of International Investment Agreements', (2005) 12 *UC Davis Journal of International Law and Policy* 257.
12 UNCTAD, ibid., p. 2.

480   INTERNATIONAL COMMERCIAL ARBITRATION

10.8   As mentioned previously, the first ever BIT signed was the 1959 Pakistan-Germany BIT. However, the number of BITs entered into during the following decade was modest – fewer than eight BITs were signed per year during that period.[13] Thereafter, the numbers of BITs gradually increased until the 1990s, when a dramatic rise took place. In that decade, an average of 146 BITs were signed each year.[14] The upturn in BIT numbers during the 1990s has been attributed to the end of the Cold War, the movement of many Central and Eastern European nations from socialist to free market economies and the rapid economic development of East Asian countries.[15] From an Asian standpoint, the recent growth of BITs has led Dolzer and Schreuer to observe:[16]

> The most significant trends in the evolution of BIT practice in the past decade concerns the negotiation of BITs by Asian states. China has concluded 117 treaties between 1982 and 2006. India concluded its first BIT in 1994, had already entered into 26 BITs by 1999, and in 2006 was a party to 56 such treaties. Japan has decided to join the practice of other OECD countries and in 2006 was a party to 12 investment agreements.

10.9   BITs were originally signed between developed states and developing states, with the intention that this would promote the flow of investment from the former to the latter. More recently, an increasing number of BITs have been signed between developing countries.[17] Additionally, case law shows that investor claimants are now not simply from developed countries. A number of cases can be found in which investors from developing countries are invoking BITs to institute claims against developed or developing countries.[18]

10.10   Free trade agreements (FTAs), unlike BITs, are treaties that are not solely dedicated to investment protection. For example, the 2009 Agreement Establishing the ASEAN-Australia-New Zealand Free Trade Area[19] (the ASEAN-ANZ Treaty) contains 18 chapters on a diverse range of subjects, including customs procedures, electronic commerce, intellectual property, trade in goods and movement of persons. Only Chapter 11 is devoted to investment protection.[20] Combined trade and investment agreements often contain investment protection provisions

---

13 KJ Vandevelde, 'The Political Economy of a Bilateral Investment Treaty', (1998) 92 *American Journal of International Law* 621, at pp. 627–628.
14 See UNCTAD, *International Investment Rule Making: Stocktaking, Challenges and the Way Forward*, UNCTAD Series on International Investment Policies for Development (2008), UN Doc. UNCTAD/ITE/IIT/2007/3, at p. 23.
15 See Vandevelde, op. cit. fn 13, at p. 628; and UNCTAD, ibid., at p. 15.
16 Dolzer and Schreuer, op. cit. fn 1, pp. 20–21.
17 Ibid., p. 21 (noting that in the past decade more than 600 BITs have been negotiated between developing states).
18 See, e.g. *Maffezini v Spain*, ICSID Case No. ARB/97/7 (Maffezini was an Argentine investor); and *MTD Equity Sdn Bhd & MTD Chile SA v Chile*, ICSID Case No. ARB/01/7 (MTD Equity was a Malaysian investor).
19 Signed on 27 February 2009, but not yet in force.
20 An important multilateral treaty relevant to this region that is entirely devoted to investment protection is the ASEAN Comprehensive Investment Agreement, signed on 26 February 2009 by members of the Association of Southeast Asian Nations (ASEAN). See generally I Maxwell and K-J Wegner, 'The New ASEAN Comprehensive Investment Agreement', (2009) 5(2) *Asian International Arbitration Journal* 167.

similar to those found in BITs.[21] At the end of 2007, 254 of these treaties were in existence and at least 75 more were under negotiation.[22]

10.11 A vital element of investment treaty arbitration is the dispute settlement clause found in investment treaties. It grants investors a right to institute arbitration proceedings directly against a state. This type of clause represents a change from traditional international law practice whereby an investor was generally dependent on its home state to pursue a diplomatic protection claim on behalf of the investor. As will be seen below, the latter system of dispute resolution has many drawbacks for the investor.[23]

10.12 Several different options may be provided in investment treaty dispute settlement clauses. Article 21(1) of Chapter 11 of the ASEAN-ANZ Treaty contains a good sample of the alternatives:

> A disputing investor may submit a claim ... at the choice of the disputing investor:
> (a) where the Philippines or Viet Nam is the disputing Party, to the courts or tribunals of that Party, provided that such courts or tribunals have jurisdiction over such claim; or
> (b) under the ICSID Convention and the ICSID Rules of Procedure for Arbitration Proceedings, provided that both the disputing Party and the non-disputing Party are parties to the ICSID Convention; or
> (c) under the ICSID Additional Facility Rules, provided that either of the disputing Party or non-disputing Party are a party to the ICSID Convention; or
> (d) under the UNCITRAL Arbitration Rules; or
> (e) if the disputing parties agree, to any other arbitration institution or under any other arbitration rules,
> provided that resort to one of the fora under Subparagraphs (a) to (e) shall exclude resort to any other.

10.13 The phrase that follows sub-para (e) is frequently referred to as a 'fork in the road' provision. It is not as simple to apply as it first appears. Whether the election of one option precludes recourse to another may depend on a number of factors, including the juridical nature of the claims made in the different fora (e.g. were they both treaty-based claims?) and the parties involved in the two proceedings (e.g. were they identical in both instances?).[24]

10.14 Usually, investment treaty dispute settlement provisions would be conditional upon the expiry of a certain period of time for amicable settlement. For example,

---

21 See, e.g. Economic Partnership Agreement concluded between Japan and Thailand 2007; Free Trade Agreement between the US and the Republic of Korea 2007; NZ-China Free Trade Agreement 2008; Australia-US Free Trade Agreement 2004; Comprehensive Economic Cooperation Agreement between India and Singapore 2005 and Agreement between Malaysia and Japan for an Economic Partnership 2005. Note that some, such as the Australia-US FTA and the Agreement between Japan and the Republic of the Philippines of an Economic Partnership 2007 do not contain investor-state dispute settlement provisions. An informative compilation of Asian trade and investment treaties is set forth in the Asia Pacific Trade and Investment Agreements Database created by the United Nations Economic and Social Commission for Asia and the Pacific (UNESCAP), at www.unescap.org/tid/aptiad/AllAgreementsGrid.aspx (accessed 17 May 2009).
22 UNCTAD, op. cit. fn 14, p. 26.
23 See Section 5.3.1.
24 See McLachlan, Shore and Weiniger, op. cit. fn 1, p. 103, paras 4.75 et seq.

in Chapter 11 of the ASEAN-ANZ Treaty, Article 19 requires amicable resolution through consultation but if the dispute cannot be settled amicably within 180 days, Article 20 permits the investor to refer the dispute to arbitration.[25]

4 The International Centre for Settlement of Investment Disputes (ICSID)

4.1 Background and structure of ICSID

10.15 A short history of the ICSID Convention is provided in Chapter 1, Section 2.3.2. ICSID is an international institution established pursuant to Article 1 of the ICSID Convention. It is based in Washington DC, USA. The centre offers special, autonomous procedures for administering investment arbitrations between a state (i.e. a government) or state entity and a foreign private investor. ICSID was created as an independent international organisation[26] but it is structurally linked to the World Bank. The bank's governors sit *ex officio* on ICSID's Administrative Council (described below), the Chairman of the Administrative Council is the World Bank's President and the ICSID Secretariat (described below) is funded through the World Bank.[27]

10.16 The two constituent bodies of ICSID are its Administrative Council and Secretariat. The Administrative Council is composed of all ICSID Convention contracting states. Essentially, it functions as the governing body of ICSID, possessing the power to adopt and approve the Centre's budget, administrative regulations and rules of arbitral procedure.[28] The ICSID Secretariat, on the other hand, provides the day-to-day administrative and support functions for arbitrations, much like most arbitral institutions.

10.17 Initially, the number of case registrations at ICSID was low. In the five years that followed the ICSID Convention's entry into force in 1966, no case was registered with ICSID[29] and between 1966 to 1996, only 35 ICSID cases were registered – an average of approximately one per year.[30] Today, the picture is fundamentally different. From 1996 through 2005, 166 ICSID cases were registered and in November 2009, a total of 121 cases were pending before

---

25 This is analogous to multi-tiered dispute resolution clauses discussed in Chapter 4, Section 9.4 of this book. Some ICSID tribunals have not required strict compliance with these negotiation periods. See, e.g. *SGS Société Générale de Surveillance SA v Pakistan*, 6 August 2003, 8 ICSID Reports 406, at para 184 and *Bayindir Insaat Turizm Ticaret Ve Sanayi AŞ v Pakistan*, 14 November 2005, at para 100. But see *Generation Ukraine Inc v Ukraine*, 16 September 2003, 10 ICSID Reports 240, at para 14.3.
26 Article 18 of the ICSID Convention states: 'The Centre shall have full international legal personality. The legal capacity of the Centre shall include the capacity: (a) to contract; (b) to acquire and dispose of movable and immovable property; (c) to institute legal proceedings'.
27 See ICSID Convention Articles 2, 4, 5; and The World Bank, *A Guide to The World Bank*, 2003, p. 44.
28 See ICSID Convention Article 6; and CH Schreuer, *The ICSID Convention: A Commentary*, Cambridge University Press, 2001, pp. 22–31.
29 *Holiday Inns S.A. v Morocco* (ICSID Case No. ARB/72/1) was the first case to be registered at ICSID on 13 January 1972. It was settled and discontinued on 17 October 1978.
30 See http://icsid.worldbank.org (accessed 23 November 2009) and G van Harten, *Investment Treaty Arbitration and Public Law*, Oxford University Press, 2007, p. 30.

ICSID.[31] Several more investment treaty arbitrations are pending at other arbitral institutions.[32] Two major reasons for this rise in investment treaty arbitration are the proliferation in the 1990s of bilateral investment treaties (most of which contained ICSID dispute settlement clauses) and Argentina's financial crisis.[33]

4.2 ICSID jurisdiction

Article 25(1) of the ICSID Convention is central to ICSID arbitrations. It defines ICSID's jurisdiction in the following terms:

10.18

> The jurisdiction of the Centre shall extend to any legal dispute arising directly out of an investment, between a Contracting State (or any constituent subdivision or agency of a Contracting State designated to the Centre by that State) and a national of another Contracting State, which the parties to the dispute consent in writing to submit to the Centre. When the parties have given their consent, no party may withdraw its consent unilaterally...

The key jurisdictional criteria under this provision relate to:

10.19

(i) the nature of the dispute (*ratione materiae*) – it must be legal and arise out of an investment;
(ii) the parties (*ratione personae*) – the claimant must be a national of an ICSID contracting state and the respondent must be another ICSID contracting state; and
(iii) the consent of the parties to have the dispute resolved in accordance with ICSID procedure.

Jurisdictional issues pertaining to the meaning of an investment, the nationality of the claimant and the consent of parties to resolve disputes under the ICSID Convention will be addressed in the following section. ICSID's Additional Facility will also be discussed, which may be used for certain claims falling outside the scope of Article 25.

10.20

4.3 Requirement of an 'investment'

As this book generally indicates, international commercial arbitration may be utilised to resolve a broad range of disputes.[34] In contrast, the subject matter of the disputes that may be resolved in investment treaty arbitrations is far more circumscribed. Article 25(1) of the ICSID Convention limits the jurisdiction

10.21

---

31 See http://icsid.worldbank.org (accessed 5 June 2010). The ICSID publication, *The ICSID Caseload – Statistics*, Issue 2010-1, indicates that 19 cases were registered during the fiscal year of 2002, 31 in 2003, 27 in 2004, 27 in 2005, 23 in 2006, 37 in 2007, 21 in 2008, and 25 in 2009. These figures do not indicate foreign investment arbitrations conducted outside ICSID's auspices. See also van Harten, ibid., pp. 30–31.
32 Two of the other arbitral institutions that administer a number of investment treaty arbitrations are the Stockholm Chamber of Commerce and the ICC International Court of Arbitration. See UNCTAD, *Latest Developments in Investor State Dispute Settlement*, IIA Monitor No. 1, 2009, UN Doc. UNCTAD/WEB/DIAE/IIA/2009/6, p. 2. The non-ICSID investment treaty arbitration figures are uncertain due to their confidential nature.
33 More than 40 investment treaty arbitrations were instituted against Argentina as a result of the government's response to the Argentine financial crisis of 2000–2001.
34 See generally Chapter 4, Section 8 in this book.

of ICSID arbitrations to 'legal disputes arising directly out of an investment' between an ICSID contracting state and an investor who is a national of a different ICSID contracting state. To exercise jurisdiction over ICSID claims, many ICSID tribunals have had to determine whether an 'investment' existed within the meaning of Article 25. No definition of the term is provided in the Convention. In the words of the World Bank's Executive Directors:[35]

> No attempt was made to define the term 'investment' [in the ICSID Convention] given the essential requirement of consent by the parties, and the mechanism through which Contracting States can make known in advance, if they so desire, the classes of disputes which they would or would not consider submitting to the Centre (Article 25(4)).

10.22 This statement indicates that it was left to contracting states to define in separate instruments the scope of an investment for the purposes of the Convention. Nonetheless, and despite the fact that almost every bilateral or multilateral investment treaty expressly defines an 'investment', the question as to what constitutes an 'investment' for the purpose of Article 25 has led to considerable debate.

10.23 A number of ICSID tribunals have, independently of any definition of 'investment' in the BIT invoked, assessed that term on the basis of four criteria.[36] A leading case in this regard is *Salini v Morocco* in which it was said that:[37]

> The doctrine generally considers that investment infers: contributions, a certain duration of performance of the contract and participation in the risks of transaction. In reading the [ICSID] Convention's preamble, one may add the contribution to the economic development of the host State of the investment as an additional condition.

10.24 A different position was taken in *Malaysian Historical Salvors Sdn Bhd v Malaysia*,[38] which gives importance not to the meaning of 'investment' in Article 25 but to the definition of an investment as found in BITs.[39] The majority of the 'ad hoc committee' there annulled the original tribunal's award because it failed to take into account the ICSID Convention drafters' intention that 'investment' in Article 25 was to be defined by states in their instrument providing recourse to ICSID, e.g. a BIT. In contrast to *Salini v Morocco* it considered that the ICSID Convention's drafters rejected imposing any specific duration or pre-set monetary value in respect of the investment. It also held that the need for an economic contribution to the host state was not a jurisdictional condition that would exclude small contributions from the coverage of the ICSID Convention.

---

35 Report of the Executive Directors on the ICSID Convention, 18 March 1965, reprinted in 1 ICSID Reports 28, at para 27. In 1965 the World Bank's name was the International Bank for Reconstruction and Development. See also G Delaume, 'ICSID Arbitration in Practice', (1984) 2 *International Tax and Business Lawyer* 58, at p. 65.
36 These criteria have been based in large measure on Schreuer's understanding of the meaning of investment. See Schreuer, op. cit. fn 28, p. 140; and Dolzer and Schreuer, op. cit. fn 1, p. 68.
37 Decision on Jurisdiction, 23 July 2001, 6 ICSID Reports 400, at para 52.
38 Decision on the Application for Annulment, 16 April 2009.
39 BITs usually define 'investments' broadly, such as including 'all assets' or 'every kind of investment' in the territory of one contracting party by nationals of another contracting party. In relation to BITs signed by South Asian states, see P Ranjan, 'Definition of Investment in Bilateral Investment Treaties of South Asian Countries and Regulatory Discretion', (2009) 26 *Journal of International Arbitration* 217.

Also relevant to this discussion is the view of some ICSID arbitral tribunals that the term 'investment' is different from 'ordinary commercial transactions,' for example, a contract for the sale of goods. They have held that disputes as to the latter fall outside the scope of the ICSID regime.[40] Concrete examples of 'investments' held to fall within the scope of Article 25 of the ICSID Convention include the construction of dams and highways, the running of hotels, the provision of pre-shipment inspection services, shareholdings in privatised government entities and resources spent to salvage a shipwreck.

A final point to be made here is that certain BITs signed by countries in the Asia-Pacific region contain not only a descriptive definition of protected investments, e.g. 'every kind of asset,' but additionally include an added requirement that those investments must be invested in government 'approved projects' or be approved by a designated authority.[41] In *Gruslin v Malaysia*,[42] the investor claimed under the BIT between Malaysia and the Belgo-Luxemburg Economic Union, which required pursuant to Article 1(3) that the 'investment' be 'invested in a project classified as an 'approved project' by the appropriate Ministry in Malaysia'. The arbitral tribunal held that it lacked jurisdiction to hear the claim because the investment – securities listed on the Kuala Lumpur Stock Exchange – was not duly authorised as an 'approved project'.[43]

4.4 Nationality

Nationality is important for ICSID arbitration for two principal reasons. First, pursuant to Article 25(1) the claimant's nationality must be that of a state that is a party to the ICSID Convention. Second, if a claimant seeks to rely on consent to ICSID arbitration under a BIT, it ordinarily must have the nationality of one of the two state parties to that bilateral treaty.

If claimants are individuals, their nationality will usually be determined by the law of the country of which the claimant is (or claims to be) a national. But the question of nationality may not be straightforward, particularly where the claimant has more than one nationality. For example, under some national laws an individual may lose his or her original nationality if another nationality is subsequently acquired.[44] Also, under Article 25(2)(a) of the ICSID Convention, claimants are not permitted to institute an ICSID arbitration if they have the nationality of both the home state and host state.

The nationality of corporations is usually determined by their place of incorporation or registered office or, alternatively, the effective seat of the business

---

40 See, e.g. *Fedax N.V. v Venezuela*, Decision on Jurisdiction, 11 July 1997, 5 ICSID Reports 186, (1998) 37 *International Legal Materials* 1378, at para 42.
41 See the examples given in relation to the BITs of Malaysia, Singapore, Pakistan, Indonesia, The Philippines and Thailand in DC Abraham, 'Arbitration of Investment Disputes: A Malaysian Perspective', (2009) 75 *Arbitration* 206, at pp. 208–209.
42 *Philippe Gruslin v Malaysia*, Final Award, 27 November 2000, 5 ICSID Reports 484.
43 Ibid., at pp. 507–508, para 27.5.
44 See, e.g. *Soufraki v United Arab Emirates*, Award on Jurisdiction, 7 July 2004, 12 ICSID Reports 158.

(*siège social*).⁴⁵ Where a BIT provides that the nationality of a company is to be determined by incorporation, arbitral tribunals have generally denied applications to pierce the corporate veil and look at the nationality of its shareholders or ultimate owners.⁴⁶ Company shareholders are also usually entitled to institute arbitration proceedings under BITs. Article 25(2)(b) of the ICSID Convention and some BITs also provide that a 'national' of a home state may be a legal entity that is incorporated in the host state but is controlled by nationals of the home state.⁴⁷

10.30 Corporations have been known to locate themselves deliberately in a particular country for the purpose of obtaining benefits or protection under a BIT or other treaty. This strategy appears to have gained general acceptance in international investment law. The arbitral tribunal in *Aguas del Tunari SA v Bolivia*, for example, has said:⁴⁸

> ... it is not uncommon in practice, and – absent a particular limitation – not illegal to locate one's operations in a jurisdiction perceived to provide a beneficial regulatory and legal environment in terms, for examples, of taxation or the substantive law of the jurisdiction, including the availability of a BIT.
>
> ... The language of the definition of national in many BITs evidences that such national routing of investments is entirely in keeping with the purpose of the instruments and the motivations of the state parties.

10.31 Accordingly, the arbitral tribunal rejected Bolivia's contention that the 'migration' of the relevant company from one state to another constituted an abuse of corporate form or fraud.

4.5 Choice of law

10.32 Article 42(1) of the ICSID Convention deals with the applicable substantive law:

> The Tribunal shall decide a dispute in accordance with such rules of law as may be agreed by the parties. In the absence of such agreement, the Tribunal shall apply the law of the Contracting State party to the dispute (including its rules on the conflict of laws) and such rules of international law as may be applicable.

10.33 The principle of party autonomy concerning the choice of applicable law as encapsulated in Article 42(1) is consistent with international commercial

---

45 See generally, A Sinclair, 'The Substance of Nationality Requirements in Investment Treaty Arbitration', (2005) 20 *ICSID Review – Foreign Investment Law Journal* 367.
46 See, e.g. *Tokois Tokelės v Ukraine*, Decision on Jurisdiction, 29 April 2004, 11 ICSID Reports 313. This was a rare case in which the president of the arbitral tribunal dissented from the other two arbitrators. The president was in favour of piercing the corporate veil. See also Chapter 4, Section 4.1.1 of this book.
47 See, e.g. *TSA Spectrum de Argentina SA v Argentina*, Award, 19 December 2008, at para 160 ('in the application of the second part of Article 25(2)(b) [of the ICSID Convention] it is necessary to pierce the corporate veil and establish whether or not the domestic company was objectively under foreign control'); and *Aguas del Tunari SA v Bolivia*, Decision on Jurièsdiction, 21 October 2005, (2005) 20 *ICSID Review – Foreign Investment Law Journal* 450, paras 203–323.
48 *Aguas del Tunari*, ibid., at paras 330 and 332.

arbitration practice.[49] If the parties have not chosen the applicable law,[50] the arbitral tribunal must apply the law of the state party to the dispute and 'such rules of international law as may be applicable.' Although there is debate as to the meaning of the latter phrase, it appears that both the host state's law and international law will be applicable where lacunae exist in the choice of law. And where there is a conflict between those two bodies of law, international law seems to prevail over the domestic law.[51] The arbitral tribunal in *LG&E Energy Corp v Argentina* drew attention to the reasoning behind this point when it stated:[52]

> International law overrides domestic law when there is a contradiction since a State cannot justify non-compliance of its international obligations by asserting the provisions of its domestic law.

4.6 Consent to ICSID arbitration

Similar to international commercial arbitration, ICSID arbitration is available only if all parties have consented to it. Article 25(1) of the ICSID Convention speaks of 'consent in writing'. As we saw in Chapter 4, written consent to international commercial arbitration usually arises from a clause in a contract or from an independent arbitration agreement signed by all parties stipulating that any or certain disputes will be submitted to arbitration. In investment arbitration, agreements submitting present or future disputes to ICSID arbitration concluded directly between the investor and host state are likewise recognised as consent within the meaning of Article 25 of the ICSID Convention, so long as all the jurisdictional criteria are satisfied. 10.34

Alternatively, the claimant and respondent need not be privy to an arbitration agreement as is traditionally the case. In a claim made under an investment treaty, the ICSID system has developed a consensual basis for arbitration that does not fall within the usual understanding of mutual 'consent in writing' to arbitration. No direct agreement between the investor and the host state is required under the ICSID regime. Rather, consent is achieved in two separate acts. The host state may express its consent through its domestic legislation[53] or in an investment treaty dispute settlement clause (as discussed above). The investor's consent 10.35

---

49 See Chapter 3, Section 3.1.
50 This situation may arise, for example, when a claim is brought under a BIT that does not contain a provision on applicable law. In these circumstances, some tribunals have held that arguing the case on the basis of the BIT is conduct that demonstrates that the parties' choice of law is the BIT. See, e.g. *Asian Agricultural Products Ltd v Sri Lanka*, Award, 27 June 1990, 4 ICSID Reports 245, at para 20.
51 See Y Banifatemi and E Gaillard, 'The Meaning of 'and' in Article 42(1), Second Sentence of the Washington Convention: The Role of International Law in the ICSID Choice of Law Process', (2003) 18 *ICSID Review – Foreign Investment Law Journal* 375; and Dolzer and Schreuer, op. cit. fn 1, pp. 269–271. But see the views expressed in M Riesman, 'The Regime for *lacunae* in the ICSID Choice of Law Provision and the Question of its Threshold', (2000) 15 *ICSID Review – Foreign Investment Law Journal* 362 (submitting, among other points, that the absence of a remedy in the chosen law of a state is not a lacuna: it may be a consequence of a state's decision not to regulate a certain matter and, moreover, the domestic law chosen may itself provide for a method to overcome lacunae).
52 *LG&E Energy Corp v Argentina*, Decision on Liability, 3 October 2006, (2007) 46 *International Legal Materials* 36, at para 94.
53 For an example of such a domestic law, see Article 8 of Egypt's Law No. 43 that was in dispute in *Southern Pacific Properties (Middle East) Ltd v Egypt*, Decision on Jurisdiction, 3 ICSID Reports 112, at para 70.

is deemed to be provided at a later point in time, namely, through its act of instituting ICSID proceedings against the host state based on that domestic law or dispute settlement clause. The institution of a claim completes the 'written' consent required for ICSID arbitration. As the arbitral tribunal in *Generation Ukraine v Ukraine* explained:[54]

> it is firmly established that an investor can accept a State's offer of ICSID arbitration contained in a bilateral investment treaty by instituting ICSID proceedings. There is nothing in the BIT to suggest that the investor must communicate its consent in a different form directly to the State ...
>
> ... It follows that the Claimant validly consented to ICSID arbitration by filing its Notice of Arbitration at the ICSID Centre.

10.36 This particular consensual process has famously been described by Jan Paulsson as 'arbitration without privity'.[55]

4.7 Additional facility

10.37 Aside from arbitration conducted under the ICSID Convention and the ICSID Rules, it is worth adding that since 1978 a set of Additional Facility Rules authorise the ICSID Secretariat to administer disputes between states and foreign nationals that fall outside the jurisdictional ambit of the ICSID Convention. Often, cases brought under the Additional Facility Rules are ones in which either the investor's home state or the host state is not a party to the ICSID Convention.[56] An important point to note is that proceedings under the Additional Facility Rules are not governed by the ICSID Convention. Consequently, Additional Facility arbitrations do not benefit from the advantages of arbitration conducted under the ICSID Convention, particularly the Convention's exclusion of domestic court involvement and its annulment and enforcement mechanisms (addressed below). The Additional Facility is frequently used to determine investor-state arbitrations under the North American Free Trade Agreement because, unlike the US, Canada and Mexico are not parties to the ICSID Convention.[57]

5 Assessment of the ICSID Convention

10.38 This section takes a closer look at the advantages and disadvantages of the ICSID Convention, particularly from the point of view of investors, and also highlights some of the Convention's innovative features.

---

54 *Generation Ukraine Inc v Ukraine*, 16 September 2003, 10 ICSID Reports 240, at paras 12.2 and 12.3.
55 J Paulsson, 'Arbitration without Privity', (1995) 10 *ICSID Review – Foreign Investment Law Journal* 232.
56 See Article 2 of the Additional Facility Rules. This Article also permits arbitration or conciliation proceedings to be administered by the ICSID Secretariat in relation to legal disputes that 'do not arise directly out of an investment, provided that either the State party to the dispute or the State whose national is a party to the dispute is a Contracting State ...'
57 Canada signed the ICSID Convention on 15 December 2006 but has not ratified it. Mexico has not signed the Convention.

5.1 Advantages

Foreign investment usually requires the commitment of substantial amounts of capital for a long period of time, without any return on the investment for years. Such long-term ventures in foreign countries carries concomitant political risks for the investor, particularly the potential for expropriation of property rights or other negative governmental interference. The architects of the ICSID Convention believed that its arbitration mechanism could provide a safeguard against such risk and enhance the security of foreign investments.

In addition to providing investors with direct rights of arbitration against host states, thereby bypassing the need to seek diplomatic protection, the ICSID Convention grants several advantages to investors, particularly when compared with the practice and procedure common to international commercial arbitration.[58]

The advantages of ICSID arbitration include:

(i) an insulated procedural system that is the most delocalised form of arbitration in the world;[59]
(ii) the right of investors to file arbitration claims directly against the host state – this may exist even if it has not concluded an arbitration agreement or has no working relationship with the government of the host state;
(iii) the application of international substantive rights and protections, rather than those found under domestic law; and
(iv) an enforcement procedure under which the losing party cannot invoke any ground, such as under Article V of the New York Convention, to resist enforcement.

5.2 Disadvantages

ICSID arbitration also has disadvantages for certain investors when compared with international commercial arbitration.[60] One of the more obvious drawbacks for investors desiring confidentiality is the fact that ICSID awards are usually made public.[61] Another drawback for investors may be the 2006 amendment to the ICSID Arbitration Rules empowering ICSID arbitral tribunals to allow a 'non-disputing party' to submit written submissions regarding matters within the scope of the dispute. Further, given ICSID's jurisdictional limitations, which

---

58 For a comparison between international commercial arbitration and investment treaty arbitration, see N Blackaby, 'Investment Arbitration and Commercial Arbitration (or the Tale of the Dolphin and the Shark)', in LA Mistelis and JDM Lew (eds), *Pervasive Problems in International Arbitration*, Kluwer Law International, 2006, p. 217.
59 It is far more delocalised than international commercial arbitration between private entities that has been the main subject of this book. For discussion of delocalisation in that context see Chapter 2 Section 5. For instance, it is not possible under any circumstances for a domestic court to set aside an ICSID award or play any role in an ICSID arbitration.
60 For an overview of the disadvantages from a developing state's perspective, see M Sornarajah, 'A Coming Crisis: Expansionary Trends in Investment Treaty Arbitration', in K Sauvant (ed), *Appeals Mechanism in International Investment Disputes*, Oxford University Press, 2008, p. 39.
61 Even though Article 48(5) of the ICSID Convention provides that the 'Centre shall not publish the award without the consent of the parties', in practice, most decisions are made public. Additionally, in 2006, the ICSID Arbitration Rules were amended to require that the centre 'promptly include in its publications excerpts of the legal reasoning of the Tribunal' (Article 48(4)).

were discussed in Section 4, lengthy and complex jurisdictional disputes are a common feature in ICSID arbitrations. Additional problems may be encountered in choosing an arbitrator due to the nationality requirements and other criteria stipulated in Articles 38–40 of the ICSID Convention.

10.43 Moreover, it may be difficult to predict the outcome of a case for lack of consistency in previously decided arbitral awards. This has become a significant issue because most investment treaty arbitral tribunals are required to interpret a specific investment treaty provision, say in a BIT between state A and state B. That provision is often materially similar to provisions found in other investment treaties. Consistency issues arise when these similar treaty provisions have been subject to prior interpretation by other arbitral tribunals. A burning question in investment treaty arbitration is whether an arbitral tribunal interpreting the BIT between A and B should follow prior interpretations of similar provisions in the same or other BITs.[62] There have been a number of instances where arbitral tribunals have not followed prior tribunal interpretations of similar treaty provisions.[63] Some commentators have made strong calls for more consistency in investment treaty arbitral tribunal awards.[64]

10.44 Finally, the amount of legal costs involved in ICSID arbitrations may also prove to be a disadvantage. One reason for the high costs of ICSID arbitrations is linked to the consistency issue discussed above. The public availability of numerous investment arbitration awards on similar issues and treaty provisions may require extensive analysis of them in the legal submissions of both sides. This process has the potential to increase legal costs significantly. The annulment process (discussed below) may also be costly because, if successful, the original award cannot be revised – it, or parts thereof, may only be annulled and the matter must be resubmitted to a new arbitral tribunal that is constituted specifically for that purpose. This process would therefore require three separate arbitral tribunals to resolve the same case – the original arbitral tribunal, the ad hoc annulment committee and the new arbitral tribunal determining the annulled points. Further, the possibility exists for the award of the new tribunal also to be

---

62 See G Kaufmann-Kohler, 'Interpretation of Treaties: How do Arbitral Tribunals Interpret Dispute Settlement Provisions Embodied in Investment Treaties?', in Mistelis and Lew, op. cit. fn 58, p. 256, at p. 258. See also R Weeramantry, 'The Future Role of Past Awards in Investment Treaty Arbitration', *ICSID Review – Foreign Investment Law Journal* (forthcoming 2010).
63 See, e.g. *Lauder v Czech Republic*, Final Award, 3 September 2001, 9 ICSID Reports 62; and *CME Czech Republic BV v Czech Republic*, Partial Award, 13 September 2001, 9 ICSID Reports 121. These were two investment treaty arbitrations brought separately by Mr Lauder in London under the US-Czech Republic BIT and his investment vehicle (CME) in Stockholm under the Netherlands-Czech Republic BIT. The dispute and factual issues were essentially the same in both cases but the outcomes were different. For example, although the two BIT provisions on expropriation were similar, the *CME* arbitral tribunal held the Czech Republic responsible for expropriation whereas the *Lauder* arbitral tribunal did not. See also the divergent findings by different arbitral tribunals in relation to Argentina's plea of necessity as a ground to exempt it from liability for its acts during the 1999–2002 Argentine financial crisis in *LG&E Energy Corp v Argentina*, Decision on Objections to Jurisdiction, 30 April 2004, 11 ICSID Reports 414, at paras 226–261 and *CMS Gas Transmission Company v Argentina*, Award, 12 May 2005, (2005) 44 *International Legal Materials* 1205, at paras 353–378. See also *CMS Gas Transmission Company v Argentina*, Annulment Proceeding, 25 September 2007, at paras 119–136. The *SGS* cases discussed in Section 6.7 have gained fame for taking different approaches to similar BIT provisions.
64 See, e.g. SD Franck, 'The Legitimacy Crisis in Investment Treaty Arbitration: Privatizing Public International Law Through Inconsistent Decisions', (2005) 73 *Fordham Law Review* 1521. See generally E Gaillard and Y Banifatemi (eds), *Precedent in International Arbitration*, Juris Publishing, 2008.

subject to the annulment process.⁶⁵ The length of time to resolve a dispute if all (or even some) of these procedures are invoked may also be inordinate.

5.3 Innovative features

The ICSID Convention introduced a number of innovative features into arbitrations between investors and states. This section will deal with three: the exclusion of diplomatic protection, the self-contained procedure established by the ICSID Convention and the absence of a requirement to exhaust domestic remedies. Two other major innovations – concerning the annulment and enforcement of ICSID awards – are discussed in the final two sections of this chapter.

5.3.1 Exclusion of diplomatic protection and investor's direct rights

Traditionally, investors depended on their home states to pursue claims on their behalf against host states before an international court or tribunal. This process, known as diplomatic espousal or protection, has been circumvented by the ICSID Convention. The International Court of Justice summarised the difficulties individuals or corporations face under the practice of diplomatic protection in the *Barcelona Traction* case:⁶⁶

> The Court would here observe that, within the limits prescribed by international law, a State may exercise diplomatic protection by whatever means and to whatever extent it thinks fit, for it is its own right that the State is asserting. Should the natural or legal persons on whose behalf it is acting consider that their rights are not adequately protected, they have no remedy in international law. . . .
>
> The State must be viewed as the sole judge to decide whether its protection will be granted, to what extent it is granted, and when it will cease. It retains in this respect a discretionary power the exercise of which may be determined by considerations of a political or other nature, unrelated to the particular case. Since the claim of the State is not identical with that of the individual or corporate person whose cause is espoused, the State enjoys complete freedom of action.

A monumental shift away from these difficulties has been facilitated by the ICSID Convention's grant to investors of direct arbitration rights against states, even if the investor has no direct agreement with that state.⁶⁷ Aggrieved foreign investors who can harness rights under the ICSID Convention (or for that matter under most non-ICSID dispute settlement provisions found in modern investment treaties) are no longer subject to the considerable limitations traditionally inherent in a state's exercise of diplomatic protection.

---

65 Annulment of ICISD awards is discussed in Section 8 below.
66 *Barcelona Traction, Light and Power Company Ltd* (Belgium v Spain), Judgment, (1970) ICJ Reports 3, at p. 44, paras 78 and 79. See also Dolzer and Schreuer, op. cit. fn 1, pp. 211–212.
67 If the investor has a contract with a state that includes an arbitration agreement, private commercial arbitration also provides a solution to this problem – the arbitration agreement is considered to constitute an implied waiver of state immunity from suit. See P Dunham and S Greenberg, 'Balancing Sovereignty and the Contractor's Rights in International Construction Arbitration Involving State Entities', (2006) 23(2) *International Construction Law Review* 130, at p. 147. This is to be contrasted with waiver of immunity from execution. See Section 9 below.

10.48   In addition to granting investors direct access to arbitration against states, the ICSID Convention expressly excludes diplomatic protection unless a respondent state fails to comply with an ICSID award. On this point, Article 27(1) of the Convention provides:

> No Contracting State shall give diplomatic protection, or bring an international claim, in respect of a dispute which one of its nationals and another Contracting State shall have consented to submit or shall have submitted to arbitration under this [ICSID] Convention, unless such other Contracting State shall have failed to abide by and comply with the award rendered in such dispute.

5.3.2 ICSID's self-contained procedure

10.49   In contrast with other arbitral institutions, ICSID procedure is self-contained and insulated from domestic court involvement during the arbitral process. This should be compared to non-ICSID forms of investment treaty arbitration, which are subject to domestic court supervision.[68]

10.50   As we have seen in previous chapters, laws and arbitral rules enable domestic courts in certain circumstances, especially at the seat of arbitration, to intervene in international commercial arbitrations. This has benefits and drawbacks. Courts can offer assistance, for example issuing subpoenas to compel recalcitrant witnesses to attend or ordering the production of documents. On the other hand, domestic courts may sometimes interfere in the arbitral process if one party to the arbitration uses the courts to frustrate the arbitration. In sharp contrast, ICSID procedure is free from such domestic court interference. As Professor Schreuer has observed, the seat of arbitration 'has little legal relevance'.[69]

10.51   The insulation of ICSID arbitral procedure from the influence of domestic courts is achieved through a number of provisions in the ICSID Convention. Under the ICSID Convention regime, domestic courts have no power to set aside ICSID awards. The only means to challenge an ICSID award is to invoke ICSID's internal annulment process in accordance with ICSID Convention Article 52. Any default appointment of arbitrators is made by the chairman of the ICSID's Administrative Council pursuant to Article 38 of the Convention. The chairman also has the power under Article 58 to disqualify arbitrators if they are challenged and the other arbitral tribunal members cannot agree on the challenge or if the challenged arbitrator is a sole arbitrator. Moreover, under Article 54, ICSID awards are automatically enforceable in a contracting state's domestic courts without any possibility of objection to enforcement as is possible under Article V of the New York Convention. None of these internal features of the ICSID arbitration process are granted to arbitrations conducted under the Additional Facility Rules or non-ICSID investment treaty arbitrations.

---

[68] The following are examples of domestic court decisions that involve court review of non-ICSID investment treaty arbitral awards: *Czech Republic v CME Czech Republic BV*, Svea Court of Appeal (Sweden) (2003), 9 ICSID Reports 439; and *United Mexican States v Metalclad Corporation*, British Columbia Supreme Court (2001) BCLR (3rd) 359, 5 ICSID Reports 236.
[69] Schreuer, op. cit. fn 28, p. 1242.

However, domestic courts may have a role to play in relation to provisional measures in ICSID arbitrations. Rule 39(6) of the 2006 version of the ICSID Arbitration Rules enables domestic courts to order provisional measures if the parties have so agreed in the document providing consent to ICSID arbitration.

5.3.3 Exhaustion of domestic remedies not required

Under general principles of international law, the submission of a private party's claim against a state before an international tribunal (by way of diplomatic protection or otherwise) requires that party first to exhaust the domestic legal remedies available to it in the respondent state's domestic courts or tribunals. The ICSID Convention reverses this traditional international law position; it presumes that parties to the Convention have waived the requirement of exhaustion of domestic remedies unless otherwise indicated.[70] Article 26 of the ICSID Convention provides:

> Consent of the parties to arbitration under this Convention shall, unless otherwise stated, be deemed consent to such arbitration to the exclusion of any other remedy. A Contracting State may require the exhaustion of local administrative or judicial remedies as a condition of its consent to arbitration under this Convention.

Although the language of Article 26 permits states to require that domestic remedies be exhausted, most BITs do not contain such a requirement. The absence of a need to pursue domestic remedies presents the investor with significant advantages.[71] Some investment treaties may, however, require investors first to seek redress in the courts or administrative tribunals of the host state for a certain duration of time.[72]

6 Substantive rights and protections under investment treaties

This section contains a short overview of the main types of substantive rights or protections that a host state offers to a foreign investor under investment treaties. One problem with these rights or protections is that they are expressed in general terms (e.g. 'fair and equitable treatment'), which makes them susceptible to a

---

[70] There may be exceptions to this general position, for example, where a denial of justice is alleged against a state, claimants have been required to show that all legal appeals available in the respondent state were made. See *Loewen v United States*, Award, 26 June 2003, 42 *International Legal Materials* 540, at paras 142–217. See also the commentary on this decision by R Weeramantry in www.investmentclaims.com.
[71] Some of the significant advantages of the ICSID system, in comparison with domestic legal systems, is set out in Section 5.1 above.
[72] See, e.g. Article 8 of the Agreement between the Government of the Republic of Korea and the Government of the Republic of Argentina on the Promotion and Protection of Investments, signed at Seoul on 17 May 1994 and entered into force on 24 September 1996. Pursuant to Article 8(3) a dispute may be submitted to international arbitration only in the following circumstances:
  (a) if one of the parties so requests, where, after a period of eighteen (18) months has elapsed from the moment when the dispute was submitted to the competent tribunal of the Contracting Party in whose territory the investment was made, the said tribunal has not given its final decision, or where the final decision has been made but the parties are still in dispute;
  (b) where the Contracting Party and the investor of the other Contracting Party have so agreed.

range of different interpretations. A significant part of a given case will therefore turn on the facts at issue but may also depend on the arbitral tribunal's approach to interpretation of the treaty provisions and its attitude toward other arbitral awards that have determined similar issues.

10.56 Before discussing substantive rights, a short point on the international law of state responsibility needs to be made. A state is not automatically responsible for any conduct that is in breach of that state's investment treaty. That conduct must also be attributable to the state. The acts of state organs, such as police, army or the judiciary, are attributable to states without much controversy. Private citizens' acts may also be attributable to states in certain circumstances, for example, where they are acting under directions of the state or the state acknowledges that conduct as its own.[73] A state may also assert certain defences, such as necessity and *force majeure*.[74]

6.1 Expropriation

10.57 International law recognises that a host state may under certain conditions legitimately expropriate foreign property. Investment treaties confirm this position. The legality of the expropriation depends on whether a state's conduct is:[75]

(i) for a public purpose;
(ii) non-discriminatory;
(iii) in accordance with due process principles; and
(iv) accompanied by prompt, adequate and effective compensation.

10.58 If one or more of these conditions are not satisfied, the conduct of the state may constitute an unlawful expropriation that violates the investment treaty in question.

10.59 Expropriations are classified into two groups: direct and indirect. The former involves the physical seizure of the foreign investor's property or transfer of the legal title to that property to a person who is not the rightful owner. In an indirect expropriation, the title of the property may remain in the name of the investor but its use and enjoyment is deprived or significantly affected. This latter form of expropriation is more prevalent though it is usually more difficult to prove than the direct taking of property. A frequently quoted award that examined indirect expropriation is *Metalclad Corporation v Mexico*, in which the arbitral tribunal observed that expropriation could include:[76]

---

[73] See, e.g. the public international law rules as to attribution codified in Articles 4–11 of the International Law Commission's 'Articles on Responsibility of States for Internationally Wrongful Acts' ('ILC Articles on State Responsibility'), in *Report of the International Law Commission on the Work of Its Fifty-third Session*, UN GAOR, 56th Sess, Supp No. 10, at 43, UN Doc A/56/10 (2001).
[74] See, e.g. Articles 23 and 25 of the ILC Articles on State Responsibility.
[75] See, e.g. (with slight variations) Article 13(1) of the ASEAN Agreement for the Promotion and Protection of Investments, signed on 15 December 1987, (1988) 27 *International Legal Materials* 612; Article 4 of the China Model BIT and Article 6 of the US Model BIT. These Model BITs are reproduced in Dolzer and Schreuer, op. cit. fn 1, Annexes 4 and 8.
[76] *Metalclad Corporation v Mexico*, Award, 30 August 2000, 5 ICSID Reports 209, at para 103. It is sometimes asserted that this test for indirect expropriation is more lenient than what is referred to as the more 'orthodox' approach. See, e.g. M Ewing-Chow, 'Thesis, Antithesis and Synthesis: Investor Protection in BITs, WTO and

covert or incidental interference with the use of property which has the effect of depriving the owner, in whole or in significant part, of the use or reasonably-to-be-expected economic benefit of property even if not necessarily to the obvious benefit of the host State.

Nonetheless, a good deal of debate still exists as to the circumstances that may constitute an unlawful expropriation. Finally, it should be mentioned that in addition to assets, contractual rights may also be expropriated, e.g. the contractual right to develop a housing project.[77]

10.60

6.2 Fair and equitable treatment

Although fair and equitable treatment is a substantive provision found in most investment treaties, it has no authoritative definition. An example of the term is found in Article III of the 1988 Australia-China BIT,[78] which provides that '[a] Contracting Party shall at all times... ensure fair and equitable treatment in its own territory to investments and activities associated with such investments'. The content of this type of treatment has tended to evolve over time, particularly through the jurisprudence of investment treaty arbitration awards. The general nature of this provision enables it to be invoked in a broad range of circumstances. One of the most detailed expositions of fair and equitable treatment was articulated in *Tecnicas Medioambientales Tecmed SA v Mexico*:[79]

10.61

> The Arbitral Tribunal considers that this provision of the Agreement, in light of the good faith principle established by international law, requires the Contracting Parties to provide to international investments treatment that does not affect the basic expectations that were taken into account by the foreign investor to make the investment. The foreign investor expects the host State to act in a consistent manner, free from ambiguity and totally transparently in its relations with the foreign investor, so that it may know beforehand any and all rules and regulations that will govern its investments, as well as the goals of the relevant policies and administrative practices or directives, to be able to plan its investment and comply with such regulations. Any and all State actions conforming to such criteria should relate not only to the guidelines, directives or requirements issued, or the resolutions approved thereunder, but also to the goals underlying such regulations. The foreign investor also expects the host State to act consistently, i.e. without arbitrarily revoking any preexisting decisions or permits issued by the State that were relied upon by the investor to assume its commitments as well as to plan and launch its commercial and business activities. The investor also

---

FTAs', (2007) 30 *University of New South Wales Law Journal* 548, at p. 557 (the 'orthodox approach requires a deprivation of the fundamental rights of ownership, all that the *Metalclad* approach apparently requires is that the government measure deprived the investor of a significant part of their anticipated profits, or significantly affected their business plans').
77 See, e.g. *Starrett Housing Corp v Iran*, Interlocutory Award, (1983) 4 Iran-US CTR 122, at pp. 156–157.
78 Agreement between the Government of Australia and the Government of the People's Republic of China on the Reciprocal Encouragement and Protection of Investments, signed and entered into force on 11 July 1988.
79 *Tecnicas Medioambientales Tecmed SA v Mexico*, Award, 29 May 2003, 10 ICSID Reports 133, (2004) 43 *International Legal Materials* 133, at para 154. See also the test articulated in *Metalclad Corporation v Mexico*, Award, 30 August 2000, 5 ICSID Reports 209, at para 76, in which the tribunal discussed NAFTA's fair and equitable treatment standard by taking into account the reference to transparency in Article 102(2) of NAFTA.

10.62 Some argue that this is a standard that most states would find difficult not to contravene. Generally, however, concepts of legitimate expectations, transparency, predictability, consistency and denial of justice[80] have become prominent criteria in determining fair and equitable treatment. Given the broad nature of this standard of treatment, its breach is largely dependent on the specific facts and circumstances of each case.

6.3 Full protection and security

10.63 A common example of a full protection and security (FPS) protection provision is contained in Article 2(2) of the 1994 Cambodia-Malaysia BIT,[81] which provides that 'Investments of investors of either Contracting Party . . . shall enjoy full protection and security in the territory of the other Contracting Party'.

10.64 The traditional understanding of this standard of treatment was that it protected a foreign national from physical violence directed against his or her person or property. The standard does not create strict liability on the part of a state for any physical harm suffered by an investor or an investment. It establishes a state's responsibility in circumstances where it fails to exercise due diligence and take reasonable measures to protect the affected investor from acts of others. A well-known regional case in this respect is *Asian Agricultural Products Ltd v Sri Lanka*.[82] In that case, Sri Lankan government security forces destroyed a shrimp farm during a military operation against rebel forces. Although the arbitral tribunal was not able to determine whether the rebels or the government forces were responsible for the destruction, Sri Lanka was held responsible for failing to provide adequate precautions to prevent the destruction from taking place.

10.65 As is the case with a number of these investment treaty standards, the meaning of FPS has evolved over the years. Arbitral tribunals now consider that it extends beyond physical security and applies to intangible assets. This standard of treatment may therefore be breached even if no physical violence or damage has been incurred.[83]

6.4 Arbitrary or discriminatory treatment

10.66 To some extent, provisions prohibiting arbitrary or discriminatory treatment may overlap with fair and equitable treatment provisions[84] but most treaties

---
[80] As to the denial of justice and its relation to fair and equitable treatment, see particularly Article 143(2) of the NZ-China Free Trade Agreement, signed on 7 April 2008 and entered into force on 1 October 2008.
[81] Bilateral Agreement for the Promotion and Protection of Investments between Cambodia and Malaysia, signed on 17 August 1994.
[82] Award, 27 June 1990, 4 ICSID Reports 246, at para 85(B).
[83] See, e.g. *CME Czech Republic BV v Czech Republic*, Partial Award, 13 September 2001, 9 ICSID Reports 121, at para 613, which observed that the amendment of laws or actions of administrative bodies could breach full protection and security standards.
[84] Article 143 of the NZ-China Free Trade Agreement (signed 7 April 2008, entered into force 1 October 2008), for example, is headed 'Fair and Equitable Treatment' but it includes an 'unreasonable and discriminatory measures' provision (Article 143(4)).

have accorded both standards a separate and distinct status. An example of an arbitrary or discriminatory treatment provision is found in Article 2(3) of the China-Germany BIT:[85]

> Neither Contracting Party shall take any arbitrary or discriminatory measures against the management, maintenance, use, enjoyment and disposal of the investments by the investors of the other Contracting Party.

10.67 In the absence of a definition of 'arbitrary measures' in the relevant BIT, the arbitral tribunal in *Lauder v Czech Republic* relied on the *Black's Law Dictionary* definition of arbitrary: 'depending on individual discretion; ... founded on prejudice or preference rather than on reason or fact'.[86]

10.68 It needs to be borne in mind that discriminatory standards in investment treaties are founded on international law, not domestic law. Accordingly, a violation of domestic law is not required to prove that conduct is discriminatory under an investment treaty. Local laws may in fact permit discrimination against foreigners but a state cannot rely on its own law to avoid its international obligations.[87]

6.5 National treatment

10.69 The national treatment standard compares the treatment accorded to the host state's investors with that provided to foreign investors. Article 4(1) of the 1999 Australia-India BIT[88] declares:

> Each Contracting Party shall, subject to its laws, regulations and investment policies, grant to investments made in its territory by investors of the other Contracting Party treatment no less favourable than that which it accords to investments of its own investors.

10.70 Overlaps may also occur in respect of this standard, particularly with the arbitrary and discriminatory treatment standard. Some investment treaties, especially those signed by the US, tend to include the proviso that the host state must accord to foreign investors no less favourable treatment than that it accords 'in like circumstances' to its own investors.[89] Case law on this point is not fully settled. On the one hand, the arbitral tribunal in *Feldman v Mexico* narrowed the 'like circumstances' comparative exercise to firms involved in the specific line of business as the claimant.[90] *SD Myers Inc v Canada* on the other hand indicates a broader approach that may take into account the relevant 'economic sector' in which the investor at issue is involved.[91]

---

[85] Agreement between the People's Republic of China and the Federal Republic of Germany on the Encouragement and Reciprocal Protection of Investments, signed on 1 December 2003 and entered into force on 11 December 2005.
[86] *Lauder v Czech Republic*, Final Award, 3 September 2001, 9 ICSID Reports 66, at para 221.
[87] Ibid., at para 220.
[88] Agreement between the Government of Australia and the Government of the Republic of India on the Promotion and Protection of Investments, signed on 26 February 1999 and entered into force on 4 May 2000.
[89] See, e.g. NAFTA Article 1102.
[90] Award, 16 December 2002, 7 ICSID Reports 341, at para 171.
[91] Partial Award, 13 November 2000, 8 ICSID Reports 18; 40 *International Legal Materials* 1408, at para 250.

6.6 Most favoured nation treatment

10.71 The scope of most favoured nation (MFN) treatment may vary depending on the wording of the investment treaty. Article 3(2) of the 1994 Malaysia-Indonesia BIT[92] provides:

> Each Contracting Party shall not in its territory subject investors of the other Contracting Party, as regard their management, use, enjoyment or disposal of investment, as well as to any activity connected with these investments, to treatment less favourable than that which it accords to investors of any third State.

10.72 From the perspective of a Malaysian investor, the effect of this provision is to enable it to claim rights that Indonesia has afforded to non-Malaysian foreign investors that are more favourable, usually under other investment treaties concluded by Indonesia with other states.

10.73 It is generally accepted that MFN clauses apply to standards of substantive treatment afforded to investors from third states. For example, in *Bayindir v Pakistan*, the arbitral tribunal used an MFN clause to import a fair and equitable treatment clause in another treaty.[93] In contrast, a good deal of debate has taken place as to whether a MFN clause may also entitle the importation into a treaty of more favourable dispute settlement procedures. The arbitral tribunal in *Maffezini v Spain* triggered the debate when it applied the MFN clause in the Argentina-Spain BIT[94] to import from the Chile-Spain BIT[95] a more favourable provision, namely, a dispute resolution clause that enabled a claimant to commence investment treaty arbitration after a six-month negotiation period and without having to seek relief in the Spanish courts.[96] The Argentina-Spain BIT required the claimant to resort to Spain's domestic courts for 18 months prior to instituting proceedings.

10.74 In the opposing camp is *Plama Consortium Ltd v Bulgaria*.[97] The arbitral tribunal in that case held that the MFN provision in the Bulgaria-Cyprus BIT[98] did not clearly indicate that it applied to dispute settlement provisions and therefore it could not be invoked to import the ICSID arbitration provision contained in the Bulgaria-Finland BIT.[99]

10.75 The prevalent view in this area appears to be that the determination as to whether an MFN provision can be invoked will hinge on the language of that

---

[92] Agreement between the Government of Malaysia and the Government of the Republic of Indonesia for the Promotion and Protection of Investments, signed on 22 January 1994.
[93] *Bayindir Insaat Turizm Ticaret Ve Sanayi AŞ v Pakistan*, Decision on Jurisdiction, 14 November 2005.
[94] Acuerdo para la Promoción y Protección Recíprocas de Inversiones Entre el Reino de España y la República Argentina, signed on 3 October 1991.
[95] Acuerdo entre la República de Chile y el Reino de España para la Protección y Fomento Recíprocos de Inversiones, signed on 2 October 1991.
[96] This decision was followed by a number of other arbitral tribunals including *Siemens v Argentina AG*, Decision on Jurisdiction, 3 August 2004, 44 *International Legal Materials* 138. See Dolzer and Schreuer, op. cit. fn 1, p. 254.
[97] Decision on Jurisdiction, 8 February 2005, 44 *International Legal Materials* 721.
[98] Agreement between the Government of the Republic of Cyprus and the Government of the People's Republic of Bulgaria on Mutual Encouragement and Protection of Investments, signed in 1987.
[99] Agreement between the Government of the Republic of Finland and the Government of the Republic of Bulgaria on the Promotion and Protection of Investments, signed on 3 October 1997. See also *Telenor v Hungary*, 13 September 2006.

provision and, as *Plama* suggests, whether it leaves no doubt that an external dispute settlement provision may be imported.[100]

6.7 Umbrella clauses

Umbrella clauses are investment treaty provisions that may be described as 'observance of obligations' clauses.[101] A typical example is Article X(2) of the Swiss-Philippines BIT:[102]

10.76

> Each Contracting Party shall observe any obligation it has assumed with regard to specific investments in its territory by investors of the other Contracting Party.

Clauses such as these raise the question whether they enable contractual breaches to be 'elevated' to the status of treaty violations. The two most famous cases at the forefront of this debate have strong connections with this region: *SGS v Pakistan*[103] and *SGS v Philippines*.[104]

10.77

In *SGS v Pakistan*, the arbitral tribunal expressed concern about the number of potential claims that could be made under an umbrella clause if it were interpreted to include contract breaches. For this and other reasons, it refused to hold that a contractual breach constituted a treaty violation under the umbrella clause in the Swiss-Pakistan BIT. Only a few months later, the *SGS v Philippines* arbitral tribunal held that the umbrella clause in the Swiss-Philippines BIT could give rise to a breach of that treaty if the host state failed to observe its contractual commitments or obligations.[105] This latter case appears to represent the dominant view.[106] However, a point that bears emphasis is that not every breach of a contract will trigger an umbrella clause.[107]

10.78

---

100 See Rubins and Kinsella, op. cit. fn 1, p. 233; and McLachlan, Shore and Weiniger, op. cit. fn 1, p. 257.
101 In a 2006 OECD study, it was suggested that approximately 40% of BITs included an umbrella clause. K Yannaca-Small, 'Interpretation of the Umbrella Clause in Investment Agreements' OECD Working Papers on International Investment, Number 2006/3, available online at www.oecd.org/dataoecd/3/20/37579220.pdf (accessed 16 May 2007), p. 5. This study examines umbrella clauses in the BITs of many of the countries that are the specific focus of this book. In Turner, Mangan and Baykitch, op. cit. fn 6, at p. 119, the interesting observation is made that only four Australian BITs contain umbrella clauses.
102 Agreement between the Swiss Confederation and the Republic of the Philippines on the Promotion and Reciprocal Protection of Investments, signed on 31 March 1997 and entered into force on 23 April 1999.
103 *SGS Société Générale de Surveillance SA v Pakistan*, Decision on Jurisdiction, 6 August 2003, 8 ICSID Reports 406.
104 *SGS Société Générale de Surveillance SA v Philippines*, Decision on Objection to Jurisdiction, 29 January 2004, 8 ICSID Reports 518.
105 The ICSID tribunal added that the umbrella clause at issue related only to the *performance* of a state's contractual obligations, not the *extent* or *scope* of those obligations. In applying this interpretation to the facts, it held that the determination as to how much money payable by the Philippines to the claimant (i.e. the *scope* of obligation) was a matter to be determined by the parties or by the Philippines courts (as was required under the investment contract between the claimant and the Philippines). The ICSID tribunal further held that only when this amount was determined could it decide if the Philippines had breached the umbrella clause, i.e. whether it had paid the amount due under the contract (i.e. *performed* its obligations). The ICSID proceedings were therefore stayed pending the determination of the amount payable. *SGS Société Générale de Surveillance SA v Philippines*, Decision on Objection to Jurisdiction, 29 January 2004, 8 ICSID Reports 518, at paras 126–128 and 174–176. A settlement was agreed between the parties and an award embodying this agreement was rendered on 11 April 2008.
106 See, e.g. Turner, Mangan and Baykitch, op. cit. fn 6, at p. 121; and Rubins and Kinsella, op. cit. fn 1, pp. 237–240.
107 See *MTD Equity Sdn Bhd & MTD Chile SA v Chile*, Award, 25 May 2004, 44 *International Legal Materials*, at para 187.

7 Remedies

7.1 Compensation for expropriation

10.79　A vexed issue in international law has been the identification and application of the standard of compensation for an expropriation. In most investment treaties, the compensation standard is expressed as 'prompt, adequate and effective',[108] which is also known as the Hull formula.[109] It is generally understood today in international investment law that inclusion of the Hull formula is a reference to the fair market value of the asset at the time of the expropriation.[110]

10.80　Nonetheless, a difference of opinion exists as to the amount of compensation to be paid in the event of an unlawful expropriation. One school of thought asserts that a higher amount may be awarded for an unlawful expropriation compared with the compensation due for a lawful expropriation of the same property.[111] Others take the view that (unlike a lawful expropriation) an unlawful expropriation enables the arbitral tribunal to order restitution of the expropriated property and award compensation for the increase in the value of the property from the date of taking until the decision awarding compensation.[112]

7.2 Compensation for non-expropriatory treaty breaches

10.81　Investment treaties generally do not specify the standard of compensation that should be awarded if a host state breaches a non-expropriatory investment treaty provision. Because a treaty breach is a violation of international law, the guiding principle for compensation in such cases must also come from international law. In a well-accepted passage in the *Chorzów Factory* case, the Permanent Court of International Justice (the predecessor to the International Court of Justice) articulated the principle as follows:[113]

---

[108] See McLachlan, Shore and Weiniger, op. cit. fn 1, p. 317, para 9.09
[109] Hull was the US Secretary of State who in 1938 referred to the formula in a series of diplomatic exchanges with the Mexican Ambassador to the US. For the text of these exchanges, see G Hackworth, *Digest of International Law*, US Government Printing Office, 1942, vol. III, pp. 655–661.
[110] See, e.g. Dolzer and Schreuer, op. cit. fn 1, p. 91. Another problem associated with this issue is determining the type of valuation method to be used to ascertain the fair market value. This matter is complex, particularly when lost profits are claimed. Valuation is an area that is beyond the scope of this book. For a detailed discussion of methods of valuation in investment treaty arbitration, see I Marboe, *Calculation of Compensation and Damages in International Investment Law*, Oxford University Press, 2009; and McLachlan, Shore and Weiniger, op. cit. fn 1, p. 319 et seq.
[111] It has been observed by Dolzer and Schreuer that damages for an illegal act take into account the subjective position of the victim whereas compensation for a legal act of expropriation is based on an objective standard that takes account of what a hypothetical, willing buyer would normally pay to a willing seller. Dolzer and Schreuer, op. cit. fn 1, p. 274.
[112] See, e.g. *Funnekotter v Zimbabwe*, Award, 22 April 2009, para 111; and *Phillips Petroleum Co Iran v Iran* (1989) 21 Iran-US CTR 79, at para 122.
[113] *Factory at Chorzów* (Germany v Poland), Merits, (1928) PCIJ Series A, no. 17, p. 47. See also Articles 31 and 36 of the International Law Commission's 'Articles on Responsibility of States for Internationally Wrongful Acts', in *Report of the International Law Commission on the Work of Its Fifty-third Session*. UN GAOR, 56th Sess., Supp No. 10, at 43, UN Doc. A/56/10 (2001).

> The essential principle contained in the actual notion of an illegal act ... is that reparation must, in so far as possible, wipe out all the consequences of the illegal act and re-establish the situation which would, in all probability, have existed if that act had not been committed.

Accordingly, the aim of compensation for an 'illegal act' is that the claimant is 'placed financially in the position in which it would have found itself, had the [treaty] breaches not occurred'.[114]

10.82

7.3 Costs

Article 61(2) of the ICSID Convention gives the arbitral tribunal the discretion to apportion the costs of the arbitration. Many investment treaty arbitrations require that the fees and expenses of ICSID and the arbitrators to be shared and for each party to bear their own expenses.[115] However, the practice is not uniform. Costs have been awarded against parties where their conduct has so warranted[116] and, increasingly, arbitral tribunals award costs in favour of the successful party.[117]

10.83

7.4 Interest

Interest is an area in which investment treaty arbitration is developing a practice that is distinct from the traditional position in public international law. The issue relates to whether investment treaty arbitral tribunals are empowered to award simple or compound interest.

10.84

The traditional international law view was expressed in 1943 by Marjorie Whiteman: '[t]here are few rules within the scope of the subject of damages in international law that are better settled than the one that compound interest is not allowable.'[118] Her view has had a considerable influence on investor-state arbitrations in the second half of the 20th century, which tended to deny awarding compound interest.[119]

10.85

In contrast, the dominant trend in contemporary investment treaty arbitration is to award compound interest. A leading case in this regard is *Santa Elena*, in which the arbitral tribunal observed:[120]

10.86

---

114 *Petrobart Ltd v Kyrgyz Republic*, Award II, 29 March 2005, 13 ICSID Reports 387, at p. 467. See generally Kaj Hobér, 'Compensation: A Closer Look at Cases Awarding Compensation for Violation of the Fair and Equitable Treatment Standard' in Yannaca-Small, op. cit. fn 1, at p. 573 et seq.
115 See McLachlan, Shore and Weiniger, op. cit. fn 1, p. 346, para 9.135.
116 See, e.g. *Generation Ukraine Inc v Ukraine*, Award, 16 September 2003, 10 ICSID Reports 240, para 24.2 et seq where the arbitral tribunal was extremely dissatisfied with the claimant's submissions (e.g. describing the claimant's written presentation of its case as 'convoluted, repetitive, and legally incoherent') and awarded all costs the respondent paid into ICSID as well as a contribution of US$100 000 towards the respondent's legal fees.
117 See, e.g. *ADC v Hungary*, Award, 2 October 2006, at para 531 et seq.
118 MM Whiteman, *Damages in International Law*, Washington, US Department of State, 1943, vol. 3, p. 1997.
119 See, e.g. *RJ Reynolds Tobacco Co v Iran* (1984) 7 Iran-US CTR 181, at pp. 191–192; and *Autopista Concesionada de Venezuela, CA v Venezuela*, Award, 23 September 2003, 10 ICSID Reports 309, para 396.
120 *Compañía del Desarrollo de Santa Elena, SA v Costa Rica*, Award, 17 February 2000, 5 ICSID Reports 153, at para 104.

where an owner of property has at some earlier time lost the value of his asset but has not received the monetary equivalent that then became due to him, the amount of compensation should reflect, at least in part, the additional sum that his money would have earned, had it, and the income generated by it, been reinvested each year at generally prevailing rates of interest. It is not the purpose of compound interest to attribute blame to, or to punish, anybody for the delay in the payment made to the expropriated owner; it is a mechanism to ensure that the compensation awarded [to] the Claimant is appropriate in the circumstances.

8 Annulment of ICSID awards

10.87 Pursuant to Article 53 of the ICSID Convention, all awards are binding on the parties and are not subject to appeal or other remedies except as provided in the Convention. The only recourse available under the ICSID Convention is by way of the annulment process. Any party may make an annulment application. On receipt of such an application, the Chairman of ICSID's Administrative Council must appoint a three-person ad hoc committee to decide whether the impugned award should be annulled. Members of the ad hoc committee cannot have (1) the nationality of any members of the tribunal that rendered the impugned award; (2) the nationality of the state party to the dispute; or (3) the nationality of the investor.[121] The ad hoc committee's review is limited to the five narrow grounds listed in Article 52(1):

> Either party may request annulment of the award by an application in writing addressed to the Secretary-General on one or more of the following grounds:
> (a) that the Tribunal was not properly constituted;
> (b) that the Tribunal has manifestly exceeded its powers;
> (c) that there was corruption on the part of a member of the Tribunal;
> (d) that there has been a serious departure from a fundamental rule of procedure; or
> (e) that the award has failed to state the reasons on which it is based.

10.88 An application for annulment must be made within 120 days from the date on which the award was rendered. The duration of an annulment procedure is variable. It generally ranges from about a year, if everything goes well, to around three years if complex issues arise.[122] The function of the ad hoc committee is not to amend or otherwise review the award. It has power only to annul the award in full or in part. In the event an ad hoc committee annuls an award, under Article 52(6) of the ICSID Convention, the dispute cannot be resubmitted to the original tribunal but must be submitted to a newly constituted tribunal.

---

[121] ICSID Convention Article 52(3).
[122] The process is therefore considerably longer than annulment procedures of international commercial arbitration awards in sophisticated jurisdictions (for example Singapore or Hong Kong). At the extreme end of prolonged ICSID cases are *Klockner Industrie-Anlagen GmbH v Cameroon* and *Amco Asia Corp v Indonesia*. They involved annulment procedures and lasted for nine years and 11 years, respectively. See A Redfern, M Hunter, N Blackaby and C Partasides, *Law and Practice of International Commercial Arbitration*, 4th edn, Sweet & Maxwell, 2004, para 9–10 (citing the two mentioned cases but noting that more recently the ICSID annulment mechanism appears to be becoming more efficient).

9 Enforcement of ICSID awards

Article 54 of the ICSID Convention imposes an automatic duty on a contracting state to recognise and enforce any pecuniary obligations under an ICSID award as though it were a final judgment of a court of that contracting state. Domestic courts are not empowered to review ICSID awards even during the enforcement process and no refusal grounds such as those provided in Article V of the New York Convention can be invoked by the losing party to prevent enforcement. This feature of ICSID provides an advantage over international commercial arbitration where state courts may refuse to enforce a foreign award pursuant to Article V of the New York Convention.[123] Article 54 is, however, limited to the enforcement of 'pecuniary obligations'. Restitution or other forms of specific performance are thus not covered within the scope of this provision.[124]

10.89

Once an order for enforcement of an ICSID award is granted, this is not the end of the matter. Execution of this order may need to be carried out against a specific asset, such as a bank account or other property. At this stage, Article 54 of the ICSID Convention allows the domestic court determining the execution request to apply the 'laws concerning the execution of judgments in force in the State in whose territory such execution is sought'. This position is supported by Article 55, which adds:

10.90

> Nothing in Article 54 shall be construed as derogating from the law in force in any Contracting State relating to immunity of that State or of any foreign State from execution.

This latter provision has been described by Professor Schreuer as the 'Achilles' heel of the [ICSID] Convention'.[125] He continues:[126]

10.91

> The self-contained nature of the procedure which excludes the intervention of the domestic courts does not extend to the stage of execution.... The Convention does not enjoin the courts of States parties to the Convention to enforce ICSID awards if this would be contrary to their law governing the immunity from execution of judgments and arbitral awards. Therefore, a State whose courts refuse execution of an ICSID award for reasons of State immunity is not in violation of Art. 54.

The foregoing sections demonstrate that from the commencement of an ICSID arbitration right up to the enforcement of the award, the arbitral process is in considerable measure insulated from domestic court involvement.[127] It is thus with a touch of irony that at the ultimate stage of the ICSID process, a domestic court is finally permitted to intervene and apply its domestic law pertaining to state immunity. This potential legal obstacle detracts somewhat from the advantages of the self-contained nature of ICSID arbitration. Notwithstanding

10.92

---

123 This provision of the New York Convention is discussed in Chapter 9, Section 6.
124 Schreuer, op. cit. fn 28, p. 1124 et seq.
125 Ibid., p. 1144.
126 Ibid.
127 There are exceptions, for example, if an agreement enables a party to request interim measures from a domestic court pursuant to Rule 39(6) of the 2006 version of the ICSID Arbitration Rules.

that Articles 54 and 55 of the ICSID Convention may prove to be a stumbling block at the finish line of the ICSID arbitral process, the ICSID system remains relatively effective. A factor often identified as enhancing the effectiveness of the ICSID process is seen to be the reluctance of states to be looked on disfavourably by the World Bank, particularly because of its links with ICSID and the bank's ability to provide (or withhold) significant amounts of funding for states. The veracity of this hypothesis is open to debate.[128]

[128] See, e.g. G Born, *International Commercial Arbitration*, Kluwer Law International, 2009, p. 2328, n 7 ('States are often very reluctant to be seen to flout awards made by ICSID tribunals, given the World Bank's importance as a lender'); and E Baldwin, M Kantor and M Nolan, 'Limits to Enforcement of ICSID Awards', (2006) 23 *Journal of International Arbitration* 1, at p. 22 ('the World Bank's Operational Procedures (and the bank's articles of agreement) do not directly address the situation where a member country refuses to honor an ICSID arbitration award. Additionally, the World Bank has not, to the authors' knowledge, spoken publicly about the consequences (if any) for new loans to a Contracting State if that state refused to honor its obligations under the award and the ICSID Convention.').

APPENDIX 1

Asia-Pacific arbitral institutions at a glance

The tables in this section provide a basic overview of some arbitral institutions established in or relevant to the Asia-Pacific region.

Australian Centre for International Commercial Arbitration – ACICA

Website	www.acica.org.au
Where headquartered	Sydney, Australia.
Year established	1985
Administrative structure	ACICA has a Board of Directors, a Secretary-General, and two Deputy Secretaries-General.
	Decisions made by ACICA are made by the ACICA Board of Directors, or by any person(s) to whom the Board of Directors has delegated decision-making authority.
Current Rules	2005 ACICA Arbitration Rules.
Default appointment process	ACICA appoints arbitrators where a party, or the parties' agreed process, fails. ACICA has no list of arbitrators and may appoint any person it wishes.
Arbitrator challenge adjudication	ACICA determines challenges.
Terms of Reference/Memorandum of Issues	Not specifically required by the rules.
Award scrutiny	Not provided in the rules.
Costs	Arbitrators are paid an agreed hourly rate. Where a rate cannot be agreed ACICA will fix an hourly rate.
	Non-refundable ACICA registration fee.
	ACICA administrative fees are calculated as a regressive percentage of the amount in dispute.

Beijing Arbitration Commission – BAC

Website	www.bjac.org.cn
Where headquartered	Beijing, China.
Year established	1995
Administrative structure	BAC has a Standing Committee and a Secretary-General.
	The Chairman of BAC or, with the authorisation of the Chairman, one of the Vice-Chairmen or the Secretary-General, performs BAC's functions.
Current rules	2008 Beijing Arbitration Commission Arbitration Rules.
Default appointment process	The BAC Chairman appoints arbitrators where a party, or the parties' agreed process, fails. Parties are expected to appoint arbitrators from the BAC list of arbitrators, but can appoint persons not on the list in international arbitrations subject to BAC's confirmation.
Arbitrator challenge adjudication	The Chairman of BAC determines challenges.
Terms of Reference/Memorandum of Issues	Not specifically required by the rules.
Award scrutiny	Not provided in the rules.
Costs	Arbitrators' fees are included in the fees charged by BAC. However, it is possible for parties to agree to increase an arbitrator's compensation where the arbitration is international.
	BAC case acceptance fees and case handling fees are calculated as a regressive percentage of the amount in dispute.

Indonesian National Arbitration Board – BANI

Website	www.bani-arb.org
Where headquartered	Jakarta, Indonesia.
Year established	1977
Administrative structure	BANI has a Governing Board whose Chairman exercises powers under the rules. BANI also has a Secretariat.
	The BANI Chairman may appoint a Vice-Chairman or other Member of the Board to perform the duties of the Chairman.
Current rules	2003 Rules of Arbitral Procedure of the Indonesia National Board of Arbitration.
Default appointment process	Parties are expected to select arbitrators from the Panel maintained by BANI except in exceptional circumstances and approval of the BANI Chairman.
	The BANI Chairman appoints arbitrators where a party, or the parties' agreed process, fails.
Arbitrator challenge adjudication	BANI composes a special team to determine challenges.
Terms of Reference/Memorandum of Issues	If the tribunal deems it necessary, it may draw up Terms of Reference to be signed by the tribunal and the parties.
Award scrutiny	Not provided in the rules.
Costs	Arbitrators' fees are included in the fees charged by BANI.
	BANI charges a registration fee.
	BANI fees are calculated as a regressive percentage of the amount in dispute.

Chinese International Economic and Trade Arbitration Commission – CIETAC

Website	www.cietac.org
Where headquartered	Beijing, China.
Year established	Antecedent organisation (Foreign Economic and Trade Arbitration Commission) established in 1956.
Administrative structure	CIETAC has a Chairman, Vice-Chairmen and advisors. Each sub-commission has its own Secretariat.
	The Chairman of CIETAC or, with the authorisation of the Chairman, one of the Vice-Chairmen, performs the duties and obligations stipulated by the CIETAC Arbitration Rules.
Current rules	2005 CIETAC Arbitration Rules.
Default appointment process	CIETAC maintains a panel of arbitrators and it is expected parties will appoint persons from that panel. A person not on the CIETAC panel can be appointed subject to the CIETAC Chairman's confirmation.
	The CIETAC Chairman appoints arbitrators where a party, or the parties' agreed process, fails.
Arbitrator challenge adjudication	The Chairman of the CIETAC determines challenges.
Terms of Reference/Memorandum of Issues	Referred to in the rules but not specifically required.
Award scrutiny	Yes.
Costs	Arbitrators' fees are included in the fees charged by CIETAC.
	CIETAC charges an additional registration fee.
	CIETAC arbitration fees are calculated as a regressive percentage of the amount in dispute.

Hong Kong International Arbitration Centre – HKIAC

Website	www.hkiac.org
Where headquartered	Hong Kong SAR, China.
Year established	1985
Administrative structure	HKIAC has a Council, a Secretary General and Secretariat.
	Decisions taken by the HKIAC Council are made by the Council of the HKIAC or a sub-committee or other body specially designated by the Council to perform the functions. Other functions in the rules are referred to the HKIAC Secretariat.
Current rules	2008 HKIAC Administered Arbitration Rules.
Default appointment process	HKIAC appoints arbitrators where a party, or the parties' agreed process, fails.
	HKIAC maintains a list of arbitrators but parties are not required to select arbitrators from that list. Before making a final decision on the appointment of an arbitrator, or on the number of arbitrators that are appropriate for any particular dispute, the HKIAC Council consults with at least three available members of the Appointment Advisory Board. The HKIAC Council is not bound to follow the Advisory Board's advice.
	A sole arbitrator or the chairperson of a three-member arbitral tribunal cannot be the same nationality as any of the parties unless otherwise agreed by all parties in writing.
Arbitrator challenge adjudication	The HKIAC Council determines challenges. Pursuant to the HKIAC Challenge Rules (separate document) a sub-committee of no more than three people can be appointed to consider the evidence and submissions in order to assist the HKIAC Council in coming to its decision.
Terms of Reference/Memorandum of Issues	Not specifically required by the rules.
Award scrutiny	Not provided in the rules.
Costs	Arbitrators' fees are calculated as a regressive percentage of the amount in dispute.
	Non-refundable HKIAC registration fee.
	HKIAC administrative fees calculated as a regressive percentage of the amount in dispute.

Indian Council of Arbitration – ICA

Website	www.ficci.com/icanet
Where headquartered	New Delhi, India.
Year established	1965
Administrative structure	The ICA has a Governing Body of the Council and a Registrar. An Arbitration Committee is formed from the Governing Body to perform the functions prescribed to the Governing Body under the Rules. The Committee can delegate certain responsibilities to the Registrar.
	The Registrar may delegate to any officer of the Council, Chambers of Commerce or Trade Association at the premises of which the arbitration proceedings are taking place, to discharge such of the functions and administrative duties of the Registrar as are deemed proper and necessary from time to time, with reference to a particular case or cases.
Current rules	1998 Rules of Arbitration of the Indian Council of Arbitration.
Default appointment process	Parties are expected to appoint arbitrators from the ICA list of arbitrators. The Registrar in conjunction with the Chairman of the Committee appoints arbitrators where a party, or the parties' agreed process, fails.
Arbitrator challenge adjudication	The Committee determines challenges.
Terms of Reference/Memorandum of Issues	Not specifically required by the rules.
Award scrutiny	Not provided in the rules.
Costs	Arbitrators' fees are calculated as a regressive percentage of the amount in dispute.
	Non-refundable ICA registration fee.
	ICA administrative fees calculated as a regressive percentage of the amount in dispute.

Japanese Commercial Arbitration Association – JCAA

Website	www.jcaa.or.jp
Where headquartered	Tokyo, Japan.
Year established	1953
Administrative structure	The JCAA has a Secretariat that administers its arbitrations.
Current rules	2008 JCAA Commercial Arbitration Rules.
Default appointment process	JCAA appoints arbitrators where a party, or the parties' agreed process, fails. JCAA has no list of arbitrators and may appoint any person it wishes.
Arbitrator challenge adjudication	JCAA's Committee for the Review of Challenges to Arbitrators determines challenges.
Terms of Reference/Memorandum of Issues	Not specifically required by the rules.
Award scrutiny	Not provided in the rules.
Costs	Arbitrators' fees are calculated by JCAA in accordance with the Regulations for Arbitrators Remuneration (separate document).
	Non-refundable JCAA request fee.
	JCAA administrative fees calculated as a regressive percentage of the amount in dispute.

APPENDIX 1: ASIA-PACIFIC ARBITRAL INSTITUTIONS AT A GLANCE 509

Korean Commercial Arbitration Board – KCAB

Website	www.kcab.or.kr
Where headquartered	Seoul, South Korea.
Year established	1966
Administrative structure	The KCAB maintains a Secretariat from which a secretary is appointed to administer each arbitration. An International Arbitration Committee advises the KCAB/Secretariat in respect of the decisions it makes regarding challenges to and replacement of arbitrators.
Current rules	2007 KCAB International Arbitration Rules.
Default appointment process	KCAB maintains a list of arbitrators but is not required by the KCAB International Arbitration Rules to appoint from that list. Similarly parties choosing their own arbitrators are not restricted to that list. For those arbitrations governed by the older 2004 'Arbitration Rules' default appointment is made using a list procedure. On the request of one party the KCAB, when appointing a sole arbitrator or the chairperson of a three-member arbitral tribunal will not appoint a person of the same nationality as any of the parties.
Arbitrator challenge adjudication	The Secretariat in consultation with the International Arbitration Committee determines challenges.
Terms of Reference/Memorandum of Issues	Not specifically required by the rules.
Award scrutiny	Not provided in the rules.
Costs	Unless otherwise agreed arbitrators are paid an hourly rate determined by the KCAB and within a range based on a regressive percentage of the amount in dispute. Non-refundable KCAB registration fee. KCAB administrative fees calculated as a regressive percentage of the amount in dispute.

Kuala Lumpur Regional Centre for Arbitration – KLRCA

Website	www.rcakl.org.my
Where headquartered	Kuala Lumpur, Malaysia.
Year established	1978
Administrative structure	KLRCA has a Secretariat operated under the guidance of its Director.
Current rules	KLRCA Arbitration Rules 2010 incorporating UNCITRAL Arbitration Rules 2010.
Default appointment process	KLRCA appoints arbitrators where a party, or the parties' agreed process fails. A panel of arbitrators is maintained from which KLRCA will appoint arbitrators if required to do so. Parties are not restricted to the panel.
Arbitrator challenge adjudication	KLRCA determines challenges.
Terms of Reference/Memorandum of Issues	Not specifically required by the rules.
Award scrutiny	Not provided in the rules.
Costs	Arbitrators' fees are calculated as a regressive percentage of the amount in dispute. Non-refundable KLRCA registration fee. KLRCA administrative costs calculated as a regressive percentage of the amount in dispute.

Singapore International Arbitration Centre – SIAC

Website	www.siac.org.sg
Where headquartered	Singapore.
Year established	1991
Administrative structure	SIAC has a Board of Directors, Chairman, Deputy Chairman, Registrar and Secretariat. The Chairman of SIAC or the Deputy Chairman, performs the duties and obligations stipulated by the SIAC Rules.
Current rules	2007 SIAC Rules (2010 SIAC Rules effective 1 July 2010).
Default appointment process	SIAC appoints arbitrators where a party, or the parties' agreed process, fails. SIAC maintains a list of arbitrators but parties are not restricted to that list.
Arbitrator challenge adjudication	The Committee of the Board determines challenges to arbitrators.
Terms of Reference/Memorandum of Issues	A Memorandum of Issues was required by the 2007 Rules, but is not required under the 2010 Rules.
Award scrutiny	Yes.
Costs	Arbitrators' fees are calculated as a regressive percentage of the amount in dispute. Non-refundable SIAC filing fee. SIAC administrative costs are calculated as a regressive percentage of the amount in dispute.

ICC International Court of Arbitration – ICC

Website	www.iccwbo.org/court/arbitration
Where headquartered	Paris, France, but with a case-administration office in Hong Kong for Asian cases.
Year established	1923
Administrative structure	The ICC International Court of Arbitration consists of 126 court members from 88 different countries. The ICC Court is supported by a Secretariat headed by the Secretary-General and Deputy Secretary-General. The Chairman of the ICC Court has the power to make urgent decisions on behalf of the ICC Court. The ICC Court may delegate decision-making power to one or more committees. The Secretary-General and Deputy Secretary-General are empowered by the Rules to make certain decisions.
Current rules	1998 ICC Rules of Arbitration (revised version expected in early 2011).
Default appointment process	Parties are free to appoint any person they wish as arbitrator. The ICC Court appoints arbitrators where a party, or the parties' agreed process, fails. There is no list but the appointment is usually made upon the proposal of one of the ICC's National Committees. Where a National Committee is not to be used, the ICC Court can appoint any person it wishes. The ICC Court will not appoint a sole arbitrator or the chairperson of a three-member arbitral tribunal who has the same nationality as any of the parties unless otherwise agreed by the parties. However where the parties appoint the arbitrator, this rule does not apply.
Arbitrator challenge adjudication	The ICC Court determines challenges to arbitrators.
Terms of Reference/Memorandum of Issues	Terms of Reference are required by the rules.
Award scrutiny	Yes.
Costs	Arbitrators' fees are calculated as a regressive percentage of the amount in dispute. Non-refundable ICC filing fee. ICC administrative expenses are calculated as a regressive percentage of the amount in dispute.

London Court of International Arbitration – LCIA

Website	www.lcia.org
Where headquartered	London, England.
Year established	1892
Administrative structure	The LCIA is a company with a Board of Directors. However, the ultimate arbitration administrative decisions are made by the LCIA Court, assisted by a Secretariat. The functions of the LCIA Court are performed by the President or a Vice-President of the LCIA Court or by a division of three or five members of the LCIA Court appointed by the President or a Vice President, as determined by the President. The Registrar is empowered in the Rules to make some decisions.
Current rules	1998 LCIA Arbitration Rules.
Default appointment process	Unless otherwise agreed, parties vest the power to appoint arbitrators in the LCIA Court in all circumstances when choosing the LCIA Rules, however parties are encouraged to nominate potential arbitrators for the LCIA Court's consideration.
Arbitrator challenge adjudication	The LCIA Court determines challenges to arbitrators
Terms of Reference/Memorandum of Issues	Not specifically required by the rules.
Award scrutiny	Not provided in the rules.
Costs	Arbitrators are paid an agreed hourly rate. Non-refundable LCIA registration fee. The LCIA Secretariat charges are similarly based on an hourly rate calculation.

APPENDIX 2

Selected arbitral institutions

The following list comprises major arbitral institutions and other organisations in the Asia-Pacific and other regions, including some institutions that predominantly administer domestic arbitrations.

Asia-Pacific	Website
Arbitrators' and Mediators' Institute of New Zealand Inc (AMINZ)	www.aminz.org.nz
Asia Pacific Regional Arbitration Group (APRAG)	www.aprag.org
Australian Centre for International Commercial Arbitration (ACICA)	www.acica.org.au
Australian Commercial Disputes Centre (ACDC)	www.acdcltd.com.au
Bangladesh Council for Arbitration (BCA)	www.fbcci-bd.org
Beijing Arbitration Commission (BAC)	www.bjac.org.cn
China International Economic and Trade Arbitration Commission (CIETAC)	www.cietac.org.cn
Hong Kong International Arbitration Centre (HKIAC)	www.hkiac.org
ICDR-Singapore	www.adr.org/about_icdr
Indian Council of Arbitration (ICA)	www.ficci.com/icanet/
Indonesian National Arbitration Board (BANI)	www.bani-arb.org
Institute of Arbitrators and Mediators Australia	www.iama.org.au
International Arbitration Centre at the Chamber of Commerce and Industry of Vietnam	www.vcci.com.vn
Japan Commercial Arbitration Association (JCAA)	www.jcaa.or.jp
Korean Commercial Arbitration Board (KCAB)	www.kcab.or.kr
Kuala Lumpur Regional Centre for Arbitration (KLRCA)	www.rcakl.org.my
London Court of International Arbitration (LCIA), India	www.lcia-india.org
Philippine Dispute Resolution Center, Inc. (PDRCI)	www.pdrci.org
Singapore International Arbitration Centre (SIAC)	www.siac.org.sg
Vietnam International Arbitration Centre (VIAC)	www.viac.org.vn

A more extensive list of Asia-Pacific arbitral and ADR institutions is found on the APRAG website: www.aprag.org/members/index.html

Other regions

	Website
American Arbitration Association (AAA) and its International Centre for Dispute Resolution (ICDR)	www.adr.org www.adr.org/icdr
Belgian Centre for Arbitration and Mediation (CEPANI)	www.cepani.be
Cairo Regional Centre for International Commercial Arbitration	www.crcica.org.eg/
Chartered Institute of Arbitrators International Arbitration Centre	www.arbitrators.org
Deutsche Institution für Schiedsgerichtsbarkeit ev (DIS) (German Institution for Arbitration)	www.dis-arb.de
Dubai International Arbitration Centre	www.diac.ae
International Arbitral Centre of the Austrian Federal Economic Chamber	www.wko.at/arbitration
International Centre for Settlement of Investment Disputes (ICSID)	www.worldbank.org/icsid
International Court of Arbitration of the International Chamber of Commerce (ICC)	www.iccarbitration.org
London Court of International Arbitration (LCIA)	www.lcia-arbitration.com
Madrid Chamber of Commerce and Industry, Court of Arbitration	www.camaramadrid.es
Milan Chamber of National and International Arbitration	www.camera-arbitrale.com
Permanent Court of Arbitration (PCA) International Bureau	www.pca-cpa.org
Swiss Chambers' Court of Arbitration and Mediation	www.sccam.org/sa/en/
Stockholm Chamber of Commerce (SCC)	www.sccinstitute.se
United Nations Commission on International Trade Law (UNCITRAL)	www.uncitral.org
World Intellectual Property Organisation (WIPO) Arbitration and Mediation Center	www.arbiter.wipo.int

A more extensive list of arbitral and ADR institutions from around the world is found on the ICCA website: www.arbitration-icca.org/related-links.html

APPENDIX 3

List of UNCITRAL Model Law countries

Arbitration legislation based on the UNCITRAL Model Law on International Commercial Arbitration has been enacted in:

Armenia
Australia
Austria
Azerbaijan
Bahamas
Bahrain
Bangladesh
Belarus
Bermuda
Bulgaria
Cambodia
Canada
Chile
Croatia
Cyprus
Denmark
Dominican Republic
Egypt
Estonia
Germany
Greece
Guatemala
Honduras
Hong Kong Special Administrative Region
Hungary
India
Iran
Ireland*
Japan
Jordan
Kenya
Lithuania
Macao Special Administrative Region
Macedonia

Madagascar
Malta
Mauritius*
Mexico
New Zealand*
Nicaragua
Nigeria
Norway
Oman
Paraguay
Peru*
Philippines
Poland
Russia
Rwanda*
Serbia
Singapore
Slovenia*
South Korea
Spain
Sri Lanka
Thailand
Tunisia
Turkey
Uganda
Ukraine
Within the United Kingdom of Great Britain and Northern Ireland: Scotland
Within the United States of America: California, Connecticut, Florida,* Illinois, Louisiana, Oregon and Texas
Venezuela
Zambia
Zimbabwe

* Incorporating the amendments to the UNCITRAL Model Law on International Commercial Arbitration as adopted in 2006.

The above information with updates can be found on the UNCITRAL website: www.uncitral.org/uncitral/en/uncitral_texts/arbitration/1985Model_arbitration_status.html

APPENDIX 4

List of parties to the New York Convention 1958

The following 144 states are parties to the 1958 New York Convention on the Recognition and Enforcement of Foreign Arbitral Awards, as at 4 July 2010:

Afghanistan	Czech Republic	Laos
Albania	Denmark	Latvia
Algeria	Djibouti	Lebanon
Antigua and Barbuda	Dominica	Lesotho
Argentina	Dominican Republic	Liberia
Armenia	Ecuador	Lithuania
Australia	Egypt	Luxembourg
Austria	El Salvador	Macedonia
Azerbaijan	Estonia	Madagascar
Bahamas	Finland	Malaysia
Bahrain	France	Mali
Bangladesh	Gabon	Malta
Barbados	Georgia	Marshall Islands
Belarus	Germany	Mauritania
Belgium	Ghana	Mauritius
Benin	Greece	Mexico
Bolivia	Guatemala	Moldova
Bosnia and Herzegovina	Guinea	Monaco
Botswana	Haiti	Mongolia
Brazil	Holy See	Montenegro
Brunei Darussalam	Honduras	Morocco
Bulgaria	Hungary	Mozambique
Burkina Faso	Iceland	Nepal
Cambodia	India	Netherlands
Cameroon	Indonesia	New Zealand
Canada	Iran	Nicaragua
Central African Republic	Ireland	Niger
Chile	Israel	Nigeria
China	Italy	Norway
Colombia	Jamaica	Oman
Cook Islands	Japan	Pakistan
Costa Rica	Jordan	Panama
Côte d'Ivoire	Kazakhstan	Paraguay
Croatia	Kenya	Peru
Cuba	Kuwait	Philippines
Cyprus	Kyrgyzstan	Poland

Portugal	South Africa	Ukraine
Qatar	South Korea	United Arab Emirates
Romania	Spain	United Kingdom of Great Britain and Northern Ireland
Russia	Sri Lanka	
Rwanda	Sweden	United States of America
Saint Vincent and the Grenadines	Switzerland	Uruguay
San Marino	Syria	Uzbekistan
Saudi Arabia	Tanzania	Venezuela
Senegal	Thailand	Vietnam
Serbia	Trinidad and Tobago	Zambia
Singapore	Tunisia	Zimbabwe
Slovakia	Turkey	
Slovenia	Uganda	

For detailed information on the signature, ratification, accession, succession and entry into force of the New York Convention, see www.uncitral.org/uncitral/en/uncitral_texts/arbitration/NYConvention_status.html

APPENDIX 5

Selected list of Asia-Pacific arbitration legislation and instruments

Australia	*International Arbitration Act 1974* (Cth)
Bangladesh	*Arbitration Act 2001*
Brunei	*Arbitration Act 1994* (Cap 173)
China (Mainland China)	*Arbitration Law 1994* Interpretation of the Supreme People's Court on Certain Issues Relating to Application of the Arbitration Law of the PRC of 23 August 2006 Notice of the Supreme People's Court on Handling by People's Courts of Relevant Issues Pertaining to Foreign-Related Arbitration and Foreign Arbitration of 28 August 1995 Notice of the Supreme People's Court on Matters Relating to Setting Aside of Foreign-Related Arbitral Awards by the People's Courts of 23 April 1998 Notice of the Supreme People's Court on the Implementation of China's Accession to the Convention on the Recognition and Enforcement of Foreign Arbitral Awards of 10 April 1987
Hong Kong SAR (China)	*Arbitration Ordinance 1963* (Cap 341) (this act may be replaced in 2010)
India	*Arbitration and Conciliation Act 1996*
Indonesia	*Arbitration and Dispute Resolution Act* (No 30 of 1999)
Japan	*Arbitration Law* (No 138 of 2003)
Korea (Republic of)	*Arbitration Act 1999*
Malaysia	*Arbitration Act 2005*
New Zealand	*Arbitration Act 1996*
North Korea	*External Economic Arbitration Law 1994*
Philippines	*Alternative Dispute Resolution Act 2004*
Singapore	*International Arbitration Act 2002* (Cap 143A)
Sri Lanka	*Arbitration Act* (No 11 of 1995)
Taiwan	*Arbitration Law* (2002)
Thailand	*Arbitration Act* BE 2545 (2002)
Vietnam	*Ordinance on Commercial Arbitration* (No 08/2003/PL-UBTVQH of 25 February 2003). Vietnam passed a new arbitration law in mid-2010, which takes effect from January 2011.

The above information is valid as at 4 July 2010. The year provided is the year the legislation first became law. In nearly all cases these laws have been amended from time to time.

Glossary

This glossary defines common arbitration terms and acronyms used in this book. A reference in this book to institutional arbitration rules is a reference to the version as defined in this glossary, unless stated otherwise.

AAA American Arbitration Association.
AAA Rules American Arbitration Association International Arbitration Rules in force as of 1 March 2008. Also referred to as the ICDR Rules – see ICDR.
ACICA Australian Centre for International Commercial Arbitration.
ACICA Rules Rules of arbitration of the Australian Centre for International Commercial Arbitration in force as of 12 July 2005.
Ad hoc arbitration An arbitration which is not an administered or institutional arbitration. Ad hoc arbitrations are commonly conducted under the UNCITRAL Arbitration Rules.
Adjudication The process of hearing and resolving a dispute. It may possess a more specific meaning particularly in disputes relating to the construction industry. In this field, an adjudicator (usually an industry expert) may be appointed when construction work is still taking place. The adjudicator provides an opinion on a technical dispute relating to the construction. Typically, the adjudicator's decision is binding (effectively facilitating continuation of the construction work) but a final determination of the dispute may be made later in court or by arbitration.
Administered arbitration See institutional arbitration.
ADR Alternative Dispute Resolution. Sometimes also referred to as 'Amicable Dispute Resolution'.
AFIA Australasian Forum for International Arbitration.
Amiable compositeur An arbitral tribunal expressly authorised by the parties to act as *amiable compositeur* is not bound to determine a dispute through the application of any particular law, rather it may found its decision on what to it seems just and right. The tribunal must still adhere to inalienable notions of fairness, such as equal treatment of the parties. See also *ex aequo et bono*.
Amicus submission A submission made by a third party for the purposes of assisting the arbitral tribunal in deciding a matter before it.
Anti-suit injunction An order by a court or arbitral tribunal to restrain a party from initiating or continuing proceedings in another jurisdiction or forum.

Appointing authority An authority designated by the parties to appoint one or more arbitrators. In some circumstances an appointing authority may be designated by an arbitral institution or national law.

APRAG Asia Pacific Regional Arbitration Group.

Arb-Med Arb-Med is a hybrid of arbitration and mediation allowing an arbitrator to act as a mediator during the arbitral process.

Arbitral tribunal The arbitrators, once confirmed or appointed.

Arbitration agreement An agreement between two or more parties to submit disputes to arbitration which may take the form of a clause in a contract.

Award A decision of an arbitral tribunal which resolves one or more of the substantive matters in dispute. See also partial award.

Award on agreed terms An award based on terms that have been agreed to by the parties. Also called an award by consent or consent award.

BAC Beijing Arbitration Commission.

BAC Rules Beijing Arbitration Commission Arbitration Rules in force as of 2008.

BANI Indonesian National Arbitration Board.

BANI Rules Rules of Arbitral Procedure of the Indonesia National Board of Arbitration in force as of 1 March 2003.

BCA Rules Rules of Arbitration of the Bangladesh Council of Arbitration in force as of 2001.

BIT Bilateral investment treaty, being a treaty between two states with a view to encouraging and protecting foreign private investment.

Bona fides In good faith.

CAS Court of Arbitration for Sport.

CEPANI Belgian Centre for Arbitration and Mediation.

CEPANI Rules Belgian Centre for Arbitration and Mediation Rules in force as of 1 January 2005. Different rules apply depending on the amount in dispute.

Chairperson of arbitral tribunal Sometimes referred to as 'the presiding arbitrator'. The chairperson may be chosen by the parties, the co-arbitrators or an appointing authority.

CIETAC China International Economic and Trade Arbitration Commission.

CIETAC Rules China International Economic and Trade Arbitration Commission Arbitration Rules in force as of 1 May 2005.

CISG United Nations Convention on Contracts for the International Sale of Goods, Vienna 1980.

Co-arbitrator The expression used to describe any member of the arbitral tribunal other than the chairperson. In some cases this may also be referred to as a 'party-appointed' or 'party-nominated' arbitrator.

Competence-Competence A legal doctrine which provides that an arbitral tribunal is competent to determine its own competence (jurisdiction) to hear the dispute. It is found in most international arbitration laws and rules, although its application varies across jurisdictions.

Conciliation A non-binding process through which disputing parties are guided by an independent third party, with the goal of reaching a settlement agreement. The independent third party may provide recommendations to that end and in some circumstances may issue a direction. Conciliation is often used as a synonym for mediation.

Conflict of laws rules Legal principles that determine the law to be applied. Sometimes referred to as 'private international law rules'.

Consent award See award on agreed terms.

Consolidation Merging two or more arbitration proceedings.

Culpa in contrahendo A tort that arises in the course of negotiating a contract that never comes into existence. This is a doctrine best known to the civil law, but is recognised in varying degrees within common law systems as well.

De novo hearing A fresh hearing conducted as if any earlier hearing had not occurred. Additional or different evidence may be presented at a de novo hearing.

DIAC Dubai International Arbitration Centre.

DIAC Rules Dubai International Arbitration Centre Arbitration Rules in force as of 7 May 2007.

Dispositive The dispositive part of an arbitral award is the operative part, usually found at the end of the award, which contains the arbitral tribunal's final decisions on the parties' claims and any orders that it makes as a consequence of those decisions.

Dispute review board A panel of technical experts retained to make an independent recommendation to the parties as to the settlement of their dispute. The recommendations of a dispute review board are generally non-binding.

Domestic arbitration Some countries distinguish between 'domestic' and 'international' arbitrations. Where there is a distinction it may be significant because the arbitration legislation applying to domestic arbitrations is often quite different from that applying to international arbitrations. See also international arbitration.

Enforcement of the award The act of realising an award, usually involving domestic court procedures applying the New York Convention.

Equity clause A clause authorising the arbitral tribunal to determine the dispute as *amiable compositeur* or *ex aequo et bono*. See also *amiable compositeur*.

Ex aequo et bono See *amiable compositeur*.

Exclusion agreement The exclusion of certain rights by agreement, for example the right to challenge or appeal decisions of the arbitral tribunal.

Execution of enforcement order The process of putting into action an enforcement order of the domestic courts in the state where a party is seeking to enforce a foreign arbitral award.

Expert determination A process where a dispute is referred to an expert for determination, not usually involving an opportunity to present formal arguments or make formal submissions.

Expert witness A witness possessing expertise in a particular field due to education and/or experience. May be appointed by the parties or an arbitral tribunal. Is usually permitted to give opinion-based evidence.
Fast track arbitration Terminology used to describe an expedited arbitration.
Fork in the road provision A provision that is commonly contained in investment treaties that requires the investor to choose between international arbitration and domestic court litigation.
Functus officio No longer having any power due to the expiry of the mandate.
HKIAC Hong Kong International Arbitration Centre.
HKIAC Challenge Rules The rules used by the HKIAC when handling a challenge to an arbitrator.
HKIAC Rules Hong Kong International Arbitration Centre Administered Arbitration Rules in force as of 1 September 2008.
Home state A term employed in investment treaty arbitration that refers to the country from which a foreign investor originates.
Host state A term employed in investment treaty arbitration that refers to the country where the foreign investor makes its investment.
IBA International Bar Association.
IBA Guidelines IBA Guidelines on Conflicts of Interest in International Arbitration approved by the IBA Council on 22 May 2004.
IBA Rules of Ethics IBA Rules of Ethics for International Arbitrators, published in 1987.
IBA Rules of Evidence International Bar Association Rules on the Taking of Evidence in International Commercial Arbitration adopted by the IBA Council on 1 June 1999. These were revised and updated with a new version released in 2010.
ICA Indian Council of Arbitration.
ICA Rules Rules of Arbitration of the Indian Council of Arbitration in force as of 1 March 1998.
ICC International Chamber of Commerce.
ICC Rules ICC International Court of Arbitration Rules of Arbitration in force as of 1 January 1998. A revised version is expected in early 2011.
ICCA International Council for Commercial Arbitration.
ICDR International Centre for Dispute Resolution, being the international branch of the AAA.
ICJ International Court of Justice, also known as the 'World Court'.
ICSID International Centre for Settlement of Investment Disputes.
ICSID Additional Facility Rules International Centre for Settlement of Investment Disputes Additional Facility Rules, as amended and in effect from 10 April 2006.
ICSID award An award rendered by an ICSID arbitral tribunal.
ICSID Convention Convention on the Settlement of Investment Disputes between States and Nationals of Other States, Washington 1966. Sometimes also referred to as the Washington Convention.

ICSID Rules International Centre for Settlement of Investment Disputes Rules of Procedure for Arbitration Proceedings in force as of 10 April 2006.

INCOTERMS Abbreviated international commercial terms which describe the allocation of various responsibilities and liabilities relating to transportation. Although INCOTERMS have differed over time, modern references to INCOTERMS are usually understood to be a reference to the INCOTERMS published by the International Chamber of Commerce.

Infra petita Where an arbitral tribunal terminates the arbitration (e.g. by the issuance of a final award) without having determined all of the claims submitted to it. See also *ultra petita*.

Institutional arbitration Arbitration proceedings conducted under the auspices of an arbitration institution. See the arbitration institutions listed in Appendix 2.

Inter alia Among other things.

Interim measures A decision of the arbitral tribunal which may be made as an order or award but which does not finally determine any issue, but grants temporary relief.

International arbitration Arbitration proceedings defined as international according to the law of the place of arbitration. Many Asia-Pacific countries have adopted the definition set out in Article 3 of the Model Law. See also domestic arbitration.

Intervention The process by which a non-signatory to the arbitration agreement attempts to participate in the proceedings on its own initiative.

Investment treaty arbitration Arbitration proceedings between a foreign investor and a host state which arise out of an investment treaty. Also referred to as 'investor-state arbitration', 'investment arbitration' or 'foreign investment arbitration'.

JCAA The Japanese Commercial Arbitration Association.

JCAA Rules The Japanese Commercial Arbitration Association Commercial Arbitration Rules in force as of 1 January 2008.

Joinder of a party The addition of another party to arbitration proceedings after the proceedings have commenced. In some instances joinder may be ordered by a court, or agreed by the parties.

KCAB The Korean Commercial Arbitration Board.

KCAB Rules The International Arbitration Rules of the Korean Commercial Arbitration Board as approved by the Supreme Court on 25 January 2007.

KLRCA The Regional Centre for Arbitration Kuala Lumpur.

KLRCA Rules Rules for Arbitration of the Regional Centre for Arbitration Kuala Lumpur 2008.

Kompetenz-Kompetenz See competence-competence.

LCIA The London Court of International Arbitration.

LCIA Rules The London Court of International Arbitration Rules in force as of 1 January 1998.

Lex arbitri The law governing the arbitration proceedings at the seat of the arbitration.

Lex contractus The law applicable to the contract.

Lex fori The law of the forum.

Lex mercatoria The law of merchants, derived from customary rules and practices established in international trade and commerce.

Lis pendens Parallel proceedings in different forums (e.g. an arbitral tribunal and a court) involving the same parties and the same cause of action.

Mandatory law Laws or rules from which the parties cannot derogate.

Mediation A non-binding alternative dispute resolution process where a third party assists the parties to mutually resolve their dispute.

Memorandum of issues See terms of reference.

Model Law Model Law on International Commercial Arbitration adopted by UNCITRAL in 1985 and revised in 2006. See the list of countries that have based their national arbitration law on the Model Law in Appendix 3.

Most favoured nation clause A clause commonly used in investment treaties requiring the host state to treat foreign investors of the home state no less favourably than it treats investors of other countries. This allows home state foreign investors to benefit from treaty protections granted by the host state to foreign investors from other states.

Multi-party arbitration An arbitration having more than two parties.

NAFTA North American Free Trade Agreement.

New York Convention The 1958 New York Convention on the Recognition and Enforcement of Foreign Arbitral Awards. There are currently 144 state parties to the Convention. See the list provided in Appendix 4.

Notice to arbitrate See request for arbitration.

Order A direction made by an arbitral tribunal to the parties.

Ordre public See public policy.

Pacta sunt servanda The principle that contractual agreements must be honoured.

Partial award An award that finally determines individual issues but not all of the remaining issues in dispute.

Party-appointed arbitrator An arbitrator appointed or nominated by a party. See also co-arbitrator.

Party autonomy A fundamental principle of international arbitration that allows parties to choose the seat of arbitration, arbitral procedure, applicable law and most other aspects of how the arbitration will be conducted.

Pathological arbitration agreement An arbitration agreement that is inoperable or gives rise to ambiguity as to its operation.

PCIJ Permanent Court of International Justice.

PDRCI Rules International Commercial Arbitration Rules of the Philippine Dispute Resolution Centre set out in Chapter 4 of the Philippines Alternative Dispute Resolution Act.

Place of arbitration See seat of arbitration.

Prima facie On first appearance.

Procedural timetable A document prepared in the early stages of the arbitration to be used as a time line for compliance with certain procedural steps. The document normally takes the form of an order of the arbitral tribunal and can be amended at any time.

Public policy Fundamental principles of morality and justice of a state that override otherwise applicable law. The application of public policy may impact upon the arbitrability of certain disputes and the challenge or enforcement of awards.

Quantum meruit An action for payment of the reasonable value of services performed in the absence of a contractual right to payment.

Rationae materiae By reason of the matter involved.

Rationae personae By reason of the person (or entity) concerned.

Rationae temporis By reason of the timing.

Recognition of award The acknowledgement by a domestic court of an award. In some countries, the recognition of an award is separate to enforcement.

Remission The return of an arbitral award, ordinarily by a domestic court, to the original arbitral tribunal for reconsideration.

Renvoi A situation which occurs when the conflict of laws rules of the designated law are applied and these conflict rules require that a law different to the designated law be applied.

Request for arbitration A request served on an arbitral institution to act as an appointing authority or administer an arbitration. A request for arbitration is to be distinguished from a notice to arbitrate that is ordinarily served directly on the respondent.

Res judicata The principle that once an issue between the given parties is validly determined by a court or arbitral tribunal it cannot be revisited.

Restitution Restoring something to its rightful owner.

Rome Convention Convention on the Law Applicable to Contractual Obligations Rome 1980.

SCC Stockholm Chamber of Commerce.

SCC Rules Stockholm Chamber of Commerce Rules in force as of 1 January 2007.

Seat of arbitration Also referred to as the place of arbitration. This is the legal location of the arbitration proceedings and is to be distinguished from the physical location or venue of the arbitration hearings. The law of the seat of arbitration may have important consequences in respect of the procedural conduct of the arbitration.

Separability The principle that an arbitration agreement is separate from the main contract in which it is contained. The principle ensures that an arbitral tribunal can still have jurisdiction where there are allegations that the main contract is void or does not exist. Its application varies across jurisdictions.

Setting aside The annulment of an award by a domestic court at the seat of arbitration.
SIAC Singapore International Arbitration Centre.
SIAC Rules Singapore International Arbitration Centre Rules in force from 1 July 2007 to 30 June 2010.
2010 SIAC Rules The Singapore International Arbitration Centre Rules in force as of 1 July 2010.
Sole arbitrator An arbitral tribunal consisting of only one arbitrator.
Sovereign immunity A public international law principle granting immunity to states and their agencies from the jurisdiction of domestic courts, and execution against that state's assets. In some jurisdictions, these immunities may not apply to commercial activities of a state or may be waived in certain circumstances.
Stay of court proceedings An order to suspend domestic court proceedings on the ground that a valid arbitration agreement exists between the parties.
Stop-clock arbitration A procedure that limits each party's time to present its case at a hearing. Also known as 'chess clock arbitration'.
Sua sponte Of its own accord.
Submission agreement An agreement to refer an existing dispute to arbitration. A submission agreement may be necessary if parties do not have a pre-existing arbitration agreement; that is, an arbitration agreement entered into prior to the dispute arising. See also arbitration agreement.
Terms of Reference A document signed by the parties and the arbitral tribunal outlining certain particulars of the arbitration such as the issues in dispute and remedies sought. Also sometimes referred to as 'Memorandum of Issues'.
Truncated arbitral tribunal An arbitral tribunal which is no longer comprised of all its members due to death, removal or resignation. In special circumstances, a truncated arbitral tribunal may continue to function and make decisions.
Ultra petita Where an arbitral tribunal has made decisions beyond what the parties have requested of it. See also *infra petita* and Article V(1)(c) of the New York Convention.
Umbrella clause A clause contained in an investment treaty by which a state undertakes to observe any obligations it has entered into with regard to the investments of nationals of the other signatory state(s). The effect of these clauses may elevate contractual breaches to the status of treaty breaches.
UNCITRAL United Nations Commission on International Trade Law, based in Vienna.
UNCITRAL Arbitration Rules United Nations Commission on International Trade Law Arbitration Rules as adopted on 28 April 1976.
2010 UNCITRAL Arbitration Rules United Nations Commission on International Trade Law Arbitration Rules in force as of 15 August 2010.
UNCTAD United Nations Conference on Trade and Development.

UNIDROIT United Nations Institute for the Unification of Private Law, based in Rome. UNIDROIT is particularly known for the UNIDROIT Principles of International Commercial Contracts (1994 and 2004) which have been seen as an attempt to codify the *lex mercatoria*. See also *lex mercatoria*.
Venire contra factum proprium A party should not be allowed to contradict its own previous conduct.
VIAC Vietnam Arbitration Centre at the Chamber of Commerce and Industry of Vietnam.
VIAC Rules Arbitration Rules of the Vietnam Arbitration Centre at the Chamber of Commerce and Industry of Vietnam 1993.
Washington Convention See ICSID Convention.
WIPO World Intellectual Property Organisation.
WIPO Rules World Intellectual Property Organisation Rules in force as of 1 October 2002.

Index

Abu Dhabi oil case   8–9
ACICA (Australian Centre for International Commercial Arbitration)   37
  on IBA Rules of Evidence   313
  overview   505
  sample multi-tiered clause   198
ACICA Rules   55, 63–5, 81, 134, 195
  amendment of claims   328
  appropriate time to decide jurisdiction   209–10
  arbitrators in multi-party disputes   255
  avoiding delay and expense   317
  on chairpersons   261
  finality of awards   390
  formal appointment of arbitrators   267
  interim measures   361
  misconduct of arbitrators   296
  number of arbitrators   248
  representation   324
  types of costs   403–4
  witness confidentiality   377
ad hoc arbitration   27–8, 195–7
  arbitration rules   310
  notification or deposit of award   392
ad hoc rules   197
ADR *see* amicable dispute resolution
Agreement Establishing the ASEAN–Australia–New Zealand Trade Area (2009)   30, 480, 481, 482
Alabama Claims Arbitration   5, 6
Alexander VI (Pope)   4
alter ego doctrine   165–7
alternative dispute resolution *see* amicable dispute resolution
amendment of claims   328–9
amiable compositeur   138–43
amicable dispute resolution (ADR)
  differences from arbitration   19–20
  history in Asia   45–7
Aramco case   10–11
arb-med
  arbitral proceedings   333–7
  CIETAC Rules   334–5

  and impartiality   293–4
  nature of   46–7
arbitrability of a dispute
  determination of   182–9
  objective arbitrability   186–9
  subjective arbitrability   182–6
arbitral awards: challenge and enforcement
  balance between autonomy of arbitral process and control of national courts   411–12
  challenging awards   415–26
  consequences of challenge   426
  enforcement   7–8
  enforcement of New York Convention awards   427–46
  enforcement refusal grounds   447–68
  enforcement under Model Law   94–5
  execution of awards   420
  finality of awards   412–15
  forum non conveniens   471
  international enforcement   24–5
  non-New York Convention enforcement   416
  recognition of awards   427
  recognition under Model Law   94–5
  setting aside   94, 417–24
  state control over awards at seat of arbitration   415–17
  state immunity   473–6
  state responsibility for illegal court interference   471–3
  time limits   424–6
arbitral awards: content and form
  consent awards   398–9
  content, form and effect   382–92
  correction and interpretation   409–10
  costs   403–8
  decisions   393
  default awards   399
  definition   392–5
  domestic awards   400–1
  drafting   388–9
  final awards   395

527

arbitral awards (cont.)
  finality 390–2
  foreign awards 400–1
  formalities 382–3
  interim awards 396–8
  international awards 400–1
  majority decisions 401–3
  non-domestic awards 400–1
  notification or deposit of award 392
  orders or measures 396–8
  partial awards 396
  payment of costs 404–6
  provisional awards 396–8
  reasons for award 383–5
  scrutiny of draft award 389–90
  separate and dissenting opinions 401–3
  signature, place and date 386
  time limits 386–7
  types 395–403
arbitral institutions
  in Asia-Pacific region 37–8, 505–11, 512
  assessment of impartiality and independence 280–2
  choosing 28
  confidentiality provisions 377–8
  cost of services 26–7
  decisions on arbitrator misconduct 297–8
  in early 20th century 6–8
  examination of jurisdiction 230–3
  listed by region 512–13
  procedural rules 310
  related associations and organisations in Asia-Pacific 38–9
  role 25–6
  rules as sources of procedural law and practice 31
  versus ad hoc arbitration 27–8
arbitral jurisdiction
  appropriate time to decide jurisdiction 209–11
  competence-competence rule 214–30
  consensual nature 202
  effect of a court or arbitral institution's prima facie examination 233–4
  effects of jurisdictional decisions 233–44
  ex officio examination by arbitral institution 208–9
  examination by arbitral institution 230–3
  jurisdictional objections raised by a party 206–8

  multi-contract arbitrations 233
  multiparty arbitrations 231–2
  negative jurisdictional decisions 237–40
  overview of objections raised 203–5
  partial and absolute jurisdictional objections 205–6
  preliminary issues 205–14
  recourse against an arbitral tribunal's jurisdictional decision 234–40
  scope of court review of tribunal's jurisdictional decisions 240–2
  subsidiary orders with negative jurisdictional decisions 242–4
  waiver of right to invoke an arbitration agreement 211–14
arbitral procedural law see procedural law; procedural law and practice: sources
arbitral procedure
  amendment of claims 328–9
  arb-med 333–7
  bifurcation and trifurcation 330
  choosing the law to govern arbitral procedure 99
  expedited arbitration procedures 332–3
  hearings and written proceedings 93
  initiating the arbitration 323–4
  institutional v ad hoc arbitration procedure 310
  interim measures 361
  on-site inspections 329–30
  overview of typical procedural steps 322–3
  party default and non-participating parties 330–2
  preliminary meeting 325–6
  representation 324–5
  termination of proceedings 337
  terms of reference 326
  written submissions 326–8
  see also procedure of arbitration
arbitral tribunals
  absence of court interference in conflict of laws decisions 105, 106
  agreements to replace arbitrators 302
  challenges to arbitrators 273–301
  choice of lex mercatoria 134–5
  choosing an arbitrator 256–66
  competence-competence rule 214–30
  conflict of laws rules of seat of arbitration 107–8
  constitution of 246–56
  cumulative application of conflict of rules laws connected to dispute 108–9

INDEX

deciding cases without law 138–43
deliberations and decision-making 379–82
ex officio examination of jurisdiction 208–9
formal appointment of arbitrators 266–7
and general principles of private international law 109–10
and law with closest connection to the dispute 110–11
and mandatory laws 122–5
multiparty arbitrations 253–6
need for high quality arbitrators 251
number of arbitrators 246–50
obligations of arbitrators 267–73
orders 379
positive jurisdictional decisions 235–7
procedure for constituting 250–3
recourse against jurisdictional decision 234–40
replacement of arbitrators 302–3
resignation of arbitrators 301–2
scope of court review of jurisdictional decisions 240–2
selecting a set of conflict of laws rules 112
substantive law of seat of arbitration 106–7
and trade usages 129–31
arbitrary treatment, under international investment treaties 496–7
arbitration
  and 'amicable' (alternative) dispute resolution 19–20
  birth of modern international law 3–17
  definitions 2
  domestic v international arbitration 20–1
  and expert determination 191–2
  finality of outcomes 23–4
  history 3
  key features 21–8
  and litigation 18–19, 23–4
  overview 21–8
  party autonomy and procedure 23
  prior to 20th century 3–6
  seat of 22
  types 2
arbitration agreements
  ad hoc or institutional arbitration 195–7
  advisable elements to include 194–5
  alter ego and group of companies 165–7

arbitrability 182–9
assignment 168–9
attaching conditions 181–2
capacity of a party to enter into an agreement 169–70
certainty of the seat if designated 193
choice of which law governs the agreement 99
consolidation 172–5
and defined legal relationship 170–2
definition and formal requirements 146–50
definition under 1985 Model Law 90–1, 146–7
definition under 2006 Model Law 147–9
determining existence of a dispute 180–1
doctrine of separability 155–64
drafting 189–201
enforcement 179–82
essential elements 189
estoppel 167–8
identity of parties 163, 164–70, 189
and incorporation by reference 151–5
international enforcement 24–5
and investor-state arbitration 145–6
joinder and intervention 172–4, 175–8
law governing 159–63
multi-tiered arbitration clauses 197–8
nature and function 21, 144
need for 145–6
New York Convention requirements 147, 149
non-signatories 164–5
obligation to arbitrate 189–93
pathological agreements 199–201
subject matter and scope of arbitration 193
submission agreements 146
and substantive claims 91
third party notices 172–4, 178–9
types 146
validity 158–9
validity when determined independently of national laws 163–4
waiver of right to invoke 211–14
what not to include 198–9
writing requirement 150
arbitration education 43
arbitration legislation, in Asia-Pacific region 517
arbitration and mediation *see* arb-med

arbitration proceedings
  delocalisation and international relations
    theory 71–2
  delocalisation and relevant legal
    provisions 72–8
  delocalised view of link to seat of
    arbitration 68–70
  traditional view of link to seat of
    arbitration 66–7
arbitration rules
  applicable version of rules 311
  choice of 276, 308–9, 452
  failure to object to non-compliance with
    procedural rules 310–11
  function 59
  nature and function 59
  and procedural law 63–5
  relationship to procedural laws and *lex
    arbitri* 65–6
arbitration support associations 39
arbitrators
  agreements to replace 302
  appointment under Model Law 91–2
  chairpersons and sole arbitrators 261–2
  challenges for misconduct 294–301
  challenges for partiality or lack of
    independence 274–94
  challenges to 274–6
  choosing 256–66
  conflict of laws methodology 105–13
  difference between qualifications and
    qualities 256
  discerning parties' implicit choice of law
    111–12
  disclosure obligations 270
  duty to avoid delay and expense 316–18
  eligibility and role 21–2
  fees 299–300, 407–8
  formal appointment 266–7
  general obligations and potential liability
    268–70
  general principles of disclosure 270–1
  grounds for challenge of appointment 92
  impartiality and independence 274–6
  main principle guiding appointment
    246
  need for cultural understanding 51–2
  obligations 267
  party-nominated co-arbitrators 262–5
  pre-appointment interviews 265–6
  procedural aspect of challenge process
    276–9
  qualifications of an international arbitrator
    256–60

  qualities 260–1
  quality 245
  replacement of 273, 296–7, 302–3,
    472
  resignation 301–2
  standard for party-nominated
    co-arbitrators 292–3
Arbitrators and Mediators Institute of New
  Zealand (AMINZ), Arbitration Appeal
  Tribunal (AAT) 38
Argentina, bilateral treaty with Spain 498
ASEAN–ANZ Treaty 30, 480, 481, 482
Asia-Pacific region
  arbitral institutions 37–8, 505–11,
    512
  difficulties in enforcement of New York
    Convention awards 431
  national arbitration legislation 517
Asia-Pacific Regional Arbitration Group
  (APRAG) 38
Asian Chapter of ICC Young Arbitrators'
  Forum 39, 265
Asian culture
  and dispute resolution 44
  and international arbitration 43
  and social, religious and political diversity
    43–4
Asian legal systems, colonial legacies 47–8
AT & T case 283–4
Australasian Forum for International
  Arbitration (AFIA) 38, 265
Australia
  adoption of 2006 amendments to the
    Model Law 35
  adoption of the Model Law in
    state/territory laws 35
  bilateral treaty with China on the
    Reciprocal Encouragement and
    Protection of Investments 145, 495
  bilateral treaty with India on the
    Promotion and Protection of
    Investments 497
  difficulties in enforcement under New York
    Convention 431, 432
  International Arbitration Amendment Bill
    2009 64, 65, 150, 285, 291
  misapplication of arbitration principles
    42
Australian Centre for International
  Commercial Arbitration *see* ACICA
awards *see* arbitral awards: challenge and
  enforcement; arbitral awards: content
  and form; foreign arbitral awards;
  international arbitral awards

BAC (Beijing Arbitration Commission)
  Arbitration Rules   37, 226–7
  overview   506
Bangladesh, difficulties in arbitration legal environment   41, 472–3
Bangladesh Council of Arbitration, Rules of Arbitration   80, 175, 258, 301
BANI (Indonesian National Arbitration Board)
  overview   506
  Rules of Arbitration   37, 230, 325
Barcelona Traction case   491
Beijing Arbitration Commission *see* BAC
Bhatia case   77, 225, 366, 418
bifurcation   46, 210–11, 330
bilateral enforcement agreements   436–7
bilateral investment treaties (BITs)   42, 479–80
Bulgaria
  bilateral treaty with Cyprus on Mutual Encouragement and Protection of Investments   498
  bilateral treaty with Finland on Mutual Encouragement and Protection of Investments   498

Cambodia, bilateral treaty with Malaysia for Promotion and Protection of Investments   496
Cambodian Arbitration Council   39
Cambodian National Arbitration Centre   15–17
CENTRAL Transnational Law Database   136
chairpersons (tribunals)   261–2
challenging arbitrators   26, 92, 195, 273–301, 492
challenging awards
  consequences of challenge   426
  setting aside awards   417–24
  state control over awards at seat of arbitration   415–17
  time limits   424–6
Chartered Institute of Arbitrators
  establishment   7
  Practice Guidelines on the Pre-Appointment Interview of Prospective Arbitrators   265–6
Chile, bilateral treaty with Spain   498
China (Mainland)
  agreements with Hong Kong and Macau on mutual enforcement of arbitral awards   9

bilateral investment treaties   42, 145, 479
bilateral treaty with Australia on Encouragement and Reciprocal Protection of Investments   495, 497
bilateral treaty with Germany on the Encouragement and Reciprocal Protection of Investments   497
difficulties in arbitration legal environment   40, 42
history of arbitration   3–4
see also BAC
Chorzów Factory case   500–1
Chromalloy case   69–70, 74, 78, 460
CIETAC (Chinese International Economic and Trade Arbitration Commission),
  overview   507
CIETAC Rules
  for arb-med   334–5
  arbitral institution's examination of jurisdiction   230
  arbitrators in multi-party disputes   256
  awards   139
  on chairpersons   261
  disclosure obligations of arbitrators   271
  drafting awards   388
  existence and validity of arbitration agreements   227
  finality of awards   390
  initiating the arbitration   323–4
  misconduct of arbitrators   296
  pathological clauses   226
  scrutiny of draft award   389–90
  time limits on awards   387
  update   38
  witness confidentiality   377
civil law procedures   318–22
civil law traditions   48
claims, characterisation as contractual or otherwise   114–15
Coke, Edward (Sir)   5
colonial empires, use of third party sovereigns as arbitrators   4
comity principle, in New York Convention   10
commercial arbitration   2
commercial reservation   441–3
common law procedure   318–22
common law tradition   48
compensation
  for expropriation in investment treaties   500
  for non-expropriatory treaty breaches   500

competence-competence rule
  arbitral tribunal's determination of
    jurisdiction 214–30
  and extent of domestic court intervention
    218–28
  China–New Zealand FTA 42
  importance of 228–30
  in JCAA Rules 216
  in Model Law 216, 219, 220
  nature and function 215–17
  role of institutions 231
  in SIAC Rules 216
compulsory arbitration 145
conciliation 45–7, 333–7
Conference on International Commercial
  Arbitration 1958 (New York
  Conference) 9–10
confidentiality and privacy 371–8
conflict of law issues
  arbitral procedure 99
  arbitration agreements 99
  individual reference or instance of
    arbitration 99
  in international arbitration 98–100
  in international litigation 97–8
  parties' substantive rights 100
  party's legal capacity 99–100
  rules and direct approaches 103–4
  supervisory, supportive and enforcement
    measures 99
  types of 96–100
conflict of laws rules
  in absence of party choice 103–4
  cumulative application 108–9
  general principles of private international
    law 109–10
  of the seat of arbitration 104–5,
    107–8
  selecting 112
consent awards 398–9
consolidation, in arbitration proceedings
  172–8
costs
  of arbitration v parties' costs 404
  arbitrators' fees 407–8
  awarding 403–8
  in ICSID arbitration 501
  payment by which party and in what
    proportion 404–6
  sealed offers 406–7
  security for 369–70
  taxation of costs 408
Court of Arbitration for Sport 56
Cyprus, bilateral treaty with Bulgaria on
  Mutual Encouragement and Protection
  of Investments 498

default awards 399
deliberations 128–9, 246, 379–82, 386,
  388
deliberations and decision-making
  379–82
delocalisation
  attitudes in Asia-Pacific court decisions
    77–8
  and conflict of laws rules 107–8
  diluted or hybrid form 79
  guidance for common law jurisdictions
    78
  and ICSID Convention 78
  influence on international arbitration
    practice 79
  and international relations theory
    71–2
  and liberal internationalism 72
  and mandatory laws 69
  and New York Convention
    73–5
  pure form 78–9
  relevant legal provisions 72–8
delocalised/contractual conception of
  arbitration 68–70
diplomatic protection 13, 481, 489,
  491–3
discriminatory treatment, under
  international investment treaties
  496–7
dispute resolution
  arbitration v expert determination
    191–2
  in Asian history and culture 44
dissenting opinions 401–3
doctrine of separability
  of arbitration agreements 151, 155–64,
    216
  consequences of application
    158
  criticisms 156
  and disputed existence of the contract
    156–8
  importance of 155–6
  law governing main contract and
    arbitration agreement 159–63
  as a legal fiction 156
  in Model Law 155
  validity of arbitration agreement
    determined independently of national
    laws 163–4
  validity of main contract and arbitration
    agreement 158–9
document requests, procedures under
  common law, civil law and international
  arbitration 320

documentary evidence
  adverse inferences drawn from non-
    production 345–6
  court assistance in document production
    342–3
  document production in arbitral practice
    341
  document production in domestic courts
    340–1
  electronic documents 346
  IBA Rules of Evidence and document
    production 343–6
  in international arbitration 339–46
  procedures under common law, civil law
    and international arbitration 319–20
domestic arbitration 2, 20–1
domestic awards 400–1
domestic courts
  assessment of impartiality and
    independence of arbitrators 282–92
  assistance in issuing interim orders
    363–8
  decisions on arbitrator misconduct
    298–301
  document production 340–1
  inappropriateness of using the same bias
    test for judges and arbitrators 291–2
  selected decisions on partiality and lack of
    independence 287–91
  state responsibility for illegal court
    interference with awards 471–3
  tests for assessing impartiality and
    independence of judges and arbitrators
    283–7
Draft Convention on the International
  Responsibility of States for Injuries to
  Aliens (1961) 12
due process 306–7, 313–6, 453–5, 494
  violation of 453–5
Dutco case 254–5

East Asian Branch of the Chartered Institute
  of Arbitrators 39, 512
Egypt, ancient history of arbitration 4
electronic documents 346
enforceability of international arbitration
  1, 99
enforcement of arbitral awards 62
enforcement of ICSID awards 503–4
enforcement of New York Convention awards
  advantages of international commercial
    arbitration over international litigation
    427–30
  application of the New York Convention
    437–44
  at the seat of arbitration 436

  bilateral and multilateral enforcement
    agreements 436–7
  commercial reservation 441–3
  delays in enforcement 445–6
  difficulties in Asia-Pacific region 431
  documents required 443–4
  implementation of New York Convention
    431–5
  need for improvements 430–1
  reciprocity reservation 440–1
  retroactivity of New York Convention
    444
  temporal issues 444–6
  time limits 444–5
enforcement refusal
  adjournment of enforcement proceedings
    467–8
  arbitrability 461
  Article V(1) of New York Convention
    451–60
  Article V(2) of New York Convention
    460, 461–7
  award not yet binding or set aside
    459–60
  in China 449–50
  excess of jurisdiction 455–7
  ICSID Convention internal annulment
    mechanism 450
  irregularity in procedure or composition of
    arbitral tribunal 457–9
  overlap of New York Convention with
    Articles 34, 35 and 36 of Model Law
    450–1
  overview 447–68
  party incapacity or agreement invalidity
    451–3
  public policy 461–7
equal treatment, right to 315–16
estoppel 167–8, 201, 204, 231, 311, 375
European Community Regulation on the Law
  Applicable to Contractual Obligations
  (Rome I Regulation) 120–1
European Community Regulation on the Law
  Applicable to Non-contractual
  Obligations (Rome II Regulation) 116,
  117–18, 125
European Convention on Human Rights
  476
European Convention on International
  Commercial Arbitration (1961) 30
evidence
  burden and standard of proof 316
  categories 338
  document production in domestic courts
    340–1
  documentary evidence 339–46

evidence (cont.)
  expert evidence   350–4
  IBA Rules of Evidence   312–13
  witness evidence   346–8
ex aequo et bono   138–43
ex parte preliminary orders   361–3
execution of awards   470–3
expedited arbitration procedures   332–3
expert determination v arbitration   191–2
expert evidence
  in arbitral proceedings   350–4
  need for   350
  party-appointed experts   350–1
  tribunal-appointed experts   351–2
  witness conferencing   352–4
expert witnesses, procedures under common law, civil law and international arbitration   321
expropriation
  compensation for   500
  under international investment treaties   494–5

fair and equitable treatment, under international investment treaties   495–6
final awards   395
finality of arbitral awards   390–2, 412–15
finality of international arbitration   1, 23–4
Finland, bilateral treaty with Bulgaria on Mutual Encouragement and Protection of Investments   498
flexibility of international arbitration   1
foreign arbitral awards   7–8, 400–1, 418–19
forum non conveniens   471
France, position on validity of arbitration agreements   163–4
free trade agreements
  nature of   480–1
  as sources of procedural law and practice in international arbitration   30–1
full protection and security, under international investment treaties   496

Geneva Convention on the Execution of Foreign Arbitral Awards (1927)   8, 30, 34
Geneva Protocol on Arbitration Clauses (1923)   7–8, 30, 34
German Institution of Arbitration, DIS Rules   278
Germany, bilateral treaty with China on the Encouragement and Reciprocal Protection of Investments   497

globalisation, and international law in early 20th century   6–9
Gough test   283, 286–7
Grain Feed Trade Association, arbitration rules   412
group of companies doctrine   165–7

The Hague Convention (1899)   6
The Hague Convention (1907)   6
The Hague Convention on Choice of Court Agreements (2005)   11, 428
hearings
  in arbitral proceedings   354–7
  common law, civil law and international arbitration procedures compared   320–1
HKIAC Electronic Transaction Arbitration Rules   357
Hilmarton case   69–70, 74, 460
HKIAC (Hong Kong International Arbitration Centre), overview   507
HKIAC Electronic Transaction Arbitration Rules   357
HKIAC Rules
  amendments   37
  challenges against arbitrators   280
  choice of lex mercatoria   134
  on deliberations of tribunals   380
  failure to object to non-compliance with procedural rules   310
  number of arbitrators   248–9
  procedural rules   308
  replacement of arbitrators   303
  seat of arbitration   55, 81
  time limits on awards   387
HKIAC Schedule of Fees and Costs of Arbitration   392
Hong Kong
  adoption of 2006 amendments to the Model Law   35
  agreement with China on mutual enforcement of arbitral awards   9
  importance as an arbitration jurisdiction   36, 37

IBA (International Bar Association), self-regulation   32
IBA Guidelines on Conflicts of Interest in International Arbitration   32–3
  arb-med   336
  disclosure obligations   270, 271–3
  pre-appointment interviews for arbitrators   265

INDEX 535

IBA Rules of Ethics for International
    Arbitrators 267, 380
IBA Rules of Evidence 32, 312–13
  and document production 343–6
  hearings 354
  on-site inspections 329
  party-appointed experts 350–1
  tribunal-appointed experts 351–2
  witness conferencing 352–4
  witness evidence 348–50
ICA (Indian Council of Arbitration), overview
    508
ICA Rules 80, 175, 249, 399
ICC (International Chamber of Commerce)
  Congress, Rome 1923 7
  establishment 7
  role in lobbying for international arbitral
      award 9
ICC Commission on Arbitration
  Report on Drafting Arbitral Awards 32,
      394
  Task Force on time and costs in arbitration
      317–18
ICC Court (ICC International Court of
    Arbitration)
  assessment of independence of arbitrators
      280–2
  establishment and mission 7
  on joinder of parties to arbitration
      agreements 177–8
  multi-contract arbitrations 233
  multiparty arbitrations 231–2
  office of Secretariat established in Hong
      Kong 37
  overview 510
  removal of arbitrators 297–8
  resignation of arbitrators 301–2
ICC Rules
  amendment of claims 328–9
  arbitral institution's examination of
      jurisdiction 230–1
  on arbitrator misconduct 297–8
  avoiding delay and expense 316
  consolidation 175
  disclosure obligations of arbitrators
      271
  formal appointment of arbitrators 267
  institutional arbitration 195
  right to equal treatment 315
  scrutiny of draft award 389–90
  seat of arbitration 82
  waiver of right to invoke arbitration
      agreement 214
ICC Young Arbitrators' Forum, Asian Chapter
    39, 265

ICSID (International Centre for the
    Resolution of Investment Disputes)
  arbitration claims against states from the
      Asia-Pacific 36
  background and structure 482–3
  establishment and operation 13
  self-contained procedure 492–3
ICSID Additional Facility Rules 488
ICSID arbitration
  advantages 489
  applicable substantive law 486–7
  consent to 487
  contrasted to international commercial
      arbitration 3
  disadvantages 489–91
  jurisdiction 483
  and nationality 485–6
  and requirement of an 'investment'
      483–5
ICSID awards
  annulment 502
  enforcement 503–4
ICSID Convention (Washington Convention
    on the Settlement of Investment
    Disputes between States and Nationals
    of Other States 1965)
  assessment of 488
  and choice of law 486–7
  and delocalisation 78
  exclusion of diplomatic protection and
      investor's direct rights 491–2
  on exhaustion of domestic remedies
      493
  formulation and acceptance 11–13
  and ICSID arbitration 3–17
  innovative features 491–3
  internal annulment mechanism
      450
ICSID Rules
  on appropriate time to decide jurisdiction
      210
  arbitral institution's examination of
      jurisdiction 230, 231
  separate opinions 401
impartiality and independence
  and arb-med or med-arb 293–4
  of arbitrators 274–6
  assessment by arbitral institutions
      280–2
  assessment by domestic courts 282–92
implied intent 111–12
implied negative choice theory 111
in rem rights 189
independence of arbitrators, v impartiality
    274–6

India
  bilateral treaty with Australia on the Promotion and Protection of Investments 497
  difficulties in arbitration legal environment 40–2, 418
  history of arbitration 4
Indian Council of Arbitration (ICA)
  overview 508
  Rules of Arbitration 80, 175, 249, 399
Indonesia
  bilateral treaty with Malaysia for the Promotion and Protection of Investments 498
  difficulties in arbitration legal environment 40–1, 443
  dispute resolution culture 47
Indonesian National Arbitration Board (BANI) 37, 230, 325, 506
industry self-regulation, as a source of procedural law and practice in international arbitration 32
Inter-American Convention on International Commercial Arbitration (1975) 30
interest, awards in ICSID arbitration 501
interim awards 396–8
interim measures
  in arbitral proceedings 357–68
  arbitral rules 361
  court assistance 363–8
  ex parte preliminary orders 361–3
  national laws 358–61
  nature and function of 357
  tribunal-ordered interim measures 357–63
international arbitral awards, as sources for procedural law and practice 33
international arbitration
  and Asian culture 43
  Asian variation of 51–3
  barriers in certain Asia-Pacific countries 40–3
  definition 20
  differences from domestic arbitration 20–1
  enforceability of 1
  enforcement of agreements and awards 24–5
  evolution in the West 48–50
  finality of 1
  flexibility of 1
  growth in number of cases in Asia-Pacific 39–40

  history and growth in the Asia-Pacific 33–43
  influence of delocalisation 79
  influence of preferences of transnational companies 52
  juridical conception 107
  need for procedures that are culturally acceptable to both sides 51–2
  neutrality of 1
  popularity of 1
  sources of procedural law and practice 28–33
  and state sovereignty 66–7
  Western influence on Asian international arbitration culture 50–1
  witness statements or affidavits 319–20
international awards 400–1
International Bar Association see IBA
International Chamber of Commerce see ICC
international commercial arbitration
  advantages over international litigation 427–30
  first case in modern era 5–6
  states as parties 3
  v commercial arbitration 2
  v ICSID arbitration 3
international conventions, as the source of procedural law and practice 30
International Council for Commercial Arbitration's (ICCA) Yearbook of Commercial Arbitration 31
International Court of Justice 491, 500
  breaches of investment treaty obligations 30
  inspiration for 6
international investment law, and investment treaty arbitration 478–9
international law, development in early 20th century 6–9
International Law Association, International Commercial Arbitration Committee taskforce on content of applicable law 127–9
international litigation
  conflict of law issues 97–8
  and law governing the procedure 98
  and law governing the parties' substantive rights 98
international relations theory
  and delocalisation 71–2
  liberal internationalism 72
  realism 71–2
investment arbitration see investment treaty arbitration

investment treaties
  bilateral investment treaties   479–80
  dispute settlement clauses   481
  fork in the road provisions   481
  free trade agreements   480–1
  nature of   479–82
  as sources of procedural law and practice in international arbitration   30–1
investment treaty arbitration   3
  advantages of ICSID Convention   489
  annulment of ICSID awards   502
  and arbitrary or discriminatory treatment   496–7
  and background and structure of ICSID   482–3
  and choice of law   486–7
  compensation for expropriation   500
  compensation for non-expropriatory treaty breaches   500–1
  and consent to ICSID arbitration   487
  costs   501
  disadvantages of ICSID Convention   489–91
  dispute settlement clauses in treaties   481
  enforcement of ICSID awards   503–4
  and exclusion of diplomatic protection and investor's direct rights   491–2
  and exhaustion of domestic remedies   493
  and expropriation   494–5
  and fair and equitable treatment   495–6
  full protection and security   496
  and ICSID Convention (1965)   11–13
  and ICSID jurisdiction   483
  and ICSID's self-contained procedure   492–3
  and individual's nationality   485
  interest   501
  and international investment law   478–9
  investment treaties   479–82
  key features of   477–8
  and most favoured nation treatment   498–9
  and national treatment   497
  and nationality of corporations   485–6
  nature and significance   477
  remedies   500–2
  and requirement of an 'investment'   483–5
  substantive rights and protections   493–9
  umbrella clauses   499

investor-state arbitration   413–14
  and arbitration agreements   145–6
  in the Asia-Pacific region   36
Iran–United States Claims Tribunal   15, 314–15, 328, 338, 339, 345, 351, 401, 409, 500

Japan
  arbitrators   257
  disinterest in arbitration   43
  preference for negotiation and settlement over law   45–6
  reciprocity reservation   441
Japanese Commercial Arbitration Association (JCAA) overview   508
JCAA Administrative and Procedural Rules for Arbitration under the UNCITRAL Arbitration Rules   309
JCAA Rules
  arbitral tribunals   175, 178
  arbitrators in multi-party disputes   255
  competence-competence rule   216
  interim measures   361
  number of arbitrators   247, 248
  update   37
joinder and intervention, in arbitration agreements   172–4, 175–8
Joint Venture Agreements (JVAs)   177–8
judges, oath of office   291
judicial review   233–44, 415–26
jur novit curia principle   127

Karachi Centre for Dispute Resolution   39
KCAB (Korean Commercial Arbitration Board)   37, 509
KCAB International Arbitration Rules
  avoiding delay and expense   316
  choice of *lex mercatoria*   134
  document production   341
  misconduct of arbitrators   296
  number of arbitrators   247, 248
  procedural steps   323
  seat of arbitration   81
  time limits on awards   387
KLRCA (Kuala Lumpur Regional Centre for Arbitration)
  Arbitration Rules   37, 75
  overview   509
Korea (Republic of)
  arbitrators   258
  bilateral treaty with Argentina on the Promotion and Protection of Investments   493
  incorporation by reference   153

Korean Commercial Arbitration Board *see* KCAB
Kuala Lumpur Regional Centre for Arbitration *see* KLRCA

LCIA (London Court of International Arbitration)
　establishment　6–7
　office in India　38, 39
　overview　511
LCIA Rules　176
League of Nations
　adoption of 1923 Geneva Protocol on Arbitration Clauses　7–8
　inspiration for　6
legal systems, colonial legacies in Asia　47–8
lex arbitri
　defined　58
　function of　58–9
　and *lex fori*　23, 59, 97, 98, 105, 114, 125
　mandatory laws　125–6
　relationship to procedural law and arbitration rules　65–6
　v arbitral procedural law　60–3
lex fori
　defined　97
　and *lex arbitri*　23, 59, 97, 98, 105, 114, 125
　and supervisory, supportive and enforcement measures in international arbitration　99
lex mercatoria
　choice by arbitral tribunal　134–5
　as choice of the parties　132–3
　content and codification　135–8
　and non-national rules of law　131–8
lex personum　99
liberal internationalism, in international relations theory　72
litigation, differences from arbitration　18–19
London Chamber of Arbitration *see* LCIA
London Court of International Arbitration *see* LCIA

majority decisions　401–3
Malaysia
　bilateral treaty with Cambodia for Promotion and Protection of Investments　496
　bilateral treaty with Indonesia for the Promotion and Protection of Investments　498
　see also KLRCA (Kuala Lumpur Regional Centre for Arbitration)
mandatory laws
　and arbitral tribunals　122–5
　categories　125
　constraints on party autonomy　306–7
　and delocalisation　69
　and freedom of parties to choose applicable law　102
　of *lex arbitri*　125–6
　public policy and limitation on choice of applicable law　119–26
med-arb *see* arb-med
Memorandum of Understanding on the Arrangement Concerning the Mutual Enforcement of Arbitral Awards (China and Hong Kong 1999)　37
misconduct
　arbitral institution decisions on　297–8
　challenges for　294–301
　court decisions on　298–301
　definition and procedure of challenges　294–7
Model Law
　application for setting aside as exclusive recourse against arbitral awards　93–4
　appointment of arbitrators　91–2
　appropriate time to decide jurisdiction　209
　arbitration agreement and substantive claim before court　91
　arbitrator challenge procedure　278
　Article 19(1) on choosing institutional rules　64
　Article 20(2) on seat of arbitration　56–7
　attaching conditions to agreements　182
　avoiding delay and expense　316
　on chairpersons　261
　on changing the seat of arbitration　84
　on choosing seat of arbitration　81
　competence-competence rule　216, 219, 220
　consent awards　398–9
　correction and interpretation of awards　409
　court assistance in issuing interim orders　363–5

definition of arbitration agreements in 1985 version   90–1, 146–7
definition of arbitration agreements in 2006 version   147–9
and delocalisation   75–7
on determining the applicable substantive law   100–1
development in 1985   15–17, 87
disclosure obligations of arbitrators   270–1
doctrine of separability   155
elaboration or qualification of setting aside grounds of Article 34   421–3
enforcement of agreements   180
equal treatment of parties   93
on *ex aequo et bono*   139
ex parte preliminary orders   361–3
formal requirements for awards   382
grounds for challenge   92
hearings and written proceedings   93
interim measures in 1985 version   358
interim measures in 2006 version   358–60
and *lex mercatoria*   132, 134
list of countries where legislation based on Model Law has been enacted   514
mandatory provisions of 1985 text   88–95
on misconduct of arbitrators   295
negative jurisdictional decisions   237–40
number of arbitrators   248
on objections raised by a party   207
on-site inspections   330
opt-out provisions in national statutes   64
overlap of Articles 34, 35 and 36 with New York Convention   450–1
party-nominated co-arbitrators   262–5
positive jurisdictional decisions   235–7
procedure for constituting tribunals   251
recognition and enforcement of arbitral awards   94–5
revision in 2006   17, 87
role in the Asia-Pacific   86–7
scope of application   89–90
security for costs   369–70
setting aside grounds and their exclusivity   419–21
written submissions   327
most favoured nation treatment, in international investment treaties   498–9

multi-contract arbitrations, arbitral jurisdiction   233
multi-tiered arbitration clauses   197–8
multilateral enforcement agreements   436–7
multiparty arbitrations
  arbitral jurisdiction   231–2
  composition of tribunals   253–6

national arbitration legislation, in Asia-Pacific region   517
national laws, as interim measures   358–61
national treatment standard, under international investment treaties   497
negative jurisdictional decisions, arbitral jurisdiction   237–40
neutrality of international arbitration   1
New York Conference (1958)   9–10
New York Convention arbitration   2
New York Convention on the Recognition and Enforcement of Foreign Arbitral Awards (1958) ('New York Convention')
  on adjournment of enforcement proceedings   467–8
  on arbitrability   460, 461–7
  arbitration agreements   147, 149
  Article V(1) and enforcement refusal   451–60
  Article V(2) and enforcement refusal   460, 461–7
  and award not yet binding or set aside   459–60
  on changing the seat of arbitration   84
  and commercial reservation   441–3
  on delocalisation (Articles I, V & VII)   73–5
  development and adoption   9–10
  documents required for enforcement   443–4
  effectiveness   427–30
  enforcement of agreements and awards   24–5, 179–80
  on excess of jurisdiction   455–7
  impact on international arbitration   11
  implementation   431–5
  importance for international commercial arbitration   30
  incorporation of arbitration clause by reference   154–5
  on irregularity in procedure or composition of arbitral tribunal   457–9

('New York Convention') (*cont.*)
  list of states that are party to convention 515–16
  and 'New York Convention arbitration' 2
  overlap with Articles 34, 35 and 36 of Model Law 450–1
  parties to 10
  on party incapacity or agreement invalidity 451–3
  principle of comity 10
  pro-enforcement bias 10
  on public policy 461–7
  and reciprocity reservation 440–1
  refusal of enforcement (Article V) 62
  retroactivity 444
  scope of application 437–40
  on violation of due process 453–5
New Zealand, adoption of 2006 amendments to the Model Law 35
non-contractual claims
  characterisation 114–15
  law applicable 113–14
  law applicable to torts claims in absence of choice 116–19
  parties' choice of law applicable 115–16
non-domestic awards 400–1, 438–9
non-national rules of law, and the *lex mercatoria* 131–8
non-participating parties 330–2
North American Free Trade Agreement 145

objective arbitrability 60, 186–9, 229, 461
OECD, Draft Convention on the Protection of Foreign Property (1962) 12
on-site inspections 329–30

Pakistan
  bilateral treaty with Switzerland on promotion and protection of investments 499
  difficulties in arbitration legal environment 41
partial awards 396
parties to arbitration, equal treatment under Model Law 93
party autonomy 305–8
  choices 23
  and non-contractual claims 115–16
party default 330–2
pathological arbitration agreements 199–201
PDRCI (Philippines Dispute Resolution Centre Inc) Rules 81, 249, 303
Peace of Westphalia (1648) 66–7

People's Republic of China *see* China (Mainland); Hong Kong
Permanent Court of Arbitration 6
Pertamina case 60, 62–3, 70, 77–8, 418, 460
Philippines
  bilateral treaty with Switzerland on promotion and protection of investments 499
  difficulties in arbitration legal environment 40, 41–2, 466
  doctrine of separability 155, 162
Philippines Dispute Resolution Centre Inc (PDRCI), Rules 81, 249, 303
place of arbitration *see* seat of arbitration
pleadings, procedures under common law, civil law and international arbitration 319, 320–2
Porter v Magill test 284, 285–6, 287
post-hearing, procedures under common law, civil law and international arbitration 321
Practice Guidelines on the Pre-Appointment Interview of Prospective Arbitrators 265–6
preliminary order 358, 361–3
privacy and confidentiality 371–8
private international law, application of general principles 109–10
procedural law
  choosing a foreign procedural law 61–2
  function 59
  relationship to arbitration rules and *lex arbitri* 65–6
  v arbitration rules 63–5
  v *lex arbitri* 60–3
procedural law and practice: sources
  expert publications 31
  free trade agreements 30–1
  industry self-regulation 32
  international conventions 30
  international sources 30
  investment treaties 30–1
  national or domestic sources 29–30
  published international arbitral awards 33
  regional conventions 30
  rules of arbitral institutions as sources 31
  seminal cases from national jurisdictions 32–3
  supranational and quasi-legal sources 31–3
  types 28–33

procedural pyramid 65–6
procedural rights and duties
  arbitrators' duty to avoid delay and
    expense 316–18
  right to equal treatment 315–16
  right to present a case 313–15
procedural rules *see* arbitration rules
procedure of arbitration
  arbitral proceedings 322–37
  arbitration rules 308–11
  balancing common law and civil law
    procedure 318–22
  core procedural rights and duties
    313–18
  evidence 337–54
  flexibility 304
  hearings 354–7
  IBA Rules on taking of evidence
    312–13
  interim measures 357–68
  party autonomy 305–8
  privacy and confidentiality 370
  security for costs 369–70
  see also arbitral procedure
provisional awards 396–8
public policy, and mandatory laws limiting
  choice of applicable law 119–26

realism
  in international relations theory
    71–2
  and state sovereignty 71–2
reasonable apprehension test 283, 287
reasonable suspicion test 283, 285–6
reciprocity reservation 440–1
recognition of awards 427
regional conventions, as sources of
  procedural law and practice in
  international arbitration 30
Rome Convention on the Law Applicable to
  Contractual Obligations (1980) 110
Rome I Regulation 120–1
Rome II Regulation 116, 117–18, 125

Saw Pipes case 77, 420, 422–3, 465
seat of arbitration
  application of substantive law 104,
    106–7
  changing 83–6
  conflict of laws rules 104–5, 107–8
  default mechanisms for choosing 81–2
  defined 55
  delocalisation and international relations
    theory 71–2
  delocalisation and relevant legal
    provisions 72–8
  delocalised view of link to arbitration
    proceedings 68–70
  distinguished from venue of hearings
    55–8
  enforcement options 436
  factors to consider in choosing 82–3
  function of 22
  general principles for choosing 80
  and geographic and infrastructure
    convenience 83
  neutrality 83
  state control over awards 415–17
  traditional view of link to arbitration
    proceedings 66–7
  versus place of arbitration 55
security for costs 369–70
separability *see* doctrine of separability
separate opinions 401–3
setting aside awards
  at seat of arbitration 417
  elaboration or qualification of Model Law
    Article 34 grounds 421–3
  failing to make a timely objection 424
  foreign awards 418–19
  Model Law setting aside grounds and their
    exclusivity 419–21
  setting aside jurisdictional decisions
    424
SIAC (Singapore International Arbitration
  Centre), overview 510
SIAC Rules
  applicable version of rules 311
  arbitrator challenge process 277
  avoiding delay and expense 316
  competence-competence rule 216
  confidentiality 376
  drafting awards 388–9
  enforcement 469
  formal appointment of arbitrators
    267
  general obligations and potential liability
    of arbitrators 268
  institutional involvement and supervision
    195
  joinder 176
  number of arbitrators 248
  procedure for constituting tribunals
    250–1
  replacement of arbitrators 303
  scrutiny of draft award 389–90
  seat of arbitration 55, 82, 176
  updated 37

Singapore
  adoption of 2006 amendments to the Model Law 35
  bilateral treaty with Indonesia on the Promotion and Protection of Investments (2005) 30
  importance as an arbitration jurisdiction 36–7
  International Arbitration (Amendment) Bill (2009) 35, 150
Singapore International Arbitration Centre see SIAC
Singapore–Australia Free Trade Agreement (2003) 30
'soft laws' 31
sole arbitrators 261–2
South Korea see Korea (Republic of)
sovereign immunity 473–6
Spain
  bilateral treaty with Argentina 498
  bilateral treaty with Chile 498
state immunity 473–6
state sovereignty
  challenges to 72
  and international arbitration 66–7
  in realism 71–2
states, as parties to international arbitration 3
subjective arbitrability 182–6
submission agreements 146
substantive law applicable
  in absence of party choice 102–5
  conflict of laws methodology adopted by international arbitrators 105–13
  and conflict of laws rules of seat of arbitration 104–5, 107–8
  content of applicable law 126–9
  freedom of parties to choose the applicable law 101–2
  and law with closest connection to the dispute 105, 110–11
  and law of seat of arbitration 104, 106–7
  mandatory laws and public policy 119–26
  non-national rules of law and the lex mercatoria 131–8
  and substance of the dispute 100–19
  to non-contractual claims 113–14
  and trade usages 129–31
  types of conflict of law issues 96–100
  where parties have not agreed 102
Swiss Rules of International Arbitration 176–7

Switzerland
  bilateral treaty with Pakistan on promotion and protection of investments 499
  bilateral treaty with Philippines on promotion and protection of investments 499

Taiwan, reciprocity reservation 441
terms of reference 326
third party notices, arbitration agreements 172–4, 178–9
time limits
  for enforcement 444–5
  for setting aside action 424–6
tort law
  law applicable to torts claims in absence of choice 116–19
  nature of 115–16
Tractoroexport case 85–6
trade usages, and applicable law 129–31
Treaty of Washington (1871) 5
trifurcation 330

umbrella clauses, in international investment treaties 499
UNCITRAL (United Nations Commission on International Trade Law)
  development of Model Law in 1985 15–17, 87
  establishment and operation 14
  revision of Model Law in 2006 17, 56
UNCITRAL Arbitration Rules
  appropriate time to decide jurisdiction 209
  arbitrator challenge process 277
  avoiding delay and expense 317
  on chairpersons 261
  initiating the arbitration 324
  majority decisions 401
  number of arbitrators 249–50
  on objections raised by a party 207
  procedural rules 309
  replacement of arbitrators 303
  revision of 171–2
  right to equal treatment 315
  right to present a case 313
  significance of 14–15, 31
  use as ad hoc rules 197
  writing requirement for arbitration agreements, 150
UNCITRAL Model Law on International Commercial Arbitration see Model Law
UNCITRAL Notes on Organising Arbitral Proceedings

on confidentiality 378
on-site inspections 330
UNCITRAL Working Group
  negative jurisdictional decisions 239
  revision of Arbitration Rules 171–2
UNIDROIT Principles of International Commercial Contracts 133, 135
United Nations
  Conference on International Commercial Arbitration 1958 (New York Conference) 9–10
  inspiration for 6
United Nations Commission on International Trade Law, *see* UNCITRAL
United Nations Compensation Commission 351
United Nations Economic and Social Council (ECOSOC) 9
United Nations General Assembly, Resolution 1803 Permanent Sovereignty over Natural Resources (1962) 12
United States, early lack of legal recognition of arbitrator's decisions 5

Venture Global case 77, 225, 366, 418, 423
venue of hearings, distinguished from seat of arbitration 55–8

Vietnam, commercial reservation 442–3
Vietnam Arbitration Centre, Arbitration Rules 195, 278
Vis (East) Moot Competition 38–9

waiver 92, 204, 206, 211–14, 293–4, 310–11, 424, 474–6
Washington Convention on the Settlement of Investment Disputes between States and Nationals of Other States (1965) *see* ICSID Convention
Washington, George 5
Western States
  early critics of arbitration 4–5
  early recourse to arbitration 4
witness conferencing 352–4
witness evidence
  in arbitral proceedings 346–8
  IBA Rules of Evidence 348–50
witness statements or affidavits, procedures under common law, civil law and international arbitration 319–20
World Bank, and 1965 ICSID Convention 12–13, 482, 484, 504
written submissions
  arbitral proceedings 326–8
  common law, civil law and international arbitration procedures compared 319, 320–2

For EU product safety concerns, contact us at Calle de José Abascal, 56–1°, 28003 Madrid, Spain or eugpsr@cambridge.org.